GW01418500

A CATALOGUE OF THE WORKS OF SIR ARNOLD BAX

A CATALOGUE OF THE WORKS OF

SIR ARNOLD BAX

Graham Parlett

CLARENDON PRESS · OXFORD
1999

Oxford University Press, Great Clarendon Street, Oxford OX2 6DP

Oxford New York
Athens Auckland Bangkok Bogotá Buenos Aires Calcutta
Cape Town Chennai Dar es Salaam Delhi Florence Hong Kong Istanbul
Karachi Kuala Lumpur Madrid Melbourne Mexico City Mumbai
Nairobi Paris São Paulo Singapore Taipei Tokyo Toronto Warsaw

and associated companies in
Berlin Ibadan

Oxford is a registered trade mark of Oxford University Press

Published in the United States
by Oxford University Press Inc., New York

First published 1999

British Library Cataloguing in Publication Data
Data available

Library of Congress Cataloging in Publication Data
Data available

ISBN 0–19–816586–2

1 3 5 7 9 10 8 6 4 2

Typeset by the author
Printed in Great Britain
on acid-free paper by
Bookcraft Ltd.
Midsomer Norton, Somerset

To my brother

DAVID PARLETT

PREFACE

'Beware, sir, of acquiring the habit of reading catalogues; you will never get any good from it, and it will consume much of your time.'

Dr Martin Routh (1755–1854)

The late President of Magdalen College, Oxford, was quite right in his belief that catalogues are time-consuming, to compile as well as to read; but the suggestion that no good derives from them cannot be allowed to pass unchallenged. Musicologists from Schmieder and Köchel to Threlfall and Craggs have laboured hard to compile work-lists, source-books and bibliographies that provide a wealth of fascinating and useful information, and nobody with a real interest in the composers represented can afford to be without them. A full-scale catalogue devoted to the works of Arnold Bax was long overdue, and this volume contains the most comprehensive documentary survey of his music yet compiled. It is of course inevitable that some minor scores still await discovery. Bax may not have been as meticulous as Holst in preserving his 'Early Horrors' but there is no evidence that he deliberately destroyed any of his works, and it may be only a matter of time before further juvenilia, occasional pieces or abortive sketches come to light. At least forty scores known to have been composed remain untraced, including a few early orchestral pieces, and the original manuscripts of nearly eighty published scores are missing. But the likelihood of there being any completely unknown works of significance is remote, and this catalogue purports to be a substantially complete record of the composer's vast musical and literary output.

Arnold Bax was a prolific writer of music in most of the traditional forms, opera being the principal exception. His earliest work was written in the summer of 1896, when he was twelve; his last dates from February 1953, eight months before his death at nearly seventy. Like Sibelius, who was granted a life pension early in his career, Bax's independent wealth meant that he was not obliged to teach, conduct or even compose for a living; and yet, like Sibelius, we find that throughout his working life ambitious scores such as the seven symphonies are interspersed with lesser pieces in undisciplined profusion. Determining precisely how many works he composed depends of course upon what criteria are used to define a single 'work', whether revisions and arrangements count as separate pieces, and so forth; but the main, chronological section has 386 entries, and there are well over 400 separate movements, of which nearly a quarter employ an orchestra. There are nearly fifty chamber works, more than sixty pieces for solo piano, twenty-five choral settings and over 130 songs. As well as music, Bax found the time to write four plays, at least thirty short stories, more than 300 poems, and over sixty miscellaneous articles, reviews and programme notes.

Much of the information in this catalogue has been collated from a wide range of published sources; but many of the details, such as precise wording of titles, dating inscriptions, dedications, foliation, paper types, and so on, derive from a study of Bax's original manuscripts, including unfinished scores and sketches. These constitute a large body of primary material held in public institutions and private collections that has scarcely been explored by previous researchers, and most of the information given here has not been documented elsewhere. Full details of verses set to music by Bax have also been included, and it has been possible for the first time to identify some of the more obscure texts to be found amongst the juvenilia and the early settings of German poetry as well as a few later pieces such as 'Dream Child' and the *Five Greek Folksongs*.

In the main part of the catalogue, Bax's works are arranged as far as possible in chronological order, thus providing a conspectus of the composer's creative life from which one can gain a clearer view of the areas of composition on which he concentrated at specific periods. His earliest works, for example, consist largely of songs, a medium that he virtually abandoned after 1927; there appear to be no works for solo piano written between 1900 and 1910 and few after the late 1920s; while the symphonies are concentrated into an eighteen-year period ending in 1939. The chronological arrangement also disposes of the myth that Bax wrote very little after his appointment as Master of the King's Music: 'He disconcerted everyone by writing hardly another note,' claimed one critic. This is complete nonsense. I have not counted the precise number of notes written by Bax after February 1942, but he certainly composed almost as much during the last decade of his life as in the previous one, though nobody could deny that most of his later works make for pleasant rather than compulsive listening.

Appendices to the chronological part of the Catalogue include a classified index of scores, information about unfulfilled commissions and projected works (much of it deriving from unpublished and oral sources), a concordance of all Bax's extant manuscripts, a bibliography and a discography. In the Introduction I have tried to offer a balanced view of the composer's achievement and reputation, but elsewhere the emphasis is on facts, and the only opinions expressed about individual scores will be found in quotations from other writers.

My interest in Bax's music dates from 1964, and I shall always be grateful to my elder brother, David Parlett, for introducing it to me in the first place. Two years later I met Lewis Foreman, the doyen of Baxographers, who was even then gathering material for his biography of the composer, and we have been comparing notes and exchanging information ever since. I am most grateful to him for his enthusiastic encouragement at all times and for his selfless generosity in sharing the results of his own investigations.

Research has extended over many years, and I am deeply indebted to the following people (some of them now deceased) who kindly allowed me access to manuscripts in their possession, answered questions about Bax, or provided valuable information:

Richard R. Adams, Mary Alwyn, Dennis Andrews, Lady Evelyn Barbirolli, Rob Barnett, †Judge Rodney Bax, John Bishop, †Sir Arthur Bliss, †Dr William Cole, Professor Stewart Craggs, †Anne Crowley, †Norman Del Mar, Dr Jeremy Dibble, Valérie Emery, †Professor Aloys Fleischmann, Dr Clifford Gillam, Sidonie Goossens, Alice Grant, Chloë Green, Elizabeth Gregory, †Julian Herbage, †Imogen Holst, Malcolm Hunter, †Maria Korchinska, John Legard, Stephen Lloyd, Dr Paul R. Ludden, Francis Marshall, †Frank Merrick, Jessica Morton, Oliver Neighbour, †Lord Olivier, Tully Potter, †Dr Edmund Rubbra, †Thelma Reiss, Anthony Rye, Lionel Salter, Christoph Schlüren, Phyllis Sellick, Maureen Sheridan, †John Simons, Peter Thompson, †Myra Verney, Richard Westwood-Brookes, David Wright.

Extracts from correspondence in the BBC Written Archives are reproduced by permission of the BBC. Extracts from the correspondence between Bax and Sir William McKie are reproduced by courtesy of the Dean and Chapter of Westminster. Bax's correspondence with May and Beatrice Harrison appears by courtesy of David Candlin of the Harrison Sisters Trust, whose archive is on permanent loan to the Royal College of Music. Other extracts from Bax's unpublished writings appear by permission of the Trustees of the Sir Arnold Bax Royalty Trust. Acknowledgements are due to the staff of the manuscript repositories listed on pp. 24-5 and of the following institutions: BBC Written Archives, Caversham; British Transport Films; Humanities Research Center, Austin (University of Texas); Muniment Room and Library, Westminster Abbey; National Film Archive (British Film Institute); Royal Archives, Windsor Castle; Royal College of Music; Theatre Museum, Covent Garden.

My thanks specifically to Outi Ahava, Sibelius Academy; John Ahouse, University of Southern California; Chris Banks, Department of Manuscripts, British Library; Professor Paul Banks, Dr Jenny Doctor, Judith LeGrove and Rosamunde Strode, The Britten-Pears Library; Dilys Bateman and Virginia Teehan, Boole Library, University College, Cork; M. Camilleri, National Library of Malta; Pamela Clark, The Royal Archives, Windsor Castle; John Cresswell, Streatham Society; Margaret Crum, Bodleian Library, Oxford; Pat Daniels, BBC Script Library; Luned Davies, Balliol College, Oxford; Suzanne M. Eggleston, Yale University; Jane Gottlieb, Juilliard School; P. J. Harbord and E. M. Rainey, University of Durham; Anthony Hodges, Royal Northern College of Music; Marita Holm and Kitty von Wright, Sibelius Museum; Norma Jessop and Fiona Tipple, University College, Dublin; Marc Joanis and Monique Lecavalier, University of Montreal; Mike Kitcatt, Victoria and Albert Museum; Rachel Ladyman, Nazlin Bhimani, John Wagstaff and Peter Linnitt, BBC Music & Gramophone Library; Kathleen McMorrow, University of Toronto; Dr Robert Manning, BBC Music Documentation; Francis Marshall, Russell-Cotes Art Gallery and Museum; Catherine Massip, Bibliothèque nationale de France, Paris; Edwin M. Matthias and Charles Sens, Library of Congress, Washington; Jane Maxwell, Trinity College Library, Dublin; Brian Payne, former BBC Popular Music Library; R. W. Sanders and J. A. Meikle, Royal Military School of Music; David Sanjek, BMI Archives; Alessandro Servadei, Grainger Museum; Anne Surfling, Alwyn Archive; Alan

Thurlow, Chichester Cathedral; Peter Todd, Karen Trudgeon, Tony Auchover and Robin Norman, Music Sales Ltd. (formerly Chester Music Ltd.); Dr Tony Trowles, Westminster Abbey; Peter Waddington, Hallé Orchestra; Rainer Weber, Breitkopf & Härtel; Marlene Wehrle, National Library of Canada; Sandie Williams, Maecenas Europe; and the following staff of Bax's principal publisher, currently known as Warner Chappell Music Limited: Ray Ayriss, Clive Bright, Daniel Inman, Robert James, Cathy Kopisarow, Ray Lee, Alison Nicholls, Tracy Smith and Caroline Underwood.

I owe a particular debt of gratitude to Professor Arnold Whittall of King's College, London, without whom I should never have completed the doctoral thesis from which this catalogue partly derives. I am also very grateful to Dr Lionel Pike and Professor Stephen Banfield for the trouble they took in reading the thesis and for their most helpful comments; to Ian Gregory and the Trustees of the Sir Arnold Bax Trust for generously providing a subvention in support of publication; to Bruce Phillips, Helen Foster, Janet Moth and Paul Cleal of OUP for their professional expertise; to Colin Scott-Sutherland for kindly allowing access to much unpublished material in his possession and for his warm encouragement at all times; to the late Christopher Whelen for putting his collection of letters from Bax at my disposal and for many illuminating conversations; and to the late Mary Gleaves, Sir Arnold's closest companion during the last twenty-three years of his life, for unique insights into the composer's mind.

Although I partly disagree with the advice given by Dr Routh that heads this preface, another of his famous aphorisms has much to commend it: 'You will find it a very good practice always to verify your references, sir!' The reader is justified in demanding accuracy from a volume of this kind ('accuracy is a duty and not a virtue', wrote Professor Housman), and wherever possible I have collated information at first hand rather than put my trust in published sources. Lewis Foreman and Stephen Lloyd very kindly scrutinized the catalogue before publication and made many valuable comments; but errors of fact or judgement will inevitably come to light, and for these I follow the traditional practice of accepting sole responsibility. I should be delighted to hear from anyone who can provide amendments or additional information.

Graham Parlett — August 1998

The Sir Arnold Bax Trust (registered charity no. 326841) exists to promote knowledge and performance of the composer and his work. Address: 14 Barlby Road, London W10 6AR.

CONTENTS

LIST OF PLATES

Between pages 210 and 211

INTRODUCTION

In his inaugural lecture as Kennedy Professor of Latin at the University of Cambridge, A. E. Housman suggested that a scholar should have no more concern with the merits of the literature with which he deals than Linnaeus or Newton with the beauties of the countryside or the starry heavens. As if to prove his point, he devoted much of his academic life to editing the work of a comparatively obscure Latin poet for whose gifts he admitted having little regard. It is quite possible, of course, to comment objectively on a writer of whom one has a higher opinion than Housman had of Manilius, and yet, as Peter Evans has pointed out, the choice of subject for investigation itself presupposes some kind of initial intuitive response even in those who would claim total objectivity: 'How many Hummel analyses', he asks, 'have been printed to how many of Mozart?'[1] Substitute Bax for Hummel and Britten for Mozart and the relative paucity of writings on the subject of this catalogue is brought into relief.

While it is true that my researches derive ultimately from an intuitive response to a performance of *Tintagel*, it cannot be denied that Bax was an uneven composer whose output includes moments of disconcerting banality as well as pages of tremendous power and beauty. It is also clear that Bax's musical aesthetic, like that of many other conservative composers from the first half of the twentieth century, is regarded with the utmost contempt by those to whom more radical modes of expression represent the only true path of progress, an attitude that, taken to extremes, can result in the wholesale rejection of even such widely acclaimed figures as Britten and Shostakovich, both dismissed by Boulez as 'irrelevant'. But all extremes are a bore, and there is much evidence in these pluralistic days that such attitudes are less rigid. Boulez has even faintly praised Vaughan Williams for at least trying to be 'deeper than the French divertimento culture',[2] and it is possible that Charles Ives's sensible dictum about appreciating the musical mountains and oceans in equal measure may yet be heeded. There is certainly no reason why in principle Bax and Webern, for example (born within a few weeks of each other), should not be appreciated for their individual, diametrically opposed qualities.

Bax's international status has never been in the same category as that of Shostakovich, nor is his historical significance remotely comparable with that of Webern, but his reputation has fluctuated considerably over the years between the extremes of adulation and disdain. It was at its peak during the inter-war years, and after a performance of his Third Symphony (a work admired by Rakhmaninov) a German music critic acclaimed Bax as 'the head of the modern English school'.

[1] Peter Evans, *The Music of Benjamin Britten* (London, 1979), p. 5.
[2] *The Gramophone* (August 1990), p. 359.

Bartók thought highly of his Piano Quartet;[3] Hamilton Harty called him 'the most absolute genius among all our young writers';[4] Henry Wood referred to him as 'a really great composer';[5] Britten commented that he was 'one of the few British composers who wrote successfully in the symphonic form';[6] Sibelius is reported to have called him 'one of the great men of our time'[7] and 'my son in music'[8] and wrote of his 'great admiration for the music of the English Maestro';[9] and Julius Harrison even went so far as to publish the startling opinion that Bax was 'possibly one of the most original composers the world has ever seen'.[10]

In view of his subsequent reputation as the purveyor of a spurious 'Celtic Twilight' in music—a notion that Bax himself dismissed as 'bunk'[11] but that still hangs like an albatross round his neck—it should be remembered that in the period before the Great War he was regarded as a 'difficult' composer who wrote 'ultra-modern' music and appeared 'to have no other ambition than to keep up-to-date in phraseology'.[12] His creative energies were prodigious and for two decades he continued to pour forth an unending torrent of works in most of the traditional forms, of which the vast majority are abstract compositions having nothing whatsoever to do with the Celtic world: '. . . many works of mine have been called Irish or Celtic when I supposed them to be purely personal to the British composer Arnold Bax.'[13] At some point during the mid-1930s, however, his inner compulsion to compose became less intense. Writing to Vaughan Williams at the end of 1935 he complained of being unable to concentrate on composition.[14] The following year in fact proved to be very productive, but by September 1937 he was lamenting to Beatrice Harrison: 'I am quite idle and have written nothing all this year. I must be getting senile!' Although this was again only a temporary lull, by the time that he had completed his Seventh Symphony, in January 1939, the signs were unmistakable. He considered the epilogue of this work to be 'as far as I can go',[15] and in a letter to Edwin Evans dated 24 July he complained that 'the perpetual political tension is scarcely conducive to concentration upon creative work'. Similar

[3] Harriet Cohen, *A Bundle of Time* (London, 1969), p. 228.

[4] Quoted in a catalogue issued by Murdoch, Murdoch & Co. (*c.* 1922).

[5] From a letter to Harriet Cohen dated 31 October 1937.

[6] Quoted in *The Cork Examiner* (5 October 1953). However, Britten had little empathy with Bax's music, and his remark was presumably an off-the-cuff comment prompted by the sudden news of his death rather than a deeply considered opinion.

[7] Quoted in Harold E. Johnson, *Sibelius* (London, 1960), p. 159.

[8] Cohen, *A Bundle of Time*, p. 182.

[9] From a letter to Clifford Gillam dated 10 August 1955 in which Sibelius feels 'deeply honoured' to be asked to accept the presidency of the Arnold Bax Society.

[10] 'The British symphonists', A. L. Bacharach (ed.), *The Musical Companion* (London, 1934), p. 258.

[11] In an undated letter to Christopher Whelen (*c.*1950).

[12] For the sources of these pronouncements see **145**, **152** and **188** in the Catalogue.

[13] From a talk recorded for the BBC in 1949.

[14] From a letter quoted in Michael Kennedy, *The Works of Ralph Vaughan Williams* (London, 1964), pp. 247-8.

[15] Christopher Whelen, 'A Tribute to Sir Arnold Bax', *Music and Musicians* (December 1953), p. 12.

messages were received by others of his friends:[16] 'I feel that my next work—if any—will be "Through Savage Sussex with machine-gun and camera".'[17] In January 1942 he wrote: 'I am sick of being idle, but feel no impulse towards any sort of creation'; and although he occasionally toyed with the idea of writing an Eighth Symphony, he told Christopher Whelen that he had retired—'like a grocer'.

This creative block coincided with a slump in his reputation that continued into the 1940s, and by the time of his death he was looked upon in many quarters as an antediluvian survival whose significance had been grossly inflated by the reactionary views of the British musical press during the previous decades. 'Bax's music', pronounced one dissenting critic, 'is not worth the paper it's written on.'[18] However, whether one adheres to Donald Mitchell's view that Bax reveals 'a most embarrassing glimpse of one aspect of English musical culture'[19] or to Anthony Payne's that he was a 'crippled genius',[20] the mere fact that a composer can provoke such extreme differences of opinion among eminent musicians suggests that his work might have at least a spark of individuality. Indeed the use of the adjective 'Baxian', which is sometimes applied by commentators to the works of other composers, indicates that his music is perceived by some as having distinctive characteristics. His flamboyant use of orchestral colour, his ability to conjure up atmosphere, the powerful emotional intensity of his music, the contours of his melodies, the richness of his harmonies: they all combine to produce a musical language which, at its best, is instantly recognizable and distinct from those of other composers. This is not meant to suggest that Bax sprang 'like Minerva, fully armed from the brain of Jove' (to borrow a phrase from his radio talk of 1949), and it is easy to detect the influences at work on his development: the Austro-German and Chopin-Liszt traditions as revealed in his earliest works; Wagner and Strauss; the spiritual and musical influence of Celtic culture, and especially the poetry of Yeats and Irish folk music; the influence of Glazunov and the Russian nationalist composers, together with Impressionism; the spiritual influence of the North (Scotland, Scandinavia) and the specific impact of Sibelius. Nevertheless, it is the unique combination of these various elements that produces Bax's highly individual sound-world and sets him apart from his contemporaries.

Bax's place in the history of music is impossible to assess absolutely, if for no other reason than that all historical judgments are inevitably provisional, subject to changing fashion and to the reaction of one generation against the opinions of its

[16] Boult, for example: see Jerrold Northrop Moore (ed.), *Music and Friends* (London, 1979), p. 128; also Lewis Foreman, *Bax: A Composer and his Times* (London, 1983), pp. 307, 322-4.

[17] From an undated letter (*c.*1940) to an anonymous addressee, probably Gladys Lees (Harrison Sisters Archive).

[18] Oral communication to Paul Podro. See 'Bax and his Critics', *Bax Society Bulletin*, 1 (February, 1968), p. [4].

[19] 'Crowds kept away by British music', *The Daily Telegraph* (31 January 1962).

[20] Speaking on Radio 3 in response to Mark-Anthony Turnage's dismissal of Bax as worthless (from *A Vaughan Williams Evening*, broadcast on 23 April 1990).

predecessor. In 1922, under the heading 'A BRITISH MUSICAL GENIUS', a leading music critic wrote:

There is no doubt that the outstanding event of the autumn musical season has been the emergence into popularity of Mr. Arnold Bax . . . We must go back to the time when Sir Edward Elgar was composing his great works to find a parallel to the interest excited in the musical world by the first production of his [First] Symphony . . .

With so many works to his credit, and displaying such an infinite variety of qualities, Mr. Bax's position among the leading composers of the world would seem to be securely established.[21]

Time has proved this assessment to have been somewhat wide of the mark.

'How swiftly', wrote Sophocles, 'the reputation of a dead man is forgotten';[22] and Clifford Bax, writing about John Ruskin in 1908, noted that 'In the ten years that follow the death of a prominent man his achievements undergo the severest of criticism. People imagine that the works he left must somehow have lost a portion at least of their original life.'[23] The works of Arnold Bax were not entirely forgotten during the decade following his death; but the apathy of his principal publisher, the inaccessibility of material held by Harriet Cohen and the hostility of certain BBC officials combined to cause a reduction in the number of performances, and it is only during the last two decades that his music has again become familiar. What Bayan Northcott has called 'the retrogressive fashions for minimalism, neotonality and sacred primitivism'[24] has certainly provided a more receptive atmosphere for the rediscovery of Bax than at any time since his death. The availability of a large part of his output in commercial recordings means that there is no longer any justification for dismissing his music en bloc without at least becoming familiar with it, as has often been done in the past. The critic who remarked that Bax's music was so much scrap paper admitted, when challenged, that he was not acquainted with any of the composer's symphonies; there would be no excuse for this today.

In conceding that Bax's work is extremely uneven, it is necessary to put aside a large proportion of his output that does not aspire to great musical heights and that it would be unfair to criticize using the same criteria applicable to works of more serious intent: one should no more judge Bax from the insipid *Mediterranean* than Wagner from his *American Centennial March* or Schoenberg from *Die eiserne Brigade*. A sound assessment must be based on those scores in which his contribution to music is at its most individual: the symphonies, the tone-poems (especially *The Garden of Fand*, *November Woods*, *Tintagel* and the *Second Northern Ballad*), and a few other large-scale pieces, notably *Winter Legends* for piano and orchestra, as well as the best of the chamber works, such as the Piano Quintet and Viola Sonata.

[21] Alfred Kalisch, *Daily News* (5 December 1922).

[22] *Aias*, line 1267.

[23] John Ruskin, *The Crown of Wild Olive and the Cestus of Aglaia*, with an introduction by Clifford Bax (London, 1908), p. x.

[24] From notes for a commercial recording of works by Elisabeth Lutyens (NMC D011).

As the twentieth century draws to a close our knowledge of composers who were writing during its first half has increased enormously through musicological research and the omnivorous appetites of the more adventurous recording companies, and Bax's fortune has undoubtedly improved as a direct result. Nevertheless, it seems doubtful whether his achievements will ultimately be regarded as comparable with those of his beloved Sibelius, as Robert H. Hull and an anonymous writer in *The Radio Times* once suggested (angrily refuted by Boult).[25] And despite extravagant claims made during the 1920s and '30s by the xenophobic British press, it can be seen with hindsight and from a broader perspective that Bax is not a giant of twentieth-century music in the innovative mould of Bartók, Schoenberg or Stravinsky. The less revolutionary but equally notable achievements of Nielsen, Shostakovich or Vaughan Williams perhaps offer closer parallels, and there are many who vehemently maintain that he deserves a place among such figures. But there is no denying the patent failure of Bax's music to achieve anything like their reputation either with the musical academic establishment, to most of whom he is anathema, or with those concert-goers who (to quote Archibald Rowan-Hamilton) 'like their Beethoven and little comforts regular as the clock.' Nor, with few exceptions, does his music make much of an appeal to a younger generation of composers, although the recent curious sight of Peter Maxwell Davies, a former standard-bearer of the avant-garde, conducting John Ireland's Piano Concerto indicates that almost anything is possible.

Despite the existence of a Bax Society in Japan, his music lacks the international status of Elgar, Britten or Walton, and he is often still grouped with certain other British composers of lesser achievement who are regarded by those out of sympathy with their musical languages as being of only parochial appeal and lacking the qualities necessary for a wider audience. One would have thought that Bax's greater emotional range and more cosmopolitan style would have made more of an international appeal, and in view of their modest demands in time and resources as compared with the much-played Mahler it is puzzling that his orchestral works are not more frequently performed. *Tintagel* is certainly still his most famous work, even maintaining a tenuous hold on the concert repertoire, but the vast bulk of his orchestral work seems destined to remained unheard in live performance.

Attention has been drawn to the existence of a musical subculture deterred from attending concerts by promoters understandably more concerned with profit than with widening horizons, whose cravings can only be satisfied by recordings. As Stephen Walsh has put it: 'Bax is an extreme case of those secret musical passions which rule the lives of thousands of music lovers around the country, and which can usually be gratified only through the gramophone.'[26] This is undoubtedly true, and if it were not for the activities of record companies even listeners with powerful

[25] See Lewis Foreman (ed.), *From Parry to Britten: British Music in Letters 1900-1945* (London, 1987), pp. 184-5.

[26] 'Not for the Celtic fringe', *Observer Review* (5 June 1983), p. 32.

urges in that direction would be familiar with only a small proportion of his enormous output. But there is often little consensus about his worth even among those in sympathy with his musical values. Some believe that the chamber works contain his best music, others have a high opinion of the unaccompanied choral works, while others regard his mastery of the orchestra as his long suit. The composer and conductor Christopher Whelen felt strongly that the greater part of Bax's output was of little account and that his reputation should rest on a handful of top-quality scores, especially the Sixth Symphony. He deplored the dissemination of what he regarded as second-rate works, believing that they seriously undermined Bax's general acceptance as an important composer, and had no time for those dewy-eyed enthusiasts who greet everything with indiscriminate rapture.

Arnold Bax thus remains a contentious figure, quite inappropriately for such a self-effacing 'monster of mildness', as he once described himself. Reviled by some, eulogized by others, his life's work will certainly never be consigned to total oblivion—his best scores contain too much of value for that—but it does seem doubtful whether he will ever play more than what he described as 'my own modest part in the world's music'. In view of the rich rewards to be derived from studying, playing and listening to it, many would maintain that Bax's finest work deserves a better fate.

CHRONOLOGY

1883 Arnold Edward Trevor Bax born at 8.30 a.m. on Thursday, 8 November, at 'Heath Villa', Angles Road, Streatham, Surrey (now called 13 Pendennis Road, London SW16): eldest son of Alfred Ridley Bax (1844–1918) and Charlotte Ellen Lea (1860–1940).

1884 A brother, Alfred Aubrey Vernon, born (died 1895).

1886 Another brother, Clifford Lea, born: became a notable poet, playwright, biographer and essayist (died 1962).

1887 Could read simple sentences from newspapers at the age of four. A sister, Evelyn Mabelle Ellen, born (died 1984).

1889 First conscious apprehension of beauty: sunset in Arundel Park.

1891 Could read Beethoven and Brahms on the piano at sight by the age of eight.

1893 Attends a preparatory school in Balham and excels at algebra.

1896 Family moves to Hampstead in North London. Takes violin and piano lessons and attends chamber music concerts. Acts as accompanist to father's private choral society. Begins composing. First visit to a Promenade Concert in September.

1898 Enrols at the Hampstead Conservatoire, studying piano, theory and counterpoint with Dr Arthur James Greenish. A piano sonata ('Op. 1') completed. Receives private tuition in other subjects from Francis Colmer.

1900 Enters the Royal Academy of Music in September. Studies piano with Tobias Matthay and composition with Frederick Corder.

1901 Visits Elgar at Birchwood in August.

1902 Discovers the Celtic world through reading W. B. Yeats's 'The Wanderings of Oisin'.

1903 Wins the Battison Haynes Prize and a Macfarren Scholarship. Visits Ireland for the first time. Discovers the village of Glencolumcille in Donegal, which becomes almost a second home. Acts as accompanist at student performances of operas by Gluck, Weber and Mascagni.

1904 Wins the Charles Lucas Medal for composition with a set of variations, his first orchestral work. Earliest published work, *A Celtic Song Cycle*, written. Earliest extant examples of his poetry date from December.

1905 First public performance of an orchestral work (*A Connemara Revel*) at Queen's Hall on 4 April. Shares the Macfarren Prize for piano playing. Conducts for the first and last time at the Royal College of Music in May. *Cathaleen-ni-Hoolihan* completed in July. Leaves the RAM. A visit to Norway with his mother may date from this year.

1906 Visits Dresden in Saxony during the spring. Hears Strauss's opera *Salome*. Writes a Trio in one movement (later disowned).

1907 Visits Dresden again. Has an affair with Dorothy Pyman. *Fatherland* completed in March. A Symphony in F sketched in April.

1908 String Quintet in G performed in July.

1909 *In the Faery Hills* completed in June. Meets Debussy, d'Indy and Sibelius at gatherings of the 'Music Club'.

1910 Visits Russia and the Ukraine in pursuit of a girl, Natalia Skarginska. Sees the Russian Imperial Ballet for the first time. Meets Sir Henry Wood in September. First Piano Sonata, First Violin Sonata and *Enchanted Summer* completed.

1911 Marries Elsa Luisa Sobrino on 28 January. Honeymoon in Connemara during April. Settles in Rathgar, on the outskirts of Dublin. *Festival Overture* and the ballet *Tamara* composed.

1912 A son, Dermot Colum, born on 11 January (died 1976). *Christmas Eve on the Mountains* written.

1913 A daughter, Maeve Astrid, born on 11 January, exactly a year after her brother (died 1987). Visits the Mediterranean with Holst, Balfour Gardiner and Clifford Bax. *Spring Fire* completed. *The Garden of Fand* sketched. Meets Schoenberg at a 'Music Club' concert.

1914 Returns to live in England. Meets Harriet Cohen (1895-1967), for whom he subsequently leaves his wife and children. *The Bard of the Dimbovitza* completed in December.

1915 The Piano Quintet completed in April, the Second Violin Sonata in August.

1916 Profoundly affected by the Easter Rising. *The Garden of Fand* orchestrated.

1917 *November Woods* orchestrated. *Tintagel* and the *Symphonic Variations* sketched.

1918 Father dies in June. Nominally on the staff of the International Conservatoire of Music as a composition teacher. *A Dublin Ballad and Other Poems* widely circulated in Dublin and promptly banned by the British censor in Ireland.

1919 *Tintagel* orchestrated in January. Visits Queenstown (Dun Laoghaire) and Rathgar with Harriet Cohen in March. Second Piano Sonata completed in July.

1920 *The Truth about the Russian Dancers* first performed on 19 March at the Coliseum. Original version of *Summer Music* orchestrated in the spring.

1921 *Mater ora Filium* written and *The Happy Forest* orchestrated.

1922 Viola Sonata completed in January and the First Symphony in October. Important concert of his music held at Queen's Hall on 13 November. Première of First Symphony on 4 December at Queen's Hall.

1923 *To the Name above every Name* completed in March, the Cello Sonata in November and *St Patrick's Breastplate* in December.

1924 In London at the beginning of the year. Visits Delius in Rapallo during January and February, and Monaco, Naples, Sicily, Turkey and the Greek islands during April. Visits Prague in June for a performance of the First Symphony and meets Janáček. Travels to Spitsbergen and Salzburg during the summer. A visit to north Africa may also date from this year.

1925 Goes to Geneva with Harriet Cohen in November and orchestrates *Cortège* there.

1926 Second Symphony completed in March. Visits Paris and Geneva in April. Stays with E. J. Moeran and Philip Heseltine at Eynsford and writes the *Romantic Overture*. In London during the General Strike. Visits Iceland in mid-July. Meets Mary Gleaves (1904-95) in August, the beginning of a deep and passionate relationship lasting until his death. Third Piano Sonata finished in November.

1927 *Overture, Elegy and Rondo* written in the summer. *Prelude for a Solemn Occasion* and *First Northern Ballad* sketched in October and November. Made a Fellow of the RAM in the summer. Records Delius's First Violin Sonata with May Harrison. Plays at the Blackpool Festival in a performance of his own Piano Quintet. Meets Kodály in London.

1928 Sonata for flute and harp completed in April. Goes to Cork to judge at the annual Féis.

1929 Third Symphony written in London and Arisaig, Inverness-shire. Records his own Viola Sonata with Lionel Tertis on 27 May (not issued until 1980). Visits Glencolumcille in September. First performance of Second Symphony on 13 December in Boston.

1930 Nonet completed in January, *Winter Legends* in April. Visits Cork during April and May for the Féis. First London performance of Second Symphony on 20 May at Queen's Hall. Goes to Morar, Inverness-shire, during the autumn. Briefly visits Glencolumcille, where the Fourth Symphony is started. Returns to Morar to complete the *Overture to a Picaresque Comedy.*

1931 Fourth Symphony completed in February. Takes part in the memorial concert for Philip Heseltine at Wigmore Hall on 23 February. *First Northern Ballad* orchestrated. Works on *The Tale the Pine-Trees Knew* and the Fifth Symphony at Morar during December. Presented with the Gold Medal of the Royal Philharmonic Society and the Cobbett Medal for Chamber Music.

1932 Fifth Symphony completed in March. First performance of Fourth Symphony on 16 March in San Francisco. Visits Stockholm at the end of June with Harriet Cohen and Balfour Gardiner, going on to Helsinki to meet Sibelius again. Cello Concerto completed in Morar during November. First London performance of Fourth Symphony on 5 December at Queen's Hall.

1933 String Quintet completed in January and the *Prelude for a Solemn Occasion* at Morar in February. Visits Paris, Fontainbleau, Venice, Yugoslavia and Greece during April and May.

1934 First performance of Fifth Symphony on 15 January at Queen's Hall. Visits Paris and Cannes, meeting Delius at Grez-sur-Loing in April. Spends the summer in London. Receives honorary D.Mus. from Oxford University on 20 June.

1935 Sixth Symphony completed in February at Morar. Receives honorary D.Mus. from Durham University. First performance of Sixth Symphony on 21 November at Queen's Hall.

1936 *Rogue's Comedy*, *Threnody and Scherzo*, Third String Quartet and *Overture to Adventure* all completed. Important concert of his recent chamber music held on 11 December, the day of King Edward VIII's abdication.

1937 Violin Concerto begun at Morar. Has an affair with Christine Ryan. Knighted at Buckingham Palace on 11 June.

1938 Violin Concerto completed in London. Seventh Symphony begun.

1939 Seventh Symphony completed in January and the *Rhapsodic Ballad* for solo cello in June. First performance of Seventh Symphony on 9 June in New York. A Concertino for piano and orchestra abandoned because of the tense political situation.

1940 Visits Morar in January and begins his autobiography, *Farewell, my Youth.* Goes to Devon and Cornwall during June and July. His mother dies at the beginning of November. Settles in Storrington, Sussex, at The White Horse Hotel. Nothing composed during 1940 and 1941.

1942 Appointment as Master of the King's Music announced on 3 February. Audience at Buckingham Palace on 13 March. Completes his first film score, *Malta, G.C.*, in September.

1943 *Farewell, my Youth* published. *Legend-Sonata* for cello and piano completed in February. First London performance of Seventh Symphony on 22 August at Royal Albert Hall. *Work in Progress* completed in November.

1944 *A Legend*, his last tone poem, finished in May.

1945 *Suite on the Name Gabriel Fauré* completed in June and the *Victory March* in September. Writes incidental music for Clifford Bax's play *Golden Eagle.*

1946 Piano Trio in B♭ completed in January. Visits Dublin in August to teach at a summer course. Returns to Storrington at the end of September and then goes back to Dublin to examine at the university. Goes on to Cork. Admitted to the Honorary Freedom of the Worshipful Company of Musicians on 8 October. *Morning Song* written for the twenty-first birthday of Princess Elizabeth.

1947 Receives honorary Mus.D. from the National University of Ireland on 8 July. Elsa, his wife, dies in September. Visits Cork and Killarney. A pageant-play, *St George*, written with the Poet Laureate, John Masefield, abandoned in October. Writes three fanfares for the wedding of Princess Elizabeth and attends the ceremony in Westminster Abbey on 20 November.

1948 Music for the film *Oliver Twist* composed. Goes to Ireland in August.

1949 Concertante for three solo instruments with orchestra completed on New Year's Day. Concertante for piano (left hand) and orchestra finished in June, and the *Variations on the name Gabriel Fauré* in August.

1950 The 'left-hand' Concertante first performed on 4 July at the Cheltenham Festival. Nothing composed this year.

1951 Appears on the BBC radio programme 'Records I like' in January. Two fanfares written for the radio programme 'Show Business'. Writes music for the short documentary film *Journey into History.* Acts as accompanist at a memorial concert for Balfour Gardiner on 23 April in London.

1952 Attends the funeral of King George VI at Windsor on 15 February. His last work for orchestra, the *Coronation March*, completed on 29 November.

1953 His final composition, the unaccompanied part-song *What is it like to be young and fair?*, written in February for a coronation concert on 1 June. Awarded the KCVO in the coronation honours list. Goes on holiday to the Isle of Wight with Mary Gleaves. Visits his brother, Clifford, for the last time in September and travels to Cork to act as an examiner at University College. Attends a concert of his own works in Dublin on 29 September that concludes with *The Garden of Fand.* Returns to Cork on 1 October and examines at the university on the following day. Dies of a pulmonary embolism at some time between 9.30 and 10 p.m. on Saturday, 3 October, after returning from a visit to the Old Head of Kinsale. Interred in St Finbarr's Cemetery, Cork, on 6 October.

PRELIMINARY NOTES

Anyone familiar with composer catalogues will find that the present work follows many of the usual conventions. The following notes are intended to provide a more detailed guide to its layout and the criteria on which it is based.

1. Scope and Arrangement

All known titles of musical works composed or arranged by Bax are set out by the date of completion in as strict a chronological order as can be deduced from the evidence available. It should be emphasized that the length of a catalogue entry depends entirely on the amount of collatable information about the work in question and has no qualitative significance. Details of published works and of extant unpublished scores are set out in the following order:

Catalogue number: This number (in **bold**) precedes the main title in each entry. For multi-movement works that are intended to be performed complete, such as symphonies, concertos and sonatas, each movement is prefixed by a roman numeral. Works comprising two or more movements that may legitimately be played on their own (such as suites, song cycles, etc.) are nevertheless treated as single entities if they were published or otherwise intended as such, but each individual title has a lower case letter appended to the collective number. Thus the *Four Orchestral Pieces* of 1912–13 are collectively **152**, the individual components numbered **152a**, **152b**, **152c** and **152d**: Bax clearly intended them as a set but, unlike the integrally related movements of a symphony, there is no reason why they should not be performed separately, as indeed they were during the composer's lifetime. An apparent exception is the *Seven Selected Songs* published in 1919, which are listed individually; this is because they were not written as a cycle but, as the title implies, were gathered together several years after composition for the purpose of publication.

Works that Bax produced for more than one medium or in one or more revised versions are noted under the years in which they appeared in their different guises. Thus the *Scherzo* for piano is **154**, the first orchestration is **187**, the pianola arrangement is **212**, and the revised orchestration is **322**, and they are listed under 1913, 1917, *c.* 1918 and 1933 respectively. Works that are complete or of which substantial portions are known to have been composed are listed in the main sequence. But there also exist many unidentifiable sketches and fragments of ideas that either never came to fruition or of which more developed workings have not been traced. These have also been incorporated into the main chronological sequence if they can be dated through their association with the manuscript of a known work. In most cases this procedure is sound, but the danger of automatically assuming that a rough sketch is contemporary with the work on whose manuscript it can be found is exemplified by a draft for part of *Walsinghame* (1926) written on a leaf later borrowed for the short score of the Third Symphony (1928–9), or the trio melody from the *Malta, G.C.* march (1942), which is found jotted down at the foot of the first page of the Sinfonietta (1932).[1] Moreover, it is often impossible to tell whether unrecognizable material associated with drafts was really intended to be part of the same work or derives from a quite different project that may or may not have been completed elsewhere. Sketches that have no obvious relationship to the rest of the music on the manuscript and are likely to have been intended for another work have separate entries, since there is always a remote possibility that related material may eventually be found. Sketches that are thematically unrelated to the main work but seem from their position on the manuscript to be associated with it are not accorded a separate entry. Sketches that occur on isolated sheets of paper and can only be vaguely dated from the handwriting, musical style or type of manuscript paper are listed at the end of the chronological sequence (**Add. 1-20**).

Title: The main title in **bold** upper case letters is the one by which the work should properly be known. Where this differs in wording or spelling from any that may appear on particular copies or states of the score the details are given in a separate title entry. The title is always found at the head of the first page of the score (a few works also having a separate title page), except in the case of sketches and some short scores, when it is absent altogether. A few early songs are also untitled but here the presumed title—that of the poem set—is given in brackets. Bax's extant settings of German and Scandinavian poetry usually have the title in the original language, but for 'lost' songs the English titles have been preferred, since this is how they appear in published lists of works drawn up by himself. For works in more than one movement, the individual titles (if any) and principal tempo indications are listed immediately after the main title, Bax's misspellings of Italian words having been silently corrected. A dash between movements indicates that one follows on from the other without a break.

Date: The wording and punctuation of a dating inscription are given within inverted commas but are otherwise transcribed precisely as they appear on the manuscript, except for the use of the normal epigraphic device for indicating the start of a new line (e.g. 'London | March 14th | 1936'); [*sic*] is used sparingly and only to obviate the suspicion of a printing error. A date can sometimes be found at the end of the published score, copied by the engraver from the manuscript. A few works are dated in Irish Gaelic, usually written in Irish script, but these inscriptions are here transliterated into roman script (with original superscript dot—the mark of aspiration—transcribed as 'h', in the usual way), and are followed by a translation in brackets: thus cpíoċ > 'críoch' [finished]. Most works have some kind of date written on them, and some also have the place in which they were composed or

[1] There is a logical explanation in this instance since there exists a photograph of Bax posing with the Sinfonietta manuscript early in 1942, shortly before *Malta, G.C.* was composed: the score was clearly the first piece of music paper to hand when the melody occurred to him.

orchestrated.[2] Some have only the year, usually at the head of the score; some have the month and the year, usually at the end; some are precisely dated, and in these cases the ordinal suffixes are invariably superscript with a dot or dash below, but the latter are not reproduced in transcription. Evidence for the dating of the comparatively few totally undated scores is given under this heading. Works that can be assigned to nothing more specific than a year are listed alphabetically at the end of that year. In the handful of cases where there is no documention whatsoever (the revised version of *Christmas Eve* (**249**), for instance) a rough date can be inferred from the handwriting and the type of manuscript paper used and from circumstantial evidence.

Dedication: This is usually found at the head of the holograph manuscript to the left of the title, though published scores often have dedications not found on the manuscripts, indicating that Bax added them at proof stage. Dedications on printed scores normally appear on the wrappers, title page and first page, often with variants in typeface and punctuation. In this catalogue, dedications of published works are transcribed from the manuscript if it is extant, otherwise from the first page (not title page) of the printed score, with upper case letters used as appropriate, though to avoid large swathes of italics the many italicized superscriptions have been put into roman. In the few cases where reprints have different typography from the original issue, the first version has been preferred. Any significant discrepancies between the wording on the manuscript and the printed score are noted. The absence of this heading in a catalogue entry means that the work bears no dedication.

Orchestra: Instruments are listed in the usual order with doubling instruments indicated in parentheses. Thus 3(1) 2+1 3(E♭)+1 2+1 = three flutes (the third doubling on piccolo), two oboes + separate cor anglais, three clarinets (the third doubling on E♭ clarinet) + separate bass clarinet, and two bassoons + separate double bassoon. Bax always writes for separate bass clarinet and double bassoon players, and for a separate cor anglais except in the Violin Concerto (**342**); but the piccolo (never more than one) is always played by the second, third or (exceptionally) fourth flute player, and the E♭ clarinet by the third clarinettist except in *The Song of the Dagger* (**160f**), which requires an additional player.[3] It should be noted that horns—usually four of them but occasionally six, three or two—are always in F, and that trumpets—never more than three but occasionally two or one—are in

[2] Bax led a somewhat nomadic existence, but the four commonest place-names actually noted down on his manuscripts are Glencolumcille (with variant spellings) in Donegal (1907–34), Morar in Inverness-shire (1928–39), London (1909-39), and Storrington in Sussex (1942–9).

[3] In Chappell's *Orchestral Hire Library* catalogue of October 1971 the following works were advertised as being 'available with reduced wind': **191**, **213**, **220**, **257**, **277**, **288**, **339**, **364**, **374**. In the catalogue for 1990 these reductions were no longer listed, and according to a former Hire Librarian they existed more in theory than in practice, though the orchestral parts for **220** do have cross-cueing indicated.

C unless otherwise indicated: a few early scores use trumpets in F, but Bax never writes for the B♭ instrument, although he occasionally employs cornets in B♭. When trombones are used Bax always writes for two tenors and one bass, except in *Into the Twilight* (**110**), where four are required to play just a few bars at the climax. 'Tuba' usually means the bass tuba in F, but a euphonium is specified for *Tintagel* (**213**), and a tenor tuba in B♭ for the *Overture to a Picaresque Comedy* (**305**). In the Second and Fourth Symphonies (**276, 307**) both tenor and bass tubas are used, and in *A Song of War and Victory* (**79**) three are specified, in E♭, B♭ and F. The number of percussionists given is the minimum required, the instruments they are to play being listed in parentheses.

Text: The name of the author and title of the text relating to choral and vocal works are given here. For a list of poets and their dates see Appendix 4.

Manuscript: Unless otherwise stated it may be assumed that all manuscripts noted are holograph (i.e. written entirely in Bax's hand, apart from later additions such as engravers' and conductors' markings) and bear the composer's signature, usually to the right of the main title at the head of the score.[4] Most of the juvenilia are signed 'A. E. T. Bax'. From 1902 until *c.* 1905 he emphasized his Welsh (and thus Celtic) third forename: 'Arnold E. Trevor Bax'; thereafter always 'Arnold Bax'. For orchestral works, the final full score was preceded by a short score, with two or three staves to a system and usually containing notes for the intended orchestration. Only a small quantity of these short scores survives, and even fewer preliminary sketches. If more than one manuscript exists of a work in the same state, *A* refers to the first copy, *B* to the second, and so forth. Separate manuscript instrumental parts are not in Bax's hand except for the violin parts of the Sonata in G minor (**49**) and *Concert Piece* (**60**), the cello part of the *Folk-Tale* (**198**), and the parts of the Two Songs with string quartet (**250**).

Details in the **Manuscript** section include the following:

(1) The type of score (short, full, 2-piano, etc.), unless this is obvious (e.g. solo piano works). The subheading *Transcript* refers to a signed excerpt from a score written out by Bax at a later date for a friend or admirer.

(2) The manuscript repository, if an academic or public institution or a publisher's archive, plus any catalogue or inventory number. The names of private owners are published only if they have given their permission; otherwise 'Privately owned'. For abbreviations used see pp. 24-5.

(3) Details of foliation, following the usual conventions: f. 8 = recto of folio 8, f. 8^{v} = the verso; 10 ff. = 10 in all; ff. 1-10^{v} = the first ten of a larger manuscript. Manuscripts not foliated by the institution that owns them have the numbers in square brackets. Since foliation may include cancels (i.e. amendments on scraps of

[4] Only three mature scores do not bear a signature: *Cortège* (**274**), in which the dedication is, exceptionally, written to the right of the title; the arrangement of a Vivaldi Concerto (**286**); and the pastiche Sonata in B♭ (**341**).

paper pasted by Bax over the original) or parts of pages tipped in, pagination is sometimes a clearer guide to the length of a manuscript.

(4) The number of pages with writing on them plus any separate title pages and any that are blank. If Bax has not done the pagination himself, the number of pages is given in square brackets. In multi-movement works, the pagination of each movement is added in parentheses.

(5) The number of bars in the work if fifty or fewer.

(6) 'Incomplete' means that part of the manuscript is missing; 'unfinished' means that Bax obviously broke off without finishing the score.

(7) The writing medium: pencil, ink or (for a few late pieces) ballpoint pen. The colour of ink is usually black or dark blue; exceptions are noted. Juvenilia are written with a stylus pen, later manuscripts with a fountain pen.[5]

(8) Details of the manuscript paper, including the imprint of the manufacturer. The paper most commonly used by Bax was made by Augener Ltd. (Augener & Co.). The different types of identifiable paper are listed under **Abbreviations** below. If the paper has no imprint, the number of staves is given (e.g. '14-staff paper'). The page measurements are given in millimetres (height × width), '*c.*' being used where an original bifolium has been torn in half, leaving a ragged edge, or where a score has been trimmed and tightly bound so that the precise width of a leaf is impossible to determine. Unless otherwise stated, the paper is of an upright format, and it should be observed that for no apparent reason Bax sometimes used sheets of manuscript paper upside down.

(9) Details of bindings are given, where appropriate; otherwise it should be assumed that the manuscript was unbound when inspected. A few scores were bound during Bax's lifetime, and many of those in the British Library have been bound since their bequest by Harriet Cohen, invariably quarter bound in claret-coloured cloth and morocco lettering-piece with gold lettering, usually with a vellum spine. Most others are unbound, often loosely inserted into manilla wrappers or folders and even (in one major repository) carelessly stuffed into padded bags.

(10) If the work is not published in any form, this is indicated here ('Unpublished'); otherwise see under **Publication** below.

Further comments on the manuscript may follow, including details of marginalia, inscriptions, etc.[6] Nearly all manuscripts of published works bear engravers' marks. Passages in scores are cited either by cue numbers or letters or by page numbers and bars: e.g. 149:3 (i.e. the third bar of p. 149).

[5] Some of Bax's writing implements, including a gold 'USA' ballpoint pen, are in University College, Cork.

[6] Words underlined by Bax are printed in italics, and double inverted commas reduced to single.

Publication:[7] Bax wrote nearly 400 works, of which fewer than fifty per cent have been published.[8] The latter word is used in its proper sense, referring to something that is or has been available in print for purchase; publishers' hire material and commercial recordings are not deemed to constitute publication.[9] Only details of works published complete or substantially complete are noted in this section; scores from which short excerpts have been printed in books or articles are not counted. If a work is published in any form, brief details under this heading include the publisher,[10] the plate number in parentheses,[11] the copyright date (usually, but not always, the year of publication), the format—folio (fo.), quarto (4to), octavo (8vo)—and the number of paginated pages. In the case of orchestral scores it may be assumed, unless otherwise stated, firstly that 'fo.' indicates a full score and '8vo' a miniature score,[12] and secondly that sets of parts were printed at the same time and were available for purchase. Likewise the publication of chamber works implies the simultaneous issuing of parts.[13] Publishers are generally able to supply printed orchestral parts for published scores or hand-written ones for unpublished works assigned to them. Orchestral material for some of the unassigned pieces is available through the Sir Arnold Bax Trust. If a score is not published in any form, this is indicated at the end of the **Manuscript** entry. For details of Bax's principal publisher see pp. 19-20; for a list of other publishers see pp. 25-6.

In examining the manuscripts of published works, discrepancies between what Bax wrote and what was printed are often to be found, evidence of careless proof-reading on the composer's part, supported by occasional references in letters to his

[7] The *Catalogue of Printed Music in the British Library to 1980* (London, 1981) lists works published by five other composers named Bax: D. Bax, Ernest Belfort Bax (Arnold's uncle), F. Lincoln Bax, Leonard H. Bax and Saint Yves Bax.

[8] No precise figure can be set down: it depends upon one's definition of a single 'work'; and there must presumably have been lost compositions of which we know nothing.

[9] John Carter, *ABC for Book Collectors*, 6th edn. (New Castle, Delaware, 1992), p. 167: 'The crucial factor in publication remains the offering of the book for sale to the public'. Some music publishers seem to regard a work as 'published' merely if it is assigned to them, regardless of whether it is available in print for purchase or in manuscript for hire only.

[10] In 1943 Chappell took over the scores published by Murdoch and reprinted many of them with new numbers; but no new impressions were issued of titles of which there were still stocks left over (including most of the orchestral works). If the Murdoch details are listed alone, it may be assumed that, although assigned to Chappell, the work in question was not reprinted.

[11] The absence of a plate number indicates that the publisher did not use such a system. On the other hand, the occasional lack of a number for a publication by Murdoch is specifically noted. Current Warner Chappell stock codes (WC prefix) are also given.

[12] There is a tendency nowadays for the older miniature or pocket scores to be replaced by larger 'study scores', and Warner Chappell currently advertise a number of orchestral works as being available in this format as well as in A3 and A4 size.

[13] There are no exceptions to this rule, but one work—the Vivaldi Concerto arrangement (**286**)—has been published only in the form of a set of parts containing many inaccuracies.

dislike of the task.[14] But such details are more appropriate for a critical edition of his works and are outside the scope of this Catalogue.

Performance: Details of the work's first performance (public unless otherwise noted) include the name(s) of the performer(s), the venue and the date. Unless otherwise stated, the venue is in London. If the first performance took place abroad, the British première is also noted. In many cases this heading is omitted for songs and short piano pieces, which were often first played at recitals of which the details have not been traced or, indeed, which may never have been publicly performed at all (e.g. most of the unpublished songs). The non-performance of larger works, on the other hand, is specifically noted. Similarly, it may be assumed, unless otherwise stated, that juvenilia composed before 1903 have never been played in public. Bax's mother used to organize private recitals in her home at 7 Cavendish Square and later at 10 Frognal Gardens, at which it is likely that some works received their first performance, but the printed programmes for only two of these events are known to be extant (see **64**). Titles of conductors (Sir, Dr) follow the usage current at the time of the performance. Press comments are sometimes quoted here if they provide information that would otherwise be lost, such as the encoring of a work or the reception accorded the composer, or remarks by Bax himself on the quality of the performance.

Arrangement: This indicates an arrangement by someone other than Bax for a medium different from the original. The composer's own arrangements of his works have separate catalogue entries.

Adaptation: This appears in a few entries for scores that have been used for purposes other than those for which they were written, such as concert works employed as music for ballets. Television and radio ephemera that have incorporated brief passages as incidental music are not included (e.g. the 1969 BBC TV production of *Treasure Island*, featuring *Tintagel* and *November Woods*).

Duration: A timing given without qualification represents the duration of an actual performance.[15] An estimated duration based on a reading or play-through of the score is qualified by '*c.*' and is meant as a rough guide only. Durations are not provided for incomplete pieces. For multi-movement works that should be played complete, a total timing is given. For scores of which the separate parts may legitimately be played individually, each has its own duration.

Note: This section contains further information about the work, commentaries on aspects of the preceding sections, background information, circumstances of composition, programme notes written by Bax (omitting any musical examples),

[14] 'I am being snowed under with proofs of orchestral parts, and they nearly drive me mad—the tediousness and lack of relief from them is quite appalling.' (From a letter to Francis Colmer dating from January 1932 and presumably referring to the Fourth Symphony.)

[15] For a wider range of timings see the work list in Lewis Foreman, *Bax: A Composer and his Times.*

and occasional anecdotes. Also included are comments deriving from the composer's enormous correspondence with friends, performers and institutions. Words underlined in Bax's original texts are here italicized; unusual or old-fashioned spellings (e.g. 'extasy', 'to-day') are of course retained. Reviews of premières are sometimes quoted, especially for early works. These are included not for their literary or critical merits, which are usually minimal, but either for any light they may throw on the work in question or to indicate how Bax's music was received by his contemporaries. In the case of scores that have eluded all efforts to locate them, documentary evidence is adduced in this section.

Synopsis: This is provided for dramatic works (ballets, plays, films).

2. *Primary Sources: Manuscripts*

The autograph manuscript is naturally the primary source for information about a work, and in collating details for this Catalogue nearly 300 holograph manuscripts have been inspected; in only a comparatively few cases has it been necessary to resort to photocopies. During Bax's lifetime, most of the unpublished manuscripts were retained by him, though some orchestral and chamber works were assigned to publishers, who hired out performing materials. The fate of manuscripts of published works seems to have varied: some were handed back to the composer and some were kept by the publisher, but many have disappeared, perhaps never returned by the engraver. The existence of both versions of unpublished works such as *Christmas Eve* and the *Festival Overture* suggests that Bax was not in the habit of destroying his manuscripts and that many of these lost scores will one day reappear. It seems unlikely that the early pieces printed by Breitkopf & Härtel will come to light,[16] but the survival of many holograph scores published by Murdoch and Chappell encourages the hope that the others may eventually be found.

During the last thirteen years of Bax's life, when he was living at The White Horse Hotel in Storrington, Sussex, most of the manuscripts that he owned were kept in a large trunk in his room. In his will of 10 February 1950 Bax bequeathed all these manuscripts to Harriet Cohen, but in a second codicil dated 18 December 1951 he revoked the bequest. Writing to me on 1 September 1975, the late Julian Herbage reported that after Bax's death his solicitors, Rye, Lawrence & Leman, had asked him to examine the composer's manuscripts; but on doing so he discovered that they were all compositions by E. J. Moeran, for whom Bax had been the literary executor, and he later heard that Miss Cohen had already taken possession of Bax's own scores. Between 1953 and her death in 1967 she distributed a number of these manuscripts to various institutions and individuals at home and abroad, but unfortunately she seems not to have kept a list of what went where. In 1960 she loaned nine autograph scores to the Department of Manuscripts of the British

[16] The staff of Breitkopf & Härtel in Leipzig made a thorough search in January 1991 without success. Much material was lost in a bombing raid in December 1943.

Museum (renamed the Department of Manuscripts of the British Library in July 1973).[17] In her will, dated 11 May 1966, she bequeathed 'to the British Museum all the remainder of the manuscripts . . . presented [*sic*] to me by Sir Arnold Bax (including those which Messieurs Chappell . . . hold and which are my property).'[18] The autograph scores of a few other works, including the Seventh Symphony, can now also be found in the British Library.

Bax's principal publisher, currently known as Warner Chappell Music Ltd., holds the second largest collection of his manuscripts. The rest are to be found in private ownership, such as the families of dedicatees, or in the collections of various institutions for which they had originally been written, such as the BBC, or to which they had been given by Harriet Cohen, such as the two English universities that bestowed honorary degrees on Bax.

3. Secondary Sources: Printed Material

Some printed scores bear the date of composition, and for works of which the manuscripts have not been traced this may be the only source of information. The scores of certain unpublished works of which the titles are known have not been located, and evidence for dating derives from lists of works published or compiled during the composer's lifetime. The principal ones are detailed in the **Abbreviations** below, but it is important to bear in mind that even those compiled by Bax himself or issued with his approval are all incomplete for the dates at which they appeared and contain errors of all kinds. Some, it is true, include titles of works that are quite unknown from other sources and accuracy must be taken on trust in the absence of more reliable information. In the case of some early works details have been confirmed by the resurrection of the manuscripts themselves long after they had ceased to be included in subsequent lists. On the other hand the fifth edition of *Grove's Dictionary*, for example, contains over seventy errors of fact in its far from complete list of Bax's music.

In addition to the sources noted above, other lists were published during Bax's lifetime, such as those that appeared in *Who's Who*, but they do not throw any additional light on his output. References in letters and concert reviews have established approximate dates for several otherwise undatable works.

Bax's principal publisher from 1920 onwards was Murdoch, Murdoch & Co.[19] In 1943 the company was bombed out and taken over by Chappell & Co. Ltd., a publisher mainly of light and popular music, who issued many of the composer's later works and maintained stocks of publications by their predecessors until 6 May

[17] Add. MSS 50173–81. See Pamela J. Willetts, 'Autograph music manuscripts of Sir Arnold Bax', *British Museum Quarterly*, XXIII (1960-1), pp. 43-5.

[18] Chappell's disputed the last clause and still hold the manuscripts to which Miss Cohen refers in her will.

[19] Printed by Augener and issued in the U. S. A. under the imprint of OUP, New York. Their first Bax issue (plate number 1) was the song 'Green grow the Rashes O!' (**203**), published in 1920; their last was the Third String Quartet (**338**), published in 1943.

1964, when a fire at their New Bond Street premises destroyed most of them.[20] From then until Bax's centenary (1983) Chappell's were able to provide only a small number of printed scores (through Francis Music Supply), though they did publish two works that had hitherto remained in manuscript: the *Rhapsodic Ballad* (**345**) for unaccompanied cello in 1968 and the Seventh Symphony (**344**) in 1972. In 1983 Chappell Music Ltd. (as it had become in 1978) reprinted most of the choral works and several chamber pieces in a 'Centenary Edition';[21] and in 1990, as Warner Chappell Music Ltd. (since 1988), they issued a catalogue in which most of the Bax material previously published by themselves and Murdoch was described as being once again in print.

In 1998 the situation is much the same, though some hitherto unpublished works are now advertised as being available for purchase (and thus in a broad sense 'published') in the form of reproductions of the original manuscripts. In the 1980s I collated printed scores of the last three symphonies and a few other works with the holograph manuscripts specifically for the recordings made by Chandos Records Ltd.; but the publishers have never shown any interest in such matters, and little attempt has been made to edit the scores when reissuing them or to correct the numerous misprints they contain.[22] A 'Collected Edition' of Bax's works based on the manuscripts is urgently needed but is unlikely to appear in the foreseeable future. In the meantime performances and recordings will continue to be disfigured by wrong notes.

Queries about the current availability and prices of scores published by or assigned to Warner Chappell Music Ltd. should be addressed to the distributor: Maecenas Europe, 5 Bushey Close, Old Barn Lane, Kenley, Surrey CR8 5AU, England (telephone: +44 (0)181 660 3914; fax: +44 (0)181 668 5273). The hire library is administered by Concord Music Hire Library at the same address (telephone: +44 (0)181 660 4766; fax: +44 (0)181 668 5273). The selling agent for many Warner Chappell publications (including chamber and choral works and study scores of the symphonies) is the Studio Music Company, 77-79 Dudden Hill Lane, London NW10 1BD (telephone: +44 (0)181 830 0110; fax: +44 (0)181 451 6470). These details were correct in August 1998.

[20] Most were printed by Lowe and Brydone Ltd., a few by Symphony Reproductions Ltd. Murdoch publications of Bax's music were issued in medium grey wrappers except for **163**, which had pictorial covers, and some of the songs, which were wrapperless. Chappell publications and reprints were mostly in similar wrappers, but some later issues were mustard, pale yellow or light blue.

[21] Printed by the Arnold Reproduction Co. through the Studio Music Co.

[22] A half-hearted attempt was made by somebody to correct the misprint in the timpani part on p. 18 of the study score of the Third Symphony currently on sale; but the 'correction' is itself incorrect. The published score of the Seventh Symphony is full of mistakes, including two bars repeated.

ABBREVIATIONS

1. Manuscript Papers

Details of paper used by Bax are set out in two categories: (i) Paper manufactured by Augener Ltd. (Augener & Co. until 1904); (ii) Paper manufactured by other companies. Each entry is arranged as follows:

(1) Abbreviation used in this catalogue.
(2) Precise wording of imprint and details of any device.
(3) Number of staves on each page.
(4) Years in which it was used.
(5) Catalogue numbers of the works written wholly or partly on the paper.

A third category (iii) lists details of paper used only by copyists, with the approximate years in which they were probably written out. Odd bifolia used as wrappers are not listed as they may not be contemporary with the manuscript itself. Since the imprint on the paper may be of use for dating purposes, close attention has been paid in examining manuscripts to the precise punctuation and variants in typeface that occur in the imprints of the commonest papers used, those manufactured by Augener. Papers with an AL or ALP abbreviation have a device depicting a galleon within a circle printed above the lettering.[1]

(i) *Paper manufactured by Augener*

A&C 14 'A & Co.'s | Manuscript Music | No. 14.'; 20 staves; 1905, 1908: **72 107.**

AL 8 'AL | No. 8'; 14 staves; post-1912: **69 71.**

AL 10 'AL | No. 10'; 16 staves; *c.* 1921: **250.**

AL 12 'AL | No. 12.';18 staves; 1914-19, 1921-3, 1926-9, 1931, 1934, 1937: **105 133 160c 161-3 165-6 174 176-8 180 183 184 186 188 191 198 206 209-10 215-16 239 242 243 251 253-6 258 265 267-8 279 284 289-90 297 299 301 309 313 320 328 330 336 341 344 + Add. 12-14 16 19.**

AL 12a 'AL | No. 12'; 18 staves; 1924, 1926, 1936-8: **276 338 341-2 344.**

AL 14 'AL | No. 14.'; 20 staves; 1915, 1928, 1930-4, 1938: **158 167 170-3 291-2 302-3 307 313 316-17 319 321 323 325 329-30 337 344 + Add. 8, 18.**

AL 14a 'AL | No. 14'; 20 staves; *c.* 1921, 1923-5, 1928: **249 264 269 273 295.**

AL 14b 'A.L. | No. 14.'; 20 staves; 1917, 1919-21: **188 191 213 215a, c 218 228 235 237 250 273.**

AL 14c 'A.L. | No. 14'; 20 staves; 1924-6, 1928: **271-3 276-8 297 309 + Add. 6-7, 9.**

AL 16 'A.L. | No 16.'; 22 staves; 1914, *c.* 1920: **158b 220 + Add. 1.**

AL 16a 'A.L. | No. 16.'; 22 staves; 1916: **179.**

AL 16b 'AL | No. 16.'; 22 staves; 1916: **179.**

[1] See plate 5, where it is visible in the bottom left-hand corner of the manuscript illustrated.

AL 18 'AL | No 18.'; 24 staves; 1913-14, 1918-20: **134 154 160d, f 187 209-12 220 + Add. 4, 5.**
AL 18a 'AL | No. 18'; 24 staves; 1921-2, 1932: **245 249 260 315.**
AL 29 'AL | No. 29.'; 30 staves; 1913-14: **153 160f.**
AL 29a 'AL | No. 29'; 30 staves; 1922-34: **256 264 267 274 276-8 286 297 303 307 309-10 313 326b.**
AL 29b 'A.L. | No. 29'; 30 staves; 1933-9: **320 322 325-27a 329 330-2 334-5 340 344.**
[AL] 29 'N°· 29.';[2] 30 staves; 1914-17: **160f 164 179 187.**
ALM 8 'AL | Manuscript Music | N°· 8.'; 14 staves; 1914: **159 + Add. 11.**
ALM 10 'AL | Manuscript Music |N°· 10.'; 16 staves; 1904, 1914: **60 158a, c.**
ALM 12 'AL | Manuscript Music | N°· 12.'; 18 staves; 1905-8, 1911-14, 1916, 1919: **66 84-5 95 106 110 138 146 148 153 156a, c 160d 175 + Add. 10.**
ALM 14 'AL | Manuscript Music | N°· 14.'; 20 staves; 1905-11, 1915: **67 72 77 81 100 102-3 105-8 113 124 128 134 138 166.**
ALM 16 'AL | Manuscript Music | N°· 16.'; 22 staves; 1905, 1908, 1919, 1931: **70 108 217 310.**
ALM 18 'AL | Manuscript Music | N°· 18.'; 24 staves; 1905, 1911-14, 1918, *c.*1931: **79 98 134 136 145 152d 157 170 220 + Add. 17.**
ALM 29 'AL | Manuscript Music | N°· 29.'; 30 staves; 1910, 1912-14: **128-9 145 152a-c 153 160a, b, e.**
ALM 30 'AL | Manuscript Music | N°· 30.'; 21 staves with names of orchestral instruments printed in left margin; 1945: **364.**[3]
ALP 12 'A.L. No 12 | Printed in England'; 18 staves; *c.* 1935, 1939: **334 345-6 364.**
ALP 14 'A.L. No 14 | Printed in England'; 20 staves; 1942: **347.**
ALP 16 'A.L. No. 16 | Printed in England'; 22 staves; 1918: **70 100 108.**
ALP 18 'A.L. No 18 | Printed in England'; 24 staves; 1936, 1938: **336-8 342 344 370d.**
ALP 29 'A.L. No. 29 | Printed in England'; 30 staves; 1938-9, 1948: **343-4 346 374.**
ALP 30 'A.L. No. 30 | Printed in England'; 21 staves with names of orchestral instruments printed in left margin; 1943-5, 1948: **354 356-7 364 374.**
AMM 10 'Augener's | Manuscript Music | N°· 10.'; 16 staves; 1900-1: **42-6.**
AMM 12 'Augener's | Manuscript Music | N°· 12.'; 18 staves; 1901-3: **49 55 57 67.**
AMM 14 'Augener's | Manuscript Music | N°· 14.'; 20 staves; 1903-5: **56 61 67.**
AMM 18 'Augener's | Manuscript Music | N°· 18.'; 24 staves; 1905: **79.**

[2] The stop is actually printed beneath the superscript 'o' on this and other similar papers.

[3] The names of the instruments are printed in the same typeface as for ALP 30, but the lettering of the Augener imprint resembles those on the other ALM papers, suggesting a much earlier date for the manufacture of the paper.

RC 1 'R.C.1 | Printed in England';[4] 12 staves; 1945: **352 362**.

(ii) *Paper manufactured by other companies*

AC '"ACME." P & W.'; 12 staves; 1900-2, 1943:[5] **28 40 48a 50 52 54 354**.
BC 5 [Bosworth & Co., Ltd] 'B.C. | No. 5.' [the letters over a lyre as part of a device];[6] 18 staves; 1907: **95**.
BC 8 [Bosworth & Co., Ltd.] 'B.C. | No. 8.' + device as for BC 5; 24 staves; 1908-9: **110 114**.
BH 12 [Breitkopf & Härtel] 'B.& H.Nr.12.C.' + device of a bear holding a caduceus in its left hand, resting on a shield bearing the head of Athena; below: '1719'; 20 staves; 1901-22: **49 55**.
BH 43 [Breitkopf & Härtel] 'B.& H.Nr.43.C.' + device as for BH 12; 32 staves; 1918: **210**. Unused sheets also found with MSS of **243 370**.
CH 26 'Chappell 26'; 26 staves; 1952: **385**.
HKS 'HAWKES | LONDON | & SON' [in a circle, the whole embossed not printed]; 24 staves; 1948: **374**.
IM '"Impervious" M & C°.'; 24 staves; 1944: **356-7**.
JH 'J. HARWOOD, [space] LONDON.'; 12 staves; 1896-8: **6-8, 17-22**.
JWC 14 'J & W | CHESTER [in a wreath] | LONDON & BRIGHTON | N°. 14'; 24 staves; 1932: **313**.
JWC 18 'J & W | CHESTER | LTD [in a circle] | LONDON | N°. 18'; 18 staves; 1942: **347**.
PO 'The "Portland."'; 12 staves; 1913: **175**.
1507 '1507' [manufacturer unknown]; 18 staves; 1931: **308**.

(iii) *Paper used by copyists only*

A&C 28 'A[ugener] & Co.'s | Manuscript Music | No.28.'; 12 staves; *c.* 1904: **59**.
AL 8a 'AL | No.8.'; 14 staves; *c.* 1915: **162**.
ARCO 'ARCO No 5'; 24 staves; *c.* 1953: **385**.
BBC 'BBC | MUSIC | MSS | PAPER | 12 stave | Plain'; 12 staves; early 1930s(?), 1951: **303 380**.
BC 6 [Bosworth & Co., Ltd.] 'No.6' + device as for BC 5 and 'Printed at Leipzig.' on the right of the page; 20 staves; 1910: **131**.
BC 7 'No. 7 (22 Staves)' + device as for BC 6 and 'Made and Printed in England by BOSWORTH & Co., LTD.' on the right of the page; 22 staves; *c.* 1944: **354**.

[4] Identifiable as being made by Augener through the use of the same galleon device as for the AL and ALP papers.

[5] See **354** in the Catalogue for an explanation of this late use of early paper.

[6] Unlike all other imprints, which appear on both leaves of a conjugate pair, this one is found only on the obverse of the first leaf.

BH III [Breitkopf & Härtel] 'III. | 6.11.' + device as for BH 12; 12 staves; *c.* 1907-10: **93 101 102 109 116**.
C 'C PAPER'; 12 staves; post-1935: **334**.
HLE 'H. Lard Esnault | Ed. Bellamy SR. | PARIS.'; 12 staves; *c.* 1905: **65**.
SC 'G. Schirmer, Inc., New York | Style No.6—24 Staves | Printed in the U.S.A.'; 24 staves; post-1921(?): **117**.
TP 'T.P.12-2'; transparency paper; 12 staves; 1950s or '60s: **378**.
2a '2a'; 12 staves; *c.* 1924: **265**.

2. Manuscript Repositories[7]

These are in England except as noted.

BBC British Broadcasting Corporation (Music Library), London.
BDL Bodleian Library (University of Oxford), Oxford.
BL British Library (Department of Manuscripts), London.
BMI Broadcast Music Inc. Archives, New York, USA.
BNF Bibliothèque nationale de France, Paris, France.
BNM Bibljoteka Nazzjonali [National Library of Malta], Valletta, Malta.
BPL Britten-Pears Library, Aldeburgh, Suffolk.
EFC Edwin Fleisher Collection, Philadelphia, Pennsylvania, USA.
GM Grainger Museum, University of Melbourne, Victoria, Australia.
JNUL Jewish National and University Library, Jerusalem, Israel.
KB Kongelige Bibliotek [Royal Library], Copenhagen, Denmark.
LC Library of Congress, Washington DC, USA.
ML Memorial Library, Stanford University, California, USA.
NYPL New York Public Library, New York, USA.
RAM Royal Academy of Music, London.
RMSM Royal Military School of Music, Kneller Hall, Twickenham, Middlesex.
SA Sibelius-Akatemia [Sibelius Academy], Helsinki, Finland.
SB Statsbiblioteket [State and University Library], Århus, Denmark.
SM Sibeliusmuseum [Sibelius Museum], Åbo (Turku), Finland.
TCD Trinity College Library, Dublin, Republic of Ireland.
UCC University College, Cork (Boole Library), Republic of Ireland.[8]
UCD University College, Dublin, Republic of Ireland.
ULC University Library, Copenhagen, Denmark.
ULD University Library, Durham.

[7] For publishers' archives see next section (3). Since this catalogue is not intended primarily for librarians, the queer-looking *RISM* sigla (e.g. 'Lam' for the Royal Academy of Music Library) have been avoided.

[8] In 1954 Harriet Cohen agreed to present the College with a selection of manuscripts and personalia to be housed in the Bax Memorial Room in the east wing, which was opened by Vaughan Williams on 15 October 1955. As part of the Music Department, the Memorial Room was later transferred to another building, but in 1988 the material was rehoused in the Boole Library.

ULL	University Library, London.
ULSC	University Library, Southern California, USA.
ULY	University Library, Yale (New Haven), Connecticut, USA.
WML	Westminster Music Library, London. (Formerly known as the Central Music Library Ltd.)

3. Publishers

These are London-based except as noted.

AFM	Anglo-French Music Co. Ltd. (1916). Taken over by OUP in 1925.
AHC	Ascherberg, Hopwood & Crew Ltd. (1906). Taken over by Chappell & Co. Ltd. in 1970.
AUG	Augener Ltd. (1855). Augener & Co. until 1904; taken over by Galliard Ltd. in 1962, by Stainer & Bell Ltd. in 1972, and subsequently by Music Sales Ltd., Bury St Edmunds.
BSY	Boosey & Co. (1816). Boosey & Hawkes Ltd. from 1930.
CA	Charles Avison Ltd. (1905-18). The Avison Edition was the publishing section of the Society of British Composers, published by Breitkopf & Härtel, Novello & Co. Ltd. and, from 1914, L. J. Cary & Co.; taken over by J. & W. Chester in 1918.
CF	Carl Fisher Inc., New York (1872).
CH	Chappell & Co. Ltd. (1810). Chappell Music Ltd. from 1978, Warner Chappell Music Ltd. from 1988. The current address and telephone and fax numbers for Bax's main publisher are given on p. 20, paragraph 3.
EA	Edwin Ashdown Ltd. (1860). Ashdown & Parry until 1891; taken over by Music Sales Ltd., Bury St Edmunds.
EME	Éditions Max Eschig, Paris (1907). Through United Music Publishers Ltd.
EN	Enoch and Sons. Taken over by Edwin Ashdown Ltd. in 1927.
FI	Fatrock Ink, Los Angeles. Selling agent: Theodore Presser Company, Bryn Mawr, PA, USA (through Universal Edition in the UK).
FMP	Fand Music Press. Distributed by Blumlein's, Petersfield, Hampshire.
JW	Joseph Williams (1808). Taken over by Augener Ltd. in 1961, by Stainer & Bell Ltd. in 1972; Bax scores assigned to Chappell & Co. Ltd. in 1975.
JWC	J. & W. Chester (1860). Founded in Brighton; refounded, London, 1915; J. & W. Chester Ltd. 1920; J. & W. Chester/Edition Wilhelm Hanson London Ltd. 1972; Chester Music Ltd. 1992 (division of Music Sales Ltd., Bury St Edmunds).
LM	Lyra Music Company, New York.
MM	Murdoch, Murdoch & Co. (Music Department: *c.* 1884). Taken over by Chappell & Co. Ltd. in 1943.
MMP	Masters Music Publications, Inc., Boca Raton, Florida.
NOV	Novello & Co. Ltd. (1811).
OUP	Oxford University Press (Music Department: 1923-4).

SB Stainer & Bell Ltd. (1907). Bax material assigned to Chappell & Co. Ltd. in 1975.
SMC Studio Music Company. Sole selling agents for many CH publications.
SMP Saga Music Publishing Ltd., Harlington, Middlesex (division of TP).
SR Sidney Riorden, Soho. Taken over by J. & W. Chester *c.* 1918; but the only Bax work published (**129**) was assigned to Murdoch & Murdoch.
TP Thames Publishing (1970). See also SMP above.
WC Warner Chappell Music Ltd. (see CH). Abbreviation used only as part of stock code numbers currently in use by this publisher (e.g. WC0464).

4. Published Sources

BMSA *The British Music Society Annual* (London: The Society of British Composers, 1920), pp. 157-9.
CSS Colin Scott-Sutherland, *Arnold Bax* (London: J. M. Dent, 1973).
FMY Arnold Bax, *Farewell, my Youth* (London: Longmans, Green and Co., 1943).[9]
FMY2 Lewis Foreman (ed.), *Farewell, my Youth and Other Writings by Arnold Bax* (London: Scolar Press, 1992; now Aldershot: Ashgate Publishing Ltd.).[10]
Gr2 J. A. Fuller Maitland (ed.), *Appendix to Grove's Dictionary of Music and Musicians*, 2nd edn. (London: Macmillan Publishers Ltd., 1914), p. 612.
Gr3 H. C. Colles (ed.), *Grove's Dictionary of Music and Musicians*, I, 3rd edn. (London: Macmillan Publishers Ltd., 1927-8), pp. 248-9.
Gr5 Eric Blom (ed.), *Grove's Dictionary of Music and Musicians*, I, 5th edn. (London: Macmillan & Co. Ltd., 1954), pp. 511-12; Supplement (1961), p. 27.[11]
LF Lewis Foreman, *Bax: A Composer and his Times* (London: Scolar Press, 1983); 2nd edn. (1988; now Aldershot: Ashgate Publishing Ltd.).
MGG F. Blume (ed.), *Musik in Geschichte und Gegenwart*, I (Kassel: Bärenreiter, 1949-51), pp. 1428-9.
MT Edwin Evans, 'Modern British Composers. II. Arnold Bax', *The Musical Times* (1 April 1919), pp. 154-6.
WWC W. W. Cobbett, *Cobbett's Cyclopedic Survey of Chamber Music*, I, 2nd edn. (Oxford University Press, 1963).
YB1 *Year Book of the Society of British Composers* (1906-7), p. 28.
YB2 *Year Book of the Society of British Composers* (1912), p. 28.

[9] Page references are to this original edition rather than to Lewis Foreman's illustrated version (next entry), which has different pagination.
[10] References to this publication will be found only in Appendix 7.
[11] The list in the fourth edition of *Grove's Dictionary* (1940) contains nothing of significance, and the one in *The New Grove* (1980) was based on an earlier catalogue that I had compiled in 1972. Neither is cited in the present work.

5. Instrumental and Vocal

A	altos	ob.	oboe
anv.	anvil	org.	organ
B	basses	perc.	percussion(ists)
bar.	baritone	pf.	piano
b.d.	bass drum	qt.	quartet
b.fl.	bass flute	ratt.	rattle
bn.	bassoon	S	sopranos
b.ob.	bass oboe	sarr.	sarrusaphone
br.	brass	s.d.	side drum
c.a.	cor anglais	sext.	sextet
cast.	castanets	sop.	soprano
cel.	celesta	str.	strings
chor.	chorus	T	tenors
cl.	clarinet	tamb.	tambourine
crnt.	cornet	tbn.	trombone
cym.	cymbal(s)	t.d.	tenor drum
d.b.	double bass	ten.	tenor
euph.	euphonium	timp.	timpani
fl.	flute	tpt.	trumpet
gl.	glockenspiel	Tr	trebles
gtr.	guitar	tri.	triangle
heck.	heckelphone	va.	viola
hn.	horn	vc.	(violon)cello
hp.	harp	vn.	violin
hpd.	harpsichord	w.m.	wind machine
m.d.	military drum	w.w.	woodwind
mezz.	mezzo-soprano		

6. Bibliographical and General

Add. MS	Additional Manuscript	fo.	folio format
arr.	arranged by; arrangement	f.sc.	full score
attrib.	attributed to	introd.	introduction; introductory
br.	broadcast	maj.	major mode
comp.	compiler	min.	minor mode
cond.	conductor	min.sc.	miniature score
dedic.	dedication; dedicatory	movt.	movement
ed.	editor	MS(S)	manuscript(s)
edn.	edition	n.d.	no date of publication
f(f).	folio(s)	opp.	opposite
fl.	*floruit* [flourished]	orch.	orchestrated; orchestration

p(p).	page(s)
pagin.	paginated; pagination
pf.sc.	piano score
pl.no.	plate number
pseud.	pseudonym
rev.	revised; revision
sh.sc.	short score
st.sc.	study score
t.p.	title page
trans.	translator
unpag.	unpaginated
vol(s).	volume(s)
v.sc.	vocal score
4to	quarto format
8vo	octavo format

CATALOGUE OF MUSIC (1896–1953)

1896

1 BUTTERFLIES ALL WHITE for voice and piano

Note: According to Bax himself, his first composition was a piano sonata written at the age of twelve (see **2** below); but his sister, Evelyn, maintained that it was a song called 'Butterflies all White'. Although no poem with this title appears to have been published, there is a translation by John Davidson of François Coppée's play *Pour la couronne* that includes an untitled poem beginning:

At sixteen years she knew no care;
How could she, sweet and pure as light?
And there pursued her everywhere
Butterflies all white.[1]

The fourth line, which is repeated with variants in subsequent verses, was also used as the title for the only published setting of the poem, by Olga Rudd (BSY, 1907). Davidson's translation of the play was used for a successful production that opened on 27 February 1896 at the Lyceum Theatre, the verses in question being recited by Mrs Patrick Campbell. Assuming that this really is the source of the title, it is possible that a member of Bax's household may have had a copy of the play that he used for his setting; or he may have come across the poem in one of the numerous magazines that reviewed the production.[2]

2 SONATA for piano

Note: 'My pristine attempt at composition was coincident (very fittingly my enemies might snarl) with an attack of sunstroke when I was twelve. A sonata of course, no less! I continued to pour forth sonatas for two years until my father came to the decision that something ought to be done about it . . .' (*FMY*, p. 16). This event must have occurred in the summer of 1896, shortly after the Bax family had moved from South London to Hampstead, and this is confirmed by J. A. Forsyth: 'His first composition was perpetrated when he was 12, and was written in bed after an attack of sunstroke caught whilst playing cricket at Hampstead.'[3] The same story can also be found in Clifford Bax's memoir of his brother.[4] The score is untraced.

[1] *For the Crown. A Romantic Play, in Four Acts* (London, 1896, the British Library's copy bearing a date stamp of 6 March 1896). The poem is recited near the start of Act II (p. 22) by Militza, a slave. See also Andrew Turnbull (ed.), *The Poems of John Davidson*, 2 (Edinburgh and London, 1973), p. 469.

[2] See, for example, *The Sketch*, 165, XIII (25 March 1896), p. 388, in which the second verse of the poem is quoted in full. It was not published separately from the play until 1902.

[3] 'Pen Pictures of Personalities Past & Present . . . No. 4 Arnold Bax', *R. A. M. Magazine*, 78 (June 1927), pp. 3-4.

[4] This was written for Christopher Whelen and first published in Lewis Foreman (ed.), *Farewell, my Youth and Other Writings by Arnold Bax*, pp. xxiii-xxx.

3-5 SONATAS for piano

Note: The passage from *FMY* quoted in **2** above suggests that Bax had produced a torrent of sonatas after his initial attempt. But since it is impossible to know precisely how many, the minimum of three implied by **15** below ('No. 5') is adopted here. None appears to be extant.

1897

6 [UNTITLED]: Fragment for violin and piano

Date: Undated but immediately preceding **7**.
Manuscript: UCC; f. [13]; [1] p.; 11 bars (unfinished); JH paper (289 × 238); f. [12ᵛ] contains a preliminary sketch for the opening two and a half bars only. Unpublished.
Performance: Bernard Partridge (vn.), Andrew Pledge (pf.); British Music Information Centre; 21 April 1983 (lecture-recital by Graham Parlett, *et al.*).
Note: This MS book and the volume of *Clavierstücke* (**9-16** below) contain Bax's earliest extant compositions, although it is impossible to tell which is the earlier. *Clavierstücke* contains fair copies of pieces dating from '1897-8', while this volume has pieces individually dated between 31 October 1897 and 27 February 1898. It may therefore be that some of the entries between **9** and **16** should precede works numbered **6-8**.

The MS book in UCC is an unfoliated volume bound in dark green leather with 'MUSIC | BOOK' embossed in gold on the upper cover and a harp on the lower. There are 30 pages of MS (289 × 238), of which ff. [11], [12], [20], [21ᵛ] and [22] to [29ᵛ] are blank; ff. [1ᵛ] and [30] are the reverse and obverse respectively of the marbled free endpapers, f. [1ᵛ] having a pencilled price (2/-) in the top left-hand corner. It also contains choral and vocal pieces written in three different hands (*A*, *B* and *C*), none of them Bax's. Details of only one of the texts set (No. 5 below) are identified in the MS:
1. 'Two Barks [barques] met on the deep mid-sea' for sopranos, basses and piano (*A*; ff. [1ᵛ-4]): These words do not appear in any poetical or vocal indexes that have been consulted.
2. 'Blow gentle gales' for two sopranos and one bass (*A*; ff. [4-7ᵛ]): This unidentified glee has words by Thomas Morton and comes from Sir Henry Bishop's three-act opera *The Slave*, first published in 1817.
3. 'Come unto me' for SATB (written in a very neat hand: *B*; ff. [8ᵛ-10]): Unidentified setting of words from St John's Gospel, VI, 37 ff.
4. 'Lead kindly light' for TrATB (pf. sc. only) (*C*; f. [10ᵛ]): Unidentified setting of words by Cardinal Newman.
5. 'Castles in the Air' for voice and piano (*C*; f. [11ᵛ]): This is identified on the score as being by James Ballantine, arranged by George Croal. The original version comes from Ballantine's *One Hundred Songs . . . with Melodies Original and Selected* (Glasgow, 1866), pp. 12-13. Ballantine wrote the words, which are printed on the

page opposite the melodic line, adapted by R. Adams, which Croal has harmonized.

The presence of these transcriptions in Bax's notebook is explained by the fact that from the age of thirteen (1895-6) he had acted as the accompanist for his father's private choral society, which was then under the direction of John Post Attwater, in whose hand it may be that some of the pieces are written. According to *FMY*, p. 18, they 'studied long-outmoded British works from the back shelves of Messrs. Novello's store, all by composers who by virtue of their mildness might well have been described as "sheep in sheep's clothing",' a description that is in accord with the music to be found in the notebook.

At the foot of f. [5^{v}] Bax has transcribed (incorrectly) the first few bars of the fugato from Beethoven's Quartet in F minor, Op. 95. At the foot of f. [6^{v}] he has rewritten the first five bars of the same piece. At the top of f. [8] there is a two-bar cadence in Bax's hand on two staves with 'Page 19.' written above them, which must refer to another, unidentified, score.

7 VARIATIONS ON AN AIR IN G MINOR for piano

Date: 'Oct 31. 1897.'
Manuscript: UCC; f. [13^{v}] of the MS book described in **6** above; [1] p.; 43 bars (unfinished), consisting of the theme (26 bars) and part of a first variation marked 'poco piu moto'. Unpublished.

8 VARIATIONS IN G MINOR for piano

Date: Undated but immediately following **7** above.
Manuscript: UCC; f. [14] of the MS book described in **6** above; [1] p.; 36 bars (unfinished), consisting of the theme (16 bars), 'Var 1. | Alla chorale' (16 bars), and the beginning of a second variation (6 bars). Unpublished.
Note: Despite their similar titles, **7** and **8** are thematically unrelated.

1897–8

9–16 CLAVIERSTÜCKE for piano (except 15)

Title: 'Clavierstücke. by A.E.T. Bax 1897-8.' (title/contents page).

'Minuetto in E minor' (**9**)
'2 Hungarian Dances': 'No 1. B♭ minor' (**10a**); 'No 2. A minor' (**10b**)
'3. Mazurkas.': 'No 1 A minor' (**11a**); 'No 2 B minor' (**11b**); 'No 3. C minor' (**11c**)
'2 Scherzi': 'No 1. A major' (**12a**); 'No. 2 E major' (**12b**)
'Prelude in G major' (**13**)
'Nocturne in B major' (**14**)
'Sonate in D minor' (**16**) (for **15** see below)

Variant titles that appear at the head of each piece:

'Minuet in E minor' (**9**)

'2 Hungarian Dances. Ra's dance.' **(10a)**
'2 Hungarian Dances | No 2 On the Mountains' **(10b)**
'Menuet in E minor' **(15)** (this is **9** arr. for w.w. and str.; not listed on t.p.)
'Sonata D.minor | No 5.' **(16)**

Date: '1897-8'.
Manuscript: BL (Add. MS 54768); 15 ff. + 4 blank; t.p. + 28 pp. (1-21, [22-3], 24-7, [28]) + 8 blank); 12-staff paper (292 × 235). The MS book has limp, faded lavender cloth covers with 'Music' in gold on the upper cover; the pages are sewn in. Formerly the property of Ian Colvin, it was sold at Christie's on 18 December 1968 (lot 22) to Bernard Quaritch Ltd. and acquired for £90 by the BL in 1979. *Foliation*: title/contents p. (f. 1^{v}); **9**: f. 2-2^{v}; **10a**: ff. 2^{v}-3; **10b**: ff. 3^{v}-4; **11a**: f. 4^{v}; **11b**: f. 5; **11c**: ff. 5^{v}-6; **12a**: f. 6-6^{v}; **12b**: ff. 6^{v}-7^{v}; **13**: f. 7^{v}; **14**: ff. 8-9^{v}; **15**: ff. 10-12; **16**: ff. 12^{v}-15^{v}.
Publication: *Nocturne* **(14)** *only*: In Connie Mayfield (ed.), *Arnold Bax. Selected Works for Piano* (TP, 1986), 4to, pp. 7-12.
Performance: *Bars 1-11 of* **14** *and 1-6 of* **10b** *only*: David Owen Norris (pf.); British Music Information Centre; 3 February 1983 (lecture-recital given by Lewis Foreman, *et al.*).
Note: The contents of this MS book are obviously fair copies of existing works and may well have been among the pieces shown to Sir Frederick Bridge in 1898, when Bax's father was considering the possibility of a musical career for his son (*FMY*, p. 16). The *Menuet* **(15)** is scored for flute, oboe, 'clarionet', bassoon (one of each) and two violins, viola and cello. The absence of double bass suggests that the work is for an octet rather than a chamber orchestra.

1898

17 SONATA, Op. 1 for piano

Date: 'Feb. 27, 1898'.
Manuscript: UCC: ff. [14^{v}-18] of the MS book described in **6** above; 8 pp., consisting of a complete first movement (pagin. 1-7) and the first three bars of an Adagio (p. 8). Unpublished.
Note: Although designated 'op. 1' this sonata is obviously not his 'pristine attempt at composition' (see **2** above). Only three other extant works bear opus numbers: *Trio in One Movement*, Op. 4 **(87)**, *Fatherland*, Op. 5 **(92)**, and Symphony in F, Op. 8 **(95)**. It is not known to which scores Opp. 2, 3, 6 and 7 were assigned, although there are far more than four substantial works dating from between 1898 and 1907. But in any case it is probable that by the time Bax came to ascribe numbers to works written during his twenties he had discounted this immature sonata and started the sequence from another, unspecified, score. Since Op. 5 was written in March 1907 and Op. 8 was completed on 3 April, with no works apparently intervening (except possibly the song 'The Fiddler of Dooney' **(93)**, which also dates from March), it is clear that Bax's use of the system was erratic, and he soon abandoned it.

18 [UNTITLED]: Fragment for piano

Date: Undated but immediately following **17**.
Manuscript: UCC; f. [18^{v}] of the MS book described in **6** above; [1] p.; 27 bars (unfinished). Unpublished.
Note: This fragment is headed 'solo' and is of a bravura character: perhaps an excerpt from an imaginary piano concerto.

19 [UNTITLED]: Fragment for piano

Date: Undated but immediately following **18** above.
Manuscript: UCC; f. [19] of the MS book described in **6** above; [1] p.; 21 bars (unfinished). Unpublished.

20 [UNTITLED]: Fragment for piano

Date: Undated but immediately following **19** above.
Manuscript: UCC; f. [19^{v}] of the MS book described in **6** above; [1] p.; 45 bars consisting of a Scherzo (32 bars) and Trio (13 bars) with 'da capo' marked at the end. Unpublished.
Note: The Scherzo is in the same key (F minor) as the first movement of the Sonata above (**9**), but it is impossible to tell whether or not the two pieces are related. The pen used by Bax to write out this piece and **21** below is different from that used for the previous scores.

21 SYMPHONISCHE DICHTUNG NACH RUBAIYAT VON OMAR KHAYYAM for orchestra (short score only)

Title: '"SYMPHONISCHE DICHTUNG" nach "RUBAIYAT" von Omar Khayyam.'
Date: Undated but following **20** above.
Orchestra: The only instruments indicated are 'corni', timpani and flute.
Manuscript: UCC; ff. [20^{v}-21] of the MS book described in **6** above; [2] pp.; 56 bars (one crossed through). Unpublished.
Note: This is Bax's earliest extant attempt at a work for orchestra, written when he was fourteen. The music ends on a dominant 7th of A major followed by a silent bar with double bar lines, suggesting that it is the completed introduction to the main, unwritten, part of the symphonic poem.

22 [UNTITLED]: Fragment

Manuscript: UCC; f. [30] of the MS book described in **6** above; [1] p.; 12 bars of a melodic line, the seventh crossed through. Unpublished.

1899

No manuscripts dating from this year have been traced.

1900

23 WANTING IS—WHAT? for voice and piano

Title: '"Wanting is—what"'.
Date: 'March 25. 1900' (to left of title).
Dedication: '(dedicated to my dear m[. . .])': this has been partly erased but is still legible, except for most of the last word (probably 'mother').
Text: Robert Browning, 'Wanting is—what?'
Manuscript: BL (Add. MS 54776); ff. 1-6 (verso of each leaf blank); [6] pp. + 6 blank interspersed; 12-staff paper (trimmed to 293 × 226). Unpublished. Add. MS 54776, which contains most of the songs detailed in the next few pages, was unbound when I first inspected it in 1973, and the inner edge of each separate leaf was ragged, the pages clearly having been torn from a MS book. By 1996 the volume had been bound by the BL with the pages tipped in, and the measurements given here are of the leaves in their new, trimmed state.
Duration: 2'45.

24 TO DAFFODILS for voice and piano

Date: 'April 4th 1900' (to right of title, below signature).
Dedication: '(To ' [*sic*].
Text: Robert Herrick, 'Daffodils' from *Hesperides. A Country Life.*
Manuscript: BL (Add. MS 54776); ff. 7-8 (8v blank); [3] pp. + 1 blank; 12-staff paper (trimmed to 286 × 226). Unpublished.
Duration: 1'43.

25 A SERENADE OF SPRING-TIME for voice and piano

Date: 'April 7. 1900' (to right of title, below signature).
Dedication: '"To my dear Nannie [Quaritch]"'.
Text: The poem begins 'Come out with me, come out with me, | The spring-time laughs in ev'ry tree'. The author's name is not given on the MS, and these lines do not appear in any index of poetry consulted.
Manuscript: BL (Add. MS 54776); ff. 9-12 (12v blank); [7] pp. + 1 blank; 12-staff paper (trimmed to 293 × 226). Unpublished.
Duration: 3'33.

26 MARCIA TRIONFALE for piano

Title: 'MARC~~H~~IA [*sic*] TRIONFALE'.
Date: 'April 26 1900 | Sea-View Bay | I.W.' The Bax family had also stayed on the Isle of Wight in April 1896 and 1897.
Manuscript: BL (Add. MS 54769); [2] ff.; [4] pp.; 20-staff paper (367 × 269). The MS has been folded in half horizontally so that f. [1] is now in two separate pieces, and f. [2] very nearly so. Unpublished.
Duration: 10'04.
Note: It was during this holiday on the Isle of Wight that Clifford Bax first read Keat's 'Lamia' and 'discovered himself to be a poet' (*FMY*, p. 41; Clifford Bax, *Inland Far*, London, 1925, p. 18; id., *Ideas and People*, London, 1936, pp. 29-30).

27 I LOVE THEE! for voice and piano

Date: 'May 13 1900' (to right of title, below signature).
Text: Anonymous English translation of Hans Christian Andersen, 'Jeg elsker Dig' from *Hjertets Melodier*.
Manuscript: BL (Add. MS 54776); f. 13-13^{v}; [2] pp.; 48 bars; 12-staff paper (trimmed to 290 × 225). Unpublished.
Duration: 1'40.

28 CYTHEREA'S DAY for voice and piano

Date: 'May 25th 1900' (to right of title, below signature).
Text: Thomas Gray, 'The Progress of Poesy. A Pindaric Ode', I, 3.
Manuscript: BL (Add. MS 54776); ff. 14-15^{v}; [4] pp.; AC paper (trimmed to 294 × 232). Unpublished.
Duration: 2'32.
Note: 'At sixteen he composed a charming setting for Gray's "The Progress of Poesy," certain phrases from which I still find myself sometimes murmuring in the bathroom.' (From 'Clifford Bax on Arnold Bax', *Crescendo*, 12, November 1948, p. 5.) Francis Colmer, who was private tutor to Arnold and Clifford Bax in the late 1890s and outlived them both, mentions in his unpublished memoirs that this setting was made for the singer Nannie Quaritch, daughter of Bernard Quaritch the bookseller. She later took part in a 'Programme of Entertainment . . . to be given by Mr. A. Trevor Bax and friends' on 24 November 1906 at Lyndhurst Hall, Warden Road, Kentish Town. See also **23** and **25** above.

29 TO THE MOON for voice and piano

Date: 'Aug 10. 1900' (to right of title; signature to left of title).
Text: Percy Bysshe Shelley, 'To the Moon'.

Manuscript: BL (Add. MS 54776); f. 16-16^{v}; [2] pp.; 12-staff paper (trimmed to 290 × 230). Unpublished.
Duration: 1'13.

30 [ARCHY'S SONG] for voice and piano

Title: None on MS.
Date: 'Aug 10 1900' (to right of title, above signature).
Text: Percy Bysshe Shelley, 'Archy's Song' ('A widow bird sate mourning for her love') from the play *Charles the First*, scene V.
Manuscript: BL (Add. MS 54776); f. 17-17^{v}; [2] pp.; 12-staff paper (trimmed to 292 × 227). Unpublished.
Duration: 1'16.

31 TO THE CUCKOO for voice and piano

Date: 'August. 14. 1900' (to right of title, below signature).
Text: William Wordsworth, 'To the Cuckoo'.
Manuscript: BL (Add. MS 54776); ff. 18-19 (19^{v} blank); [3] pp. + 1 blank; 12-staff paper (trimmed to 290 × 227). Unpublished.
Duration: 1'18.

32 [IF I BUT KNEW] for voice and piano (sketch)

Title: None on MS; title of poem not known.
Date: Undated but written out on the last folio of the preceding song.
Text: The verse begins: 'If I but knew the harp of fire were mine'. Neither the title nor the author's name is given on the MS, and this line does not appear in any index of poetry consulted.
Manuscript: BL (Add. MS 54776); f. 19^{v}; [1] p.; 10 bars written in pencil on three single-line staves (in 4/4 time, but some bars containing more, some fewer than four crotchets); 12-staff paper (trimmed to 290 × 227). Unpublished.

33 AN INDIAN SERENADE for voice and piano

Title: Bax misquotes the original title of the poem, writing the indefinite instead of the definite article.
Date: 'Aug 15. 1900' (to right of title, above signature).
Text: Percy Bysshe Shelley, 'The Indian Serenade'.
Manuscript: BL (Add. MS 54776); ff. 20-22 (22^{v} blank); [5] pp. + 1 blank; 12-staff paper (trimmed to 290 × 231). Unpublished.
Duration: 2'20.

34 TO PHYLLIS for voice and piano

Date: 'Aug 20. 1900.' (to right of title, above signature).
Text: Thomas Lodge, 'Phillis I'. Words erroneously attributed by Bax (or his source) to Sir Edward Dyer (1550-1607), misspelt 'Dyers' on the MS.
Manuscript: BL (Add. MS 54776); ff. 23-4^{v}; [4] pp.; 12-staff paper (trimmed to 290 × 220). Unpublished.
Duration: 1'57.

35 PHILLIDA AND CORYDON for voice and piano

Title: Bax (or his source) amends the author's sixteenth-century spelling of 'Coridon' (a character from Virgil, *Eclogues*, II, 1).
Date: 'Aug 20. 1900.' (to right of title, below signature).
Text: Nicholas Breton, 'Phillida and Coridon'.
Manuscript: BL (Add. MS 54776); ff. 25-6^{v}; [4] pp.; 12-staff paper (trimmed to 291 × 218). Unpublished.
Duration: 2'17.

36 [WHY WE LOVE AND WHY WE HATE] for voice and piano

Title: None on MS.
Date: '23rd August 1900'.
Text: Ambrose Philips, 'Why we love and why we hate'.
Manuscript: BL (Add. MS 54776); f. 27-7^{v}; [2] pp.; 12-staff paper (trimmed to 292 × 220). Unpublished.
Duration: 0'53.

37 [SAY, MYRA!] for voice and piano

Title: None on MS.
Date: Undated but almost certainly written shortly after the preceding song.
Text: George Lyttleton, 'Song' ('Say, Myra!').
Manuscript: BL (Add. MS 54776); f. 28-8^{v}; [2] pp.; 12-staff paper (trimmed to 292 × 217). Unpublished.
Duration: 0'51.

38 MUSIC WHEN SOFT VOICES DIE for voice and piano

Date: Undated but almost certainly written shortly after the preceding song.
Text: Percy Bysshe Shelley, 'Music when soft voices die'.
Manuscript: BL (Add. MS 54776); f. 29 (29^{v} blank); [1] p. + 1 blank; 12-staff paper (trimmed to 293 × 230). Unpublished.
Duration: 0'55.

39 THE SOLDIER'S DREAM for voice and piano

Date: Undated but almost certainly written shortly after the preceding song.
Text: Thomas Campbell, 'The Soldier's Dream'.
Manuscript: BL (Add. MS 54776); ff. 30-2^{v}; [6] pp.; 12-staff paper (trimmed to 291 × 226). Unpublished.
Duration: 2'59.

40 FANTASIA IN A MINOR for two pianos

Title: *MS A*: 'Fantasia ~~Sonata~~ [*sic*] for 2 pianos | A minor'. *MS B*: 'Fantasie in A minor | PIANO II'.
Date: *A* only: 'October 1900' (at head of score); 'Fine October 28th 1900' (at end).
Manuscript: *A*: RAM (MS 317); [10] ff.; [20] pp.; 12-staff paper (293 × 237); proprietary music book with black cloth wrappers; ff. [1-7] and [10] have been torn out leaving just the stubs; both piano parts are included. *B*: RAM (MS 318), [5] ff.; [10] pp.; AC paper (368 × 260); in an acid-free pocket, the MS having been folded in half horizontally at some time; this contains the second piano part only. Unpublished.
Duration: *c.* 8'00.
Note: This work was written shortly after Bax's admission to the RAM in September 1900 and is his earliest composition for two pianos, a medium to which he did not return until 1916.

41 [FUNERAL] MARCH for piano

Title: '"   March"' [*sic*].
Date: 'October 29th 1900.' (at head of score); 'Nov 3 1900' (at end of score).
Dedication: 'In Mem. P.I.T' (at end of score; see **Note** below).
Manuscript: RAM (MS 317) (see also **40**); [6] ff.; [11] pp. (non-autograph pagin. 21-31); 12-staff paper (293 × 237); f. 6^{v} contains five single-line staves with material that is not obviously related to the march. Unpublished.
Duration: 17'10 (observing the 51½-bar cut at 29:2).
Note: The initials P. I. T., in whose memory the work was written, obviously stand for Pyotr Ilyich Tchaikovsky, who had died seven years before, on 6 November 1893, two days before Bax's tenth birthday. This is confirmed by a quotation from the Tsarist national anthem (composed by Alexei Lvov and used in the overture *1812*) that occurs on the last page of Bax's march.

42 SONATA IN D MINOR for piano

Date: Undated but handwriting and style similar to **40-1** above.
Manuscript: RAM (MS 319); [3] ff. + 1 blank (the lower outer corner cut away); [6] pp. + 2 blank; AMM 10 paper (360 × 265); in an acid-free pocket. Unpublished.
Duration: *c.* 6'00.

Note: This work, which is in a single movement (or of which only the first survives), bears no thematic relationship with the earlier Sonata in D minor (**16** above).

43 [TO THE VIRGINS]: Fragment for voice and piano

Title: None on MS.
Date: Undated but paper the same as for the preceding work and handwriting similar.
Text: Robert Herrick, 'To the Virgins, to make much of Time' ('Gather ye rosebuds while ye may').
Manuscript: BL (Add. MS 54780); f. 10^{v} (10 blank); [1] p. + 1 blank (unfinished); AMM 10 paper (360 × 265). This MS, which was acquired together with Add. MS 54768 (**9-16** above), contains the second verse (of four) only, beginning: 'The glorious lamp of heaven the Sun . . .'.

44 [UNTITLED]: Fragment for orchestra (short score only)

Date: Undated but paper the same as for the preceding song and handwriting similar.
Manuscript: BL (Add. MS 54780); ff. 11 (11^{v} blank) and 12^{v} (a bifolium; for f. 12 see next entry); [2] pp.; AMM 10 paper (360 × 265). The score is written in pencil and ink with notes for orchestration.

45 [UNTITLED]: Fragment for two high voices and piano

Date: Undated but written on one side of the bifolium listed in the preceding entry.
Text: Details untraced. The only words written under the vocal line are 'majesty attend' and 'elevation [?] yellow jacket', the latter faintly recalling the yellow and red coat worn by the Pied Piper in Browning's poem (see **53** below for Bax's setting), though that does not include these two phrases.
Manuscript: BL (Add. MS 54780); f. 12 (for 12^{v} see the preceding entry); [1] p.; AMM 10 paper (360 × 265). This comprises two vocal lines and two piano lines.
Note: There is no obvious relationship between **44** and **45**, but they may be connected.

1901

46 INTERMEZZO for clarinet and piano

Date: 'April. 1901.'
Manuscript: Privately owned; [6] ff.; t.p. + 1 blank + 9 pp. + 1 blank; AMM 10 paper (360 × 265). Unpublished.
Performance: None traced.
Duration: *c.* 10'00.

Note: This work was written during Bax's first year at the RAM. At the head of the first page of the score is the numeral '2', which suggests that it may originally have been intended as the second movement of a larger work, though the fact that it has a separate title page suggests (without proving) that the plan was not carried through. The score is almost entirely devoid of phrasing and expression marks, and the clarinet part is written at its actual pitch.

47 TRIO IN B♭ MINOR for violin, cello and piano

Date: 'Fine September 1 1901 Colwyn Bay. North Wales'.
Manuscript: Lewis Foreman; [6] ff. ; t.p. + 1 blank + 9 pp. + 1 blank; 12-staff paper (302 × 237). Unpublished.
Duration: *c.* 4'00 [*sic*].
Note: This work was completed when Bax was nearly eighteen, shortly before the start of his second year at the RAM. The separate title page is inscribed:

TRIO in B♭ minor | No 1. Allegro Appassionata [*sic*] | No. 2. Scherzo | No. 3. Elegy. | No. 4. Allegro Vivace. | NO I.

The numeral 'I' on the first page of the score has been crossed through, and it seems likely that Bax's original plan of writing a four-movement work was not realized.

48 SONGS OF THE FOUR SEASONS for voice and piano

Title: a. '2 Songs of the Springtime "It was a lover and his lass" No 1.' **b.** 'Songs of the four Seasons No 3 "In Summer-time"'.[5]
Date: a. Undated. **b.** 'Fine November 4th | 1901'.
Texts: a. William Shakespeare, 'Song. It was a lover and his lass' from *As you like it*, V, iii. **b.** The poem begins: 'Thro' meadowland and dingle, where brooklets tell of May'. The author's name is not given on the MS, and these lines do not appear in any index of poetry consulted.
Manuscript: a. BL (Add. MS 54776); ff. 33-4v; [4] pp; AC paper (298 × 233). **b.** BL (Add. MS 54776); ff. 35-8 (38v blank); [7] pp. + 1 blank; 12-staff paper (297 × 236); there is a cancel over bars 7-10 on f. 36v, the four bars replaced by five; f. 39-9v, [2] pp., contains another copy of the vocal line of **48a** only. Unpublished.
Duration: a. 3'15. **b.** 2'43.
Note: There is no proof that **48a** is part of the *Songs of the Four Seasons*, but it seems likely. The numbering included in the titles implies that other songs in the series existed or were planned; but since the intended order of the two extant ones is not certain, it is impossible to tell how many songs are missing; the two songs preceding 'No. 3 "In Summer-time"' may or may not have been the '2 Songs of the Springtime'.

[5] When I first inspected this MS, in 1973, the title was complete. By April 1996, the contents of Add. MS 54776 having been bound, the word '-time"' had been 'conserved' out of existence.

49 SONATA IN G MINOR for violin and piano

Title: *MS A* (holograph): 'First movement of a Sonata for Piano & Violin'. *MS B* (first holograph violin part): 'Sonata in G minor | Violin & Pianoforte'. *MS C* (second holograph violin part): 'Sonate | Violin and Piano'. At the private performance listed below, the title appears on the programme as 'Sonata in B flat (First movement)'; since B♭ is the relative major of G minor, it seems reasonable to assume that the two titles refer to the same piece. See also **60** below for the possibility of its having been renamed *Phantasie*.
Date: *A* and *B* only: 'November 1901'.
Dedication: '(To G.N.L)' (Gladys Lees).
Manuscript: Privately owned (formerly by Judge Rodney Bax); *A*: [6] ff.; [12] pp.; BH 12 paper (359 × 273). *B*: [4] ff.; 7 pp. + 1 blank; AMM 12 paper (363 × 264). In the left margin of p. 2 Bax has written: 'The bowing of this part the same as before, of course but I don't remember it'. *C*: [2] ff.; 3 pp. + 1 blank; 16-staff paper (356 × 270). *Copyist's score and part*: Graham Parlett. Unpublished.
Performance: (1) *Private:* Gladys Lees (vn.), Arnold Bax (pf.); Ivy Bank (the Bax family home), Hampstead; 29 April 1903. (2) *Public:* Ivy L. St Aubyn Angove (vn.), Arnold Bax (pf.); Æolian Hall; 4 June 1907.[6]
Duration: 9'39.
Note: The dedicatee, Gladys Lees, is the girl referred to on p. 24 of *FMY* who held Bax in thrall during his first term at the RAM. In Clifford Bax's autobiographical volume *Inland Far*, p. 20, we find the following passage descriptive of an evening in the Bax family home when he and Arnold were in their teens: 'After supper we would break up into groups. My brother and a girl-visitor would play, perhaps, a sonata for violin and piano: and most of the household remained in the music-room to hear it.' Reviews of the first public performance were not favourable: '. . . it cannot be said that the work proved of any very great musical interest,' wrote the critic of *The Queen* (15 June 1907), p. 1095; and it was all too much for the critic of *The Daily Telegraph* (5 June 1907), p. 13:

> . . . a more tiresome work we cannot recall. Restless and rhapsodical, the music wandered on, showing no trace of inspiration, and nothing definite in the way of a theme, for a full quarter of an hour. Not by such means can young English composers expect to gain the ear of the public. Like many others, Mr. Trevor Bax is on the wrong road, and he should make up his mind to retrace his steps forthwith.

50 BALLET SUITE for orchestra (short score only)

Title: **a.** 'Ballet Suite No 2 Humoreske'. **b.** 'Ballet Suite Russian Dance'.
Date: Undated but probably late 1901 (see **Note** below).

[6] It cannot be proved conclusively that **49** is the work performed on this occasion, but reviews refer to its being in one movement, and there is no other known violin sonata by Bax antedating 1907.

Manuscript: BL (Add. MS 54732); ff. 1-6^{v}; [12] pp. ([1-7], [8-12]); AC paper (300 × 236). Unpublished.
Performance: None.
Duration: a. 5'07. **b.** 3'00 (movement incomplete).
Note: This attempt at writing an orchestral work never progressed beyond the short-score stage. In *FMY*, p. 31, Bax mentions that at the time of his visit to Elgar in the autumn of 1901 he had 'no experience whatever of the Egyptian labour that is orchestration'. That the suite was intended for orchestra from the first, rather than being a piano piece that he decided to orchestrate as an afterthought, is evident from figurations high up on the keyboard that are repeated for bars on end with both hands busy down below, a feat beyond even Bax's pianistic dexterity.

The *Humoreske* is virtually complete in short score (there are some blank bars in the left hand) and has instrumental indications for the following: picc., fl., ob., c.a., cl. and str. Since it is marked 'No. 2' there was presumably at least one other movement of the suite that is now lost (if it was ever written). It is conceivable that Bax took the German title *Humoreske* from a piano piece of the same name by his uncle, Ernest Belfort Bax (1854-1926), which had been published in 1877. The *Russian Dance* also has some blank bars in the left hand but the only instruments indicated are tamb. and '2 violin'. At the end is the note 'Segue il Trio', but the trio is not extant.

Although the score is undated, the work is roughly contemporary with the *Love-Song* (**54**), which dates from February 1902. The whole of Add. MS 54732 consists of a single MS book, with staples on the spine but no cover, containing the *Ballet Suite*, *Tegnér's Drapa* (incomplete) and *Love-Song* on eleven folios. The first extant folio of the suite is a singleton, the opening movement evidently having been removed, and the rest is in one complete stapled section of conjugate leaves (f. 3 detached) as far as the extant ending of *Tegnér's Drapa* (**52**), but with three leaves torn out at the end of the *Russian Dance* (presumably the missing trio). The *Love-Song*, which is complete, is written on four separate folios loosely inserted at the end of the book.

At the end of the *Humoreske* there are two fragmentary vocal lines in F♯ pencilled in with the words 'I will dream'. The completed version of this song, untitled and in E, is listed below (**51**). Although undated, it can be ascribed to late 1901, which tallies with the conjectured date for the *Ballet Suite*.

51 [I WILL DREAM] for voice and piano

Title: None on MS.
Date: Undated but handwriting similar to that of the preceding work.
Text: Probably by Clifford Bax (see **Note** below).
Manuscript: BL (Add. MS 54776); ff. 40-3^{v}; [8] pp.; 12-staff paper (290 × 232). A fragment of the opening vocal line (but in F♯ instead of E) can be found on f. 4 of Add. MS 54732 (**50** above). Unpublished.
Duration: 3'16.

Note: The suggestion that Clifford Bax is the author of the words derives from a piece of light blue writing paper (Add. MS 54776, f. i; 226 × 175) containing a 'List of [eight] songs sent to Storrington. AETB.' (not in Bax's hand but obviously dating from the period when he was living in the village: 1940-53). It is conceivable that these early songs had been found amongst the papers of Bax's mother, who had died in November 1940, and were being restored to the composer. The opening lines of this song ('I will dream, I will dream in my boat') are quoted in the list, followed by the initials 'CLB', i.e. Clifford Lea Bax, implying that he wrote the words. No published edition of his poetry contains a poem with these opening lines, but in view of its date this is hardly suprising; nor does the title appear in a privately owned collection of unpublished 'Early Poems & Fragments' by Clifford Bax written out in Francis Colmer's hand.[7]

52 TEGNÉR'S DRAPA for chorus and orchestra (fragment of vocal score)

Date: Undated but contemporary with the preceding song.
Orchestra: The only instruments indicated on the score are br., tbn. and str.
Text: Henry Wadsworth Longfellow, 'Tegnér's Drapa' from *The Seaside and the Fireside.*
Manuscript: BL (Add. MS 54775); f. 7; [2] pp.; 49 bars (counting the two consecutive bars of 2/4 as an error for a single bar of 4/4; incomplete); AC paper (300 × 236). Unpublished.
Note: All that exists of this projected work for chorus and orchestra (Bax's first extant attempt) are the introduction (forty-five bars) and the first four bars of the initial unison choral entry starting at bar 46 ('I heard a voice that cried . . .'). The rest of the work must have been written on the missing right-hand side of the gathering, whose left-hand side, which is loose, contains the first page of the *Ballet Suite* (**50**). From this it can be deduced that the work was never completed even in vocal score, unless of course it was rewritten and finished as a separate MS no longer extant.

c. 1901

53 THE PIED PIPER OF HAMELIN: Cantata

Text: Robert Browning, 'The Pied-Piper of Hamelin; A Child's Story'.
Note: This is known only from its mention in the memoirs of Francis Colmer (see **28**). It is impossible to date precisely, but since it is not included even in the earliest lists of Bax's music maybe it comes from about the same time as *Tegnér's Drapa* (**52**).

[7] The earliest poem by Clifford Bax to be published is 'Fantasia' (1903), in *Gleanings* (London, 1921; privately printed limited edn. of 40 copies). The earliest known unpublished poems date from January 1901.

It is unlikely ever to have been orchestrated or perhaps even completed in short score.

1902

54 LOVE-SONG for orchestra (short score only)

Date: 'Feb 21 1902' (to right of title; Bax's name does not appear).
Orchestra: A few instruments are indicated: bn., br., 'drum', vn. solo, vc. solo, wind, str., etc.
Manuscript: BL (Add. MS 54732); ff. 8-11 (11ᵛ blank); [7] pp. + 1 blank; AC paper (300 × 236). Unpublished.
Performance: *Bars 22-30 only*: David Owen Norris (pf.); British Music Information Centre; 3 February 1983 (lecture-recital by Lewis Foreman, *et al.*).
Duration: *c.* 5'00.
Note: As explained under **50** above, this work is written out on four separate folios loosely inserted into the back of Add. MS 54732.

55 STRING QUARTET IN A

I. Allegro con fuoco ma moderato in tempo. II. Andante con moto e cantabile. III. Scherzo Finale. Allegro furiante.

Title: 'String Quartett in A major'.
Date: *Movt. II only:* 'Fine November 25 | 1902'.
Manuscript: Privately owned; [30] ff.; [59] pp. (1-21; 2 pp. pagin. '20', the first crossed through: 22 pp. in all), [22-37], [38-58] (non-autograph pagin.) + 3 blank; pp. 1-10, [38-59] + 3 blank: BH 12 paper (355 × 270); pp. 11-[21]: 20-staff paper (355 × 268); pp. [22-37]: AMM 12 paper (360 × 265); stitched into brown paper wrappers but now loose. Unpublished. *Parts for movt. II*: Graham Parlett.
Performance: *Movt. II only:* Ivy L. St Aubyn Angove (vn.), Edward Rowsby Woof (vn.), Emily Wingfield (va.), Bertram Walton O'Donnell (vc.); St James's Hall; 23 November 1903.
Duration: *c.* 25'00.
Note: The following quotation appears at the head of the score:

> "Be thou Spirit Fierce,
> My Spirit! Be thou me, impetuous one!"
> (Shelley, Ode to the West Wind [V. 2]).

Movt. III is prefaced by the following note: 'This movement is intended | to serve both as Scherzo & | Finale so that the Quartett | will consist of three movements | instead of the customary four,' an early indication of Bax's predilection for writing large-scale works in three movements with scherzo and finale combined. The score has numerous pencil markings in the hand of Frederick Corder, Bax's composition teacher at the RAM. There are cue letters in red ink throughout, which suggests that it may originally have been intended to perform all three movements of the work at the concert that took place in 1903. The following review of that performance comes from *The Musical Times* (December 1903), p. 808: 'An Andante in A [actually in D] from a MS. String Quartet by Mr Arnold E. T. Bax proved somewhat vague in character, but showed musicianly feeling.' *The Musical News* (28 November 1903), p. 460, thought it 'a composition of considerable merit, but has not sufficient strength, and is too indefinite in form and treatment.' According to the *R. A. M. Club Magazine*, 11 (January 1904), p. 18, two movements of the quartet were played, but there is no other documentary evidence to support this statement.

1903

56 THE GRAND MATCH for baritone and piano

Date: 'June 29th 1903' (on t.p.).
Text: Moira O'Neill, 'The Grand Match' from *Songs of the Glens of Antrim*, pp. 49-50.
Manuscript: Privately owned; [7] ff.; t.p. + 1 blank + [10] pp. + 1 blank; AMM 14 paper (360 × 264). Unpublished.
Performance: George Clowser (bar.), Arnold Bax (pf.); St James's Hall; 23 July 1903 ('Students' Chamber Concert'). 'A clever Irish dialect song . . . was very spiritedly sung . . .' (*The Queen*, 1 August 1903, p. 166). '. . . not of particularly interesting musical value.' (*The Musical Times*, 1 August 1903, p. 96). As far as can be ascertained, this was the first public performance of a work by Bax.
Duration: 3'23.

57 STRING QUARTET IN E

I. Allegro molto vivace. II. Adagio ma non troppo. III. Allegro con vivacità.

Title: 'Quartett in E major'.
Date: Undated but see **Note** below.
Manuscript: Privately owned; [25] ff. + 1 blank; 49 pp. (1-20 + 2 blank, [21-31] + 1 blank, [33-49] (pagin. 1-15, [16-18] + 2 blank); AMM 12 paper (trimmed to 347 × *c.* 258); bound in dark green cloth with gold lettering on upper cover; there are cancels on pp. [24, 31, 43, 45, 46]. Unpublished. *Parts for movt. II*: Graham Parlett.
Performance: *Movt. II only*: Delmé Quartet: Galina Solodchin (vn.), John Trusler (vn.), John Underwood (va.), Jonathan Williams (vc.); Wigmore Hall; 13 July 1989.
Duration: *c.* 25'00.
Note: In 1905 Bax orchestrated the second movement of this work as the tone-poem *Cathaleen-ni-Hoolihan* (**72**), the score of which provides the only clue to the date of the quartet, since it is headed 'December 1903 | July 1905'. (See also **64**.) Like the tone-poem, the slow movement of the quartet is prefaced by a quotation from Yeats's poem 'To Ireland in the Coming Times', in which Bax has made a few small slips (amended here in brackets):

Know[,] that I would accounted be
True brother of that company [a company]
That sang[,] to sweeten Ireland's wrong[,]
Ballad and story, rann and song.

When *Cathaleen-ni-Hoolihan* was first broadcast, the announcer misread 'rann' ('verse' or 'stanza') as 'poem' since Bax writes a long-stemmed Irish 'r' on both scores (see also **252**). Like the Quartet in A (**55**) this work contains cue numbers in red ink and pencil comments in Frederick Corder's hand.

c. 1903–4

58 [UNTITLED]: Two fragments for piano

Note: These are to be found quoted in an undated letter written by Bax to a girl-friend, 'Jean' (later Mrs Thornton), and reproduced in LF, p. 23. The first fragment (**58a**) consists of two bars, the second (**58b**) of four, and they were either composed on the spur of the moment while Bax was writing the letter or derive from an otherwise unknown score. The conjectured date is based on the handwriting. The second fragment (in A♭, 3/4 time) was adapted in 1912-13 for the opening of *In the Hills of Home*, the third of the Four Orchestral Pieces (**152c**), where it appears in E, 4/4 time.

1904

59 CONCERT PIECE for viola and piano

Title: *Copyist's score*: 'Concert-Piece' (unhyphenated in Bax's programme note). See also **Note** below.
Date: Score undated but written in the spring of 1904, according to Bax's programme note.
Dedication: None on the extant score but written for Lionel Tertis.
Manuscript: *Holograph*: Not traced. *Copyist's score*: UCC; [18] ff. ; t.p. + [11] pp. + 1 blank + [21] pp. + 2 blank; A&C 28 paper (357 × 260); sewn into greyish brown wrappers. The t.p. bears a note in Bax's handwriting: 'If lost return to Arnold E. Trevor Bax', followed by his Ivy Bank address. Unpublished.
Performance: Lionel Tertis (va.), Arnold Bax (pf.); Æolian Hall; 6 December 1904 (Second Patron's Fund [chamber music] Concert).
Duration: 11'44.
Note: This was one of sixty-three chamber, instrumental and vocal works submitted to the selection committee for the second Patron's Fund Concert (see **Note** under **61** below), from which sixteen were chosen for a 'trial rehearsal'. Of these, seven were by RCM students, eight by RAM students, and one by J. B. McEwen, at that time professor at the RAM. The committee consisted of Bax's composition teacher, Frederick Corder, Edward Dannreuther (1844-1905, professor

of piano at the RCM), and Dr Eaton Faning (1850-1927, former professor at both the RCM and RAM), who finally selected Bax's work together with pieces by Frank Bridge, Clive Carey, Paul Corder, George Dyson (his also called Concert Piece), William Hurlstone and J. B. McEwen. For the first performance Bax wrote a programme note:

This piece was written in the spring of the present year for the artist who brings it forward on this occasion.
The work consists of but one movement, cast in the usual sonata form as recognized by the older composers, though certain modifications are adopted necessary to the requirements of modern art.
Throughout the composition it will be observed that a Celtic element predominates, free use being made of the flattened seventh, the falling intervals of the pentatonic scale, and other features peculiar to Irish folk music. [Followed by a descriptive 'analysis' with musical examples.]

The following comment appeared in both the *Royal College of Music Magazine* (January 1905) and *The Musical Times* (January 1905), p. 369: 'There were some effective passages, and one particular expressive theme of Irish idiom . . . but vagueness of form marred the composition.' This review also mentioned that the concert was poorly attended. Another review, by 'P. S.' (perhaps Percy Scholes), was published in *The Musical Standard* (10 December 1904), p. 369:

. . . it breathes a spirit almost of rebellion and violence throughout its fervid pages. Brilliantly written for both instruments, the work was strikingly played. . . . If the composition is a little overdone, the excess of zeal is refreshing and even infectious, and it reveals gifts and force which look well for the future of Mr. Trevor Bax.

The *Concert Piece* is listed in *YB1* and *YB2* but is omitted from *BMSA*. In *MT* there is a reference to a *Fantasy* for viola and piano dated 1904, which appears to be included in place of the *Concert Piece* and is clearly the same work. It is also listed in WWC, p. 67, as *Phantasy*, and likewise in the programme note for performances of Bax's Second Symphony by the Boston Symphony Orchestra in December 1929. *YB1*, however, lists both the *Concert Piece* and a *Phantasie* for violin and piano, but it is impossible to be certain whether the second title is the violin arrangement of the *Concert Piece* (60 below), another name for the one-movement Sonata in G minor of 1901, or an otherwise unknown score.

60 CONCERT PIECE for violin and piano

Title: 'Concert Piece for Violin and Piano | 1904'.
Manuscript: *Holograph violin part only*: UCC; [4] ff.; t.p. + 1 blank + [5] pp. + 1 blank; ALM 10 paper (355 × 257). Unpublished.
Note: This is an arrangement of the work in the preceding entry. It is unlikely that Bax ever wrote out a separate piano score for it, and the handwriting and general appearance of the autograph part suggest that it is more or less contemporary with the original version.

61 VARIATIONS for orchestra

[Theme] Moderato Allegro (pp. 1-4). Var. 1: Allegro Moderato (pp. 4-13). Var. 2: [L'istesso tempo] (pp. 13-20). Var. 3: Andante con moto (pp. 20-31). Var. 4: Tempo di Valsero (pp. 32-53). Var. 5: Burlesque. Allegretto scherzando (pp. 53-70). Var. 6: Allegretto e semplice (pp. 71-80). Finale: Allegro vivace (pp. 81-115).

Title: 'Variations for Orchestra. (Improvisations). | Variations.' Listed in *YB1* as 'Variations on an Original Theme'.
Date: 'Fine June 10th 1904'.
Orchestra: 3(1)222, 43(in F)31, timp., 2 perc. (s.d., tamb., cym., tri.), org., hp., str.
Manuscript: Lewis Foreman; [58] ff.; 115 pp. + 1 blank; pp. 1-70, 107-115: AMM 14 paper; pp. 71-104: 20-staff paper (all trimmed to 350 × *c.* 259); bound in black leather with gold tooling and marbled endpapers. The legend 'A.E.T.B. | 8 NOV. 1904.' embossed on the front cover suggests that the MS was bound for the composer as a twenty-first birthday present. Bax has written his name and Ivy Bank address on the front free endpaper. One folio, immediately before the start of the finale (p. 81), has been torn out, but since there is no break in the pagination it was presumably removed by Bax during the course of writing out the score; a note at the top of p. 80 reads: 'Segue finale'. Unpublished.
Performance: [Student Orchestra], Arnold Bax; RCM; *c.* 26 May 1905.[8]
(public rehearsal only).
Duration: *c.* 20'00.
Note: This is Bax's earliest completed orchestral work, written during his fourth year at the RAM, where it won the Charles Lucas Medal for composition. In February 1905 Frederick Corder submitted the score to the selection committee of the Patron's Fund, which had been established by Sir Ernest Palmer in 1903 with a capital of £20,000 to finance the copying out of parts and rehearsal of works by young British composers with a view to having them publicly performed at one of the London concert halls.[9] Fifty-nine other orchestral works were submitted to the committee, which on this occasion consisted of Francis Davenport (1847-1925, composer and former professor at the RAM), Dr Charles Lloyd (1849-1919, Precentor of Eton College and former professor at the RCM), and the composer Edward German (1862-1936), who individually looked through each work and then decided whether it was worthy of being rehearsed by the student orchestra. In the examiners' reports both Davenport and Lloyd agreed that Bax's *Variations* should be given a run-through. On 28 February Lloyd wrote: 'A good deal of this work is more curious than beautiful, but it ought to be tried. The finale should be very

[8] The records of the Patron's Fund in the RCM do not divulge the precise date; but in *FMY*, p. 26, Bax mentions that the rehearsal coincided with 'the beginning of a blistering heat-wave'. London temperatures in May 1905 were low until Thursday 25th, when they began to rise. The maximum temperature recorded was 84° F. on Monday 29th.

[9] See Guy Warrack, 'Royal College of Music: The First Eighty-Five Years (1883-1968)—and beyond—', 1, unpublished MS in the Parry Room Library, RCM, p. 81. In *FMY*, p. 25, Bax mistakenly gives Palmer's forename as 'Edward' instead of 'Ernest' ('Samuel Ernest' in full).

effective.' German, who submitted his report on 8 March, was less certain and at first wrote 'No' against the title; but he later changed his mind and altered it to 'Possibly', adding (in imitation of Dickens's Mr Jingle): 'Eccentric very!' Davenport was the last to inspect the score and on 15 March wrote 'Yes' against the work without further comment.

Together with fifteen other pieces Bax's score was subsequently submitted for a 'trial rehearsal' during May 1905, and in *FMY*, pp. 26-7, the composer relates how he arrived at the RCM at the start of a heatwave and discovered to his horror that he was expected to conduct the thing himself, the only occasion on which he ever wielded a baton in front of an orchestra. His amusing account of this humiliating fiasco is too long to quote, but the upshot was that he vowed never to conduct again.

Not surprisingly the *Variations* were rejected, together with eight of the other works played through at the rehearsals. The seven selected for performance at the fourth Patron's Fund Concert, which took place at Queen's Hall on 29 June 1905, were by Hubert Bath, Harry Farjeon, Gustav Holst, John W. Ivimey, Harold Moore, Frank Tapp and Haydn Wood. Apart from Tapp (who played the solo piano part of his *Variations on 'Tom Bowling'* under Stanford's direction), all the works were conducted by their respective composers, and it may well have been Bax's incompetence with the baton that led to the rejection of his score. On the other hand, a statement issued to the musical press before the rehearsals mentioned that several of the composers recommended (including Bax) had already had works performed at a Patron's Fund concert and that preference ought therefore to be given to those who had not.

62 TO MY HOMELAND for voice and piano

Date: 'July 1904'.
Text: Stephen Lucius Gwynn, 'Ireland'.
Manuscript: Privately owned (formerly by Judge Rodney Bax); [2] ff. (a bifolium); 2 pp. + 2 blank; 20-staff paper (380 × 274). Unpublished.
Duration: 2'08.

63 A CELTIC SONG CYCLE for voice and piano

a. Eilidh my Fawn. **b.** Closing Doors. **c.** Thy dark eyes to mine. **d.** A Celtic Lullaby. **e.** At the last.

Title: *Printed score*: 'A Celtic Song-Cycle' [hyphenated]. In the notebook detailed under **88** below, **63c** is listed as 'A Falling Star', which is the final line of the poem.
Date: *Printed score*: 'July–August 1904'. Partly revised in 1922 (see **259**).
Dedication: *Original edition*: None. *Revised edition*: 'To Miss Gladys Lees' (printed on each song).

Text: Fiona Macleod, 'Eilidh my Fawn', 'Mo-lennav-a-chree', 'Thy Dark Eyes to Mine', 'Lullaby' from *From the Hills of Dream*; and 'At the Last' from *Closing Doors*. Bax himself also wrote a poem called 'At the last' (1907).
Manuscript: Not traced. For the revision of 1922, Bax made amendments in red ink on a copy of the CA edition.
Publication: CA (Avison Ed. 12), 1906, fo., 29 pp. *Revised edition*: JWC (3869 A–E), fo., 1922, 29 pp.
Performance: (1) **63a, b** *and* **e** *only*: Ethel M. Lister (sop.), Arnold Bax (pf.); Queen's (Small) Hall; 21 November 1904 (RAM Concert). '. . . we have listened to more pleasant themes from the pen of this gentleman.' (*The Musical News*, 26 November 1904, p. 470). (2) *Complete (earliest traced)*: Ethel M. Lister (sop.), Arnold Bax (pf.); Queen's (Small) Hall; 14 June 1907.
Duration: a. 2'23. **b.** 5'18. **c.** 2'03. **d.** 6'54. **e.** 3'58.
Note: 63d was orchestrated in 1914 (see **156a** below). After hearing an early performance of the cycle, Parry 'expressed the opinion that "Young Bax's stuff sounds like a bevy of little devils!"' (*FMY*, p. 27).

64 CATHALEEN-NI-HOOLIHAN for two violins and piano

Title: *Printed programme for first performance*: '"CATHALEEN-NI-HOOLIHAN," Poem for two Violins with Piano Accompaniment'.
Date: Probably written during the months leading up to the first performance on 9 November 1904.
Manuscript: Not traced.
Performance: *Private*: Gladys Lees (vn.), Evelyn Bax (vn.), Arnold Bax (pf.); The Music Room, Ivy Bank (Bax family home), Hampstead; 9 November 1904.
Note: The title of this work is an Anglicization of the Irish 'Caitlín Ní Uallacháin' ('C. daughter of U.'), one of the personifying epithets of Ireland. The music was probably an arrangement of the slow movement of the String Quartet in E of 1903 (**57**), which in 1905 was recast as an orchestral tone-poem also called *Cathaleen-ni-Hoolihan* (**72**). It is known only from the programme for the first performance, which took place on the day after Bax's twenty-first birthday. A few months later, in a letter addressed to 'Eilidh Aroon', i.e. Isobel Hodgson, who studied piano and singing at the RAM (1903-6), Bax alluded to the occasion:

I hope, my dear one, this will reach you on your birthday . . . As it is your twenty-first birthday,[10] of course it is perfectly hopeless to wish you a happy day. I shall never forget mine which took place last November, which to my infinite sorrow was crowned with a party or an 'at home' or something on the following evening. I felt on that occasion not meringuey [*sic*] but rather the reverse as I got the hump badly, like a camel in fact, whose back was broken by the last straw in the shape of the at-home. I hope for your sake you will be spared that, du lieber [*sic*].

[10] This fell on 29 April 1905. The letter was obviously written a few days earlier, from Achill, off the coast of Co. Mayo in Ireland.

The 'at home' also included songs and violin pieces by Franck, Schumann, Massenet, Brahms, Quilter and others.

1905

65 WHEN WE ARE LOST for voice and piano

Title: *MS*: '"When we are lost" (Roundel)'. *Copyist's score*: '"When we are lost"'.
Date: *MS*: 'Jan 27th | 1905.'
Text: 'Dermot O'Byrne' (Arnold Bax), 'When we are lost' (not otherwise published).
Manuscript: *Holograph*: BL (Add. MS 54778); ff. 45-6v; pp. 55-8; 47 bars; 20-staff paper (trimmed to 330 × 260). Add. MS 54778 is a volume bound in dark green cloth with 'SONGS. VOL. I.' embossed on the upper cover (the lettering piece on the spine having been added by the BL) and containing printed copies of all the songs published by CA (ff. 1-18v) and then the holograph MSS of twelve songs in the following order: 'From the Uplands to the Sea' (**66**), 'The Garden by the Sea' (**115**), 'Marguerite' (**113**), 'The Fiddler of Dooney' (**93**), 'A Lyke-Wake Dirge' (**105**), 'I fear thy kisses, gentle maiden' (**82**), 'A Lullaby' (**126**), 'A Christmas Carol' (**116**), 'When we are lost' (**65**), 'Landskab' (**108**), 'The Flute' (**97**), 'Du Blomst i Dug' (**99**). The pagination is continuous, and some songs start on the reverse of the last folio of the preceding one, indicating that the contents are fair copies. On f. 19 (19v blank) Bax has written: 'Songs (Poems by Various Authors) | Arnold Bax (1905-1910)'. *Copyist's score*: Lewis Foreman; [3] ff. + 1 blank; t.p. + [6] pp. + 2 blank; HLE paper (353 × 267); stitched into brown wrappers.
Publication: In Lewis Foreman (ed.), *Dermot O'Byrne: Poems by Arnold Bax*, TP, 1979, 8vo, pp. 75-9. Also in *Five Songs [by] Arnold Bax (Heritage of English Song 4)*, TP, [1985], 4to., pp. 7-11. Also in *Arnold Bax: Six Songs*, TP (THA 978047), 1994, 4to, pp. 5-9.
Performance: (1) *Public*: Jeff Weaver (ten.), David Owen Norris (pf.); British Music Information Centre; 3 February 1983 (lecture-recital by Lewis Foreman, *et al.*). (2) *Broadcast*: Anthony Roden (ten.), Geoffrey Parsons (pf.); br. on Radio 3, 20 November 1983.
Duration: 3'56.

66 FROM THE UPLANDS TO THE SEA for voice and piano

Title: Bax has misquoted the original title of the poem (writing 'Uplands' for 'Upland').
Date: 'February | 1905.'
Text: William Morris, 'From the Upland to the Sea' from *Poems by the Way*.
Manuscript: BL (Add. MS 54778); ff. 20-6v; pp. 1-14; ALM 12 paper (trimmed to 330 × 260); bound with 11 other songs (see **65** above). Unpublished.

Performance: None in this form (but see **67** below).
Duration: *c.* 13'00.

67 FROM THE UPLANDS TO THE SEA for voice and two pianos

Date: *MS A*: 'February | 1905'. *MS B*: Undated.
Manuscript: *A*: Lewis Foreman; [12 ff.]; [23] pp. + 1 blank; AMM 14 paper (360 × 262). *B*: Privately owned; [9 ff.]; 13 pp. + 5 blank (unfinished); ALM 14 paper (360 × 262); the first piano part is written in red ink, the second in black. Unpublished.
Performance: (1) *Broadcast*: Michael Goldthorpe (ten.), Howard Shelley (pf.), Hilary Macnamara (pf.); br. on Radio 3, 23 November 1983. (2) *Public*: Alasdair Elliott (ten.), Keith Williams and Clive Williamson (pfs.); Institute of Contemporary Arts; 24 March 1984.
Duration: 12'57.
Note: In this version of the song—Bax's longest—the heading 'PRELUDE (A Spring Morning)' is written above the initial tempo marking. The prelude lasts for seventy-one bars before the voice enters. See also **66** above.

68 A CONNEMARA REVEL (An Irish Overture) for orchestra

Performance: (1) RAM Orchestra, Sir Alexander Mackenzie; Queen's Hall; 4 April 1905.[11] (2) Bournemouth Municipal Orchestra, Dan Godfrey; Winter Gardens, Bournemouth; 13 December 1906.
Note: This work is known only from reviews of the two performances listed above. After the first, a reviewer in *The Musical Times* (1 May 1905), p. 330, wrote:

> The students . . . gave an excellent account of themselves at their concert . . . [and] entered with zest into the humour and spirit of a neatly-written overture called 'A Connemara Revel' by their fellow-student, Arnold E. T. Bax.

Another reviewer, in *The Musical News* (8 April 1905), p. 318, mentioned that the concert was well attended and divulged the fact that the work included some ethnic Irish material:

> Chief interest was attached to a new Overture . . . This consisted, as was to be expected, of the adaptation of Irish airs, and the result is a cleverly-scored work of a delightfully fresh and optimistic nature.

For the Bournemouth performance in the following year, Bax apparently changed the title to *An Irish Overture*, which is described in the programme booklet as an 'Allegro vivace in E minor'. It was being played for the 'first time at these concerts'

[11] Four days after this performance Bax was at Aranmore in Ireland writing two poems ('A Sea-dream' and 'Perpetuum Mobile').

(implying that it had already been performed elsewhere) and was to be conducted by the composer, a curious statement in view of Bax's vow that he would never do so again after the traumatic rehearsal of his *Variations* in May 1905 (see **61** above). The concert was reviewed in *The Bournemouth Guardian* (15 December 1906) and in *The Bournemouth Observer* (22 December 1906). The former states unequivocally that Bax did conduct his work, but it seems likely that the review was written before the concert and possibly by the same person ('D.H.') who wrote the programme note, since he quotes whole phrases from them. The other review is of more interest:

This young composer's name is unfamiliar to me, and I believe this is the first time that it has appeared on one of our Concert programmes. His Overture is described as 'a brilliant and light-hearted representation of several sides of Irish character', but I am fain to confess that neither of these definitions would occur to me as very appropriate. The beginning of the work brought Stanford's Irish Symphony at once to my mind, but only because some of the same native material is utilised in both, for as regards treatment of such material there was but little resemblance, and I am afraid the comparison was not in favour of the young writer. There are in the work, no doubt, many pleasing and well-wrought parts, and some which struck me as piquantly original, but there are also others to which the epithet 'chaotic' might, I think, almost be applied, and the general impression left on my mind was not particularly favourable. I should suppose the work to be a difficult one to interpret, and I daresay [*sic*] it required more rehearsal than Mr. Godfrey could afford to give it.

The inference to be drawn from the last sentence is that it was Dan Godfrey who conducted, and this was confirmed by Frank Merrick in 1969, sixty-three years after he had given the first British performance of Dvořák's Piano Concerto on the same occasion: 'I remember that concert in 1906 dimly, the first time I heard of and saw Bax. He did not conduct his work.'[12]

Apart from the press reviews there is no mention anywhere else of *A Connemara Revel*, while *An Irish Overture* is otherwise known only from its inclusion in *YB1* and *YB2*; but it seems probable that they are one and the same. Both reviews quoted refer to *A Connemara Revel* as an overture, and the *Musical News* writer mentions that it contained 'adaptations of Irish airs', which tallies with the information given in the programme note for *An Irish Overture*:

A brilliant and lighthearted representation of several sides of Irish character, this Overture has much in it that is interesting. The composer is already favourably known as the writer of several Celtic pieces, based more or less upon Folk melodies. In the Overture played to-day only two actually Irish tunes are used; the well known 'Emer's farewell to Cuchullin' and one of the traditional 'Caiones' (or Keens) a kind of wailing chant sung for hours together to the word 'Ochone' by mourners at wakes—at least in former days. The Overture is intended to represent for the most part the lighter side of Irish life, but besides that and the touches of

[12] From a postcard sent to me on 25 November 1969 in response to an enquiry.

pathos which always underlie, there are indications of the fiery and warlike side of the Irish nature.

The first section of the Music is founded on a theme in typical Irish tonality.

The middle section (in the major) introduces the hearer to a delightful melody, on the first violins; further on the Caione will be recognised by the descending triplets with which it begins, and by its being given out by Bassoon and 'Cello.

The merrier tune soon regains its sway, and the Overture proceeds happily on its way through a clever series of subject management, to its brilliant ending.

As well as Dvořák's Piano Concerto the concert included Cyril Scott's *Aubade* and Schumann's Second Symphony.

The 'folk tune' referred to in the programme note as 'Emer's Farewell to Cuchullin' is better known as the 'Londonderry Air' and 'Danny Boy', first published by George Petrie in 1855; it was one of Bax's favourite tunes. It is strange that the opening of the work should have reminded the *Bournemouth Observer* critic of Stanford's *Irish Symphony* for its use of 'the same native material' since the symphony does not include either the 'Londonderry Air' or a *caoineadh* (keen) in any of its movements, and the programme note makes it clear that these were the only two Irish tunes used in Bax's overture. The writer may have been confusing it with Stanford's *Irish Rhapsody No. 1*, written in 1902, which does include 'Emer's Farewell', although of course this would not have appeared at the opening of Bax's work, which began with a 'merry tune'.

69 LEAVES, SHADOWS AND DREAMS for voice and piano

Title: 'Leaves Shadows and Dreams.'
Date: 'May 1905'.
Text: Fiona Macleod, 'The Old Bard's Song' from the play *The Immortal Hour*.
Manuscript: BL (Add. MS 54776); ff. 44-5^{v}; [4] pp.; AL 8 paper (362 × 263). That this is a fair copy of another MS, now lost, is proved by the style of the imprint on the paper, which was not in use until *c.* 1913. Unpublished.
Duration: 2'56.

70 IN THE SILENCES OF THE WOODS for voice and piano

Date: *MS A*: 'June 2nd | 1905.' *MS B*: 'June 1905'.
Text: Fiona Macleod, 'In the Silences of the Woods'.
Manuscript: *A*: BL (Add. MS 54777); ff. 23-4; pp. 13-15; 20-staff paper (trimmed to 330 × *c.* 259). Add. MS 54777 is a volume bound in dark green cloth with 'CELTIC SONGS | ARNOLD BAX' embossed in gold on the upper cover and containing a printed page headed 'INDEX' (f. 1), the printed score of *A Celtic Song-Cycle* (ff. 2-16), and then the holograph MSS of 11 songs with words by Fiona Macleod (ff. 17-36^{v}) in the following order: 'A Milking Sian' (**101**), 'Viking-Battle-Song' (**77**), 'A Hushing Song' (**81**), 'In the Silences of the Woods' (**70**), 'Heart o'Beauty' (**103**), 'Isla'

(**111**), 'Green Branches' (**71**), 'Shieling-Song' (**109**), 'The White Peace' (**102**), 'Longing' (**96**), 'From the Hills of Dream' (**100**). The pagination is continuous, and some songs start on the reverse of the last folio of the preceding one, indicating that the contents are fair copies. *B*: BL (Add. MS 54776); ff. 46-7ᵛ; [4] pp.; ALM 16 paper (359 × 270). Several details suggest that *B* is a later copy than *A*: the handwriting is slightly maturer; the paper is of a type not used by Bax in 1905; the date ('June 1905') abbreviates that on *A*; the piano part has minor amendments tending towards simplification. Unpublished.
Duration: 1'19.

71 GREEN BRANCHES for voice and piano

Date: *MS A*: 'June 6th | 1905.' *MS B*: '1905.'
Text: Fiona Macleod, 'Green Branches'.
Manuscript: *A*: BL (Add. MS 54777); ff. 29-30ᵛ; pp. 25-8; 20-staff paper (trimmed to 330 × *c.* 259); bound with 10 other songs (see **70** above). *B*: UCC; [2] ff.; [4] pp.; AL 8 (365 × 268). In this copy bars 21, 40 and 41 of the piano part are blank. In *MS A*—the earlier of the two—the song is in E major; in *B* it is in D. The handwriting and imprint of the paper indicate that *B* was copied out no earlier than *c.* 1913. Unpublished.
Duration: 2'06.

72 CATHALEEN-NI-HOOLIHAN for orchestra

Title: 'Orchestral Poem | "Cathaleen-ni-Hoolihan"'.
Date: 'December 1903 | July 1905.'
Orchestra: 2221, 2100, timp., hp., str.
Manuscript: UCC; [19] ff.; [38] pp.; ff. [1-7]: A&C 14 paper; ff. [8-19]: ALM 14 paper (trimmed to 347 × 253); bound in dark green cloth with the title and composer's name embossed in gold on the upper cover; Bax's name and Ivy Bank address handwritten on the free front endpaper. Many of the dynamics are written in red ink (cf. **61**). Unpublished. *Parts*: BBC; Lewis Foreman.
Performance: (1) *Amateur*: Students' Association Orchestra, David Chatwin; RCM; 22 October 1970. (2) *Professional*: BBC Concert Orchestra, Ashley Lawrence; BBC Studios, Golders Green; 30 October 1974; br. on Radio 3, 7 November 1974.
Duration: 12'20.
Note: This was originally written as the slow movement of the Quartet in E (**57**) and probably later arranged for two violins and piano (**64**). Both the quartet and orchestral versions bear the same misquotation from Yeats's poem 'To Ireland in the Coming Times' at the head of the score (p. 1).

73 THE FAIRIES for voice and piano

Date: *Printed score*: 'October 1905'.
Dedication: 'To "LITTLE BRIDGET".' (a character in the poem, not otherwise identified).[13]
Text: William Allingham, 'The Fairies (A Child's Song)'.
Manuscript: Not traced.
Publication: CA (Avison Ed. 55), 1907, fo., 11 pp.; JWC, [1919?].
Performance: Luisa Sobrino (sop.), Carlos Sobrino (pf.); Bechstein Hall; 20 June 1908.
Duration: 4'57.
Note: The first performers became Bax's parents-in-law in 1911, when he married their daughter, Elsa (Elsita) Sobrino.

74 GOLDEN GUENDOLEN for voice and piano

Title: *Printed score*: 'Golden Guendolen | A Pre Raphaelite [*sic*] Song'.
Date: 'Nov. 1905'.
Dedication: 'To CHRISTABEL MARILLIER.'
Text: William Morris, 'Golden Guendolen'.
Manuscript: Not traced.
Publication: CA (Avison Ed. 54), 1907, fo., 11 pp.; JWC, [1919?].
Duration: 5'10.

75 THE SONG IN THE TWILIGHT for voice and piano

Date: *Printed score*: 'Dec. 8th 1905.'
Dedication: 'To FREDA.' (Winifred Ada Bax).
Text: 'Verses by Freda Bax' (not otherwise published).
Manuscript: Not traced.
Publication: CA (Avison Ed. 57), 1907, fo., 7 pp.; JWC, [1922?]. Also in *Five Songs [by] Arnold Bax (Heritage of English Song 4)*, TP, [1985], 4to, pp. 12-16. Also in *Arnold Bax: Six Songs*, TP (THA 978047), 1994, 4to, pp. 10-14.
Duration: 4'31.

76 RUNE OF AGE for voice and piano

Note: This is the original, untraced version of the first of the Two Songs for voice and orchestra (see **80** below).

[13] In *Inland Far*, p. 145, Clifford Bax mentions that in about 1905 he and his brother stayed at a farmhouse in Donegal and were attended by 'a large, sweet-natured, guileless girl' called Bridget; perhaps the dedication is ironic. Padraic Colum, however, once observed that to Bax 'all little girls in cottages were Bridgiheen.'

77 VIKING-BATTLE-SONG (Mircath) for baritone and piano

Title: *MS A*: 'Mircath.' *MS B*: '"Viking-Battle-Song"'. Both versions differ from the title of the original poem.
Date: *A*: Undated. *B*: '1905'.
Text: Fiona Macleod, 'The War-Song of the Vikings'.
Manuscript: *A*: Lewis Foreman; [2] ff. (1 bifolium); [4] pp.; ALM 14 paper (357 × 257). *B*: BL (Add. MS 54777); ff. 18^v-20^v; pp. 4-8; 20-staff paper (trimmed to 330 × *c.* 259); bound with 10 other songs (see **70** above). *MS B* is clearly later than *A*, and the piano part is slightly simplified. Unpublished.
Performance: *MS B*: John Hancorn (bar.), John Thwaites (pf.); Big School, Christ's Hospital, Horsham; 18 May 1996 (second day of 'The Bax Weekend': part of the 'Horsham and District Arts Fanfare Weekend 1996').
Duration: 4'21.
Note: The Irish Gaelic word 'mircath' means 'battle champion'. At the words 'high in Valhalla' Bax quotes the 'Walhalla' motive from Wagner's *Ring*. For the orchestrated version see **80** below.

78 A SONG OF LIFE AND LOVE for orchestra

Note: The score of this unperformed work has not been traced and the only published references to it in Bax's lifetime appeared in *YB1* and *YB2*, where it is described as a 'Tone-poem for full orchestra'. No date is given, but doubtless it was roughly contemporary with *A Song of War and Victory* (**79**), which was written in 1905. The title echoes Cowen's *Phantasy of Life and Love* (1901) and foreshadows Delius's *A Poem of Life and Love* (1918-19).

79 A SONG OF WAR AND VICTORY for orchestra

Date: '1905'.
Dedication: 'To Godwin H. Baynes' (it should properly be 'H. Godwin Baynes').
Orchestra: 2(1) 2 + 1 (alto oboe) 2 +1 20, 42(in F)31 + tba.(in E♭) + tba.(in B♭), timp., 2 perc. (b.d., s.d., cym., tri.), str.
Manuscript: Lewis Foreman; [37] ff.; 1 blank + [74] pp.; ALM 18 paper (trimmed to 346 × *c.* 251); bound in blue-grey linen.
Publication: *Editor and publisher*: Paul R. Ludden, 1994, fo., 81 pp. (copyright by the Sir Arnold Bax Estate).[14]

[14] Score and parts currently available from Dr Paul R. Ludden, 3113 Ethel Avenue, Muncie, Indiana 47304, USA, or c/o Orchestral Department, Ball State University, Muncie, Indiana 47306, USA.

Performance: (1) *With cut:*[15] Windsor Sinfonia, Robert Tucker; School Hall, Eton College; 24 September 1994 (Twenty-third Annual Concert of The Broadheath Singers). (2) *Complete*: Ball State Symphony Orchestra, Paul R. Ludden; Pruis Hall, Ball State University, Muncie, Indiana, USA; 9 October 1997 (part of a lecture-recital: 'Elgar to Bax: influences on the creation of the 1905 *Song of War and Victory*').
Duration: 14'39.[16]
Note: During Bax's lifetime the only published references to this work were to be found in *YB1* and *YB2*.The theme beginning on p. 31 was adapted thirty-two years later for use in the trio of *London Pageant* (**340**). The E♭ and B♭ tuba parts are written in the treble clef, the former ascending at one point to a written F above the staff. At the first performance the parts were played by euphoniums in E♭ and B♭, although some of the higher notes were difficult to obtain.

1905–6

80 TWO SONGS for voice and orchestra

a. Rune of Age. **b.** Viking-Battle-Song.

Date: See **Note** below.
Text: **a.** Fiona Macleod, 'Rune of Age'. **b.** Fiona Macleod, 'The War-Song of the Vikings'.
Note: The scores of these songs have not been traced. They are listed in *YB1* as 'Two Songs with orchestral accompaniment', but no year of composition is given. However, since the original voice-and-piano version of **80b** is dated 1905 (see **77** above) and *YB1* was published in 1906-7, they can probably be ascribed to 1905-6. It is conceivable that the orchestration of the songs existed only in theory and that Bax never wrote out full scores (cf. **83**).

1906

81 A HUSHING SONG for voice and piano

Date: 'March | 1906.'
Dedication: '(To D.P)' (Dorothy Pyman).
Text: Fiona Macleod, 'A Hushing Song'.

[15] Following a rehearsal four days before the concert, the conductor decided to make a seventeen-page cut at the first performance, the final bar of p. 48 being followed immediately by the first bar of p. 66.
[16] This is the duration of the complete performance. The cut version was 10'40.

Manuscript: BL (Add. MS 54777); ff. 21-2^{v}; pp. 9-12 + 2 blank; ALM 14 paper (trimmed to 330 × *c.* 259); bound with 10 other songs (see **70** above). Unpublished.
Duration: 3'02.

82 I FEAR THY KISSES, GENTLE MAIDEN for voice and piano

Date: 'Fine | June 15th | 1906'.
Text: Percy Bysshe Shelley, 'To —' (posthumous).
Manuscript: BL (Add. MS 54778); ff. 40^{v}-1 (41^{v} blank); pp. 42-3 + 1 blank; 20-staff paper (trimmed to 330 × 260); bound with 10 other songs (see **70** above). Unpublished.
Duration: 1'21.

83 THE BLESSED DAMOZEL for speaker and orchestra

Note: The existence of this score is dubious. See **Note** in next entry.

84 THE BLESSED DAMOZEL for speaker and piano

Title: 'The Blessed Damozel | A Musical illustration for performance during the | recital of D. G. Rossetti's poem'.
Date: Undated but doubtless contemporary with 'The Twa Corbies' (**85**).
Dedication: '(Dedicated to Miss Dorothy Pyman).'
Text: Dante Gabriel Rossetti, 'The Blessed Damozel'.
Manuscript: Lewis Foreman; [7] ff.; [14] pp. + 2 blank; ALM 12 paper (360 × 265). Unpublished.
Duration: *c.* 12'00.
Note: To the left of the title Bax has written 'Piano Arrangement', but there is no evidence that an orchestral version existed, and it is listed in *YB1* as being with piano accompaniment. It is possible that Bax's two recitations (**84-5**) may have been prompted by the efforts of Stanley Hawley (1867-1916), who composed many such pieces (see Joseph Holbrooke, *Contemporary British Composers*, London, 1925, pp. 273-4; also *FMY*, p. 57); and Frederick Corder, Bax's composition teacher, was an enthusiast for this art form. But a more immediate source of inspiration was undoubtedly Mary Field, one of Bax's girl-friends, who, to judge from three letters that he wrote to her, seems to have had some skill in recitation (see Maggs Brothers, catalogue 956, March 1974, Music, part 3, item 26). In one letter he wrote that recitation was 'the most intimate of interpretative arts' and 'nearest allied to that of 'story-telling' of old times and all its lovely romantic associations of firelight and the rhapsodic interludes on the harp or some other simple instrument, now developed (not altogether to the betterment of the emotional effect) into the Enoch Arden of Richard Strauss and similar complexities.' In another letter Bax wrote of 'that hideous abortion, the English poetic drama.' See also Clifford Bax, *Inland Far*, pp.

216-7, in which Arnold discusses recitation with Gustav Holst and Balfour Gardiner.

85 THE TWA CORBIES for speaker and piano

Title: 'Ballad. | The Twa Corbies'.
Date: 'Sept 20th 1906'.
Dedication: 'To Roland Bocquet.'
Text: Traditional words 'From "Border Minstrelsy"'. No volume with this precise title has been traced. Perhaps Andrew Lang, *Border Ballads* (1895) is meant, or Walter Scott, *Minstrelsy of the Scottish Border* (1902).
Manuscript: Lewis Foreman; [2] ff.; [3] pp. + 1 blank; ALM 12 paper (355 × 258). Unpublished.
Duration: 5'09.
Note: Erroneously listed as a song in *MT*. Balfour Gardiner read through this piece in his capacity as an adviser for CA, but it was not published (see Stephen Lloyd, *H. Balfour Gardiner*, Cambridge, 1984, pp. 49-51). See also under **84** above.

86 MAGNIFICAT for voice and piano

Title: Printed score: 'Magnificat. | (After a picture by D. G. ROSETTI [*sic*].)' (see **Note** below).
Date: 'Xmas 1906.'
Dedication: 'TO DOROTHY PYMAN.'
Text: St Luke's Gospel, I, 46-55.
Manuscript: Not traced.
Publication: CA (Avison Ed. 56), 1907, fo., 9 pp.; JWC [1919?].
Duration: 4'46.
Note: It is not known which picture Bax had in mind when composing this song but it was presumably one of Rossetti's three portraits of the Virgin Mary.[17] In *FMY*, p. 40, Bax mentions that during 1907-8 his life 'took on a slightly pre-Raphaelite tinge, for I was a frequent guest at Kelmscott House . . . [where] the flowered walls were hung with engravings by pre-Raphaelite artists . . .' Bax's composition teacher, Frederick Corder, was an avid collector of Kelmscott Press books. For the arrangement of this song for SATB and organ see **376**. Other works with Pre-Raphaelite connections are 'The Blessed Damozel' (**84**) and *Spring Fire* (**153**).

[17] See Virginia Surtees, *The Paintings and Drawings of Dante Gabriel Rossetti . . . A Catalogue Raisonné* (Oxford, 1971), Nos. 51, 110, 689.

87 TRIO IN ONE MOVEMENT for piano, violin and viola (or clarinet[18])

Title: *Printed score*: 'Trio in one movement, op. 4'.
Date: '1906' (*YB1*, etc.).
Dedication: 'To A. J. ROWAN-HAMILTON.'
Manuscript: Not traced.
Publication: CA (Avison Ed. 40), 1907, fo., 33 pp.; JWC (248), *c.* 1925, 4to.
Performance: *Earliest traced*: Albert Sammons (vn.), Alfred Hobday (vla.), Ethel Hobday (pf.); Æolian Hall; 9 November 1915.
Duration: 18'22.
Note: In later life Bax regretted having submitted this work for publication:

> An early trio of my own which I madly allowed to appear in the catalogue of the 'S.B.C.' [Society of British Composers] has become the very bane of my life; for the firm of J. & W. Chester, which took over all the publications of the Society upon the latter's official demise, has ever been the principal musical link between ourselves and the Continent, and whenever application is made to them from abroad for an example of my work that early derivative and formless farrago is inevitably sent out, with the natural result that European interest in me is stillborn. I cannot blame Messrs. Chester & Co. (who do not pay rent in Great Marlborough Street for the good of their health), since this trio is the only extended work of mine in their list; but I wish the devil would fly away with the whole remaining stock of the damned thing, and give himself ptomaine poisoning by eating it! (*FMY*, pp. 88-9.)

c. 1906

88 ECHO for voice and piano

Note: This is known only from *YB1* and from a list of thirty-five song titles written out by the composer on ff. [7^{v}-8] of a notebook in UCC that otherwise contains mostly cricket scores and batting averages (see Appendix 7, section V (i)). The list is headed 'Fiona M^c^Leod Songs', which refers, however, only to the first thirteen titles. The remaining twenty-two songs have the poet's name written against each, this song (No. 33) being listed as 'Come to me in the silence of the night', with the words ascribed to Christina Rossetti, namely 'Echo' from *Goblin Market and Other Poems* (1862).

No dates are given against any of the songs in the notebook. The earliest datable title is 'The Grand Match' (**56**), which was completed on 29 June 1903, while the latest is 'A Lyke-Wake Dirge' (**105**), dated 25 January 1908, which is the last of the thirty-five song titles in the notebook. No later songs are listed except possibly 'Der Waldsee', which is attributed to 1908 in *MT*. But other songs definitely finished later in 1908 are lacking, suggesting that the list may have been made out early that year.

[18] The clarinet alternative is noted in *YB1* but is not found in any other source (including *YB2*). The set of parts does not include one for clarinet.

89 FOR LOVE'S SAKE for voice and piano

Note: This is known only from the list detailed in **88** above (No. 23), the words being ascribed to Ben Jonson. The title given by Bax is actually from the opening line of the poem 'Begging Another, on Colour of Mending the Former' from *From Underwoods consisting of Diverse Poems, II. A Celebration of Charis in Ten Lyric Pieces*, 7.

90 GARDEN SONG for voice and piano

Note: This is known only from the list detailed in **88** above (No. 15), the words being ascribed to 'A. E. T. B.' (i.e. the composer himself), though the poem is not otherwise attested. It is conceivable that the title is a generic one (like 'A Song by Rückert', which also occurs in the list) and that Bax is simply referring to a song about a garden.

91 SUMMER NIGHT for voice and piano

Note: This is known only from the list detailed in **88** above (No. 24), the words being ascribed (like **90**) to 'A. E. T. B.', though the poem is not attested elsewhere.

1907

92 FATHERLAND for tenor, chorus and orchestra

Title: The NOV edition appends 'Op. 5' to the title, but this is omitted in later reprints. The work was described as a 'cantata' at its first performance. In the list of songs detailed in **88** above, there appears the title 'Finland' with words ascribed to J. L. Runeberg, who appears not to have written a poem with this title. It seems quite likely that Bax is referring to *Fatherland*, written in praise of Finland: perhaps he originally wrote it as a song for voice and piano.
Date: *Printed score*: 'March 1907' (but see **Note** below).
Dedication: *NOV edition*: 'TO ARNE VON ERPECUM.' The JWC reprints and the holograph f.sc. of the revised version bear no dedication.
Orchestra: Not traced (for revised version see **325**).
Text: Johan Ludvig Runeberg, 'Vårt land' ['Our Land'] from *Fänrik Ståls Sägner* ['Tales of Ensign Steel'], translated from the Swedish by Clifford Bax (not otherwise published).
Manuscript: Not traced.
Publication: *Vocal score only*: NOV (Avison Ed. [no pl. no.]), copyright by Arnold Bax, 1909, 8vo, 18 pp.; JWC (9719), 1922 (plates purchased in January 1921 and destroyed in 1962). *Proof of printed score*: JWC; this is corrected in Bax's hand and date-stamped 7 December 1921. Assigned to CH in 1982 in exchange for Lord Berners' film score *Nicholas Nickleby*.

Performance: (1) John Coates (ten.), Liverpool Welsh Choral Union, Members of the Hallé Orchestra and Liverpool Philharmonic Orchestra, Harry Evans; Philharmonic Hall, Liverpool; 25 September 1909 (First Festival of the Music League). (2) Spencer Thomas (ten.), Edward Mason Choir, New Symphony Orchestra, Edward Mason; Queen's Hall; 22 March 1911.
Duration: *c.* 8'00.
Note: For the first performance the following information in Bax's own words was incorporated into the programme note:

'Although these poems' says the composer, 'and the hymn that precedes them have a very particular local significance, it is clear that the latter might appropriately voice the sentiments of any small and oppressed nationality'. His idea in the composition is 'a strolling ballad-singer chanting by a smoking hearth on some northern winter night, and surrounded by an entranced audience of young and old. The emotional appeal gradually increases, the listeners participating more and more actively in the music, until finally, with linked hands and eyes flashing in the flickering firelight, the whole company bursts forth into the song of the fatherland's approaching freedom and glory.'

Although 'March 1907' is given at the end of the printed v.sc., Bax's original copyright is dated 1909, the year of its first performance, and it is possible that the orchestration was not completed until that year. Runeberg's poem comprises eleven verses, of which Bax sets five in the order 1, 10, 2, 3, 11; the words had been set in 1843 by Frederick Pacius, whose version became the Finnish national anthem. The published v.sc. of Bax's setting has the text in both Swedish and English but the revised f.sc. has the English version only. The orthography of the Swedish words is naturally that of the language before the spelling reforms of 1906, but the use of Dano-Norwegian *aa* for *å* (the latter introduced in 1526) is probably for typographical convenience. On the title page of the NOV edition, for example, 'Fänrik Ståls Sägner' appears as 'Pänrik Staal's Saagner' ('Pänrik' is corrected to 'Fänrik' in the JWC reprint). 'Saagner' for 'sägner' (tales) is a double error, perhaps through confusion with 'sånger' (songs), which occurs in the subtitle of Runeberg's collection: *En samling sånger*.

In a letter published in *The Irish Statesman* (11 September 1926), p. 11, about a proposed Irish national anthem, Bax described 'Vårt land' as 'unquestionably the most moving national poem ever composed.'

93 THE FIDDLER OF DOONEY for voice and piano

Date: *Holograph MS*: 'Dresden. | March 1907'.
Dedication: *Copyist's score* (but dedication in Bax's hand): 'To | J.B. M[c]Ewen.'
Text: W. B. Yeats, 'The Fiddler of Dooney'.
Manuscript: *Holograph*: BL (Add. MS 54778); ff. 34-6; pp. 29-33; 20-staff paper (trimmed to 330 × 260); bound with 11 other songs (see **65** above). *Copyist's score*:

JWC; [4] ff.; [8] pp.; BH III paper (356 × 264). Bax has added the dedication and '(W.B. Yeats)' under the title.
Publication: Pages 1 and 3 of corrected proofs reproduced in Lewis Foreman (ed.), *Dermot O'Byrne: Poems by Arnold Bax*, pp. 19-20;[19] not otherwise published with these words (see **Note** below).
Performance: Janet Linsé[20] (sop.), David Owen Norris (pf.); British Music Information Centre; 14 October 1983 (lecture-recital by Lewis Foreman, *et al.*).
Duration: 2'09.
Note: After this song had been set up in print by JWC, but before it was issued, Bax decided to change the words (see next entry for details). He had a deep veneration for the poetry of Yeats and considered it too good to be set to music. In a radio talk recorded on 6 May 1949 he claimed never to have set any of Yeats's verse and expressed the opinion that 'Poetry has its own precise rhythms and intrinsic melody, and at its highest should be reverently let alone.'

94 THE ENCHANTED FIDDLE for voice and piano

Title: Erroneously listed in *MT* as 'The Magic Fiddler'.
Date: The music was composed in 1907 but the words in this form were not added until 1918 (see **Note** below).
Dedication: 'To | J.B. McEwen.'
Text: *Printed score*: 'Anon.' (words written by Bax himself).
Manuscript: JWC: The proofs of 'The Fiddler of Dooney' (**93** above) were altered by Bax in red ink with the new text replacing Yeats's original; a typescript of Bax's poem is pinned to it.
Publication: [No.5] (3778) in *Album of Seven Songs*, JWC, 1919, 4to, pp. 18-23 (proofs sent to Bax on 1 January 1918). The front cover of this edition has the title *Seven Selected Songs | Chester Series No. 44.* A reprint issued in the late 1970s has the title *Seven Bax Songs* on the front cover. Each song has its own pl. no., and they were issued separately in 1922. For details of the other six songs see **101, 102, 109, 116, 132, 158a.**
Performance: John Coates (ten.), Anthony Bernard (pf.); Queen's (Small) Hall; 23 June 1919.
Duration: 2'09.
Note: For details of the original version see previous entry. The words were written by Bax himself exactly following the scheme and metre of Yeats's 'The Fiddler of

[19] Unfortunately the printer of Foreman's book mistook the purpose of the exercise and obeyed some of Bax's handwritten instructions believing them to have been made by the editor. Thus the original printed title of this song has been replaced by the revised version.

[20] Not Jeannette Wilson, as indicated in the printed programme.

Dooney'. A similar parody, called 'The Song of the Old Fiddler', is published in Lewis Foreman (ed.), *Dermot O'Byrne: Poems by Arnold Bax*, p. 36.

95 SYMPHONY IN F for orchestra (short score only)

I. Allegro molto vivace. II. Andante con moto. III. Intermezzo: Tempo di valsero. IV. Finale: Molto vivace.

Title: *I-II*: 'Symphony in F minor'. *III-IV*: 'Symphony in F op. 8.' *Gr2*: 'Symphony in F minor and major'.
Date: 'Fine April 3rd 1907'.
Manuscript: UCC (movts. I-II formerly owned by Colin Scott-Sutherland); [33] ff.; [64] pp. ([1-19] + 1 blank, [21-8], t.p. + 1 p. with 'Note' (see below) + [31-40], [41-65] + 1 blank; III and IV have non-autograph page numerals in ballpoint pen); I-II: ALM 12 paper (360 × 265), III-IV: BC 5 paper (342 × 267). Unpublished.
Performance: *Movt. III only*: David Owen Norris (pf.); British Music Information Centre; 3 February 1983 (lecture-recital by Lewis Foreman, *et al.*).
Duration: *c.* 60'00.
Note: This is Bax's earliest attempt at writing a symphony and is his longest composition apart from the unorchestrated ballet *Tamara* (**138**). The work is referred to in *FMY*, pp. 37-8, in the chapter describing Bax's second visit to Dresden during the first three months of 1907: 'I was engaged upon a colossal symphony which would have occupied quite an hour in performance, were such a cloud-cuckoo dream to become an actuality. (Happily, it never has!).' In March, after completing *Fatherland* (**92**) and 'The Fiddler of Dooney' (**93**), Bax left Dresden with 'a tall, calm-eyed Scandinavian girl' (Dorothy Pyman), and the short score of this symphony was finished a few weeks later. The MS contains very few notes for orchestration, and we can be certain that Bax never prepared a full score. On f. [15v], at the start of movt. III, the composer has written the following note:

The motif of this intermezzo was suggested by, and to some extent based upon, the central idea of 'Der Tor und der Tod' by Hugo von Hoffmannsthal [*sic*]. The central figure of this author's play, Claudio (der Tor) is the impersonation of the overcivilized and hypersensitive modern man, the tragedy of whose destiny is to be traced to the super-subtlety and complexity of his emotional life. At the end of life he realizes that he has not really lived in the fullest sense of the word. A perverse demon has haunted him throughout the whole course of his earthly existence preventing him from sounding the depths of any of the great spiritual experiences and mingling them together in such a manner that joy has become confused with sorrow and love with hate and so forth. It is this central conception that this intermezzo sets forth to illustrate. In the scherzo section the demon of unrest and perversity is represented and in that part of the movement usually occupied by the Trio three motivs are introduced symbolizing respectively (a) Love (b) Religion or Philosophy (c) The battle of life. Each of these is interrupted and broken to pieces by the theme of the Sche[r]zo. In the coda the subject of the programme dies returning with a broken sigh to the love of his youth.

Immediately following the end of this movement there are eight staves containing the melodies of four Irish folk songs: 'Irish Molly O', 'The Bed of Green Rushes', 'Musha, woman I think you're mad', and 'Maidean óg [Early Morning]'. At the end of movt. II Bax has written out the melody of 'The Boys of Wexford' (unidentified on the score), also known as 'The Flight of the Earls' and 'Granuaille'.

96 LONGING for voice and piano

Title: Listed in *YB1* as 'The Multitudes of the Wind' (a phrase from the poem).
Date: 'May 8th | 1907.'
Dedication: '(To D.P)' (Dorothy Pyman).
Text: Fiona Macleod, 'Longing'.
Manuscript: *Holograph*: BL (Add. MS 54777); ff. 33-4^{v}; pp. 33-6; 20-staff paper (trimmed to 330 × *c.* 259); bound with 10 other songs (see **70** above). *Copyist's score*: Privately owned; [4] ff.; [7] pp. + 1 blank; 12-staff paper. Unpublished.
Duration: 2'41.

97 THE FLUTE for voice and piano

Title: *MS*: '"Ideala"'. *Printed score*: 'The Flute' (t.p.); 'The Flute. | (Ideala.)' (p. 1).
Date: *MS*: 'July 8th | 1907'. *Printed score*: '1908'.
Dedication: *MS*: '(To G.N.L.)' (Gladys Lees). *Printed score*: 'To Madame Elisabeth Munthe-Kaas.'
Text: Bjørnstjerne Bjørnsen, untitled poem from the peasant tale *Arne*, end of chapter 14, introduced by the words: 'Han sang det stilt, som han havde gjørt det' ('He sang it quietly as he had composed it'). Translated by Sir Edmund Gosse 'and printed by his kind permission.'[21] A footnote in the printed score states that 'the music of the voice-part was originally set to the Norwegian words.'
Manuscript: BL (Add. MS 54778); ff. 49-50^{v}; pp. 63-6; 20-staff paper (trimmed to 330 × 260); bound with 11 other songs (see **65** above).
Publication: MM (10), 1923, fo., 7 pp.
Performance: *Earliest traced*: John Coates (ten.), Arnold Bax (pf.); Wigmore Hall; 15 June 1920.
Duration: 4'14.
Note: Although the title on the MS is 'Ideala', the main title on the printed score is 'The Flute', with the original given as a subtitle. It is listed in *MT* (1919) as 'The Flute', but on the lower wrappers of songs published by MM in 1921—fourteen years after its composition and two years before it was issued—it still appears as 'Ideala' alone, and it was performed under this title in 1920. (The word does not

[21] Not to be confused with the translation by Walter Low in *The Novels of Bjørnstjerne Bjørnsen*, II (London, 1894), pp. 187-8, which was edited by Gosse.

appear in Bjørnsen's original text.) For details of other works entitled 'Ideala' see **122** and **177**.[22] In the MS the words are written in the original Dano-Norwegian (Riksmål) alone. The published score has this 'Norse Original' and an English translation by Edmond Gosse printed on separate staves. The MS gives the author's name as 'Björnstjerne Björnsen' and the printed score substitutes *ö* for *ø* throughout the otherwise accurate text, presumably for typographical convenience since none of the varieties of Norwegian actually uses this letter. The date given on the printed score ('1908') is probably that of another, untraced MS containing both the original and the English words from which it was engraved.

98 CARNIVAL: Sketches (in short score)

Title: 'Carnival' appears at the head of each of the two bifoliated MSS.
Date: Undated, but the presence on one of the sheets of a draft for the song 'From the Hills of Dream' (**100**) suggests that these sketches may pre-date 6 September 1907, the day on which the song was finished. Since there is nothing dating from between 8 July and 2 September, they have been tentatively assigned to that seven-week period, though they may of course have been written earlier or later, the MS perhaps having already been used for the song draft.
Manuscript: Clifford Gillam (MS formerly owned by Harriet Cohen); *A*: [2] ff.; [4] pp.; ALM 18 paper (272 × 361). *B*: [2] ff.; 3 pp. + 1 containing the ten-bar ink sketch for 'From the Hills of Dream'; ALM 18 paper (272 × 361). Each MS has two-staff systems with writing in pencil and ink.
Note: The MSS contain a few indications of the intended orchestration (cor anglais, muted trumpets, etc.) but the material is not sufficiently developed for it to be regarded as constituting a final short score. The music is in an appropriately jovial, unbuttoned vein, and above a staff on f. 2 of MS *A* appears the word 'laughter', suggesting that it may have been intended as incidental music for some kind of stage work (cf. 'whooping and laughter' on sketches possibly for the projected opera *Red Owen* (**170**)). None of the material appears in any other extant work.

99 DU BLOMST I DUG for voice and piano

Title: *MS*: '"Du blomst i Dug"'. *MT*: 'O dewy flower'.
Date: 'Sept. 2nd | 1907.'
Text: J. P. Jacobsen, 'Du Blomst i Dug' from *Mogens*. (Bax has erroneously written the author's initials as 'J. B.' on the MS.)

[22] John Foulds's *Dichterliebe* for piano (1898) is dedicated to 'Ideala', which has been interpreted by Malcolm MacDonald as either a girl's name or the 'Feminine Ideal'—presumably a pseudo-feminine form of late Latin 'idealis' (*John Foulds and his Music: An Introduction*, London, 1989, p. 4). In a book written anonymously by Sarah Grand (*Ideala: A Study from Life*, London, 1888) it is the name of a woman.

Manuscript: BL (Add. MS 54778); ff. 51-2 (52^{v} blank); pp. 67-9 + 1 blank; 20-staff paper (trimmed to 330 × 260); bound with 11 other songs (see **65** above). Unpublished.
Duration: 1'25.

100 FROM THE HILLS OF DREAM for voice and piano

Title: *MS B* has 'Celtic Songs | No ' [*sic*] to the left of the title.
Date: *A*: 'Sept 6th | 1907.' *B*: 'Sept 6th 1907.'
Dedication: *A*: '(To G·N·L)' *B*: '(To G.N.L.)' (Gladys Lees).
Text: Fiona Macleod, 'From the Hills of Dream'.
Manuscript: *A*: BL (Add. MS 54777); ff. 35-6^{v}; pp. 37-40; 20-staff paper (trimmed to 330 × *c.* 259); bound with 10 other songs (see 70 above). *B*: Lewis Foreman; [2] ff. (1 bifolium); [4] pp.; ALM 14 paper (361 × 267). Unpublished.
Duration: 2'54.

101 A MILKING SIAN for voice and piano

Title: 'Sian' is the Irish Gaelic for a chant or cry.
Date: 'Sept 23rd 1907.'
Dedication: *MS*: '(To D. P)' (Dorothy Pyman). No dedication on copyist's or published scores.
Text: Fiona Macleod, 'Milking Sian' from *Foam of the Past*.
Manuscript: *Holograph*: BL (Add. MS 54777); ff. 17-18; pp. 1-3; 20-staff paper (trimmed to 330 × *c.* 259); bound with 10 other songs (see 70 above). *Copyist's score* (annotated by Bax): JWC; [4] ff.; 5 pp. + 3 blank; BH III paper (356 × 264).
Publication: [No. 6] (3774) in *Album of Seven Songs*, JWC, 1919, 4to, pp. 24-8. For reprints see **94** above.
Performance: *Earliest traced*: Ethel Lister (sop.), Arnold Bax (pf.); Æolian Hall; 16 July 1908. This concert also included Bax's Quintet in G (**107**) and no fewer than fourteen of his songs, most of which were settings of Fiona Mcleod.[23] Since no copy of the programme booklet has yet come to light, it is impossible to know precisely which songs were performed, apart from 'A Milking Sian' and 'Closing Doors' (**63b**), which are mentioned in reviews.
Duration: 3'07.

102 THE WHITE PEACE for voice and piano

Date: *MS A*: 'Sept 26th 1907'. *MS B*: 'Fine | 1906.' *Printed score*: '1907' (see **Note** below).
Dedication: *A*: 'To Dorothy [Pyman]'. *B*: None. *Printed score*: 'To | my Mother.'

[23] Information from *The Daily Telegraph* (16 July 1908) and *The Musical News* (25 July 1908).

Text: Fiona Macleod, 'The White Peace' from *Closing Doors*.
Manuscript: *A*: Lewis Foreman; [1] f.; [2] pp.; 28 bars; ALM 14 paper (360 × *c.* 264). *B*: BL (Add. MS 54777); f. 32-2^{v}; pp. 31-2; 20-staff paper (trimmed to 330 × *c.* 259); bound with 10 other songs (see 70 above). *Copyist's score*: JWC; [2] ff.; 3 pp. + 1 blank; BH III paper (356 × 264). The dedication to his mother and the name of the author are in Bax's hand. There are also a few annotations, and the three bars containing the words 'moonlight of a perfect peace floods heart and' are entirely in Bax's hand, having been pasted over the copyist's version.
Publication: [No. 1] (3769) in *Album of Seven Songs*, JWC, 1919, 4to, pp. 2-4. For reprints see **94** above.
Performance: *Earliest traced*: John Coates (ten.), Harriet Cohen (pf.); Wigmore Hall; 15 June 1920.
Arrangement: For solo piano by Ronald Stevenson (unpublished).
Duration: 2'14.
Note: MS *B* is obviously a fair copy of *A*, and '1906' written at the end is presumably a mistake, the correct year being found on the printed score.

103 HEART O'BEAUTY for voice and piano

Title: *MS A*: 'Celtic Songs. No ' [*sic*], written to the left of the title.
Date: *A*: 'Sept 30 1907'. *B*: 'Sept 30th | 1907'.
Dedication: *A*: None. *B*: '(To G.N.L)' (Gladys Lees).
Text: Fiona Macleod, 'Heart o'Beauty'.
Manuscript: *A*: Lewis Foreman; [4] ff.; t.p. + 1 blank + [5] pp. + 1 blank; ALM 14 paper (360 × 267). *B*: BL (Add. MS 54777); ff. 24^{v}-26^{v}; pp. 16-20; 20-staff paper (trimmed to 330 × *c.* 259); bound with 10 other songs (see 70 above). Unpublished.
Duration: 2'40.

104 THE KINGDOM for voice and piano

Note: The score of this song has not been traced. It is listed in *MT* with the words attributed to Friedrich Rückert, presumably his 'Das Reich und sein König' from *Pantheon*, 2, or possibly 'Mein Reich' from *Mailieder in sechs Büchern*, 2. This is probably the work listed vaguely as 'A song by Rückert' in the notebook detailed under **88**.

1908

105 A LYKE-WAKE DIRGE for voice and piano

Title: *MS A*: 'A Lyke-Wake Dirge'. *MS B*: 'A Lyke-Wake | (Border Ballad)'. A lyke-wake is the watch (wake) kept at night over a dead body (lyke, lych or lich).
Date: *A*: 'Jan 25th | 1908.' *B*: Undated.

Text: Anonymous 15th-century Scottish border ballad.
Manuscript: *A*: BL (Add. MS 54778); ff. 36^{v}-40; pp. 34-41; 20-staff paper (trimmed to 330 × 260); bound with 11 other songs (see **65** above). *B*: ULL (MS 435); [4] ff.; 8 pp. (incomplete: lacking p. 9); AL 12 paper (360 × 265). The handwriting and imprint of the paper suggest that this MS was probably written out in 1934, shortly before it was orchestrated. Unpublished.
Performance: Jeff Weaver (ten.), David Owen Norris (pf.); British Music Information Centre; 3 February 1983 (lecture-recital by Lewis Foreman, *et al.*).
Duration: 6'18
Note: For the orchestrated version see **326a.**

106 DEIRDRE: Opera (unfinished)

Title: The name can be spelt 'Deirdre' or 'Déirdre'; Bax generally prefers the version without an acute accent.
Title: *Typescript libretto*: 'DÉIRDRE. | A Saga-drama in Five Scenes and a Prologue.' *MS A*: '"Eiré" [*sic*] | Prologue' [originally 'Deirdre | Prologue'; see **Note** below]. *MS B*: '"Deirdre" Scene II | "The Gathering of the Chiefs"' (t.p.); 'Deirdre. [in Irish script] Scene II | "The Gathering of the Chiefs"'. *MS C*: 'Deirdre | Cuid [scene] 5' [in Irish script].
Date: 'Glencolumcille, Co. Donegal, | Nov. 18th 1907.' (end of foreword to typescript libretto). The music sketches are undated, but Bax is known to have been working on them in 1908.
Dedication: 'TO THE SPIRITS ON THE ULSTER MOUNTAINS.' (libretto).
Manuscript: *Libretto*: Privately owned typescript with annotations in Bax's hand; [62] ff.; dedic. p. + t.p. + 11 pp. (pagin. [i], ii-xi) of a foreword + half-t.p. + 107 pp. + 2 pp. of notes at the end. The dedicatory page has a motto typed above the dedication: '"Old unhappy far-off things, | And battles long ago."'; this is from William Wordsworth's 'The Solitary Reaper' in *Memorials of a Tour in Scotland* (1803). The contents are attached by clips to a limp cover with a paper label on the front with 'DEIRDRE.' typed on it. Inside the front cover Bax has written his Ivy Bank address, which is crossed through and replaced by his Fellows Road address. Plain paper unmarked except for last folio: 'W.S.& B*RECENT LINEN | MADE IN U.S.A.', on the reverse of which there is a pencilled sketch, presumably by Bax, of the rear view of a portly conductor seated on a stool with his arms outstretched, a baton in his right hand. Unpublished.

Three short-score MSS: *A*: UCC; [3] ff.; [5] pp. + 1 blank; ALM 12 paper (357 × 265). There are a few instrumental indications, and above the antepenultimate bar is written 'Curtain rises'. *B*: UCC; [4] ff.; t.p. + 1 blank + [6] pp.; ALM 14 paper (360 × 267); in a manila envelope. There are a few instrumental indications, and at the end Bax has pencilled in the initials 'A. B. B. G. V. W. W. H. B.' (i.e. Arnold Bax, Balfour Gardiner, Vaughan Williams and W. H. Bell). *C*: UCC; [2] ff.; [3] pp.

+ 1 blank; ALM 12 paper (358 × 266); in a manila envelope. There is a single instrumental indication ('Oboe') at bar 25. All unpublished.
Arrangement: *MS C* edited and orchestrated by Graham Parlett (as *On the Sea-shore*): 3(1) 2 +1 2 +1 2 +1, 4331, timp., 3 perc. (b.d., s.d., cym., gong), str.: t.p. + introd. note + pp. 3-21 + 1 blank; D24 Panopus 24-staff paper (413 × 294). Unpublished. *Parts*: Graham Parlett. *Performance*: (1) Kensington Symphony Orchestra, Leslie Head; St John's, Smith Square; 7 February 1984. (2) Ulster Orchestra, Vernon Handley; Ulster Hall, Belfast; 26 March 1986 (recording session for Chandos Records Ltd.).[24]
Note: In 1907 Yeats published a three-act play based on the story of Deirdre, which is first found in the twelfth-century *Book of Leinster*. It also provided the basis for plays by George Russell (AE) and J. M. Synge, and the inspiration for poems by several Irish writers including Bax's own literary alter ego, 'Dermot O'Byrne' ('To Deirdre', first published in *Orpheus*, 13, January 1911, p. 249; the MS of the poem is dated 'In Russia June 12th 1910').

The characters in the projected opera are listed on the title page of the libretto:[25]

Concobar (Connachor) McNessa: High King of Ulster and Eire.
Naoisi (Neeshé), Ardan and Ainnle: the sons of Usnach.
Fergus Mac Roigh: who abdicates the throne of Emain in favour of Concobar.
Cuchullain of Muirthemne: 'the Hound of Uladh'.
Connall Cearnach.
Cathbad: the Arch-druid.
A Bard.
Another Druid.
An old fisherman.
Deirdre: Daughter of Fedlimid the harper.
Levarcam: Nurse to Déirdre and formerly nurse to Concobar.
Fedlimid: the harper.

After finishing his play, Bax set about writing the music, and in an undated letter to Mary Field he wrote: 'At present I am in my usual condition in that I have too much work on hand, all of which is clamouring to be accomplished! As it is I am concentrating on the Deirdre music by main force . . .'. In the end, however, all that he appears to have composed are the three non-vocal sections listed above, and he eventually abandoned the project. 'I have no particular gift for opera', he later remarked in his BBC talk of 1949, 'nor any technical theories about it, and on the whole I do not think it is a medium suited to us as a nation.' The *Prologue* (MS *A*) was orchestrated in the winter of 1908 as the first part of the *Éire* trilogy, *Into the Twilight* (**110**), the title 'Deirdre' being scratched out on the MS short score and

[24] The scoring was slightly revised between the two performances.
[25] This is not a precise transcription: the original typography has been modified.

'Eiré' [*sic*] substituted. 'The Gathering of the Chiefs' (MS *B*) was intended as a march accompanying the arrival of King Conchobar and his retinue at a feast during scene II:

The sound of distant horns is heard, heralding the approaching company. . . . A barbaric march tune is heard, and the heroes and nobles of the Red Branch [i.e. the Craobh ruadh, the king's warriors, the fiercest in Ireland] enter in procession. With them come a number of bards with beautifully carven harps, trumpet players with great curved instruments fashioned of bronze with decorated mouthpieces, tympan-players, ollavs (the administrators of law), druids and other dignitaries.

After the play had been abandoned, however, Bax orchestrated the march in 1910 as *Rosc-catha* (**128**), the third part of the *Éire* trilogy. The third sketch (MS *C*), which was intended as the opening of scene V, was orchestrated as *On the Sea-shore* (see **Arrangement** above), the title being taken from the heading of the scene in the play. Towards the end of this piece there occurs a theme that also appears in the *Prologue* and has all the hallmarks of being Deirdre's thematic motive.

There is a further offshoot from *Deirdre* to be found in 'The Well of Tears' from the song cycle *The Bard of the Dimbovitza* (**160**), where there appears to be a direct quotation of another theme from *Into the Twilight*. The title of the song inevitably brings to mind the fact that Deirdre's most common epithet is 'sorrowful', and it is tempting to postulate that the theme was somehow associated in Bax's mind with the notion of sadness. For details of Bax's other operatic aspirations see **170**. See also Graham Parlett, 'The Unwritten Operas of Arnold Bax', *BMS News*, 67 (September, 1995), pp. 152-5.

107 QUINTET IN G for 2 violins, 1 viola and 2 cellos

I. Allegro vivace. II. Lento espressivo. III. Scherzo. Allegro vivace. IV. Allegro molto vivace.

Title: 'Quintett for strings in G.' (the key designation has been added later in ink of a lighter colour).
Date: I. 'Gleann- | Columcille | Bealtainne | 1908.' [Glencolumcille, May 1908]. II. 'Glencolumcille | Beltaine 1908' [this inscription in roman script, the others in Irish]. III. 'GleannColumcille, Eire. | Bealtainne 1908'. IV. Undated.
Manuscript: Privately owned; [35] ff.; 70 pp. (1-20 + 1 blank, 21-31, 32-47 + 1 with Bax's name and Ivy Bank address (not in his hand) + 1 blank, t.p. + 1 blank + [20] pp.); A&C 14 paper (359 × 262); stitched into brown wrappers with 'Finale | Quintett | A.T. Bax' on upper cover in blue pencil (not in Bax's hand). Unpublished but see **261** for revised version of movt. II.
Performance: (1) Wessely Quartet: Hans Wessely (vn.), Spencer Dyke (vn.), James Lockyer (va.), B. Patterson Parker (vc.), with R.W. Tabb (vc.); Æolian Hall; 16 July 1908 (part of a concert attended, according to *The Musical News* for 25 July 1908, pp. 76-7, by a 'large and interested audience' that also included fourteen Bax songs sung by Ethel Lister with the composer at the piano). 'An elaborate but dull and diffuse

Quintet . . . has some musical merits, but it failed to make a very favourable impression.' (*The Musical Standard*, 25 July 1908, p. 68.) (2) Movts. I and II were repeated by the same performers in November 1908 and at the Bechstein Hall on 3 February 1909.
Duration: *c.* 40'00.
Note: 'At the outbreak of war [4 August 1914] the only MS. copy had been sent for performance to Germany, where it naturally remained. The composer regarded it as lost, but at the end of the war period it suddenly returned to him.' (Edwin Evans in WWC, p. 67.) For details of the revision of movt. II see **261**. There is a separate set of parts for movt. III in which the second cello part is noted as being adaptable as an ad lib. double bass part, suggesting that the movement might be played by a string orchestra. The melody that occurs in movt. I, 3:4 ff. also appears in *A Hill Tune* for piano (**232**).

108 LANDSKAB (LANDSCAPE) for contralto or baritone and piano

Title: *MSS A and B*: '"Landskab" | (Landscape)'. *MS C*: 'Landscape'.
Date: *A and B*: 'July 15th | 1908'. *C*: Undated.
Text: J. P. Jacobsen, 'Landskab' (one of two poems with the same title: that beginning 'Stille, du elskede Kvinde!').
Manuscript: *A*: KB (CI. 370); [2] ff.; 3 pp. + 1 blank; ALM 14 paper (363 × 264). *B*: BL (Add. MS 54778); ff. 47-8v; pp. 59-62; 20-staff paper (trimmed to 330 × 260); bound with 11 other songs (see **65** above). *C*: KB (CI. 370); [1] f.; [2] pp. (unfinished); ALM 16 paper (360 × 271). MS *A*, the earliest version, has the Danish words 'Digt af [poem by] | J. B. [*sic*] Jacobsen.' to the left of the title and 'Musik af | Arnold Bax | contralto Voice.' to the right. The words 'Contralto | or | Baritone' occur at the start of the vocal line. There are no tempo markings or dynamics. *MS B*, the second version, has the marking 'Lento e tranquillo' at the beginning and includes dynamic markings. *MS C*, which is marked 'Molto tranquillo', is unfinished, the vocal line continuing to the end of p. 2, stopping at the word 'spille', but the piano part finishing three bars before, which suggests that Bax abandoned rewriting the score at this point rather than that a third page is missing. The handwriting of *C* indicates a later date than that of the other two MSS. Unpublished.
Duration: 3'15.

109 SHIELING SONG for voice and piano

Title: *MS*: '"Shieling-Song"'. *Printed score*: 'Shieling Song'. The word 'shieling' or 'shealing' (misspelt 'sheiling' by the poet) means grazing-land for cattle.
Date: 'July 30th | 1908'.
Dedication: *Printed score only*: 'To | Mrs William Sharp.'

Text: Fiona Macleod (i.e. William Sharp, the dedicatee's late husband), 'Sheiling Song' from *From the Hills of Dream*.
Manuscript: *Holograph*: BL (Add. MS 54777); f. 31-1ᵛ; pp. 29-30; 20-staff paper (trimmed to 330 × *c.* 259); bound with 10 other songs (see **70** above). *Copyist's score*: JWC; 3 pp. + 1 blank; BH III paper (356 × 264). '(Fiona Macleod)' is written under the title in Bax's hand.
Publication: [No. 3] (3771) in *Album of Seven Songs*, JWC, 1919, 4to, pp. 10-12; issued separately in December 1923. For reprints see **94** above.
Duration: 1'34.

110 INTO THE TWILIGHT for orchestra

Title: *Short score*: '"Eire"' (t.p.); 'Into the Twilight' followed by Yeats's poem (next p.); '"Eiré" [*sic*; written over an erasure, probably 'Deirdre'] | Prologue' (p. 1). *Full score* (t.p.): '"Éire" No I | "Into the Twilight" | (after the poem of the same name | by W.B. Yeats)'; (p. 1): '"Eire" [in Irish script] Part I | Into the Twilight.'
Date: *Short score*: Undated. *Full score*: 'Críoch | GleannColumcill | Geimhreadh 1908' [finished at Glencolumcille, winter 1908].
Orchestra: 3 2 + 1 3 + 1 2 + 1, 4040, timp., 1 perc. (cel.), 2 hps., str. This is the only work in which Bax uses four trombones (clearly indicated in the margin of p. [28] of the full score), though they play only for a few bars at the climax; a tuba is usually substituted for the fourth trombone.
Manuscript: *Short score*: UCC; [4] ff.; t.p. + 1 p. containing Yeats's poem + [5] pp. + 1 blank; ALM 12 paper (357 × 265). *Full score*: UCC; [18] ff.; t.p. + p. containing Yeats's poem + 33 pp. + 1 blank; BC 8 paper (332 × 270); bound in light green cloth, with the title and composer's name embossed in gold on the upper cover; on the free front endpaper appear Bax's name and his Ivy Bank address (not in his hand). Unpublished. *Parts*: BBC.
Performance: Beecham Orchestra, Thomas Beecham; Queen's Hall; 19 April 1909. '[It] showed all the ability in harmonization and orchestration normally possessed by the young English composer, and more than the usual intellect and restraint.' (*The Musical Times*, 1 May 1909, p. 327). '. . . of only moderate musical interest . . . was well received, and Mr. Bax received the compliment of a call to the platform.' (*The Queen*, 24 April 1909, p. 696.)
Adaptation: Part of the score was used for the ballet *Oscar* (based on the life of Oscar Wilde), choreographed by Domy Reiter-Soffer. *Performance*: Cornel Crabtree (Oscar), Pieter-Paul Blok (Bosie), John Kavanagh (speaker), Radio Telefís Éireann Concert Orchestra, Gareth Hudson; Opera House, Cork; 11 February 1989 (final production of the Irish National Ballet (Ballet Náisiúnta na hÉireann), which was disbanded after the work had later been performed in Dublin and Belfast).
Duration: 12'52.

Note: This work is the first in the *Éire* trilogy of tone-poems, all based on Irish subjects, the others being *In the Faery Hills* (**114**) and *Rosc-catha* (**128**). In *Gr2* the trilogy is described as 'three symphonic pictures after W. B. Yeats and J. C. Maugan [*sic*]' (i.e. Mangan, who published 'The Fair Hills of Eire, O!', a translation of Donnchadh (Ruadh) Mac Con-Mara's poem 'Ban-chnoic Éireann O!'). On the second of the two preliminary pages of the full score Yeats's poem 'Into the Twilight' is quoted in full, though Bax makes several mistakes in his transcription. In a programme note, he wrote that the work 'seeks to give a musical impression of the brooding quiet of the Western Mountains at the end of twilight, and to express something of the sense of timelessness and hypnotic dream which veils Ireland at such an hour.' The only published allusion to the work by Bax himself occurs in *FMY*, p. 90, where he refers to it as 'a mild and rather hesitant essay in Celticism . . .'. He goes on to describe how the orchestral parts for the first performance were full of mistakes and how Beecham ploughed through the rehearsal 'without comment and utterly unperturbed'; the actual performance went 'tolerably well'. For the connection between this work and the projected opera *Deirdre* see **106**.

111 ISLA for voice and piano

Title: On the MS 'Isla' replaces another title, perhaps that of the original poem, which has been erased, probably with an ink rubber.
Date: Undated but listed as '1908' in *MT* and clearly contemporary with the other songs in Add. MS 54777.
Text: Fiona Macleod, 'The Monody of Isla the Singer'.
Manuscript: *Holograph*: BL (Add. MS 54777); ff. 27-8^{v}; pp. 21-4; 20-staff paper (trimmed to 330 × *c.* 259); bound with 10 other songs (see **70** above). *Copyist's score*: Privately owned; [4] ff.; t.p. + 1 blank + [6] pp.; 12-staff paper. Unpublished.
Duration: 1'47.

112 THE WOOD-LAKE for voice and piano

Note: The score of this song has not been traced. It is listed in *MT* with the words attributed to Heinrich Leuthold, namely his poem 'Der Waldsee'.

1909

113 MARGUERITE for voice and piano

Date: 'June 8th 1909.'
Text: William Morris, 'The Eve of Crécy'.
Manuscript: BL (Add. MS 54778); ff. 31-3^{v}; pp. 23-8; ALM 14 paper (trimmed to 330 × 260); bound with 11 other songs (see **65** above). Unpublished.
Duration: 4'15.

114 IN THE FAERY HILLS for orchestra

Title: *Full score* (front cover): '"EIRE" Nº II | "AN SLUAGH SIDHE"'. *Full score* (t.p.): '"Eire" | Cuid [part] 2 | "An sluagh sidhe" [all in Irish script] | ("The Hosting of the Shee".)'. *Full score* (p. 1): '"Eire" Part II | "In the Faery Hills" "~~The Hosting of the Shee~~" [*sic*]'.
Date: 'Críoch. GleannColmcill. Samhradh 1909. [finished at Glencolumcille, summer 1909] | Fine | June 28th'.
Orchestra: 3(1) 2 +1 3 +1 20, 43(in F)31, timp., 3 perc. (b.d., tamb., cym., gong, gl., cel.), 2 hps., str.
Manuscript: BL (Add. MS 54733); [42] ff.; t.p. + 1 p. containing pencilled note (see below) + 71 pp. + 11 blank; BC 8 paper (332 × 269); bound in green cloth *c.* 1909. On a flyleaf Bax has written his name and his Ivy Bank address, crossed through and replaced by his Marlow address; and underneath there is a label giving details of performances of the work by the Boston Symphony Orchestra under Monteux on 17 and 18 December 1920. There are conductors' blue pencil marks, and pencil and red pencil marks, some in Bax's hand; and he seems to have made later additions with a different pen; the original ink is often faded to sepia. One folio of writing paper (250 × 198; with a 'MONTEVRAIN | B.F. | IMPORTE D'ANGLETERRE' and crown device watermark) is loosely inserted bearing the word 'Bunting' (a pet name for Harriet Cohen), but not in Bax's hand. Unpublished in this form.
Performance: Queen's Hall Orchestra, Sir Henry Wood; Queen's Hall; 30 August 1910 (Promenade Concert). '. . . he gave a beautifully balanced rendering of a piece which was at that time considered dangerously modern and uncomfortably difficult to play.' (Arnold Bax, 'He is a National Institution', *Sir Henry Wood: Fifty Years of the Proms*, London, [1944], p. 29.)
Duration: *c.* 15'30.
Note: This work was written at the request of Sir Henry Wood, who had invited Bax to submit an orchestral piece for the 1910 series of Promenade Concerts. Bax's name had been brought to Wood's attention by Elgar, whom the young composer had first met in the summer of 1901 (see *FMY*, pp. 28-32).

On the reverse of the title folio Bax has written the following in pencil:

This work is an attempt to suggest the riots of the Hidden People in the hills of Ireland after twilight. The composer has endeavoured also to shadow forth the atmosphere of mystery and almost of terror with which the Irish people regard their faery compatriots. The middle section was to some extent suggested by a passage in Mr. Yeats' 'Wanderings of Oisin' in which a human bard having strayed among the host of the Sidhe is asked by them to sing a song for their pleasure. But when he sings a song of human joy the faeries declare it the saddest song that was ever sung and throw the harp away in sorrow and anger while the harper is swept away into their revel.

N.B It would be well if all *pianos* in this work were treated as *pianissimos*.

For the first performance Bax wrote a longer programme note:

> 'In the Faery Hills' attempts to suggest the revelries of the 'Hidden People' in the inmost deeps of the hollow hills of Ireland. At the same time I have endeavoured to envelop the music in an atmosphere of mystery and remoteness akin to the feeling with which the people of the West think of their beautiful and often terrible faeries—beings very different from the lightsome folk of 'A Midsummer-Night's Dream'. The middle section of the work is based to some extent on a passage in W. B. Yeats's poem 'The Wanderings of Oisin'. In this he tells how the Danaan host give the human bard a harp and bid him sing. The latter sings a song of human joy, which the immortals declare to be the saddest thing they have ever heard. One of them, weeping, snatches the harp from Oisin's hand and flings it away into a pool, whereupon the host surround the harper and whirl him away in a tumult of laughter and dancing.
>
> The piece is heralded by a faery horn-call,[26] used throughout the work in various forms. The gates of the hills are opened, and the revelries of 'the wayward twilight companies' begin in a maze of shadows and sudden flashings of opal and rainbow light. In the middle section, referring to the incident of the harper, the gloomy caoine-like melody must be understood not as the actual 'song of human joy', but rather as that singing as it sounded in the ears of those 'who fear no dawning morrow', and 'dance like shadows on the mountains'.

In a letter to Tilly Fleischmann (postmarked 1 May 1931) Bax wrote: 'This is the work that came to me in the Dingle peninsula—from Brandon mountain in fact'. In another letter, to Anne Crowley, he went on to explain: 'I got this mood under Mount Brandon with all W. B. [Yeats]'s magic about me, and I know there is no piece quite like it—no credit to me of course because I was possessed by Kerry's self'. For details of the revised, published version, in which Bax made a few cuts and other changes, see **245** below; and for details of the *Éire* trilogy, of which this is a part, see **110** above.

115 THE GARDEN BY THE SEA for voice and piano

Title: Bax misquotes the original title of the poem, writing the definite instead of the indefinite article.
Date: 'Fine Oct 26th 1909.'
Dedication: 'To G.' (perhaps Gladys Lees). Bax's collection of poems *Seafoam and Firelight* (The Orpheus Press, [1909]), published under the pseudonym 'Dermot O'Byrne', also bears a dedication 'To G.'
Text: William Morris, 'A Garden by the Sea (The Nymph's Song to Hylas)' from *The Life and Death of Jason*, 1. 577.

[26] Apparently quoting from Elgar's incidental music to *Diarmuid and Grania* ('Grania and Diarmid'), the play by George Moore and W. B. Yeats (1901).

Manuscript: BL (Add. MS 54778); ff. 27-30^{v}; pp. 15-22; 20-staff paper (trimmed to 330 × 260); bound with 11 other songs (see **65** above). Unpublished.
Duration: 7'02.

116 A CHRISTMAS CAROL for voice and piano

Date: 'Christmas 1909'.
Dedication: *Holograph*: None. *Copyist's score* (but dedication in Bax's hand): 'To | my sister Evelyn.' (also on printed score).
Text: Anonymous 15th century.
Manuscript: *Holograph*: BL (Add. MS 54778); ff. 43^{v}-4^{v}; pp. 48-50; 20-staff paper (trimmed to 330 × 260); bound with 11 other songs (see **65** above). *Copyist's score*: JWC; [4] ff.; 6 pp. + 2 blank; BH III paper (356 × 264). The dedication and '(15th Century)' are written in Bax's hand.
Publication: [No. 2] (3770) in *Album of Seven Songs*, JWC, 1919, 4to, pp. 5-9. For reprints see **94** above. Published separately on 31 October 1921.
Performance: *Private*: Elsita Bax (sop.), Arnold Bax (pf.); Ivy Bank (Bax family home), Hampstead; Christmas 1909 (family gathering).
Arrangement: For boys' voices and organ. Unpublished but recorded (see Appendix 3 for details).
Duration: 4'12.
Note: For the orchestrated version see **156b**.

117 ASPIRATION for voice and piano

Date: *Printed score*: '1909'.
Dedication: '(To Paul Corder.)'
Text: Richard Dehmel, 'Erhebung' from *Weib und Welt: Ein Buch Gedichte*, I. Words translated and adapted by Clifford Bax (not otherwise published).
Manuscript: Not traced.
Publication: MM (209), 1921, fo., 3 pp.; CH (37304), [1945], 4to.
Arrangement: For voice with piano trio (vn., vc., pf.) accompaniment: UCC, [1] f.; [2] pp.; SC paper (340 × 267), which has been folded in eight at some time. It is not known whether this arrangement is by Bax or not, but the MS, with the words written in pencil, is not in his hand. *Performance*: Janet Linsé[27] (sop.), Bernard Partridge (vn.), Elizabeth Wilson (vc.), David Owen Norris (pf.); British Music Information Centre; 14 October 1983 (lecture-recital by Lewis Foreman, *et al.*).
Duration: 2'28.

[27] Not Jeannette Wilson, as indicated in the printed programme.

118 BELOVED, EVEN IN DREAMS for voice and piano

Note: The score of this song has not been traced. It is listed in *MT* with the words attributed to Friedrich Rückert, obviously the verses beginning 'O Liebster! nie hab'ich geahnt in Träumen' from *Liebesleben*, 5, 61. This is confirmed by a list of songs on f. [63v] of the notebook detailed under **88**, where it appears in garbled form as 'Geliebter nie hab ich geahnt'.

119 THE DANCE RING for voice and piano

Note: The score of this song has not been traced. It is listed in *MT* with the words attributed to Otto Julius Bierbaum, suggesting that it is a setting of part of his long poem 'Die Tanzgilde (nach Arne Garborg)' from *Fremde Blumen*. However, on the free front endpaper of Bax's copy of Will Vesper (comp.), *Die Ernte aus acht Jahrhunderten deutscher Lyrik* (Düsseldorf and Leipzig, 1907),[28] which is in UCC, he has pencilled in the titles of five poems contained in the book, four of which he certainly set to music. The fifth is Bierbaum's 'Tanzlied', suggesting that this, and not 'Die Tanzgilde', may be the title listed in *MT*.

120 ENLIGHTENMENT for voice and piano

Note: The score of this song has not been traced. It is listed in *MT* with the words attributed to Richard Dehmel, namely his poem 'Erleuchtung' from *Erlösungen: Gedichte Sprüche*, 1.

121 HOME for voice and piano

Note: The score of this song has not been traced. It is listed in *MT* with the words attributed to Richard Dehmel, namely his poem 'Heimat' from *Erlösungen: Gedichte Sprüche*, 1.

122 IDEALA for voice and piano

Note: This song is listed in *MT* with the words attributed to Richard Dehmel, who appears, however, to have written no poem with this title. 'Ideala' is the original title of the song 'The Flute' (**97**), but since 'The Flute (Björnsen)' and 'Ideala (Dehmel)' appear separately in the *MT* list, it is possible that the second title is an error for 'Das Ideal', a poem by Dehmel (from his collection *Weib und Welt*, 1), or possibly his 'Ideale Landschaft' (from *Weib und Welt*, 2). To add to the confusion, *Ideala* is also the original title of the piano piece *Nereid* (**177**) and is listed as such in *MT*. The earliest use by Bax of 'Ideala' as a title is for a poem that he wrote in January 1905.

[28] Bax's name and the date 8 November 1907 are written on the flyleaf (not in his hand), indicating that the book was given to him as a twenty-fourth birthday present.

123 LOVE-ODE for voice and piano

Note: The score of this setting of Otto Erich Hartleben's 'Liebesode' has not been traced in this form, although it is listed as such in *MT*. For details of the version for voice and orchestra see **136b**.

1910

124 SONATA NO. 1 for violin and piano (first version)

I. Moderately slow and very Tranquilly. II. Slow and sombre. III. Allegro molto vivace.

Date: I. 'Fine Feb 2nd 1910.' II. 'Fine. | Feb 8th'. III. Undated.
Dedication: 'à M'selle | Natalia Skarginski [*sic*] 1910.' (the girl referred to in *FMY*, pp. 63-79, as 'Loubya Korolenko'). For the dedication on the revised version see **166**.
Manuscript: BL (Add. MS 54765); ff. 1-27v; 54 pp. + 2 blank (1-16, 17-24, [pagin. 49-78: not in Bax's hand]); movts. I and II: ALM 14 paper; III: 12-staff paper (all trimmed to 358 × 265); bound by the BL with brown wrappers bound in at front and after movt. II. The composer has pencilled in his Ivy Bank and Dublin addresses on p. 1. Movt. III is not in Bax's handwriting, and the pagination suggests that the copyist may also have written out the other movements. As with the MSS of **154** and **217**, several pages of the score have been rendered almost illegible by careless conservation; a microfilm exists of the score in its original, unconserved state. *Copyist's score and vn. part of movts. II and III*: Graham Parlett. Unpublished in this form.
Performance: (1) *Movt. I only*: Winifred Smith (vn.), Myra Hess (pf.); Steinway Hall; 18 June 1914. (2) *Movt. II only*: Bernard Partridge (vn.), Andrew Pledge (pf.); British Music Information Centre; 21 April 1983 (lecture-recital by Graham Parlett, *et al.*). A proposed first performance in 1914 at a Music Study Union Conference in Brittany did not take place (see M. Montagu-Nathan, 'Reminiscences of Arnold Bax', *The Musical Times*, November 1953, p. 507).
Duration: *c.* 30'00.
Note: There are four versions of this sonata: **124:** Original version of 1910; **166:** Version of 1915 with movts. II and III replaced by new ones; **236:** Version of 1920—the first published (1921) version—basically the same as **166** but with some revisions, a few passages removed from movts. I and III, and the violin part edited by Paweł Kochański, who introduced certain features to be found in the printed score but not marked in Bax's MS, such as the 'quasi glissando' at 43:13. Since the MS of movt. I of the second version contains no printers' marks (unlike II and III) Bax may have written out another version, either in 1915 or in 1920, which is missing; the printed

score contains too many differences for it to have been engraved from the 1910 MS. Movts. II and III of the 1915 version contain a pianist's markings (fingering, etc.) but no public performance before publication other than by Bax has been traced; **361:** Version of 1945—the second published version—basically the same as **236** but with a few cuts in I and III.

Movts. II and III of this original version were discarded when the work came to be revised in 1915 (see **166** for details). The holograph score of III has not been traced, but the extant copyist's score contains remarks in Bax's handwriting and can otherwise be confirmed as belonging to the sonata through its use of the motto theme that occurs in the other two movements.

In a letter to Rosalind Thornycroft dated 16 February 1912 (and presumably alluding to a private performance) Bax wrote:

> . . . I would like you to have heard my sonata (one of my most intimate and Bax-y compositions . . . I was very pleased with my sonata. It did not sound at all like anything else, and I realized for the first time that my harmonic scheme is unlike that of other modern composers—an interesting thought. Also I realized an illuminating paradox, i.e. that one cannot know one's own work until one gets entirely outside it, which I did then as I listened to it from the next room.

In an undated letter to May Harrison, Bax commented: 'I am *very* pleased to hear that you like my sonata and that you find a spring mood in it, because that is exactly what I meant when I wrote it.' In another undated letter to her (possibly 1927), he wrote: 'The old slow movement of the "Spring" sonata is rather too juvenile for public performance I fancy, besides being a movement which could not very well be played by itself.'

125 CONCERT VALSE IN E♭ for piano

Title: *Copyist's score*: 'Two Valses. | I.' There is no physical or documentary evidence for a second waltz implied by this heading. Listed in *MT* as 'Valse de Concert'.
Date: *Copyist's score* (but date in Bax's hand): 'Feb 16th 1910.'
Dedication: *Copyist's score* (but dedication in Bax's hand): 'To Myra Hess, most poetical of pianists | with admiration and sympathy | from A.B.' *Printed score*: 'To Miss Myra Hess.'
Manuscript: *Holograph*: Not traced. *Copyist's score*: WML; [8] ff.; dedic. p. (in Bax's hand) + 13 pp. + 2 blank; 12-staff paper (349 × 278); sewn into brown wrappers.
Publication: BSY (H 7002), 1911, fo., pp. 13.[29]

[29] Submitted to BSY by Tobias Matthay (see Jessie Henderson Matthay, *The Life and Works of Tobias Matthay*, London, 1945, p. 40).

Performance: Myra Hess; Broadwood Rooms; 18 March 1910 (Society of British Composers Concert).
Duration: 6'15.

126 A LULLABY for voice and piano

Title: *MS*: '["]Lullaby"'. *Printed score*: 'A Lullaby'.
Date: 'March 22nd | 1910'.
Dedication: *Printed score only*: 'To Gladys Ross [née Lees].'
Text: 'Sheila MacCarthy' (pseud. of Arnold Bax), 'A Lullaby'. The privately owned typescript of the poem is dated 'March 21st 1910', the day before it was set to music. The words differ slightly from those of the published setting. On the MS of the song, 'Shiela McCarthy' (thus spelt) has been written over another name that has been erased (perhaps 'Dermot O'Byrne').
Manuscript: BL (Add. MS 54778); ff. 42-3; pp. 45-7; 20-staff paper (330 × 260); bound with 11 other songs (see **65** above).
Publication: No. 2 (5346) in *Three Songs for Medium Voice and Pianoforte* [with **201** and **207**], EN, 1920, 4to, pp. 9-12; EA' (later assigned to CH). Reprinted in *Five Songs [by] Arnold Bax (Heritage of English Song 4*, TP, [1985], 4to, pp. 17-20. Also in *Arnold Bax: Six Songs*, TP (THA 978047), 1994, 4to, pp. 15-18.
Duration: 2'11.
Note: For the orchestrated version ('Slumber-Song') see **156c**.

127 SONATA NO. 1 in F♯ MINOR for piano (first version)

Title: (1) Originally performed under the title 'Romantic Tone-Poem'. (2) Renamed 'Sonata'. (3) Performed again under the title 'Symphonic Phantasy'. (4) Performed again under the title 'Sonata'. (5) Revised and published under the title 'Sonata in F♯ minor'.
Date: *Printed score* (final version): 'Written in Russia | Summer 1910 | Revised 1917-1921'.
Manuscript: Not traced.
Performance: Myra Hess; Bechstein Hall (later renamed Wigmore Hall); 25 April 1911. 'It was played very picturesquely and loudly applauded.' (Alfred Kalisch).
Note: The title *Romantic Tone-Poem* appears in *YB2* but is not found in later lists of Bax's music. Its first performance was reviewed in *The Queen* (6 May 1911), p. 781:

> As a technical exercise one could wish for nothing more exacting than the 'Romantic Tone Poem' . . . The composer presumably had some 'programme' in his mind when he wrote it, but since no clue was afforded of its meaning, the audience was left to imagine the romance that had inspired music so rhetorical as this proved to be. It presented no difficulties to Miss Hess, who played it . . . with complete success.

Eight years later, on 9 October 1919, Myra Hess played a *Symphonic Phantasy* by Bax at the Wigmore Hall, and, although it cannot be proved conclusively, there is every likelihood that it was identical with the *Romantic Tone-Poem*. One of the reviews of this performance, from *The Pall Mall Gazette* (10 October 1919), was written by 'E. E.' [Edwin Evans] and is of particular interest:

Some years ago Mr. Arnold Bax wrote a pianoforte sonata, which was played by Miss Myra Hess. With the musicianly insight that distinguishes her among pianists, she suggested that it should be renamed a 'Symphonic Phantasy', under which title it reappeared in her programme last night. She might have gone further and described it as an episode from a projected epic.

That the *Symphonic Phantasy* was a version of the First Piano Sonata (originally written, according to the revised score, in 1910) is confirmed by the review of the same concert printed in *The Times* (10 October 1919):

The phantasy is full of striking musical ideas, freely and richly developed, and culminating in a climax in which the terse main theme seems to thread its way through a riot of pealing bells.

This description tallies exactly with Harriet Cohen's comments on the ending of the sonata in A. L. Bacharach (ed.), *British Music of Our Time*, 2nd edn. (London, 1951), p. 124: 'The finale . . . [has] a suggestion of the multi-rhythmed jangles of Slavonic church bells during the Easter Festival.' It is obvious that Bax's experience of arriving in St Petersburg on the eve of Easter Day in 1910 had been the catalyst for this musical effect: 'Bells thundered and jangled from every church . . .', he wrote in *FMY*, p. 67. In her description of the sonata, Harriet Cohen also mentions that this ending had been composed ten years after the rest of the piece. A further performance of (presumably) the same work ('a manuscript pianoforte sonata in one movement') was given by Miss Cohen at the Wigmore Hall on 15 June 1920. This seems to have been its last public outing before the final revisions of 1921.

Since the *Symphonic Phantasy* was originally called a sonata (according to Edwin Evans), there is a further possibility that the work may be identifiable with the otherwise unknown Sonata in D minor (**137**), which was played by Myra Hess at the Æolian Hall on 2 June 1911 as part of the Fourth Congress of the International Musical Society. According to the official report of the congress (p. 42) only the first movement of the sonata was played, which could mean that Bax may originally have been considering the possibility of adding further movements rather than that it was performed incomplete. An obstacle to equating the Sonata in D minor with the First Sonata is the fact that, in its published version at least, it rarely strays into the key of D minor; perhaps it was originally written in this key. Watson Lyle, writing in *The Musical Standard* (25 October 1919), found the *Symphonic Phantasy* 'incoherent and blatantly noisy', while another critic in *The Music News* for 10 June 1911 found the Sonata in D minor to be 'a work abounding in dissonance and not always logical in its construction'. For details of the published version of the Piano Sonata No. 1 see **240**.

Summary of versions and performances:

First version:
1. *Romantic Tone-Poem*: Myra Hess; 25 April 1911.
2. Possibly as Sonata in D minor ('first movement'): Myra Hess; 2 June 1911.

Second version (revised from 1917 onwards):
3. *Symphonic Phantasy*: Myra Hess; 9 October 1919.
4. Sonata: Harriet Cohen; 15 June 1920.

Third version (final revision of 1921):
5. Sonata No. 1 in F♯ minor: Harriet Cohen; 12 April 1921.

128 ROSC-CATHA for orchestra

Title: 'Eire No. III | Rosc-catha [in Irish script] (Roscatha)'. 'Rosc-catha' (pronounced roughly like the English words 'rusk-*car*-huh') is the Irish Gaelic for 'battle hymn' or 'battle song'.
Date: 'Críoch GleannColumcille | Samhain 1910' [finished, Glencolumcille, November 1910].
Dedication: 'To the "mountainy men" of Glencolumcille.' The significance of the epithet 'mountainy' is probably connected with the old Irish saying 'Pós bean ó'n tsléibh is pósfair an tsliabh go léir' ('Marry a "mountainy" woman and you marry the whole mountain!'), the point being that mountain-dwellers are renowned for their friendliness. Perhaps also influenced by the title of Seosamh Mac Cathmhaoil's book *The Mountainy Singer* (Dublin, 1909), of which Bax owned a copy.
Orchestra: 3+1 2+1 3+1 2+1, 43(in F)31, timp., 4 perc. (b.d., m.d., s.d., cym., gl.), str.
Manuscript: *Short score*: UCC; [4] ff.; t.p. + 1 blank + [6] pp.; ALM 14 paper (360 × 267); in a manila envelope. *Full score*: BL (Add. MS 54734); [32] ff.; [57] pp. + [7], of which [1] and [4-7] are blank, [2] has a pair of treble clefs and single-sharp key signatures at the top, and [3] (used upside down) has 'Prometheus Unbound Act II Scene 2.' at the top with 18 instruments in the left margin (from fl./picc. to hp. II), most with clefs and key signatures, the rest blank: Bax clearly began to write out the full score of *Enchanted Summer* (**129**) here but abandoned it; ALM 29 paper (360 × 266).
Publication: *Edited by Graham Parlett*: SMP (THA 978449), 1994, 8vo, 55 pp. (copyright by the Sir Arnold Bax Estate).

Performance: (1) *Semi-professional*: Kensington Symphony Orchestra, Leslie Head; St John's, Smith Square; 5 March 1974. (2) *Professional play-through*:[30] BBC Welsh Symphony Orchestra, Vernon Handley; Studio 1, Broadcasting House, Llandaff; 20 June 1983. (3) *Professional:* Ulster Orchestra, Bryden Thomson; Ulster Hall, Belfast; 10-12 February 1985 (recording session for Chandos Records Ltd.). (4) Allentown Symphony Orchestra, Diane M. Wittry; Symphony Hall, Allentown, Pennsylvania, USA; 8 November 1997.
Duration: 10'49.
Note: *Rosc-catha* is an orchestrated version of 'The Gathering of the Chiefs', one of the three extant extracts from the projected opera *Deirdre* (see **106** for a description of the scenario). The full score shows evidence of having been hastily completed, the last few pages having no dynamics or phrasing whatsoever, and there is a trombone passage originally written out on the trumpet staves. For details of the *Éire* trilogy, of which this is part, see **110**.

129 ENCHANTED SUMMER for two sopranos, chorus and orchestra

Title: '"Prometheus Unbound" Act II Scene II'. The final title does not appear on the MS.
Date: 'Fine. | Glencolmcille | C$^{o.}$ Donegal. December | 1910.'
Dedication: *Printed score*: 'To F. Corden [i.e. Corder], Esq. F.R.A.M. my ever-true friend.'
Text: Percy Bysshe Shelley, 'Prometheus Unbound', II, 2.
Orchestra: 3+1 2+1 3+1 2+1, 43(in F)31, timp., 3 perc. (b.d., tamb., cym., tri., gl., cel.), 2 hps., str.
Manuscript: *Full score*: BL (Add. MS 54771); [46] ff.; 91 pp. + 1 blank; ALM 29 paper (360 × 265); 2 non-staved pp. at front, the first with pencilled notes not in Bax's hand, including the name of the conductor Arthur Fagge; bound in light green cloth with title and composer's name embossed in gold on the upper cover. Bax has not numbered the first 28 pages (the page-numerals are pencilled in another hand); he has inked in '25' on p. [29] and thus misnumbered all the rest, so that his p. 87 is really p. 91; the correct page-numerals have been pencilled in by the same hand that did 1-28. There are cue numbers in red and conductors' pencilled markings. For a false start on writing out the full score see *Rosc-catha* above (**128**). *Parts*: CH.
Publication: *Vocal score only*: SR, copyright by Arnold Bax, 1911, 42 pp. Later assigned to MM and then to CH but not reprinted. The f.sc. was not published, but announcements that it was 'in the press' can be found on the lower wrapper of, for example, the MM edition of *Red Autumn* (published 1933).

[30] It was intended to record the work for broadcasting, but the project was abandoned after a single play-through because some of the parts were illegible.

Performance: Caroline Hatchard, Carrie Tubb (sops. representing the two fauns),[31] London Choral Society, New Symphony Orchestra, Balfour Gardiner; Queen's Hall; 13 March 1912.
Duration: 28'01
Note: For the first performance Bax wrote the following note:

In this first section the composer has tried to render the continual interchange of light and shadow among the green forest-aisles, and the eternal youth and Theocritan serenity of the woodland in its early summer foliage.

In the second division of the work, illustrative of the strange and enchanted mood occasioned by the midday singing of the nightingales, the music becomes more impassioned, and the swooning peace and drowsiness is disturbed by the eternal pain of Philomela's age-long complaint [i.e. 'Sick with sweet love'].

The third part (Allegro Vivace—and here the full chorus enters for the first time) is chiefly concerned in suggesting the glitter and glory of the strengthening sunlight and the vernal force and surge of the youth of the year.

As inland boats are driven to Ocean
Down streams made strong with mountain-thaw.

Finally the Spirits, intoxicated with their own voices, rush headlong and laughing through the leaves into the distances of the forest. Silence falls again. The two little Fauns, astonished by what they have seen and heard, approach one another shyly, and one of them who appears somewhat wiser than his companion tells what he has heard of the invisible woodland singers. Finally they remember that the goats of Silenus are not yet milked, and run off to perform their duties, lest they shall miss the tales of the origin of the world and the gods that are their delight.

As regards the general character of the music, it may perhaps be added that the composer has endeavoured to combine the impressionistic manner with a melodic scheme freer in scope than that commonly used in choral writing, and yet of a definite cantabile character. It seemed that an attempt at a musical translation of poetry so spontaneous, and inherent with a quality of ecstasy possibly unequalled in English literature, required a mingling of two elements of music usually divorced from one another.

130 FRÜHLINGSREGEN (Spring Rain) for voice and piano

Date: 'Dec 21 | 1910' (in Paul Corder's hand; the '10' is written over an illegible erasure).
Text: Friedrich Rückert, 'Frühlingsregen'.
Manuscript: *Mostly non-autograph*: UCC; [2] ff.; 3 pp. + 1 blank; 20-staff paper (340 × 272). The music and the original German words are in the handwriting of Paul Corder, but Bax has added the English words below the vocal line as well as the English title. He has also written his signature and

[31] It is not clear why Bax allotted these parts to two sopranos: fauns, like satyrs, are normally represented as ithyphallic Pan-like figures with horns and goats' legs, though Shelley's specimens are, admittedly, more refined than usual.

the words 'divisi ad lib' above the penultimate bar of the piano part and has pencilled a note at the top left of p. [1] that has been erased but is still just legible: 'German words can be eventually dispensed with'. The score is paginated from 16 to 18, suggesting that it was intended as part of a cycle or collection of songs, but whether with others by Bax or Corder is not known. See also 'Treue Liebe' (**131**).
Publication: In *Five Songs [by] Arnold Bax (Heritage of English Song 4)*, TP, [1985], 4to, pp. 21-4. Also in *Arnold Bax: Six Songs*, TP (THA 978047), 1994, 4to, pp. 19-22.
Performance: Jeff Weaver (ten.), David Owen Norris (pf.); British Music Information Centre; 3 February 1983 (lecture-recital by Lewis Foreman, *et al.*).
Duration: 2'21.

131 TREUE LIEBE for voice and piano

Title: 'Treue Liebe (Volkslied)' (in Paul Corder's hand).
Date: 'Dec 23. 1910' (in Paul Corder's hand).
Text: Volkslied from the Thuringer Wald (some sources specify Hildburghausen), with an English translation written under the German words.
Manuscript: *Mostly non-autograph*: Privately owned (formerly by Eva Pain and then by her son, Sam Matheson); [2] ff.; 3 pp.; BC 6 paper (292 × *c.* 231). Like 'Frühlingsregen' (**130**), this MS is mostly in the hand of Paul Corder, with annotations by Bax. Unpublished.
Performance: Peter Savidge (bar.), David Owen Norris (pf.); Christ's Hospital, Horsham, Sussex; 7 October 1983 (recording session for Triad Press).
Duration: 2'45.
Note: Since it is subtitled 'Volkslied', it seems likely that this song is to be equated with the otherwise unknown 'Folk Song' that is ascribed to 1910 in *MT*, even though the English and German terms are not entirely synonymous. The words were adapted by Helmine von Chézy, the librettist of Weber's *Euryanthe*, and at least three tunes are associated with them. One is based on a Thuringian folk melody; another is described as a 'neuere Volksweise' ('newer folktune') but was apparently composed by Friedrich Kücken in 1827, although it was included by Granville Bantock in one of his collections of folksong arrangements. However, Bax's melody bears no resemblance to any of these and may be a pastiche.

132 TO EIRE for voice and piano

Title: Erroneously listed in *MT* as 'To Eve'.
Date: *Printed score*: '1910'.
Text: James H. Cousins, 'To Eire'.
Manuscript: Not traced.

Publication: [No. 4] (3772) in *Album of Seven Songs*, JWC, 1919, pp. 13-17. For reprints see **94** above.
Duration: 3'42.

1911

133 DAS TOTE KIND for voice and piano

Date: 'Jan. 5 | 1911.'
Text: Conrad Ferdinand Meyer, 'Das tote Kind'. The author's name is erroneously given as 'JP Meyer' on the MS, perhaps through confusion in Bax's mind with J. P. Jacobsen, whose poetry he had also set.
Manuscript: BL (Add. MS 54779); ff.1-2^{v}; [4] pp.; AL 12 paper (trimmed to 356 × 261). The handwriting and the imprint of the paper (not otherwise attested for Bax before 1914) suggest that this is a fair copy or a reworking of an original version now lost. Unpublished. Add. MS 54779 is a volume bound by the BL and containing the holograph MSS of 15 songs in the following order: 'Das tote Kind' (**133**), 'The Splendour falls on castle-walls' (**186**), 'Three Rondels' (**158**), 'Spinning-Song' (**160d**), 'The Song of the Dagger' (**160f**), 'A Rabelaisian Catechism' (**227**), 'Glamour' (**239**), 'I heard a soldier' (**268**), 'Eternity' (**273**), 'Three Songs from the Norse' (**285**), 'My eyes for beauty pine' (**237**).
Duration: 2'14.

134 FESTIVAL OVERTURE for orchestra (first version)

Date: *Short score*: Undated but 'autumn of 1909' (see **Note** below). *Full score:* 'Composed: | London | Oct 1909. | Orchestrated: | Renvyle | Connemara | Feb:- March | 1911'.
Dedication: 'To H Balfour Gardiner.'
Orchestra: 3+1 2+1 3+1 2+1, 4331, timp., 6 perc.[32] (b.d., s.d., tamb., cym., tri., gl.), hp., str.
Manuscript: *Short score:* BL (Add. MS 50173); [6] ff.; [10] pp. + 1 p. of sketches + 1 blank (unfinished); ALM 14 paper (356 × 266); bound by BL. Mostly in ink but a few passages in pencil, with pencil and ink notes for orchestration. The last bar of f. 5^{v} is blank, the score stopping ten bars before the end of the work; f. 6 contains sketches for an unidentified work (**135**). *Full score*: BL (Add. MS 50174); ii + 37 ff. (37^{v} blank); 73 pp. + 1 blank; ALM 18 paper (trimmed to 359 × 265); bound in light green cloth with the title and composer's name embossed in gold on the upper cover, and a red leather label in the centre declaring that it was presented by

[32] The largest number of percussionists called for in any of Bax's works.

Harriet Cohen. There are conductors' blue pencil marks throughout. Bax's signature and his parents' Cavendish Square address are on f. i, the original front free endpaper, the binder having inserted a new leaf in front of it. The next two pages are blank; on f. ii^v there is a non-autograph note requesting 'W. C. S' to copy all the parts except for the 3rd flute. Unpublished.
Performance: New Symphony Orchestra, Balfour Gardiner; Queen's Hall; 27 March 1912. '. . . a depraved version of Smetana and Dvořák—with a spice of Byng[33] in his best Alhambra mood.' (*The Musical Standard*, 6 April 1912, p. 215).
Arrangement: For 2 pianos, possibly by Bax but MS not in his hand: Lewis Foreman (MS formerly owned by Vivian Langrish—perhaps the arranger); [13] ff. + 1 blank; t.p. + 25 pp. + 2 blank; BC 4 paper (339 × 267) stitched on the spine. *Publication (photocopy of MS)*: WC0134. *Performance*: Howard Shelley, Hilary Macnamara; Broadcasting House; 9 August 1983; br. on Radio 3, 16 December 1983.
Duration: *c.* 16'00.
Note: The wording at the end of the full score clearly reveals the distinction that Bax made between composition and orchestration. Although he often orchestrated works several years after they were completed in short score, usually when a performance was in the offing, he would refer to the date of the short score as the date of composition. For details of the revised version, see **209**. For the first performance Bax wrote the following note:

> This work, composed in the autumn of 1909, shows little formal deviation from the scheme employed by classical writers in compositions of its genre. The only divergence from accepted lines will be noticed in the middle of the piece, where in place of the usual short development section, a new melody is introduced of a more serious and sustained character than that of the remainder of the work, and appearing again in still broader and more triumphant guise towards the close. With the exception of this passage, the Overture may be said to present the festal spirit in somewhat riotous mood.

135 [UNTITLED]: Fragment (in short score)

Note: Ink and pencil sketches on f. 6 of the *Festival Overture* (**134**) but apparently unrelated to it. One phrase resembles the opening horn call from 'The Gathering of the Chiefs' from *Deirdre* (**106**).

136 THREE NOCTURNES for soprano and orchestra (incomplete)

a. 'No 1. "Aufblick"'. **b.** 'No. 2. | "Liebesode"'. **c.** [Not extant].

Title: 'Three Nocturnes | for soprano voice | with orchestral accompaniment'.

[33] George W. Byng, composer of musical comedies.

Date: **a.** 'Fine | April 18th | 1911.' **b.** 'Orchestrated | Caina Connemara. | April 1911.'
Orchestra: **a.** 2+1 2+1 2+1 20, 4231, timp., 2 perc. (gong, gl., cel.), hp., str. **b.** 3 20 2+1 20, 4200, timp., 1 perc. (cel.), hp., str.
Text: **a.** Richard Dehmel, 'Aufblick'. **b.** Otto Erich Hartleben, 'Liebesode'.
Manuscript: *Holograph*: BL (Add. MS 54772); [13] ff.; [26] pp. ([1-14], [15-26] + 2 blank); ALM 18 paper (361 × 272). *Copyist's score*: BBC; **a.** 6 ff.; 12 pp.; **b.** 8 ff.; 15 pp.; both on 28-staff paper (413 × 292); both in orange-brown wrappers. Unpublished. *Parts*: BBC.
Performance: Rita Cullis (sop.), BBC Northern Orchestra, Edward Downes; Studio 7, New Broadcasting House, Manchester; 23 September 1982; br. on Radio 3, 18 November 1983.
Arrangement: **136a** arr. for voice and piano by Stephen Banfield. *Performance*: John Potter (ten.), Stephen Banfield (pf.); University of Keele; 6 November 1980.
Duration: **a.** 3'47. **b.** 3'24.
Note: These two songs were orchestrated while Bax was on his honeymoon in Connemara in 1911. There is no trace of the third nocturne implied by the collective title, and it is not known whether it was ever completed or even what the title of the song might have been. The most likely candidate is the untraced song listed in *MT* as 'The Bridal Prayer' (words by Richard Dehmel; see **139**), whose original German title is 'Nachtgebet der Braut' (set by Webern in 1899-1903). In a letter to Christopher Whelen dating from the early 1950s, Bax wrote: 'I stayed at Caina very often in my youth—always in the spring. I don't think I ever wrote any new music there, but I spent some time revising early (and Straussian) songs . . .'.

137 SONATA IN D MINOR for piano

Date: See **Note** below.
Manuscript: Not traced. Unpublished.
Performance: *Movt. I only*: Myra Hess; Æolian Hall; 2 June 1911 (Fourth Congress of the International Musical Society).
Note: This work does not appear in any lists of Bax's music published during his lifetime, and the only record of its existence is the programme for the congress at which it was performed. See **127** above for the suggestion that it may be the original version of the First Sonata for piano.

138 TAMARA: Ballet (unorchestrated)

Title: 'TAMARA' (first t.p.); 'Tamara. | A Little-Russian fairy tale in action and dance.' (second t.p.); '~~TAMARA~~ [*sic*] King Kojata.' (p. 1). The title appears as 'King Kojata' in early editions of *Who's Who in Music* but is absent from the main lists of music published during Bax's lifetime.
Date: 'Fine. Rathgar C° Dublin. | July–November | 1911.'

Dedication: 'To the divine dancer | Mdme. Tamara Karsavina | whose wonderful art inspired this work. | Arnold Bax. Autumn 1911'.
Manuscript: UCC; [52] ff.; 2 unstaved introd. pp. + 1 containing an illustration + 5 blank (unstaved) + 92 pp. + 4 blank (unstaved); pp. 1-24, 57-92: ALM 14 paper; pp. 25-56: ALM 12 paper (all trimmed to 344 × 264); bound in dark blue cloth, with the title and composer's name embossed in gold on the upper cover; on the front paste-down endpaper appear Bax's name and his parents' address. *Synopsis*: List of section titles (headed 'King Kojata'): Privately owned; written in pencil on the upper and lower paste-down endpapers of a black-covered notebook from which all the pages have been removed (see Appendix 7, section V). Unpublished.
Duration: *c.* 120'00.
Note: The inspiration for this work is explained by the elaborate dedication on p. 2 of the MS, though Karsavina never even knew of its existence until several years after Bax's death. Professor Aloys Fleischmann, who first brought the work to her attention, suggests that Bax may have been waiting for an opportunity to present her with the score when in May 1912, a few months after its completion in short score, she appeared as the eponymous vampire queen in Diaghilev's ballet *Thamar*, which was based on Balakirev's symphonic poem *Tamara*.[34] Although the two scores are based on entirely different stories, Bax may have felt that the unfortunate clash of titles would militate against his own work, and this would account for his decision to alter the title to *King Kojata*, even though that character plays a comparatively subordinate rôle in the plot. Karsavina became a close friend of the composer in 1920, when he was involved with Barrie's play *The Truth about the Russian Dancers* (see **220** for details), but he never even mentioned to her the existence of this earlier ballet, although he did use some of its thematic material in the later work as well as in the ballet *From Dusk till Dawn* (**188**). In a letter to Rosalind Thornycroft, Bax wrote: 'I am full of dreams about my ballet—as to the possibility of the Russians taking it up—if only I knew how to get hold of them.' The piano score (thus designated on the MS) contains a few indications of the intended orchestration, but it is certain that he never wrote out a full score.

The first title page of the MS contains an elaborate pictorial representation of the two principal characters, Tamara and Igor.[35] Although it is not signed, the picture was undoubtedly done by Bax's brother Clifford, who studied art at the Slade and Heatherley Schools before abandoning it in favour of literature. Examples of Clifford's work appear in issues of *Orpheus*, the theosophical magazine that he edited between 1909 and 1917

[34] Aloys Fleischmann, 'Arnold Bax', *Recorded Sound: The Journal of the British Institute of Recorded Sound*, 29–30 (January–April 1968), pp. 275–6.

[35] It is reproduced (back to front) on the cover of the booklet for the 1992 Continuum recording of Benjamin Dale's Sonata in D minor (CCD 1044).

(see, for example, No. 22, April 1913), and a comparison between the human figures there and on the MS of *Tamara* leaves no room for doubt. It is known, furthermore, that Clifford visited his brother in Rathgar, on the outskirts of Dublin, at about the time the ballet was being written, Arnold and his wife having moved there shortly after their honeymoon in Connemara.[36]

The ballet is in two acts with a prologue and contains thirty numbers: Bax's longest score by far. The second page of the MS bears the title and dedication, followed by a detailed account of the plot, which is based on a Little-Russian (Ukrainian) folktale.[37] Throughout the score Bax has written in details of this scenario at the relevant points, providing the music with its own continuous narrative summary of the story.

Synopsis:[38]

Prelude

Lento—Allegro vivace—Tempo primo (pp. 1-3): 'Curtain rises. The depths of a pine forest in Eastern Russia towards evening. To the left is a pool with mist-hung Trees overhanging it.'

No. 1. Lento malincolo [*sic*] (pp. 4-5): 'King Kojata enters weary and thirsty. He is alone . . . He peers about everywhere . . . but does not see the pool . . . Sinks down despondently upon the mossy bole of a tree.' Allegro vivace (pp. 5-7): 'He suddenly notices the haunted pool . . . He takes a few impetuous steps towards the pool . . . He makes a gesture of repudiation . . . Overcome with exhaustion he sinks to the ground and falls asleep.'

No. 2. Allegro (p. 7); 'The scene begins to glow with a strange green light . . .'.

No. 3. Allegro vivace (pp. 8-10): 'A number of water spirits . . . etc. appear from the pool and dance temptingly before King Kojata.'[39]

No. 4. Vivace (pp. 10-11): 'King Kojata stirs in his sleep and wakes . . . He crouches at the edge of the pool, his immense beard becoming submerged . . . His beard is seized by invisible hands . . . A hoarse laughter from the depths.' Lento (pp. 11-12): 'The magician appears, a horny beaked creature of horrible aspect . . . Kojata, in order to escape, must swear to deliver . . . after twenty years whatever new thing he finds on his return home. The king swears . . . ' . Allegro vivace ed agitato (pp. 12-13): 'The king rises . . . and hurries from the place . . . Total darkness.' Lento ma non troppo (pp. 13-14): 'A beautiful light appears over the pool revealing a vision of the Princess Tamara . . . End of Prologue.'[40]

[36] In *FMY*, p. 95, Bax writes: 'No sooner was I settled in than Clifford was invited to stay with me.'

[37] Bax's text is published in LF, pp. 383-4.

[38] The use of '. . .' in this synopsis indicates gaps between words or sentences in the MS; it does not mean that words are missing.

[39] This passage was later used in the ballet *From Dusk till Dawn* (**188**).

[40] 'Scene 1' is indicated but no other scene numbers appear in the score.

Act I[41]

No. 5. Lento marcato—Allegro vivace (pp. 15-17): 'Same scene as Prologue. Spring morning. The princess Tamara stands by the pool listening to the sound of hunting horns which gradually approach . . . Igor enters. Tamara can scarcely contain herself with delight . . .' .
No. 6. Non troppo Allegro (pp. 17-19): ' . . . she runs out suddenly and dances a graceful dance on the grass often glancing at the prince . . . but pretending not to see him.'
No. 7. Molto vivace (p. 19): 'Igor has already fallen in love with her and now advances . . . She pretends to be surprized [*sic*] and terrified . . .'. Presto vivace: ' . . . but does not long resist the prince's advances.' Tempo I.
No. 8. Allegretto (pp. 20-2): 'Tamara laughs joyously . . .'.
No. 9. [L'istesso tempo] (pp. 22-3): 'But the Prince's destiny must be fulfilled . . . [He] will be obliged to choose from among the thirty daughters of the magician, who are exactly alike.' Valse tempo (p. 23): 'But he will know her from her sisters . . . because he will see a tiny fly upon her left cheek as he passes her. The Princess runs away.'
No. 10. Lento languido (p. 24): 'The scene becomes hazy . . . ondines and naiads appear beckoning to Igor . . .' . Andante con moto (pp. 25-7): 'Igor is drawn down into the arms of the naiads into the water . . .'[42]
No. 11. Allegro vivace (pp. 27-8): 'The hall of the magician's palace beneath the water . . . a multitude of grotesque and bizarre forms crowd the scene . . .'.
No. 12. Allegro furioso (pp. 28-33): 'Dance of the slaves and subjects of the enchanter . . . Tamara drifts through the crowd, dancing . . . languidly as though bewitched. She does not seem to recognize Igor.'.
No. 13. Tempo di Mazurka (pp. 34-5): 'Un danseur et une danseuse'.
No. 14. Moderato—Allegro vivace (pp. 36-9): 'Dance. Variations (Tamara).'[43]
No. 15. Allegretto (pp. 40-1): 'Variations I. (Une danseuse).'
No. 16. Allegretto grazioso (pp. 42-3): 'Variation 2. (Danseuse II).'[44]
No. 17. Allegro marcato (p. 43): 'A blare of trumpets announces the . . . enchanter . . . He makes a menacing gesture . . . signifying that the prince's ordeal shall begin.'
No. 18. Moderate Valse Tempo (pp. 44-50): 'The dance of the Enchanter's thirty beautiful daughters.'
No. 19. Vivace (pp. 51-2): 'Igor rushes forward . . . He takes Tamara . . . and leads her from among her sisters. Dance (Igor and Tamara).'
No. 20. Tempo di valsero languido (pp. 53-8): 'Valse d'Amour. (Igor and Tamara and the girls.)'[45]
No. 21. Allegro vivace (p. 58): 'The Enchanter starts up . . . in uncontrollable fury. [Igor and Tamara] pause as though spellbound.' Più Lento e marcato—Lento (pp. 58-9): 'Tamara looks up at the enchanter with entreaty in her eyes. He . . . makes several

[41] This passage was later expanded as the 'Dance of Motherhood' in *The Truth about the Russian Dancers* (**220**).

[42] This passage, preceded by the final four bars of the previous section, was later arranged as *Naiad*, the third of the Four Pieces for flute and piano (**149**).

[43] This dance was later used in *From Dusk till Dawn*.

[44] This was arranged as *The Princess dances*, the second of the Four Pieces for flute and piano.

[45] This waltz was later used in *From Dusk till Dawn*.

strange gestures over her with a magic wand . . .' . Lento semplice (pp. 59-60): ' . . . and all that is left of her is a little blue water flower . . .'.
No. 22. Allegro molto vivace (pp. 60-1): 'The servants of the enchanter dance in savage triumph.' Grazioso e expressivo [*sic*] (pp. 61-2): 'The Girls'. Un poco più Lento (p. 62): 'Une danseuse seule. One of the sisters . . . grieves for the loss of her beautiful sister.'
Tempo Primo—Da capo al Signo [*sic*] (pp. 62-3): 'The solitary mourner unperceived . . . picks up the blue flower and hides it . . . Curtain falls. End of Act I.'

Act II

No. 23. Tempo di Polacca (pp. 64-9): 'Introduction and Polonaise. Curtain rises. The great hall of King Kojata's palace . . . Great assemblage of princes, boyars and ladies to celebrate the safe return of Prince Igor . . .'.[46]
No. 24. Lento ma non troppo (pp. 69-70): 'The melancholy of Prince Igor.'
No. 25. Allegro Vivace e molto rythmico [*sic*] (pp. 71-5).
No. 26. Tempo di Mazurka (pp. 76-8): 'Une danseuse.'[47]
No. 27. Allegretto marcato (pp. 79-80): 'Buffoon's Dance.'[48]
No. 28. [No tempo indicated] (p. 81): 'Suddenly a knocking is heard at the great door of the hall.' Tempo molto moderato (pp. 81-2): 'A little old woman dressed in green enters, carrying a basket of flowers . . .'.[49] Tempo Moderato (Andante) (pp. 82-4): 'She is old and lonely and miserably poor.'[50] 'She . . . brings out a little blue flower . . . Igor . . . rushes forward . . . He embraces the old woman [who] changes into a beautiful water nymph . . . She waves [a wand?] over the flower . . . Tamara appears laughing joyously.' Allegro Agitato (pp. 84-5): '[Igor] snatches her up in his arms.'
No. 29. Allegro molto (pp. 86-91): 'General rejoicing.' Tempo di Galop: 'The light fades . . . Darkness . . .'.
No. 30. [No tempo indicated] (pp. 91-2): 'Apotheosis'[51].

For further details of thematic material from *Tamara* that was later used in *From Dusk till Dawn* and *The Truth about the Russian Dancers* see **188** and **220**.

139 THE BRIDAL PRAYER for voice and piano

Note: The score of this song has not been traced. It is listed in *MT* with the words attributed to Richard Dehmel, namely his poem 'Nachtgebet der Braut' from *Erlösungen: Gedichte und Sprüche*, 2. See also **Note** under **136.**

[46] Part of this section—from 66:26 to 67:17—was used in the overture to *The Truth about the Russian Dancers.*

[47] This passage was later arranged as *Shadow Dance*, the first of the Four Pieces for flute and piano.

[48] This was arranged as *Grotesque*, the fourth of the Four Pieces for flute and piano.

[49] This passage occurs in *The Truth about the Russian Dancers* as an interlude during the 'Storm' sequence.

[50] The first fifteen bars of this section were used in *From Dusk till Dawn* (pp. 102-4).

[51] Based on the theme used at the end of the Prologue, which reappears in 'The Dance of Motherhood' from *The Truth about the Russian Dancers.*

140 FAITH for voice and piano

Note: The score of this song has not been traced. It is listed in *MT* with the words attributed to Friedrich Rückert, namely his poem 'Vertrauen' from *Mailieder in sechs Büchern*, 2.

141 FLIGHT for voice and piano

Note: The score of this song has not been traced. It is listed in *MT* with the words attributed to Richard Dehmel, namely his poem 'Im Fluge' from *Erlösungen: Gedichte und Sprüche*, 1.

142 FREIMUND for voice and piano

Note: The score of this song has not been traced. It is listed in *MT* with the words attributed to Friedrich Rückert, who does not appear, however, to have written a poem with this title, although in 1814 he devised a cycle of 'Deutsche Gedichte' ascribed to a pseudonymous 'Freimund Reimer'; it may have been one of these that Bax set to music—perhaps 'Geharnischte Sonette', which is the best known.

143 THE JOURNEY for voice and piano

Note: The score of this song has not been traced. It is listed in *MT* with the words attributed to Richard Dehmel, namely his poem 'Die Reise' from *Der Kindergarten: Gedichte Spiele und Gedichten für Kinder und Eltern jeder Art.*

c. 1911

144 SYMPHONIETTA for orchestra (part of short score only)

Title: 'Symphonietta | Finale'.
Date: Undated (see **Note** below).
Manuscript: Richard Westwood-Brookes (MS formerly owned by Harriet Cohen, then by Colin Scott-Sutherland);[52] [4] ff.; [8] pp. (incomplete); 14-staff paper (355 × 274). Unpublished.
Note: This work has no connection with the Sinfonietta of 1932 (**314**) and is not mentioned in the literature on Bax. There is no trace of the previous movements, and none of the material appears to have been used in any later works. It is assigned here to *c.* 1911 on the basis of style and handwriting, which closely resemble that of *Tamara* (**138**): the opening bars, for example, are very similar to a passage on p. 16 of the ballet score.

[52] See Sotheby's catalogue of Continental Manuscripts and Music, 26 May 1995, lot 118.

1912

145 CHRISTMAS EVE ON THE MOUNTAINS for orchestra (first version)

Date: *Short score*: Undated. *Full score*: 'Fine. | Jan 1912'.
Orchestra: 3+1 3+1 3+1 2+1, 4331, timp., 2 perc. (b.d., cym., gl., cel.), org., 2 hps., str.
Manuscript: *Short score*: UCC; [2] ff.; [4] pp. (ff. [1] and [3] only; f. [2] is missing); ALM 18 paper (360 × 267); inserted into a manila card folder. *Full score*: BL (Add. MS 54736); [27] ff.; 52 pp. + 1 blank; ALM 29 paper (360 × 266). The score contains cuts and revisions that Bax incorporated into the revised version (see **249** for details). Unpublished.
Performance: New Symphony Orchestra, Balfour Gardiner; Queen's Hall; 4 March 1913.
Duration: *c.* 19'00.
Note: For the first performance Bax wrote the following note:

> The motif of this tone-poem occurred to me whilst wandering one frosty evening last winter [i.e. 1911-12] in the beautiful and legended Gleann na Smól, in county Dublin. I hope that the rather mystical mood of which this piece is the outcome may be sufficiently evident in the music to carry its own explanation . . . [It] is based principally on two leading themes. The first is a slow passage of six notes (woven polyphonically through the whole composition) which will be recognised, by those familiar with ecclesiastical music, as an old Magnificat tone of the Roman Catholic Church.

The chant used by Bax is actually a setting of the Credo that also occurs in Bach's *Mass in B minor* and is quoted by Strauss in *Also sprach Zarathustra* (p. 10 of the Eulenburg score). The first performance is described in some detail in *FMY*, pp. 80-8, although some of the facts have been altered for literary purposes. Its companion pieces were not Berlioz's overture *Benvenuto Cellini* and Schumann's Piano Concerto but Vaughan Williams's *Fantasia on Christmas Carols*, Holst's *The Cloud Messenger*, McEwen's *Grey Galloway*, and two folk-tune arrangements by Percy Grainger. (Clifford Bax mentions in *Inland Far*, p. 208, that he also attended this concert.) A critic in *The Musical Standard* (22 March 1913), p. 245, gave the work short shrift: 'Other items were an unattractive tone-poem . . . by Mr. Arnold Bax, who appears so far to have no other ambition than to keep up-to-date in phraseology.'

146 TWO RUSSIAN TONE-PICTURES for piano

a. Nocturne. **b.** Gopak.

Title: a. *MS*: 'No. 2 "Nocturne" for Pianoforte Solo. | May night in the Ukraine (after Gogol)'. *Printed score* (p. 2): 'N°. 1. "NOCTURNE." | "MAY-NIGHT IN THE UKRAINE."' [unhyphenated on front cover].

b. *MS*: '"Russian Country Dance" | "Gopak"'. *Printed score* (p. 2): 'N°· 2. "GOPAK." | (NATIONAL DANCE.)' [on front cover: 'RUSSIAN | NATIONAL DANCE']. At its first performance it was called 'Barbarian Dance'.

Date: a. 'Fine Feb 10th 1912'. **b.** Undated.

Dedication: *Printed scores only*: **a.** '(To OLGA [Antonietti] and NATASHA [Natalia Skarginska]. 1910.)' **b.** '(To Tobias Matthay affectionately dedicated.)'

Manuscript: Privately owned (MS formerly owned by Dame Myra Hess); [9] ff.; [18] pp. ([1-8], t.p. + 1 blank + [1-7] pp. + 1 blank); ALM 12 paper (trimmed to 358 × *c.* 261); bound in green cloth with green leather spine; lettering in gold down spine.

Publication: JW (15418, 15419), 1913, 11 pp. each. Assigned to CH in May 1975.

Performance: a. Myra Hess; Royal Academy Musical Union; 2 *or* 12 November 1912.[53] **b.** Myra Hess; Bechstein Hall; 9 April 1913.

Arrangement: 146a. Arr. for orchestra by Graham Parlett (see *Russian Suite*, **215**, for details). **146b.** Arr. for violin and piano by Louis Godowsky; published JW (W. 180), 15 pp. Assigned to CH in May 1975. For Bax's own orchestration of **146b** see **215**.

Duration: a. 8'17. **b.** 5'42.

Note: In the original MS **146a** is labelled 'No. 2' but the pieces were published in reverse order. The programmatic source for **146a** is Nikolai Gogol's *Evening on a Farm near Dikanka* (see LF, pp. 99-100).

147 PRELUDE TO ADONAIS for orchestra

Performance: [Theatre Orchestra], Norman O'Neill; Haymarket Theatre; 25 June 1912 (repeated on 28 June: 'Special Matinées', starting at 3 p.m., for the Keats-Shelley Memorial House in Rome).

Note: The score of this work has not been traced and the title does not appear in any of the lists published during Bax's lifetime. In 1953 Clifford Gillam, one of the founders of the now defunct Bax Society, came across the printed programme for the two matinées that included this work. He wrote to Bax for information about it, and in what proved to be one of his last letters (dated 31 August 1953) the composer replied as follows:

> The Prelude to Adonais was an orchestral piece. Norman O'Neill, who conducted, asked me to write it for the occasion. I could not attend as I was in Ireland and do not know much about the performance. I believe that Marie Löhr recited Shelley's 'Skylark'. The score of my piece has completely disappeared, but that is no loss as it was very much a pièce d'occasion.

[53] No reviews of this performance have been traced, and the date written by Myra Hess in her notebook (BL Add. MS 57730A) is indistinct.

The matinées were arranged and organized by Frederick Harrison and also included works specially written for the occasion by Parry and Coleridge-Taylor (who died a few months later). Bax's piece was the first item on the programme and preceded a reading by Genevieve Ward of seven stanzas from Shelley's 'Adonais'. In the absence of the score or parts the only conclusions one can draw about the work are that it must have been scored for a theatre orchestra, and that it was presumably of a sombre nature befitting Shelley's poem. Bax may have been asked to write the piece on the strength of his setting of part of Shelley's 'Prometheus Unbound' (*Enchanted Summer*, **129**). For Parry's account of the matinées see Jeremy Dibble, *C. Hubert H. Parry: His Life and Music* (Oxford, 1992); pp. 449-50.

148 NYMPHOLEPT for piano

Title: '"Nympholept." Poem for piano.' The title derives from Greek νυμφόληπτος—one who suffers from nympholepsy, a state of rapture inspired in men by nymphs.
Date: 'Fine | July 1912.'
Dedication: 'To Tobias Matthay affectionately dedicated.'
Manuscript: BL (Add. MS 54737); 11 ff. (11^v blank); [11] pp. (only pp. 2 and 3 are numbered) + 1 blank; ff. 3-6 and 8 are passages revised for the orchestration of 1915 and glued over the original, but now detached except at the inner margins of the versos and the outer margins of the rectos: ff. 3 and 4 are attached to f. 2; 5 and 6 to 2^v; and 8 to 7; ALM 12 paper (360 × 265); there are pencil notes for the orchestration of 1915. Unpublished.
Performance: *Edited by Connie Mayfield*: Martin Roscoe; BBC Studios, New Broadcasting House, Manchester; 17 September 1986; br. on Radio 3, 14 February 1987. A computer-generated score of Dr Mayfield's edition was considered for publication in 1995 but has not yet appeared.
Duration: 11'05.
Note: Beneath the title Bax has written:

> The tale telleth how one walking at summer-dawn in haunting woods was beguiled | by the nymphs, and, meshed in their shining and perilous dances was rapt | away for ever into the sunlight life of the wild-wood.

In preparing his orchestral version (**164**) Bax rewrote several passages, which appear as cancels in this MS. For a connection with 'Roundel' see **158a**.

149 FOUR PIECES for flute and piano

a. Shadow Dance. **b.** The Princess Dances. **c.** Naiad. **d.** Grotesque.

Title: First performed as 'Four Dances'. **149c** is erroneously listed in *Gr5* as 'Nereid', and **149d** as 'Clown's Dance'.
Date: *Printed score*: 'Dublin 1912'.

Dedication: 'Dedicated to Joseph Slater' (see **Note** below).
Manuscript: Not traced.
Publication: CH (38539), 1947, 4to, 19 pp.
Performance: Albert Fransella (fl.), Harriet Cohen (pf.); Æolian Hall; 28 June 1916.
Duration: **a.** 3'08. **b.** 1'21. **c.** 4'16. **d.** 1'45.
Note: These are arrangements of four numbers from Bax's unorchestrated ballet *Tamara* (**138**): **149a** = No. 26; **149b** = No. 16; **149c** = No. 10; **149d** = No. 27. The dedication to the flautist Joseph Slater was probably added when the pieces were published in 1947, the original performer (Albert Fransella) having committed suicide in 1935.

150 MASK for piano

Note: The score of this piece has not been traced. The title appears in *BMSA* (1920) and in a much later list, *MGG* (1949), but there are no other known references to it. Whether the title is the variant spelling of 'masque' or has some connection with Yeats's 'The Mask' (1910), a 'lyric for an unpublished play', it is impossible to tell. There is even a remote possibility that there may be a connection with Richard Dehmel's poem 'Masken', which appears in a collection of his verse owned by Bax and now in UCC (Berlin, 1908). It is conceivable, in view of its date, that *Mask* may be the original version of *Red Autumn* for two pianos (**311**), which, according to *Gr5*, was composed as a piano solo in 1912 (see **151** below), but there is no evidence to support this suggestion.

151 RED AUTUMN for piano

Note: As mentioned in the previous entry, this title is listed in *Gr5* as a work for piano solo, but the score has not been traced. For Bax's later arrangement for two pianos see **311**.

1912–13

152 FOUR ORCHESTRAL PIECES for orchestra

a. 'Pensive Twilight'. **b.** 'Dance in the Sun'. **c.** ['In the Hills of Home'] or ['From the Mountains of Home']. **d.** 'The Dance of Wild Irravel'.

Title: The title page has 'Four Orchestral Pieces', and this is repeated on the first page of music, where it has been written over an erasure and in darker ink; the titles of **152a** and **b** (but not the roman numerals that precede them) are also in darker ink, as are many dynamics throughout. The work was called 'Four Orchestral Sketches' at its first performance, and when **152a** and **152d** were performed separately they were called 'Two Orchestral Sketches'. **152b** is erroneously listed in *MGG* as a song. **152c** has no title on

the MS, but in his programme note for the first performance Bax calls it 'In the Hills of Home' (see **Note** below), although in the copyist's score in UCD he has written in 'From the Mountains of Home', which is how it is listed in *Gr5* and elsewhere.
Date: '1912-13', the '-13' being in a slightly darker ink, as if added later.
Orchestra: **a.** 3+1 203020, 2000, hp., str.
b. 3(1)232, 4000, timp., 2 perc. (tamb., cym., gl.), hp., str.
c. hp., str.
d. 3+1 2+1 3+1 2+1, 4331, timp., 4 perc. (b.d., cym., cast., gl.), hp., str.
Manuscript: *Holograph*: BL (Add. MS 50175); iii + [44] ff.; 81 pp. (t.p. + 1 p. with non-autograph annotations + 1-12, 13-37, 38-44, 45-81 + 5 blank); **152a–c**: ALM 29 paper; **152d**: ALM 18 paper (trimmed to 356 × 262); bound in dark green cloth with a red leather label on the front declaring that it was presented by Harriet Cohen. A new front free endpaper has been inserted by a BL binder in front of the old one, the latter (f. i) bearing Bax's signature and his Chester Terrace address; the reverse is blank; f. ii is a piece of lined paper headed 'INDEX' (perhaps torn from a ledger), the plain reverse blank; f. iii is the t.p., which includes Bax's parents' address (not in his hand); f. iii^{v} contains non-autograph notes. The final page has a non-autograph pencilled note up the left side with instructions for the binder. There are many cancels pasted over the original, and non-autograph blue pencil markings throughout. *Copyist's score*: UCD (MS 26/6); [49 ff.]; 98 pp. (t.p. + p. with list of individual titles + pp. 1-14, 15-48, 49-56, 57-95 + 1 blank); 32-staff paper (348 × 268); bound in limp red leather with the title and composer's name embossed in gold up the spine. The copyist was J. Collins of 142 Sheepcote Lane, Battersea, [London] SW (from a sticker on the title page). There are additions in Bax's hand, including the title of **152c** on p. 49. Unpublished. *Str. parts for* **152d**: Graham Parlett.
Performance: (1) **a** *and* **d** *only*: Queen's Hall Orchestra, Sir Henry Wood; Queen's Hall; 23 September 1913 (Promenade Concert). (2) *Complete*: Queen's Hall Orchestra, Geoffrey Toye; Queen's Hall; 20 March 1914 (F. B. Ellis Concert of Modern Orchestral Music).
Arrangement: **147c**: Piano reduction by Philip Heseltine: Privately owned; [3] ff.; [6] pp.; red and purple ink on 12-staff paper.
Adaptation: Part of **152d** was used for the ballet *Oscar* (see **110** for details).
Duration: **a.** 7'27. **b.** *c.* 5'30. **c.** 9'03. **d.** 5'25.
Note: In *The Musical Standard* for 27 September 1913, p. 303, Bax was interviewed about these 'Celtic' and 'ultra-modern' pieces, and in reply to a query about the title of the fourth he is quoted as saying: '"Wild Irravel" is merely the personification of a gipsy mood. I was trying to get some name which suggested no nationality.' Bax implies here, and in his programme note to the first complete performance, that he coined the name 'Irravel', and it can indeed be analysed as a lexically unattested Irish Gaelic word: *rámhail* (*mh* pronounced *v*), meaning hallucinative dreaming or delirium—

cognate with 'rave'—plus the intensive prefix *ir–*; thus: **irrámhail* (cf. *Nympholept*, **148**). Bax wrote to Arthur Alexander: ' . . . it will sound like Armageddon—a complete battery of percussion, and castanettes [*sic*] clucking like a self complacent hen . . . [and] the gentle and refined melancholy of the first piece will set it off well.' In his programme note for a performance on 7 January 1915 Ernest Newman quotes Bax:

> The subjects are all dance rhythms yet the composer has endeavoured to invest the music with a somewhat veiled and atmospheric quality, and to convey the suggestion of unreality and strangeness. Attention may be drawn to the melody of the middle section, which it will be noticed is really in 4/4 time against a persistent pulsation in triple measure. At the close the music becomes more and more remote in mood and harmonically bizarre, as though the vision were gradually fading away.

The opening melody of **152c** appears to have been composed considerably earlier: it appears in a letter addressed to a girl-friend ('Jean', later Mrs Thornton) dating from *c.* 1903-4 (reproduced in LF, p. 23; see **58**). The title used at the first performance of **152c** (*In the Hills of Home*) may have been taken from Stuart McLean's book *Hills of Home*, which appeared in 1914, the year of the first complete performance (cf. Robert Louis Stevenson's sequence of poems *The Hills of Home*). For details of Bax's revision of **152a–c** as *Three Pieces for Small Orchestra* see **295**.

1913

153 SPRING FIRE for orchestra

Title: *Short score*: '"Spring-Fire". | Symphonic Poem'. *Full score*: 'Spring Fire'.
Date: *Short score*: 'Fine Jan 23rd | 1913.' *Full score*: Undated.
Dedication: 'To Sir Henry J. Wood' (full score only).
Orchestra: 3(1) 2+1 3+1 2+1, 6 (or 4)331, timp., 5 perc. (b.d., tamb., cym., gl., cel.), pf., 2 hps., str.
Manuscript: *Sketches*: Privately owned; [6] ff.; [12] pp. (incomplete at both ends); ALM 12 paper (360 × 277). These comprise an undated piano score with a few instrumental indications containing material used in *Spring Fire.* The opening two bars, marked 'accelerando', lead into an 'Allegro vivace' in A minor. The first bar has a 'segno' ($) written above it, which Bax uses elsewhere to indicate the beginning and end of a cut (see, for example, p. 5 of the MS of *In the Night* (**159**) and pp. 8-9 of the short score of *November Woods* (**191**), where it is used at both the start and end of passages crossed through). A figuration in the treble at the beginning closely resembles the flute ostinato starting at bar 3 of *Spring Fire.* The rest of the material is not used elsewhere except for a passage beginning at 7:20, in which 'Horn 1.' has the theme starting in *Spring Fire* at bar 13. The score is therefore either an unfinished work from which Bax later borrowed material for *Spring Fire* or

part of an early draft containing a discarded version of (presumably) the 'Full Day' section. It is not part of the short score, which is complete in itself, but it is written on the same kind of MS paper.

Short score: BL (Add. MS 54738); 14 ff.; [27] pp. (1-23 non-autograph pagin.; 24-7 unpag.) + 1 blank; ALM 12 paper (360 × 267).

Full score: BL (Add. MS 54739); [62] ff.; 123 pp. + 1 blank; pp. 1-80, 99-114: AL 29 paper (360 × 262: the earliest use by Bax of Augener paper with the galleon imprint); pp. 81-98, 115-123: ALM 29 (360 × 265). The date noted above appears at the end of the second system of f. 14^r; Bax then rewrote the final 13 bars adding an extra 5 bars, as in the final f.sc. He has written his name and his parents' Cavendish Square address on the front free endpaper. There is a pencilled list of instruments to be used for the orchestration at the foot of p. [1]. The MS contains comments and queries in the hand of a copyist, presumably the person who wrote out the parts and another version of the full score. *Copyist's score A*: This dated from *c.* 1914; it was destroyed by fire on 6 May 1964. *Copyist's score B*: This dates from 1983: CH.

Publication: *Full score (photocopy of copyist's score B)*: CH, 1990, 124 pp. (pagin. 1-67a, 67b-123): WC0477C (A3 size); WC 0148C (A4 size).

Performance: (1) *Semi-professional*: Kensington Symphony Orchestra, Leslie Head; Kensington [Old] Town Hall; 8 December 1970. (2) *Professional*: BBC Symphony Orchestra, Norman Del Mar; Royal Festival Hall; 5 October 1983 (Royal Philharmonic Society Concert). (3) Same performers; br. on Radio 3, 8 October 1984 (studio recording). (4) Royal Philharmonic Orchestra, Vernon Handley; St Andrew's Hall, Norwich; 11 October 1985 (Forty-seventh Norfolk and Norwich Festival of Music and the Arts).

Duration: 31'28.

Note: For a projected performance on 28 February 1916 Bax wrote the following note:[54]

This work was written three years ago, and was to have received its first performance at the Norwich Festival of 1914, an event postponed on account of the War.

The music is an attempt to depict the first uprush and impulse of Spring in the woods, and though derived primarily from Nature itself, the formal scheme of the composition was influenced in a large measure by the beautiful first chorus in 'Atalanta in Calydon' ('When the hounds of spring are on winter's traces'). Indeed, the exuberant and pagan qualities of much of the earlier writings of Swinburne colour the musical content of the fantasy throughout.

'Spring Fire' may be regarded as a kind of freely-worked symphony, the four sections linked together without a break.

[54] The fussy layout and punctuation of the original have been slightly modified.

SECTION I (Introduction).

(a) In the Forest before day.

The composer wishes to suggest the uncertain and pensive hour immediately before daybreak in the woodland. It has been raining. The branches drip softly, and a damp, delicate fragrance rises from the earth.

(b) Daybreak and Sunrise.

The rippling and dripping sounds cease suddenly, and there is a strange hush. Then—very remotely—wind instruments begin to sound short, capricious figures, as though the beautiful and quaint denizens of antique woods were awakening from their winter sleep, and were calling to one another through the brakes and long distances of rainy leaves.

The light spreads rapidly, and soon the whole forest is astir. The nymphs stretch their languid arms in the copse, and fauns and satyrs, and bizarre half-human shapes skip with mad antics down the deep glades. The sun rises on a glittering and dazzling earth.

SECTION II (Allegro)

Full Day.

Swinburne's lines:—

> 'With a noise of winds and many rivers,
> With a clamour of waters and with might'

will best convey the mood of this movement. Succeeding a headlong climax, the tempo slackens, and a new episode occurs which may be taken to suggest the newly-blown daffodils and other woodland flowers. The tumultuous movement reasserts itself for a short time, and then definitely subsides in preparation for—

SECTION III (Slow movement)

Woodland Love.

The whole of this section is very quiet in character, and, finally, almost dies away in some strange harmony, as though the forest-lovers had become drugged with their own ecstatic dream. But their self-absorption is suddenly dissipated by the approach of a turbulent rout of satyrs and maenads.

SECTION IV (Finale).

Maenads

The dryads, maenads, and bassarids fly dancing and screaming through the woods, pursued relentlessly by Bacchus and Pan and their hordes of goat-footed and ivy-crowned revellers. Gradually elements from earlier parts of the composition become mingled into the thematic weft of this musical Daphnephoria.[55] It is as though the whole of Nature participated in the careless and resistless riot of youth and sunlight.

The occasion for which Bax wrote this note was a Royal Philharmonic Society Concert under Thomas Beecham at Queen's Hall. *Spring Fire* was cancelled because of the work's 'exceptional difficulty . . . and the insufficiency of time available for proper rehearsal,' and *In the Faery Hills* was played instead. After two disappointments Bax appears to have abandoned the idea of having the work performed. A copyist's score, together with all but a few of the orchestral parts (those not returned by the players after the rehearsal of 1916), was deposited with MM, and in 1964 it was loaned out to Lewis Foreman, who returned it a few days before it was destroyed in Chappell's disastrous fire of 6 May. Although the incomplete set of parts survived, the work was considered unperformable in its entirety until 1968, when the holograph MS came to light among the scores bequeathed to the British Museum by Harriet Cohen.

Thematic material from *Spring Fire* was later used in other works. Bars 3-35 recur in transcription at the beginning of the slow movement of the Cello Sonata of 1923 (**265**); and the passage beginning at fig. 18 of 'Woodland Love' may also be found later in the same movement of the sonata (pp. 20 ff.). The strident fanfare theme that is first clearly heard at fig. 5 was later used in the first of the two fanfares written for the Red Army Day celebrations of 1943 (**351**) and the first of the two written for the wedding of Princess Elizabeth in 1947 (**373**; see also **348**).

154 SONATA for piano (only SCHERZO extant)

Title: 'Sonata | No 2 Scherzo'.
Date: 'Oct 17th 1913'.
Manuscript: BL (Add. MS 54767); ff. 1-8; 2 blank pp. + [12] pp. + 2 blank; AL 18 paper (trimmed to 358 × 264) but bound inside a bifolium of BH paper (353 × 217 and 263), on the last side of which there are blue pencilled marks including four clumsy crotchets in a childish scrawl;[56] bound by the BL. In the left margin of p. 1 Bax has listed in pencil the names of the instruments intended for his orchestration of 1917. Unpublished.
Performance: Malcolm Binns; EMI No. 1 Studio, Abbey Road, London; 9 September 1981 (recording session for Pearl Records).
Duration: 9'07.

[55] 'Laurel-bearing': a Boeotian festival in honour of Apollo at which a laurel-bedecked staff was carried in procession. Bax may have come across this word in J. G. Frazer's *The Golden Bough*, I, 'The Magic Art . . .', II, 3rd edn. (London, 1907), p. 63, where it appears in a footnote to an Irish May Day custom; but his use of the name of an Apollonian rite in a rampantly Dionysiac context seems inappropriate.

[56] Perhaps in the hand of Bax's son, Dermot, or his niece, Undine (both born in 1911).

Note: This Scherzo in F is the only extant movement from an otherwise unknown, unnumbered sonata. The indication 'No 2' clearly refers to the title of this separate movement rather than to the work as a whole, and the reference to a 'Sonata in F' in LF (p. 449) is incorrect. It is conceivable, since it is in the relative major, that there may be some connection with the lost Sonata in D minor of 1911 (**137**). A fragment of melody at 7:1-6 is identifiable as part of what became the motto theme from the Second Violin Sonata (**171**), also used in *November Woods* (**191**). For details of Bax's 1917 orchestration see **187**, and for his pianola arrangement see **212**.

155 TOCCATA for piano

Title: Listed in *MT* as 'Capriccio'.
Date: *Gr5*: '1913'.
Dedication: *Printed score*: 'To Hamilton Harty.'
Manuscript: Not traced.
Publication: MM (136), 1920, fo., 15 pp. ; CH (40901), [1951], 4to.
Duration: 5'24.

1914

156 THREE SONGS WITH ORCHESTRA for high voice and orchestra

Title: No collective title on MSS. The title given above derives from the programme for the first performance. **a.** 'A Celtic Lullaby'. **b.** 'A Christmas Carol'. **c.** 'Slumber-Song' (called 'Lullaby' at its first performance).
Date: a. Undated. **b.** 'Fine | Orchestrated | Dublin Feb 1914'. **c.** 'Fine | Feb 26th | 1914 Dublin'.
Dedication: a. '(To Gladys Lees 1904.)': added in different ink (now faded) from the rest of the score. **b.** 'To my sister Evelyn'; **c.** None.
Text: a. Fiona Macleod, 'A Celtic Lullaby'. **b.** Anonymous, 15th century. **c.** 'Sheila McCarthy' (pseudonym of Bax; the text differs very slightly from that of the original poem of 1910).
Orchestra: a. 2020 2+1 20, 4000, hp., str. **b.** 2222, 4000, str. **c.** 2022, 0000, hp., str.
Manuscript: a. BL (Loan 75/1 (M178)); [12] ff.; 24 pp.; ALM 12 paper (trimmed to 336 × 259); stuck with brown gummed paper into dark green paper wrappers ('Chester's Circulating Music Library'). **b.** JWC; [8] ff.; 15 pp. + 1 blank; 18-staff paper (305 × 230). **c.** BL (Add. MS 54772); [6] ff.; 12 pp.; ALM 12 paper (357 × 265). Unpublished. *Parts*: JWC.
Performance: Dilys Jones (sop.), Queen's Hall Orchestra, Francis Bevis Ellis; Queen's Hall; 27 March 1914 (F. B. Ellis Concert of Modern Orchestral Music). 'The vocalist hardly did justice to [the songs] or showed off their fine possibilities.' (*The Musical Standard*, April 1914, p. 327); 'Miss

Dilys Jones evidently did not find the songs very singable.' (*The Musical News*, 4 April 1914, p. 320).
Duration: a. 7'00. **b.** 4'06. **c.** 3'56.
Note: For details of the original voice-and-piano versions of these songs see **63d, 116** and **126.** The concert at which they were first played was notable for including the first performance of Vaughan Williams's *London Symphony* (original version).

157 THE HAPPY FOREST for piano

Title: 'The Happy Forest.' 'After a prose poem by | Herbert Farjeon.' (to left of title).
Date: 'May 13th 1914'.
Dedication: 'To Herbert Farjeon'.
Manuscript: *Sketches*: Clifford Gillam (MS formerly owned by Harriet Cohen); [1] f. (f. 1 of a bifolium also containing unidentifiable sketches: see **Add. 16**); [2] pp.; ALM 18 paper (361 × 272); in pencil. *Complete*: BL (Add. MS 50176); 4 ff.; [8] pp.; ALM 18 paper (trimmed to 355 × 265); bound by BL with manila wrappers bound in bearing Harriet Cohen's writing. There are pencil and ink notes for orchestration. Bax was obviously pleased with the antepenultimate bar of p. [4]: the note 'This bar is exactly right' is pencilled underneath it (bar 1 of p. 26 in the published orchestral version). Unpublished in this form.
Performance: None.
Duration: *c.* 10'00.
Note: This is better known in its later orchestration as a 'Nature-Poem' (**260**); there are no structural differences between the two versions. Farjeon's prose poem, on which the score is based, is reproduced in LF, pp. 385-6.

158 THREE RONDELS for voice and piano

Title: 'Three Rondels by Chaucer'.
a. 'Roundel'. **b.** 'Welcome Somer'. **c.** 'Of her mercy'.
Date: a. *MS A*: 'Aug 14th 1914.' *MS B*: 'August 1914.' (written, unusually, to the left of the title); **b.** 'Oct 20th 1914.'; **c.** 'Oct 31st 1914.'
Dedication: a. 'To Tania' (Harriet Cohen): on MS *A* only; not on printed score. **b.** '(To Joan Thorneycroft [*sic*]) .' **c.** None.
Text: Attributed to Geoffrey Chaucer: **a.** 'Merciles Beautè: I Captivity.' **b.** 'Welcome Somer' from 'The Parlement of Foules'. **c.** 'Merciles Beautè: II Rejection'.
Manuscript: *MS A* (three songs): BL (Add. MS 54779); ff. 1-6 + 1 unfol. + 7-14 (14v blank); [17] pp. (t.p. + 1 blank + [4] pp., [5] pp. + 1 blank, [5] pp. + 1 blank); **a.** ALM 10 paper (trimmed to 359 × 266); **b.** AL 16 paper (trimmed to 360 × 265); **c.** ALM 10 paper (trimmed to 359 × 266); all bound with 14 other songs (see **133** above). *MS B* (**158a** only): BL (Loan 75/2

(M188)); [2] ff.; [4] pp.; AL 14 paper (360 × 266); with engravers' marks. **158b** and **c** unpublished.
Publication: 158a *only*: [No. 7] (3775) in *Seven Selected Songs*, JWC, 1919, 4to, pp. 29-32. For reprints see **94** above.
Duration: a. 3'31. **b.** 2'17. **c.** 3'12.
Note: The opening words of **158a** ('Your eyen two wol slay me sodenly') are set to a melody also found in *Nympholept* (beginning on brass, 11:3 of f.sc.). This song is the earliest work by Bax to be dedicated to Harriet Cohen, who had already joined his circle of friends by the summer of 1913.

159 IN THE NIGHT (Passacaglia) for piano

Title: 'In the Night | (Passacaglia)'. Listed in *Gr3* as 'Passacaglia' only.
Date: 'Nov 6th | 1914.'
Manuscript: BL (Add. MS 54769); [4] ff.; [6] pp. + 2 blank; ALM 8 paper (359 × 267). Eight bars are crossed through on p. [5]. Unpublished.
Performance: Martin Roscoe; BBC Studios, New Broadcasting House, Manchester; 17 September 1986; br. on Radio 3, 14 February 1987.
Publication: *Edited by Richard G. Hallas*: FMP, 1995, 4to, 9 pp.+1 p. of editorial notes; introductory note by Graham Parlett.
Duration: 5'39.
Note: The main title is derived either from Fiona Macleod's poem 'In the Night' (from *Through the Ivory Gate*) or from Bax's own poem with the same title, written on 29 January 1910 and published in *Love Poems of a Musician* (London, 1923), p. 15; also in Lewis Foreman (ed.), *Dermot O'Byrne: Poems by Arnold Bax*, p. 47.

160 THE BARD OF THE DIMBOVITZA for mezzo-soprano[57] (160f for bass) and orchestra (first version)

Title: 'The Bard of the Dimbovitza': **a.** 'The Well of Tears'. **b.** 'Gipsy Song'. **c.** 'My girdle I hung on a Tree Top Tall'. **d.** 'Spinning-Song'. **e.** 'Misconception'. **f.** 'The Song of the Dagger' (titles given as on f.sc. MS).
Date: b. 'Fine | Dec 14th | 1914'. **d.** 'Oct. 1914.' (sh.sc. dated 'Oct 15th | 1914'). **f.** '1914' (in blue pencil, possibly not in Bax's hand). The other songs are undated.
Dedication: None on original version (see **368** for revision).
Orchestra: a. 3(1) 2+1 3+1 20, 4000, hp., str. **b.** 1111, 0000, hp., str. **c.** 3(1) 2+1 3+1 20, 3000, hp., str. **d.** 3(1) 20 2+1 20, 3000, hp., str. **e.** 3 2+1 2+1 20, 3000, hp., str. **f.** 3(1) 3+1 2+1+E♭ 2+1, 4331, timp., 3 perc. (b.d., tamb., cym.), hp., str.

[57] On the MS full score 'soprano' is specified for **160d**, 'contralto' for **160e**.

Text: Poems from Hélène Vacaresco, *The Bard of the Dimbovitza: Roumanian Folk-Songs collected from the Peasants*, trans. by Carmen Sylva [Queen Elizabeth of Romania] and Alma Strettell, 2nd edn. (London, 1908), pp. 49, 15-16, 241-2, 221-2, 225-6, 50-1 respectively. On the flyleaf of Bax's own copy of this volume (now in UCC) he has pencilled in the titles of five of the poems set.
Manuscript: *Vocal scores of* **160d** *and* **f** *only*: BL (Add. MS 54779); ff. 15-20^{v}, 21-2^{v} (incomplete); t.p. + 1 blank + [10] pp., [4] pp. (incomplete); **d.** ALM 12 paper (trimmed to 358 × 263); **f.** AL 18 paper (trimmed to 360 × 265); both bound with 14 other songs (see **133** above). *Full scores of* **160a** *and* **c–f**: BL (Add. MS 54773); **a.** ff. 1-16 (14^{v} and 15^{v} (i.e. pp. 27 and 28) are glued back to back, the composer having presumably made a mistake on his original p. 28; 16^{v} blank); 29 pp. + 1 blank; **c.** ff. 17-30 + 2 blank; 28 pp. (mispaginated by Bax: p. 26 unpag., p. 27 pagin. '26', p. 28 pagin. '27') + 4 blank; **d.** ff. 31-48 (48^{v} blank); 35 pp. + 1 blank; **e.** ff. 49-64^{v}; 30 pp.; **f.** ff. 65-89 (89^{v} blank) + 6 blank; 47 pp. (1-15, [16-47] + 13 blank); **a.** and **e.** ALM 29 paper; **c.** AL 12 paper; **d.** AL 18 paper; **f.** [AL] 29 (pp. 1-[18] and [43-7]), AL 29 (pp. [19-42]); the whole trimmed to 359 × 266; bound *c.* 1915 in maroon cloth with gold lettering (title and composer's name) up spine. *Full score of* **160b**: CH (MS 241); [8] ff.; 15 pp. + 1 blank; ALM 29 paper (359 × 266); torn out of bound volume when the other songs were revised in 1946. Unpublished in this form.
Performance: **160b** *only (with piano)*: Gladys Moger (sop.), Harold Samuel (pf.); Æolian Hall; 9 November 1918 (third in a series of six 'recital-lectures' by Edwin Evans on 'Modern English Song'). **160a–e** *only (with orchestra)*: Ethel Fenton (mezz.), 'A Specially Selected Orchestra' (including Barbirolli among the cellos), Edward Clark; Queen's Hall; 8 April 1921. Several of the songs were later performed individually with piano accompaniment (e.g. **160c** sung by Violette Browne, as noted in *The Musical Times*, January 1929, p. 71). 'The Song of the Dagger' (**160f**) remains unperformed.
Duration: *c.* 43'00.
Note: For details of the revised version see **368**. For details of thematic material common to 'The Well of Tears' and *Into the Twilight* see **110**.

1915

161 THE PRINCESS'S ROSE GARDEN (Nocturne) for piano

Title: *MS*: '"Berceuse"'. *Printed score*: 'The Princess's Rose Garden | NOCTURNE' ('Rose-Garden' hyphenated on p. 1).
Date: *MS*: 'Jan 9th / Jan 13th } 1915.' *Printed score*: 'Jan. 10th 1915'.

This discrepancy suggests that the printed score may have been engraved from another, untraced MS.

Dedication: *MS*: 'To Tania.' *Printed score*: 'To Miss Harriet Cohen'.
Manuscript: BL (Add. MS 54769); [4] ff.; 6 pp. (p. 6 unpag.) + 2 blank; AL 12 paper (362 × 266).
Publication: AUG (14923), 1915, fo., 7 pp.
Performance: Myra Hess; Grafton Galleries; 29 April 1915 (Music Club Concert).
Duration: 8'17.

162 IN A VODKA SHOP for piano

Date: 'Jan 22nd | 1915.'
Dedication: *MS*: 'To Tania.' *Printed score*: 'To Miss Myra Hess'.
Manuscript: *Holograph*: BL (Add. MS 54769); [4] ff.; [6] pp. (only p. 6 pagin.) + 2 blank; AL 12 paper (362 × 266). Non-autograph fingering and other markings in pencil. *Copyist's score*: WML (035719); [6] ff.; t.p. + 8 pp. + 3 blank; AL 8a paper (trimmed to 344 × 265).
Publication: AUG (14921), 1915, fo., 7 pp. *Proof sheets corrected by the composer*: BL (H.403.aa.(2.)), 7 ff. (imperfect: lacking f. 3).
Performance: Myra Hess; Grafton Galleries; 29 April 1915 (Music Club Concert).
Duration: 3'27.
Note: Many years after he had written this piece, the composer learned that a writer in the *Contemporary Musical Journal* (Petrograd, 1916) had expressed the opinion that

> . . . Mr. Bax might just as well have based his 'alcoholic slander' upon the behaviour of frequenters of any beer-house in the East End . . . Early last year Bax told me that he had never been aware of this indictment, and expressed anxiety 'lest I may be arraigned before an international court on the count of "alcoholic slander"'.

(M. Montagu-Nathan, 'Reminiscences of Arnold Bax', *The Musical Times*, November 1953, p. 508.) For details of the orchestrated version see **215.**

163 THE MAIDEN WITH THE DAFFODIL (Idyll) for piano

Title: *MS A*: '"Idyll" "The Maiden with the Daffodil"'. First performed as 'To a Maiden with a Daffodil'.
Date: *A*: 'Jan 23rd | 1915.' *B*: 'Jan 23rd 1915'.
Dedication: 'To Tania.' (Harriet Cohen).
Manuscript: *A*: BL (Add. MS 54769); [2] ff. (1 bifolium); [4] pp.; AL 12 paper (362 × 266). *B:* WML (035718); [2] ff.; [4] pp.; AL 12 paper (362 × 265).
Publication: JW (15543), 1915, fo., 5 pp. Also in Connie Mayfield (ed.), *Arnold Bax: Selected Works for Piano,* TP, 1986, 4to, pp. 13-17.
Performance: Myra Hess; Æolian Hall; 24 March 1915 (Classical Concert Society Concert).

Duration: 4'26.
Note: According to Harriet Cohen, Bax wrote this piece after she had attended a tea-party at the home of Frederick Corder with a single daffodil as her only decoration (see *A Bundle of Time*, London, 1969, p. 30). The piano piece was presented to her together with a poem, which is probably identical with an eight-line verse beginning 'This for the maiden with the daffodil' that he later wrote into her autograph album, where it is dated 10 May 1918; the complete poem is reproduced in CSS (p. 49).

164 NYMPHOLEPT for orchestra

Title: 'Nympholept | (Nature-poem for Orchestra).'
Date: 'Feb 1915'.
Dedication: 'To Constant Lambert' (see **Note** below).
Orchestra: 3(1) 2+1 3+1 2+1, 4331, timp., 4 perc. (b.d., tamb., cym., tri., xyl., gl., cel.), 2 hps., str.
Manuscript: *Short score*: The original piano version (see **148**). *Full score*: CH (MS 244); [30] ff.; end papers + 57 pp. + 3 blank; [AL] 29 paper (trimmed to 354 × 264); bound in dark blue linen boards (now loose and unstitched) with the title and composer's name embossed in gold on the upper cover.
Publication: *Photocopy of MS*: WC0455.
Performance: (1) *Semi-professional*: Strolling Players Orchestra, Terence Lovett; RAM; 31 May 1961. (2) *Professional*: BBC Welsh Symphony Orchestra, Vernon Handley; Studio 1, Broadcasting House, Llandaff; 2 October 1983; br. on Radio 3, 23 December 1983.
Duration: 17'49.
Note: The recto of the free front end paper has Bax's name followed by his Regent's Park address (1a Chester Terrace) and then the following note:

> The title of this short tone-poem comes from Swinburne [his poem 'A Nympholept'], and the quotation from [George] Meredith's 'The Woods of Westermain'. Both poems derive from the same central idea—that of a perilous pagan enchantment haunting the sunlit midsummer forest.

The verso has the quotation mentioned above: '"Enter these enchanted woods | You who dare....." | (Meredith)'. Bax also wrote a poem called 'Nympholept', published anonymously in *Love Poems of a Musician*, pp. 12-13; see also Clifford Bax, *Evenings in Albany* (London, 1942), pp. 38 ff. The dedication was clearly added at a later date: the ink used is of a lighter shade and the pen is slightly thicker (almost certainly the same pen used to write the title on the MS of **295b**); and Constant Lambert was only ten years old at the time of composition (see **333** for a plausible explanation). In a letter to Adrian Boult dating from April 1935, Bax wrote that '[Nympholept] was never played in those days on account of its elaborate difficulties.' For details of the original piano version see **148**.

165 LEGEND for violin and piano

Date: 'Feb | 1915.'
Dedication: 'To Winifred Smith.'
Manuscript: BL (Add. MS 54395); 5 ff. (foliated 18-22) + 1 blank; 9 pp. + 3 blank; AL 12 paper (359 × 266); loose in a packet with MSS by other composers published by Augener or Galliard.
Publication: AUG (14984), 1915, fo., 12 pp.
Performance: Winifred Small[58] (vn.), Harriet Cohen (pf.); Æolian Hall; 28 June 1916. Bax was impressed by this performance and wrote to the violinist: 'All throughout . . . the variety of tone was really remarkable.'
Duration: 8'48.
Note: In a letter to May Harrison dated 7 April 1941, Bax wrote:

> I am very pleased to hear that you played the old Legend again and that 'R.V.W.' [Vaughan Williams] liked it. That piece is always associated in my mind with the last war and came straight out of the horror of that time—like much of the second violin sonata.

166 SONATA NO. 1 for violin and piano (second version of 124)

I. Moderately slow and very Tranquilly. II. Allegro Vivace. III. Moderate Tempo. Smooth and serene.

Date: I. 'Fine Feb 2nd 1910.' (this movement may not have been revised until 1920). II. Undated. III. 'March 1915'.
Dedication: 'à M'selle | Natalia Skarginski 1910.' (i.e. the same dedication as on the original version).
Manuscript: BL (Add. MS 54765); ff. 1-8v,[59] 29-58v; (1-16, [1-16], t.p. + 1 blank + [1-26] pp.); Movts. I and II: ALM 14 paper (trimmed to 356 × 261); III. AL 12 paper (trimmed to *c.* 354 × *c.* 271); bound by BL with brown wrappers bound in. III is headed with a quotation: '"A pity beyond all Telling is | hid in the heart of love" | (W.B. Yeats)'.[60] Unpublished (but see **Note** below).
Performance: None.
Duration: *c.* 35'00.
Note: This version of the sonata, with its new second and third movements, is substantially the same as the first published version (1920-1; see **124** and **236** for details).

[58] Not to be confused with the dedicatee, who was also a violinist (see **124**).
[59] Ff. 9-28v contain the original movts. II and III of 1910 together with the brown wrappers.
[60] Several pages from this MS have been poorly conserved.

167 QUINTET IN G MINOR for piano and strings

I. Moderately fast. Passionate and rebellious. II. Slow and serious. III. Moderate Tempo–Allegro vivace.

Date: I. 'July 16th 1914'. II. 'July 19th | 1914'. III. 'April | 13th | 1915.'
Dedication: *Printed score only*: 'To Edwin Evans.'
Manuscript: BL (Add. MS 54761); [42] ff.; 84 pp. (1-34, 35-51, 52-84: this is the original pagin. in pencil, with most page-numerals shaved off by the binder; bound with gold lettering on front cover; AL 14 paper (trimmed to 335 × *c.* 247) bound in dark green cloth with title and composer's name on the upper board; the front free endpaper has been cut out leaving a stub. I: The last bar of p. 42 is crossed through in pencil and p. 43 has a new page pasted over the original; pp. 44-5 are tied together with three strips of glued paper, the passage in between having been cut; thus the penultimate bar of p. 42, from 8 after (C), is followed by bar 1 of p. 46. III: There is a cut of 67 bars from 61:6 to bar 67:1, an episode in B♭ being deleted; a reprise of the same episode is cut and the last system of p. 76 has a new lead into the epilogue pasted over the top; pp. 77-8 and the first bar of p. 79 are crossed through in pencil. It is not possible to tell whether these cuts were made before the first performance (1917) or just before publication (1922).
Publication: MM (304), 1922, fo., 70 pp.; CH (37975), [1947].
Performance: (1) *Private*: Harriet Cohen (pf.), English String Quartet: Marjory Hayward (vn.), Edwin Virgo (vn.), Frank Bridge (va.), Ivor James (vc.); Savoy Hotel, London; 19 December 1917 (Music Club Concert). (2) *Public*: Fanny Davies (pf.), Bohemian String Quartet; Wigmore Hall; 12 May 1920.
Duration: 36'20–46'14.[61]
Note: In a letter to Philip Heseltine dating from Easter 1915, Bax wrote: 'I have also written a piano quintet and finished off . . . 'Nympholept' [**164**] both of which I believe to be representative of the best I can do at present.' In reply to a query from Vivian Langrish about a dubious note in the score, Bax remarked that 'odd notes did not matter so long as the style and atmosphere were right'. (From an interview between Lewis Foreman and the pianist in 1975.)

168 APPLE-BLOSSOM-TIME for piano

Date: *Printed score*: 'May 1915'.
Dedication: 'To S.H. Braithwaite'.
Manuscript: Not traced.
Publication: AUG (14939), 1915, fo., 5 pp. *Proof sheets corrected by the composer*: BL (H.403.cc.(4.)), 5 ff.

[61] These are the times of the fastest and slowest performances noted.

Performance: Phyllis Emanuel; Steinway Hall; 18 November 1915 (War Emergency Entertainments All-British Concert).
Duration: 3'17.

169 SLEEPY-HEAD for piano

Title: *Printed score*: 'Sleepy-head' (front cover); 'Sleepyhead' (advertisement page); 'Sleepy Head' (p. 1 of score).
Date: *Printed score*: 'May 24th 1915'.
Dedication: 'To Elsita'. Apart from his collection of short stories *Children of the Hills* (Dublin, [1913]), this is the only work that Bax dedicated to his wife.
Manuscript: Not traced.
Publication: AUG (14938), 1915, fo., 5 pp. *Proof sheets corrected by the composer*: BL (H.403.cc.(3.)), 5 ff. Also in Connie Mayfield (ed.), *Arnold Bax: Selected Works for Piano*, TP, 1986, 4to, pp. 18-22.
Duration: 5'36.

170 RED OWEN: projected opera

Date: Undated, but some of the pages containing musical fragments also have sketches for the Second Violin Sonata, which was completed in the summer of 1915 (see **171** below).
Text: Dermot O'Byrne [Arnold Bax], *Red Owen: A Play in 3 Acts* (Dublin: The Talbot Press, 1919).
Manuscript: *Sketches for libretto*: Privately owned (formerly by Colin Scott-Sutherland); [11] pp.; pencil. These sketches for the beginning of Act II are written upside down on the reverse of folios in a black notebook on the obverse of which there is an unpublished story called *The Horseman*. The latter is undated but previous pages in the notebook evidently once contained another story, *The Sisters*, which was written in St Petersburg in April–May 1910; this has been torn out, presumably for publication in 1912, but the t.p. is still extant. *Sketches for music*: *MS A*: Privately owned; verso of one f. + recto of another; [2] pp.; pencil; AL 14 paper (331 × 246). The first page contains a sketch for the last ten bars of III from the Second Violin Sonata (**171**) followed by a three-line fragment in 6/8 time, headed 'In a Donegal kitchen'. This is followed by a variant in 3/4 time, with another variant in 2/4 time at the foot of the page. Between the last two variants there is an untitled three-bar fragment in a Mixolydian F on a two-line system. The second page contains a single line marked 'senza tempo' that is clearly intended to represent a violin tuning up, followed by an extended (but incomplete) 32-bar version of the previous reel-like material on six two-staff lines. The assigning of this sketch to *Red Owen* is based on two pieces of evidence: the title 'In a Donegal kitchen' is similar to the setting of the play, which in the 1919 publication is described as 'a kitchen in western

Connemara' (the location may have been changed between its composition and its publication); and the suggestion of a fiddle being tuned, leading to an Irish dance, is in accordance with the stage instruction on p. 7 of the play, in which a fiddler tunes his instrument and launches into the reel 'Silvermines'. This title has not so far been traced among genuine Irish reels and may have been made up by Bax. For the recto of f. [1] and the verso of [2] see **171** below.

MS B: Privately owned; [1] f.; [1] p. + 1 blank; AL 14 paper (331 × 246). Four two-staff systems containing seventeen bars of a lyrical variant of the reel tune in A above. *MS C*: Privately owned; [2] ff. (1 bifolium; [2v] blank; [3] pp. + 1 blank; ALM 18 paper (331 × 247); f. [1] contains seven two-staff systems including a waltz-like melody that was later used in 'Karissima's Dance of Joy' from *The Truth about the Russian Dancers* (**219**); f. [1v] has similar material on eight systems, and at one point the words 'whooping and laughter' appear above the staff, suggesting a scene of revelry in a dramatic context; since there is no extant dramatic work by Bax other than *Red Owen* in which such a scene might have occurred, the draft has been tentatively assigned to this score (but cf. the sketches headed 'Carnival', **98**); f. [2v] contains five systems with more of the waltz melody upside down at the bottom of the page.

Note: In his radio talk of 1949 Bax described *Red Owen* as a 'folk comedy rather in the manner of J. M. Synge' based on the Irish tale *The Twisting of the Rope*.[62] It concerns the itinerant, picaresque poet Red Owen Hanrahan, who, in the first act, gate-crashes a party and is finally ejected by means of a ruse, whereby he is invited to help with the twisting of a hempen rope and manoeuvred in such a way that while he is occupied with this task he is unwittingly backed out through the open door, which is then bolted against him. During the course of the play Bax provided himself with ample opportunity for musical participation. In the opening scene the reel called 'Silvermines' is played by a fiddler, who is interrupted by the entrance of Red Owen carrying a harp slung over his shoulder (p. 7). A little later (p. 22) Owen half declaims, half sings a song as he is slowly and unwittingly removed from the scene. In the second act he sings the folk song 'Casadh an tSúgáin' ('Twisting of the Rope') in counterpoint with the dance music inside the house (pp. 26 ff.), and shortly afterwards (pp. 35 ff.) there is a 'fever-dream', which would have provided an opportunity for some Straussian 'Fieberträumerisch Musik'. Finally, in the third act, the shade of Oisin appears and at one point (p. 46) chants his lines. And when he has at last disappeared 'a strange music is heard' (p. 49) and a 'wild solemn dance' takes place before Red Owen eventually expires.

[62] See W. B. Yeats, *Stories of Red Hanrahan* (Dundrum, 1904), pp. 15-25. Douglas Hyde's Gaelic play *Casadh an tSúgáin* is also based on this story.

For further details of Bax's operatic aspirations see **106** above; and for a curious sidelight see Clifford Bax, 'The British Composer in the Theatre', *The Radio Times* (5 January 1934), p. 11, together with Eugene Goossens's riposte in a later issue (23 February 1934), p. 539.

171 SONATA NO. 2 for violin and piano (first version)

I. Introduction—Fantasy—II. 'The Grey Dancer in the Twilight'—III. Interlude—Lento espressivo—IV. Allegro feroce—Epilogue.

Date: 'In Summer. | 1915.' (at head of MS); 'The End. | August 13th | 1915.' (at end).
Manuscript: *Sketch*: Privately owned; [2] ff.; [3] pp.; pencil; AL 14 paper (331 × 246). F. [1r] contains twelve bars on four three-staff systems + a system blank except for the clefs: I, 6:2-11 in the published version; [1v] contains the last ten bars of I (10:19-28) followed by sketches for **170**; [2r] contains more sketches for **170**; [2v] contains nineteen bars on five systems: I, 9:15 to 10:18 in the published version (omitting the six bars after 10:6). *Complete*: BL (Add. MS 54766); ff. 1-28; 49 pp. (pagin. in pencil: 1-10, 11-25, 26-36, 36-49 + 3 blank); AL 14 paper (362 × 266); loosely inserted in brown paper wrappers bearing Harriet Cohen's writing on the front. Unpublished in this form. See **248** for the revised version, which was achieved by pruning and overpasting of new material on to the original MS.
Performance: This version unperformed.
Duration: *c.* 35'00.

172 A MOUNTAIN MOOD (Melody and Variations) for piano

Title: *MS A*: 'A Mountain Mood. | Melody and three Variations'. *MS B*: 'A Mountain Mood. | Melody and Variations.'
Date: *A*: 'Sept 2nd | 1915 | Críoch [finished]'. *B*: 'Sept 2nd | 1915.'
Dedication: *A*: 'To Tania [Harriet Cohen] | who plays it perfectly.' *B*: None. *Printed score*: 'To | Miss Harriet Cohen.'
Manuscript: *A*: BL (Add. MS 54769); [2] ff. (1 bifolium); [4] pp.; AL 14 paper (361 × 266). *B*: BL (Loan 75/3 (M189)); [2] ff.; [3] pp. + 1 blank; AL 14 paper (361 × 267).
Publication: JWC (2020), 1918, fo., 7 pp. (issued May 1918). Also published with *Dream in Exile* (**176**), MMP (M 2224, 'Master Piano Series'), [1994], 4to, 18 pp.
Duration: 4'34.

173 WINTER WATERS (Tragic Landscape) for piano

Title: '"Winter Waters". | Tragic Landscape.'
Date: *Original ending*: 'Sept 5th | 1915.' *Revised ending*: 'Sept 5th. | 1915'.
Dedication: 'To Arthur Alexander.'

Manuscript: BL (Loan 75/4 (M184)); [3] ff.; [5] pp. + p. [6] stuck over the top of p. [5] containing the revised ending[63] + 1 blank; AL 14 paper (361 × 267).
Publication: JWC (2024), 1918, fo., 11 pp. (issued May 1918).
Performance: Harriet Cohen; Æolian Hall; 6 June 1919.
Duration: 6'44.

c. 1915

174 [UNTITLED]: Sketch (in short score)

Date: Undated and assigned to *c.* 1915 on the basis of handwriting and the fact that the MS was found with that of the First Violin Sonata (**166**). The paper type is not otherwise attested before 1914.
Manuscript: BL (Add. MS 54780); f. 9 (the first side of a bifolium of which the remaining three sides are blank); [1] p. (24 bars on six two-staff lines); AL 12 paper (362 × 266).
Note: That this is part of a draft for an orchestral work rather than for a piano piece is indicated by the presence of a melodic line high up in the treble unplayable by a pianist in conjunction with the harmonies in both hands below; there are no indications of the orchestration. Stylistically the music is in a Russian pseudo-Oriental vein reminiscent of *Tamara* (1911), the opening phrase being similar to the motive with which the ballet score begins, and it could quite easily be the opening of a work.

1916

175 THE GARDEN OF FAND for orchestra

Date: In a written answer to an enquiry from Christopher Whelen, Bax gave '1913' as the year of composition and 'Dublin' as the location. In a letter to Arthur Alexander dated 'Oct 10th or thereabouts [1915]', he wrote: 'I am now going gently crazy in an attempt to orchestrate the "Garden of Fand".' In a letter to Anne Crowley he wrote: 'I can't remember any work connected with it at all except the orchestration . . . I remember feeling how almost uncanny it was; I did it partly in Dublin and partly in London but there was no break in the continuity.'[64] Since *Gr5* gives '1916' as the date of completion, it seems likely that the orchestration took Bax several months, and the work has been allocated to the beginning of this year on the assumption that the work was carried out more or less continuously and because nothing else can be ascribed to January.
Orchestra: 3+1 2+1 3+1 2+1, 4331, timp., 4 perc. (b.d., tamb., cym., gl., cel.), 2 hps., str.

[63] Both endings are reproduced in LF, pp. 134-5.
[64] Bax lived at 'Yeovil', 10 Bushy Park Road, Rathgar, Co. Dublin, from 1911 to 1914.

Manuscript: *Short score*: UCC; [16] ff.; 26 pp. + 6 blank; pp. 1-16: ALM 12 (361 × 265); pp. 17-26 + 6 blank: PO paper (295 × 237). *Full score*: Not traced.
Publication: MM (8), 1922, fo. and 8vo (min.sc.), 80 pp.; CH (38071), [1948], 8vo (st.sc.). *Printer's pulls*: CH (MS 807).
Performance: (1) Chicago Symphony Orchestra, Frederick Stock; Orchestra Hall, Chicago; 29 October 1920. (2) British Symphony Orchestra, Adrian Boult; Kingsway Hall; 11 December 1920 (Quinlan Concert).
Adaptation: As a ballet entitled *Picnic at Tintagel*, with choreography by Frederick Ashton and costumes by Cecil Beaton. *Performance*: New York City Ballet; New York Center; 28 February 1952. 'All slightly bewildering', commented Bax in a letter to Christopher Whelen. For details of the scenario see Walter Terry, *Ballet Guide* (London, 1976), pp. 253-5. A brief excerpt from the ballet is available on film in The Performing Arts Research Center (New York Public Library).
Duration: 15'19.
Note: The short score contains several passages that were cut when it was orchestrated. The published score is prefaced with the following note:

The Garden of Fand is the sea. The ancient Saga called 'The sick-bed of Cuchulain' tells how that hero (the Achilles of the Gael) was lured away from the world of deeds and battles by the Lady Fand, daughter of Manannan,[65] lord of the ocean; and how in the time of his country's direst need he forgot all but the enchantments of an immortal woman. The tale goes on to relate that Cuchulain's wife, Emer, pursued him to that wonder-land and pleaded with the goddess for her husband's return. Then, with one of those touches of modern romanticism which are continually occurring in the Irish pagan tales, the Saga ends with Fand's pitying renunciation of her human love, and we read that Manannan shook his 'Cloak of Forgetfulness' between Cuchulain and Fand, that the memory of each might be utterly blotted out from the mind of the other.

This tone-poem has no special relation to the events of the above legend. In the earlier portion of the work the composer seeks to create the atmosphere of an enchanted Atlantic completely calm beneath the spell of the Other World. Upon its surface floats a small ship adventuring towards the sunset from the shores of Eirinn, as St. Brendan and the sons of O'Corra are said to have sailed in later times. The little craft is borne on beneath a sky of pearl and amethyst until on the crest of an immense slowly surging wave it is tossed on to the shore of Fand's miraculous island. Here is unhuman revelry unceasing between the ends of time, and the voyagers are caught away, resisting, into the maze of the dance. A pause comes, and Fand sings her song of immortal love enchaining the hearts of her hearers for ever. The dancing and feasting begin again, and, finally, the sea rising suddenly overwhelms the whole island, the immortals riding in rapture on the green and golden waves, and laughing carelessly amidst the foam at the fate of the over-rash mortals lost in the depths. Twilight falls, the sea subsides, and Fand's garden fades out of sight.

In an undated letter to Rosalind Thornycroft, Bax wrote that while writing the principal melody of the middle section he had 'wept in his Dublin room'.[66] In a

[65] Actually his wife, not his daughter.
[66] This room still exists and has a splendid view of the Dublin mountains.

brief interview with Eamonn Andrews broadcast on Irish radio in 1947, Bax cited *The Garden of Fand* as his favourite amongst his works; and it was the last piece of his own music that he heard, at a concert in Dublin four days before his death.

176 DREAM IN EXILE (Intermezzo) for piano

Title: *MS*: '~~Capriccio~~. ~~Intermezzo~~.' (both crossed through). *Printed score*: 'DREAM IN EXILE | INTERMEZZO'.
Date: 'Feb | 1916.'
Dedication: *Printed score only*: 'affectionately dedicated to | Tobias Matthay.'
Manuscript: JWC; [4] ff.; 8 pp.; AL 12 paper (360 × 265). Bax has written his name and Marlow address on the score.
Publication: JWC (2022), 1918, fo., 12 pp. Also published with *A Mountain Mood* (**172**), MMP (M 2224, 'Master Piano Series'), [1994], 4to, 18 pp.
Duration: 8'17.

177 NEREID for piano

Title: *MS A*: 'Ideala.' *MS B*: 'Nereid.' 'When he wrote this piece . . . he had vaguely in mind some sort of water nymph of Greek mythological times.' (Harriet Cohen, *Music's Handmaid*, London, 1936, p. 153; she discusses the work on pp. 153-60.)
Date: *A*: 'March. 24th 1916.' (on f. 8) and 'March 24th 1916.' (on f. 10). *B*: Undated. *Printed score*: '1916'.
Dedication: *A*: None. *B*: '(To Harriet Cohen)'.
Manuscript: *A*: BL (Add. MS 54769); [11] ff.; 22 pp. (partly numbered); AL 12 paper (361 × 266). This MS contains two very similar versions of the work (hereafter α and β, the latter incomplete) plus a single folio (γ) disposed in the following order: **α**: ff. [1-5] ([5^{v}] blank); [9] pp. + 1 blank; **β**: ff. [6-9] ([9^{v}] blank) + 1 blank; pp. 3-7 + 1 unpagin. + 3 blank; β is a copy of α with minor modifications and with the same date appended; the first folio (pp. 1-2) is missing and the music begins at the equivalent of bar 2 on p. [3] of α; **γ**: f. [11] ([11^{v}] blank); 1 p. + 1 blank. This contains eight bars in E♭/C minor that do not appear in the other versions (unless they appeared in the two pages of α which have had leaves pasted over the top and are therefore inaccessible).
B: BL (Loan (75/6)); [2] ff. (1 bifolium); 3 pp. + 1 containing sketches (see below); AL 12 paper (361 × 266). Folio [2^{v}] contains a four-bar sketch on three staves of part of the third verse ('Our echoes roll . . .') from the song 'The splendour falls on castle-walls' (1917); it differs slightly from the final version (see **186**). This is followed by a list of works in Bax's handwriting in which he distinguishes between scores written for or played by Myra Hess and Harriet Cohen ('Tania'):

Myra
2 Violin Sonatas.
Two Capriccios [i.e. *Toccata* (**155**) and *Dream in Exile* (**176**)]
Moy Mell
Symphonic Phantasy [i.e. original version of the First Piano Sonata (**127**)] |

Tania
A Mountain Mood.
Winter Waters.
Ideala [i.e. *Nereid* (177)]
Quintett. [i.e. the Piano Quintet (167)]

MS *A* ('Ideala') is the original version of this work, MS *B* ('Nereid') is the final, published version. The two versions are more or less identical as far as 5:4 of the published score. Thereafter the five bars that conclude the printed version replace 87 bars in *A*, of which bars 21-34 are crossed through in pencil in α, while bars 24-46 are on two separate leaves pasted over an earlier version.
Publication: JWC (2054), 1919, fo., 5 pp. (issued April 1920). Also in Connie Mayfield (ed.), *Arnold Bax: Selected Works for Piano*, TP, 1986, 4to, pp. 23-7.
Performance: *Earliest traced*: Harriet Cohen; Wigmore Hall; 15 June 1920.
Duration: 4'29.
Note: For other works entitled 'Ideala' see **97** and **122**.

178 ELEGIAC TRIO for flute, viola and harp

Date: *MS*: 'April–May 1916.' (t.p.); 'Fine | May 1916.' (at end).
Manuscript: *Holograph*: BL (Loan 75/5 (M185)); [8] ff.; t.p. + 1 blank + 14 pp.; AL 12 paper (361 × 265). Twelve bars are crossed through (eight on p. 7, four on p. 8) and are omitted from the printed score (they would have come between bars 8 and 9 on p. 12). *Copyist's score*: JWC; [14] ff.; 12 pp. + 2 blank + separate parts; 16-staff paper. The cover of the score is a standard grey printed JWC cover of the period with a lyre in the centre, in the middle of which Bax has written: 'ARNOLD BAX | Elegiac Trio | for | Flute, Viola & Harp'.
Publication: JWC (218), 1920, fo., 18 pp.
Performance: Albert Fransella (fl.), H. [Harry] Waldo Warner (va.), Miriam Timothy (hp.); Æolian Hall; 26 March 1917.
Duration: 9'21.
Note: Debussy's sonata for the same group of instruments was completed early in October 1915, six months or so before Bax's trio, though it was not performed until December 1916, and not publicly until March 1917. It seems too coincidental, however, that Bax should have chosen to write for such a combination unaware of the existence at least of Debussy's work.

179 IN MEMORIAM for orchestra

Date: *Short score*: 'Aug 9th 1916.' *Full score*: Undated.
Dedication: *Short score*: 'I gcuimhne ar bPadraig mac Piarais' [in Irish script] ['In memory of Patrick Pearse'].[67] *Full score*: None.

[67] This is almost certainly a dedication, not an alternative title.

Orchestration: 3(1) 2+1 2+1 2+1, 4231, timp., 3 perc. (b.d., s.d., cym.), hp., str.
Manuscript: *Short score*: UCD; [4] ff.; [8] pp.; [AL] 29 paper (362 × 268); in brown folder with a note indicating that the MS was presented by Harriet Cohen in October 1955. There are indications of the orchestration written in ink, although in the full score Bax has sometimes disregarded his original annotations and scored for different instruments. *Full score*: Privately owned; [30] ff. + 6 blank; 59 pp. + 13 blank + free endpapers; pp. 1-34: AL 16a paper; pp. 35-57 + blank: AL 16b paper (trimmed to 365 × 266); bound in red cloth *c.* 1916 with gold lettering (title and composer's name) up the spine. Bax has paginated the score in blue pencil but has accidentally omitted the page numerals on a double spread between the two pages numbered '17' and '18'; his final page should thus be '59' not '57'. Other blue-pencilled markings also appear to be in the composer's hand rather than that of a conductor (cf. the pencilled 'sfz' on p. '25' (properly '27') with the trombones' marking in ink); there are no cue letters or numbers. Unpublished. *Parts*: BBC; Graham Parlett.
Performance: BBC Philharmonic Orchestra, Vernon Handley; BBC Studio 7, Manchester; 16 June 1998 (first play-through); 17 June 1998 (public performance); 18 June (recording session for Chandos Records Ltd.); br. on Radio 3, 1 July 1998.
Arrangement: Orchestrated by Graham Parlett: 3(1) 2+1 2+1 2+1, 4331, timp., 3 perc. (b.d., s.d., m.d., cym., gl., tri.), org. (*ad lib.*), hp., str. Unpublished.[68]
Duration: 14'48.
Note: The execution of Pádraig Pearse after the Easter Rising affected Bax profoundly, although they had met only once (see *FMY*, pp. 105-6). In addition to this work he wrote *In Memoriam (1916)* (**190**), which is thematically unrelated, the song 'A Leader' (**183**), and a poem 'In Memoriam Patrick H. Pearse', which was published in *A Dublin Ballad, and Other Poems* (Dublin, 1918). In *The Musical Quarterly* (April 1923), p. 173, Edwin Evans referred to the orchestral work as having 'so far remained in the composer's portfolio', and it seems never to have been played during Bax's lifetime; perhaps the score's political undertones prevented performance. In 1948 Bax borrowed the main theme for the finale of his music for the film *Oliver Twist* (**374**). For many years it was believed that Bax had left the work in short score; but in November 1993 the full score MS came to light in a music publisher's basement.

180 MOY MELL (The Happy Plain) for two pianos

Title: *MS*: '"Moy Mell." | for two pianos.' (t.p.); '"Moy Mell." | (The Happy Plain).' (p. 1). *Copyist's score B* (but title in Bax's hand): 'Moy Mell (An Irish Tone Poem) | The Happy Plain.' Listed in *MT* as 'Magh Mell', which is also the title of a poem by Bax written on 8 May 1909.
Date: 'August 25th 1916.'

[68] This orchestration was made before the discovery of Bax's own version.

Dedication: *MS*: 'To Miss Irene Sharrer [*sic*] | and Miss Myra Hess.'
Manuscript: *Holograph*: BL (Add. MS 53735); i (front wrapper) + 9 ff. (f. 8 is a four-bar cancel on p. [12]) + 2 unfoliated; t.p. + 1 blank + [14] pp. + 4 blank; AL 12 paper (trimmed to 356 × 266); bound by BL with brown wrappers bound in with a note on the front cover in Howard Ferguson's handwriting indicating that the score was 'given in 1916 to Myra Hess' and bequeathed to himself in 1965. *Copyist's score A*: JWC; [8] ff.; 16 pp.; 12-staff paper; at top of p. 1 the title has been added by Bax himself. *Copyist's score B*: WML; [10] ff.; t.p. + 16 pp. + 3 blank; 20-staff paper (355 × 275), but staves erased between systems (excluding t.p. and blank pp.).
Publication: JWC (2903), 1918, fo., 21 pp.; reprinted 30 November 1927 and 23 September 1938.
Performance: Myra Hess, Irene Scharrer; Æolian Hall; 5 December 1916.
Arrangement: For 2 pianos, 3 hands by Lionel Salter; commissioned by Phyllis Sellick and completed on 17 December 1967. Unpublished but assigned to JWC. *Earliest performance traced*: Cyril Smith, Phyllis Sellick; br. on Radio 3, 31 August 1970.
Duration: 10'05.
Note: In a letter to the *The Gramophone* (February 1928, p. 397), Bax included information on the background to this piece:

Moy Mell (properly Magh Mell) means 'The Pleasant Plain', one of the three ideas connected with the ancient Irish conception of the 'Happy Otherworld' or Pagan paradise. The other two are the enchanted island in the Atlantic (to which St. Brendan and many others are said to have adventured in their corracles) and the faery world of the Hollow Hill. I have treated both of these in two orchestral works, *The Garden of Fand* and *In the Faery Hills*. There is no definite story attached to *Moy Mell* apart from this poetic basis.

181 BALLAD for violin and piano (first version)

Title: *Advertisement for an abortive JWC edition* (first version): 'Ballade'. *Printed score* (second version): 'Ballad'.
Date: *Printed score*: '1916'.
Dedication: *Printed score*: 'To Winifred Small'.
Manuscript: Privately owned. It has not been possible to inspect this MS or to ascertain whether it is of the original or the revised version.
Publication: Advertised by JWC in 1922 (priced at 5/-) but never printed (see **Note** below). For publication details of revised version see **300**.
Performance: Winifred Small (vn.), Harriet Cohen (pf.); Æolian Hall; 28 June 1916. Thus listed in LF, p. 432; but reviews of this concert only mention the *Legend* (**165**), and in the letter of 1948 to May Harrison quoted in the **Note** below Bax states that he had never heard the work played in public.
Duration: 7'49.
Note: In an undated letter to the dedicatee Bax wrote:

I have just been looking at that 'Ballad' I wrote for you in 1916. It was lost for seven years or it would have been published by Chester long ago. (It was down on their list in fact and people used to enquire about it at the shop.) Then it turned up two years ago and I revised it heavily and put it in a drawer and never thought of it again. To-day I believe it is rather good—it's a wild stormy thing.

The fact that he describes the work and then goes on to ask if she would look through the violin part might suggest (unless he was simply refreshing her memory) that Winifred Small was unfamiliar with it and had not played it in 1916, perhaps because the MS had disappeared before a performance could be arranged, in which case the revision would date from *c.* 1923. But it seems unlikely that JWC would have advertised the work in 1922 if the MS was not extant at that time, and a date *c.* 1929 is more probable (see **300**). In an undated letter to May Harrison after a performance of the piece, Bax wrote: 'It sounded a little strange to me as I had practically forgotten the little work. . . . I seem to remember that it was once longer with a distinct middle section, but I have no memory of any details.' In another letter to Miss Harrison, dating from January 1948 and perhaps referring to the same performance as in the previous letter, Bax remarked that he had never before heard the *Ballad* played at a concert. These letters suggest that cuts were made when it was revised and that it had not been played at the 1916 concert noted in **Performance** above.

182 I KNOW MYSELF NO MORE, MY CHILD for voice and piano

Note: The score of this song has not been traced. It is listed in *MT* with the words attributed to AE (George Russell) and is clearly a setting of his poem 'A New Being', which opens with the above line.

183 A LEADER for baritone and piano

Date: *MS*: Undated. *MT*: '1916', and obviously written after the suppression of the Easter Rising early in May of that year.
Dedication: 'In memory of | certain Irish patriots'.
Text: AE (George Russell), 'A Leader'.
Manuscript: UCD (MS 26/3); [2] ff.; [4] pp.; AL 12 paper (360 × 265). Presented to UCD by Harriet Cohen on 11 December 1959. Loosely inserted into the MS is a postcard (MS 26/3a) from Padraic Colum addressed to Bax from Hawaii, postmarked 21 March 1923.[69] Unpublished.
Performance: John Hancorn (bar.), John Thwaites (pf.); Big School, Christ's Hospital, Horsham; 18 May 1996 (second day of 'The Bax Weekend': part of the 'Horsham and District Arts Fanfare Weekend 1996').
Duration: 4'06.
Note: Bax has written '(C·S·P)' above the opening bar, followed by a brace extending over the first five bars, suggesting a melodic quotation. The initials

[69] Colum later published a book called *Legends of Hawaii* . . . (New Haven, 1937).

perhaps stand for Charles Stewart Parnell (1846-91), leader of the Irish Nationalist Party, but the melody has yet to be identified.

184 O MISTRESS MINE for voice and piano

Title: 'O mistress mine where are you roaming?'
Date: *MS*: Undated. *MT*: '1916'.
Text: William Shakespeare, 'O Mistress mine! where are you roaming?' from *Twelfth Night*, II, iii, 42 ff.
Manuscript: BPL; [2] ff.; [3] pp. + 1 blank; AL 12 paper (360 × 265); loosely inserted into a protective bifolium of 18-staff paper (368 × 272) together with **250**. Unpublished.
Duration: 2'00.
Note: This version of the song is in A♭; an arrangement with string quartet accompaniment (**250b**) is in A.

185 PARTING for voice and piano

Date: *Printed score*: '1916'.
Text: AE (George Russell), 'Parting'.
Manuscript: Not traced.
Publication: MM (208), 1921, fo., 7 pp. Also in *Twelve Songs for Medium/High Voice and Piano*, TP, 1984, 4to, pp. 20-5.
Performance: *Earliest traced*: John Coates (ten.), Arnold Bax (pf.); Wigmore Hall; 15 June 1920.
Duration: 4'25.
Note: For details of the melodic connection between this song and the *Symphonic Variations* see CSS, pp. 53-4.

1917

186 THE SPLENDOUR FALLS ON CASTLE-WALLS for voice and piano

Date: 'Nov 1912– | Jan 1917' (at the end, with Bax's signature written immediately above it instead of at the head of the score, the usual place).
Text: Alfred, Lord Tennyson, 'Blow, bugle, blow' from *The Princess*, iv.
Manuscript: BL (Add. MS 54779); ff. 3-5v; [6] pp.; AL 12 paper (365 × 263); bound with 14 other songs (see **133** above). A four-bar sketch on three staves of the second part of verse 3 ('Our echoes roll . . .') appears on f. 2v of the MS of *Nereid* (see **177**); it differs slightly from the final version. Unpublished.
Performance: Jenevora Williams (sop.), John Thwaites (pf.); Big School, Christ's Hospital, Horsham; 18 May 1996 (second day of 'The Bax Weekend': part of the 'Horsham and District Arts Fanfare Weekend 1996').
Duration: 4'44.
Note: For a projected orchestral version see **326**.

187 SCHERZO for orchestra (first version)

Date: 'June 7th | 1917.'
Orchestra: 3(1) 2+1 3+1 2+1, 4331, timp., 5 perc. (b.d., s.d., tamb., cym., gl., cel.), hp., str.
Manuscript: *Short score*: BL (Add. MS 54767); [6] ff.; 12 pp.; AL 18 paper (see **154**). *Full score*: Lewis Foreman; [39] ff. + 1 blank; 78 pp. + 2 blank; [AL] 29 paper (trimmed to 357 × *c.* 258); bound in crimson cloth. Unpublished. *Parts*: CH.
Performance: Queen's Hall Orchestra, Sir Henry Wood; Queen's Hall; 3 September 1919 (Promenade Concert).
Duration: *c.* 8'00.
Note: On a blank leaf bound in at the back of the score, Bax has written: 'For Mary | Dec 5th 1933 | Morar.', indicating that the MS of this original version was given to Mary Gleaves as a present on the occasion of Bax's finishing his 1933 revision (see **322**).

188 FROM DUSK TILL DAWN: Ballet

Title: *Short and full scores*: '"Between twelve and three".' First performed as 'From Dusk till Dawn'. Listed in *Gr5* as 'Between Dusk and Dawn'.
Date: *Short score*: Undated. *Full score*: 'June | 1917.'
Text: Scenario by Mrs Christopher Lowther.[70]
Orchestra: 2(1)122, 4230, timp., 3 perc. (s.d., tamb., cym., w.m.), hp., str.
Manuscript: *Short score*: RAM (MS 533); [11] ff.; [22] pp.; AL 12 paper (360 × 265); loosely inserted in front of the f.sc. *Full score*: RAM (MS 533); [60] ff.; 116 pp. + 4 blank; AL 14b paper (361 × 266); bound in cardboard covered in marbled black paper with light brown linen backstrip: now completely detached from binding, with sh.sc. loosely inserted in front, the whole in a manila-covered solander box. Unpublished. *Parts*: RAM (given by Viscount Ullswater).
Performance: (1) *Complete ballet*: Mrs Christopher Lowther (The Dancer), Donald Calthrop (The Chelsea Figure and producer), Ernest Thesiger (The Clown), Mrs F. Mackay (The Wind), Geraldine Worcester (Cupid), [Orchestra], Herman Finck;[71] Palace Theatre, London; 7 December 1917 (Princess Christian's Matinée). Revived in July 1918. (2) *Concert performance ('Prelude and Dances' only)*:[72] London Symphony Orchestra, Adrian Boult; Queen's Hall; 4 March 1918. Bax wrote to Boult: 'It went excellently, except for the fact that the side drum was apparently seized with a maenad fury, so much so that he was unable to contain himself and poured out his dithyrambic soul in places where his entry was merely on the horizon.' (3) *Semi-professional concert performance (complete work)*:[73]Southern Philharmonia,

[70] For whom Elgar composed his ballet *The Sanguine Fan*.
[71] Not Norman O'Neill, as sometimes stated; Finck was the Palace Theatre's resident conductor.
[72] Namely 'Prelude—Summer Night at the Window'; 'Dance of the Wind in the Garden'; 'Midnight strikes'; 'The Awakening'; 'The Russian Dancer and the Clown'.
[73] The important harp part was omitted, the player having failed to appear at the concert.

Aaron Tighe; St Mary's Parish Church, Petworth, Sussex; 25 September 1982 (penultimate day of the Petworth Festival of English Music and Art). (4) *Professional*: London Philharmonic Orchestra, Bryden Thomson; St Jude's Church, Golders Green; 6 March 1990 (recording session for Chandos Records Ltd.).
Duration: 22'20.
Note: 'I am doing some extremely interesting work scoring a little ballet I have been asked to write . . .'. (From a letter to Arthur Alexander.) The score was commissioned by Mrs Christopher Lowther for a charity matinée that also included a 'comedietta', a series of tableaux, and a light-music selection. A review of the performance appeared in *The Stage* (13 December 1917), p. 20, in which the critic thought that Bax had written 'some very clever music on the ultra-modern side'. The concert performance of excerpts conducted by Boult was reviewed in *The Musical Times* (April 1918): 'Although presenting ample variety of colour and movement, it cannot be said that it was especially attractive on the concert platform.' In a letter to Boult after the performance, Bax asked what had happened to the parts (see Jerrold Northrop Moore (ed.), *Music and Friends: Letters to Adrian Boult*, London, 1979, p. 30); it was not until the late 1970s that they were discovered by Viscount Ullswater among the papers of his mother, the former Mrs Lowther, who had married Lord George Cholmondeley in 1921.
Synopsis: The ballet is in one continuous act and concerns the nocturnal activities of Dresden china figures. The short score, which Bax obviously devised with Mrs Lowther's scenario in front of him, is the most detailed source for the plot since he has written in stage directions (e.g. 'The curtains flap', 'Business with handkerchief etc.') that do not appear in the full score. In the following synopsis the titles derive from the short score, with full score variants added in brackets:

Slow: Prelude. Summer night. [Summer-night at the window.] . . . 'Curtain rises'. Più mosso: Wind's dance in garden. [The Wind dances in the garden.] . . . The moonlight gradually enters the room. . . . The curtains flap. . . . The wind dies away. . .
Clock strikes twelve: The figures on table stir. The flowers gradually awake one by one. . . . The flowers shake out their petals. . . . Flowers dance. . . .The dancer and clown embrace. . . . They dance together. . . .The wind as before. The clock strikes one. The flowers dance again. . . . The Dresden figure passes below where the clown and dancer are sitting. Business with handkerchief etc. Flirtation dance. Faster. The Dresden figure becomes more and more excited. The D.F. kisses her violently. She boxes the figure's ears. The clock strikes two. She falls weeping into the clown's arms. He thrusts her aside and scolds at her fiercely. They quarrel whilst the D.F. eggs on the clown. The wind enters violently and boisterously. The Dresden figure falls over with a crash. She goes up to the clown humbly drawing his attention to the sad fate of his rival. He makes an angry movement. She tiptoes to the Dresden figure . . . finds him too broken to speak. She turns back to the clown trying to cajole him out of his ill humour. The clown rejects her advances peevishly and sulkily. Dawn. The clock steps forward. They return to their stands as the clock strikes three. Everything is still. A sad silence reigns. The wind thrusts his head through the window. . . tip-toes mischievously . . . behind the dancer . . . with a great puff he blows the dancer into the clown's arms. The wind dances wildly. He points mischievously at the couple. Curtain falls quickly.

A full list of alternative titles is printed in the booklet that accompanies the Chandos recording (CHAN 8863).

189 GO, LOVELY ROSE for voice and piano

Note: The score of this song, with words by Edmund Waller, is listed in *MT* but has not been traced.

190 IN MEMORIAM (1916) for cor anglais, harp and string quartet

Title: The year in parentheses is part of the title. First performed and listed in *MT* as 'Irish Elegy'.
Date: *Gr5*: '1917'.
Manuscript: Not traced.
Publication: MM (647), 1935, 4to, 16 pp.; WC0421.
Performance: (1) *Private*: Eugène Dubrucq (c.a.), Gwendolen Mason (hp.), Philharmonic String Quartet: Arthur Beckwith (vn.), Frederic Holding (vn.), Raymond Jeremy (va.), Cedric Sharpe (vc.); 32 Holland Park, London (the home of George Davison); 10 March 1918 (Plough Club Concert). 'We rehearsed the sextet on Monday. I think it will be all right, though that is the only rehearsal we shall get.' (From a letter dated 6 March 1918 from Bax to his brother.) (2) *Public*: Same performers; Wigmore Hall; 13 February 1919.
Duration: 8'11.
Note: For another work connected with Pádraig Pearse and the Easter Rising see **179** (cf. **183**).

191 NOVEMBER WOODS for orchestra

Date: Short score undated. In a written answer to an enquiry from Christopher Whelen, Bax gave the date as '1914', which, following his usual practice, was probably the year of composition.[74] A resemblance between the opening bars and those of the epilogue to Vaughan Williams's *London Symphony* suggests that it may have been started after 27 March 1914, the date of the symphony's first performance, which Bax attended (the concert also included his own *Three Songs*, **156**). All the published lists of his music give '1917', presumably the year of orchestration, though this does not appear on the printed score. Bax also stated that the work was written 'altogether in London'.
Orchestra: 3(1) 2+1 3+1 2+1, 4331, timp., 2 perc. (b.d., cym., gl., cel.), 2 hps., str.
Manuscript: *Short score*: BL (Add. MS 54743); [11] ff.; [20] pp. + 2 blank; pp. 1-6, 11-22: AL 14b paper (362 × 266); pp. 9-10: AL 12 paper (362 × 266). Mostly on two-staff systems, but a few three-staff; p. 6 is crossed through in pencil, and there

[74] Lewis Foreman believes that this year must be wrong since it would pre-date the 'certain rather troublous experiences' that Bax mentions in his letter to Newman (see **Note**).

are pencilled notes for the orchestration; there is an eighteen-bar cut in blue pencil from 8:14 to 9:5; p. 1 of this MS is reproduced in CSS, p. [94]. *Full score*: Not traced.
Publication: MM (4), 1921, fo. and 8vo, 94 pp.; WC0038C (f.sc.).
Performance: (1) Hallé Orchestra, Hamilton Harty; Free Trade Hall, Manchester; 18 November 1920. (2) Orchestra of the Royal Philharmonic Society, Hamilton Harty; Queen's Hall; 16 December 1920.
Duration: 18'25.
Note: The inspiration for this tone-poem came to Bax on a stormy November day in a beech wood in Buckinghamshire, probably the one near Amersham Station through which he would have passed on his way home to Beaconsfield. (Stephen Lloyd has suggested a structural and thematic parallel between *November Woods* and Bax's poem 'Amersham'.) In a letter to Ernest Newman, who was drafting the programme note for the first performance, Bax wrote:

> I don't want it to be considered too seriously in the light of objective programme music. It may be taken as an impression of the dank and stormy music of nature in the late autumn, but the whole piece and its origins are connected with certain rather troublous experiences I was going through myself at the time and the mood of the Buckinghamshire wood where the idea of this work came seemed to sound a familiar chord as it were. If there are sounds in the music which recall the screaming of the wind and cracking of strained branches, I hope they may suggest deeper things at the same time. The middle part may be taken as a dream of happier days, such as sometimes come in the intervals of stress either physical or mental.

In February 1951, referring to a recent performance by Boult, Bax wrote to Christopher Whelen: 'I thought that Adrian's performance of "November Woods" was very much better than any the work has received in the past. He was much amused when I remarked to him at rehearsal—"this is probably the worst storm that has ever visited Buckinghamshire".'

1918

192 I HAVE HOUSE AND LAND IN KENT: Arrangement for voice and piano

Date: Probably February 1918.
Text: Thomas Ravenscroft, 'A wooing Song of a Yeoman of Kents Sonne' from *Melismata. Musicall Phansies. Fitting the Court, Citie, and Countrey Humours. To 3, 4, and 5. Voyces* (London, 1611).
Manuscript: The MS of this song and the others by Bax included in the Répertoire Collignon series were seen at JWC's premises in the early 1980s by Lewis Foreman but have subsequently been mislaid. I am grateful to him for the information that most of the arrangements dated from February 1918.
Performance: *Earliest traced*: Raymonde Collignon (sop.), Harriet Cohen (pf.); Æolian Hall; 6 June 1919.
Publication: JWC (3846), 1920, fo., 7 pp. (Répertoire Collignon No. 12) (issued 9 October 1920).

Duration: 2'36.
Note: JWC's 'Répertoire Collignon' series comprises ten folksong arrangements by Bax (Nos. 3, 10, 11 and 12), Goossens (Nos. 2 and 6) and Howells (Nos. 4, 5, 7 and 8);[75]one folksong arrangement by Bax, Bridge, Goossens and Ireland in collaboration (No. 1); and an arrangement by Bax of Thomas Campion's 'Jack and Jone' (No. 9). They were all made especially for the French light soprano Raymonde Collignon. New cover designs for the series by Paul Nash were issued in 1928 (see *The Chesterian*, IX, 68, January–February 1928, p. 134).

193 JACK AND JONE by Thomas Campion: Arrangement for voice and piano

Date: Probably February 1918.
Text: Thomas Campion, 'Jacke and Jone they thinke no ill', from *Two Bookes of Ayres, the First contayning Divine and Morall Songs*, I (London, 1613?).
Manuscript: JWC (see **192**).
Publication: JWC (3843), 1920, fo., 3 pp. (Répertoire Collignon No. 9).
Performance: Raymonde Collignon (sop.), Edwin Evans (pf.); Æolian Hall; 27 April 1918. 'Collignon gave one of her unique recitals of "acted" songs . . . [and] Evans interspersed interesting explanatory remarks.' (*The Musical Times,* 1 June 1918, p. 267).
Duration: 2'39.

194 THE MAID AND THE MILLER: Arrangement for voice and piano

Date: Probably February 1918.
Text: Traditional English.
Manuscript: JWC (see **192**).
Publication: JWC (3844), 1920, fo., 3 pp. (Répertoire Collignon No. 10) (issued June 1919).
Performance: *Earliest traced*: Raymonde Collignon (sop.), Andrée Conti (pf.); The Coliseum; 16 December 1918.
Duration: 0'45.

195 O DEAR! WHAT CAN THE MATTER BE?: Arrangement for voice and piano

Date: Probably February 1918.
Text: Traditional English.
Manuscript: JWC (see **192**).
Publication: JWC (3845), 1920, fo., 5 pp. (Répertoire Collignon No. 11) (issued 9 October 1920).

[75] Howells later set 'I have house and land in Kent' as part of *A Kent Yeoman's Wooing Song*.

Performance: Raymonde Collignon (sop.), Edwin Evans (pf.); Æolian Hall; 27 April 1918. See review under **193**.
Arrangement: (i) For violin, cello and piano by Gilbert Stacey. This unpublished 'light music' version of Bax's arrangement is listed in the *BBC Music Library: Orchestral Catalogue I* (BBC, 1982), though it is believed to have been for piano trio. The work was apparently transposed from E♭ to B♭. The score and parts (LM G 4436) have not been traced and were probably jettisoned by the BBC. (ii) For voice and wind band by Leonard B. Smith (available from the Bovaco Catalog, The Detroit Concert Band, Inc.). *Earliest performance traced*: Barbara Ziegler (sop.), The Community Band of Brevard, Marion A. Scott; BCC Fine Arts Auditorium, Cocoa, Florida, USA; 16 May 1997 ('Music of the British Isles').
Duration: 1'19.

196 TROIS ENFANTINES: Arrangements for voice and piano

a. 'Jean, p'tit Jean, prends ta serpette' ('Reaper John, come take thy sickle!').
b. 'Berceuse' ('Petit enfant, déjà la brume') ('Babe of my heart, the dew is falling').
c. 'Une petite fille' ('While her parents were a-praying').

Date: Probably February 1918.
Text: Traditional French with English translations by Edward Agate. He was paid five guineas for these and other translations for the Répertoire Collignon series.
Manuscript: JWC (see **192**).
Publication: JWC (3837), 1920, fo., 13 pp. (Répertoire Collignon No. 3). **196b** also published separately as 'Musical Supplement No. 5' to *The Chesterian* (June 1923), inserted between pp. 244 and 245.
Performance: Raymonde Collignon (sop.), Edwin Evans (pf.); Æolian Hall; 27 April 1918. See review under **193**.
Duration: **a.** 2'00. **b.** 3'15. **c.** 0'45.
Note: According to LF, p. 154, the order in which the songs were published differed from that on the MS.

197 VARIATIONS SUR 'CADET-ROUSSELLE': Arrangement for voice and piano in collaboration with Frank Bridge, Eugene Goossens and John Ireland

Title: *Printed score*: 'Variations sur Cadet Roussel [*sic*]' (t.p.); 'Variations sur Cadet-Rousselle' (p. 1). 'Harmonisées par Arnold Bax, Frank Bridge, Eugène Goossens, John Ireland.'
Date: Probably February 1918.
Dedication: 'To our good friend, Edwin Evans, who suggested this collaboration'.
Text: Traditional French.
Manuscript: *Holograph*: Not traced. *Copy in Eugene Goossens's hand*: JWC (see **192**).

Publication: JWC (3835), 1920, fo., 11 pp. (Répertoire Collignon No. 1) (issued 9 October 1920).
Performance: Raymonde Collignon (sop.), Harriet Cohen (pf.); Æolian Hall; 6 June 1919.[76]
Duration: *c.* 3'45 (complete); 2'30 (omitting variations 8-11).
Arrangement: (i) For orchestra without voice, omitting four variations, Op. 40, by Eugene Goossens ('Dec. 1930 | Cincinnati'): 2121,[77] 2100, timp., 1 perc. (s.d., tamb., tri., gl., xyl., cym., bells), hp., str. *Publication*: JWC, [1931], 28 pp. This arrangement, with the title 'VARIATIONS | ON | "CADET ROUSSELLE" | (FRENCH FOLK-SONG)', was made 'to while away the tedium of an American railway journey' (quoted in *The Musical Times*, April 1932, p. 360). *Performance*: (1) Bournemouth Municipal Orchestra, Sir Dan Godfrey; The Pavilion, Bournemouth; 4 November 1931. (2) Subsequently played as an orchestral interlude during ballets of the Camargo Society: [Orchestra], Constant Lambert; Savoy Theatre; 28 February 1932. (ii) For solo male voice, men's chorus and small orchestra by Max Saunders: w.w. (1121), pf., hp., str. On hire from JWC.
Note: The initials of each composer are printed in the score above the staff at the point where each began his part of the arrangement. There is an optional cut from bar 123 to bar 199. If the cut is not made, bars 199-201 are omitted.

198 FOLK-TALE (Conte Populaire) for cello and piano

Title: *MS*: 'Folk-Tale for Cello and Piano'. The subtitle 'Conte Populaire', found on the printed score, is written on the MS but not in Bax's hand. *Holograph part*: 'Folk Tale | for | Cello and Piano. | Arnold Bax' ('Conte Populaire' again added in another hand).
Date: 'April 3rd 1918' (on both score and part).
Dedication: '(to Felix Salmond)' (on score only; written with a different pen and obviously added later).
Manuscript: BL (Loan 75/7 (M 187)); *score*: [6] ff.; [9] pp. + 3 blank; AL 12 paper (359 × 265); *part*: [4] ff.; t.p. + 5 pp. + 1 blank; AL 12 paper (359 × 265); loose in fawn paper wrappers. The imminence of the première so soon after the work's completion probably led Bax, unusually, to write out the separate cello part himself.
Publication: JWC (916), 1920, fo., 11 pp. (issued September 1920).
Performance: Felix Salmond (vc.), Arnold Bax[78] (pf.); Wigmore Hall; 27 April 1918.
Duration: 9'07.
Note: On 3 January 1938, in answer to a query from Beatrice Harrison, Bax wrote: 'No, the folk-tale is not orchestrated. I don't think it is very suitable, though of course *anything can* be scored.'

[76] Possibly performed earlier, on 27 April 1918 (with **197**).
[77] One oboe, not two as listed on the reverse of the title page.
[78] Not, as sometimes asserted, Geoffrey O'Connor-Morris, who accompanied songs at the same concert; reviews make it clear that the composer played the piano part in his own work.

199 STRING QUARTET NO. 1 IN G MAJOR

I. Allegretto semplice. II. Lento e molto espressivo. III. Rondo (Allegro vivace).

Title: *Printed score*: 'String Quartet | in G major' ('No. 1' not added on later impressions even after the completion of Bax's other two published quartets).
Date: *Gr5*: '1918'. Before 7 June, the date of the first performance.
Dedication: *Printed score*: 'To Sir Edward Elgar, O.M.'
Manuscript: Not traced.
Publication: MM (150), 1921, 8vo, 45 pp.; *parts*: fo.; CH (47077), [1945], 4to.; *parts*: WC00133; *extra part*: WC00133E).
Performance: Philharmonic Quartet: Arthur Beckwith (vn.), Frederic Holding (vn.), Raymond Jeremy (va.), Cedric Sharpe (vc.); Æolian Hall; 7 June 1918.
Duration: 24'42.
Note: In *FMY*, p. 32, Bax commented that after sending the dedicatee the score of his quartet, Elgar wrote that he 'liked the look of it' but never came to hear it. The letter that Bax sent to Elgar offering him the dedication is quoted in Percy Young, *Elgar O. M.: A Study of a Musician* (London, 1955), p. 214. The Irish folk tune 'The Fanaid Grove' or 'Ban Cnuic Éireann Óg' appears to be alluded to in the finale.

200 DANCE PRELUDE and LAMENT OF THE SWAN-PRINCESS: Arrangement for orchestra of piano pieces by Anatol Liadov

Date: Orchestrated between the Paris (1917) and London (December 1918) productions of the ballet *Children's Tales* (see **Note** below).
Performance: [Orchestra], Henry Defosse; London Coliseum; 23 December 1918.
Note: The scores of these two orchestrations have not been traced. They were commissioned for the 1918 season of Diaghilev's Ballets Russes and formed part of the 'people's play' *Children's Tales* by Leonid Massine. This ballet had first been produced under the title *Kikimora* in San Sebastian in 1916; it was later enlarged and produced in Rome under the revised title *Contes Russes*, in which form it was given in Paris in 1917. For the London season of 1918 it was revised again and, at the suggestion of Edwin Evans, enlarged by the addition of Bax's two orchestrations. The first, a prelude to the ballet, used Liadov's *Prelude*, Op. 11 No. 1; the second, an interlude between a 'Peasant Dance' and the tale of Bova Korolevich, used his *Sur la prairie*, Op. 23. (See Edwin Evans, 'Ballets based on Existing Compositions', *Columbia Record Guide*, 3, 11, November 1943, p. 10.) The ballet was revived in May 1919 at the Alhambra Theatre, with Ernest Ansermet conducting, and was repeated at the Empire Theatre in October under Adrian Boult, at the Coliseum Theatre in December, and under Ansermet at the Royal Opera House, Covent Garden, in July 1920. Referring, presumably, to the *Dance Prelude* as orchestrated by Bax, C. W. Beaumont writes: 'The ballet commences with an overture whose simple folk tunes, set to the accompaniment of drums and tambourines, radiate the spirit of peasant holiday.' (*Impressions of the Russian Ballet 1919: Children's Tales*, London, n.d., p. 6; this book describes the plot of the ballet.)

201 FAR IN A WESTERN BROOKLAND for medium voice and piano

Date: *MT*: '1918'.
Dedication: *Printed score*: '(To Frederic Austin.)'
Text: A. E. Housman, *A Shropshire Lad*, LII.
Manuscript: Not traced.
Publication: No. 1 (5346) of *Three Songs for Medium Voice and Pianoforte* [with **126** and **207**], EN, 1920, 4to, pp. 2-7; EA (later assigned to CH). Also in *Twelve Songs for Medium/High Voice and Piano*, TP, 1984, 4to, pp. 7-11.
Duration: 4'12.

202 THE FROG-SKIN: Ballet

Note: The score of this work has not been traced. It is listed in *MT* and elsewhere, with the date given as 1918, but nothing else is known about it. It appears not to have been performed and, like *Tamara* (**138**), it may never even have been orchestrated. The date of composition suggests the possibility that, like *From Dusk till Dawn* (**188**), it may have been commissioned for one of the charity matinées that were common at the time but was then abandoned owing to the ending of the war; writing in *The Musical Times* (June 1919), p. 154, Edwin Evans implied that it had not then been performed. Nothing is known about the plot of the ballet, but there is a Georgian folktale called 'The Frog's Skin', about a man 'married' to a beautiful maiden disguised as a frog, on which it might conceivably have been based (see Marjory Wardrop (trans.), *Georgian Folk Tales*, London, 1894, pp. 15-21). A similar folktale, common throughout Europe and Asia, in which a frog turns into a handsome prince when kissed by a beautiful princess, has a variant in which the metamorphosis is accomplished by burning the frog's skin.

203 GREEN GROW THE RASHES O! (Character Sketch) for voice and piano

Date: *MT*: '1918'.
Dedication: *Printed score*: 'To John Coates.'
Text: Robert Burns, 'Green grow the Rashes'. These lyrics were written to an old Scottish tune that Bax would have known from its use in the finale of Alexander Mackenzie's *Scottish Concerto* of 1897; but he has set them to a tune of his own.
Manuscript: Not traced.
Publication: MM (1), 1920, fo., 7 pp. (two issues: E minor and G minor).
Duration: 2'57.

204 MIDSUMMER for voice and piano

Note: The score of this song has not been traced. It is listed in *MT* with the words attributed to Clifford Bax, but there is no published poem by him with this title. There may be some connection with his *Midsummer Madness*, a 'play for music' published in 1923, which was later performed with a score by Armstrong Gibbs.

205 ON A MAY EVENING for piano

Date: *MT*: '1918'.
Dedication: *Printed score*: 'To C Albanesi Esq.'
Manuscript: Not traced.
Publication: AHC (10118), 1919, 4to, 13 pp. (No. 8 in G. H. Clutsam and T. F. Dunhill (eds.), *The Repertoire Series of Pianoforte Music by Modern British Composers*).
Duration: 6'37.

206 A ROMANCE for piano

Title: Erroneously listed in *MT* as 'Love Song'.
Date: *MS*: None. *Gr5*: '1918'.
Dedication: *MS*: None. *Printed score*: 'To Miss Harriet Cohen.'
Manuscript: BL (Add. MS 50178); f. i (front wrapper) + 3 ff. + 1 unfoliated; [5] pp. + 3 blank; bound by BL with wrappers bearing Harriet Cohen's handwriting bound in; AL 12 paper (trimmed to 357 × 265).
Publication: AHC (10119), 1919, 4to, 7 pp. (No. 10 in G. H. Clutsam and T. F. Dunhill (eds.), *The Repertoire Series of Pianoforte Music by Modern British Composers*). Also in an *Album of Piano Music by Distinguished Modern Composers*, AHC, 1919, 4to, pp. 27-32 (with pieces by Thomas Dunhill, Norman O'Neill, Balfour Gardiner and Julius Harrison).
Duration: 5'42.
Note: Much of this work was incorporated into the slow movement of the Fourth Symphony (307).

207 WHEN I WAS ONE-AND-TWENTY for voice and piano

Date: *Gr5*: '1918'.
Dedication: *Printed score*: '(To Harriet Cohen.)'
Text: A. E. Housman, *A Shropshire Lad*, XIII.
Manuscript: Not traced.
Publication: No. 3 (5348) of *Three Songs for Medium Voice and Pianoforte* [with **126** and **201**], EN, 1920, 4to, pp. 13-17; EA (later assigned to CH). Also in *Twelve Songs for Medium/High Voice and Piano*, TP, 1984, 4to, pp. 12-15.
Duration: 3'00.

208 YOUTH for voice and piano

Date: *Printed score*: '1918'.
Text: Clifford Bax, 'Youth' from *Poems Dramatic & Lyrical*, The Orpheus Series IX (London: The Orpheus Press, autumn 1911), p. 62.
Manuscript: Not traced.
Publication: MM (207), 1920, fo., 7 pp.; CH (38734), [1948]. Also in *Five Songs:*

Arnold Bax (Heritage of English Song 4), TP, [1985], 4to, pp. 25-8. Also in *Arnold Bax: Six Songs*, TP (THA 978047), 1994, 4to, pp. 23-6.
Duration: 3'52.

209 FESTIVAL OVERTURE for orchestra (second version of **134**)

Date: '1909-1911 | Revision | Nov 1918.'
Dedication: None (original version dedicated to Balfour Gardiner).
Orchestra: 3(1) 2+1 3+1 2+1, 4331, timp., 5 perc. (b.d., s.d., tamb., cym., tri., gl.), hp., str.
Manuscript: CH (MS 235); [40] ff.; 79 pp. (numbered in pencil) + 1 blank; AL 18 paper (359 × 259); loose in brown card folder with purple cloth backstrip. Unpublished. *Parts*: CH.
Performance: Orchestra of the Royal Philharmonic Society, Dr Adrian Boult; Queen's Hall; 27 February 1919.
Duration: 15'34.
Note: Although the differences between this revision and the original version of 1911 are too numerous to list in detail, they are all very minor and mostly to do with the orchestration: 'Since the first production [of the overture] the scoring has been somewhat modified.' (From Alfred Kalisch's programme note.) There are also a few rhythmic modifications, from which one can tell that the two-piano arrangement that may or may not be by Bax himself (see **134**) is of the original and not this revised version.

210 SYMPHONIC VARIATIONS for piano and orchestra

Date: *Short score*: 'End. | Feb 8th 1917.' *Full score*: Undated ('Fine.' only); but at the foot of p. 170 Bax has pencilled in the note: 'Maroon announces | signing of Armistice | 11. A.M Nov 11th 1918', with a line connecting it to the E♭ semiquaver in the left hand piano part of bar 6, which he was writing as the maroon sounded.
Dedication: *Short score*: 'To Miss Harriet Cohen'. *Full score*: None in Bax's hand; 'For Harriet Cohen' in her own hand, and likewise in the copyist's f.sc. in the BL.
Orchestra: 3(1) 2+1 20 2+1, 4231, timp., 3 perc. (b.d., tamb., cym.), str.
Manuscript: *Sketch*: Privately owned; [1] f.; [1] p.; AL 18 paper (359 × 259). F.sc. pencil sketch for bars 45:17-25 in Var. V (published 2-pf.sc.). *Short score*: BL (Add. MS 54740); [40] ff.; [78] pp. + 2 blank; AL 12 paper (359 × 265); loosely inserted into fawn card wrappers. Bar 2 has an alteration in pencil agreeing with the f.sc. There is a cut marked in Var. V (part of the piano cadenza + 13 bars for orchestra alone). Starting on p. [68] there is a cut of 58 bars + 1 line (8 bars?) over which has been pasted the revised version. *Full score pencil sketch for bars 3-4 and 7-9 of Var. II*: BL (Add. MS 54731); f. 1 (verso blank); 1 p.; BH 43 paper (356 × 264). *Full score*: CH (MS 234); [104] ff.; 205 pp. (numbered in pencil) lacking pp. 20-8 (see below) + 2 blank between Parts I and II; AL 18 paper (359 × 259); bound in crimson cloth with title and composer's name up spine.

There is considerable fire damage towards the end of the bound score caused by two incendiary bombs that struck the dedicatee's house in 1940; the last few pages have been inserted into plastic pockets to prevent the charred paper from crumbling away. *Pages [20-8] of full score*: BL (Add. MS 54740); [5] ff.; 9 pp. (pagin. 20-8 in pencil); AL 18 paper (359 × 259); loosely inserted into fawn card wrappers.

Copyist's full score A: BL (Add. MS 54741); [84] ff.; tp + blank + 165 pp. + 3 blank; 22-staff paper (trimmed to 345 × 263); bound (probably in the late 1920s) in dark blue cloth with gold lettering up the spine. This MS is of the cut version. It is in the same hand as the copyist's score of *To the Name above Every Name* (**264**) and contains additions in Bax's hand; there are burn marks at the edges. A slip of paper loosely inserted has a pencilled note to the composer giving him the timing of a performance on 1 September 1938 (38 minutes exactly). *Copyist's full score B*: CH; [102] ff.; 204 pp.; AL 16 paper (317 × 233). This copy probably dates from the 1960s.

Publication: *Two-piano score*: CH (46377), 1963, fo., 69 pp. *Full score (photocopy of copyist's score B)*: WC0136.

Performance: Harriet Cohen (pf.), Queen's Hall Orchestra, Sir Henry Wood; Queen's Hall; 23 November 1920. 'There was a mighty success at the concert: I think we had about twelve recalls. All the composers, young and old, were there.' (From a letter to Colin Scott-Sutherland from Harriet Cohen.) Arnold Bennett reports in his diary that at a Promenade Concert on 18 October 1922 Miss Cohen 'gave an astonishing performance [of this work] and was recalled seven times. Such an ovation I have never before seen at a Prom.'

Adaptation: Part of the score was used for the ballet *Oscar* (see **110** for details).

Duration: 49'34 (without cuts); 38'00 (with cuts).

Note: Rosa Newmarch's programme note for the first performance is clearly based on information provided by the composer:

> The work might not inaptly be compared to some great epic poem dealing with the adventures of a hero round whose dominating figure all the minor incidents are centred. . . . the hero of the poem passing through a number of different experiences, a clue to which is given in the titles affixed to each variation. The composer wishes to disclose no more than a general outline of the various psychological aspects under which his theme appears. . . .

After the première, Bax was persuaded by Henry Wood to make certain cuts. The original version was constructed as follows:

1. Theme. 2. Variation I (Youth). 3. Variation II (Nocturne). 4. Variation III (Strife). 5. Variation IV (The Temple). 6. Variation V (Play. Scherzo). 7. Intermezzo. 8. Variation VI (Triumph).

In the revised version Var. I was discarded; hence the fact that the autograph score of these nine pages is separately located from the rest of the work.[79] In addition, 15 bars were removed from Var. III, 41 from Var. IV, 153 from Var. V, and a four-bar optional cut was introduced into Var. VI. In this truncated form the work was played, exclusively by Miss Cohen, between 1923 and 1938.

In a haphazardly typed letter to Colin Scott-Sutherland, Kaikhosru Sorabji wrote of Bax:

H He was consut bwkt unfortuhate in the ghastly nonentitities whp so inadeqiateuly nd miswrably peformed his works,notbatly the Iiano pconcerto which fell into the hands ofincompetent females if the type of the lamentable HHaroet Cohen who ruoned Bax's spllspendidi Syphonic Variatios . . . by far the best work for piano and orchext a by any Englosh compose.r.

c. 1918

211 [UNTITLED]: Sketch (in full score)

Date: Estimated from the handwriting, which is very similar to that on a sketch for the Symphonic Variations (**210**).
Instrumentation: fl., ob., c.a., cl., bn., hns., tpt., vns. 1 and 2, vas., vcs.
Manuscript: Privately owned (formerly by Colin Scott-Sutherland); [1] f. (verso blank) + 1 blank f.; [1] p. + 3 blank; pencil; AL 18 paper (359 × 259). Six bars of full score on twelve staves occupying two thirds of the page (horizontally), the remainder cut away.
Note: The music does not appear in any extant work.

212 SCHERZO: Arrangement for pianola

Date: 'In the years 1917-1918 Edwin Evans, on behalf of the Aeolian Company, approached well-known composers of the day, including Stravinsky, Bax, Eugene Goossens, Percy Grainger and York Bowen, for a series of pianola roles.' (Monica Watson, *York Bowen: A Centenary Tribute*, London: Thames Publishing, 1984, p. 23.)
Manuscript: Not traced. Unpublished in printed form; issued on pianola by the Æolian Co., 1920 (see Appendix 3 for details)
Note: This is a truncated arrangement of the Scherzo of 1913 (**154**).

[79] This variation having been cut, an extra chord for orchestra was inserted at the start of the original second variation. In the reconstruction of the full version this isolated chord was inadvertently left in and played in the first recording of the work, made in 1970 by Joyce Hatto; this error is corrected in the recording by Margaret Fingerhut.

1919

213 TINTAGEL for orchestra

Title: The title on the short score has been pencilled in by Bax, suggesting perhaps that it was added after the work had been composed.
Date: *Short score*: 'Oct 1917.' *Full score*: 'Fine. | Jan. | 1919.' In response to an enquiry from Christopher Whelen, Bax wrote that the work was written 'altogether in London'.
Dedication: *MS full score*: 'For Darling Tania | with love | from | Arnold' (in pencil on free front endpaper). *Printed score*: 'To Miss Harriet Cohen.'
Orchestra: 3(1) 2+1 2+1 2+1, 433 + euph., timp., 3 perc. (b.d., cym., gl.), hp., str.
Manuscript: *Short score*: RAM (MS 19); [7] ff.; [12] pp. + 1 p. with sketches + 1 blank; AL 14b paper (362 × 266); in acid-free pocket. The unsigned score has pencilled indications of the intended instrumentation, and on f. [7] there are pencil sketches for part of the Harp Quintet (**214**). *Full score*: RAM (MS 18); [35] ff.; 68 pp. + 2 blank; bound in crimson cloth with title and composer's name in gold lettering up the spine; AL 18 paper (355 × *c.* 260);[80] pp. [53] and [54] are the obverse and reverse respectively of two folios pasted together. The back of p. [53] contains just a single line down the left margin, the back of p. [54] a double line with the clefs for the instruments in the left margin but, as far as one can see through the paper, no notes. On the fly-leaf Bax has written his name followed by 'c/o Messrs Goodwin & Tabb' and the firm's address. There are conductors' blue pencillings and engravers' marks.
Publication: MM (329), 1923, fo. and 8vo, 55 pp.; CH (37098), 1943, 8vo (min.sc.); [1948], fo.; (38808), [1973], 8vo (st.sc.); WC0265C (f.sc.).
Performance: Bournemouth Municipal Orchestra, Dan Godfrey; Winter Gardens, Bournemouth; 20 October 1921.
Duration: 14'58.
Note: This tone-poem was inspired by a six-week holiday spent with Harriet Cohen in Cornwall during August and September 1917.[81] The passionate dedication on the autograph full score indicates Bax's mood at the time, and it is significant that he quotes the 'Sick Tristan' motive from Wagner's *Tristan und Isolde*. The printed score contains the following preface:

Though detailing no definite programme this work is intended to evoke a tone-picture of the castle-crowned cliff of Tintagel, and more particularly the wide

[80] The MS was detached from its binding when I first inspected it; by 1996 it had been tightly rebound.
[81] In September 1917 Bax also wrote a poem called 'Tintagel Castle', first published anonymously in *Love Poems of a Musician* (London, 1923).

distances of the Atlantic as seen from the cliffs of Cornwall on a sunny but not windless summer day. In the middle section of the piece it may be imagined that with the increasing tumult of the sea arise memories of the historical and legendary association of the place, especially those connected with King Arthur, King Mark, and Tristram and Iseult. Regarding the last named, it will be noticed that at the climax of the more literary division of the work there is a brief reference to one of the subjects in the first act of 'Tristan und Isolde'.

Bax also wrote a longer programme note:

This work is only in the broadest sense programme music. The composer's intention is simply to offer a tonal impression of the castle-crowned cliff of (now sadly degenerate) Tintagel, and more especially of the long distances of the Atlantic, as seen from the cliffs of Cornwall on a sunny, but not windless, summer day. The literary and traditional associations of the scene also enter into the scheme. The music opens, after a few introductory bars, with a theme, given out by brass, which may be taken as representing the ruined castle, now so ancient and weather-worn as to seem an emanation of the rock upon which it is built. The subject is worked to a broad diatonic climax, and is followed by a long melody for strings, which may suggest the serene and almost limitless spaces of the ocean.

After a while a more restless mood begins to assert itself, as though the sea were rising, bringing with it a new sense of stress, thoughts of many passionate and tragic incidents in the tales of King Arthur and King Mark and others among the men and women of their time. A wailing chromatic figure is heard, and gradually dominates the music until finally it assumes a shape which recalls to mind one of the subjects of the first Act of 'Tristan and Isolda' (whose fate was, of course, intimately connected with Tintagel). Here occurs a motif which may be taken as representing the increasing tumult of the sea. Soon after there is a great climax, suddenly subsiding, followed by a passage which will perhaps convey the impression of immense waves slowly gathering force until they smash themselves upon the impregnable rocks.

The theme of the sea is heard again, and the piece ends as it began, with a picture of the castle still proudly fronting the sun and wind of centuries.

214 QUINTET for harp and string quartet

Date: *Gr5*: '1919'.
Dedication: *Printed score*: 'To Raymond Jeremy.'
Manuscript: Not traced. Pencil sketches for the viola passage beginning at 4:5 of the printed score appear on f. [7] of the short score of *Tintagel* (see **213** for details). Bax presumably jotted them down at about the time he was orchestrating the tone-poem, in January 1919; hence the quintet is listed here rather than at the end of the year.
Publication: MM (311), 1922, fo., 22 pp.; WC0062C.
Performance: Gwendolen Mason (hp.), Philharmonic Quartet: Frederic Holding (vn.), Cecil Bonvalot (vn.), Raymond Jeremy (va.), Cedric Sharpe (vc.); Hampstead Centre; 24 February 1921.
Duration: 15'30.

215 RUSSIAN SUITE for orchestra

a. Gopak (National Dance).
b. Nocturne (May-night in the Ukraine) [orchestrated by Graham Parlett].
c. In a Vodka Shop.

Title: a. 'National Dance' ('Gopak | No.2 of Two Russian Tone Pictures', the title of the original piano piece, has been added in another hand).
Date: Undated, but commissioned for the 1919 season of Diaghilev's Ballets Russes, **215a** pre-dating May, **215c** pre-dating 25 July.
Orchestra: a. 3(1)202020, 4231, timp., 3 perc. (b.d., tamb., cym.), hp., str. **b.** 2(1)202020, 2000, timp., 2 perc. (b.d., tamb., cym.), hp., str. **c.** 3(1)20202+1 (ad lib.), 4331, timp., 4 perc. (b.d., tamb., cym., tri.), hp., str.
Manuscript: CH; **215a** and **c** (**a** formerly JW, **c** formerly the Hallé Orchestra Library): [19], [16] ff.; 38, 31 pp.; AL 14a paper (355 × 263); **214b**: [21] ff. ; 42 pp.; 18-staff paper (350 × 250). For details of the original piano pieces see **146** and **162**. Unpublished. *Parts*: CH; **215a** also BBC.
Performance: (1) **215a** *only (earliest traced)*: [Orchestra], Ernest Ansermet; Alhambra Theatre; May 1919. (2) **215c** *only*: [Orchestra], Ernest Ansermet; Alhambra Theatre; 25 July 1919. (3) *Concert performance of* **215c**: City of Birmingham Orchestra, Hamilton Harty; Town Hall, Birmingham; 15 December 1920. (4) *Complete*: London Philharmonic Orchestra, Bryden Thomson; St Jude's Church, Central Square; 3 November 1988 (recording session for Chandos Records Ltd.).
Duration: a. 5'58. **b.** 8'52. **c.** 3'47.
Note: For the 1919 season of Diaghilev's Ballets Russes at the Alhambra Theatre, four British composers—Arnold Bax, Lord Berners, Eugene Goossens and Herbert Howells—were commissioned to provide short orchestral works to serve as 'symphonic interludes' between the ballets. Bax's contribution was a *Russian Suite*, which, according to *The Musical Times* (June 1919), p. 286, was originally intended to comprise orchestrations of the three piano pieces whose titles are listed above. In the event, *Gopak* and *In a Vodka Shop* were performed separately, and the *Nocturne* appears to have remained unorchestrated. Later in the year the ballet company moved to the Empire Theatre, where 'In a Vodka-Shop' (thus hyphenated) was presented as an interlude after Massine's *Children's Tales* (see **200**). These performances took place in October and were conducted by Adrian Boult. The programme note was as follows:

> In 1910, the composer paid a brief visit to Russia. On his return he recorded his impressions in three pianoforte pieces: A National Dance (Gopak), A Nocturne, and A Humoresque, entitled 'In a Vodka-Shop'. The first and third of these have been specially orchestrated to serve as symphonic interludes for these programmes.

This implies that Bax did not orchestrate the *Nocturne* himself.

216 WHIRLIGIG for piano

Date: *MS*: 'July 1st 1919'. *Printed score*: 'Summer | 1919'. This discrepancy suggests that the printed score may have been engraved from another MS, which has not been traced.
Dedication: *Printed score*: 'To Miss Irene Scharrer.' (in parentheses on MS).
Manuscript: BL (Loan 75/8 (M 191)); [4] ff.; [5] pp. + 3 blank; AL 12 paper (359 × 265). First page reproduced in facsimile in *Arnold Bax*, Miniature Essay Series (JWC, 1921), opposite p. 10.
Publication: JWC (2053), 1919, fo., 5 pp.
Duration: 2'50.

217 SONATA NO. 2 for piano (first version)

Title: 'Sonata', above which Bax has added '2nd' in fainter ink.
Date: 'July 26th | 1919.'
Dedication: *MS*: 'To Harriet Cohen' (in her own handwriting).
Manuscript: BL (Add. MS 54767); ff. 10-24v (17 comprising a thin strip of paper with the end of a system visible on the recto, 22v blank); [28] pp. (partly pagin. but incorrectly; p. 24 blank); bound by the BL with brown wrappers bearing Harriet Cohen's handwriting bound in; ff. 10-14v, 18-21v, 23-4v: AL 12 paper (trimmed to 355 × 259-263); ff. 15-16v, 22: ALM 16 (359 × 260). The last three bars of f. 14 and the whole of 14v are crossed through; likewise bars 5-9 of 20v, 1-8 of 18, and 1-10 of 23v. Unpublished in its original form, but the MS contains the numerous alterations made for the published version.
Performance: Arthur Alexander; Æolian Hall; 24 November 1919.
Duration: *c.* 25'00.
Note: For details of the revised version see **225**.

218 THE SLAVE GIRL for piano

Title: *Printed score*: 'The Slave Girl' (t.p.); 'The Slave-Girl' (p. 2). The title 'Slave Dance' found on the sleeve of the Pearl recording (SHE 565) is a mistake.
Date: *Gr5*: '1919'.
Dedication: *Printed score*: 'To Madame Tamara Karsavina.'
Manuscript: Not traced.
Publication: AFM (136), 1920, fo., 7 pp.
Performance: Harriet Cohen; Wigmore Hall; 15 June 1920.
Adaptation: As a dance work. *Performance*: Tamara Karsavina, Laurent Novikoff (dancers), Harriet Cohen (pf.); London Coliseum; 29 November 1920. The pianist wrote that Karsavina created a 'fierce and strange' dance (*A Bundle of Time*, p. 48).
Duration: 4'05.

219 WHAT THE MINSTREL TOLD US (Ballad) for piano

Title: *MS*: 'What the minstrel Told us. | (Ballad)'.
Date: *MS*: Undated, but a date stamp ('14 JAN 1920') and the printer's note 'Copies wanted by Feb 15' suggest that '1919' (*Gr5*, etc.) is correct.
Dedication: 'To Harriet Cohen'.
Manuscript: BL (Add. MS 54769); [4] ff.; [8] pp.; AL 14b paper (362 × 266).
Publication: AFM (135), 1920, fo., 11 pp.
Performance: Harriet Cohen; Wigmore Hall; 15 June 1920.
Duration: 9'34.

1920

220 THE TRUTH ABOUT THE RUSSIAN DANCERS: Incidental music to a play

Date: 'Fine Feb 5th 1920'.
Orchestra: 3(1) 2+1 2020, 4331, timp., 3 perc. (b.d., tamb., cym., bells), hp., str. A reduced orchestration is available through cross-cueing noted in the parts.
Text: J. M. Barrie, *The Truth about the Russian Dancers* (see **Note** below).
Manuscript: *Sketches*: Privately owned (formerly by Colin Scott-Sutherland): [3] ff.; [4] pp. + 1 blank + 1 with sketches that are not obviously related; pencil but 1 p. partly in ink; 1 f. of AL 16 paper (362 × 266); 2 ff. of ALM 18 paper (361 × 272). These sketches comprise: (*A*) A fragmentary two-bar pencil sketch for the opening of what became 'Karissima's Dance of Joy'. The bars occur at the end of a page of otherwise unidentifiable sketches, which were thus either material discarded from the final version of the score or were composed as part of another unfulfilled project or otherwise unknown score from which Bax borrowed this fragment. AL 16 paper is only otherwise attested in the song 'Welcome Somer' (**158b**), which dates from 1914. (*B*) Unidentified material but containing the waltz melody used in 'The Walking Lesson'. (*C*)The solo violin passage in 'Karissima appeals for Love'.

Full score: BL (Add. MS 54744); [99] ff.; 197 pp. (part I pagin. 1-90, a–o + 2 blank; part II pagin. 1-92 + 2 blank + 1 f. attached by paper clips in front of p. 61 containing a sketch for 'A Rabelaisian Catechism' (see **228**); AL 18 paper (359 × 259). At the end of 'Karissima's Farewell', on the verso of the folio clipped in, Bax has written in an alternative ending with the note 'P. 61a. | for Orchestral Suite following p. 60.', but no such suite appears to have been made. *Copyist's score*: CH (MS 306); [100] ff.; 200 pp.; 16- and 22-staff paper (destroyed by fire on 6 May 1964 but photocopy extant: *c.* 354 × *c.* 247). Unpublished, though a f.sc. and 'piano arrangement' were announced by MM in 1920 as being 'in preparation'. *Parts*: CH.

Performance: (1) Tamara Karsavina (Karissima), [Orchestra], Alfred Dove, décor by Paul Nash; London Coliseum; 15 March 1920. '. . . a piece in which the music seemed to them more notable than Barrie's whimsy . . .' (From Clifford Bax's novel *Time with a Gift of Tears*, London, 1943, p. 115.) (2) *Revival:*[82] Thamar [Tamara] Karsavina, [Orchestra], James A. Lowe; Savoy Theatre; 28 July 1926 (part of a double bill with Seymour Hicks's play *Sleeping Partners*).
Arrangement: The hire copy of CH's score contains suggestions for a truncated version, but no definitive suite exists.
Duration: 46'27 (without dialogue).
Note: The origins of J. M. Barrie's play and of Tamara Karsavina's involvement are described at length in *Dance Perspectives*, 14 (spring 1962), which also includes Barrie's otherwise unpublished text. The play was written in 1919 with Karsavina specifically in mind, and Bax was invited to write the music at the suggestion of Edwin Evans, who was the ballerina's musical adviser at the time; six weeks later, the piano score was ready for the first rehearsal. The whimsical plot concerns a prima donna from the 'Russian Ballet' called Karissima (spelt Carissima on the MS), who marries into the English nobility. While the other characters in the play converse normally, Karissima is unable to speak, and so she dances her lines instead. Bax has written in dialogue cues throughout. At the foot of many pages he has written out the clarinet parts for instruments in A instead of B♭ as in the main body of the score.

Synopsis:

PART I

Overture (pp. 1-20). Part of this was published in an arrangement for piano solo with the title *Ceremonial Dance* (see **221** for details). The Russian tune starting at bar 41 is taken from the trio section of the polonaise danced at the opening of Act II of the ballet *Tamara* (pp. 66-7; see **138**).
Moderato (pp. 21-8). This begins with a brief passage for solo violin, which in the MS is written within quotation marks. The theme is taken from Balakirev's *Tamara* (1882) and is a subtle allusion to Tamara Karsavina, who makes her first entry as Karissima at this point. The section continues with a dance in 'Rather fast Valse tempo'.
'Golf Dance' (pp. 28-44).
'The Walking Lesson' (pp. 45-62)[83].
'The Wedding Ceremony' (pp. 62-79).

[82] With the subtitle 'A Ballet-play in One Act'. It is conceivable that some minor adjustments were made to the score but there is nothing to suggest a full-scale revision.
[83] 'I think the walking lesson one of the quaintest and prettiest inventions I ever saw.' (Bax writing to Harry Farjeon in March 1920.)

'The Wedding Service' (pp. 80-4). This consists of five four-bar passages corresponding to the wedding responses, which Karissima, unable to speak, dances instead. It is followed by a modified reprise of the 'Wedding Ceremony' (pp. 85-90).
'The Storm' (pp. a–o). The storm music frames a short 'Moderato' section beginning with a melody for solo bassoon taken from No. 28 of *Tamara* (**138**).

PART II

'Dance of Motherhood' (pp. 1-19). Part of this is taken from the end of the Prologue to *Tamara*. It was published in an arrangement for piano as *Water Music* (**223**).
'The Funeral of Karissima' (pp. 20-30).
'Child's Dance' (pp. 30-46).
'Karissima's Farewell' (pp. 47-68). For an arrangement of this section for piano solo with the title *Serpent Dance* see **222**.
Finale (pp. 68-9). At figure 81 Bax quotes a melody that Lewis Foreman has identified as the English folk-tune 'To the Maypole haste away' (LF, p. 175).

221 CEREMONIAL DANCE for piano

Date: Although not published until 1929, it is likely that this arrangement of an excerpt from the Overture to *The Truth about the Russian Dancers* (**220**) was made in 1920, though Bax may have revised it shortly before publication. There is an advertisement by MM dating from 1920 for 'pianoforte solos' from *The Truth* that presumably refers to this piece and the next two entries.
Manuscript: Not traced.
Publication: MM (517), 1929, 4to, 6 pp.; CH (37717), 1943; WC0511.
Duration: 3'26.

222 SERPENT DANCE for piano

Dedication: 'To Reginald Paul.' Since the dedicatee was an unknown twenty-six-year-old in 1920, it seems likely that the dedication was added when the work came to be published nine years later.
Manuscript: Not traced.
Publication: MM (521), 1929, 4to, 6 pp.; CH (37232), [1945].
Duration: 3'22.
Note: This is an arrangement of 'Karissima's Farewell' from *The Truth about the Russian Dancers* (see **220** for details).

223 WATER MUSIC for piano

Dedication: 'To Lady George Cholmondeley'. As Mrs Christopher Lowther, the dedicatee had devised and danced in the ballet *From Dusk till Dawn* (**188**). She was divorced in 1920 and became Lady Cholmondeley in 1921, indicating that the dedication was added when the work was published.
Manuscript: Not traced.

Publication: MM (516), 1929, 4to, 7 pp.; CH (37346), [1945]; WC0472.
Duration: 4'27.
Note: This is an arrangement of the 'Dance of Motherhood' from *The Truth about the Russian Dancers* (see **220** for details). It derives ultimately from the final part of the Prologue to the ballet *Tamara* (**138**).

224 LULLABY (Berceuse) for piano

Date: *Printed score*: 'April 27th. 1920.'
Dedication: *Printed score*: 'To Madame Tamara Karsavina.'
Manuscript: Not traced.
Publication: MM (130), 1920, fo., 7 pp.; CH (35543), 1943, 4to.
Performance: Harriet Cohen; Wigmore Hall; 15 June 1920. '. . . the charming manuscript lullaby, which Miss Cohen had to repeat.' (From a review in *The Daily Telegraph*, 19 June 1920.)
Duration: 3'35.

225 SONATA NO. 2 for piano (second version of **217**)

Date: Revised between 24 November 1919 and 15 June 1920 (the dates of the first and second performances).
Dedication: *Printed score*: 'To Miss | Harriet Cohen.'
Manuscript: Revisions made on the score of the original version (see **217** for details).
Publication: MM (3), 1921, fo., 31 pp.; CH (35322), 1943, 4to.; WC0466. The CH edition includes several minor amendments by Bax, mostly to do with dynamics and tempi, but not really enough to regard it as a 'third version'.
Performance: Harriet Cohen; Queen's Hall; 15 June 1920. '. . . too big to be all taken in at a first hearing, but is plainly a remarkable piece of work.' (Ernest Newman, *The Sunday Times*, 20 June 1920.)
Duration: 24'02.
Note: Bax once told Frank Merrick that the work '. . . in some degree typified a struggle between good and evil.' (From Merrick's sleeve note to his 1963 recording [FMS Record No. 6]); and in a letter to Tilly Fleischmann (1930) Bax wrote: 'Like a great deal of my music it certainly is concerned with the warring of the forces of light and darkness but I can't say that there was anything more definite in my mind when I wrote it.'

226 LE CHANT D'ISABEAU (French Canadian Melody) 'freely arranged' for voice and piano

Date: *Printed score*: 'July 24th 1920'.
Text: 'The composer desires to thank M. Uzanne the collector of "French Songs of Old Canada" for very courteously permitting the verses and

melody of the above ballad to be printed in this arrangement.' The book referred to is *French Songs of Old Canada, pictured* [*sic*] *by W. Graham Robertson, with translations* (London: William Heinemann, 1904; limited edn. of 350 numbered copies). Robertson (not Uzanne) was the compiler, though the French edition, *Chansons de l'Ancienne France* (Paris: H. F. Floury, 1905), does have an introduction by Octave Uzanne.
Manuscript: Not traced.
Publication: MM (201), 1921, fo., 11 pp.
Performance: Anne Thursfield (sop.), Arnold Bax (pf.); The Grafton Galleries; 13 February 1921 (concert of The Music Club: 'Reception to the Representatives of the British Music Society').
Duration: 4'20.
Note: This song was first performed as No. 1 of the *Traditional Songs of France*, Nos. 2-4 being 'Femmes, battez vos marys', 'Langueo d'amours' and 'Me soui meso en danso'. The last three were published together with two other arrangements (see **227** below), but 'Le chant d'Isabeau', being the only French Canadian arrangement, was published separately. See also **228**.

227 TRADITIONAL SONGS OF FRANCE 'freely arranged' for voice and piano

a. 'Sarabande. Amours, amours, tant tu me fais de mal. (Old French Melody).'
b. 'Langueo d'amours, ma doulce fillette. (Old French Poem and Melody).'
c. 'Me soui meso en [misprinted as 'mesocu'] danso (Me suis mise en danse) (Bas Quercy).'
d. 'Femmes, battez vos Marys. (Old French).'
e. 'La Targo. (Provençal).'

Date: *Printed score* (in published order): **a.** 'July 28th 1920'. **b.** 'July 31st 1920'. **c.** 'July 27th 1920'. **d.** 'Aug. 21st 1920'. **e.** 'July 26th 1920'.
Text: **a** and **d.** French. **b.** Macaronic (French and Latin). **c** and **e.** Occitan (Provençal).
Manuscript: Not traced.
Publication: MM (202-206), 1921, 4to, pp. 1-9, 10-15, 16-21, 22-25, 26-30. Also available separately: **a** (204); **b** (202); **c** (206); **d** (205); **e** (203). No CH reprint seen.
Performance: **227a–d** *only*: Anne Thursfield (mezz.), Arnold Bax (pf.); The Grafton Galleries; 13 February 1921 (concert of The Music Club: 'Reception to the Representatives of the British Music Society'). According to *The Musical Times* (March 1921), p. 183, **227d** was repeated.
Duration: **a.** 3'30. **b.** 4'29. **c.** 1'54. **d.** 1'14. **e.** 1'37.
Note: 'Le chant d'Isabeau' (**226**) and 'A Rabelaisian Catechism' (**228**) were originally part of this cycle.

228 A RABELAISIAN CATECHISM for voice and piano

Title: 'A Rabelaisian Catechism | "La foi d'la loi"'.
Date: 'Fine Aug 16th 1920.' Although written before **227d** above, this song is listed here for convenience.
Text: Traditional chanson de série from Bassac, Charente, France.
Manuscript: *Sketch*: Inserted into the MS of *The Truth about the Russian Dancers* (BL (Add. MS 54744): [1] f. clipped in between pp. 60 and 61 of part II; see **220** above). *Complete*: BL (Add. MS 54779); ff. 23-9 (29v blank); pp. 16-28 + 3 blank; AL 14b paper (trimmed to 362 × 266); bound with 14 other songs (see **133** above). Unpublished.
Duration: *c.* 7'00.
Note: The pagination of the score suggests that this song (like 'Le chant d'Isabeau') was originally intended as part of the *Traditional Songs of France* (**226**); and this is confirmed by a note on the first page (not in Bax's hand): 'leave out this (pp. 16-28)', which suggests that it was omitted from the cycle when the other songs came to be published. This chanson de série takes the form of a dialogue between Le Prieur and Frère Grégoire in which the former asks 'La premièr' partie d'la foi d'la loi, dit'la moi, Frère Grégoire', to which the latter responds with 'Un bon farci sans os'. The question is put twelve times and the answer is given cumulatively with all the other answers, in the manner of 'The Twelve Days of Christmas'. At the twelfth and final time of asking, Le Prieur is accompanied by a quotation (thus marked) from Vaughan Williams's *Sea Symphony* ('O vast rondure swimming[84] in space') in the piano part, a jocular reference, no doubt, to the increasing rotundity of the two friars as the list of delicacies finally comes to an end.

229 BURLESQUE for piano

Date: *Gr5*: '1920'.
Dedication: *MM edn.*: None. *CH edn.*: 'To Iso Elinson' (the pianist, whom Bax met as a neighbour after settling in Storrington in 1940).
Manuscript: Not traced.
Publication: MM (131), 1920, fo., 7 pp. ; CH (37715), [1945], 4to.
Performance: *Earliest traced*: Evlyn Howard-Jones;[85] Wigmore Hall; 15 February 1922.
Duration: 3'01.

[84] Bax mistakenly writes 'dwelling'.
[85] Not 'Evelyn', as sometimes written.

230 COUNTRY-TUNE for piano

Date: *Gr5*: '1920'.
Manuscript: Not traced.
Publication: MM (260), 1921, fo., 7 pp. ; CH (37091), [1944], 4to.; WC0439. Also in Connie Mayfield (ed.), *Arnold Bax: Selected Works for Piano*, TP, 1986, 4to, pp. 28-32.
Duration: 2'02.

231 THE DEVIL THAT TEMPTED ST ANTHONY for piano

Note: The score of this version of the work has not been traced. It is listed in *Gr3* as a piece for solo piano and dated 1920. For details of the arrangement for two pianos see **293**.

232 A HILL TUNE for piano

Title: *Printed score*: 'A Hill Tune' (t.p.); 'A Hill-Tune' (p. 4).
Date: *Gr5*: '1920'.
Manuscript: Not traced.
Publication: MM (138), 1920, fo., 7 pp.; CH (35253), 1943, 4to.
Performance: *Earliest traced*: Evlyn Howard-Jones; Wigmore Hall; 15 February 1922.
Duration: 4'44.
Note: The principal melody was originally written in 1908 as part of the second thematic group in the first movement (at 3:4 ff.) of the String Quintet in G (**107**).

233 MEDITERRANEAN for piano

Date: *Gr5*: '1920'.
Manuscript: Not traced.
Publication: MM (151), 1921, fo., 7 pp.; CH (37083), 1943, 4to.
Performance: Harriet Cohen; Steinway Hall; 26 May 1921 (Guild of Singers and Players Concert). '. . . was much liked and repeated.' (*Era*, June 1921).
Arrangement: (i) For violin and piano by Jascha Heifetz: CF (MM 666), 1935, 4to, 8 pp.; CH (44159). The MM edition bears the dedication '"To Firenze"', but this is omitted on the CH reprint. The legend 'copyright 1921' by MM printed on the score refers to the original piano version. (ii) For 2 pianos, 3 hands by H. Rich: unpublished but recorded by Cyril Smith and Phyllis Sellick (HMV CLP 3563; CSD 3563).
Duration: 3'07.
Note: For details of Bax's orchestral arrangement see **257**.

234 OF A ROSE I SING A SONG: Carol for harp, cello, double bass, small choir (SATB)

Date: *Gr5*: ‘1920’.
Dedication: *Printed f.sc.*: ‘(To Leigh Henry.)’ (no parentheses on chor. part).
Text: Anonymous 15th century, according to the printed score; other sources give *c.* 1350. The words appear in Arthur Quiller-Couch (ed.), *The Oxford Book of English Verse 1250-1900* (Oxford, 1919), pp. 9-10. Since this collection contains the texts of four of Bax's choral works dating from between 1920 and 1926, it was probably his source.
Manuscript: Not traced.
Publication: *Full score*: MM (175), 1921, fo., 19 pp.; CH (38921), 1948; WC0471. *Chorus part only*: MM (262), 1921, 8vo, 14 pp.; CH (38773) [1948].
Performance: Marie Goossens (hp.), Cedric Sharpe (vc.), Victor Watson (d.b.), Oriana Madrigal Society, Charles Kennedy Scott; Æolian Hall; 7 March 1922. The work was given an instant encore; and after another performance a few months later, according to *The Queen* (15 July 1922), p. 69, ‘the shy composer was dragged, much against his will, to the front of the audience and rapturous applause’.
Duration: 6'58.

235 PHANTASY for viola and orchestra

[I.] Poco lento—Allegro moderato molto ritmico—[II.] Lento semplice—[III.] Allegro vivace.

Title: *MS*: ‘~~Concerto~~ PHANTASY for Viola & Orchestra.’, the replacement word written in pencil in an unknown hand; similarly on a printed label on the front cover. First performed as ‘Concerto, in D minor’. On the handbill and in the essay accompanying the programme notes for its second performance, in November 1922, Eric Blom still refers to it by this title, though elsewhere in the programme booklet it is called ‘Phantasy’, suggesting that the name was changed shortly before the booklet went to press.
Date: *MS*: Undated. *Gr5*: ‘1920’.
Dedication: *MS and printed vla. and pf.sc.*: ‘To Lionel Tertis’ (in upper case on printed f.sc.). The viola and piano arrangement has the following note on the reverse of the t.p.: ‘The Composer is greatly indebted to Mr Lionel Tertis for very kindly editing and fingering the Solo Viola part.’
Orchestra: 3(1) 2+1 2020, 4200, timp., 1 perc. (s.d. [*ad lib.*], cym.), hp., str.
Manuscript: *Holograph*: BL (Add. MS 54745); [54] ff.; 105 pp. + 3 blank; AL 14b paper (trimmed to 355 × *c.* 253); tightly bound *c.* 1920 in thick cardboard boards with green leather backstrip, with printed label on upper cover bearing both the original and revised titles and composer's name. Several revised viola passages appear as cancels. Bar 6 before the ‘Lento’ is in accordance with the printed f. sc., not the viola-and-piano version, though

someone has pencilled in the other version over the top. The final two bars have been altered in pencil, and there are conductors' and engravers' marks. *Copyist's score*: UCD (MS 26/5); [52] ff.; t.p. + 1 blank + 102 pp.; AL 14a paper (350 × 258); bound in green cloth, with the title and composer's name embossed in gold up the spine. The copyist's name is given on a label at the top of the t.p. as 'J. Collins, 142 Sheepcote Lane, Battersea, [London] SW' (cf. **152**). The ending is of the original version, not the published version.
Publication: *Viola and piano*: MM (312), 1922, fo., 21 pp.; CH (40911), [1951]. *Full score*: MM (695), 1938, fo., 72 pp.; WC0092.
Performance: (1) *As 'Concerto'*: Lionel Tertis (va.), Orchestra of the Royal Philharmonic Society, Albert Coates; Queen's Hall; 17 November 1921. (2) *As 'Phantasy'*: Lionel Tertis (va.), Goossens Orchestra, Eugene Goossens; Queen's Hall; 13 November 1922.
Duration: 21'34.
Note: For the first performance Bax wrote the following note:

This Concerto follows established classical tradition in that it consists of three distinct movements, though these are linked together without a break in the flow of the music. The orchestra employed is a comparatively small one, the only member of the heavier brass instruments admitted being one trumpet, occasionally used for solo purposes. [Followed by a descriptive 'analysis' with musical examples.]

In movt. II, beginning at the ninth bar before letter L, Bax makes use of the Irish folktune 'An Cailín donn deas na cíocha bána'[86] ('The Pretty Brown-Haired Girl with the White Breasts'), the only such use to which he admitted (but see *A Connemara Revel*, **68**). The melody that appears in the bass at letter (X), though not identified as such on the score or in Bax's note, is a quotation from the opening phrase of the Sinn Fein marching song 'Amhrán na bhFiann' ('A Soldier's Song'), composed by Patrick Heeney (1881-1911) to words by Peadar Kearney (1883-1942). It was first published in the monthly journal *Irish Freedom* in 1912 and adopted as the national anthem of the Irish Free State in 1926 (i.e. after Bax's *Phantasy* had been written).

236 SONATA NO. 1 for violin and piano (third version of 124)

I. Moderately slow and very Tranquilly. II. Allegro Vivace. III. Moderate Tempo. Smooth and serene.

Date: 1920 assumed from date of performance and publication.
Dedication: *Printed score only*: 'To Paul Kochanski.'

[86] This is how it is printed in the published full score. In the MS it appears (in Irish script) as '("A Cailín donn deas na gcíocha bána")'. The printed version has *An* ('The') for *A* ('O') and gives the radical form of *cíocha* ('breasts').

Manuscript: Amendments made to the MS of the 1915 version (see **124** and **166** for details). But the printed score contains further amendments made by Paweł Kochański that are not in the MS, and these were presumably devised while he was preparing the 1920 performance. *Transcript*: BMI, [1] f.; [1] p. + 1 blank; 3 bars (unfinished); plain A5 paper (280 × 219; written inside a lined border 232 × 165). This was written out by Bax for the American autograph-collector Howes Norris, Jr., whose name is printed at the top of the paper (see also **348**). The quotation is a melodic line containing the opening theme, although it does not appear in the work in this precise form. Underneath the quotation Bax has written: 'from Sonata for Violin and Piano | in E major | With good wishes | sincerely yours | Arnold Bax | Nov 18th 1928'.
Publication: MM (182), 1921, 52 pp. The CH edn. is of the 1945 revision (see **361**).
Performance: (1) *Before publication*: Paweł [Paul] Kochański (vn.), Arnold Bax (pf.); Queen's (Small) Hall; 22 November 1920. (2) *After publication*: Bessie Rawlins (vn.), Arnold Bax (pf.); Wigmore Hall; 2 November 1921.
Duration: 32'33.
Note: After performing this work with a 'worthy' lady violinist in the 1920s, Bax wrote to a friend: 'I am not sure that middle-aged and unquestionably virtuous virgins ought to play my music.'

c. 1920

237 MY EYES FOR BEAUTY PINE for voice and piano

Title: *MS*: 'My eyes for Beauty ~~yearn~~ pine [*sic*]'.
Date: Undated and not mentioned in any of the lists of Bax's works published during his lifetime. The handwriting suggests a date *c.* 1920, and the imprint of the MS paper is identical with that of, for example, 'A Rabelaisian Catechism' (1920).
Text: Robert Bridges, 'My eyes for beauty pine'.
Manuscript: BL (Add. MS 54779); ff. 54-5^{v}; [4] pp.; AL 14b paper (trimmed to 362 × 260); bound with 14 other songs (see **133** above). Unpublished.
Duration: 3'00.
Note: For details of the version for voice and string quartet see **250a**.

1921

238 FIVE IRISH SONGS for voice and piano

a. The Pigeons. **b.** As I came over the grey, grey hills. **c.** I heard a piper piping. **d.** Across the Door. **e.** Beg-Innish.

Date: *Printed scores*: **a.** 'March 1st 1921'. **b.** 'Feb.28th 1921'. **c.** Undated. **d.** 'Feb.18th 1921'. **e.** 'Feb.19th 1921'.
Text: a and **d.** Padraic Colum (spelt 'Colm' on the printed score). **b** and **c.** Joseph Campbell. **e.** J. M. Synge. The poets' original titles are precisely the same as those of the songs listed above.
Manuscript: Not traced.
Publication: MM (6), 1922, 4to, pp. 1-3, 4-8, 9-11, 12-15, 16-20; also issued separately; CH (38798; **b.** 38430, WC0281; **c.** 38530), 1943.
Performance: Dorothy Moulton (sop.), Arnold Bax (pf.); Wigmore Hall; 4 July 1921.
Arrangement: 230c arranged for flute and guitar by John Harper. Unpublished. *Earliest performance traced*: Atarah Ben-Tovim (fl.), John Harper (gtr.); Purcell Room; 29 March 1976.
Duration: a. 2'28. **b.** 3'05. **c.** 2'53. **d.** 2'32. **e.** 2'02.

239 GLAMOUR for voice and piano

Title: 'Glamour' is used here in its proper sense of magic, enchantment.
Date: 'March 11th | 1921.'
Text: 'Dermot O'Byrne' (Arnold Bax), 'Glamour', in *Orpheus*, 12 (October 1910), pp. 202-3. Also published anonymously in *Love Poems of a Musician* (London: Cecil Palmer, 1923), pp. 51-2. The poem was written in June 1910, while Bax was in the Ukraine (see *FMY*, pp. 71-9).
Manuscript: BL (Add. MS 54779); ff. 30-6v; 14 pp. + 1 blank; AL 12 paper (trimmed to 356 × 260); bound with 14 other songs (see **133** above). The MS has notes for orchestration in Bax's hand but there is no evidence that he wrote out a full score.
Publication: In Lewis Foreman (ed.), *Dermot O'Byrne: Poems by Arnold Bax*, TP, 1979, 8vo, pp. 80-95.
Performance: Anthony Roden (ten.), Geoffrey Parsons (pf.); br. Radio 3, 20 November 1983.
Arrangement: For voice and orchestra by Rodney Newton ('orchestrated | March–April | 1987'): Graham Parlett; t.p. + list of instruments + 42 pp.; D28 Panopus Score-System Transparency Paper (417 × 292); *str. parts*: Graham Parlett. *Performance*: Martyn Hill (ten.), London Philharmonic Orchestra, Bryden Thomson; All Saints' Church, Tooting; 11 April 1988 (recording session for Chandos Records Ltd.).
Duration: 8'07.

240 SONATA NO. 1 IN F♯ MINOR for piano (second version of 127)

Date: *Printed score*: 'Written in Russia | Summer 1910 | Revised 1917-1921'.
Manuscript: Not traced.
Publication: MM (7), 1922, fo., 32 pp.; CH (39287), [1949], 4to.; WC0270.

Performance: Harriet Cohen; Wigmore Hall; 12 April 1921. '. . . a work full of mice produced by mountains.' (*Musical Opinion*, May 1921, p. 681.)
Duration: 18'26.

241 BALLADE IN A♭: Piano piece by Frédéric Chopin transposed into A major and orchestrated

Performance: (1) Tamara Karsavina, Laurent Novikoff (dancers), [Orchestra], Alfred Dove; London Coliseum; 4 July 1921. (2) *Revival*: Phyllis Bedells, Harold Turner, Savoy Orchestra, Constant Lambert; Savoy Theatre; 29 November 1931; and Carlton Theatre; 15 December 1931 (Camargo Society production).
Note: The score of this orchestration has not been traced. According to Tamara Karsavina in her book *Theatre Street* (London, 1930), p. 201, it was presented to her by Bax as a gift. In an undated letter to his brother Clifford, he wrote: 'I have been bragging about your inventiveness and she is very much at a loss about some little ballets she wants to do. One is a short piece out of Schubert's 'Rosamunde' and the other a dance version of Chopin's Ballade in A♭.'

Bax's orchestral arrangement was performed during the week beginning 4 July 1921, twice daily at 2.30 and 7.45 p. m., as part of a 'balletic spectacle' designed by Claude Lovat Fraser. Other items on the programme ranged from a 'Grand March' by Elgar to a music-hall turn by Val Vett, 'The Ragtime Rag-Picking Rag-Painter'. Other specially commissioned orchestrations were also played, including Arthur Bliss's arrangement of Sinding's *Fire Dance* (also 'lost').

No synopsis appears in the printed programme, but 'What story there was to it seemed to be embodied in the pursuit, the capture, and the escape of a forest nymph from the clutches of a would-be lover.' (*The Daily Telegraph*, 5 July 1921.) It is not clear whether the 'Corps de Ballet', which appeared in the next item, was also involved in the Chopin piece, but it certainly took part in the 1931 revival with new choreography by Phyllis Bedells: there is a photograph in *The Morning Post*, 30 November 1931, p. 5 showing the two principals surrounded by eight ballerinas. The information that Bax had transposed the original into A major comes from a review in *The Musical Times* (January 1932).

242 SONATA IN E♭ for piano

I. Allegretto moderato e feroce. II. Lento con molto espressione. III. Scherzo-Finale. Largamente—Allegro molto vivace.

Title: '~~3rd Sonata~~ [*sic*] Symphony in E♭ | (Sketch)'. See **Note** below.
Date: I. 'April 27th 1921.' II. Undated. III. 'Fine June 30th | 1921'.

Manuscript: BL (Add. MS 54724); [20] ff.; 39 pp. (1-17 + 1 blank, 18-26 + 1 blank, [27-39]) ; AL 12 paper (360 × 265). The MS also has inserted in front of movt. III the replacement slow movement written when Bax decided to orchestrate the work. Unpublished.
Performance: (1) *Movt. II only*: John Simons; Bishopsgate Institute; 1982 (recording session for Whitetower Records). (2) *Complete*: Noemy Belinkaya; Purcell Room; 16 October 1983.
Duration: 34'05.
Note: After completing this sonata, Bax played it through to his friends Harriet Cohen and Arthur Alexander, who suggested to him that it was really a symphony and should be orchestrated. Before doing this, Bax wrote an entirely new slow movement to replace the original. For details of the orchestral version (Symphony No. 1) see **256**.

243 SUMMER MUSIC for orchestra (first version)

Title: *Short score*: '~~Idyll~~ [*sic*] Summer Music' (see **Note** below).
Date: According to the letter from Bax quoted below, the work was written 'last spring', i.e. the spring of 1921. The full score (which I have not seen) is apparently dated at the end: 'Sept 1921' (see **Manuscript** below). In response to an enquiry from Christopher Whelen, Bax wrote that the work was composed 'altogether in London'.
Orchestra: Not known.
Manuscript: *Short score*: BL (Add. MS 54746); 4 ff. (2 bifolia); [7] pp. + 1 blank; AL 12 paper (360 × 262) loosely inserted between a bifolium of BH 43 paper (357 × 269). There are pencilled notes for orchestration. *Full score*: Privately owned (formerly by Elizabeth Poston). It has proved impossible to gain access to this MS. Unpublished in this form.
Performance: London Symphony Orchestra, Hamilton Harty; Queen's Hall; 1 November 1921 (Margaret Collins Orchestral Concert).
Duration: *c.* 9'45.
Note: Unlike some of his tone-poems, which were originally written for piano solo (such as *The Happy Forest*), *Summer Music* was conceived as an orchestral work since the short score is written partly on three-staff systems. In a letter to F. Gilbert Webb, the author of the programme notes for the concert at which this work was first performed, Bax wrote:

> The 'Idyll', the title of which I am changing to 'Summer-Music' is in M.S and almost my latest piece. It was written last spring. The score has no trombones or tuba in it, and only one trumpet. After a few preliminary bars the principal melody appears on the cor anglais accompanied by strings. This subject is repeated, this time on viola and cellos with a wavy accompaniment in the upper register. A new theme of a pastoral character for the wood-wind follows which, after being brought to a climax, gives place to capricious allusions to the first melody tossed about among the wood instruments. This episode serves as a bridge to the middle section of the piece—a third melody of a still more serene nature. A climax built upon fragments of the first

subject leads to a broad re-statement of the latter by all the strings after which the music dies drowsily away.

This is all that can be said about this short work, I think. Would you kindly alter the title in the programme to 'Summer-Music'? 'Idyll' is not a little played out.

A revised version of this work was published in 1932 (see **314**).

244 HOSTING AT DAWN for woodwind, brass and percussion

Title: Published as 'Hosting at dawn'. Called 'Fanfare for a Hosting at Dawn' at its first performance.
Date: Probably a few months before 1 November 1921, when it was published.
Orchestra: 3 tpts., 3 tbns., timp., cym. (according to the copyist's score in the RMSM).
Manuscript: *Holograph*: Not traced. *Copyist's short score A*: RMSM; [1] f.; [1] p. (10 bars); 14-staff paper. *Copyist's short score B*: Not traced.
Publication: *Copyist's short score B* (with Bax's signature underneath): reproduced in facsimile in Leigh Henry (ed.), *Fanfare: A Musical Causerie*, 3 (London: Goodwin & Tabb Ltd., 1 November 1921), 4to, p. 50.
Performance: 'Specially Selected Orchestra', Eugene Goossens; Queen's Hall; 12 December 1921.
Arrangement: (i) For fl., 2 cls., 2 hns., 3 tpts., 2 tbns. (2nd ad lib.), tba., cym., b.d. by Arthur Cohn: EFC. (ii) For 3 tpts., 3 tbns., cym. (with final bars scored, at the conductor's request, for full orchestra) by Graham Parlett. *Performance*: Kensington Symphony Orchestra, Leslie Head; St John's, Smith Square; 2 March 1979.
Duration: 0'33.
Note: This fanfare was one of many commissioned from prominent composers, both British and foreign, to celebrate the publication of the periodical Fanfare. Other composers who contributed were Bantock, Falla, Goossens, Harrison, Harty, Holbrooke, Malipiero, Milhaud, Poulenc, Prokofiev, Roussel, Satie, Wellesz and Felix White.

245 IN THE FAERY HILLS for orchestra (second version of 114)

Title: 'In the Faery Hills. | 1908-1909'.
Date: 'Revised Score. 1921.' (to left of title).
Orchestration: 3(1) 2+1 2+1 2+1, 4331, timp., 3 perc. (b.d., tamb., cym., gong, gl., cel.).
Manuscript: UCC; [43] ff.; 83 pp. (pagin. in pencil) + 1 blank + 1 p. containing 3½ bars of non-autograph pencil sketches upside down on two staves + 1 blank; AL 18a paper (355 × 262); inserted into a manila folder with an undated presentation inscription (*c.* 1955?) in Harriet Cohen's handwriting. The MS contains engravers' marks, including the pl.no. 426, although it was eventually published with a different number.

Publication: *Full score*: MM (441), 1926, fo., 78 pp.; WC0456. *Min.sc.* (8vo): *c.* 1934.
Performance: Orchestra of the Royal Philharmonic Society, Frank Bridge; Queen's Hall; 24 February 1927.
Duration: 15'17.
Note: In revising this work, Bax made a ten-bar cut before letter K and rewrote sixteen bars at letter N. Philip Heseltine, with whom Bax was staying while correcting the proofs, regretted the discarding of these original bars, and when the score appeared in print he transcribed the excised passage and pasted it into the flyleaf of his copy with the note: 'This is where the trombones came in with the excellent tune which Bax cut out in revision because he thought it was "vulgar"! The passage, which was a gay and brilliant climax to the first movement of the piece, is now merely thick and commonplace.'

246 MATER, ORA FILIUM: Carol for unaccompanied double choir (SSAATTBB)

Title: The comma is inserted after 'Mater' in an early MM catalogue of Bax's music but is wrongly omitted on the printed score.
Date: *Gr5*: '1921'.
Dedication: *Printed score*: 'To C. Kennedy Scott.'
Text: *Printed MM score*: '(Carol from a manuscript at Balliol Collage [corrected to 'College' on CH reprints]. Oxford.)'. The MS is *A Boke of dyueris tales and balettes and dyueris Reconynges etc.*: the Memorandum-book of Richard Hill, citizen and grocer, London, 16th century (Balliol MS 354, f. 177^{v}: see R. A. B. Mynors, *Catalogue of the Manuscripts of Balliol College Oxford*, Oxford, 1963, pp. 352-4). Hill's book contains the words of several carols written out *c.* 1504. They are reproduced in Roman Dyboski (ed.), *Songs, Carols, and other miscellaneous Poems from the Balliol MS. 354, Richard Hill's Commonplace-book*, Early English Text Society, extra series, ci (Oxford, 1908). The words are macaronic (partly in Latin, partly in English).
Manuscript: Not traced.
Publication: MM (183), 1921, fo. and 8vo, 20 pp.; CH (38731), 1947, 8vo, 23 pp. The MM edition includes a piano arrangement for rehearsal only; the CH edition was printed from new plates without the arrangement.
Performance: Oriana Madrigal Society, Charles Kennedy Scott; Queen's Hall; 13 November 1922 ('Concert of Recent Works of Arnold Bax'). 'Its first performance', according to the conductor, 'was the best I ever gave.' (CSS, p. 57.)
Duration: 10'21.
Note: Bax was prompted to write this work (his first for unaccompanied choir) after hearing, for the first time, a performance of Byrd's Mass for five

voices, which was sung by the Tudor Singers at one of Harriet Cohen's musical evenings. The concert at which it was first performed was a landmark in Bax's career: 'It may be that the future historian of music in England will write down the event that took place . . . last night in red letters. . . . At the end of the concert the hero of the evening was presented with a laurel wreath.' (*The Daily Telegraph*, 14 November 1922.) 'At the concert . . . [Bax] appeared in various disguises—as a Russian, as a Spaniard, as a Bergerette, and even in a job lot of ecclesiastical vestments. . . . Mr. Bax uses such ecclesiastical tags as he finds attractive, and decorates them with all sorts of fantastic ideas. The result on paper looks an almost unsingable jumble. In performance it was admirably calculated, full of the most adorable surprises . . .' (Edward Dent, 'Arnold Bax', *The Nation*, 25 November 1922). 'I am looking forward so much to hearing "Mater Ora Filium" again, for I feel very happy about this work, although I should not say so aloud perhaps. . . . The success [of the concert] exceeded my most sanguine expectations . . .' (Letter from Bax to 'Miss Waddington').

247 NOW IS THE TIME OF CHRISTYMAS: Carol for men's voices (TTBB), flute and piano

Date: *Gr5*: '1921'.
Dedication: *Printed score*: '(To Hamilton Harty.)'
Text: Anonymous 15th century. The words (in modernized form) are taken from the same source as those of *Mater, ora Filium* (**246**): Balliol MS 354, f. 223^{v} (see Dyboski, op. cit., p. 15, and Richard Leighton Green (ed.), *The Early English Carols*, Oxford, 1977, p. 6).
Manuscript: Not traced.
Publication: MM (269), 1921, fo. and 8vo, 11 pp.; CH (38398), 1943, fo. and 8vo.
Performance: (1) [Choir],[87] E. Swingler (fl.), Granville Hill (pf.);[88] Opera House, Blackpool; 21 October 1922 (Blackpool Festival). '. . . the unmistakable popular success of the evening.' (*The Manchester Guardian*, 23 October 1922, p. 13). (2) Robert Murchie (fl.), Arnold Bax (pf.), Oriana Madrigal Society, Charles Kennedy Scott; Queen's Hall; 13 November 1922 ('Concert of Recent Works by Arnold Bax').
Duration: 3'02.
Note: The voice and piano parts in this score have the key signature for G major (an F♯), but the flute part has an F♮, creating a Mixolydian/Ionian bimodal effect.

[87] Sung as a test piece at the festival; it has not been possible to determine which choir sang it first.

[88] These, at any rate, were the instrumentalists at an evening performance after the competition; they may not necessarily have accompanied the first choir which sang the piece.

248 SONATA NO. 2 IN D for violin and piano (second version of **171**)

I. Introduction—Fantasy—II. 'The Grey Dancer in the Twilight'—III. Interlude—Lento espressivo—IV. Allegro feroce—Epilogue.

Title: Published with the above title. In a letter to the BBC dated 21 June 1930, Bax indicated that he wanted a broadcast of the work announced as 'Sonata in four linked movements'.
Date: Undated, but date of first performance suggests 1921 (see **Note** below).
Manuscript: BL (Add. MS 54766). This is the MS of the original version, which Bax has extensively amended to produce his revision (for further details see **171**). The principal alterations are as follows: in movt. II a cut is made from 17:7 to 23:23, a further 5 (?) bars with the new version (4 bars) pasted over the top; in movt. III a cut is made from 26:13 to 27:2 (a six-bar cut), and 39 bars are crossed through from 34:7 to 36:2; in movt. IV, 54 bars are crossed through from 36:1 to 41:15, with six new bars pasted over, leading to the 'Slow and serious' interlude (pp. 28-9 of printed score).
Publication: MM (325), 1923, fo., 34 pp.
Performance: Bessie Rawlins (vn.), Arnold Bax (pf.) ('whose very kind consent to play is occasioned by Miss Harriet Cohen's illness.'); Wigmore Hall; 25 April 1922.
Duration: 30'34.
Note: The following note—unsigned but almost certainly by Bax—appeared in the programme for the first performance of this revised version:

This Sonata was written in 1915, but for various reasons has hitherto been withheld by the composer. Recently it has been considerably revised. The work is in four distinct movements, though the whole is played without a break. The end of each of the first three divisions of the sonata is designed to create an impression of pause and expectancy, so that the plan of the various movements should be clear to the listener. The work is in cyclic form, and the principal motive which dominates the whole sonata is used also in the same composer's orchestral piece, 'November Woods.'. . . (The second movement, which might also be called 'The Dance of Death', was influenced in a particular degree by the events of 1915).

c. 1921

249 CHRISTMAS EVE for orchestra (revised version of **145**)

Title: 'Christmas Eve (revision)'.
Date: Undated. The imprint of the MS paper is only otherwise to be found on the revised version of *In the Faery Hills* (1921) and the Sinfonietta (1932), and since the handwriting is similar to that of the former, it has been tentatively assigned here to *c.* 1921.
Orchestration: 3(1) 2+1 2+1 2+1 (ad lib.), 4331, timp., 2 perc. (b.d., cym., cel., gl.), org., hp., str.

Manuscript: BL (Add. MS 54735); 28 ff.; 55 pp. + 1 blank; AL 14a paper (355 × 263). Unpublished.
Performance: (1) *Semi-amateur*: Kensington Symphony Orchestra, Leslie Head; St Peter's Church, London; 8 November 1979. (2) *Professional*: London Philharmonic Orchestra, Bryden Thomson; All Saints' Church, Tooting; 5 March 1986 (recording session for Chandos Records Ltd.).
Duration: 17'53.
Note: The principal differences between the original and the revised versions are noted on the MS of the original: bars 9-16 are marked 'cut' and do not occur in the revision; bars 12-14 after (2) are replaced by two bars that are sketched out in this original version; bars 9-10 are altered slightly and the next 24 bars are replaced by five new bars sketched at the bottom of the page; bars 31-35 after (19) are marked 'cut'. There are innumerable minor changes of harmony, rhythm and instrumentation.

250 TWO SONGS for tenor[89] and string quartet

a. 'My eyes for Beauty pine'. **b.** 'O Mistress mine'.

Title: '2 songs for voice | and String Quartet'.
Date: Undated. Handwriting and imprint of MS paper suggest *c.* 1921.
Text: **a.** Robert Bridges, 'My Eyes for Beauty pine'. **b.** William Shakespeare, 'O Mistress mine! where are you roaming?' from *Twelfth Night*, II, iii, 42 ff.
Manuscript: *Scores*: **a.** BPL; [4] ff.; t.p. + [5] pp. + 1 blank; AL 14b paper (362 × 266). **b.** BPL; [2] ff.; [4] pp.; AL 14b paper (362 × 266). *Parts* (in Bax's hand): BPL, [1] f. for each of the four parts, 'My eyes for beauty pine' on the recto, 'O Mistress mine' on the verso; AL 10 paper (360 × *c.* 263), the vn. I and va. parts on a bifolium torn in two, the vn. II and vc. parts on another pair of leaves. There are players' markings in blue pencil. The scores and parts are loosely inserted into a protective bifolium of 18-staff paper (368 × 272) together with the original version of 'O Mistress Mine' (**184**). Unpublished.
Performance: (1) *Private*: The existence of parts written out by Bax with players' markings suggests that the work may have been privately performed, perhaps at one of Harriet Cohen's musical evenings. (2) *Public*: Janet Linsé[90] (sop.), Bernard Partridge (vn.), Antonina Balos (vn.), Michael Ponder (va.), Elizabeth Wilson (vc.); British Music Information Centre; 14 October 1983 (lecture-recital by Lewis Foreman, *et al.*).
Duration: **a.** 3'10. **b.** 2'00.
Note: For details of the versions for voice and piano see **184** and **237**.

[89] Although Bax specifies only a high voice, the words are more appropriate for a tenor. 'Tenor Voice' is pencilled at the top of the title page, probably by Harriet Cohen, who presented the scores to Peter Pears after Bax's death.
[90] Not Jeannette Wilson, as indicated in the printed programme.

1922

251 SONATA for viola and piano

I. Molto moderato—Allegro. II. Allegro energico ma non troppo presto. III. Molto Lento.

Date: I. 'Dec 9th | 1921.' II. Undated. III. 'Fine. | Jan 9th 1922.'
Dedication: *Printed score only*: 'To Lionel Tertis.', followed by the note: 'The thanks of the composer are due | to Mr Lionel Tertis for his kindness | in editing the Viola part of this work.'
Manuscript: ULD (Add. MS 814; formerly BL (Loan 53/26)); [18] ff.; 35 pp. (1-13, 14-27, 28-35 + 1 blank); AL 12 paper (362 × 266); in brown wrappers with Harriet Cohen's handwriting on the front. Also attached is a letter from her solicitors explaining that it had been selected by her trustees to fulfil a bequest in her will. Received by ULD on 29 November 1968.
Publication: MM (355), 1923, fo., 27 pp.; CH (38180), [1946], 4to.
Performance: Lionel Tertis (va.), Arnold Bax (pf.); Æolian Hall; 17 November 1922.
Duration: 20'31 (timing of the performance recorded in 1929 by Tertis and Bax).

252 THREE IRISH SONGS for voice and piano

a. Cradle Song. **b.** Rann of Exile.[91] **c.** Rann of Wandering.

Date: *Printed score*: 'FEB.1922' (on each song).
Text: Padraic Colum (spelt 'Colm' on the score), 'A Cradle Song', 'Rann of Exile', 'Rann of Wandering'.
Manuscript: Not traced.
Publication: MM (295), 1922, 4to, pp. 3-7, 8-11, 12-15; also issued separately; CH (37350; **a.** 37075), [1945], fo. **252b** and **c** also in *Twelve Songs for Medium/High Voice and Piano*, TP, 1984, 4to, pp. 26-9, 30-3.
Performance: *Earliest traced*: Eleanor Charter (sop.), Arnold Bax (pf.); Liberty Buildings, School Lane, Kingston-upon-Thames, Surrey; 5 November 1926 ('A Recital of Mr. Arnold Bax's Works' given by The Sandon Music Group).
Duration: **a.** 2'52. **b.** 2'45. **c.** 1'29.
Note: The name 'Mavoureen' on p. 4 of 'Cradle Song' is a misprint for 'Mavourneen'. 'Rann of Exile' begins with a senza misura melodic line on the piano labelled '*In the manner of a Caoin* [keen].'—an Irish lament.

[91] *Rann* is the Irish Gaelic for 'verse' or 'stanza' (see also **57**).

253 DERMOTT DONN MacMORNA for voice and piano

Title: *MS*: 'Dermot Donn McMorna'. *Printed score*: 'Dermott Donn MacMorna' (the poet's spelling).
Date: 'March 1st 1922.'
Text: Padraic Colum, 'Dermott Donn MacMorna'.
Manuscript: Clifford Gillam (MS formerly owned by Harriet Cohen); [4] ff.; [6] pp. + 2 blank; AL 12 paper (359 × 262); two bifolia, one within the other, the outer edge Sellotaped.
Publication: In *Arnold Bax: Six Songs*, TP (THA 978047), 1994, 4to, pp. 27-32.
Duration: 2'35.
Note: The title of this song does not appear in any of the lists of Bax's music published during his lifetime.

254 THIS WORLDES JOIE: Motet for unaccompanied chorus (SATB)

Title: *MS*: '"This World's Joy."' *Printed score*: 'This Worldes Joie'.
Date: 'March 14th | 1922'.
Dedication: 'To W.G. Whittaker.'
Text: Anonymous, *c.* 1300. From MS Harley 2235 in the BL; printed in Arthur Quiller-Couch (ed.), *The Oxford Book of English Verse 1250-1900*, p. 7.
Manuscript: UCC; [9] ff.; 18 pp.; AL 12 paper (357 × 267); inserted into a manilla card folder.
Publication: MM (324), 1923, fo. and 8vo, 12 pp. With 'piano for rehearsal'. *Corrected proofs*: UCD (MS 26/4); in brown folder; final page (p. 12) missing; corrections in Bax's hand in red ink and pencil; the proofs have a date stamp ('9 FEB 1923') on them and are charred at the edges; presented by Harriet Cohen on 4 September 1961. The Middle English words originally appeared alone on the reverse of the title folio, but Bax has written in a modernized version, which appears on the printed score.
Performance: Oriana Madrigal Society, Charles Kennedy Scott; Æolian Hall; 2 November 1923 (Gerald Cooper Chamber Concert).
Duration: 5'50.

255 QUARTET IN ONE MOVEMENT for piano, violin, viola and cello

Date: 'Summer | 1922'.
Dedication: *Printed score only:* 'To Miss Bessie Rawlins.'
Manuscript: BL (Add. MS 54762); [13] ff.; 26 pp. (pagin. in pencil); AL 12 paper (362 × 266); loosely inserted into brown wrappers with Harriet Cohen's writing on the front. Engravers' marks in pencil and red pencil, and a date stamp '27 NOV 1923'.

Publication: MM (368), 1924, fo., 27 pp.; CH (37286), [1946], 4to.; WC 0464.
Performance: Meredyll Piano Quartet: Marguerite Meredyll (pf.), Bessie Rawlins (vn.), Raymond Jeremy (va.), Émile Dœhaerd (vc.); Æolian Hall; 9 February 1923.
Duration: 11'53.
Note: For Bax's arrangement of this work as *Saga Fragment* see **317**.

256 SYMPHONY NO. 1 for orchestra

I. Allegro moderato e feroce. II. Lento solenne. III. Allegro maestoso—Allegro vivace ma non troppo presto.

Title: *Short score*: Movts. I and III were originally part of the Sonata in E♭ (see **242**), the title of which is crossed through on the piano score and replaced by 'Symphony in E♭ | (Sketch)'. *Full score*: 'Symphony in E♭'. *Printed score*: 'Symphony in E flat' (original issue); 'First Symphony' (reissues after the publication of the Second Symphony).
Date: *Short score*: I. 'April 27th 1921'; II. 'April 1, 1922' [*sic*]; III. 'Fine June 30th 1921'. *Full score*: I and II undated; III. 'Fine | Oct 8 th | 1922.' (the '8' perhaps altered from a '7'). In response to an enquiry from Christopher Whelen, Bax wrote that the work was composed 'altogether in London'.
Dedication: *Full score only*: 'To John Ireland'.
Orchestra: 4(1)+b.fl. 2+1 (heck. or b.ob.) 3(E♭)+1 2+1 (contrabass sarr. or d.bsn.), 4331, timp. (doubled if possible at 74:2ff in movt. II), 5 perc. (b.d., t.d., s.d., tamb., cym., gong, tri., bells, xyl., gl., cel.), 2 hps., str.
Manuscript: *Short score*: BL (Add. MS 54724); [20] ff.; 39 pp. (1-17 + 1 blank, [1-8], [1-13]); AL 12 paper (360 × 265). Annotations for orchestration throughout. *Full score*: BL (Add. MS 54725); 93 ff.; 127 pp. (1-59, 60-84, 85-127) + 5 blank; AL 29a paper (trimmed to 359 × 260); bound by the BL with upper cover of brown wrappers bearing Harriet Cohen's writing bound in. There are conductors' marks in blue pencil and cues for instruments replacing b.fl. and heck. added by Bax in red ink. The foliation (ff. 1-93) includes numerous cancels, most of them minor amendments on scraps of paper pasted over the original.
Publication: MM (335), 1923, fo. and 8vo, 122 pp.; CH (37133), 1943; WC0143C (A3 size); WC0143CX (A4 size); SMC (st.sc.).
Performance: London Symphony Orchestra, Albert Coates; Queen's Hall; 2 December 1922. 'MUSIC OF NOBLE HATRED. GRIEF AND TRAGEDY IN NEW BAX SYMPHONY. AUDIENCE MOVED. FIRST IMPRESSIONS MARKED AND POWERFUL' (*Pall Mall Gazette* headline, 5 December 1922). 'Wonderful New Work Performed at Queen's Hall' (*Daily Chronicle* headline, 5 December 1922).
Adaptation: Part of the score was used for the ballet *Oscar* (see **110** for details).

Duration: 36'44.
Note: For details of the origins of this work see **242**. In a programme note for a Cleveland Orchestra performance in January 1926, Bax wrote that 'the fierce, almost defiant character of the first two themes colours the music of this introductory section, and seems to suggest some conflict. . . . In the development section the music seems to express in still more emphatic a fashion the idea of strife.' Of the second movement he wrote: 'Here the mood is both mystic and elegiac. . . . At the outset two clashing tonalities are sounded faintly . . . with an accompanying rhythm from side drum (played with snares loosened, as at a military funeral). Then the cellos and basses give out a lamenting phrase; the principal subject follows, announced by muted trombones and tuba, with a continuation, a dirge-like phrase for trombones, over a rhythm in lower strings.' In a letter to Julian Herbage dating from April 1934, Bax unwisely sanctioned a cut 'between the second bar p 37 to the fifth bar p 40 as the composer believes that the shape of the first movement is thereby considerably improved.' In a letter to Adrian Boult dated 5 November 1942, Bax wrote: 'I rather think that funeral march is one of my best slow movements.'

257 MEDITERRANEAN for orchestra

Date: Orchestrated specifically for the concert at which it was first performed.
Dedication: *Printed score*: 'To Gustav Holst.'
Orchestra: 20 2+1 2020, 4000, timp., 3 perc. (tamb., cast., gl.), hp., str.
Manuscript: Not traced.
Publication: MM (334), 1923, fo., 19 pp.; CH (40846), [1943].
Performance: Goossens Orchestra, Eugene Goossens; Queen's Hall; 13 November 1922 ('Concert of Recent Works by Arnold Bax').
Duration: 3'05.
Note: For details of the original piano version see **233**.

258 QUINTET for oboe, 2 violins, viola and cello

I. Tempo molto moderato—Allegro moderato. II. Lento espressivo. III. Allegro giocoso.

Date: I. 'Nov 1st 1922'. II. Undated. III. 'Christmas | 1922'.
Dedication: '(To Leon Goossens)'.
Manuscript: UCC; [16] ff.; 30 pp. (1-9, 10-17, 18-29) + 1 blank except for the five clefs in the left margin: Bax intended to write the final bar on this page but decided to squeeze it on to the end of the previous page instead; AL 12 paper (357 × 260); inserted into a manila card folder.
Publication: MM (*score*: 384; *parts*: 385), 1925, 4to, 19 pp. Two impressions were issued, the earlier with a Celtic design in place of the AB ligature used

on nearly all other MM issues of Bax's music; CH (39493), [1950]; *score*: WC0009C; *parts*: WC0009; *extra part*: WC0009E.
Performance: Léon Goossens (ob.), Kutcher Quartet: Samuel Kutcher (vn.), George Whitaker (vn.), James Lockyer (va.), Ambrose Gauntlett (vc.); Hyde Park Hotel; 11 May 1924 (Mrs Adèle Maddison Chamber Concert).
Arrangement: By Sir John Barbirolli as a Concerto for oboe and string orchestra (unpublished). There is no full score: Barbirolli appears to have conducted from a printed score of the quintet, and the string-players from the original printed parts, with original double-stopping played 'divisi'. The extra bass part, copied out by hand, is held in the Royal Northern College of Music, Manchester. *Performance*: Evelyn Rothwell (ob.), Hallé Orchestra, Sir John Barbirolli; Free Trade Hall, Manchester; 21 April 1968.
Duration: 18'06.
Note: When Barbirolli suggested the idea of arranging this work, Bax was delighted and, according to Lady Barbirolli, 'did not even wish to see the arrangement but said he would leave it entirely to my husband.' However, it was not until about fourteen years after Bax's death that the arrangement came into being, and Lewis Foreman recalls that Harriet Cohen was 'very bothered by the proposal'. Léon Goossens had previously asked Bax to arrange the quintet as a concerto himself, but nothing came of it (see Carole Rosen, *The Goossens: A Musical Century*, London, 1993, p. 127).

259 A CELTIC SONG CYCLE for voice and piano (second version of 63)

Date: 1922 inferred from the date of publication.
Dedication: *Printed score*: 'To Miss Gladys Lees' (on each song).
Manuscript: Bax's minor revisions made on a set of pulls from the original plates: JWC. 'A Celtic Lullaby' has no alterations.
Publication: JWC (3869 A—E), 1922, fo., 29 pp. Also issued separately. 'New edition, carefully revised, and in some passages slightly altered, by the composer' (advertisement in *The Chesterian*, 28, January 1923, pp. 122-3).

260 THE HAPPY FOREST for orchestra

Title: *Piano score*: 'The Happy Forest.' 'After a prose poem by | Herbert Farjeon.' *Full score*: 'Nature-Poem | The Happy Forest'.
Date: *Piano score*: 'May 13th 1914'. *Full score*: Undated, but listed as 1922 in *Gr5*, etc. The programme note for the first performance (July 1923) mentions that it 'was only recently completed'.
Dedication: *Piano score*: '(To Herbert Farjeon)'. *Full score*: 'To Eugene Goossens' (written in a different kind of ink—now faded—from the rest, suggesting that it was added later).

Orchestra: 3(1) 2+1 2+E♭+1 2+1, 4331, timp., 4 perc. (b.d., tamb., cym., xyl., gl., cel.), hp., str.
Manuscript: *Piano score*: see **157** for details. *Full score*: BL (Add. MS 50177); 23 ff. (+ f. i: a blank leaf with an old printed label stuck on bearing the title and composer's name); 43 pp. + 1 blank + 1 with f.sc. pencil sketches for the passage from bars 5-10 (incl.) after fig. (6) + 1 blank; AL 18a paper (trimmed to 348 × 257); bound by the BL. There are conductors' and engravers' marks throughout.
Publication: MM (392), 1925, fo., 43 pp.
Performance: The Goossens Orchestra, Eugene Goossens; Queen's Hall; 3 July 1923 (concert in aid of the funds of the Great Ormond Street Hospital for Sick Children).
Adaptation: As a ballet with choreography by Bice Bellairs. *Performance*: Bellairs Ballet, Guildford Municipal Orchestra, Vernon Handley; Civic Hall, Guildford, Surrey; 19 March 1964.
Duration: 9'52.
Note: For details of the original piano version see **157**. Henry Coates's programme note to the first performance is clearly based on material supplied by Bax:

> This work by Mr. Arnold Bax was only recently completed. It was inspired by a fantastic prose-poem of the same name by Mr. Herbert Farjeon, the composer intending his score to be a 'musical counterpart', to use his own expression, of the poem.
>
> The latter is too long for reproduction here, and in any case Mr. Bax prefers the music to be listened to apart from the poet's lines, and to tell its own tale.
>
> The piece was first planned as a work for pianoforte, but never appeared in this form and was eventually evolved into an orchestral work. It takes the form of a Scherzo and Trio, and is so simple in construction that its composer deems any detailed analysis unnecessary.
>
> The sub-title of the work, 'A Nature Poem', sufficiently indicates the scope of the music, and one may add that its aim is to depict the delicate charm of the early days of May in woodland country. . . .

261 LYRICAL INTERLUDE for 2 violins, 2 violas, 1 cello (second version of movt. II from Quintet in G (107))

Title: The above title was given to this movement when it was revised.
Date: *Originally version*: 'Glencolumcille | Beltaine [May] 1908'. Revised version assigned to 1922 on the strength of the publication date (1923).
Dedication: *Printed score*: 'To R. Vaughan Williams'.
Manuscript: Revised version not traced.
Publication: MM (333), 1923, fo., 10 pp.
Performance: Believed to have been played *c.* 1930. *Earliest traced*: Music Group of London; br. on Radio 3, 15 September 1972.
Duration: 11'50.

262 THE MARKET GIRL for voice and piano

Date: *Gr5*: '1922'.
Text: Thomas Hardy, 'The Market-Girl' (hyphen omitted on printed score).
Manuscript: Not traced.
Publication: MM (296), 1922, 4to, 7 pp.; CH (46449). Also in *Twelve Songs for Medium/High Voice and Piano*, TP, 1984, 4to, pp. 40-3.
Duration: 1'47.

263 THE BOAR'S HEAD for men's voices (TTBB)

Date: *Printed score*: 'Jan. | 1923'.
Dedication: 'Dedicated to the Blackpool Festival Committee.'
Text: Anonymous, 15th century (according to the score) or 16th century (according to Green, *The Early English Carols*, p. 380). The words (in modernized form) are taken from the same source as those of *Mater, ora Filium* (**246**) and *Now is the Time of Christymas* (**247**), viz. Balliol MS 354 (f. 228). The carol has verses partly in Latin, partly in English, and is associated with the feast held in The Queen's College, Oxford, at which a boar's head is brought in on a silver salver. This commemorates the occasion when a student is said to have been confronted by a wild boar, which he asphyxiated by shoving his volume of Aristotle down its throat.
Manuscript: Not traced.
Publication: MM (328), 1923, 8vo, 7 pp.; CH, 1943(?) (3841).
Performance: [Choir];[92] Old Opera House, Blackpool; 20 October 1923.
Duration: 2'31.
Note: This was written for the male-voice choirs class (tenor lead) at the Blackpool Festival, which was won by the Warrington Male Choral Union.

264 TO THE NAME ABOVE EVERY NAME for soprano solo, chorus (SATB) and orchestra

Date: *MS vocal score*: 'March | 16th 1923'. *MS full score*: 'Fine | May | 1923' (the '3' almost illegible).
Text: Richard Crashaw, 'To the Name above every Name'.
Orchestra: 3(1) 2+1 2+1 2+1, 4331, timp., 3 perc. (b.d., s.d., cym., gong, tri., gl.), org., hp., str.
Manuscript: *Vocal score*: BL (Add. MS 50179); 20 ff.; 31 pp. (pp. 1-27 are paginated, p. 27 having only one system on it, as far as bar 3 after (34); the next page (f. 17v) is blank; f. 18 is paginated 17; ff. 18v-19v are paginated 29-31 in pencil (not by Bax); f. 20 is paginated 11 by Bax and contains the original

[92] Sung as a test piece at the festival; it has not been possible to determine which choir sang it first.

version of the passage from bar 1 before (14) to 9 after (14) but written in D♭ instead of C♯, the revised version being on f. 8ᵛ (p. 10); f. 20ᵛ is blank); AL 14a paper (355 × 263). There are instructions from Bax to the engraver in red ink about 'small notes' for subsidiary parts and for unaccompanied choral passages doubled in the piano part for rehearsal purposes; these are also written out in red on pp. 13-14. *Full score*: SA; [38] ff.; 74 pp. + 2 blank; AL 29a paper (360 × 262); bound. *Copyist's full score*: BL (Document Supply Centre (formerly Lending Division) acquired from CH); [48] ff.; t.p. + 1 blank + 93 pp. + 1 blank; 32-staff paper. *Parts*: CH.
Publication: *Vocal score only*: MM (no pl.no.) [1923], 8vo, 36 pp.
Performance: Agnes Nicholls (sop.), Combined Choirs of Worcester, Hereford and Gloucester, London Symphony Orchestra, Sir Ivor Atkins; Worcester Cathedral; 5 September 1923 (Three Choirs Festival).
Duration: 20'12.

265 SONATA for cello and piano

I. Moderato—Allegro passionato. II. Poco lento. III. Molto vivace ma non troppo.

Title: *MS*: 'Sonata for violincello [*sic*] | and Piano'.
Date: 'Nov 7th 1923.'
Dedication: *MS and MM score*: 'To Beatrice Harrison'. In the late 1940s Bax wrote to the Dutch cellist and composer Henri van Marken telling him that he was going to rededicate the sonata to him, but neither the MS nor copies of the printed score were altered.
Manuscript: BL (Add. MS 50180); 31 ff. (ff. 8, 19, 22, 24, 25, 27, 28 and 31 are cancels, amendments that Bax has stuck over the original; f. 30ᵛ is blank); t.p. + 43 pp. (1-17, 18-27, 28-43 + 1 blank); AL 12 paper (trimmed to 360 × 263); bound by the BL, with brown wrappers bound in; there is a pencilled note in Bax's hand below the title asking the engraver not to put in bowing marks for the first proof. Also bound in at the back is a copyist's cello part: foliated 32-6; 10 pp.; 2a paper (335 × 272); there are pencilled notes in German.
Publication: MM (388), 1925, 4to, 38 pp.; CH (37932), [1946]; WC0295.
Performance: Beatrice Harrison (vc.), Harriet Cohen (pf.); Wigmore Hall; 26 February 1924. 'The Sonata was finely played, and a large audience called the artists and the composer several times.' ('Crescendo', *The Star*, 28 February 1924). '. . . the composer was no less warmly recalled at the end than his admirable interpreters.' (*The Manchester Guardian*, 27 February 1924). 'At its close the players received an ovation, and so many floral and other offerings that the attendants in the end grew tired of handing them on to the stage, and disappeared with them through the swing doors.' (*The Morning Post*, 27 February 1924).
Duration: 33'54.

Note: Bax was delighted with Beatrice Harrison's playing at the first performance:

I want to write you a line to thank you again for your *perfect* playing on Tuesday. You are quite an inspiring person and I should really like to write more music for the cello if *you* will play it. I never can tell about my own works—and with regard to the sonata I went through many different moods. Sometimes I very nearly tore it up and then I would feel sorry for it—as it were—and affectionate towards it. It gave me so much trouble that I could not tell, when it was finished, what kind of first impression it would make—and whether it would be difficult to follow or not. . . . I wonder what he [the *Daily Telegraph* critic] means by that allusion to 'The [*sic*] Shropshire Lad'. For me this passage is darkly and densely obscure.

The opening of movt. II is a transcription of bars 3-35 of *Spring Fire* (**153**).

266 I SING OF A MAIDEN: Part-song for five unaccompanied voices (SAATB)

Date: *Gr5*: '1923'.
Dedication: *Printed score*: '(To J.B. McEwan.)' (corrected on reprints to 'McEwen').
Text: Anonymous, 15th century. From MS Sloane 2593 in the BL; printed in Arthur Quiller-Couch (ed.), *The Oxford Book of English Verse 1250-1900* (Oxford, 1919), pp. 34-5.
Manuscript: Not traced.
Publication: MM (440), 1926, 8vo, 14 pp.; CH (38732), [1948?]. With piano for rehearsal only.
Performance: Not traced.
Duration: 5'13.
Note: Although apparently written for five solo voices, this work is more often sung by five-part chorus.

1924

267 ST PATRICK'S BREASTPLATE for chorus (SATB) and orchestra

Title: *MS vocal score*: 'St. Patrick's Breastplate | (Lúireach Naoimh Pádraig)' [the Gaelic part in Irish script] | Chorus and Orchestra.' *MS full score*: 'St Patrick's Breastplate.'
Date: *MS vocal score*: 'Dec 1923.' *Full score*: Undated, but presumably 1924.
Text: 'From the Irish Gaelic' (MS v.sc. and printed sc.), perhaps translated by Bax himself (see **Note** below). The Gaelic text dates from the eighth century and, although usually referred to as 'St Patrick's Lorica [breastplate]', has no direct connection with the patron saint of Ireland.
Orchestra: 3(1) 2+1 2+1 2+1, 4331, timp., 3 perc. (b.d., s.d., cym., gl.), hp., str.

Manuscript: *Vocal score*: UCD (MS 26/2); [15] ff.; 30 pp.; AL 12 paper (360 × 263). The pages are loose except for pp. 21-4, and there are pencilled notes for the orchestration; the piano part doubling the chorus for rehearsal only is in red ink, and there is a date stamp of 4 June 1924. *Full score*: CH (MS 242); [31] ff.; 59 pp. + 5 blank; AL 29a paper (360 × 262); bound in mid-green cloth with composer's name and title down spine, but pages no longer stitched in.
Publication: *Vocal score only*: MM (no pl.no.), [1924], 8vo, 34 pp.; CH (39281), [1949]; WC0269.
Performance: Philharmonic Choir, Orchestra of the Royal Philharmonic Society, Charles Kennedy Scott; Queen's Hall; 21 May 1925.
Duration: 15'06.
Note: Since no ackowledgement is made on the published score to a translator, Bax may have translated the text himself. The extent of his knowledge of Irish Gaelic is summarized in an unpublished letter, probably dating from the early 1930s, in The Pierpoint Morgan Library, New York (MFC B355.X (3)). 'Keith', to whom it is addressed, is clearly a Gaelophone since Bax includes several sentences in Irish. 'I am not an Irish-speaker, alas, though I ought to be for I began to study the language in 1907. An incurable (inherited) shyness has always prevented me from making a fool of myself in the presence of bi-lingual people. I can read Irish Gaelic quite easily . . . but I am no scholar, I assure you.' In an interview broadcast on Irish radio in 1947, Bax told Eamonn Andrews: 'I never got very far with it in the matter of speaking, but I can read it pretty easily', and this is confirmed by the large number of Gaelic books owned by Bax that are now in the library of UCD. He was able to take down folksongs sung in the Donegal dialect—the MS of 'Na bearta cruach' is in UCC—and there is a holograph Gaelic–English vocabulary book in private possession. Another MS in UCC contains the first nine pages of a translation into Irish by Bax ('Ardhghail Bacs') and Donnall Gillespie of Synge's *The Shadow of the Glen* (see Appendix 7, section I). The reference in LF, p. 91, to Bax's irritating George Russell by speaking in Gaelic is spurious (see *FMY*, p. 97).

268 I HEARD A SOLDIER for baritone or mezzo-soprano and piano

Date: 'March 31st | 1924'.
Dedication: *Printed score only*: 'To W. Grant Oliver.'
Text: Herbert Trench, 'I Heard a Soldier'.
Manuscript: BL (Add. MS 54779); ff. 37-40 (40v blank); [5] pp. + 1 blank + 1 p. with titles (see below) + 1 blank; AL 12 paper (330 × 243); in brown wrappers with Harriet Cohen's writing on the front. On f. 40 there is a list of ten poems with their authors' names written in Bax's hand that has been crossed through: '"Glamour" | (Dermot O'Byrne) | "I heard a Soldier" |

(Herbert Trench) | "Morfydd" | (Lionel Johnson)[93] | A Patriot | (Æ) | "Dermot Donn McMorna" | (P. Colm) | "To an Isle in the Water" | (W.B. Yeats) | "A New Being" | (Æ) | "The Splendour falls on Castle-walls" | (Tennyson) | A Lyke Wake Dirge | (Traditional) | Wild Almond (Herbert Trench)'. It is not possible to determine whether this is a list of poems or, since seven of the ten titles had been set by Bax, a list of songs that he had written, of which three have not been traced. The first suggestion seems more probable since the three 'missing' titles do not appear in any lists of works published during Bax's lifetime.
Publication: MM (436), 1926, 4to, 7 pp. Also in *Twelve Songs for Medium/High Voice and Piano*, TP, 1984, 4to, pp. 34-9.
Duration: 3'33.

269 WILD ALMOND for voice and piano

Title: 'Wild Almond (Scherzo)'.
Date: 'April 1924'.
Text: Herbert Trench, 'Wild Almond'.
Manuscript: BPL; [4] ff.; 6 pp. (p. 1 unpag.) + 1 blank + 1 with pencil sketches for an unidentified orchestral work; AL 14a paper (355 × 263); loosely inserted into a brown folder with an inscription to 'Ben & Peter' (Britten and Pears) on the front in Harriet Cohen's hand. Unpublished.
Performance: Jenevora Williams (sop.), John Thwaites (pf.); Big School, Christ's Hospital, Horsham; 18 May 1996 (second day of 'The Bax Weekend': part of the 'Horsham and District Arts Fanfare Weekend 1996').
Duration: 3'11.
Note: For details of the orchestrated version see **326**.

c. 1924

270 [UNTITLED]: Sketches

Note: These are to be found on p. [8] of 'Wild Almond' (**269**). They seem to have no connection with any extant work.

1925

271 STRING QUARTET NO. 2

I. Allegro. II. Lento molto espressivo. III. Allegro vivace—Lento.

Date: I. 'Glencolumcille Dec 18th 1924'. II. 'Jan 13 th 1925'. III. 'Feb 5 th | 1925.'

[93] This could refer to one of two poems by Johnson: 'To Morfydd' or 'To Morfydd dead'.

Dedication: *Printed score only*: 'To RALPH VAUGHAN WILLIAMS.'
Manuscript: BL (Add. MS 54763); [20] ff.; 40 pp. (1-18, 19-27, 28-40); AL 14c paper (353 × 263); loosely inserted into brown wrappers with Harriet Cohen's writing on the front cover. Most of movt. I is written in light blue ink but some passages are in a darker ink and were obviously filled in later. Four bars in movt. II (7-10 after fig. 8) have been crossed through.
Publication: MM (462), 1927, 4to, 35 pp.
Performance: New Philharmonic Quartet: Bessie Rawlins (vn.), Christopher Southward (vn.), Winifred Stiles (va.), Brenda Sichel (vc.); Grotrian Hall (called Steinway Hall until 1925); 15 March 1927. 'It is rather a turgid work.' (*The Times*, 18 March 1927.) 'It had the advantage of an excellently vivid performance, and the composer was twice called to the platform.' ('Crescendo' in *The Star*, 16 March 1927.) '. . . intonation and ensemble were all that could be desired,' (*The Daily Telegraph*, 16 March 1927). '[There was] a certain disturbance of the perfect balance necessary to the ideal playing of chamber music.' (*The Morning Post*, 18 March 1927.) 'It was extremely well played, and very cordially received.' (*The Daily News*, 16 March 1927.)
Duration: 30'47.
Note: After hearing a performance of this work in 1951, Bax wrote to Christopher Whelen:

> My second quartet was an outstanding adventure to me the other day. I had not heard it nor thought of it for about twenty years and had almost entirely forgotten it—and had no idea what was coming next. It was like listening to a new work by someone. I must say I enjoyed it . . .

272 CARREY CLAVEL for voice and piano

Title: *MS*: 'Carry [*sic*] Clavel.'
Date: 'August 6th | 1925.'
Dedication: *Printed score only*: 'To W. Grant Oliver.'
Text: Thomas Hardy, 'To Carrey Clavel'.
Manuscript: BL (Add. MS 50181); 2 ff.; [4] pp.; AL 14c paper (354 × 262); bound by the BL with brown wrappers bound in bearing Harriet Cohen's writing on the front.
Publication: MM (427), 1926, 4to, 7 pp. Also in *Twelve Songs for Medium/High Voice and Piano*, TP, 1984, 4to, pp. 52-6.
Duration: 1'40.

273 ETERNITY for voice and piano

Date: *MS*: 'Sept 6th 1925.'
Dedication: *Printed score only*: 'To W. Grant Oliver.'
Text: Robert Herrick, 'Eternity'.

Manuscript: *Sketch*: Privately owned (formerly by Colin Scott-Sutherland); [1] f.; [2] pp. (the second mostly full of unidentifiable material); pencil; AL 14c paper (354 × 262). These are clearly Bax's initial jottings for the song; there are no words written down. *Complete*: BL (Add. MS 54779); ff. 41-2^{v}; 4 pp.; AL 14a paper (trimmed to 355 × 260); bound with 14 other songs (see **133** above) and with the original brown wrappers bearing Harriet Cohen's writing on the front bound in.
Publication: MM (433), 1926, 4to, 7 pp.; CH (38529), [1947]. Also in *Twelve Songs for Medium/High Voice and Piano*, TP, 1984, 4to, pp. 57-61.
Duration: 3'39.
Note: For details of the version for voice and orchestra see **330**.

274 CORTÈGE for orchestra

Title: 'Cortége' [*sic*]. In 1935 Bax referred to the work as 'Barbaric Cortege' (see **Note** below).
Date: 'Geneva | 1925.'
Dedication: 'To Herbert Hughes' (written, unusually, to the right of the title in place of Bax's name, which does not appear on the score).
Orchestra: 3(1) 2+1 3+1 2+1, 4331 2 crnts. in B♭, timp., 4 perc. (b.d., s.d., tamb., cym., gong, tri.), hp., str.
Manuscript: CH (MS 237); [18] ff.; 33 pp. (p. 1 unnumbered) + 3 blank; AL 29a paper (360 × 262); bound in mid-green cloth with composer's name and title in gold up spine (bound in March 1926, according to a note tipped in at the end). Unpublished. *Parts*: CH.
Performance: (1) *Semi-professional*: Kensington Symphony Orchestra, Leslie Head; St John's, Smith Square; 29 January 1972 (Vaughan Williams Centenary Concert). (2) *Professional*:[94] London Philharmonic Orchestra, Bryden Thomson; All Saints' Church, Tooting; 10 January 1986 (recording session for Chandos Records Ltd.).
Duration: 5'43.
Note: Unusually for Bax, only the year of composition is given on the MS, but since it was completed in Geneva it must date from November or December of 1925; he is known to have been in Switzerland at that time with Harriet Cohen, who had gone there for medical treatment. In a letter to his brother Clifford he wrote: 'My imagination seems to be chloroformed . . . my one resource is an endless (and I fear unsatisfactory) piece of orchestration.' *Cortège* is thus the only orchestral work by Bax completed outside the British Isles. (The Second Symphony was partly written in

[94] The first professional performance advertised as part of the 'Great British Music Festival', with the LPO conducted by Vernon Handley at the Royal Festival Hall on 14 November 1983, did not take place; Bax's *London Pageant* was played instead.

Geneva but mostly in London.) In a letter to Adrian Boult dated 3 March 1935, Bax wrote:

By the way, would you care to do a first performance of a very short thing of mine called 'Barbaric Cortege' sometime next season? It is all *the d[euce]*[95] *of a row* (with two cornets added to the wind orchestra), but it may sound exhilarating, and is the kind of piece for the beginning or end of a concert. I would rather you did it than anyone else, because it will want care in the arrangement of the din!

Boult replied that he would be delighted to arrange a performance—'It all sounds exciting!'—but nothing seems to have come of it.

c. 1925?

275 BLOW NORTHERN WIND for voice and piano

Note: The score of this song has not been traced. The title is listed only in *MGG*, but with no further details given. A translation by Clifford Bax of this Old English poem was made in 1925 ('Old Song' in *Farewell my Muse*, London, 1932, pp. 86-7), and the dating of the song to *c.* 1925 is based solely on the supposition that this is the version set. But it may equally well have been another version, perhaps the one in Quiller-Couch (ed.), *The Oxford Book of English Verse*, pp. 5-7, which immediately precedes the poem 'This World's Joy', set by Bax in 1922 (**254**).

1926

276 SYMPHONY NO. 2 IN E MINOR AND C for orchestra

I. Molto moderato—Allegro moderato. II. Andante. III. Poco largamente—Allegro feroce.

Title: *Short score*: 'Symphony in E minor.' *Full score MS*: 'Second Symphony'. *Printed score*: 'Second Symphony in E minor and C'.
Date: *Short score*: 'Oct 10th 1924.' *Full score*: 'London | March 1926.' In response to an enquiry from Christopher Whelen, Bax wrote that the work was composed in 'London and Geneva' (see under *Cortège*, **274**).
Dedication: *Printed score only*: 'To Serge Koussevitsky [*sic*]'.
Orchestra: 3(1) 2+1 3+1 2+1, 4331 ten. tba. in B♭, timp., 4 perc. (b.d., s.d., tamb., cym., gong, xyl., gl., cel.), org., pf., 2 hps., str.
Manuscript: *Short score*: BL (Add. MS 54726); 29 ff.; for pagin. see below; AL 14c paper except f. 25, which is AL 12a paper (all trimmed to 354 × 260); bound by the BL with front brown wrappers with Harriet Cohen's

[95] Or '*d[evil]*': the word has had a hole punched through it in attaching the paper to the file.

writing bound in at the front. There are notes for the orchestration, and there are many erasures and additions tipped in or pasted over. Movt. I is paginated 1-8, followed by a folio (f. 5) tipped in (verso blank); then pp. 9-12 followed by ¾ of a folio tipped in (verso blank); then pp. 13-17; ff. 8, 10-12, 14-16 are scraps of paper tipped in bearing amendments in ink, ff. 8, 15 and 16 having pencil sketches on the versos (8 and 16 for passages in movt. II, obviously torn from an earlier pencil draft for the symphony). Movt. II is paginated 18-24 (in pencil, not by Bax). Movt. III (again not pagin. by Bax) begins on the fourth system of p. 24; the fourth system of p. 32 ('Tempo di Marcia') and first seven bars of p. 33 are crossed through; p. 33 has another folio (f. 25) tipped in in front of it (verso blank) that contains the beginning of the epilogue; f. 27 has pencil sketches for the epilogue; ff. 27^v, 28 and 29 are blank; ff. 28^v and 29^v contain a few unidentifiable pencil sketches written upside down.

Full score: BL (Add. MS 54727); 86 ff.; unstaved free front endpaper with a list of instruments required written on the reverse + 150 pp. (1-73 + 1 blank, 74-107, 108-50 + 3 blank); AL 29a paper (360 × 262); bound, with a label pasted on to the last page indicating that the score was originally bound in March 1929; the present binding was done by the BL. There are conductors' marks. The violin solo starting on p. 149 of the printed score does not appear in the MS and was obviously added at proof stage.

Publication: MM (510), 1929, fo., 153 pp.; *c.* 1934, 8vo.; CH (37134), 1943, 8vo.; WC0139C (A3 size); WC0139CX (A4 size); SMC (st.sc. in preparation). *Printer's pulls*: CH (MS 780).

Performance: (1) Boston Symphony Orchestra, Serge Koussevitzky; Symphony Hall, Boston; 13 December 1929. (2) An *ad hoc* orchestra drawn from the BBC Symphony Orchestra, the London Symphony Orchestra and the Philharmonic Orchestra,[96] Eugene Goossens; Queen's Hall; 30 May 1930. 'Debonair Eugene Goossens triumphed . . . yesterday afternoon with a "nameless" orchestra of 110 performers, magnificent quality and unusually superb balance.' (*The Daily Express*, 31 May 1930.) '. . . a disgracefully small audience . . . [It] had a very warm reception.' (Alfred Kalisch, *The Star*, 31 May 1930).

Adaptation: A proposed ballet by Walter Gore based on the symphony was advertised for the London Festival Ballet's 1972 season at the London Coliseum, but it failed to materialize.

Duration: 41'42.

Note: In an undated letter to Holst—the only one from Bax found among his papers after his death—he wrote:

[96] Sometimes referred to as the Royal Philharmonic Orchestra. There is no connection with the present orchestra of that name, which was founded in 1946.

It interests me that you feel you like No III the better of the two [symphonies]—because just now I can't compare them.[97] No II is associated with so much trouble and unhappiness that I felt very grateful to Eugene for his brilliant performance of it, which lifted it at last for me into a purely abstract world. So for the moment I feel perhaps unduly tender towards its grim features. No III is the outcome of a much calmer state of mind.

On 5 November 1931, Barbirolli played the work at a Royal Philharmonic Society concert in which Bax was presented with the Society's gold medal, prompting the composer to reflect: 'Personally I rather think that symphony is the most sustained and concentrated that I have done, but it is too oppressive in mood ever to become popular.' (Letter to May Harrison.) To Richard Church he confided: 'I was going through absolute *hell* when I wrote it . . . I was certainly not remembering emotion in tranquillity'.

277 ROMANTIC OVERTURE for chamber orchestra

Title: *Short score*: 'Romantic Overture for | Small Orchestra'. *Full score*: 'Romantic Overture for | Chamber Orchestra'.
Date: *Short score*: Undated. *Full score*: 'April 1926' (crossed through in blue pencil by the engraver).
Dedication: *Printed score only*: 'To Frederick Delius.'
Orchestra: 2(1)122, 2100, pf., str.
Manuscript: *Short score*: BL (Add. MS 54748); [6] ff.; 11 pp. + 1 p. containing pencil sketches on six two-bar systems: Nos. 1 and 4-6 are unidentifiable, No. 2 is bars 18-22 of the overture, and No. 3 is bars 5-11 of movt. II from the *Fantasy Sonata* for viola and harp (**284**); AL 14c paper (354 × 262); loosely inserted in a bifolium of ALP 18 paper (355 × 262). Bar 2:4 (1 after (C)) is a cancel taped over the original. Bar 3 after (E) is an afterthought pencilled above the surrounding bars. Bars 5:12-13 are crossed through in blue pencil, and bars 5:14-20 (2 after (H)) are on a cancel glued at the edges over the original. The score contains a few pencilled notes for the orchestration. *Full score*: BL (Add. MS. 54749); 15 ff.; 29 pp. + 1 blank; AL 29a paper (360 × 262); loosely inserted within a bifolium of ALM 16 paper (359 × 270). The engravers' marks are in pencil, blue pencil and ink.
Publication: MM (463), 1928, fo., 35 pp.
Performance: Rae Robertson (pf.), Chenil Chamber Orchestra, John Barbirolli; New Chenil Galleries, Kings Road; 18 January 1927. Three days later Bax wrote to Armstrong Gibbs: 'The performance was fine, and I think that if he remains as enthusiastic and conscientious as he is at present

[97] The Third Symphony had been premièred over two months before the first British performance of the Second Symphony.

Barbirolli is going to be a very important figure in the conducting world.' (From a letter in BPL.)
Duration: 12'26.
Note: This work was composed while Bax was staying with Philip Heseltine at Eynsford. In a letter received at the BBC on 11 September 1935 he wrote: 'I am glad you like the Romantic Overture, for I enjoyed writing it I remember.' At letter H there is a two-bar allusion to the motto theme from Franck's Symphony, which Heseltine had lampooned in 'The Old Codger', the fourth of his *Codpieces* for piano (1916-17).

278 WALSINGHAME for tenor, soprano obbligato, chorus (SATB) and orchestra

Date: *Vocal score*: 'Fine| May 1926.' *Full score*: 'May | 1926'.
Dedication: *Printed score only*: 'To Philip Heseltine.'
Text: 16th century. There seems to be some doubt about the attribution to Sir Walter Raleigh, which appears on the printed score. On the MS v.sc. Bax has written '16th century' only, and it is listed as anonymous in Quiller-Couch (ed.), *The Oxford Book of English Verse*, pp. 51-3, and in Clifford Bax (ed.), *Vintage Verse* (London, 1945), pp. 38-9; but *The Oxford Dictionary of Quotations*, 2nd edn. (Oxford, 1985), ascribes it to Raleigh. It was Philip Heseltine who introduced Bax to the poem when he was staying at Eynsford writing the *Romantic Overture* (**277**).
Orchestra: 2222, 4331, timp., 2 perc. (tamb., cym., cel.), hp., str.
Manuscript: *Sketch*: BL (Add. MS 54728); f. 19^v; [1] p.; AL 14c (355 × 262). This page is the verso of the last leaf in the short score of the Third Symphony (**297**) and contains sketches for the lines beginning 'Of womenkind such indeed is the love or the word love abused'. *Vocal score*: BL (Add. MS 54774); 7 ff.; 12 pp. + ½ folio (16 staves) attached to p. 7 by a rusty pin, with writing on the recto only: the nine bars between letters K and L are written out on four staves, that in the original are on two staves only, crossed through in pencil; AL 29a paper (360 × 262); loosely inserted into brown wrappers with Harriet Cohen's writing on the front cover. There are notes for the orchestration. *Full score*: CH (MS 250), [24] ff.; 42 pp. + 6 blank; AL 29a paper (360 × 261); loose in brown paper wrappers.
Publication: *Vocal score only*: MM (447), 1927, 8vo, 24 pp. *Parts*: CH.
Performance: Stuart Wilson (ten.), Philharmonic Choir, Philharmonic Orchestra (see p. 175 n.), Charles Kennedy Scott; Queen's Hall; 6 June 1929. 'A very good performance. It was played twice at the concert—somewhat unusual, but there seemed to be no objection.' (From a letter postmarked 16 June 1929 from Bax to Tilly Fleischmann.)
Duration: 18'02.

279 SONATA NO. 3 for piano

I. Allegro moderato. II. Lento moderato. III. Allegro.

Title: '3rd Sonata for Piano Solo | in G♯ minor'.
Date: I. Undated. II. 'Nov 9th 1926'. III. 'Nov 23rd 1926'.
Dedication: *Printed score only*: 'To Miss Harriet Cohen.'
Manuscript: BL (Add. MS 54767); ff. 26-41 (41v blank); 29 pp. (1-12, 13-20, 20-29, the last movement misnumbered 15-31 by Bax + 9 blank); AL 12 paper (trimmed to 350 × 258); bound by the BL with brown wrappers bound in bearing Harriet Cohen's handwriting; f. 33 is ⅓ of a leaf tipped in, the verso blank, containing a passage replacing the last ten bars of f. 32v; f. 34 is crossed through in pencil.
Publication: MM (518), 1929, 4to, 39 pp.; CH (37249), [1945]; WC0467.
Performance: (1) Harriet Cohen; Liverpool Centre of the British Music Society; 18 November 1927. '. . . brilliantly played . . .' (*The Musical Times*, January 1928, p. 67). (2) Harriet Cohen; Court House, Marylebone Lane, London, W1; 23 January 1928 (Contemporary Music Centre Concert). 'Few composers have ever written with more mastery of piano technique. . . . Miss Harriet Cohen interpreted the sonata quite admirably.' (*The Daily Telegraph*, 24 January 1928.)
Adaptation: As a ballet entitled *Unbowed*, with choreography by Sara Patrick and costumes and masks by Hugh Stevenson. *Performance*: Antony Tudor (as Cuchullain), Charles Lynch (pf.); Mercury Theatre; 10 July 1932 (presented by Marie Rambert for The Ballet Club). Other characters in the ballet were Laeg (Cuchullain's chariot-driver), the Washer at the Ford (a banshee), three Women of the Sidhe, three Water Spirits and the Apparition of Maeve. The synopsis was as follows:

Cuchullain going to battle against Maeve the warrior Queen meets with ill-omen: the banshee wails foreboding and the Sidhe gloat over coming disaster. Mortally wounded he returns to bind himself to a monolith that he may die unbowed.

According to Harriet Cohen, 'Bax did not think this experiment a success' (quoted in Julian Herbage, 'Sir Arnold Bax', in A. L. Bacharach (ed.), *British Music of our Time*, 2nd edn., Harmondsworth, 1951, p. 125).
Duration: 25'42.
Note: In a letter to John Simons postmarked 13 May 1935, Bax wrote: '[The sonata] gave me a lot of trouble . . . and as always when work does not come easily I always felt doubtful about it.'

280 [THREE CAROLS]: Arrangements for (a) baritone and piano; (b) contralto and piano; (c) voice, piano, flute and tambourine

a. Haut, haut, Peyrot. **b.** Laisse-quy tas aiffares. **c.** Guillô, pran ton tamborin.

Date: 1926 assumed from the date of their first performance. Not mentioned in any of the lists of Bax's works published during his lifetime.
Text: Bax's source for the melodies and words was presumably H. J. L. J. Massé and Charles Kennedy Scott (eds.), *A Book of Old Carols* (London, 1907); most of the carols had not previously been published in England. **a.** 'Haut, haut, Peyrot' is a 'Béarnais carol, words by Andichon, sung to a traditional tune given by Gustave Probst in his *Mélodies Béarnaises*'; see also C. L. Hutchins, *Carols Old and New* (London, [1916]), and *The Oxford Book of Carols* (London, 1928), No. 157. **b.** 'Laisse-quy tas aiffares' is a carol 'in the Besançon patois from the collection of Th. Bellamy'; the tune is still sung in the west of France to the words 'Laissez paître vos bêtes', and in this version is published in *The Oxford Book of Carols*, No. 140. **c.** 'Guillô, pran ton tamborin' is a 'Burgundian Noel sung to the air "Ma mère, mariez moi". Words by Bernard de la Monnoye (Gui-Barozai) edited by Monsieur F. Fertiault. It is quoted by [William] Sandys [*Christmas Carols, Ancient and Modern* . . . (London, 1833)]'; see *The Oxford Book of Carols*, No. 82.
Manuscript: Not traced. Unpublished.
Performance: Oriana Madrigal Society, Charles Kennedy Scott (with Joseph Slater (fl.) in **280c**); Æolian Hall; 14 December 1926.
Note: These arrangements are known only from newspaper reports of their première and of another performance at the Wigmore Hall on 16 December 1930. The titles and details of the forces used are listed in *The Daily Telegraph* for 15 December 1926. The decision to score the final carol for flute and piano was doubtless influenced by the inclusion in the programme of Bax's *Now is the Time of Christymas* (**247**), written for men's chorus, flute and piano. Bax writes a part for a tambourine in the third carol, but the 'tamborin' of the title is a narrow Provençal drum. The programme also included Bax's *This Worldes Joie*, and carols by Foggia, Deering, Holst, Charles Wood, Benjamin Dale, Kenneth G. Finlay, and one of the Nanini brothers. Half-way through the evening there was an interval for folk-dances given by the English Folk Dance Society. Bax's 'wistful arrangements' (as the *Morning Post* critic called them) came in the second half of the programme.

281 IN THE MORNING for voice and piano

Date: *Gr5*: '1926'.
Dedication: *Printed score*: 'To W. Grant Oliver.'
Text: A. E. Housman, *Last Poems*, XXIII.
Manuscript: Not traced.
Publication: MM (435), 1926, 4to, 6 pp. Also in *Twelve Songs for Medium/High Voice and Piano*, TP, 1984, 4to, pp. 16-19. Also in *A Century of English Song: An Anthology for Singers, 2: Ten Songs for Baritone and Piano*, TP (THA 978422), 1994, 4to, pp. 26-9.

Performance: Anne Thursfield (sop.), Ivor Newton (pf.); Wigmore Hall; 30 November 1927. 'The exquisite loveliness of this song . . . made her give a rendering that brought one to the verge of tears.' (*The Manchester Guardian*, 1 December 1927.)
Duration: 2'05.

282 ON THE BRIDGE for voice and piano

Date: *Gr5*: '1926'.
Text: Thomas Hardy, 'Sitting on the Bridge (Echo of an Old Song)'.
Manuscript: Not traced.
Publication: MM (428), 1926, 4to, 10 pp.; CH (38159), 1943. Also in *Twelve Songs for Medium/High Voice and Piano*, TP, 1984, 4to, pp. 44-51.
Performance: Anne Thursfield (sop.), Ivor Newton (pf.); Wigmore Hall; 30 November 1927.
Duration: 2'45.

283 OUT AND AWAY for voice and piano

Date: *Gr5*: '1926'.
Dedication: *Printed score*: 'To W. Grant Oliver.'
Text: James Stephens, 'Out and Away'.
Manuscript: Not traced.
Publication: MM (434), 1926, 4to, 7 pp.
Duration: 3'10.

1927

284 FANTASY SONATA for viola and harp

I. Allegro molto—II. Allegro moderato—III. Lento espressivo—IV. Allegro.

Title: *MS*: 'Fantasie Sonata'. First performed as 'Sonata in four linked movements'. Subsequently published as 'Fantasy Sonata'. On the MS it is for 'viola and harp'; on the printed score it is 'harp and viola'.
Date: 'April 1927'.
Dedication: 'To Madame Maria Korchinska.' (printed score only, although the MS does have her name and address written by Bax in pencil to the left of the title).
Manuscript: UCC; [19] ff.; 37 pp. (1-9, 9-14, 15-20 + 1 blank + [9] + 7 blank); AL 12 paper (355 × 260); inserted into a manila card folder. Movts. I and II are written in dark blue ink, but the 'poco più lento' on pp. 13–4 and movt. III are in a lighter blue, suggesting that he returned to the score after an interval; a few details in I and II are also in light blue. There are blue pencil and ink marks in Maria Korchinska's hand. A pencil sketch for bars

5-11 of movt. II can be found on the reverse of p. 11 of the short score of the *Romantic Overture* (**277**).
Publication: MM (465), 1927, 4to, 39 pp.; CH, [1946]; WC0465.
Performance: Raymond Jeremy (va.), Maria Korchinska (hp.); Grotrian Hall; 10 June 1927.
Arrangement: For viola and piano by Charles Matthews. Unpublished but recorded (see Appendix 3 for details).
Duration: 21'53.

285 THREE SONGS FROM THE NORSE for voice and piano

a. Irmelin Rose. **b.** Lad Vaaren komme. **c.** Venevil.

Date: *Copyist's score*: 'Summer 1927' (t.p.). **a.** 'April 16th | 1927'. **b.** 'April 20th | 1927'. **c.** 'June 1927'. Although at least two other works (**286** and **287**) were composed between **b** and **c** in this set, the songs are listed together here for convenience.
Dedication: 'To Lydia' (almost certainly Lydia Jellinek).
Text: **a.** J. P. Jacobsen, 'Irmelin Rose'. **b.** J. P. Jacobsen, 'Lad Vaaren komme' ['Let spring come']. **c.** Bjørnstjerne Bjørnsen, 'Venevil'.
Manuscript: *Holograph*: Not traced. *Copyist's score*: BL (Add. MS 54779); ff. 43-53v + 1 blank; t.p. + 1 blank + 1-5, 6-9, 10-20 + 2 blank; 16-staff paper (trimmed to 361 × 268); all bound with 14 other songs (see **133** above). In the same hand as the copyist's score of the *Suite on the Name Gabriel Fauré* (**362**); Harriet Cohen has pencilled in 'Harriet Cohen, C.B.E.' at the top right of the t.p. Words in Danish (**a, b**) and Norwegian (**c**) only. Facsimiles of this score are in KB (I 370) and SB. Unpublished.
Performance: (1) *Semi-private*: Tracey Chadwell (sop.), Pamela Lidiard (pf.); 'Little Slyfield', Cobham Road, Stoke d'Abernon, Surrey (the home of Susan and Aidan Woodcock); 5 January 1994. (2) *Public*: Same performers; Wigmore Hall; 18 January 1994.
Duration: **a.** 3'49. **b.** 3'16. **c.** 5'17.
Note: These songs do not appear in any of the lists of Bax's works published during his lifetime. Nielsen also made a setting of 'Irmelin Rose' (1891), and Delius set all three poems (1889-90, 1897).

286 CONCERTO IN D MINOR by Antonio Vivaldi (RV 540): Arrangement for harp and string quartet

I. Moderato. II. Lento. III. Allegro risoluto.

Title: *MS*: 'Concerto Vivaldi'. First performed as 'Concerto for Violin and Harp with String accompaniment'.
Date: 'May 8th 1927'.

Manuscript: Privately owned (formerly by Maria Korchinska); [7] ff.; [13] pp. (1-6, [1-3] + 1 blank, [1-4] + 2 blank); AL 29b paper (trimmed to 354 × 263). Bax's name does not appear on the MS.
Publication: *Parts only*: LM, 1978, 4to, 10 (harp), 4, 4, 4, 4 pp.[98]
Performance: Harp Ensemble: Maria Korchinska (hp.), Sybil Eaton (vn.), Edwin Virgo (vn.), Raymond Jeremy (va.), Cedric Sharpe (vc.); Grotrian Hall; 10 June 1927.
Duration: *c.* 10'00.
Note: Vivaldi's concerto (RV 540; F. XII/38; P. 266) was the third in a set played by the girls of the Ospedale della Pietà in Venice before the Crown Prince of Poland in 1740. The original scoring is for viola d'amore, lute and strings, and the MS is in the Sächsische Landesbibliothek in Dresden (D. 2389/0/4 (c)). A copy was made in 1880 and later deposited in the British Museum (Add. MS 31305, ff. 10-23b);[99] it was from this score that Bax made his rather free arrangement in 1927. The original was published in 1960 as vol. 320 of the collected works (Istituto Italiano Antonio Vivaldi, Edizioni Ricordi).

287 HARDANGER for two pianos

Date: *Printed score*: 'May 1927'.
Dedication: 'To Ethel Bartlett and Rae Robertson.'
Manuscript: Not traced.
Publication: MM (508), 1929, 4to, 11 pp.; CH (38452), [1947].
Performance: Ethel Bartlett, Rae Robertson; Æolian Hall; 2 February 1929.
Duration: 3'35.
Note: Hardanger is a district on the west coast of Norway, and Bax's piece is in the style of a Norwegian 'halling', a reel-like dance adopted by Grieg in several of his works. The legend 'With acknowledgments to Grieg' appears at the head of the score.

288 OVERTURE, ELEGY AND RONDO for orchestra

Title: First performed as 'Three Orchestral Pieces'.
Date: Bax's programme note: '. . . the summer of 1927'.
Dedication: *Printed score*: 'To Eugene Goossens'.
Orchestra: 3(1) 2+1 2+1 2+1, 4331, timp., 3 perc. (b.d., s.d., tamb., cym., gong, xyl., gl.),[100] hp., str. The following are cued in and may be omitted: c.a., b.cl., d.bsn.

[98] These parts contain many inaccuracies.
[99] See Augustus Hughes-Hughes, *Catalogue of Manuscript Music in the British Museum*, III (London, 1909), p. 5.
[100] Although 'Tri' is indicated in the margin of the first page of the printed score, it has nothing to play.

Manuscript: Not traced.
Publication: MM (699), 1938, fo., 96 pp.; WC0363C.
Performance: 'Sir Henry Wood and his Symphony Orchestra';[101] Queen's Hall; 3 October 1929 (Promenade Concert).
Adaptation: Part of the score was used for the ballet *Oscar* (see **110** for details).
Duration: 23'37.
Note: For the first performance Bax wrote a note that begins with the statement: 'These three pieces (written in the summer of 1927) are associated with no programme whatever, and should be regarded as strictly absolute music.' (Followed by a descriptive 'analysis'.)

In 1930, the full score MS disappeared from the lounge of the Park Lane Hotel, where it had accidentally been left by John Barbirolli, who was preparing a performance. Barbirolli is said to have written out a short score from memory and conducted from it without telling the composer.[102] In a letter dated 21 August 1930 to a BBC official, Bax wrote: 'Since my unhappy experience last March when a M.S score of mine was completely lost I don't like the idea of manuscripts wandering about.' The score had presumably been found by the time it was engraved for publication eight years later (unless it was reconstructed from the orchestral parts), but its present whereabouts are unknown. In a letter to Christopher Whelen dating from 1949 Bax remarked: 'I think the Elegy is in rather an unusual mood—a little spectral!'. In another letter, he wrote: 'I am sorry to tell you that I remember nothing whatsoever about the writing of "O, E and R"! I am pretty sure that it was composed at Hampstead, but until you told me 1929 [*sic*] I had no idea even of the date. It is "absolute" music; no programme of any kind.' Further remarks in letters to Whelen suggest that Bax was fond of the piece, and he told him that it was 'amongst my brightest and most optimistic compositions.'

289 SONATA NO. 3 for violin and piano

I. Moderato. II. Allegro moderato—Lento espressivo.

Date: *MS*: Undated. *Gr5*: '1927'. Finished after 26 September (see **Note** below).
Dedication: *MS*: None. *Printed score*: 'To Emil Telmanyi.'
Manuscript: BL (Add. MS 54776); ff. 29-43; 30 pp. (1-13, 14-30 + 6 blank); AL 12 paper (355 × 260).
Publication: MM (494), 1929, 4to, 38 pp.; CH (40436), [1950].

[101] Not the BBC Symphony Orchestra, as sometimes stated; this was not founded until 1930.
[102] See Charles Reid, *John Barbirolli* (London, 1971), p. 137.

Performance: Emil Telmányi (vn.), Arnold Bax (pf.); Arts Theatre Club; 4 February 1929 (BBC Chamber Concert).
Duration: 19'41.
Note: In a letter to May Harrison postmarked 26 September 1927, Bax wrote: 'It is nice of you to want to do my—at present—only semi-existent sonata. I did some other work in the summer and have only recently begun on the violin sonata, so I am afraid it won't be finished for a long time yet.' In a letter to the BBC offering his services as pianist in a broadcast of the sonata, Bax commented that the piano part of movt. II was 'foully hard to play'. The violin passage beginning at II, 26:6 in the published score is marked '*planxty*': 'A harp tune of a sportive and animated character, moving in triplets.' (J. Stainer and W. A. Barrett, *A Dictionary of Musical Terms*, London, 1876.)

290 FANTASIA by Johann Sebastian Bach (BWV 572): Arrangement for piano

Date: *MS*: 'Xmas 1927.' (not 1932 as given in all other printed sources).
Dedication: *MS*: 'For Tania' (Harriet Cohen). Miss Cohen has bracketed 'Tania' and added 'For Harriet Cohen'. *Printed score*: 'This book is dedicated by the contributors to | HARRIET COHEN'.
Manuscript: JNUL (Music Dept. 4 MUS.2 (2)); [3] ff.; [6] pp.; AL 12 paper (355 × 260).
Publication: No. 2 in *A Bach Book for Harriet Cohen*, OUP, 1932, 4to, pp. 5-10. Published with arrangements by Bantock, Berners, Bliss, Bridge, Goossens, Howells, Ireland, Lambert, Vaughan Williams, Walton and Whittaker.
Performance: Harriet Cohen; Queen's Hall; 17 October 1932.
Duration: 5'56.
Note: Of the three other dated contributions to *A Bach Book for Harriet Cohen* the earliest is Bridge's, which is inscribed 'June 1931'. This suggests that Bax's was made independently (as a Christmas present, judging from the date), well before the idea of a collection had been mooted. See Harriet Cohen, *A Bundle of Time*, pp. 183-4.

1928

291 SONATA for flute and harp

I. Allegro moderato. II. Cavatina (Lento). III. Moderato giocoso.

Title: *MS*: 'Sonatina for | Flute and Harp'. First performed and subsequently listed in *Gr5* as 'Sonata'; but later performances also sometimes given under the title 'Sonatine' (e.g. the Midland Home Service broadcast of 29 July 1945).

Date: 'April | 15th | 1928'.
Dedication: 'To Count K. Benckendorff'.
Manuscript: Privately owned (formerly by Maria Korchinska);[103] [12] ff.; 23 pp. (1-9, 10-15, [16-23] + 1 blank); AL 14 paper (356 × *c.* 258).
Publication: LM, 1987, 4to, 37 pp.[104]
Performance: (1) *Semi-private*: Constantin [Konstantin] Kony [Count Benckendorff] (fl.), Maria Korchinska [Countess Benckendorff] (hp.); Ipswich Central Library; 19 January 1929. (2) *Public*: Same performers; Wigmore Hall; 28 January 1929. All the reviews mention the poor playing of the flute part at this performance.
Arrangement: The *Cavatina* (movt. II) was played several times with violin instead of flute. *Performance*: May Harrison (vn.), Maria Korchinska (hp.); National Gallery; 26 March 1941.
Duration: 17'51.
Note: For details of Bax's arrangement as the Concerto for seven instruments see **337**.

292 SONATA IN F for violin and piano

I. Molto moderato—Allegro. II. Allegro—Più lento, espressivo.

Title: 'Sonata in F'.
Date: 'Sept 1928' (on t.p and at end of score).
Manuscript: BL (Add. MS 54766); ff. 44-57v; 28 pp. (t.p. + 1 blank + 1-12, 12-[25] ([16-25] unpag.) + 1 blank); AL 14 paper (355 × 262). Unpublished. *Copyist's score and part*: Graham Parlett.
Performance: Bernard Partridge (vn.), Andrew Pledge (pf.); British Music Information Centre; 21 April 1983 (lecture-recital by Graham Parlett, *et al.*).
Duration: 19'54.
Note: This work—Bax's 'Violin Sonata No. 4' in all but name—is not mentioned in any of the lists of his music published during his lifetime. For the subsequent arrangement as a nonet see **302**.

293 THE DEVIL THAT TEMPTED ST ANTHONY for two pianos

Date: 1928 assumed from date of first performance. *Gr5* wrongly gives 1929.
Dedication: *Printed score*: 'To Ethel Bartlett and Rae Robertson.'
Manuscript: Not traced.
Publication: MM (489), 1928, 4to, 15 pp.; CH (37953), [1946].
Performance: Ethel Bartlett and Rae Robertson; Æolian Hall; 19 June 1928.

[103] According to LF, p. 435, the MS was destroyed, but this was based on Mme Korchinska's mistaken belief that it had been torn to shreds when her house was burgled in the mid-1970s. After her death, in 1979, it was found intact among her papers.

[104] The published score and part both contain many inaccuracies.

Duration: 6'00.
Note: This was originally written for piano solo (see **231**). The title refers to St Antony the Abbot, whom the Devil's temptations failed to deflect from the path of righteousness.[105] He was born in Upper Egypt in 251 and died at the age of 105, later becoming the patron saint of basket-makers, butchers, domestic animals, and grave-diggers.

294 PÆAN (Passacaglia) for piano

Date: *MGG*: '1928'. There seems to be no justification for the year 1920 given in *Gr5*, since the title is not mentioned in earlier editions of *Grove's Dictionary* or in other lists published before *MGG* (1949-51).
Dedication: *Printed score*: 'To Frank Merrick.'
Manuscript: Not traced.
Publication: MM (506), 1929, 4to, 6 pp.; CH (35563), 1943; WC0512.
Performance: *Earliest traced*: Frank Merrick; Houldsworth Hall, Manchester; 25 June 1929.
Arrangement: For organ by William Barr, CH (39220), 1949, 7 pp.
Adaptation: As the basis for a dance by Ted Shawn. The Performing Arts Research Center (New York Public Library) has a photograph of him in 'The Kinetic Molpai and Pæan', taken by John Lindquist and dated '[1945?]', together with a 3½-minute film and a taped commentary on the piece.
Duration: 3'07.
Note: For Bax's own arrangement for orchestra see **343**.

295 THREE PIECES for small orchestra

a. Evening Piece. **b.** Irish Landscape. **c.** Dance in the Sunlight.

Date: *MS*: Undated. *Gr5*: '1928'.
Orchestra: **a.** 2222, 2000, hp., str. **b.** hp., str. **c.** 2(1)202020, 4000, timp., 1 perc. (tamb.),[106] hp., str.
Manuscript: *Holograph*: CH (MS 247); [38] ff.; 75 pp. (1-25, 26-39, 40-75 + 1 blank); AL 14a paper (355 × 263); loose in brown paper wrappers. When I inspected this MS in the late 1970s, it contained a f.sc. pencil sketch for a passage in the *First Northern Ballad* (**309**); searches made in January 1991 and October 1995 failed to locate this loose folio. *Copyist's score*: CH; [40] ff.; 78 pp. (t.p. + 1 blank + 1-25, 26-37, 38-78). Unpublished. *Parts*: CH.
Performance: (1) **295 a** *and* c *only*: 'The Symphony Orchestra' [players drawn from London's main orchestras], Dr Malcolm Sargent; Central Hall, Westminster; 1 December 1928 (Children's Orchestral Concert). (2)

[105] The spelling 'Anthony' (as in Bax's title) is no earlier than the 16th century.
[106] Although 'Cym' is indicated in the margin of p. 36, it has nothing to play.

Complete (earliest traced): BBC Northern Ireland Orchestra, Eric Wetherell; br. on Radio 3, 6 November 1978.
Duration: **a.** 7'27. **b.** 9'03. **c.** 4'51.
Note: These pieces are revised versions of three of the Four Orchestral Pieces of 1912-13: **a.** Evening Piece > Pensive Twilight; **b.** Irish Landscape > In the Hills of Home; **c.** Dance in the Sunlight > Dance in the Sun. For details of the original versions see **152**. The revisions are minor: slight rhythmic changes, modified instrumentation, etc. There are a few structural alterations: **a.** The twelve bars from 25 after fig. 6 to 6 after fig. 7 are replaced by five new bars, and the three bars from 1 before fig. 9 to 2 after 9 are replaced by a single new bar. **c.** This movement is transposed up a tone to F major, and the 32 bars from 13 after fig. 16 to 12 after fig. 18 are cut.

In a letter to Edward Clark (BL Add. MS 52256) written shortly after the revisions, Bax commented: 'I think they have a certain freshness which might please, although of course they are unfashionably romantic. They are scored for an early 18th century orchestra with the addition of harp (no brass, except horns).'

296 THE POISONED FOUNTAIN for two pianos

Date: 1928 deduced from date of first performance. *Gr5* wrongly gives 1929.
Dedication: *Printed score*: 'To Ethel Bartlett and Rae Robertson.'
Manuscript: Not traced.
Publication: MM (490), 1928, 4to, 10 pp.; CH (37733), [1945].
Performance: Ethel Bartlett and Rae Robertson; Æolian Hall; 19 June 1928. '[It] proved such a success that the audience would not be content until it had been played again.' (*The Daily Telegraph*, 20 June 1928).
Duration: 3'53.
Note: The programme behind this work comes from Irish mythology. The fountain of the title was the Secret Well of Segais, the source of knowledge, which stood on Sídhe Nectain, the hill of the water-god Nectan. Only the god and his three cupbearers could approach the fountain without burning their eyes. According to one version of the story, Nectan's wife, Boann, scorned the danger and walked round the fountain three times anticlockwise. The waters rose up in pursuit, drowning her and forming the river Boyne.

1929

297 SYMPHONY NO. 3 for orchestra

I. Lento moderato. II. Lento. III. Moderato—Epilogue (Poco lento).

Date: *Short score*: Undated. The presence of sketches for *Walsinghame* (**278**) on the last page (f. 19^{v})—the lines beginning 'Of womenkind such indeed is the love or the word love abused'—does not mean that the symphony was composed before the completion of the choral work in May 1926 and a blank page used to jot down the sketch. The last folio of the symphony bears a different imprint from the rest (but the same as for the vocal score of *Walsinghame*), indicating that it was salvaged from sketches for the choral work and that the blank side was used at a later date for the symphonic short score. *Full score*: I. 'Arisaig and Morar | Dec 1928.' (at end of original version of movt. I). II. Undated. III. 'Morar | Inverness-shire | February | 1929' (partly obscured by the tight binding). In answer to an enquiry from Christopher Whelen, Bax wrote that the work was composed in 'London and Arisaig'.

Dedication: *Printed score only*: 'To Sir Henry J. Wood.' On the front cover of Wood's copy, kept in the RAM, Bax has written: 'With sincerest affection from Arnold Bax'.

Orchestra: 3(1) 2+1 3(E♭)+1 2+1, 4331, timp., 5 perc. (b.d., t.d. (*ad lib.*), s.d., tamb., cym., gong,[1] xyl., gl., cel., anv.), 2 hps. (2nd *ad lib.*), str.

Manuscript: *Sketch*: Privately owned (formerly by Colin Scott-Sutherland); [1] f.; [2] pp.; pencil; AL 12 paper (330 × 243). These seem to be Bax's initial jottings for the opening theme, the 'second subject', and the principal theme of movt. II, plus fragments later discarded from the symphony or intended for another, aborted work.

Short score: BL (Add. MS 54728); 19 ff.; [37] pp. ([1-16], [17-24], [25-37]); ff. 1-18: AL 12 paper (358 × 262); f. 19: AL 14c (355 × 262); bound by the BL with brown wrappers bound in bearing Harriet Cohen's writing. The MS is written in ink with pencilled additions and contains notes for the orchestration mostly in pencil but a few (such as the opening bn. solo and the hn. solo at the start of movt. II) in ink. To the left of the title, Bax has written: '"My wisdom became pregnant on lonely | mountains; upon barren stones she | brought forth her young." | Nietzche [*sic*].' (This is from *Also sprach Zarathustra*, pt. 2, ch. 1, which is also found, in a slightly different translation, as an epigraph to Fiona Macleod, *From the Hills of Dream: Threnodies, Songs and Later Poems*, London, 1907, p. xvi.) A few passages appear that were cut when the work was orchestrated: in II the passage beginning at bar 2 after fig. 6 was preceded by 31 extra bars, of which 11 are crossed through; in III bars 2 and 3 after fig. 18 are separated by a crossed-through 52-bar passage based on the fanfare figure beginning at four bars after fig. 8 and the opening 'motto' theme; there are seventeen extra bars between bar 6 after fig. 18 and 4 before fig. 19 in the published f.sc. (These bars were orchestrated but deleted from the published version.) As mentioned under **Date** above, f. 19^{v} contains pencil sketches for *Walsinghame*.

Full score: BL (Add. MS 54729); [70] ff.; 140 pp. (1-65, 66-91, 92-140); AL 29a paper (360 × 262); bound by the BL. The revised ending of movt. I consists of 47

[107] Bax, unusually, writes 'tam-tam' in the second movement, but this is crossed through in another hand and replaced by 'gong', the word used by Bax himself in the third movement.

bars. The last 11 of these are the same as the original ending, which was preceded by a further 4 bars subsequently deleted. The revised ending (with the first four bars pasted over the original) is pagin. from 64 to 69 (duplicating p. 64), II continuing from the original pagin. starting at p. 66. There is a blank folio (f. 37) inserted between the revised ending and the last seven bars of the original. The pagin. is thus as follows: pp. 1-63 (ff. 1-32) = pp. 1-54 of the printed score; p. 64 (f. 32^{v}) = the opening eight bars of the original coda crossed through (leading into f. 38); pp. 64[bis]-69 (ff. 33-36^{v}) = the revised coda, the first four bars on p. 64 pasted over the original; f. 37 = blank except for a few pencilled remarks in Wood's hand and a green label stuck on to the recto; p. 65 (f. 38) = the original final seven bars, which are identical to the printed version except for the omission of the side drum in the last two bars. In III there are 17 extra bars (pp. 120-1), mainly for strings, between the sixth bar after fig. 18 and 4 before fig. 19 in the published score. The presence of cue numbers 19 and 20 in this passage that have been crossed out in pencil suggests that the music may have been included at the first performance and subsequently cut when the score went to press late in 1930. The single anvil note at fig. 47 in movt. I appears only in Wood's hand at the foot of the page, Bax originally having written a cymbal clash on the second beat of the bar.

Transcript: Graham Parlett (bought from Richard MacNutt in 1983); [1] f.; [1] p.; 4 bars (unfinished); slip of plain, pale blue paper (58 × 115) mounted on card. This consists of the opening bars of the bassoon solo written out by Bax (the fourth bar incorrectly) and dated 'Feb 2nd 1949'.

Publication: MM (555), 1931, fo. and 8vo, 114 pp.; CH (35537), 1943, 8vo; CH [1949], fo.; CH [1990], 8vo (st.sc.); WC0144C (A3 size); WC0144CX (A4 size); SMC (st.sc.). *Page proofs corrected by Bax*: ML. *Printer's pulls*: CH (MS 415).

Performance: BBC Symphony Orchestra, Sir Henry Wood; Queen's Hall; 14 March 1930. 'H. J. W. always took particular pains over this symphony . . . and the first performance was an excitement to me because I felt the audience was more impressed by this work at a first hearing than anything else of mine.' (From a note to Christopher Whelen, 1951.)

Adaptation: (1) Movt. II was played at the coronation of King George VI at Westminster Abbey on 11 May 1937. (2) Part of the score was used for the ballet *Oscar* (see **110** for details).

Duration: 49'37.

Note: For the first performance Bax wrote a programme note that begins:

This symphony was written in 1928-29. No title or programme is attached, and the work in its formal aspect deviates little from the lines laid down by the classical composers of the past. The first movement is preceded by an introduction in which the basic idea of the music is adumbrated as through a dark haze.

In *A Handbook on Arnold Bax's Symphonies* (London, [1932]), p. 44, Robert H. Hull remarked:

. . . although the composer is emphatic in his statement that there is no programme attached, it has been suggested that the symphony possesses a mood of northern legends. Bax agrees that the interpretation is apt, allowing that subconsciously he may have been influenced by the sagas and dark winters of the North . . . [but] the second movement does not share this mood in any way.

It was at the suggestion of Vaughan Williams that Bax lengthened the ending of the first movement (see 'Arnold Bax 1883-1953', *Music & Letters*, January 1954, p. 13-14). This revision had clearly not been made by the time of the work's performance at a Promenade Concert on 25 September 1930: '. . . the first movement is as good as anything that Bax has written, its only fault being an over-abrupt ending.' (*The Musical Times*, 1 November 1930, p. 1032.) In a letter to May Harrison with an envelope postmarked 24 September 1930, Bax wrote: 'Some eminent colleagues including Vaughan Williams and Holst maintain that it is my best work.' Of the slow movement he remarked: 'I am fond of this piece myself and so was he [Henry Wood], I know.' (Letter of 7 March 1946 to Jessie Wood.)

298 SONATA for two pianos

I. Molto moderato (quasi andante)[108]—Allegretto scherzando (ma non troppo presto). II. Lento espressivo. III. Vivace e feroce (ma non troppo presto).

Date: Edwin Evans's programme note: '. . . composed in 1929 after the composer had spent the springtime in the country and by the sea.' In his radio talk of 1949, Bax mentioned that this work was written 'at about the same time' as *The Garden of Fand* (1913) and *Winter Waters* (1915); but there is no other evidence to corroborate such an early date; perhaps like other works for two pianos, such as *Red Autumn* and *The Devil that tempted St Anthony*, it is based on earlier material.
Dedication: *Printed score*: 'To Ethel Bartlett and Rae Robertson.'
Manuscript: Not traced.
Publication: MM (521), 1930, 4to, 47 pp.; CH (37228), [1945].
Performance: Ethel Bartlett and Rae Robertson; St John's Institute, Westminster; 10 December 1929 (Music Society Concert). Bax thought the performers' playing 'much too accurate' (LF, p. 252).
Duration: 22'09.
Note: The third movement is based on Hebridean dance rhythms.

299 LEGEND for viola and piano

Date: 'London | July 1929.'
Dedication: *MS*: 'To M[rs] Elisabeth [*sic*] Sprague Coolidge'. Also misspelt on printed score.
Manuscript: LC (ML29c.B34); [6] ff.; 11 pp. + 1 blank; AL 12 paper (360 × 243). Presented by Harriet Cohen on 30 December 1960.

[108] The published score prints the direction 'in a languorous, sunstained mood' at the opening; in Edwin Evans's original programme note the second adjective appears as 'sustained'. One of them is obviously a misprint, but only the missing MS could confirm which.

Publication: MM (528), 1930, 4to, 11 pp.; CH (38047), [1946]; WC0425.
Performance: Lionel Tertis (va.), Arnold Bax (pf.); Æolian Hall; 7 December 1929.
Duration: 10'31.
Note: This work was apparently 'inspired' by Herbert Read's poem 'This X'.

c. 1929

300 BALLAD for violin and piano (second version of 181)

Publication: MM (646), 1934, 4to, 12 pp.
Note: For details of the original version of this work and the reasons for assigning its revision to *c.* 1929 see **181**.

301 BALLAD for piano (or short score of orchestral work)

Manuscript: Privately owned (formerly by Colin Scott-Sutherland); [1] f.; [2] pp.; pencil; AL 12 paper (360 × 243).
Note: The melodic material resembles a theme from the Sonata for two pianos (**298**)—the passage beginning at 6:10 in the second piano—and for that reason is assigned here to *c.* 1929. The title appears in the middle of the first page.

1930

302 NONET for flute, clarinet, oboe, harp, 2 violins, viola, cello and double bass

I. Molto moderato—Allegro. II. Allegro.

Title: *MS and MM printed score*: 'Nonett' (the German spelling). *CH impressions*: 'Nonet' (the English spelling).
Date: 'Jan 1930'.
Dedication: '(To the memory of Eric Verney-Cohen)'. This is written in black ink, the rest of the MS being in dark blue, and was obviously added over a year after the work's completion, since Harriet Cohen's brother died on 10 February 1931.
Manuscript: BL (Add. MS 54760); [20] ff.; 39 pp. (1-21, 22-39 + 1 blank); AL 14 paper (355 × 262). There is an MM stamp on p. 39 and engravers' marks throughout. The blank page at the end contains a few unidentified pencil jottings and sketches for the first two thematic groups of the Fourth Piano Sonata (**318**).
Publication: MM (569), 1932, fo., 32 pp.; CH (37976; *parts*: 38830), [1946]; *score*: WC0199C; *parts*: WC0199.
Performance: (1) Joseph Slater (fl.), Léon Goossens (ob.), Ralph Clarke (cl.), Maria Korchinska (hp.), Brosa Quartet: Antonio Brosa (vn.), David Wise (vn.), Leonard Rubens (va.), Livio Mannucci (vc.), Victor Watson (d.b.); Queen's Hall, Bradford; 30 September 1930 (The Third Bradford Festival of Chamber Music: part of the Triennial Festival). '[It was] composed specially for the Festival . . . [and] gave the Festival its special interest and lustre. . . . [It] made an exceptionally good

impression, in spite of a not by any means ideal performance.' (Ferruccio Bonavia, *The Musical Times*, November 1930, p. 1034). 'Mr. Bax received an ovation after the performance.' (*The Daily Mail*, 1 October 1930.) (2) Same performers; Working Men's College, Crowndale Road, Camden Town, London NW1; 31 March 1931 (Sunday Evening Concert Society concert in memory of Eric Verney-Cohen).
Duration: 17'30.
Note: Bax's programme note for the première is mainly a descriptive 'analysis'. For details of the original version (Sonata in F for violin and piano) see **292**.

303 WINTER LEGENDS for piano and orchestra

I. Allegro. II. Lento, molto espressivo. III. Molto moderato—Allegro molto—Epilogue (molto cantabile).

Title: The subtitle 'Sinfonia Concertante' appears in the programme for the first performance but not on the MS.
Date: *Short score*: I. 'Oct 22nd 1929'. II. 'Oct 30th | 1929'. III. 'Dec. 4th 1929.' *Full score*: I. Undated. II. 'Morar Feb. 1930' III. 'April 3rd, 1930'.
Dedication: *Short score*: None in Bax's hand; 'Dedicated to Harriet Cohen' written in her own hand on a label on the front cover. *Full score*: 'To Sibelius'. Miss Cohen has erased this and replaced it with: 'Written for and dedicated to Harriet Cohen'.
Orchestra: 3(1) 2+1 3+E♭+1 2+1, 4331, timp., 4 perc. (b.d., s.d., tamb., cym., gong, xyl., gl.), hp., str.
Manuscript: *Short (2-piano) score*: BL (Add. MS 54751); 27 ff.; 51 pp. (1-19, 20-32 + 2 blank, 33-51 + 3 blank); AL 14 paper (355 × 263) loosely inserted in brown paper wrappers ('A. WEEKES & Co., Ltd. "Handy" Music Covers.') with a label on the front cover (including 'Property & copyright [*sic*] of Harriet Cohen', in her hand). There are engravers' marks on the score, but it was never published. *Full score*: BL (Add. MS 54752); [77] ff.; 153 pp. (1-64; 65 blank (except for a non-autograph 'II'), 66-99, 100-53 + 1 blank); AL 29a paper (360 × 262). *Copyist's full score*: CH (MS 252); [77] ff.; 153 pp. + 1 blank; AL 29a paper. *Copyists' 2-piano score*: BL (Add. MS 54751); ff. 28-79; t.p. + 1 blank + 90 pp. (1-35 + 5 blank, 36-58 + 3 blank, 59-60). 12-staff-paper (302 × 238) loosely inserted in brown paper wrappers; written out by two copyists, movt. I in a neater hand than II and III. *Copyist's solo piano part*: CH; 57 pp.; BBC paper. *Parts*: CH.
Publication: *2-piano score (photocopy of the 2 copyists' score)*: WC [no stock number].
Performance: (1) Harriet Cohen (pf.), BBC Symphony Orchestra, Dr Adrian Boult; Queen's Hall; 10 February 1932. (2) *Ed. by Margaret Fingerhut* (without cuts): Margaret Fingerhut (pf.), London Philharmonic Orchestra, Bryden Thomson; All Saints' Church, Tooting; 3 April 1986 (recording session for Chandos Records Ltd.).
Duration: 43'19.
Note: Bax wrote a programme note for the first performance:

This work, which is designed in three movements and on a symphonic scale, makes no pretence of being a piano concerto in the ordinary sense. The piano is not used as a means of technical display though it plays a difficult part. Neither has the piece any communicable programme. The listener may associate what he hears with any heroic tale or tales of the North—of the far North, be it said. Some of these happenings may have taken place within the Arctic circle

'Legends that once were told or sung
In many a smoky fireside nook
Of Iceland, in the ancient day
By wandering Saga-man or Scald'.[109]

There is nothing consciously Celtic about this work. [Followed by an 'analysis'.]

According to the dedicatee (*A Bundle of Time*, p. 182) Bax regarded *Winter Legends* almost as another symphony: 'Chronologically and emotionally the concerto was another Symphony in Arnold's mind—"My No 4 really", he would say.' In answer to a question about its programmatic origins, he said: '. . . any concrete ideas that may be in it of place or thing are of the North—Northern Ireland, Northern Scotland, Northern Europe—in fact, the Celtic North.' (Watson Lyle, 'Musician of the North', *The Bookman*, February 1932, p. 268.) Writing to Adrian Boult after the première, Bax commented: 'I am not sure that it is not one of my best things. (The piano is really only an important orchestral instrument, and the work is—in a way—a symphony, except that the first movement is short and rhapsodic.)'[110] The following cuts appear in the f.sc.: movt. II. The eight bars from 4 after fig. 12 to 1 after the original fig. 13 + 1 before fig. 15. III. The sixteen bars from 6 after fig. 26 to 1 after the original fig. 28.

304 FANFARE FOR A CHEERFUL OCCASION for brass and percussion

Date: Probably a month or so before 8 May, the date of the first performance.
Orchestra: 2 sop. crnts. in E♭, 4 tpts. in B♭, 3 ten. tbns., 1 b.tbn., timp., cym.
Manuscript: *Holograph*: Not traced. Unpublished.
Performance: (1) *Private*: [Twelve] Kneller Hall Trumpeters, Capt. H. E. Adkins; Savoy Hotel; 8 May 1930 (Annual Dinner of the Musicians' Benevolent Fund; repeated at the next Annual Dinner on 7 May 1931). (2) *Public*: Kneller Hall Trumpeters, brass and percussion of the Philharmonic Orchestra (see p. 175 n.) and BBC Symphony Orchestra, Capt. H. E. Adkins; Royal Albert Hall; 26 May 1932 (Concert for the Musicians' Benevolent Fund organized by *The News Chronicle*). The fanfare was 'sounded by 50 brass and percussion players . . . ' (*The Times*, 27 May 1932, p. 12.)
Arrangement: Since Bax nowhere else writes for trumpets in B♭, it is likely that the only extant score is an arrangement, probably by Capt. Adkins, who conducted the first performance and made a recording (HMV C 2445). *Copyist's score*: RMSM; [4] ff.; [8] pp.; 20-staff paper (*c.* 366 × 273).
Duration: 0'45.

[109] From Henry Wadsworth Longfellow, 'Interlude' preceding 'The Musician's Tale: The Saga of King Olaf' from *Tales of a Wayside Inn*.

[110] It is no shorter than the average timings for the first movements of the first three symphonies.

305 OVERTURE TO A PICARESQUE COMEDY for orchestra

Date: *Printed score*: 'Morar | Oct. 19th. 1930'.
Dedication: *Printed score*: 'To SIR HAMILTON HARTY' (t.p.); 'To Hamilton Harty.' (p. 1).
Orchestra: 3(1) 2+1 3+1 2+1, 433 ten. tba. in B♭, timp., 4 perc. (b.d., t.d., s.d., tamb., cym., gong, ratt., xyl., gl., cel.), hp., str.
Manuscript: Not traced.
Publication: MM (588), 1932, fo. and 8vo, 73 pp.; CH (pl.no. as for MM ed.), [1945], 8vo; [1946], fo.; WC0418C (f.sc.).
Performance: (1) Hallé Orchestra, Sir Hamilton Harty; Free Trade Hall, Manchester; 19 November 1931. 'It was so successful that it had to be repeated on December 10.' (From Edwin Evans's later programme note.) (2) London Symphony Orchestra, Sir Hamilton Harty; Queen's Hall; 15 February 1932.
Adaptation: Part of the score was used for the ballet *Oscar* (see **110** for details).
Duration: 8'36.
Note: Edwin Evans's programme note for this piece is worth quoting in part:

> Remarks overheard at the first London performance of this buoyant and exhilarating Overture make it appear not entirely superfluous to define what is meant by 'picaresque'. The word derives from Spanish picaro, a rogue, and was applied in the first place to the tales of Spanish rogues and vagabonds which had a great vogue in the seventeenth century. Since then its meaning has been extended to embrace even the modern 'crime story', one example of which bears the title 'The [*sic*] Elusive Picaroon'.[111] But the evidence of the music suggests a 'rogue's comedy' [cf. **335**] that is not definitely concerned with piracy or the Spanish Main, and certainly not with any contemporary Raffles, but perhaps with the generic idea of genial roguery. The composer denies the existence of any specific programme, so we must leave it at that.

Bax is said to have produced this overture after being challenged by someone to write a piece in the style of Richard Strauss. The composer's friend Mary Gleaves was present while he was orchestrating the work in Morar; he characterized it for her as 'high jinks!'.

306 LORD, THOU HAST TOLD US (Wonder): Hymn for SATB

Title: The printed score gives no title; 'Wonder' is the name of the tune.
Date: Composed specifically for *Songs of Praise* (1931).
Text: Thomas Washbourne, 'Lord, Thou hast told us that there be'.
Manuscript: Not traced.
Publication: No. 107 in *Songs of Praise*, OUP, 1931, 8vo, p. 129 (Lenten hymn in four verses; preceded by the note 'May be sung in unison').
Performance: *Earliest traced*: The Abbey Singers, Andrew Seivewright; Carlisle Cathedral; br. on Radio 3, 30 December 1983 (choral evensong).

[111] By Herman Landon (London, 1932). There is no article in the title.

Duration: 3'14.
Note: 'Wonder was composed by Arnold Bax especially for the enlarged Songs of Praise (1931). It is clearly founded on the style of the early psalm-tunes, but has some individual touches in rhythm and expression.' (Archibald Jacob in Percy Dearmer (ed.), *Songs of Praise Discussed*, London, 1933, pp. 69-70.)

1931

307 SYMPHONY NO. 4 for orchestra

I. Allegro moderato. II. Lento moderato. III. Allegro—Tempo di marcia trionfale.

Date: *Short score*: I. 'July 13th 1930'. II. 'August 1930'. III. 'Sept 11th 1930'. *Full score*: I. 'Morar and | Glencolumcille. | Oct–November 1930' ['Oct–' is in a lighter ink and was clearly added later]; II. Undated. III. 'Morar Feb 1931'. In response to an enquiry from Christopher Whelen, Bax wrote that the work was composed in 'London and Morar'.
Dedication: *Printed score only*: 'To PAUL CORDER'.
Orchestra: 3(1) 2+1 3+1 2+1, 6331 + ten. tba. in B♭, timp., 3 perc. (b.d., s.d., tamb., cym., gong, xyl., gl., cel.), org., hp., str.
Manuscript: *Short score*: RAM (MS 529); 18 ff.; t.p. + 1 blank + [35] pp. ([13] + 1 blank, [7] + 1 blank, [12]); AL 14 paper (354 × 262); in acid-free pocket. The t.p. has 'Sketch for | 4th Symphony' written on it in Bax's hand. There are numerous pencilled notes for the orchestration. On f. 15v there are sixteen bars that have been crossed through in blue pencil and do not appear in the orchestrated version (they come between bars 8 and 9 after fig. (18) of the printed score). On f. 18v there are some unidentifiable pencil sketches, one fragment resembling a thematic figure in the Sinfonietta (**314**).

Full score: BDL (MS Don.c.48); 77 ff.; 153 pp. (1-69 (superscript 'a' added in another hand) + 1 blank ('69b'), 70-105, 105-53 + 3 blank); AL 29a paper (trimmed to 354 × 261); bound in light blue cloth with dark blue leather backstrip and corners, with gold tooling and lettering on spine, and with brown wrappers bound in at the end (pagin. 157-60 in another hand). Page 95 ('94b' in another hand) is crossed through because Bax started to write out a passage having omitted the preceding four bars; he then renumbered his original p. 96 as '95' and p. 97 as '96'. According to the *F. O. B. Annual Report*, X (1934-5), p. 17, the holograph f.sc. was 'presented by the composer through the Friends [of the Bodleian Library]'. A letter from Bax dated 3 April 1935 is tipped in (pagin. 'v' and 'vi', the latter blank) attached to a separate stub) in front of p. 1 of the score: 'I am sending the M.S of my fourth symphony to you by the next post.[112] I am afraid that the engravers (as usual) have made it very ragged and dirty, and have also added a great many indications of their own in pencil. But this is unavoidable when music is engraved.' Marjorie

[112] In recognition of the honorary doctorate that he had received in June 1934.

McTavish and the dedicatee went through the symphony before publication simplifying the notation.
Publication: MM (568); [July] 1932, fo. and 8vo, 156 pp.; CH (no pl.no.), [1948], 8vo.; WC0145C (A3 size); WC0145CX (A4 size); SMC (st.sc. in preparation).
Performance: (1) San Francisco Symphony Orchestra, Basil Cameron; Civic Auditorium, San Francisco; 16 March 1932. (2) London Philharmonic Orchestra, Dr Malcolm Sargent; Queen's Hall; 5 December 1932 (Courtauld–Sargent Concert; repeated on 6 and 9 December). 'Magnificent continuity is the splendour of this symphony: it never sags; whilst its march-like rhythms sweep along with a rhythmic force and power that is remindful of Beethoven, Bruckner and Mahler.' (*Musical Opinion*, January 1933, p. 329).[113]
Arrangement: For piano duet by Walter Emery and William Cole. Privately owned: I. [14] ff.; 28 pp.; 20-staff paper (355 × 260); II. [8] ff.; 15 pp.; 20-staff paper (355 × 260); III. [14] ff.; 27 pp.; 14-staff paper (361 × 267). Unpublished. *Performance of movt. I only*: William Cole, Walter Emery; Duke's Hall, RAM; 5 July 1933 (first item in a 'Practice Concert' beginning at 8 p.m.). Emery arranged movts. I and II (inscribed respectively 'March 4 1933' and 'This transcription made May 24-31 1933'), while Cole arranged movt. III at about the same time. Sixty-two years later, Dr Cole wrote:

Stanley Marchant [later Principal of the RAM] thought we should play it to Bax and we did so at the RAM in room 33 on 14th September 1933. When Bax came in . . . and we were introduced to him he looked round the room, saw a portrait of Beethoven over the fire-place, walked towards it and turned himself round and with a big gesture planted his feet in front of it and asked us to begin.

He missed the orchestra but seemed pleased that we had taken the trouble to arrange the symphony. I told him that there were misprints in the miniature score from which we worked. He said that in his younger days his works were played before they were printed and thus the score was corrected. Now however his works were printed before they were played. [Extracts from two letters written to me in April 1995.]

Duration: 41'33.
Note: In *The Daily Telegraph* for 9 January 1932, Robert H. Hull wrote:

Early in 1931 it was revealed to a privileged few that Bax had completed his Fourth Symphony. Absolute reticence was enjoined upon those to whom this information was conceded. The composer desired that the new work should be neither performed nor openly discussed until his other three symphonies became better known . . . The beginning of the first movement means to him a rough sea at flood-tide on a sunny day, and most of the work is nature music.

Christopher Whelen recalled that Bax once referred to the work as 'my Sea Symphony'; but when asked to elucidate he replied that descriptive titles were for his

[113] After a performance of this work in the 1950s, Hans Keller complained that it was too long. 'It's not the symphony which is too long', remarked Harriet Cohen to Clifford Gillam, 'it's Hans Keller who's too short'.

tone poems, not his symphonies. Bax incorporated most of his piano piece *A Romance* (206) into the second movement.

308 VALSE for harp

Date: 'Sept 5th | 1931'.
Dedication: 'To Sidonie Goossens'.
Manuscript: Sidonie Goossens; [3] ff.; 6 pp.; 1507 paper (350 × 261).
Performance: Sidonie Goossens; Wigmore Hall; 21 October 1931.
Publication: *Edited by Marcia Dickstein*: FI (494-02006), 1995, 12 pp.
Duration: *c.* 4'00.
Note: This is Bax's only work for solo harp and does not appear in any of the published lists of his music compiled during his lifetime. The dedicatee first played it during a song recital by Betty Bannerman, at which she also gave the first performances of van Dieren's *Estemporale*. Writing to me sixty-five years later, on 9 March 1996, Miss Goossens recalled:

> ... he wrote [it] for me at *his wish*—not mine, although I was delighted to have it. I had just given the 2nd performance of his [Fantasy] Sonata for viola and harp and he was pleased with it, hence the reward. It has only been performed by me, and a pupil once included it in her diploma recital.

The 'key' signature is unique in Bax's output: an F♯ and a B♭, indicating a combination of the Lydian and Mixolydian modes with C as final (the work ends on a chord of C major).

309 NORTHERN BALLAD NO. 1 for orchestra

Title: *Short score*: None. *Full score*: 'Northern Ballad'; '1st' has been prefixed in ballpoint pen by another hand. First performed as 'A Northern Ballad'.
Date: *Short score*: 'Nov 1927'. *Full score*: Undated, but listed in *Gr5* as 1931.
Dedication: 'To Basil Cameron'.
Orchestra: 3(1) 2+1 2+1 2+1, 4331, timp., 3 perc. (b.d., s.d., tamb., cym., gong, gl.), 2 hps., str.
Manuscript: *Sketches*: (*A*) Privately owned (formerly by Colin Scott-Sutherland); [1] f. (the verso with unidentified fragments); [1] p.; pencil; AL 14c paper (331 × 246). This page contains a sketch on the first line for the melody at 37:5 to 38:3 in the f.sc. MS; the rest of the material on the page is unidentifiable. (*B*) CH (MS 247): In the late 1970s a f.sc. pencil sketch for the passage leading up to the 'Allegro con fuoco' was included with the MS of the *Three Pieces for Small Orchestra* (**295**); in January 1991 and October 1995 this folio could not be located. *Short score*: BL (Add. MS 54750); 6 ff.; [12] pp. (non-autograph pencilled page numerals partly erased); AL 12 paper (355 × 260). There are ink and pencil notes for orchestration, and Sellotape marks at inner edges. *Full score*: CH (MS 254); [24] ff.; 46 pp. + 2 blank; AL 29a paper (360 × 262); bound in mid-green cloth with brown paper wrappers

bound in. Bax has inserted an extra bar in pencil before the final bar (noted in the parts). Unpublished. *Parts*: CH.

Performance: (1) Scottish Orchestra, Basil Cameron; St Andrew's Hall, Glasgow; 14 November 1931. (2) Orchestra of the Royal Philharmonic Society, Basil Cameron; Queen's Hall; 3 December 1931 (played, according to *The Musical Times* for 1 January 1932, p. 68, in place of Sibelius's Eighth Symphony, which had been promised). 'The audience took the rare gift a little ordinarily: the composer has been so unstintingly generous, and that is the world's way of thanks.' (*Monthly Musical Record*, January 1932.)

Duration: 10'01.

Note: For the first performance Bax supplied the following note:

> This short work dates from about four years ago. It recounts no particular tale; there is little definite local colour, nor is any use made of traditional airs. It is simply meant as a general impression of the fiery romantic life of the Highlands of Scotland before the opening up of the country subsequent to the '45 [the Jacobite Rising of 1745], a musical counterpart of the mood permeating the dark and stormy legends of the clans and such books as the late Neil Munro's 'The Lost Pibroch' [Edinburgh, 1896].
>
> Although the musical structure is intentionally terse and concise, there should be no difficulty in following the development of the piece, as the divisions of the sections are clearly marked.
>
> The work is dedicated to Basil Cameron.

Bax's reference to the date of the work as 'about four years ago' is another example of his distinction between composing and orchestrating. In the interview with Watson Lyle published in *The Bookman* (February 1932), p. 268, Bax briefly spoke of his composition methods: '"I have known practically the complete work to come to me at once." (Later, if I remember rightly, he alluded to his [First] Northern Ballad....).' For a connection with the *Prelude for a Solemn Occasion* see **320**.

310 THE TALE THE PINE-TREES KNEW for orchestra

Title: In a letter to May Harrison dated 27 October 1932 (i.e. before publication), Bax referred to this work as 'What the Pine Trees Knew'—perhaps a mental slip, since the short score MS (completed a year earlier) bears the final title. This is written above something that has been erased, probably with an ink-rubber—an altered slur above the first staff, perhaps, rather than words.

Date: *Short score*: 'Oct 2nd 1931' (possibly begun in March: see **Note** below). *Full score*: 'Morar | December | 1931'. Finished before 18 December, the date on which he wrote to May Harrison: 'The Pine-Trees piece is done . . .'.

Dedication: *Printed score only*: 'TO JOHN BARBIROLLI'.

Orchestra: 3(1) 2+1 3(E♭)+1 2+1, 4331, timp., 4 perc. (b.d., t.d., s.d., tamb., cym., gong, xyl., gl., cel.), 2 hps., str.

Manuscript: *Short score*: BL (Add. MS 54753); [6] ff.; [12] pp.; ALM 16 paper (362 × 266); loosely inserted within a bifolium of 32-staff paper (354 × 270). There are pencilled additions (such as the violin solo that starts at bar 4 before [50]) and notes

for orchestration. *Full score*: BL (Add. MS 54754); [34] ff.; 66 pp. + 2 blank; AL 29a paper (360 × 262); loosely inserted into brown wrappers. Pencilled notes from Bax to the engraver about engraving string 'divisi' on separate staves are on pp. 43, 54 and 67.
Publication: MM (609), 1933, fo., 85 pp.; WC0149 (f.sc.).
Performance: London Philharmonic Orchestra, Sir Thomas Beecham; Queen's Hall; 12 April 1934.
Duration: 17'23.
Note: In March 1931 Bax wrote to Mary Gleaves:

I have been in rather a shadowed mood all day . . . I am trying to begin a new work, and I think it must be rather like the state of mind that a woman knows when she finds she is going to have a child. One feels all nerves and rebellion and egotism, and ready to scream at nothing! It is all such a chaotic mess at present (this piece).[114]

For the first performance Bax wrote the following note:

. . . in planning the composition I was thinking of two landscapes dominated by the pine trees—Norway and the West of Scotland—thinking, too, of the Norse sagas and of the wild traditional legends of the Highland Celt. . . . But this work is concerned solely with the abstract mood of these places, and the pine-trees' tale must be taken as a purely generic one. Certainly I had no specific coniferous story to relate, and would not have tried to tell it as music if I had, for I do not believe that such a task lies within the province of the art.

Christopher Whelen recalled Bax's telling him that there was even less of a programme to this work than to Sibelius's *Tapiola*: 'So whatever the title may suggest to you, remember it possesses only the bare beauty and mystery of any forest.' In a letter to Julius Harrison dating from the 1940s, Bax wrote that 'since the printing of the score I have altered the last chord of all to pp, only strings pizz and harps . . . this sounds much better.' Orchestral parts used by Barbirolli in the 1930s have a repeat marked for the first four bars after figure 57, perhaps sanctioned by Bax, and this is followed by David Lloyd-Jones in his Naxos recording.

311 RED AUTUMN for two pianos

Date: *Gr5*: '1931'. The same source mentions that the work was composed for piano solo in 1912 but not published in that form (see **151**).
Dedication: *Printed score*: 'To Ethel Bartlett | and Rae Robertson'.
Manuscript: Not traced.
Publication: MM (616), 1933, 4to, 12 pp.; CH (48658), [1948].

[114] It is not certain that *The Tale the Pine-Trees knew* is the piece to which Bax is referring; he may have meant the Fifth Symphony or some other work.

Performance: Ethel Bartlett, Rae Robertson; College of Nursing, Henrietta Street, WC2; 3 October 1933 (London Contemporary Music Centre Concert).[115]
Duration: 5'17.

c. 1931

312 WATCHING THE NEEDLEBOATS for voice and piano

Date: Some of the songs in the collection for which this was written date from late 1930; others, including Bax's, are ascribed to '*c.* 1931' in Stephen Banfield, *Sensibility and English Song* (Cambridge, 1985). The commissioning date of March 1932 given in LF (p. 286) is unlikely since the song was publicly performed on 16 March.
Text: James Joyce, 'Watching the Needleboats at San Sabba' from *Pomes Penyeach.*
Manuscript: Not traced.
Publication: No. 2 in Herbert Hughes (ed.), *The Joyce Book* (London: The Sylvan Press, and Humphrey Milford, OUP, [1933]), fo., pp. 21-3 (published on 2 February 1933 in a limited edition of '500 printed [copies] of which 450 for sale' at two guineas each). Published with settings of Joyce's verse by Antheil, Bliss, Carducci, van Dieren, Goossens, Howells, Hughes, Ireland, Moeran, Orr, Roussel and Sessions. (Holst, Milhaud and Walton, amongst others, declined to contribute.) Also in *Twelve Songs for Medium/High Voice and Piano*, TP, 1984, 4to, pp. 62-4.
Performance: Dorothy Moulton (sop.), William Busch (pf.); College of Nursing, Henrietta Street, WC2; 16 March 1932 (London Contemporary Music Centre Concert).
Duration: 1'40.
Note: The idea for *The Joyce Book* came about in the autumn of 1929 (see Arthur Bliss, *As I Remember*, London, 1970, pp. 100-1). In a letter to Jane Wilson, Bliss recalled that the poems were allotted to their respective composers by the editor, except for Bliss's own, which he chose himself. Each of the thirteen contributors provided his services free so that the royalties might go to Joyce, though he later complained that he had received 'netissimo—that is a net nothing.'

1932

313 SYMPHONY NO. 5 for orchestra

I. Poco lento—Allegro con fuoco—Moderato. II. Poco lento. III. Poco moderato—Allegro—Epilogue: Doppio movimento alla breve.

Date: *Full score*: I. 'Morar and | London | Dec–1931–Jan 1932'. II. Undated, but a pencilled note under 79:4-6 reads 'Salen, Mull. Jan 1932'. III. 'Dec 1931 to | March 1932'. *Piano reduction*: 'Morar November 4th 1932'.

[115] The London Contemporary Music Centre was the British Section of the International Society for Contemporary Music.

Dedication: 'To Jean Sibelius'.
Orchestra: 3(1) 2+1 3(E♭)+1 2+1, 4331, timp., 4 perc. (b.d., t.d., s.d., tamb., cym., gong, gl.), hp., str.
Manuscript: *Sketch*: Privately owned (formerly by Colin Scott-Sutherland); [1] f. (verso blank); [1] p.; pencil; five staves cut from a larger piece of MS paper (218 × 79). The music comprises four bars on four staves with a pencil sketch for bars 131:2 to 132:2 in movt. III of the published score. *Full score*: BL (Add. MS 54730); 78 ff.; 151 pp. (1-64, 65-93, 94-151 + 1 blank); pp. 1-112, 125-51 + 1 blank: AL 29a paper (pp. 1-68: 355 × 263; pp. 69-112 and 125-51: trimmed to 360 × 258); pp. 113-24 (three bifolia): JWC 14 paper (trimmed to 358 × 263); bound by the BL with brown wrappers left over from the British Empire Exhibition (1924) bound in bearing the non-autograph note 'Original Manuscript | of | Bax "Symphony, No: 5"'. *Piano reduction*: SM; [18] ff.; 35 pp. + 1 blank; AL 12 paper (356 × 263); loosely inserted in elaborate stiff leather covers of Italian make, probably dating from 1965, when the MS was donated by Harriet Cohen to mark the centenary of Sibelius's birth; it was handed over to the museum by the Finnish Minister of Education on 30 May 1965.
Publication: MM (600), 1933, fo. and 8vo, 160 pp.; CH (no pl.no.), [1946]. 8vo; CH [1996], 8vo (st.sc.); WC0146C (A3 size); WC0146CX (A4 size); SMC (st.sc.).
Performance: London Philharmonic Orchestra, Sir Thomas Beecham; Queen's Hall; 15 January 1934 (Courtauld–Sargent Concert); repeated on 16 January.
Duration: 42'48.
Note: The piano score in the Sibelius Museum is not the original short score, which is missing, but a reduction made by Bax after the work had been completed in full score. This is confirmed in a letter to May Harrison dated 17 November 1932 in which he refers to the 'enormous amount of work' on which he has been engaged while staying in Morar, including 'making a piano version of the whole of my fifth symphony.' Earlier, on 18 December 1931, while orchestrating the first movement, he had described the symphony to May Harrison as 'one of my stormiest and darkest works'. To Christopher Whelen (in an undated letter from the early 1950s), he commented that 'the most crucial part [of movt. I] is the first few pages at the beginning of the first allegro. The strings must know their notes and play with confident ferocity.' To May Harrison he wrote (*c.* 1944): 'Personally I am not sure that No 5 is not the best of my symphonies but it is very hard to judge oneself.'

314 SUMMER MUSIC for orchestra (second version of **243**)

Date: 1932 (programme note for the first performance, in May, of this revised version).
Dedication: *Printed score*: 'To Sir THOMAS BEECHAM.'
Orchestra: 3(1) 1+1 2020, 4100, timp., hp., str.
Manuscript: Not traced.
Publication: MM (592), 1932, fo., 35 pp.

Performance: Philharmonic Orchestra (see p. 175 n.) and BBC Symphony Orchestra, Basil Cameron; Royal Albert Hall; 26 May 1932 (Concert for the Musicians' Benevolent Fund organized by *The News Chronicle*). 'This piece was once played . . . with two orchestras, and it sounded grand.' (From a letter dated 9 April [1951] from Bax to Christopher Whelen.)
Duration: 9'45.
Note: In a letter to Adrian Boult written shortly after the publication of the revised version, Bax commented: 'I am rather fond of this little bit of southern England under the sun, and enjoyed revising the orchestration. It is practically a new work in a way.' And to Christopher Whelen (December 1950): 'I am always fond of this piece as it holds the "sustained" serenity for which the Bournemouth critic kindly praises me.' On 16 January 1933, Bax sent May Harrison a programme note for the first performance of this revised version:

> The score of this short work (first produced by Sir Hamilton Harty some years ago and since considerably revised) has recently appeared in print with a dedication to Sir Thomas Beecham. The orchestra is a very modest one, a single trumpet alone representing the heavier brass group.
>
> The piece, a musical description of a hot windless June mid-day in some wooded place of Southern England, is lyrical throughout.
>
> During the greater part of it the strings are occupied in providing a murmurous accompaniment to the pastoral reveries of the various wind instruments, and not until near the end is there any great climax of sound.
>
> It is hoped that these indications of the composer's scheme in this little tone-poem will prove sufficient for its understanding.

Despite the revision, there was still a point of balance which failed to come off as he had intended, as he remarked in a letter to Whelen dating from about 1951:

> There actually is one awkward moment in it, for balance, and that strangely enough is where the cor anglais theme returns on all the strings near the end, with only light wood-wind above it, and yet the attention is inclined to be directed from the tune.

A similar warning was sent to Adrian Boult (see Jerrold Northrop Moore, *Music & Friends: Letters to Adrian Boult*, London, 1979, p. 145).

315 SINFONIETTA for orchestra

I. Alla breve. Molto moderato—Allegro deciso ma moderato—II. Andante con moto—III. Allegro.

Title: *MS*: 'Symphonic Phantasy'. Referred to by Bax, and listed in *Gr5*, as 'Sinfonietta'.
Date: 'May 1932'.
Orchestra: 3(1) 2+1 3+1 2+1, 4331, timp., 2 perc. (tamb., cym., gl.), hp., str.

Manuscript: *Holograph*: Dennis Andrews (MS formerly owned by Christopher Whelen); [42] ff.; 84 pp. (1-32, 33-51, 51-84); AL 18a paper (354 × 262); loosely inserted into green paper wrappers. *Copyist's score*: BBC.[116]Unpublished. *Parts*: BBC.
Performance: BBC Welsh Symphony Orchestra, Vernon Handley; Studio One, BBC Concert Hall, Llandaff; 25 June 1983; br. on Radio 3, 23 December 1983.
Duration: 23'37.
Note: The original title of this work should not be confused with the piano piece of the same name (see **127**); and there is no connection with the Symphonietta (**144**). The work was never played during Bax's lifetime, and in a letter to Christopher Whelen he explained why: 'You ask about the Sinfonietta. I have never thought this work was quite up to the mark and so have not tried to get a performance.' Whelen visited him in Storrington on 17 July 1950, and it was on this occasion that Bax gave him the MS of the Sinfonietta, nudging him in the ribs and saying 'I don't want this done, mind.' At the foot of p. 1 Bax has written in pencil the outline of a melody that was used in the finale of the music for the film *Malta, G. C.* (**347**), and subsequently in the *Victory March* (**364**) and the *Coronation March* (**385**). A photograph of the composer taken at The White Horse in Storrington in 1942, shortly before the *Malta, G. C.* music was begun, appears in (among other publications) Jonah Barrington's autobiography *And Master of None* (London, n.d.), p. 97, and shows him posing with a MS that can be identified as pp. 4-5 of the Sinfonietta. He is holding a pen in his hand, and it seems probable that it was on this occasion that he wrote the word 'wildly' just under fig. 5, which seems to be written in a different ink from that used for the rest of the score. This pictorial evidence further suggests that Bax conceived the *Malta, G. C.* melody at about this time and wrote it down on the first piece of MS paper that came to hand.

316 CONCERTO for cello and orchestra

I. Allegro moderato—Più lento (Andante). II. Nocturne (Lento). III. Molto vivace.

Title: *MS*: 'Concerto for | Violincello [*sic*] and Orchestra'.
Date: *Full score*: I. 'Morar | Nov 12th 1932'. II. 'Morar Nov 16th 1932'. III. 'Dec 19th 1932'. Written in 'London and Morar' according to a note from Bax to Christopher Whelen (see also **Note** below).
Dedication: 'To Gaspar Cassado'.
Orchestra: 3(1) 2+1 20 2+1, 4200, timp., hp., str.
Manuscript: *Sketch*: Privately owned (formerly by Colin Scott-Sutherland); [2] ff. (1 bifolium); [2] pp. + 2 blank; in pencil; 12-staff paper with printed clefs and braces (269 × 366), not otherwise attested among Bax's MSS. This comprises a short-score sketch for movt. III, 76:15 to 80:1 in the published f.sc. *Full score*: BL (Add. MS

[116] At the time of writing, this score was not available for inspection, having been on loan to a conductor for ten years.

54755); [58] ff.; 111 pp. (1-54, 55-74, 75-111 + 5 blank); AL 14 paper (357 × 261); loosely inserted in brown paper wrappers. There are two extra bars at the end of movt. I that are crossed through in blue pencil and omitted from the published score, which ends with the unaccompanied timp. solo. There are engravers' marks and also annotations in ink, presumably written by a part-copyist, since they refer to instrumental cues.

Publication: *Full score*: MM (615), 1934, fo., 84 pp.; WC0229C. *Cello and piano*: MM (620), 1934, fo., 43 pp.; CH (38833), [1948]; WC0229.

Performance: Gaspar Cassadó (vc.), London Symphony Orchestra, Sir Hamilton Harty; Queen's Hall; 5 March 1934.

Arrangement: For viola and orchestra by Norman Carrell. *Viola part only*: Privately owned; t.p. + 16 pp.; 12-staff paper. Unpublished. Bax is reported to have shown little enthusiasm for this arrangement, and it has never been played.

Duration: 33'43.

Note: The commission to write this work came from the dedicatee, but Bax was initially unenthusiastic: 'Have you considered the horror of trying to write a cello concerto? That is my hideous fate,' he wrote to Arthur Alexander; and in another letter, to Tilly Fleischmann, he commented: 'I have been scoring part of a cello concerto I am trying to write for the Spaniard, Gaspar Cassadó. It is a tricky but interesting undertaking—though I would never have thought of writing such a thing if I had not been bullied into it.' Harriet Cohen, however, claimed that 'Arnold doted on Gaspar and promptly wrote him a cello concerto the slow movement of which was "to recall you to your naughty boy" as he called the darkly handsome Spaniard.' (*A Bundle of Time*, p. 160.) On the day after finishing the slow movement, he wrote to May Harrison from the Station Hotel in Morar: 'I have been doing an enormous amount of work whilst I have been here—in fact 73 pages of scoring the cello concerto in ten days . . .'. Beatrice Harrison performed the concerto on 2 January 1938, and in a letter written a few weeks earlier he warned her about the opening of the work: 'Be careful not to let the beginning hang about rhapsodically. It must go along with urge [*sic*] and fire. Cassado (who gave the first performance . . .) made this mistake at first, but the other day at Bournemouth it was just right.'[117] Later on, in 1947, Bax mentioned in a letter to the BBC that 'the fact that nobody has ever taken up this work has been one of the major disappointments of my musical life.'

317 SAGA FRAGMENT for piano, trumpet, strings and percussion

Title: *MS*: 'Saga-fragment.'

Date: Undated. *Gr5*: '1932'.

Dedication: 'To Harriet Cohen.' (in her handwriting only).

[117] For further correspondence between Bax and Beatrice Harrison, see David Candlin's notes for Symposium CD 1150, which contains her 1938 performance of the concerto.

Orchestra: 1 tpt., 2 perc. (b.d., s.d., cym.), pf., str.
Manuscript: *Holograph*: LC (ML96.B36); [18] ff.; 2 blank pp. (the first with a presentation inscription to LC from Harriet Cohen dated 29 December 1933) + 33 pp. (only 1-13 pagin. by Bax) + 1 blank; AL 14 paper (357 × 261). *Copyist's score*: BL (Add. MS 54747) [16] ff.; 32 pp.; 28-staff paper; facsimile held by CH. Unpublished. *Parts*: CH.
Performance: Harriet Cohen, 'The Orchestra',[118] Constant Lambert; Queen's Hall; 21 October 1933.
Duration: 10'53.
Note: This work is an orchestrated version of the Piano Quartet (**255**). The arrangement adheres quite closely to the original: the piano and string parts are altered slightly and there is an additional double bass part, as well as counter melodies for the solo trumpet and parts for three percussion instruments. In a programme note, Bax wrote:

> . . . although the music follows no detailed programme, the title, suggesting violent and passionate scenes in a Northern land, may evoke in the listener's mind the 'battles of long ago' of which the composer was thinking.

The quotation comes from Wordsworth's 'The Solitary Reaper' and can also be found as the epigraph on the title page of Bax's libretto for his projected opera *Deirdre* (**106**). In a letter to Aloys Fleischmann, Bax referred to the work as 'rather a tough pill'.

318 SONATA NO. 4 for piano

I. Allegro giusto. II. Allegretto quasi andante. III. Allegro.

Date: *Gr5*: '1932'.
Dedication: *Printed score*: 'To Charles Lynch'.
Manuscript: Not traced. Pencil sketches for the first two subject groups can be found on a blank page at the end of the MS of the Nonet (**302**).
Publication: MM (633), 1934, 4to, 34 pp.; CH (37240), [1945]; WC0468.
Performance: (1) Harriet Cohen; Town Hall, New York; 1 February 1934. (2) Harriet Cohen; Wigmore Hall; 18 May 1934.
Duration: 17'35.
Note: Apart from his eighteenth-century pastiche, the Sonata in B♭ ('Salzburg') of 1937 (**341**), this was Bax's last sonata for piano and, with the exception of the *Legend* of 1935 (**334**), his last major work for the instrument. Tilly Fleischmann drew Colin Scott-Sutherland's attention to the close resemblance between the principal melody of the slow movement and the Irish folktune 'Has sorrow thy young days shaded' (CSS, pp. 80, 112). The composer is said to have been particularly fond of this movement.

118 '. . . a small unnamed, but efficient, orchestra.' (*Musical Opinion*, December 1933, p. 236.)

1933

319 STRING QUINTET for 2 violins, 2 violas and 1 cello (in one movement)

Title: *MS*: 'String Quintett.'
Date: 'London | Jan 21st 1933'. *Gr5* wrongly lists it as 1931.
Dedication: *Printed score only*: 'To the Stratton String Quartet'.
Manuscript: CH (MS 239a); [11] ff.; 21 pp. + 1 blank; AL 14 paper (357 × 261).
Publication: MM (652), 1935, 4to, 20 pp.; *score*: WC0483C; *parts*: WC0483.
Performance: Raymond Jeremy (va.), Stratton Quartet: George Stratton (vn.), Carl Taylor (vn.), Watson Forbes (va.), John Moore (vc.); Æolian Hall; 1 March 1935.
Duration: 11'46.

320 PRELUDE FOR A SOLEMN OCCASION for orchestra

Title: *Short score*: 'III'. *Full score*: 'Prelude for a Solemn Occasion'. For the spurious title 'Northern Ballad No. 3' see **Note** below.
Date: *Short score*: 'Oct 26th | 1927'. *Full score*: 'Morar. | Feb 1933'.
Orchestra: 3(1) 2+1 2+1 2+1, 4331, timp., 2 perc. (b.d., s.d., cym., tri., gong, gl.), org.,[119] hp., str.
Manuscript: *Short score*: BL (Add. MS 54750); [6] ff.; [12] pp. (pagin. 31-42); AL 12 paper (355 × 260). There are pencil notes for orchestration and, at the foot of p. 35, pencil sketches for the ending of the first movement of the Sixth Symphony (**331**). Bars 11-15 of p. 36 and the whole of p. 37 are crossed through in pencil. The first four bars of p. 38 are also not in the orchestrated version. *Full score*: BL (Add. MS 54756); 18 ff.; 34 pp.; AL 29b paper (356 × 263). The first page of the score is preceded by a folio (conjugate with f. 18) on the recto of which are unidentified pencil sketches (**323**). *Copyist's score*: BBC; 20 ff.; 40 pp.; 28-staff paper (413 × 292); in orange-brown wrappers. Unpublished. *Parts*: BBC.
Performance: BBC Northern Orchestra, Edward Downes; Studio 7, New Broadcasting House, Manchester; 23 September 1982; br. on Radio 3, 18 November 1983.
Duration: 7'24.
Note: Since the short score of this work is headed 'III' and dates from about the same time as the short score of the *First Northern Ballad*, the orchestrated version was first broadcast as 'Northern Ballad No. 3', a title that was never used by Bax but has regrettably become attached to it, displacing the correct one on both its commercial recordings. It seems inappropriate for the ceremonial nature of much of the music and is chronologically confusing, since the full score was completed before the *Second Northern Ballad*. The short score of 'III' is paginated from 31 to 42, suggesting that it was indeed intended originally as the third movement of a larger work; but it is impossible to determine whether what became the *First*

[119] Although not marked in the score as optional, the organ is not essential; it was omitted at the first performance.

Northern Ballad was also originally intended to be part of it. However, three facts suggest that it was not: firstly, it postdates 'III'; secondly, since it was unpaginated by Bax, it is unlikely to be part of a MS containing a third movement that *is* paginated; thirdly, it occupies twelve pages, which means that the hypothetical middle movement would have been paginated from 13 to 30, making it three times as long as, for example, the piano-score slow movement of the Fifth Symphony. The pagination of 'III' certainly suggests that the work of which it was intended to form part was on a symphonic scale; but the first movement would surely have been longer than what became the *First Northern Ballad*.

321 SONATINA for cello and piano

I. Allegro risoluto. II. Andante. III. Moderato.

Title: *MS*: 'Sonatina'. First performed as 'Sonata in D minor', but subsequently as 'Sonatina'.
Date: 'Sept 27th | 1933'. The second element of the date is indistinct but looks more like '27' than '29'.
Dedication: 'To Pablo Casals' (who never played the work).
Manuscript: NYPL; [9] ff.; 18 pp. (1-6, 7-11, 12-18); AL 14 paper (357 × 261).
Publication: MM (622), 1934, 4to, 23 pp.; CH (40421), [1950]; WC0436.
Performance: (1) *As 'Sonata in D minor'*: Thelma Reiss (vc.), Harriet Cohen (pf.); Wigmore Hall; 8 March 1934. 'The Sonata was extremely well played and warmly received.' (*The Musical Times*, April 1934, p. 363.) (2) *As 'Sonatina in D minor'*: Thelma Reiss (vc.), Harriet Cohen (pf.); br. live on BBC National programme, 13 March 1934.
Duration: 15'56.

322 SYMPHONIC SCHERZO for orchestra (second version of 187)

Title: The original version of 1917 was called 'Scherzo'.
Date: '1917 | Revised 1933 | Morar'. Since the MS of the original version of 1917 bears an inscription to Mary Gleaves dated 'Dec 5th 1933 | Morar.', it seems certain that this revision was completed on or about that date.
Orchestra: 3(1) 2+1 2+1 2+1, 4331, timp., 4 perc. (b.d., s.d., tamb., cym., gl., cel.), hp., str.
Manuscript: BL (Add. MS 54742); [29] ff.; 57 pp. + 1 blank; AL 29b paper (355 × 262). Unpublished. *Parts*: CH.[120]
Performance: Royal Philharmonic Orchestra, Vernon Handley; All Saints' Church, Tooting; 3 January 1986 (recording session for Chandos Records Ltd.).
Duration: 7'18.

[120] The note 'arr Graham Parlett' against this title in Warner Chappell's 1990 hire catalogue is a mistake; I was responsible only for writing out some of the parts.

Note: The differences between this revision and the original version are mostly to do with orchestration, though there are also a number of melodic, harmonic and rhythmic alterations.

c. 1933

323 [UNTITLED]: Sketches

Note: These pencil sketches are jotted down on a folio of the full score of the *Prelude for a Solemn Occasion* (**320**) and seem to bear no relation to any of Bax's extant works.

1934

324 NORTHERN BALLAD NO. 2 for orchestra

Title: *MS*: 'Second Northern Ballad'.
Date: 'Morar | Dec-1933 | Jan 1934'.
Dedication: 'To Adam Carse'.
Orchestra: 3(1) 2+1 2+1 2+1, 4331, timp., 4 perc. (b.d., s.d., tamb., cym., gong, tri., xyl., gl.), hp., str.
Manuscript: *Sketches*: Privately owned (formerly by Colin Scott-Sutherland); [2] ff.; [4] pp.; mostly in pencil, a few lines in ink; AL 14 paper (357 × 261). These pages contain rough jottings for much of the work's thematic material, mostly on two staves but with a four-staff sketch for the transition to the middle section; there are also four systems of music not found in the f.sc. *Full score*: CH (MS 253); [32] ff.; 58 pp. + 6 blank; AL 29b paper (356 × 262); loosely inserted in brown card wrappers.
Publication: *Photocopy of MS*: WC0306.
Performance: London Philharmonic Orchestra, Basil Cameron; Royal Albert Hall; 16 February 1946.
Duration: 15'12.
Note: The origins of this work are revealed in a letter that Bax wrote to Julian Herbage in 1946, shortly before its first performance:

> [It] has no special programme attached to it—even less than its predecessor [**309**]. It suggests merely an atmosphere of the dark north and perhaps dark happenings among the mists. I have never been able to discover whether I like this piece or not—to tell you the truth.

This last remark explains why Bax waited twelve years before having the work performed (cf. his comments on the Sinfonietta (**315**); the Fourth Symphony and the Violin Concerto were also initially held back). Having heard the work, however, Bax changed his mind: 'The performance of the Ballad was certainly not perfect,[121] but all the same I liked the piece far better than I thought I did. (I wrote

[121] Elsewhere in this letter Bax mentions that the string parts were poorly copied.

it in 1933 and just put it aside as I was doubtful about it.)' (From an undated letter to May Harrison.)

325 FATHERLAND for tenor, chorus and orchestra (second version of **92**)

Date: Undated, but the front of the wrappers containing the MS has '1934 Revised Version' written on it (not in Bax's hand), and this is consistent with the appearance of the handwriting in the score. Since there was a performance on 1 May 1934, perhaps it was revised at Morar during the early months of that year. The performance was advertised in *The Musical Times* for October 1933, p. 946, but the revision may not have been started until later.
Orchestra: 3(1) 2+1 2+1 2+1, 4331, timp., 3 perc. (b.d., s.d., cym., gl.), hp., str.
Manuscript: BL (Loan 75/9); [15] ff.; 29 pp. + 1 blank; AL 29b paper (355 × 262); stitched into orange paper wrappers ('Chester's Circulating Music Library'). This revision is unpublished, the printed vocal scores of the original version being amended by hand. The work was transferred to CH from JWC in 1982 in exchange for Lord Berners' *Nicholas Nickleby*. *Parts*: CH.
Performance: Percy Manchester (ten.), Philharmonic Choir, London Symphony Orchestra, Charles Kennedy Scott; Queen's Hall; 1 May 1934.
Duration: 6'48.
Note: Since the full score of the original version is untraced, it is impossible to tell how much Bax revised the orchestration. Structurally the only difference is the excision of 27 bars (from 12:1 to 13:12 of the printed vocal score), which are replaced by ten new bars.

326 THREE SONGS for high voice and orchestra[122]

a. 'A Lyke-Wake | (Border Ballad)'. **b.** 'Wild Almond (Scherzo)'. **c.** [The Splendour falls].

Title: Collective title found only in *Gr5* as '3 Songs'. **a.** *Original (1907) title*: 'A Lyke-Wake Dirge'. **b.** *MS*: 'Wild Almond | (Herbert Trench) | Poem with Orchestra' (t.p.). 'Wild Almond (Scherzo)' (p. 1).
Date: a. 'Scored | Morar. | Feb 1934'. **b.** 'Orchestrated | Glencolumcille | April 1934'. The date '*c.* 1927' given in *Gr5* is somewhat wide of the mark.
Text: a. Anonymous 15th century Scottish ballad. **b.** Herbert Trench, 'Wild Almond'. **c.** Alfred, Lord Tennyson, 'Blow, bugle, blow', introductory song from *The Princess*, iv.
Orchestra: a. 3(1) 2+1 2+1 2+1, 4330, timp., 2 perc. (b.d., cym.), hp., str.
b. 3222, 3000, hp., str.
Manuscript: 326a: ULL (MS 435); [8] ff.; 15 pp. + 1 blank; AL 29b paper (356 × 262). **326b**: ULSC (fML 96 B35); [6] ff.; t.p. + 1 p. with an inscription in Harriet

[122] **327b** specifically for 'soprano voice'.

Cohen's hand (see below) + 9 pp. + 1 blank; AL 29a paper (360 × 262). The inscription on f. [1v] reads: 'To Ben & Peter' (Britten and Pears) offering them the MS; but in a postscript dating from 1960 Miss Cohen indicates that she will send them 'another copy' of the song (i.e. the version with piano) and give this one to ULSC. **326c**: Not traced. All unpublished. *Str. parts for* **a.** Graham Parlett.
Performance: 326a *only*: Martyn Hill (ten.), London Philharmonic Orchestra, Bryden Thomson; All Saints' Church, Tooting; 11 April 1988 (recording session for Chandos Records Ltd.). **326b** and **326c**: None.
Duration: a. 7'04. **b.** *c.* 3'00.
Note: Unlike the piano scores of the first two songs, that of 'The Splendour falls' contains no instrumental indications, although that in itself is no proof that Bax did not—as in the case of 'A Lyke-Wake'—annotate a rewritten piano score. For details of the original versions for voice and piano see **105, 269** and **186** respectively.

327 SONATA for clarinet and piano

I. Molto moderato. II. Vivace.

Title: The designation 'Sonata in B flat' found on the notes to the Chandos recording and elsewhere is a mistake, the work being in D; it is scored for a clarinet in B♭.
Date: 'June 1934'.
Dedication: 'To Hugh Prew'.
Manuscript: UCC; [9] ff.; 17 pp. (1-9, 10-17 + 1 blank); AL 12 paper (357 × 262); stitched into manila wrappers with non-autograph paper title label on upper cover. A pencilled note in Bax's hand beneath the title reads: 'Please do not engrave phrasing marks in the clarinet part at present'.
Publication: MM (653), 1935, 4to, 20 pp.; CH (37089), 1943; WC0513. In 1998 the work had been on the Syllabus of Examinations for the Advanced Certificate of The Associated Board of the Royal Schools of Music for seven years.
Performance: Frederick Thurston (cl.), Harriet Cohen (pf.); Cowdray Hall; 17 June 1935 (London Contemporary Music Centre Concert). The work was played twice at the concert, the second time in place of Lennox Berkeley's Sonatina, the score of which had been lost in the post.
Duration: 13'41.

328 [SONATA NO. 2] for viola and piano

I. [Unknown]. II. [Lento?]. III. Allegro.

Date: 'In the journal *Musical Opinion* in 1934, there appeared an announcement that Bax was writing a second viola sonata for Lionel Tertis' (LF, p. 300). I have been unable to trace this reference, but in view of its relationship to the Sixth Symphony (see **Note** below), this date is likely. I have placed it between the Sonata for clarinet (finished in June) and the Octet (drafted by 20 October) because no other work can be ascribed to this period.

1. Arnold Bax as a young man. Photograph signed by the composer: '"Teddy" 1903'

2. Arnold Bax at the age of sixty. Photograph by Howard Coster, 1944

3. A page from the manuscript of the String Quartet in E (1903)

4. A page from the manuscript of *In Memoriam* (1916)

5. A page from the manuscript of the Sinfonietta (1932)

Manuscript: Not traced except for 1 folio (pagin. 21 and 22): Clifford Gillam (MS formerly owned by Harriet Cohen); AL 14 paper (362 × 262). This consists of the final page of movt. II and, on the reverse, the first page of III. Unpublished.
Performance: *Extant fragments only*: Michael Ponder (va.), David Owen Norris (pf.); British Music Information Centre; 14 October 1983 (lecture-recital by Lewis Foreman, *et al.*).
Note: The musical material of the final page of movt. II is identical with the ending of the slow movement of the Sixth Symphony: the last six bars have been crossed through and replaced with the chords with which the symphonic movement concludes. It seems quite possible, though at present unprovable, that the missing first movement and the rest of the second were used by Bax as a short score for the symphony (see **331** for details). The material of the first page of the finale, which has been crossed through, was not reused in any later extant work.

329 OCTET for horn, piano, 2 violins, 2 violas, cello and double bass

I. Meditation (Molto moderato). II. Scherzo (Allegro).

Title: *Short score*: 'Serenade | Horn Str VI and Piano'. *Full score*: 'Octet'.
Date: *Short score*: 'London | Oct 20th 1934'. *Full score*: 'London | Oct 31st 1934'.
Dedication: 'To Mrs Elizabeth Sprague Coolidge | with kindest birthday wishes'.
Manuscript: *Short score*: LC (ML29c.B34); [6] ff.; [12] pp. ([1-5], [6-12]); AL 14 paper (357 × 261). *Full score*: LC (ML29c.B34); [18] ff.; 35 pp. (1-15, 16-35 + 1 blank; also non-autograph pagin. 13-47, pp. 1-12 referring to the sh.sc.); AL 29b paper (355 × 262). MSS received by LC from the dedicatee on 2 November 1935. Facsimiles of both scores are in the BL (MS Facs. 639). *Copyist's score A*: Dennis Andrews (MS formerly owned by Christopher Whelen); 19 ff.; t.p. + 1 blank + 35 pp. ([1]-15, 16-35) + 1 blank; 24-staff paper (365 × 272); the pencilled cue letters are almost certainly in Bax's hand. *Copyist's score B*: CH; 21 ff.; 42 pp. (1-17, 18-42); 24-staff paper.
Publication: *Photocopy of copyist's score B*: CH, 1990 (*score*: WC 0381C; *parts*: WC0381).
Performance: Aubrey Brain (hn.), Harriet Cohen (pf.), Frederick Riddle (va.), Eugene Cruft (d.b.), Griller Quartet: Sidney Griller (vn.), Jack O'Brien (vn.), Philip Burton (va.), Colin Hampton (vc.); Æolian Hall; 11 December 1936 (London Contemporary Music Centre Concert). For a review of this concert see **336** below.
Duration: 14'20.

330 ETERNITY for high voice and orchestra

Date: 'Morar Nov 16th 1934'.
Text: Robert Herrick, 'Eternity'.
Orchestra: 3 2+1 20 2+1, 4331, timp., str.
Manuscript: BL (Add. MS 54774); [5] ff.; 10 pp.; AL 29b paper (356 × 262). Unpublished in this form. *Str. parts*: Graham Parlett.
Performance: Martyn Hill (ten.), London Philharmonic Orchestra, Bryden Thomson; All Saints' Church, Tooting; 11 April 1988 (recording session for Chandos Records Ltd.).
Duration: 2'57.
Note: For details of the original version for voice and piano see **273**.

1935

331 SYMPHONY NO. 6 for orchestra

I. Moderato—Allegro con fuoco. II. Lento, molto espressivo. III. Introduction (Lento moderato)—Scherzo and Trio (Allegro vivace—Andante semplice)—Epilogue (Lento).

Date: *Short score*: Undated. *Full score*: I. Undated; II. 'Morar | Nov. 1934'; III. 'Morar Feb 10th | 1935'. Composed in 'London and Morar' according to a note from Bax to Christopher Whelen. 'I don't remember about the origins of the symphony, but the idea of the scherzo certainly [came] to me at Morar. I can even remember the exact place by the sea opposite the islands of Rum and Eigg.'
Dedication: *Full score*: '~~To Karol Szymanowski~~ Adrian Boult' (the first name in ink, the second in pencil). In a letter to the dedicatee dated 4 September 1935, Bax wrote: 'I have put "To Adrian Boult" as a dedication. It seemed more matey than "Dr." But if you prefer the latter let me know.'
Orchestra: 3(1) 2+1 3(E♭)+1 2+1, 4331, timp., 4 perc. (b.d., t.d., s.d., tamb., cym., gong, tri., gl., cel.), hp., str.
Manuscript: *Sketches*: (A) British Library (Add. MS 54750); [1] f.; [1] p.; AL 12 paper (330 × 243). Final bars of movt. I pencilled on three staves at the foot of p. 35; (B) Clifford Gillam (MS formerly owned by Harriet Cohen); [1] f.; [1] p.; AL 14 paper (357 × 261). Final page of movt. II in its original form as part of a projected viola sonata (see **328** above).

Short score (incomplete): BL (Add. MS 54731); 12 ff. (the last two unfoliated); [4] pp. + 11 + [3] pp. + 6 blank (except for f. 10^{v}, which contains a pencilled sequence of ten unidentified chords on a single staff); AL 14 paper (trimmed to 354 × 263); bound by the BL; f. 1 is the first leaf of a bifolium of BH 43 paper (356 × 264), the second leaf being f. [12]), and contains one five-staff system of six bars in pencil of the full score of bars 3-4 and 7-9 from the third variation (*Nocturne*) of the *Symphonic Variations* for piano and orchestra (see **210**), bars 5-6 (for piano solo) being omitted and the rest of the side and its reverse being blank; f. 2 is the short score of the introduction to the Sixth Symphony, with the heading 'Vorspiel Sechste Symphonie' crossed through in pencil and 'Sixth Symphony' pencilled in to the left; ff. 3-8v contain the short score of movt. III with indications of the intended orchestration in pencil; there is a cut from bar 13 of f. 7v to bar 9 (inclusive) of f. 8, a 'Più Lento' episode based on the melody of the trio having been excised; f. 9 contains a pencilled f.sc. of the epilogue beginning with the solo horn entry as far as five bars after fig. 40 in the printed score; the remainder is blank except for f. 10v (as noted above).

Full score: *Movt. I*: CH (MS 245) but currently (1998) on loan to the Bournemouth Symphony Orchestra for exhibition in the Guildhall Museum, Bournemouth; [29] ff.; 58 pp.; AL 29b paper (356 × 262); loose in brown folder. *Movts. II and III*: GM (MG C2/BAX-9-2); [41] ff.; 82pp. (59-84, 85-140); AL 29b paper (356 × 262). These two movements arrived at the Grainger Museum in July 1939, seven months after it opened. In an undated letter to Percy Grainger (30 May 1939?) Bax wrote: 'Thank you for your letter of last week. I am very pleased to fall in with your request and am leaving the m.s of part of my sixth symphony at Schott's to be delivered to you. I will send on the rest of it if it turns up.' By 1951 Bax had forgotten about this arrangement and thought the MS had been lost: "I expect it was burned in Tania's [Harriet Cohen's] house when it was destroyed by two incendiary bombs in 1942 [actually 1940].' (From a letter to Christopher Whelen.)

Publication: MM (651), 1935, fo. and 8vo, 128 pp.; CH (37849), [1945], 8vo (min.sc.); CH, [1990], 8vo (st.sc.); WC0479C (A3 size); WC0479CX (A4 size); SMC (st.sc.).

Performance: London Philharmonic Orchestra, Sir Hamilton Harty; Queen's Hall; 21 November 1935 (Royal Philharmonic Society Concert). Bax was delighted with this performance and wrote to the conductor: 'You realised everything I wanted and indeed took some of it into a world of beauty I did not know the work compassed. I am only afraid that no-one (except maybe yourself) will ever recreate tonight's experience for me. I am sure it was the best first performance any work ever had.' 'The audience, which included many of the foreign music critics now visiting this country, were moved to great enthusiasm and called the composer several times to the platform.' (Review by 'B.M.' (Basil Maine?) from an unidentified newspaper cutting.) '[It is] in all respects the most mature and powerful work of Bax that I have ever heard . . . The whole work marches irresistibly and irrevocably from point to point with the inevitability of complete mastery.' (Kaikhosru Sorabji, *The New English Weekly*, 12 December 1935, p. 174.)

Duration: 39'35.

Note: The short score as it stands consists only of the introduction to movt. I and the whole of III; but since there is evidence that II at least was originally written as part of a second viola sonata, of which only one folio has been traced (see **328** above), it is possible that movt. I (excluding the introduction), as well as II, was also intended as part of the sonata, to which Bax added the introduction when he came to turn it into a symphony; this might explain the absence of the rest of the short score and also why the last bar of the introduction, ending with the downward septuplet (last bar of p. 9 in the published score) is followed by a blank space rather than plunging straight into the 'Allegro'. The imprint of the paper is the same as that of the extant folio of the sonata.

In a letter to Christopher Whelen (1950), Bax wrote:

> I like the idea of No 6 being played at Bournemouth, as it is the symphony of mine which I know least myself. When I heard it played by Boult about two years ago there were times when I could not remember what was coming next—a very curious experience. I don't think any of my symphonies have been played more than about ten times in this country—a somewhat discouraging fact!

332 THE MORNING WATCH for chorus (SATB) and orchestra

Date: 'London | March | 1935'.
Dedication: *MS*: 'To Sir Ivor Atkins | (in memory of very old days)'. *Printed score*: 'To Sir Ivor Atkins'.
Text: Henry Vaughan, 'The Morning Watch'.
Orchestra: 3(1) 2+1 3+1 2+1, 4331, timp., 3 perc. (b.d., t.d., s.d., cym., gong, tri., gl.), hp., str.
Manuscript: *Full score*: CH (MS 256); [33] ff.; 66 pp. (pp. 1 and 2 have the top corner missing; p. 3 has the number pencilled in; the rest are numbered in ink by Bax); AL 29b paper (356 × 262); loose in brown wrappers. *Parts*: CH.
Publication: *Vocal score only*: MM (650), 1935, 8vo, 40 pp.; CH (37963), 1943.
Performance: Combined choirs of Gloucester, Hereford and Worcester, London Symphony Orchestra, Sir Ivor Atkins; Worcester Cathedral; 4 September 1935 (Three Choirs Festival). According to Harriet Cohen (*A Bundle of Time*, p. 258), this performance was 'under-rehearsed and rather ragged orchestrally . . . the choir was magnificent.'
Duration: 19'13.

333 NYMPHOLEPT for orchestra (second version of **164**)

Note: In a letter received by Adrian Boult on 23 April 1935, Bax mentioned that he was revising this tone-poem of 1915: 'I have been working hard at the revision of this little piece, and I believe there is something in it. It was never played in those days on account of its elaborate difficulties.' However, there is no trace of a revised MS. It was probably at this time that Bax inscribed the dedication to Constant Lambert, who conducted some of his works in the early 1930s (including *Saga Fragment* and *The Tale the Pine-trees knew*).

334 LEGEND for piano

Title: 'Legends | No I'.
Date: Undated, but probably started after 13 May (see **Note** below).
Dedication: 'To John Simons'.
Manuscript: *Sketch*: Privately owned; [1] f.; [1] p. + 1 blank; pencil; AL 29b paper (356 × 262). Two two-staff systems containing the ten bars from [6]:16 to [7]:5 in the final version. *Complete*: Lewis Foreman (MS formerly owned by John Simons); [4] ff.; [7] pp. + 1 blank; ALP 12 paper (355 × 263); loose in brown paper wrappers with Harriet Cohen's writing on the front; dyeline copies were circulated privately by the dedicatee. *Copyist's score A*: Privately owned; [4] ff.; 8 pp.; C paper; the copyist was Peter Washtell. *Copyist's score B*: Lewis Foreman; [7] ff.; 15 pp. + 7 blank; 12-staff 'Tudor Music Manuscript Book' with green wrappers; in ballpoint; the copyist was Patrick Piggott.
Publication: *Edited by Richard G. Hallas*: FMP, 1995, 4to, 14 pp. + 1 p. of editorial notes; introductory note by Graham Parlett.
Performance: John Simons; br. on Radio 3, 28 August 1969.
Duration: 6'24.
Note: This work was not played during Bax's lifetime, and the dedicatee knew nothing of its existence until several years after the composer's death, when Harriet Cohen presented him with the MS. Bax apparently wrote it after hearing his Third Sonata played by Simons at a private play-through less than a week before a public performance at the Wigmore Hall on 18 May 1935, which the composer was unable to attend. Bax was so impressed that he wrote to the pianist congratulating him on 'the sensitivity showed [*sic*] towards the inner meaning of the work'. This letter is postmarked 13 May, which indicates that the *Legend* was started after that date. In spite of the wording of the title, there do not appear to be any other pieces in the series.

1936

335 ROGUE'S COMEDY: Overture for orchestra

Title: The plural form *Rogues'* is sometimes written but is incorrect.
Date: 'Morar | Jan to Feb | 1936'.
Dedication: 'To Julius Harrison' (the name has been written over an illegible erasure, the 'J' seemingly altered from an 'S').
Orchestra: 3(1) 2+1 3+1 2+1, 4331, timp., 5 perc. (b.d., s.d., tamb., cym., gong, ratt., tri., gl.), hp., str.

Manuscript: CH (MS 243); [28] ff.; 54 pp. + 2 blank; AL 29b paper (355 × 262); loose in brown paper wrappers. Unpublished. *Parts*: CH.
Performance: Liverpool Philharmonic Orchestra, Sir Hamilton Harty; Central Hall, Liverpool; 13 October 1936.
Duration: 9'06.
Note: 'I have been in the west of Scotland again lately, scoring a rather rampagious [*sic*] overture—most unsuited to the lovely country!' (From a letter to Tilly Fleischmann postmarked 24 February 1936.) For the first performance Edwin Evans wrote the following note, which is clearly based on information supplied by Bax:

As the title of this work may be taken to imply the existence of a detailed underlying programme it is perhaps expedient to state that the Overture was completed before the title occurred to the composer. He considers it an apt description for a short work during the greater part of which the characteristics exhibited are swagger, braggadocio and impudence. Otherwise it has no definite programme basis . . .

Perhaps the title had been suggested by the phrase 'rogue's comedy' used in Evans's programme note for the *Overture to a Picaresque Comedy* (**305**).

336 THRENODY AND SCHERZO for bassoon, harp, 2 violins, 2 violas, cello and double bass

I. Threnody (Poco lento). II. Scherzo (Allegro).

Title: *MS*: 'Threnody and Scherzo for Bassoon Str Sextet and Harp'. First performed under the title 'Octet', but changed presumably to avoid confusion with the Octet for horn, piano and string sextet (**329**), which was premièred at the same concert. The title 'Concerto' has been crossed through on the paper wrappers containing the MS, and a note added in ballpoint pen: 'Bax calls it Threnody and Scherzo'; but it is listed as 'Concerto' in *Gr5*, probably through confusion with **337** below.
Date: I. 'London | March 3rd 1936'. II. 'London | March 14th | 1936'.
Dedication: 'To Patrick Hadley.' Someone has barbarously gone over the letters of this dedication in ballpoint pen to make them clearer, presumably for reproduction.
Manuscript: *Sketch*: Privately owned (formerly by Colin Scott-Sutherland); [1] f.; [1] p. + 1 blank; pencil; AL 12 paper (330 × 243). Fragment of a melodic line resembling the bassoon passage beginning at 10:13 in the f.sc. *Full score*: CH (MS 246); [21] ff.; 42 pp. (1-20, 21-42); ALP 18 paper (355 × 263); loose in brown paper wrappers. The harp part has pedallings marked in pencil in Maria Korchinska's hand.
Publication: CH, 1990 (*score*: WC0096C; *parts*: WC0096).
Performance: Archie Camden (bn.), Maria Korchinska (hp.), Frederick Riddle (va.), Eugene Cruft (d.b.), Griller Quartet: Sidney Griller (vn.), Jack O'Brien (vn.), Philip Burton (va.), Colin Hampton (vc.); Æolian Hall; 11

December 1936 (London Contemporary Music Centre Concert). 'At the end of the concert the lights were lowered and the audience listened to the broadcasting of Edward VIII.'s farewell.' (Jack Westrup, *The Daily Telegraph*, 12 December 1936.)
Arrangement: With full string orchestra replacing the original string sextet. *Performance*: John Millar (bn.), New Hampshire Symphony Orchestra, James Bolle; Keene, New Hampshire, USA; 1 December 1977.
Duration: 15'50.
Note: In a letter to the BBC dated 24 March 1943, Bax wrote: 'I remember scarcely a note of this piece, but I believe the bassoon part comes off well.'

337 CONCERTO for flute, oboe, harp and string quartet

I. Allegro moderato. II. Cavatina (Lento). III. Moderato giocoso.

Title: 'Concerto for, Fl. Oboe, Harp with String IVtet | accompaniment'.
Date: 'London | April 19th | 1936'.
Dedication: 'To Count K. Benckendorff'.
Manuscript: *Holograph*: CH (MS 240); [25] ff.; 49 pp. (1-20, 21-31, 32-49 + 3 blank); pp. 1-12: AL 14 paper (356 × 262); pp. 13-49 + 1 blank: ALP 18 paper (355 × 263); loose in cream card folder. *Copyist's score*: CH; [25] ff.; 50 pp. (1-21, 22-32, 33-50); 20-staff paper.
Publication: CH, 1990 (*score*: WC0482C; *parts*: WC0482).
Performance: John Francis (fl.), Helen Gaskell (ob.), Maria Korchinska (hp.), Griller Quartet: Sidney Griller (vn.), Jack O'Brien (vn.), Philip Burton (va.), Colin Hampton (vc.); Æolian Hall; 11 December 1936 (London Contemporary Music Centre Concert).
Duration: 21'26.
Note: This work is a transcription of the Sonata for flute and harp of 1928 (**291**), the only alteration (apart from additional melodic lines) occurring in the final two bars.

338 STRING QUARTET NO. 3 in F

I. Allegro. II. Poco lento. III. Scherzo and Trio (Allegro moderato). IV. Allegro.

Date: I. 'London | July 5th 1936'. II. 'London | Sept 6th | 1936'. III. 'Aug 21st | 1936 | Cúan-an-Chaislán | Ciannigh' [Cashla Bay, Co. Galway]. IV. 'London | Sept 23d [*sic*] 1936'.
Dedication: *MS*: 'To the Griller IVtet'.
Manuscript: BL (Add. MS 54763); [27] ff.; 52 pp. (1-16, 17-25 + 1 blank, 26-38, 39-52 + 1 blank; pagin. in pencil); title folio: ALP 18 paper (355 × *c.* 243); pp. 1-52 + 1 blank: AL 12b paper (355 × *c.* 262); apparently disbound (stitched at inner edges). Movts. I, II and IV are written in black ink, but III is mostly in dark blue except for the vn. solo at 34:11 and from fig. 22 to the end which are written in black, having obviously been filled in later.

Publication: MM (715), 1941, 4to, 54 pp.; *score*: WC0514C; *parts*: WC0514. A set of proofs of the parts with pencilled corrections in Bax's hand is in UCC, together with a dark green notebook containing the corrections written out in another hand, presumably that of the engraver.
Performance: (1) *Broadcast*: Griller Quartet: Sidney Griller (vn.), Jack O'Brien (vn.), Philip Burton (va.), Colin Hampton (vc.); BBC National Programme; 16 May 1937. (2) *Public*: Griller Quartet; Æolian Hall; 29 October 1937.
Duration: 38'42.
Note: The Scherzo was originally intended as movt. II; it was completed before the slow movement, and on the MS (p. 26) an extra stroke has clearly been added by Bax to the original numeral 'II' at the head of this movement. In movt. IV the opening figure on the viola, together with all its subsequent appearances, has been pasted over the original version, which can still be seen at the very end.[123] A cut of 22 bars was made in this movement between the tenth bar after fig. (9) of the printed score and fig. (10). *The Radio Times* for 14 May 1937 (p. 20) contains quotations from Bax about the quartet:

> [The first movement] was probably influenced by the coming of spring in beautiful Kenmare. . . . The third movement consists of two strongly opposed elements—a rather sinister and malicious scherzo, and a dreamy, remotely romantic trio. This contest is finally won by the scherzo, when it converts the subject of the trio to its own way of thinking. The texture of the finale is rougher and more robust than that of the rest of the work, though there is a softening of the mood towards the abrupt and impetuous closing bars.

339 OVERTURE TO ADVENTURE for orchestra

Date: *Printed score*: 'Oct. 1936 Morar-Invergarry'.
Dedication: 'To Richard Austin'.
Orchestra: 3(1)202020, 4331, timp., 3 perc. (b.d., s.d., tamb., cym., tri., gl.), str.
Manuscript: Not traced.
Publication: MM (681), 1937, fo., 34 pp.
Performance: Bournemouth Municipal Orchestra, Richard Austin; Winter Gardens, Bournemouth; 23 February 1937 (Bournemouth Music Festival). Bournemouth newspaper reviews mention that Bax took his bow from the balcony and was warmly applauded.
Duration: 8'55.
Note: Percy Whitlock wrote a note for the first performance of this work that includes the following:

[123] The resemblance of this theme to the opening of Paul Corder's *Prelude in A* (1904) is surely too close for it to be coincidental.

. . . the composer says: 'It has no programme attached to it, and follows more or less the usual form of the classical Overture: that is to say, it is in Sonata form, but in a less serious style than that of a symphony movement. The principal subjects are sharply contrasted—one being aggressive in character, and the other lyrical.' With these few words of introduction, we must let the music speak for itself.

1937

340 LONDON PAGEANT for orchestra

Title: Bax appears to have originally called this work 'London Pageantry'; but the final two letters have been crossed out on the MS. In a letter to Julian Herbage dated 6 April 1937, he still uses 'Pageantry', and this is how the title appears on a programme for a performance in Liverpool on 12 October 1937; but in answer to a query from Jessie Wood dated 10 April 1943 (BL Add. MS 56419, f. 83) he wrote: '"London Pageant" is the better title for the piece, I think.'
Date: 'Morar & | London | Fine (thank Heaven!) | February 1937'.
Dedication: 'To my friends of the B.B.C. Orchestra'.
Orchestra: 3(1) 2+1 30 2+1, 4331 2 crnts. in B♭, timp., 4 perc. (b.d., s.d., cym., gong, tri., gl., bells), org., str.
Manuscript: CH (MS 257); [28] ff.; 56 pp. + 2 blank; AL 29b paper (355 × 262); in brown cardboard wrappers.
Publication: *Photocopy of MS*: WC0278C.
Performance: (1) *Broadcast*: BBC Symphony Orchestra, Albert Coates; BBC National Programme; 4 May 1937. (2) *Concert*: BBC Symphony Orchestra, Sir Henry Wood; Queen's Hall; 2 October 1937 (Promenade Concert).
Duration: 10'08.
Note: In the letter to Herbage quoted above, Bax indicated that this work had been written 'following a hint from the B.B.C. last autumn, when I declined the suggestion that I should write music for a King Arthur fantasy for Christmas' (see Appendix 6). According to Edwin Evans's programme note, the piece 'was written last December with forethoughts of London's pending Coronation scene in the composer's mind'. His comment at the end of the score (see **Date** above) was a reference to the exhausting task of orchestrating the work,[124] and, according to Christopher Whelen, Bax was really quite fond of the piece. He later commented that 'the scoring was a very laborious affair', and in conversation with John Ireland he echoed Verdi's remark on being asked whether there would be a successor to *Falstaff*: 'Too many notes! Too many notes!' To Clarence Raybould (undated letter) he expressed the hope that it 'might make some sort of

[124] Echoing Sheridan's inscription at the end of the MS of *The School for Scandal*: 'Finished at last, thank God!'

popular success'; and in the letter to Jessie Wood quoted above he wrote: 'I am pleased that Henry is doing this again as I believe it goes down well with the public.' The broad melody used in the trio was adapted from the 1905 tone poem *A Song of War and Victory* (**79**).

341 SONATA IN B♭ ('Salzburg') for piano

I. Allegro moderato. II. Lento espressivo. III. Tempo di menuetto. IV. Rondo (Allegro vivace).

Title: *MS*: 'Sonata in B♭ major | ("Salzburg")' (t.p.); 'Sonata in B♭' (p. 1).
Date: 'Date: (conjectured) circa 1788 [*sic*]' (at head of score). Being worked on in the early summer of 1937 (see **Note** below).
Manuscript: BL (Add. MS 54767); ff. 42-53 (42^{v}, 53^{v} blank); t.p. + 1 blank + 21 pp. (1-7, 7-11, 11-15, 16-21 + 1 p. containing pencil sketches); AL 12b paper (trimmed to 348-354 × 260); bound by the BL.[125] At the top of the t.p. Bax has written 'Property of | Arnold Bax'. Unpublished.
Performance: (1) *Movt. II (and the opening paragraph of I) only*: Jonathan Higgins; British Music Information Centre; 21 April 1983 (lecture-recital by Graham Parlett, *et al.*). (2) *Movt. II only*: Eric Parkin; St Jude's Church, Central Square, NW11; 24 June 1991 (recording session for Chandos Records Ltd.).
Duration: *c.* 20'00.
Note: This work does not appear in any of the lists of Bax's music compiled during his lifetime. At the head of the MS, immediately after the title and dating superscription, are the words 'Author unknown', which ostensibly suggests that it is a transcription of an anonymous eighteenth-century work from Salzburg. In fact it was written as a pastiche, as was confirmed by Bax to a friend, Alan Richardson (1904-79), when they met on a bus some time in the early summer of 1937. The date is corroborated by the appearance in the second movement (which is marked 'Lento espressivo', an unlikely tempo indication for an eighteenth-century work) of a passage that appears in the slow movement of the Violin Concerto (**342**), which was begun in 1937, and that on the reverse of the last folio of the sonata there is a pencil sketch of the opening theme from the same movement of the concerto. It is not known why Bax embarked on a piece in eighteenth-century style. Maybe, with its simple textures, it was intended as a musical purgative after the drudgery of orchestrating *London Pageant* (**340**).

[125] Several pages from Add. MS 54767, which also contains the *Scherzo* (**154**) and the Second and Third Piano Sonatas (**217** and **279**), have been rendered almost illegible by a ham-fisted conservator. Microfilm copies of the *Scherzo* and the Sonata in B♭ had been made before this occurred.

1938

342 CONCERTO for violin and orchestra

I. Overture (Allegro risoluto)—Ballad [no tempo indicated]—Scherzo (Allegro moderato). II. Adagio. III. Allegro—Slow valse tempo.

Date: Begun in 1936 (in June, according to LF, p. 308); sh.sc. completed by the beginning of October 1937. *Full score*: I. 'Morar | Feb 27th 1938'. II. Undated. III. 'March | 1938 Morar | and London.'
Dedication: *MS*: 'To Jascha Heifetz'. *Printed score*: None.
Orchestra: 3(1) 2(1) 20 2+1, 4200, timp., 2 perc. (b.d., t.d., tamb., cym.), hp., str.
Manuscript: *Sketch* (for the opening of movt. II only): BL (Add. MS 54767); f. 53v; [1] p.; AL 12b paper (trimmed to 354 × 260). *Full score*: BL (Add. MS 54757); [68] ff.; 136 pp. ([1]-67, 68-91, 92-136); ALP 18 paper (355 × 263); loose in fawn wrappers edged with Sellotape. The vc. and d.b. parts in bars 98:3 to 99:1 are in Henry Wood's hand. *Copyist's violin part*: Graham Parlett (MS formerly owned by the violinist Orrea Pernel); t.p. + 21 pp. + 2 blank; 12-staff paper (303 × 238). This part contains annotations in Bax's hand, including expression marks that are not found in the printed score, as well as pencilled fingerings, including some in the three passages that were later cut; this suggests that it may have been the copy used by Eda Kersey when preparing for the first performance. *Transcript*: Privately owned; opening four bars + a single note on 2-staff systems; on a piece of pink paper (146 × 89); inscribed underneath: 'Yours sincerely | Arnold Bax | — Morar | Inverness-shire | Feb. 1938.' This MS was part of a collection of thirty-eight quotations written out mainly by British composers that was sold at Sotheby's on 26 May 1994 (lot 151).
Publication: *Violin and piano*: CH (37926), 1946, 4to, 51 pp. *Full score (photocopy of MS)*: WC0279C. *Study score (photocopy of MS)*: WC0325C.
Performance: *Possibly uncut*:[126] (1) Eda Kersey (vn.), BBC Symphony Orchestra, Sir Henry Wood; br. live on BBC Home Service, 22 November 1943 (St Cecilia's Day Concert). (2) *With cuts*: Eda Kersey; BBC Symphony Orchestra 'A', Sir Adrian Boult; Corn Exchange, Bedford; 23 February 1944. (3) *With second cut passage restored*: Alan Brind (vn.), University of East Anglia Student Symphony Orchestra, Mark Fleming; Norwich Cathedral; 13 June 1987. (4) *With second and third cut passages restored*: Lydia Mordkovitch (vn.), London Philharmonic Orchestra, Bryden Thomson; St Jude's

[126] Although the BBC has an archive recording of this performance, it has not been possible to listen to it to find out whether or not the cuts were made. The existence of a copyist's violin part with fingerings in the cut passages (see **Manuscript**) suggests that it was played complete at least once; perhaps the cuts were introduced at a rehearsal for the première.

Church, Central Square, NW11; 23 June 1991 (recording session for Chandos Records Ltd.).
Duration: 34'27. The first performance is noted on the full score MS as 31'00.
Note: This concerto was written for Jascha Heifetz, who apparently found it not to his taste and never played it. No evidence has so far emerged to support the suggestion in a letter to *The Gramophone* (April 1995, pp. 6 and 9), that Bax completed the first two movements of the concerto early in 1937 and that Heifetz, who was in England, made a trial recording of them with the LSO under Barbirolli and subsequently rejected the score. Having been disappointed by the reception accorded his Cello Concerto in 1934, Bax decided to withhold the new concerto until his other large-scale works had become better known. On 22 December 1942, Arthur Bliss, as Head of Music at the BBC, formally commissioned Bax to write a violin concerto, and the score was premièred exactly eleven months later.

At some time between its completion and its publication Bax made a number of cuts in movts. II and III: II. The sixteen bars from 80:5 to the 83:1 and the whole of p. 87 (12 bars) were removed. III. The forty-three bars from 118:4 to 123:4 were cut. These cuts account for the fact that letters (M) and (N) in II and (T) to (Y) in III are omitted from the printed score. Although Bax once described the concerto as being 'rather like Raff' (*Music & Letters*, XXXV, 1, January 1954, p. 11), the slow movement has a theme taken from the eighteenth-century pastiche, the 'Salzburg' Sonata (**341**). May Harrison had earlier (1932) suggested that Bax write a concerto for her, but he declined (see Appendix 6).

Julian Herbage wrote about the concerto in his article 'Hail, Bright Cecilia' in *The Radio Times* for 19 November 1943, p. 4, which includes a short programme note by Bax himself:

> Unfortunately I have had the opportunity of examining only the piano score [now missing] of the concerto . . . I asked the composer if he would in his own words give me a description of its structure, and in spite of his usual diffidence, he sent me the following brief explanatory note.
>
>> This concerto consists of the usual three movements, but it may be advisable to say a few words about the somewhat unconventional shape of the first. This actually comprises three distinct short pieces labelled respectively: Overture, Ballad, and Scherzo, and yet at the same time the whole may be counted as in sonata form.
>> The Overture contains several themes, all of a restless and energetic character; the following Ballad takes the place of a main second subject; while the Scherzo represents the development section (making mock of the themes of the first part). Finally there are triumphant restatements of the chief themes of the Overture and Ballad.

343 PÆAN for orchestra

Title: 'Paean'. The subtitle of the original piano piece ('Passacaglia') has been appended in another hand.
Date: 'April 14 | 1938 | London' (the day of the month without ordinal suffix, contrary to Bax's usual practice).
Orchestra: 3(1) 2+1 30 2+1, 4331 2 crnts. in B♭, timp., 4 perc. (b.d., s.d., tamb., cym., gong, bells), org., str.
Manuscript: CH (MS 255); [8] ff.; 14 pp. + 2 blank; ALP 29 paper (355 × 260); in fawn card folder.
Publication: *Photocopy of MS*: WC0277C.
Performance: Special orchestra drawn from the BBC Symphony Orchestra, the London Symphony Orchestra, the British Women's Orchestra, and the Royal Schools of Music, Sir Malcolm Sargent;[127] Royal Albert Hall; 24 May 1938 (Royal Command Performance).
Adaptation: Used for the ballet *Oscar* (see **110** for details).
Duration: 3'10.
Note: This orchestration of a piano piece (**294**) was made specifically for the Royal Command Performance organized by Sir Walford Davies, Bax's predecessor as Master of the King's Music.

1939

344 SYMPHONY NO. 7 for orchestra

I. Allegro. II. Lento—In Legendary Mood (Più mosso). III. Theme and Variations: Allegro—Andante—Vivace—Epilogue (Sereno).

Date: *Short score*: I. 'June 18th 1938'; II. None; III. 'Oct | 1938'. *Full score*: 'Morar | Inverness-shire | January 1939'. Composed in 'London and Invernesshire [*sic*]' according to a note from Bax to Christopher Whelen.
Dedication: A dedication to Basil Cameron was originally written below the title on the f.sc. MS but has been completely erased. As a commissioned work for the New York World Fair the final dedication, 'To the People of America', was obligatory, though it does not appear on the MS.
Orchestra: 3(1) 2+1 3+1 2+1, 4331, timp., 3 perc. (b.d., t.d., s.d., tamb., cym., gong, tri., gl.), hp., str.
Manuscript: *Short score*: LC (ML96.B36); [20] ff.; [40] pp. ([1-21], [21-9], [30-40]; non-autograph pagin.); pp. [1-32]: AL 12b paper (360 × 262); pp. [33-40]: AL 14 paper (356 × 262). Presented by Harriet Cohen on 30 December 1960. *Full score sketch* (bars 1-8 after fig. 24 in III only): UCC; [1] f. (written in pencil on the verso, the recto blank); [1] p.; ALP 18 paper (355 × 262);

[127] Not Sir Henry Wood, as originally announced.

inserted into a manila folder with 'Out and Away' (see **283**) written on it in Harriet Cohen's handwriting. *Full score*: BL (Add. MS 57523); [80] ff.; 157 pp. (1-80, 80-110, 111-157 + 3 blank); pp. 1-28, 115-157 + 3 blank: ALP 29 paper (355 × 260); pp. 29-114: AL 29b paper (355 × 261); bound by the BL. When first given to the BL, the MS was loose in a brown cover with British Council seals and a note: 'Sent to us by Midland Bank in the past for safe keeping'. *Discarded pages of full score*: UCC; [4] ff.; 8 pp. (pagin. 35-41; 52 bars); AL 29b paper (355 × 261); inserted into a manila card folder. The pagination of the MS f.sc. suggests that these pages were jettisoned immediately after they were written out rather than after the rest of the movement had been completed. The passage would have followed 41:5 of the published score. Bars 41:4-5 also appear in the discarded MS, but the cellos' last three notes were originally given to the double basses instead.
Publication: CH (1-49211), 1972, 8vo (st.sc.), 219 pp.; WC0362C (A3 size); WC0362CX (A4 size).
Performance: (1) New York Philharmonic-Symphony Orchestra, Sir Adrian Boult; Carnegie Hall, New York; 9 June 1939 (New York World Fair). (2) BBC Symphony Orchestra, Sir Adrian Boult; Colston Hall, Bristol; br. live on 21 June 1940. (3) BBC Symphony Orchestra, Sir Henry Wood; Royal Albert Hall; 22 August 1943 (Promenade Concert).
Duration: 47'34.
Note: In a letter to Beatrice Harrison dated 12 May 1939, Bax called the work 'this blasted symphony for the New York Fair'. And in a letter to Arthur Bliss dated 21 March 1943, he wrote about a proposed Prom performance: 'I still feel that I would much prefer [symphonies] 5 or 6 to be played, as they are quite unknown, and no 7 is certainly no advance upon them. In fact the first movement has never seemed satisfactory to me.' In a letter of 1949 to Christopher Whelen, however, he conceded: 'I think it is more accessible than any of the others to those who are unfamiliar with my work'. According to Harriet Cohen (*A Bundle of Time*, p. 294) Bax, 'after much heart-searching', decided not to go to New York for the première (in fact he never once set foot in the United States), but after hearing a recording of the performance he wrote to Boult: '. . . the third movement should start more deliberately—a real 18FORTY romantic wallow!' In another letter to Boult, after the second performance, he commented: 'I was particularly moved by the playing of the Second movement which expressed all the heavy summer languor which I meant to convey.'

345 RHAPSODIC BALLAD for cello

Date: 'London | June 3rd 1939'.
Dedication: 'To Beatrice Harrison'.
Manuscript: UCC; [4] ff.; 7 pp. + 1 blank; ALP 12 paper (355 × 262); inserted into a manila card folder.

Publication: CH (48143), 1968, 4to, 8 pp.; WC0138.
Performance: (1) Bernard Vocadlo; Municipal School of Music, Cork; 25 May 1966. (2) Rohan de Saram; Worcester; br. live on BBC Midland Home Service, 6 February 1967. (3) Rohan de Saram; Purcell Room, London; 10 May 1967.
Duration: 12'41.
Note: This work for unaccompanied cello was commissioned by Beatrice Harrison. In an undated letter to a mutual acquaintance,[128] Bax wrote: 'You may tell Baba [B. H.] that I am going to try, though it is a very difficult thing to write under such severe limitations.' In another letter—headed just 'Tuesday night' but clearly dating from the spring of 1939—he wrote:

As a matter of fact I have nearly finished the first draft of that solo-cello piece. It is a very, very difficult job, and I daresay some of my passages cannot be played. I rather wish that I could have seen the score of Kodaly's sonata to get some idea of what little tricks are possible. Baba plays it in a most masterly way, and I am afraid she will be very disappointed with my inexperienced effort. Anyway I am going to think it all out again . . . there's too much Hitler about this spring.[129]

On 12 May he wrote directly to Beatrice Harrison:

I have done a good bit of it—long ago too—and then I went to Ireland for a month and since I got back I have been up to my eyes (and down in the mouth!) correcting the parts of this blasted symphony [No. 7] for the New York Fair.

I think you will have to invent lots of amusing stunts and gadgets to enliven my ignorant cello writing.

And on 21 May:

I am afraid I cannot send you the Ballad just yet as it is only in a half-baked state and unfinished at that. But in about a fortnight I might get it sufficiently presentable for you to have a look at it.

The score was indeed completed a fortnight after this letter, but in the end Beatrice Harrison never played it. It has been suggested that she refrained from doing so to avoid incurring the jealousy of her sister May, who was infatuated with Bax. But it is clear that the composer himself was never wholly satisfied with the work, as he explained in a letter to Beatrice dating from 2 January 1951:

It is so sweet of you to want to include that solo cello piece in your March recital that I hate to be disappointing. But to tell you the truth I am *not* satisfied with it and cannot feel that it could be made into a success. Even sister Evelyn, who never

[128] Only the opening of the letter is extant, pasted on to another piece of paper, which is signed 'with love G', and sent to Beatrice Harrison. 'G' is probably Gladys Lees, for whom see Appendix 5.

[129] This letter begins 'My dear' and is signed 'Lorrie'. The recipient is again probably Gladys Lees, whom Bax had known since his student days; 'Lorrie' was a youthful nickname for Bax.

criticises, told me that it did not come off, and I should much dislike either of us to launch a failure upon the concert platform.

The first performance finally took place the year following Beatrice Harrison's death.

346 CONCERTINO for piano and orchestra (unorchestrated)

I. Lento. II. Lento. III. Allegro.

Date: Undated, but apparently mentioned in a letter from Bax to Edwin Evans written on 24 July 1939: 'I have been trying to perpetrate a small concerto for Tania [Harriet Cohen], but it is heavy labour.'[1] In a letter to Tilly Fleischmann dated 27 December 1939, he lamented: 'I have written nothing at all since August', which suggests that he persevered with the score for a few more weeks after his letter to Evans.
Manuscript: *Movts. I and II*: BL (Add. MS 54758); 6 ff. (ff.3ᵛ and 5ᵛ blank + 1 unfoliated blank at the end); [12] pp. ([5] + 1 blank, [3] + 3 blank); ALP 29 paper (354 × 262); ff. 1ᵛ and 5ᵛ were once joined together with sticky tape, which has been removed. This MS comprises the piano solo and orchestral parts written in pencil on a single two-staff system. *Movt. III*: BL (Add. MS 54780); ff. 1-8ᵛ; [16] pp.; ALP 12 paper (355 × 262). This is a two-piano score written in ink. Unpublished.
Arrangement: Movt. III edited and orchestrated by Graham Parlett (in preparation).
Duration: *c.* 20'00.
Note: Although it cannot be proved conclusively that the Concertino is the work referred to in Bax's letter quoted above, the handwriting and musical style leave little room for doubt. That the third movement, which is simply headed 'III', belongs with the other two is suggested by the fact that it is in the same key (A♭) as the first, as well as the Seventh Symphony, completed six months earlier.

1940–1

Bax appears to have written no music between August 1939 and the summer of 1942, his longest fallow period since the age of twelve. In January 1940 he paid his last visit to Morar, where he began work on *Farewell, my Youth*. In February he was involved as an examiner in the Dunedin Scottish Composers Competition; but then Morar became a closed area: 'I may have to clear out . . . by March 11th', he wrote to Erik Chisholm. He spent June and July in Devon and Cornwall. His mother died early in November, and in the winter he took up permanent residence at The White Horse Hotel, Storrington, Sussex. The only significant event of 1941 was a dispute with the Inland Revenue.

1942

On 3 February 1942 Bax was named Master of the King's Music,[130] his first official position of any kind and one that was to involve him in a good deal of tedious correspondence.[131] On 23 March he declined an invitation from the BBC to write a work for brass band, and during the spring he wrote eight short stories (unpublished) before his court appointment led to his being compelled to turn once again to music.

347 MALTA, G. C.: Film music for orchestra

Title: *MS*: 'Malta' (with 'G.C.' appended in another hand). The film was originally to be entitled 'Under Fire in Malta'.
Date: 'Sept 1942'. The principal theme of the 'Old Valetta [Valletta]' section is written out by Bax as a musical quotation in Gloria Bax's visitors' book and dated 'July 1942' indicating that he was working on the score at that date. The film had first been mooted on 28 February, before the island was awarded the George Cross (on 15 April).
Dedication: The bound MS bears a printed page with the following: 'THIS ORIGINAL MANUSCRIPT OF THE MUSIC SPECIALLY WRITTEN FOR THE FILM "MALTA, G.C." IS DEDICATED TO THE HEROISM OF THE MALTESE PEOPLE BY THE COMPOSER SIR ARNOLD BAX, MASTER OF THE KING'S MUSICK'. Beneath this, Bax has written 'To Heroic Malta, G.C | Arnold Bax'. The printed date 'LONDON • FEBRUARY • NINETEEN FORTY-THREE', which appears under his signature, refers to the ceremony at the Ministry of Information at which Bax presented his MS to the Governor of Malta (see **Note** below).
Orchestra: 2222, 2231, timp., 2 perc. (b.d., s.d., tamb., cym., gong), str.
Manuscript: *Sketch*: The principal theme of the final march is pencilled in at the foot of the first page of the MS of the Sinfonietta, with which Bax

[130] According to the Lord Chamberlain's Office, the spelling 'Musick' in this title 'has never at any time been the practice in Court circles'; and Leonard Duck, in his article 'Masters of the Sovereign's Music' (*The Musical Times*, June 1953, fn. on p. 255), states that the 'k' had been 'dropped in the warrants issued by Queen Victoria and her successors.' But most holders of the office, including Bax, have used the obsolete spelling, and it appears even in an official letter written to him on 17 February 1942 from Buckingham Palace. It should be noted that Bax was not appointed in 1941, as often stated; there was an interregnum following the death of Sir Walford Davies on 11 March of that year.

[131] Letters in the Royal Archives at Windsor Castle reveal that Bax was required to deal with such momentous issues as whether the Blackpool Glee and Madrigal Society should be given 'royal recognition'; whether an obscure composer of 'completely undistinguished' church anthems should be allowed to dedicate a piece to the King; and whether it would be in order for Sir Malcolm Sargent to begin the national anthem fortissimo at the opening ceremony of the 1948 Olympic Games.

posed for a photograph early in 1942 (see **315**). *Full score*: BNM (Libr. Ms. 1424); [46] ff.; dedic. p. + 91 pp. (Part I: 1-46; Part II: 1-45); bound in maroon goatskin leather, the front board cushioned, with decoration and title tooled in gold, the George Cross emblem in platinum; the MS was sewn on three parchment bands, the edges being plain. Part I, pp. 1-46 and Part II, pp. 1-10: JWC 18 paper; Part II, pp. 11-22: ALP 14 paper; pp. 23-45: 18-staff paper (all trimmed to 357 × 260). *Transcript*: Gloria Bax (see **Date** above). Unpublished except for the arrangements of the two marches listed below. *Parts*: CH. *Master copy of film* (16/35 mm, 1832 ft.): National Film Archive, British Film Institute. *Master copy of script*: Public Record Office, Kew (file EO/670/216/1 CFU 223; also files F. 383 and F. 256/760).
Performance: (1) *Soundtrack recording*: Laurence Olivier[132] (narrator), RAF Central Band, Muir Mathieson; EMI Studios, Abbey Road; December 1942. (2) *Preview of film*: Ministry of Information; 22 January 1943. (3) *Pre-release run*: The Gaumont Cinema, Haymarket; 24 January 1943 (incongruously coupled with the feature film *You were never lovelier*, starring Fred Astaire and Rita Hayworth). (4) *Complete score*: Royal Philharmonic Orchestra, Kenneth Alwyn; CBS Studios, London; 8-9 January 1986 (recording session for Cloud Nine Records).
Duration: (1) *Complete film*: 20'00. (2) *Complete music*: 24'05.
Arrangement:[133] (i) For organ by W. H. Harris of *Funeral March* (i.e. the 'Ruins' section of Part I), CH (37881), 1945, 7 pp. This arrangement was intended for the funeral of the Duke of Kent; it was also performed, by Sir William Harris, at the state funeral of King George VI in St George's Chapel, Windsor, on 15 February 1952, with Bax himself sitting in the organ loft. (ii) For piano by [William] Lloyd Webber of 'March | Malta, G.C.', CH (40729), 1951, 7 pp. (the final fifteen pages of the f.sc. score only); with introductions by A. Salomone, Commissioner General for Malta (dated 6 December 1950), and Lloyd Webber. (iii) For military band by W. J. Duthoit; condensed (conductor's) score in *Chappell's Army Journal*, 766 (41287), 1952, 5 pp.
Note: It was Muir Mathieson, Musical Director of the newly formed Crown Film Unit, who asked Bax to write the music for this documentary film about Malta, which had been awarded the George Cross on 15 April 1942 for its heroism in resisting aerial attacks from Sicily soon after Italy had entered the war in 1940. In an internal BBC memorandum dated 15 January 1943, Kenneth Wright wrote: 'You may remember that after considerable hesitancy the composer succombed [*sic*] to Muir Mathieson's pleading.' The

[132] Replacing Joseph Macleod in mid-December 1942. The narration on the copy of the film kept in the British Film Institute seems to differ slightly from that on the Imperial War Museum's copy, though both credit Olivier as the narrator.

[133] The so-called 'Malta, G.C. Suite' simply refers to concert performances of the work with a few passages cut.

film was made by the RAF, Army and Crown Film Units for the Ministry of Information (to be distributed by Warner Bros.) and combined material especially shot on Malta with newsreel footage from Pathé, G. B. News and Paramount News. It was dubbed into at least eight languages, and more than 100 prints were made for commercial distribution abroad. Like Vaughan Williams, who was working on the music for *Coastal Command* at about the same time, Bax was paid £50 and retained the rights to his music, which was fitted to the film by Mathieson.[134] On 19 February 1943, a few weeks after the première, Bax was invited to present his score to the Governor and Commander-in-Chief of Malta, Lord Gort.[135]

Several comments by Bax on his music for the film may be quoted:

> Have just finished my Malta film music. It has been nothing but a worry from beginning to end—and very hard work.[136]

> [I] do not feel that air-raids have much to do with my own particular style![137]

> I have heard the music rehearsed. It is quite commonplace.[138]

> The music I wrote (with much labour) for the "Malta" film . . . appears to be a success with the musical public. Last Friday I presented the score (magnificently bound, not by myself) to Viscount Gort . . . I don't like the limelight but everyone was very pleasant indeed and in retrospect I enjoyed the event.[139]

> I do not think the medium is at present at all satisfactory as far as the composer is concerned, as his music is largely inaudible, toned down to make way for—in many cases —quite unnecessary talk. This is, in my opinion, quite needless as it is possible to pay attention to two things at the same time if they appeal to different parts of the intelligence.[140]

This last complaint refers to an incident at the private showing of the film when Laurence Olivier asked Bax if he was annoyed at the way in which his music had been toned down for the narration:

> Yes, I jolly well am—chattering away all over my music. Bombs falling in all directions, planes crashing right and left, my music is faded down to make way for some fatuous remark like 'an air raid is in progress; it is a time of danger for the population!'.[141]

[134] Elizabeth Sussex, *The Rise and Fall of British Documentary* (California, 1975), p. 150.
[135] A photograph of the ceremony appeared in *The Illustrated London News* for 27 February 1943, p. 230.
[136] From an undated letter to May Harrison.
[137] From a letter to Sir Alan Lascelles, King George VI's private secretary, dated 8 October [1942].
[138] From a letter to May Harrison dated 1 October 1942.
[139] From a letter to Aloys Fleischmann dating from February 1943.
[140] John Huntley, 'Oliver Twist', *Film Music Notes* (September–October 1951), p. 20.
[141] John Huntley, loc. cit.

Recalling this incident many years later, Olivier remembered that he apologized for his vocal interruptions and that Bax 'accepted my apology graciously but with no hint that it was not due!'.[142] Bax also remarked to his brother Clifford that the music was 'totally unstimulated by self' and wondered whether 'it may well be different from the rest of my work . . . I can't say I derived much pleasure from the writing.' Reviewing the film in *The Sketch*, C. A. [Caroline] Lejeune commented:

> Remarkable in many ways, 'Malta' is not least remarkable for its musical score . . . This broad noble music is so full of riches that the discerning listener will want to hear the soundtrack again and again. . . . Sir Arnold is frank about it. 'I don't quite know what they wanted me to do. So I just wrote the sort of music I liked'.

William Glock, writing in *The Observer* (28 February 1943, p. 2), was not quite so impressed:

> . . . the music was far above the average. If it seemed stale, it was infinitely less so than Alfred Newman's or Addinsell's. Yet I could not feel that Bax had added much to the film, as Aaron Copland added to 'Mice and Men'.

The score is divided into two parts corresponding to the two reels of the film. The music is 'through composed' in that the sections follow on from each other without a break, so that the score can be played through complete as a two-movement suite, although in practice, when the work was performed in the concert hall during the 1940s, a number of cuts were made in Part II. In the recording preserved in the National Sound Archive (BBC Transcription 13330/9, recorded on 9 June 1943), these cuts are made; furthermore, the antique mode of recording (acetate discs) entailed the addition of a few cadential chords at the end of sections which have been pencilled into the score, presumably by Muir Mathieson. Although Bax himself wrote the titles of a few of the sections into the MS in pencil, a clearer impression of the film's structure can be derived from the titles listed when the music was performed as a concert suite.

Synopsis:

PART I

1. Opening Fanfare, p. 1.
2. 'Prelude and Convoy', pp. 1-3 and 3-12. These two continuous sections are used for the opening credits and titles and for the first scene, depicting the arrival of a convoy of ships to the island.
3. 'Old Valetta [Valletta]', pp. 13-26. This section accompanies a brief guided tour of the island.
4. 'Air Raid', pp. 26-36.
5. 'Ruins', pp. 36-46. This depicts the aftermath of the raid.

[142] From a letter to me dated 30 December 1975.

PART II

6. 'Gay March', pp. 1-6. The Maltese people are seen going about their daily business.
7. 'Intermezzo', pp. 7-10. On the soundtrack there is a cut from the bar before fig. (3) of the 'Gay March' to the beginning of this section.
8. 'Work and Play', pp. 11-30. This is divided into a number of subsections. The first 20 bars of 'Work' are omitted from the start of this passage on the soundtrack, which depicts the work of reconstruction, the music commencing at fig. (10) on p. 13. This leads into an 'Allegretto semplice' for the children of Malta. The energetic music returns at fig. (13) on p. 16, and on the soundtrack continues as far as the second bar after (14), before returning to the very opening bars of this section, which had previously been omitted. This depicts patrols of Spitfires taking off from the island to attack Sicily, and continues as far as fig. (11). A cut is now made from here to the 9th bar after (14), an 'Allegretto scherzando', which Bax has labelled 'Children's Dance'. At the end of this 11-bar section there appears the note: 'The eight bars between (13) and (14) can be repeated here if possible to the timing'. At this point on the soundtrack a repeat is made of the opening 'Gay March', this time almost complete, only the final three bars being omitted, and depicting the announcement of the news that Malta has been awarded the George Cross. From this point the film proceeds towards its peroration. The first 21 bars of the section in the score that follows on immediately from the 'Children's Dance' and begins 'Tranquillo' on p. 20 are omitted from the soundtrack, the music beginning at the second bar of p. 24 (5 after (18)) and marked 'Vivo'. This continues as far as the second bar of p. 28 (4 after (20)) and then cuts directly into the concluding march. When the suite was recorded by Muir Mathieson in June 1943, the music was cut from this point back to the final 19 bars of the 'Gay March', presumably to create a more satisfactory ending for the side break necessitated by the acetate-disc format. In both versions the 11 bars of 'Lento non troppo' (pp. 28-9) for seven solo stringed instruments were omitted.
9. March, pp. 31-45. The principal melody of this march is first found sketched on the opening page of the MS of the Sinfonietta (see **Manuscript** above). It was later used as the trio of the *Victory March* (1945) and the *Coronation March* (1952). At some time between his writing the score and the recording of the soundtrack, Bax realized that the opening bars were reminiscent of 'Men of Harlech'. He accordingly altered the fourth note of the second bar from F to C in an attempt to disguise it.

In an internal BBC memorandum dated 3 January 1945, Julian Herbage wrote: ' . . . Bax tells me that he has revised his Malta music which now ends with a new march called "Call to the Red Army".' (see **358** and **364**).

348 [FANFARE]: Fragment

Date: 'Storrington | Sussex | Sept. 1942'.
Orchestration: 'Tr. Solo'.
Manuscript: BMI; [1] f.; [1] p. + 1 blank; 6 bars (unfinished); plain A5 paper (280 × 219; written inside a lined border 232 × 165). Unpublished.
Note: This brief unharmonized melodic line, marked 'Maestoso', was written out for an American autograph-collector, probably Howes Norris, Jr. (see also **236**). There is no evidence that it derives from a completed

fanfare, but the music is taken from Spring Fire (**153**) and was later used in the first of the two 'Red Army' fanfares written in 1943 (**351**) and then in one of the royal wedding fanfares of 1947 (**373**).

349 FIVE GREEK FOLKSONGS for unaccompanied chorus (SATB)

a. Miracle of Saint Basil. **b.** The Bridesmaid's Song. **c.** In Far-off Malta. **d.** The Happy Tramp. **e.** A Pilgrim's Chant.

Date: Erroneously ascribed to 1944 in *Gr5.* The correct year is confirmed in a letter from Bax to May Harrison dating from 7 November 1942: 'I have been arranging some Greek folk-music for unaccompanied choir—at the request of dear old Calvocoressi—such queer Balkan tunes that I have got quite a lot of amusement out of treating them. And now I am asked to cope with Polish carols—not at all queer, nor interesting!' To Tilly Fleischmann he wrote on 16 December 1942: 'I have done nothing lately except some arrangements of Greek and Polish folk music by request and am getting rather bored.'
Text: 'English Translation from the Greek and Readjustment of Text by M. D. [Michel-Dmitri] CALVOCORESSI' of the following folksongs from Asia Minor and Macedonia: **a.** Presumably Ἅϊ-Βασίλη μ', πόθεν ἔρχεσαι (Cappadocia), but Bax's melody is not the one printed in a standard collection of Greek folksongs.[143] **b.** Ἦρθεν ἡ ὥρα ἡ χρυσῆ (Bithynia). **c.** Κάτω 'ς τῆς Μάλτας τὰ χωριά (Bithynia). **d.** Ἤμαν ξένος κ'ἦρθα τώρα (Macedonia). **e.** Εἴνταντε νὰ ὑπᾶμε 'ς τὸν Ἅϊ-Βασίλη (Cappadocia).
Manuscript: Not traced.
Publication: CH (38450), 1947, 4to, 31 pp.
Performance: BBC Singers, Leslie Woodgate; Cowdray Hall, Royal College of Nursing; 11 November 1946 (Contemporary Music Centre Concert).
Duration: 11'01.
Note: Calvocoressi had asked several composers to make arrangements for a Greek chorus to be formed by a wartime Greek National Committee for Broadcasting. In a letter to May Harrison dated 20 November [1945?], Bax wrote:

> They are very quaint and rather barbaric tunes but I think I made something interesting of them. Calvo's death [on 1 February 1944] hindered them from being performed and I was wondering whether you could get the B.B.C. singers and Leslie Woodgate to perform them at your Greek concert. They would need the B.B.C. singers as they are decidedly difficult.

[143] Georgios D. Pachtikos, *260 δημώδη Ἑλληνικὰ ᾄσματα ἀπὸ τοῦ στόματος τοῦ Ἑλληνικοῦ λαοῦ τῆς Μικρᾶς Ἀσίας...* (Athens, 1905, etc.), pp. 274-5, 103-5, 111-12, 302-4, 17-19 respectively. This may not have been Calvocoressi's source since Bax's arrangements are mostly in different keys from the versions printed here.

350 **FIVE FANTASIES ON POLISH CHRISTMAS CAROLS for unison trebles and string orchestra**

a. God is Born (Bóg Się Rodzi).
b. In Nightly Stillness ['In nightly shadows' on the MS] (Wśród Nocnej Ciszy).
c. In the Manger He is Lying (W żłobie leży).
d. Lullay, dear Jesus (Lulajże Jezuniu) [for solo girl's voice].
e. Merrily to Bethlehem (Przybieżeli do Betlejem).

Title: *MS*: 'Fantasies | on | Polish Christmas Carols | for | unison treble voices | and | String Orchestra | by | Arnold Bax' (t.p.); 'Polish Christmas Carols' (p. 1).
Date: a. 'Nov 11th 1942'. **b.** 'Nov 11th | 1942'. **c.** 'Nov 17th 1942'. **d.** 'Nov 21st | 1942'. **e.** 'Nov 17th 1942'. (In the MS **d** and **e** are in reverse order.)
Dedication: *Printed score only*: 'To the Children of Poland'.
Text: Words translated by Jan Śliwiński. The MS and printed f.sc. have the English words only; the printed v.sc. has both the Polish and English texts.
Manuscript: CH (MS 236); [8] ff.; t.p. + 1 blank + 15 pp. (1-4, 4-7, 8-11, 12-13, 14-15 + 1 blank); 20-staff paper (360 × 265); loose in fawn card folder; pp. 1 and 2 are glued back to back suggesting that Bax inadvertently turned over two leaves when writing out the score. There is a note on the t.p.: 'To Conductor | Please see | important note | about repeat | in Lullay dear Jesus (no 5)'.
Publication: *Chorus part:* CH (1711), 8vo, 1944, 4 pp. *Vocal score*: CH (37342), 4to, 1945, 20 pp.; with an introduction by Jan Śliwiński. *Full score*: CH (37965), 1946, 4to, 16 pp. **350b** and **d** issued separately (v.sc.): CH (**b.** 38523; **d.** 38524), [1947].
Performance: (1) *Amateur*: At a school in Glasgow; this preceded the first professional performance, but no further details are known.[144] (2) *Professional*: Joan Cross (sop. in **d** only), Leicester Philharmonic Society and Morley College Choir, London Philharmonic Orchestra, Edric Cundell;[145] Royal Albert Hall; 28 February 1945 ('Concert for the Polish Children Rescue Fund').
Duration: 15'03.
Note: This work was commissioned from Bax by Jan Śliwiński for the benefit of the Polish Children and the Polish Red Cross[146] and is his only piece written specifically for juvenile performers. As noted under **349** above, he viewed the prospect of arranging Polish carols with little enthusiasm. **350a** is not a traditional carol but a setting by an unknown composer of

[144] Information from an internal BBC memorandum.
[145] Cundell took over from an indisposed Basil Cameron at short notice.
[146] See 'London Day by Day', *The Daily Telegraph & Morning Post* (28 February 1945), p. 4.

words by Franciszek Karpiński (1745-1825). A variant of **350d** appears in the middle section of Chopin's Scherzo in B minor; and Bax's arrangement of this carol is prefaced by a quotation from Bach's Passion Chorale 'O Haupt voll Blut und Wunden', adapted from Hans Leo Hassler's song of 1601 'Mein G'müt ist mir verwirret'.

1943

351 TWO FANFARES for brass and percussion (a. also with organ)[147]

Title: a. Unknown. **b.** Programme for first performance: 'Salute to the Dead of the Red Army'. Referred to by Basil Dean (see **Note** below) as 'A Solemn Fanfare'.
Date: Composed between mid-January and mid-February.
Manuscript: Not traced. Unpublished.
Performance: Trumpeters and drums of the Life Guards, the Royal Horse Guards, and the Royal Air Force;[148] Royal Albert Hall; 21 February 1943 (Red Army Celebration: the 25th anniversary of the decree setting up a Red Army of 'workers and peasants' on 23 February 1918). Excerpts were broadcast live, and a recording of nine of them is preserved in the BBC Sound Archives (acetates: 5985-9; tape: MT 5985); a copy is in the National Sound Archive. Bax's first fanfare is heard at the start of the fourth excerpt, but the second fanfare was not recorded.
Duration: a. 0'47. **b.** Unknown.
Note: In his book *The Theatre at War* (London, 1956), pp. 304, Basil Dean describes the origins of the event for which Bax wrote these fanfares: 'Towards the middle of January 1943 the Government instructed the Campaigns' Division of the Ministry of Information to organize a mass celebration . . . to commemorate the 25th Anniversary of the founding of the Red Army.' The pageant lasted for two hours and included a specially written ode by Louis MacNeice, with music by Rawsthorne, two fanfares by Walton, and orchestrations by Norman Del Mar of Russian songs; Dr Malcolm Sargent was the conductor.

The first fanfare immediately preceded an arrangement of the Russian folksong 'A Song of Youth' and begins with a theme borrowed from *Spring Fire* (**153**) and later used in the first of the fanfares for the royal wedding of 1947 (**373**); it is also found in a fragment sent to an autograph-collector (**348**). The second fanfare was sounded towards the end of the proceedings:

[147] Instrumentation deduced from the dim recording of the first fanfare, which begins on the organ.

[148] Since the first fanfare includes an organ, it is possible that it was performed by the LPO and members of the BBCSO, who played other pieces on the programme.

Louis MacNeice's Ode is now sung . . . ending in a crescendo. The audience waits for the entrance of the Foreign Minister, some of them standing up and craning their necks, forgetting those behind them, in their excitement. Mr [Anthony] Eden stands in front of the flags. From the high gallery Bax's *A Solemn Fanfare* is sounded by the trumpeters of the Household Cavalry. Before the echoes have died away the Minister is speaking.[149]

According to *The Times* for 22 February 1943, p. 4: '[Eden] called the audience to stand in silent tribute . . . while a solemn fanfare . . . and the Last Post were sounded'.

352 LEGEND-SONATA for cello and piano

I. Allegro risoluto. II. Lento espressivo. III. Rondo (Allegro).

Title: 'Legend-Sonata in F♯ for | cello and piano'.
Date: 'Quilters | Storrington | Feb 1943'. According to Mary Gleaves, 'Quilters' was the name of a house owned by a Mr Gee (who was on Storrington Council) and situated about three miles from The White Horse Hotel; the composer sometimes went there on his own in order to be able to compose in peace.
Dedication: 'To Florence Hooton' (written over an illegible erasure).
Manuscript: BDL (MS MUS.c.370; received on 29 November 1968); [16] ff.; 32 pp. (1-13, 13-20, 21-32); 20-staff paper (359 × 264); bound in dark blue cloth. Some of the tempo markings are in pencil, and some have been inked over. In bars 32:5-6 (18-19 from the end of movt. III) there is an 'ossia' passage for the left hand, but this does not appear in the printed score. Two extra bars appear before the twenty-sixth bar from the end of movt. I which are crossed through. *Transcript*: The opening eleven bars were written out by Bax on one side of a sheet of RC 1 paper and reproduced in facsimile in Hubert Foss, 'Dots & Lines: Being some Random Examples of a Soho Industry, namely the Writing and Printing of Music', *Soho Centenary: A Gift from Artists, Writers and Musicians to the Soho Hospital for Women* (London, New York, Melbourne: Hutchinson & Co. Ltd., [1944]; also a limited edn. of 250 copies), p. [55]; the MS is dated at the bottom right of the page: 'Storrington | Aug 25th 1944'.
Publication: CH (35515), 1944, 4to, 43 pp.
Performance: Florence Hooton (vc.), Harriet Cohen (pf.); Wigmore Hall; 10 November 1943 (Boosey & Hawkes Concert).
Duration: 27'56.
Note: 'I have been quite busy again since Christmas and have finished a very romantic sonata for cello and piano which gets about as far away from present day realities as it possibly could. I enjoyed writing it and perhaps

[149] Dean, op.cit., p. 309. See also his *Mind's Eye, 1927-72* (London, 1973), pp. 283-6.

because of my long rest from responsible composition it all came very easily.' (From an undated letter to Aloys Fleischmann.) In a programme note for the first performance, Bax is quoted as saying: 'I wrote it with so much hope for a better world.'

353 SALUTE TO SYDNEY for brass and percussion

Date: 'Quilters | Storrington | March 31st | 1943'. (For 'Quilters' see **352** above.)
Orchestra: 4 hns., 3 tpts., 3 tbns., 1 tba., timp., 3 perc. (b.d., s.d., cym.).
Manuscript: BBC (Misc. 2994); [2] ff.; [4] pp. (29 bars); 22-staff paper (*c.* 370 × *c.* 250); stitched into a cardboard folder. Unpublished. *Parts*: BBC.
Performance: Anonymous performers, probably conducted by Hubert Clifford;[150] br. 19 April 1943 (BBC Overseas Broadcast 'Calling Sydney' in the series 'Calling Australian Towns').
Duration: *c.* 1'10.
Note: This was composed in response to a written request of 18 March 1943 from Arthur Bliss, then Head of the Music Department at the BBC, for a 30-second fanfare 'more dignified than the usual military flourishes' and required by 10 April. On 21 March, Bax replied: 'I will try to produce a fanfare, or something of that kind . . .'; and on 8 April he posted off the score:

> I am sending this brassy flourish (I cannot call it a fanfare) and hope it may be something like what you want. It consists of twenty-nine bars and will take rather longer than half-a-minute. I would like it to be played as it stands if this is possible, but the bars towards the end with the pencil line over them [bars 22-7] could be cut if absolutely necessary (though I think it would make rather a tame ending.).

It is not known whether Bax was paid for the piece. Bliss implies in his original letter that a fee would be forthcoming; but in a later memo another BBC official suggests that Sir Arnold should be tactfully asked if he was intending to offer his services free of charge.

354 WORK IN PROGRESS: Overture for orchestra

Date: 'Storrington | Nov | 1943'.
Dedication: 'To Walter Legge'.
Orchestra: 2(1)222, 4231, timp., 2 perc. (tamb., cym., tri.), str.
Manuscript: *Short score (incomplete)*: BL (Add. MS 54775); ff. 24 and 25 (24v and 25v blank); [2] pp. (the first numbered '5', the preceding four pages being missing; the second unpag.); AC paper (landscape format; f. 24: 263 × 369;

[150] The BBC files do not record the name of the conductor, but there is some correspondence about the score between Bliss and Clifford (who was himself Australian). Clifford thought that Bax had 'done Sydney proud'.

f. 25: 266 × 367); f. 24 contains pencil sketches for the music from bar 2 after (5) to the end, although 10 bars are marked 'cut' and do not appear in the f.sc.; they would have come immediately before (T); f. 25 contains pencil sketches for the passage from 1 to 4 after (T). The MS paper used for these sketches calls for comment since it is of a type dating from the late nineteenth century and was last used by Bax in 1902. A possible explanation is that it may have been at about this time that the MSS of Bax's early songs were sent to Storrington (see **Note** for **51**) and that he extracted some unused sheets from his juvenilia to write out the short score of this overture.

Full score: CH (MS 251); [24] ff.; 48 pp.; ALP 30 paper (355 × 263); loose in brown card wrappers. *Copyist's score*: CH, [24] ff.; 48 pp.; BC 7 paper (341 × 258). Unpublished. *Parts*: CH.

Performance: London Symphony Orchestra, George Weldon; 'New hall at a big factory in the London Suburbs' (see **Note** below); 24 February 1944.

Duration: 7'41.

Note: This overture was commissioned by the National Services Entertainments Association (ENSA) for a series of 'Symphony Concerts for War Workers'. Writing in *Hinrichsen's Year Book 1944: Music of our Time* (London, 1944), p. 175, the dedicatee, Walter Legge, who was ENSA's Director of Music from 1942 until 1945, revealed details of the commission:

> So that these concerts may begin with British works I have invited Sir Arnold Bax, Arthur Bliss, E. J. Moeran, Alan Rawsthorne and Vaughan Williams to write works of anything from six to nine minutes in length, particularly to open these concerts. The Bax work . . . is already completed, and will have its first performance in February. The Bliss and Moeran works are well on the way and have their first performances in the same month.

In the event, only Moeran's *Overture for a Masque*, Rawsthorne's *Street Corner* and Bax's piece were completed.

In a letter from Bax to John Barbirolli quoted in Donald Brook, *Conductors' Gallery* (London, 1945), p. 14, the composer refers to the overture as a 'jeu d'esprit'. His assumption that Barbirolli is due to conduct the first performance is incorrect, and it was first played under George Weldon. For reasons of national security during wartime, the precise location of the première was not mentioned in the press. According to *The Musical Times* for March 1944, p. 90, critics were especially invited and transported to the venue. The proceedings began thirty minutes after blackout, with the result that the hall was only three-quarters full; numerous performances in other London suburbs soon followed.

There is a satirical allusion to 'The Emperor's Hymn' by Haydn—in other words 'Deutschland über Alles'—at bars 1-4 of p. 12; and the 'second subject' is reminiscent of the similar theme (also introduced by a clarinet) in Balfour Gardiner's *Overture to a Comedy*.

c. 1943

355 DREAM CHILD for voice and piano

Date: See **Note** below.
Text: Val Newton, 'Dream Child' (not otherwise published).
Manuscript: Not traced.
Publication: CH (43809), 1957, 4to, 5 pp.
Performance: *Earliest traced*: Patricia McCarry (sop.), Paul Hamburger (pf.); br. on Radio 3, 28 August 1969.
Duration: 2'08.
Note: Val Newton, the author of the words, was the wife of the Director of the Food Office in which Bax's friend Mary Gleaves worked from 1941 to 1948. She had written the poem in memory of her daughter, who had died as a child, and in about 1943 asked the composer to set it to music. Although he had not written a song for over ten years Bax complied but was not pleased when Mrs Newton (or 'Mutton Dressed Lamb', as he used to call her) tried to cajole him into submitting it to the BBC for broadcasting. It was published four years after Bax's death.

1944

356 TO RUSSIA for baritone solo, chorus (SATB) and orchestra

Title: 'To Russia | (1944)'.
Date: *Vocal score*: 'Storrington | Jan | 1944'. *Full score*: 'Feb 3rd | 1944'.
Text: John Masefield, 'Ode to the Red Army', published in *The Times*, 24 February 1944.
Orchestra: 3(1)222, 4331, timp., 2 perc. (b.d., s.d., cym.), str.
Manuscript: *Vocal score*: CH (MS 249); [2] ff.; [4] pp.; 22-staff paper (370 × 275); loose in plastic pocket. *Full score*: CH (MS 249); [8] ff.; 16 pp.; pp. 1-12: ALP 30 paper (355 × 263); pp. 13-16: IM paper (358 × 262); loose in plastic pocket. *Copyist's vocal score*: [4] ff.; 8 pp.; 12-staff paper (359 × 264). Unpublished. *Parts*: CH.
Performance: Roy Henderson (bar.), Royal Choral Society, London Symphony Orchestra, Dr Malcolm Sargent; Royal Albert Hall; 23 February 1944 (concert entitled 'Salute the Red Army').
Duration: 3'51.
Note: In a letter to Adrian Boult dated 24 February 1944, excusing himself from another function, Bax wrote: 'I felt I had to hear my new little piece played at the Red Army Jamboree.' To May Harrison, however, he conceded: 'The Albert Hall Anglo-Russian Jamboree yesterday was incredibly boring and I returned here [Storrington] in the evening almost dead to the world.'

357 A LEGEND for orchestra

Date: 'Storrington | May 2nd 1944'.
Dedication: 'To Julian Livingstone Herbage'.
Orchestra: 3(1)222, 4331, timp., 3 perc. (b.d., s.d., tamb., cym., tri., gl.), hp., str.
Manuscript: *Short score*: Not traced. In a letter to me dated 1 September 1975, the dedicatee mentioned that he had 'somewhere or other' the three-staff short score of this work, but he never found the time to hunt it out; he died the following year, and his executors were subsequently unable to locate it among his papers. In June 1944 Herbage had written asking for the full score in order to compile a programme note for a proposed performance in July. Bax replied on 1 July that the parts were being copied from it:

> However there is a piano compression. As you will see there are many cuts. There is no communicable programme to the piece and listeners must put their own interpretation to it. I would much rather leave the analysis to you for I hate writing these things. I never have anything to say about my own works! . . . The bars leading to the march (p. 6) are retained in somewhat similar form to those I have crossed out, but the passage is shorter.

This short score was subsequently lent to Norman Higgins of the Cambridge Arts Theatre Trust, who passed it on to Philip Radcliffe, the note-writer for the first performance in October; it is conceivable that the score was never returned to Herbage. *Full score*: CH (MS 258); [38] ff.; 75 pp. (p. 1 unnumbered) + 1 blank; pp. [1]-67: ALP 30 paper (355 × 263); pp. 68-75 + 1 blank: IM paper (358 × 262). Unpublished. *Parts*: CH.
Performance: BBC Symphony Orchestra, Sir Adrian Boult; The Guildhall, Cambridge; 28 October 1944. 'Bax is one of my loves: but his new "*Legend*" . . . is just an old Bax-o'-tricks.' (W. R. Anderson, *The Musical Times*, December 1944, p. 372).
Duration: 13'14.
Note: This work was written at the suggestion of Julian Herbage that Bax should produce a new score for a Promenade Concert. On 25 April 1944, the composer wrote: 'I am getting towards the end of scoring an entirely new piece which may suit you for the Prom in July. It is at present called simply "Legend" . . .'. On 17 June, however, he wrote to May Harrison: 'I don't think much of the new Legend and have shelved it for the time being.' The first performance of this work—Bax's last tone-poem—was broadcast live by the BBC, preceded by a five-minute talk given by Robin Hull. In *The Radio Times* for 20 October 1944, p. 5, Ralph Hill provided a useful preview of the broadcast:

> Sir Arnold tells me that his new tone poem, which was specially written for Sir Henry Wood's Jubilee Season of Promenade Concerts, is not a musical version of a particular story. It merely purports to evoke certain characteristic elements in the tales of some northern land—a matter of the atmosphere of strangeness and

remoteness inherent in the word 'legend'. Mountainy landscapes, wild weather, windswept castles, shadowy battles, and finally triumph in a barbaric setting may perhaps be suggested by this series of musical episodes.

358 CALL TO THE RED ARMY

Note: In an internal BBC memorandum dated 3 January 1945, Julian Herbage wrote: 'Arnold Bax tells me that he has revised his Malta music [347] which now ends with a new march called "Call to the Red Army". (I am not quite sure what the connection is between Malta and the Red Army, and didn't like to ask Sir Arnold!).' For the suggestion that this may have been the original title of what became the *Victory March* see **364**.

1945

359 TE DEUM for chorus (SATB) and organ

Date: In a letter to Jessie Wood dated 27 February [1946], Bax refers to 'a "Te Deum" and "Nunc Dimittis" which the B.B.C. commissioned me to write early last year, but have never *yet* performed (!) . . .'.
Text: Canticle attributed to St Ambrose, translated from the Latin.
Dedication: *Printed score*: 'To Sir Stanley Marchant'.
Manuscript: Not traced.
Publication: CH (37332), 1945, 8vo, 27 pp. Tonic Sol-fa notation printed above voice parts.
Performance: Choir of New College, Oxford, Dr H. K. Andrews; br. on the Third Programme, 13 November 1946.
Duration: 10'17.
Note: In the letter quoted above Bax added: 'I think well of them myself . . . The BBC paid me a fee for these pieces, but their idea was to get together several new serious church works by English composers and give a series of performances. Apparently the others have not come up to scratch!' He further suggests that he should orchestrate both pieces for a concert in memory of Sir Henry Wood, who died on 19 August 1944; and on 27 February he wrote to the BBC requesting permission to do so. In reply, Jessie Wood wrote that she thought this 'an excellent suggestion'; but in another letter, dated 5 March, Bax wrote that '[Victor] Hely Hutchinson [Director of Music at the BBC] thinks the Te Deum will be sufficient by itself. . . . Whether I shall be able to score it I don't yet know. I have had an awful misfortune in that my glasses have been stolen and my spare pair is not strong enough to allow me much reading or writing . . . ' It is clear from another letter to Jessie Wood, however, that his plan to orchestrate the *Te Deum* never came to fruition: 'I am extremely sorry that the "Te Deum" is considered inappropprate because just as music it would be very suitable.' The reason given by Jessie Wood for its being considered unsuitable was the

fact that it was dedicated to Sir Stanley Marchant and was therefore 'out of the question' as a memorial piece for Sir Henry Wood.

360 NUNC DIMITTIS for chorus (SATB) and organ

Date: Erroneously ascribed to 1944 in *Gr5*.
Dedication: *Printed score*: 'To Eric Gillett'.
Text: St Luke's Gospel, ii, 29.
Manuscript: Not traced.
Publication: CH (37333), 1945, 8vo, 7 pp. Tonic Sol-fa notation printed above voice parts.
Performance: Choir of New College, Oxford, Dr H. K. Andrews; br. on the Third Programme, 13 November 1946.
Duration: 2'45.
Note: For the origins of this piece see **359** above.

361 SONATA NO. 1 for violin and piano (fourth version of 124)

I. Moderately slow and very Tranquilly. II. Allegro Vivace. III. Moderate Tempo. Smooth and serene.

Date: *Printed score*: 'Revision 1945'
Dedication: 'To Paul Kochanski.'
Manuscript: Bax undoubtedly made his revisions on a printed copy of the original published score (1922).
Publication: CH (37890), [1946], 4to, 49 pp.
Performance: *Earliest traced*: Erich Gruenberg (vn.), John McCabe (pf.); The Maltings, Snape; 17 November 1989 (recording session for Chandos Records Ltd.).[151]
Duration: 31'47.
Note: In an undated letter sent to Harry Isaacs in 1945, Bax wrote: 'I'm correcting my First Violin Sonata for a new edition. It was one of my earliest tunes to be published, and lordy what a host of errors and ambiguities I let pass.' The revision seems originally to have been mooted for a prospective performance by May Harrison, as revealed in a letter to her (undated but certainly the early 1940s): 'I don't like cutting published works as it creates a most dangerous precedent, but I have done so for this occasion as I should like you to play the old sonata again'. In another letter to Miss

[151] This is the only work by Bax to have been published in two versions. The final revision may well have been played in public before 1989, perhaps by May Harrison, as implied in the letter quoted in the **Note** below. But in view of the comparatively minor differences from the 1920 version, it is unlikely that such a performance would have been advertised as a première, and copies of the first published edition would still have been in circulation. The recording by Henry Holst and Frank Merrick issued in 1965 is of the 1920 version.

Harrison, he described the work as now being 'a good deal improved'. For the previous versions see **124**, **166** and **236**.

362 SUITE ON THE NAME GABRIEL FAURÉ for piano

I. Prelude. II. Barcarolle. III. Polka. IV. Intermezzo (Storm). V. Finale (Quodlibet).

Title: *MS*: None. *Copyist's score*: 'SUITE | ON THE NAME | GABRIEL FAURÉ', with 'Suite for Fauré' written by Harriet Cohen in pencil on the front cover. Published in France with the title 'Cinq pièces sur le nom de Gabriel Fauré'.
Date: I. 'April 25th | 1945'. II. 'Storrington | May 5th 1945'. III. 'Storrington | May 17th | 1945'. IV. 'May 24th | 1945'. V. 'Storrington | June 1st | 1945'.
Manuscript: *Holograph*: BNF (MS 9884 (1-5)); [12] ff.; [24] pp. ([1-4], [5-8], [9-13], [14-7], [18-24]); pp. [1-22]: 12-staff paper (310 × 250); pp. [23-4]: RC 1 paper (310 × 250); in wrappers with a donative inscription written by Harriet Cohen in French and dated 16 February 1955. *Copyist's score*: BL (Add. MS 54770); 16 ff. (16v blank); tp + 1 blank + 23 pp. + 3 blank (1-3, 4-7, 8-12, 12-16, 16-23); 16-staff paper (364 × 270); loose in brown paper wrappers with Harriet Cohen's handwriting on the front; in the same hand as the *Three Songs from the Norse* (**285**).
Publication: *Edited with an introduction and editorial notes by Michel Fleury*: EME (M.E. 9014), 1996, 4to, 29 pp.
Performance: Marie Catherine Girod; Église Saint Pierre, Paris; 9 October 1992 (recording session for Opès 3D).
Duration: 19'36.
Note: Bax was an admirer of Fauré, having written a sonnet about him in 1906 beginning 'O unknown elder brother across the sea | Thou singest, and magic summers linger long'. For details of Bax's arrangement for harp and string orchestra see **379**.

363 GLORIA (Communion Service) for chorus (SATB) and organ

Date: *Printed score:* 'Storrington Aug.21st 1945'.
Dedication: 'To Horace A. Hawkins'.
Text: The Lesser Doxology (Gloria Patri), translated from the Latin.
Manuscript: Not traced.
Publication: CH (38654), 1947, 8vo, 15 pp. Tonic Sol-fa notation printed above voice parts.
Duration: 5'20.

364 VICTORY MARCH for orchestra

Title: 'Victory March', with 'MALTA G.C.' written to the left; 'Victory' seems to be written over an erasure (see **Note** below).
Date: 'Storrington | Sept 8th | 1945.'

Orchestra: 2222, 2230, timp., 1 perc. (s.d., cym.), str.
Manuscript: *Holograph*: CH (MS 260); [18] ff.; 35 pp. (p. 1 unnumbered) + 1 blank; pp. 1-16: ALP 30 paper (355 × 263); pp. 17-35 (p. 35 unnumbered) + 1 blank: ALM 30 paper (360 × 262); loose in a bifolium of 'Chappell 22' paper. *Copyist's score*: [21] ff.; 41 pp. + 1 blank; ALP 12 paper. Unpublished. *Parts*: CH.
Performance: *Earliest traced*: BBC Symphony Orchestra, Muir Mathieson; non-commercial recording of unknown provenance, late 1940s. The march might conceivably have been played by the BBC Scottish Orchestra under Ian Whyte in a programme entitled 'Music for Victory Day' that was broadcast on 8 June 1946 on the Home Service and included music from *Malta, G.C.*
Duration: 7'36.
Note: The origins of this work are obscure. Since it is unlikely that Bax would have bothered to write such a work without being prompted, it was presumably commissioned to celebrate the victory of the Allies in the war, which officially ended with the defeat of Japan on 2 September 1945, six days before the score was completed. It is possible that the work was intended for, but not performed at, the 'Thanksgiving for Victory Concert' held at the Royal Albert Hall on 20 April 1946, since Bax was one of the vice-presidents on the committee for that event. Unlike Vaughan Williams's *Song of Thanksgiving*, it was not commissioned by the BBC. The material for the trio is taken directly from the concluding march in Bax's music for the film *Malta, G. C.* (**347**; see also **385**), although his inclusion of the name of the film at the head of this score is confusing, and it is best to ignore it as part of the title. It is possible that the *Victory March* was originally conceived as the *Call to the Red Army* detailed in **358**, written in short score in 1944 (to tally with the date of Herbage's note) and subsequently orchestrated, with the title changed as an afterthought.

365 O DAME GET UP AND BAKE YOUR PIES (Variations on a North Country Christmas Carol) for piano

Date: *Copyist's score*: 'Storrington | Dec 10th | 1945'.
Dedication: *Printed score*: 'To Anna and Julian Herbage in acknowledgement of | pies baked and enjoyed "on Christmas Day in the morning" 1945.'
Manuscript: *Holograph*: Not traced. It was given to Julian Herbage and Anna Instone but is now missing. *Copyist's score*: TCD (MS 4940/1); [3] ff.; 5 pp. + 1 blank; 12-staff paper (350 × 245).
Publication: CH (1961), 1947, 4to, 7 pp. Also in Connie Mayfield (ed.), *Arnold Bax: Selected Works for Piano*, TP, 1986, 4to, pp. 33-7.
Performance: Harriet Cohen; br. live on BBC Third Programme, 23 December 1945 (on 'Music Magazine').
Duration: 2'37.

Note: This was commissioned from Bax by Julian Herbage in a letter dated 5 November 1945. On 11 December he wrote: 'How are the Dame and her Christmas pies getting along?' Bax replied the following day: 'I have baked seven minute pies in the form of variations each a few bars long (including pipe-music demanded by Harriet). It only remains for Anna [Herbage's wife] to produce her counter-pies.' These were eaten by Bax, Harriet Cohen and the Herbages at Broadcasting House after the programme had come off the air, hence the dedication.

366 GOLDEN EAGLE: Incidental music for a play

Date: Begun no earlier than September 1945 and perhaps not until early December; finished by the end of December (see **Note** below).
Text: Clifford Bax, *Golden Eagle: A Drama* (London: Home & Van Thal, 1946).
Orchestra: 1 tpt., s.d., hp., hpd. and pf. (1 player), str. + sop., con., bar.
Manuscript: CH (MS 259); [12] ff.; 24 pp. (p. 22 blank); 22-staff paper (365 × 270), the ends of the lines printed very irregularly (cf. **367**). Copies by Bax of 'My faithful fair one' and 'Rizzio's Song (Ronsard)': BPL; [1] f.; [1] p. + 1 blank; [2] ff. (a bifolium); [4] pp.; 12-staff paper (295 × 238); both loose in a fawn card folder. The fact that both songs have been folded up at some stage, presumably for insertion into pockets or handbags, suggests that these were the actors' copies, from which they were required to learn their music. Unpublished. *Parts*: CH.
Performance: John Byron (bar.), Ann Farrer (con.), Mary Honer (sop.),[152] [anonymous instrumentalists]; Westminster Theatre; 29 January 1946.
Duration: (1) *Complete play*: *c.* 3¼ hours;[153] (2) *Complete music*: *c.* 16'00 (11'03 excluding the two songs and two instrumental solos).
Note: The play for which this incidental music was written dates from the autumn of 1945. On 17 August Clifford Bax sent the MS to his friend Harold Rubinstein asking for his opinion: 'Is it dull? I wrote it in a state of mild hypnotism and cannot remember fashioning the phrases: a kind of Twilight sleep!' A week later he wrote another letter to Rubinstein expressing the hope that he would not 'despise' the play and asking him to 'tell the truth about it'. These letters show that the undated score must have been started no earlier than September 1945. In a letter to Jessie Wood dated

[152] These were the actors playing David Rizzio, Mary Carmichael and Mary Beaton. '... Mr. John Byron is an admirable Rizzio, singing period songs specially set by Sir Arnold Bax most agreeably.' (From a review in *The Times*, 30 January 1946.) No mention is made of the two women, suggesting that perhaps only the baritone part was sung (see II. under **Synopsis** below).
[153] According to James Agate's review in *The Sunday Times* for 3 February 1946. This timing presumably included the two intervals.

9 January [1946], Bax wrote that he had just completed 'the second of two outstanding jobs which I had on hand'; this refers to the Trio in B♭, which is dated the same day as the letter.

On 4 December 1945, Bax wrote that he had completed the first two movements of this trio and was half way through the third, and it may be that *Golden Eagle* was composed between then and the completion of the trio. 'One of my jobs', he continued, 'was the writing and scoring of incidental music for my brother's new play which is to be produced on Jan 29th! (originally Feb 25th) so you can imagine I have had a hectic time.' In another letter, to a friend, Bax expressed the opinion that the play was, from an architectural point of view, 'most excellently designed'; but it failed to impress the drama critics and ran for only three performances. 'You missed nothing musically', he wrote to May Harrison, 'in not hearing "Golden Eagle" for nearly all my work is practically inaudible—the public prattling and gassing from beginning to end except during the action of the ill-fated play. Clifford has been so violently insulting to the critics that he is not likely ever to have a good notice again.'

Synopsis:

I. 'Prelude', pp. 1-3 (pf. and str.).
II. 'Rizzio's Song of Ronsard', pp. 3-6 (vocal soloists, hp. and str.). In the play, this song is performed during Act I Scene 1 (pp. 25-6) by David Rizzio, Mary Beaton and Mary Carmichael. A footnote on p. 25 of the play mentions that 'on the stage one verse was omitted', although all three are printed and appear in the score. In the 1946 production, this song was sung by the actors on the stage. A note in the BPL MS states: 'If the two female voices are not available Rizzio must sing the top part of this refrain in each verse'.
III. 'Dance', p. 8 (hpd. solo). This piece—the only use of a harpsichord (which he misspells 'harpsicord') in Bax's entire output—begins with an exact transcription of the first 19 bars of the Prelude, followed by a repetition of the opening four bars, leading to the original concluding four bars. In the play, the dance is performed while Mary Beaton accompanies on the virginals (p. 27). In the score, the piece is written out immediately after No. V.
IV. 'Prelude Act II Scene 1': Pavane, pp. 9-12 (hp., pf. and str.).
V. 'Rizzio preludes on the lute', p. 7 (hp. solo). This 19-bar passage is played during Act II Scene 1 of the play (p. 53): 'RIZZIO fingers his lute' and quietly strums while speaking his lines; to which Mary Carmichael responds with: 'That's a sweet sad tune you are playing . . .'. They are interrupted by the entrance of Mary Beaton, and in the score Bax has written 'Breaks off' as the music comes to a halt three-quarters of the way through a repeat of the opening four-bar phrase. The passage appears originally to have been intended as No. III, which has been crossed through and replaced by 'V'; a note at the foot of the page (p. 7) states: 'No 5 This should come after the Pavane on P9 to P12'.
VI. 'Song (Rizzio) Harp accompanying', p. 13. This consists of 10 bars in D major. In the full score there is no tempo indication nor any marks of expression, the music comprising a vocal line without any words and a bare accompaniment for solo harp;

the copy in the BPL is more complete. In the play it is performed by Rizzio almost immediately after the preceding number (p. 53): 'He begins an old Scottish love song'. The song is identified on the BPL copy as 'My faithful fair one' | Mo Rún Dileas | From the Gaelic': actually an 'Old Highland Melody' usually associated with the Gaelic poem 'Mo rùn geal, dìleas' ('My faithful fond one')[154] by Young MacLean (see Alfred Moffat (ed.), *The Minstrelsy of the Scottish Highlands*, London, n.d., p. 96; Bax's version is in the same key and uses the same notation as Moffat). Since the words postdate the sixteenth century, their use in a play about Mary Stuart is anachronistic.
VII. 'Prelude Act II Scene 2', pp. 14-16 (pf. and str.).
VIII. 'Act III Scene I', pp. 17-19 (tpt., s.d., pf. and str.). From erasures at the head of the page it is clear that this section was originally intended as a prelude to Act III Scene 2, which is set on Carberry Hill; but it was actually used as the prelude to the previous scene. In its original context the music illustrates the stage direction: 'There should be off-stage noises and murmurings in order to suggest the vicinity of two armies; and occasionally there might be distant pipe-music'; and Bax has provided appropriately martial fanfares for the trumpet and ominous side drum rolls, all of which would seem to be incongruous for the start of the scene to which it was eventually assigned: a room in Dunbar Castle.
IX. 'Prelude Act III Scene II', pp. 20-1 (pf. and str.). Above the third bar from the end Bax has written 'Side drum starts'; and on an empty staff above the final bar he has pencilled in a brief flourish for the trumpet.
X. 'Mary Stuart's Prayer', pp. 23-4 (tpt., hp., pf. and str.). This passage accompanies the queen's final prayer at the end of Act III Scene 2 (p. 99), which is followed by a slow curtain.

1946

367 TRIO IN B♭ for piano, violin and cello

I. Allegro con brio. II. Adagio (alla breve). III. Tempo moderato e molto ritmico.

Date: *MS*: 'Fine. | Jan 9th 1946 | Storrington.'
Dedication: *Printed score only*: 'To the Harry Isaacs Trio'.
Manuscript: BL (Add. MS 54764); [18] ff.; 33 pp. (1-13, 14-22 + 2 blank, 23-33 + 1 blank); 22-staff paper (365 × 270), the same paper as for **366**; loose in a bifolium of AL 18b paper (359 × 259) with non-autograph title.
Publication: CH (38363), 1946, 4to, 41 pp.; WC0343.
Performance: Harry Isaacs Trio: Harry Isaacs (pf.), Leonard Hirsch (vn.), James Whitehead (vc.); Wigmore Hall; 21 March 1946.
Duration: 26'12.
Note: This work was commissioned by Harry Isaacs for inclusion in a series of six concerts to be given at the Wigmore Hall during the early part of 1946. Bax's initial reaction was to refuse, complaining that the medium was

[154] Also set by Peter Warlock (1915).

too difficult and suggesting that Dvořák's 'Dumky' Trio, Op. 90, was the only successful example. However, the idea gradually grew on him, and in a letter to Isaacs dated 4 December 1945 he wrote: 'I was thinking that you will be pleased to hear that I have finished two movements of the trio and am in the middle of the last. I am pleased with the work so far.' After completing the score, Bax described the first two movements as 'severely classical. . . . As to the last [mostly in 5/8 time], it might have a quotation from Hamlet [III. ii. 148-9]. "This is miching mallecho—it means mischief"'.

368 THE BARD OF THE DIMBOVITZA for mezzo-soprano and orchestra (second version of 160)

a. Gipsy Song [this song was not revised]. **b.** The Well of Tears. **c.** Misconception. **d.** My girdle I hung on a tree-top tall. **e.** Spinning Song.

Date: a. 'Fine | Dec 14th | 1914.' **b** and **c.** '1914 | Revised 1946'. **d.** '1914 | Revised | 1946'. **e.** 'Oct | 1914 | Revised | 1946'.
Dedication: *Printed score only*: 'To my friend | Gou Constantinesco'.
Orchestra: a. 1111, 0000, hp., str. **b.** 2 2+1 2020, 4000, hp., str. **c–e.** 2 2+1 2020, 3000, hp., str.
Text: See details listed under **160**.
Manuscript: *Holograph*: CH (MS 241); [71] ff.; [142] pp. (1-15 + 1 blank, 1-27 + 1 blank, 1-30, 1-25, 1-29 (separately pagin.); 1: ALM 29 paper (359 × 265); 2-5: 22-staff paper (366 × 270). *Copyist's score*: CH; [72] ff.; 143 pp. + 1 blank; 18-staff paper (354 × *c.* 247). F.sc. unpublished. *Parts*: CH.
Publication: *Vocal score only*: CH (38597), 1948, 4to, 51 pp.
Performance: Emelie Hooke (mezz.), BBC Symphony Orchestra, Sir Adrian Boult; br. on the Third Programme, 26 March 1949.
Duration: 38'53.
Note: 'I believe it to be one of my better things'. (From an undated letter, *c.* 1948, to Victor Hely-Hutchinson.)

369 MORNING SONG (Maytime in Sussex) for piano and orchestra

Date: 1946 inferred from the date of publication.
Dedication: Printed score: 'To Her Royal Highness Princess Elizabeth'.
Orchestra: 2(1)222, 2000, timp., str.
Manuscript: Not traced.
Publication: *Full score*: CH (38404), 1946, 4to, 39 pp. *Piano part*: CH (38400), 1946, 4to, 11 pp.
Performance: (1) Harriet Cohen (pf.), 'Orchestra', Dr Malcolm Sargent; EMI Studios, Abbey Road; 7 February 1947 (recording session for HMV Records Ltd.; the record was issued in June, before the first concert performance). (2) Harriet Cohen (pf.), London Symphony Orchestra, Sir

Malcolm Sargent;[155] Royal Albert Hall; 13 August 1947 (Promenade Concert).
Adaptation: Part of the score was used for the ballet *Oscar* (see **110** for details).
Duration: 8'16.
Note: This work was written to celebrate the dedicatee's twenty-first birthday (21 April 1947). A piano piece with the same title by F. Lincoln Bax was published in 1909: No. 1 of *Three Original Melodies* (London: Orpheus Music Publishing Co.).

1947

370 [FOUR PIECES] for piano

a. Fantastic March. **b.** Romanza. **c.** Idyll. **d.** Phantasie.

Title: No collective title on MS. Published as 'Four Pieces'.
Date: a. 'Storrington | Jan 30th | 1947'. **b.** 'Storrington | Feb 11th 1947'. **c.** 'Storrington | Feb 19th | 1947'. **d.** 'Storrington | March 12th 1947'.
Manuscript: BL (Add. MS 54770); ff. 17-24, [16] pp. ([1-4], [1-3] + 1 p. with pencil sketches, [1-2], 1-5 + 1 p. with sketches); 22-staff paper (ff. 17-21: 365 × 271; f. 22: 355 × 261; f. 23: 370 × 274; f. 24: 365 × 270); loose in a bifolium of BH 43 inside brown paper wrappers together with the copyist's score of **362**; f. 20^{v} contains a pencil sketch for the opening of movt. II of the Concertante for three solo instruments and orchestra (**377**), which was completed on 7 December 1949. A more fragmentary sketch for part of the same movement can be found written in pencil and blue and red ballpoint pen on f. 24^{v}.
Publication: *Edited by Richard G. Hallas*: FMP, 1998, 4to, 24 pp. ([2]-8, 9-13, 14-16, 17-24)+ 2 pp. of editorial notes; introductory note by Graham Parlett.
Performance: Jonathan Higgins; British Music Information Centre; 21 April 1983 (lecture-recital by Graham Parlett, *et al.*)
Duration: a. 4'46. **b.** 5'18. **c.** 3'52. **d.** 5'01.
Note: These pieces are not individually numbered, but the chronological order given above is quite satisfactory. The only published allusion to them in Bax's lifetime is in *Hinrichsen's Musical Year Book, 1949-50* (London, n.d.), p. 121, which mentions 'Six Piano Pieces (unpublished and unperformed)' as being 'recent compositions'. The reference to six pieces instead of four suggests either an error, or that two others were written and are missing, or that other works are being referred to, although the only known

[155] Sargent had received his knighthood in the summer of 1947.

unpublished piano work written during the 1940s was the five-movement *Suite on the Name Gabriel Fauré* (**362**).

371 ST GEORGE for baritone, chorus (SATB), organ and orchestra (unorchestrated)

Title: Although referred to as the 'Pageant of St George' in LF, the MS is headed 'St. George' alone.
Date: See **Note** below.
Text: Unpublished text by John Masefield. Subsequently revised and published as *A Play of St. George* (London: William Heinemann Ltd., 1948).
Manuscript: BL (Add. MS 54775); ff. 1-13 (13^v blank); [25] pp. + 1 blank; 22-staff paper (366 × 271); loosely inserted in a bifolium of CH paper (419 × 250). Unusually for Bax, the score is written mostly in bright blue ink. Unpublished.
Duration: *c.* 15'00 (music only).
Note: This work was commissioned to celebrate the sexcentenary of the foundation of the Order of the Garter and the College of St George in 1348. It is not known at exactly what stage Bax's contribution was invited, but an advance notice was given to the press early in 1947 that the Poet Laureate, John Masefield, had been asked to write a 'Pageant-play' for performance in the nave of St George's Chapel in Windsor during the spring of the following year.[156] Bax was presumably involved in the affair during the summer of 1947; but on 24 October he wrote to a friend:

> The Windsor Pageant has been abandoned owing to the financial and political situation, so my almost completed music is a dead loss as it cannot be adapted to any other purpose. A little saddening for the time being.

And the Dean of St George's Chapel, writing in February 1948, explained that '. . . the Pageant-play . . . with all it must have involved in terms of advertisement, travel and expense would not, in this year of general hardship and financial crisis, have been justified.'[157] Although the event for which it had been written never took place, at least one other attempt was made to have the work performed. In August 1948 Bax wrote to Masefield:

> I should of course be delighted if my music could be used at the performance of St. George at Exeter. But I am afraid the matter of the expense of an orchestra has been forgotten. I went into this matter when a performance at Exeter was suggested some time ago, and found out that at least £200 would be required. I wrote to the Dean explaining this and he replied that the price was prohibitive (as I expected). The music is quite unsuited to the organ and the choral element needs women's

[156] See the Dean's letter in the *Annual Report of Windsor: Society of the Friends of St. George's* (February 1947).
[157] *Annual Report* (February 1948).

voices—so I don't see what can be done as far as the music is concerned. There are some nibblings from another cathedral and perhaps if this should come to anything, they would care for the full performance.

Although this might imply that Bax had already prepared a full score, he often deferred the chore of orchestrating his music until a specific performance was in sight, and there is certainly no trace of one.

A comparison between the text of John Masefield's published play and the words as they appear on Bax's score suggests that the author made extensive alterations before publication.

Synopsis:

I. 'Allegro moderato' (29 bars) for orchestra alone.
II. 'Ceremonial Dance' (37 bars) for orchestra alone.
III. 'Chorus of Ecclesiastics' (89 bars) for chorus with orchestra.
These first three sections appear originally to have been intended as a Prologue to the play. The words sung by the chorus in section III introduce the story of St George, which is to be enacted, but do not appear in the published version of the play.
IV. 'Allegro' (38 bars) for chorus with orchestra—Interlude (14 bars) for organ solo. The words for this untitled section appear on pp. 2-3 of the published play ('Alas, for a defenceless land'), where they are sung by the half-chorus. The music was adapted for orchestra alone early in 1948 as part of the 'Storm' sequence in Bax's music for the film *Oliver Twist*, although it was omitted from the soundtrack (see **374**). The passage for organ solo was presumably intended to accompany the entrance of Queen Artemisia immediately after that of the chorus.
V. 'Lament' (112 bars) for baritone and chorus with orchestra. This passage ('What is past hope of help or cure') is sung, according to the published play, by the two halves of the chorus alternately (pp. 4-6), although in Bax's score part of it is sung by the baritone soloist.
VI. 'Lento moderato' (49 bars) for chorus with orchestra. For some unknown reason this section is written out immediately after section IX in the MS. The words ('Once, in this land, long since . . .') can be found on pp. 13-14 of the play, where they are sung by a group of singers in procession.
VII. 'The Dragon's Song' (21 bars) for baritone with brass only. This song, in a truncated version, appears on p. 20 of the play ('O sing, and let the people know').
VIII. 'In time long past' (70 bars) for 'voice' (unspecified) with orchestra. In the play, this song is performed by Demetrius on p. 29 ('In times long past, there were delightful days . . .'). In the score, the vocal part is written out in the treble clef and was presumably intended for a tenor soloist, although the voice is not specified.
IX. 'The Coming of Spring' (44 bars) for chorus with orchestra. This song ('Dark and cruel was the winter day') is sung on pp. 37-8 of the play at the entrance of the priests, Demetrius, the Queen, Sabra and other citizens. As mentioned above, section IX is followed in the MS by VI, which itself is followed by an unnumbered, untitled passage of 42 bars. This begins with an orchestral introduction marked 'Moderato grazioso' (20 bars) leading to a song for 'a few women's voices' ('We who were Hope in human thought'), consisting of two verses with a four-bar coda for orchestra alone. In the published play this passage occurs on p. 32 (i.e. before section IX above),

where it is described by Masefield as 'The dance of the Answered Prayers' (the orchestral passage) followed by a chorus of singers.

That Bax's piano score of *St George* is incomplete can be deduced from the fact that the final apotheosis—the entrance of The Christus and the chorus of Radiant Spirits—is lacking, though whether this final section was not completed or is simply missing it is impossible to tell. In the published version of the play, at least, there are three other passages for which the stage directions demand music: on p. 11 'with a beating of time or a rude marching song, the Dragon enters'; on p. 19 there occurs 'the Dance of sad Thoughts to some slow and gentle air, pavane or waltz'; and on p. 38 'the march of the Imperial Guard is heard: military brass of sorts, with possible drums and fifes. Then a shout of "Music...Left Wheel. Music... Halt...Music...the Imperial Salute". There is a great fanfare for the Emperor's Proxy.'

372 EPITHALAMIUM for chorus (SATB) in unison and organ

Title: Bax uses a Latinized version of Spenser's original Greek title (meaning a nuptial song).
Date: *Printed score*: 'Storrington | Sept. 2nd 1947'.
Text: Edmund Spenser, 'Epithalamion', l. 204 ff.
Manuscript: Not traced.
Publication: CH (38696), 1948, 8vo, 7 pp. *Separate voice part*: CH (38735), [1947], 8vo, 3 pp.
Performance: *Earliest traced*: 'Augmented choir' of Chichester Cathedral, Anne Sheail (org.), Horace Arthur Hawkins; Chichester Cathedral; July 1948 (special service of Bax's church music).
Duration: 5'31.
Note: This work was intended for the wedding of Princess Elizabeth on 20 November 1947, as Bax explained in a letter to Dr William McKie, the Organist and Master of the Choristers at Westminster Abbey:

> I write this letter with much diffidence, and I don't want it to cause you any embarrassment whatever.
>
> So many people have asked me (until I am sick of it) what I am writing for the Royal Wedding that almost in self-defence I have made a setting for *unison* (S.A.T.B.) voices and organ of a very beautiful stanza from Edmund Spenser's 'Epithalamium'. This poem seems to me perfect for such an occasion. It would occupy about four minutes or less in performance. I should think it highly probable that all arrangements as to the music to be performed have already been made, and I shall perfectly understand if this is so.[158]

[158] Bax has misdated this letter 8 November—his birthday—instead of 8 September.

McKie replied on 13 September that he would mention it to the Dean of Westminster Abbey, who was responsible for arranging the wedding service. In a further letter, dated 2 October, McKie apologized for the fact that *Epithalamium* would not be played. Bax replied: 'I am rather disappointed that the Spenser setting cannot be included though I did not expect that it was very likely.' On 14 November, he wrote to McKie: 'Many thanks for sending me a copy of your wedding anthem, which I think very charming. In return I enclose the Spenser piece of which I spoke to you.'

373 [THREE] ROYAL WEDDING FANFARES for brass and percussion

a. Con brio. **b.** Moderato. **c.** [Unknown].

Title: *Copyist's score of* **a** *and* **b**: 'Royal Wedding Fanfares'. For a proposed performance at a Promenade Concert on 27 July 1953, the BBC asked Bax if a new title could be used; on 6 May he replied: 'I am quite agreeable to the title "Fanfares for a Royal Occasion" being used.'
Date: It was on 10 October that Bax opened the letter officially commissioning the fanfares; he wrote them during the following two or three weeks.
Orchestra: Original versions not traced (see **Arrangement** below).
Manuscript: Not traced. Unpublished.
Performance: Original versions not performed (see **Arrangement** below).
Arrangement: By Capt. Meredith Roberts of **a** and **b** for 8 tpts., 4 tbns., s.d., cym. *Copyist's score*: RMSM; [3] ff.; t.p. + [5] pp. ([2], [3]); 12-staff paper (*c.* 366 × 273). Unpublished. *Parts*: RMSM. *Performance of* **a** *and* **b** *only*: Trumpeters of the Royal Military School of Music, Capt. Meredith Roberts; Westminster Abbey; 20 November 1947 ('Marriage of H. R. H. The Princess Elizabeth with Lieutenant Philip Mountbatten, Royal Navy').
Duration: a. 0'55. **b.** 1'32. **c.** Unknown.
Note: Bax's earliest contact with Dr William McKie over the royal wedding appears to be a letter dated 14 August 1947, in which he encloses a suggestion he has received from Eugene Cruft (the double-bass player) about the music to be played:

> I told him [Cruft] at the time in reply that it was then uncertain whether the wedding would be on a grand scale or a simple ceremony at St. George's Chapel, and of course I do not know even now whether a large orchestra is to be employed.
>
> I am also sending you a letter from Mr Hubert Langley received to-day, following one in which he suggested that a wedding anthem specially composed by Handel might be included in the Service. Sir Malcolm Sargent spoke to me about this last night, and intimated that he would gladly give his services as conductor if required.
>
> The reference to E. J. Dent in Mr Langley's letter was occasioned by my telling him that Professor Dent had remarked that the original anthem suggested might be too long. But very likely you have already heard all about this.

The fact that Bax appends his court title to his signature suggests that he and McKie were not acquainted at the time. (Although appointed Organist in 1941, McKie was on war service until 1945 and may have had no occasion to meet Bax.) It was also perhaps intended to be a hint that, as Master of the King's Music, he might have expected to be approached by now about the musical arrangements. McKie replied that the music would be on a smaller scale than the composer's correspondents had thought and that proposals had already been agreed. A further hint from Bax comes in his letter of 8 September about his reasons for writing *Epithalamium* (see **372**). At last, in a letter dated 2 October 1947, McKie officially commissioned Bax to write three fanfares for the wedding:

i) an extended one, lasting about a minute, before the processional hymn at the beginning of the service. (This will be 'Praise, my God, the King of Heaven', to the Goss tune, in the key of D.) If this could be extended to provide for short flourishes between the verses of the hymn, so much the better;
ii) a shorter fanfare (up to ½ minute) after the Blessing, leading into the National Anthem (which should be sung in F, I think, so that all may join in);
iii) something very short indeed to announce the departure of the bride and bridegroom and to be followed immediately (on the organ) by—The Mendelssohn Wedding March!

Bax replied on 11 October:

Thank you for your letter which I received only last night on my return from Ireland.[159] The Precentor [of Westminster Abbey] rang me up directly after my arrival telling me of the proposed fanfares. I told him I would do my best to contribute something suitable, though I find such things rather thankless and usually sound blatant in result. (As a matter of fact they need not necessarily be noisy all the time!) . . . I should like to know as soon as possible what instruments will be available.

McKie replied two days later that twelve instruments—eight trumpets and four trombones—would be available and gave Bax the telephone number of Captain Meredith Roberts, Director of Music at Kneller Hall. On 12 November, McKie again wrote to Bax:

On Monday [10 November] we heard your fanfares in Abbey [*sic*] for the first time, and they sounded magnificent, particularly the first one; I believe you will be pleased with them. We are very grateful. Captain Roberts is bringing up his players for the Final Rehearsal on Wednesday next, 19th, at 5 p.m.; will you let me know if you would care to come, so that I can send you a pass?

I wonder if you would be willing to agree to a slight rearrangement? Last Friday we had an urgent request from Buckingham Palace to time the whole service; the King is anxious about its length, and we have been told to ensure that the whole

[159] It was here, on 27 September, that he had heard the news that his wife had died; they had been separated for nearly thirty years.

service is over inside of fifty minutes. I am afraid that I have been at fault in asking you for too much music in the fanfare to come before the National Anthem (No.2). Would you be agreeable to transferring this fanfare to the end of the service, to announce the departure of the bride and bridegroom, and to replace it before the National Anthem by a drum roll and by the playing over of the first line of the Anthem by the brass in octaves? This would mean that there would then be no place for the third fanfare, which I should be loath to sacrifice anyhow, and so I put forward the proposal with diffidence and apologies. . . . I understand the King is coming to the Final Rehearsal on the 19th, and we are particularly anxious to avoid laying ourselves open to the possibility of being commanded then that the alterations must be made.

I will telephone you at midday to-morrow to ask what you think about this.

P.S. I should have said that we should particularly like No.2 at the end because it is exactly the right length there and seems to us even better than No.3 at that point in ceremonial flavour.

On receipt of the letter the following day, the composer replied by telegram: 'FULLY AGREE WITH YOUR SUGGESTION WILL COME WEDNESDAY = BAX'.

In the event, the first fanfare, which had announced the arrival of the bride, was repeated at the conclusion of the service, just before the national anthem; the second fanfare followed the signing of the register and led straight into the wedding march; the missing third was not played.

In a letter written shortly before the ceremony, Bax commented:

I have been writing three raucous fanfares for the WEDDING at Westminster. I have scored them for ordinary orchestral brass but now they have gone to the Military School of Music at Kneller Hall so that the disintegrating din may be keyed up still further. I hope they will not cause too much damage at the ceremony.

The opening of the first fanfare uses the first part of the theme that begins at fig. (5) of Bax's Swinburne-inspired orchestral work *Spring Fire* (**153**); it also appears in a fragment sent to an autograph-collector (**348**), and in the first of the Red Army Day fanfares of 1943 (**351**). A brief article entitled 'Bax composes a Royal Fanfare' appeared in the issue of *Picture Post* for 22 November 1947, p. 47, and includes two photographs of the composer taken at Kneller Hall during the rehearsal of the fanfares. Bax attended the ceremony, and in a letter to Meta Malins he wrote:

The Royal Wedding was a sumptuous display with a real enchanted faery-tale feeling . . . I was in the Abbey and had quite a good profile view of the whole affair. The two Fanfares I wrote for the occasion was [*sic*] considered a great success—indeed I have become not a little sick of the subject. This morning I received a letter from Koussevitsky [*sic*] asking for the scores of them, although what he could do with them in Boston I don't quite know. (They [i.e. Capt. Roberts' arrangements] are not written for ordinary orchestral brass.)

On her ninetieth birthday in 1994, Mary Gleaves recalled Bax's telling her that, coming out of Westminster Abbey after the ceremony, he waited for a car with Noël Coward and was delighted to find himself surrounded by a bevy of the playwright's young female fans.[160] This is confirmed in Coward's diary entry for 20 November 1947, in which he refers to his having been 'mobbed' by crowds outside the abbey while waiting for a car, though there is no mention of Bax. The composer later referred to the fanfares as 'dreadful',[161] an opinion not shared by three 'celebrities in all walks of life' who cited them as their strongest musical impression of 1947 (see *The Music Teacher*, XXVII, 1 and 2, January and February 1948, p. 13 in each).

1948

374 OLIVER TWIST: Film music for orchestra

Date: MS undated but written between about January and March 1948, within ten weeks, according to Muir Mathieson ('Music in British films', *Film Review*, London, [1948], p. 20). Bax viewed the film twice in its entirety at Pinewood Studios before beginning work.
Orchestra: 3(1) 2+1 2020, 4331, timp., 3 perc. (b.d., s.d., tamb., cym., gong, tri., xyl., gl., cel.), pf., hp., str.
Manuscript: *Sketches*: (*A*) BL (Add. MS 54780);[162] f. 13 (13^v blank); [1] p.; 16-staff paper (torn from a larger leaf). These comprise four lines of two staves each, written in pencil. The sketches are identified by Bax underneath: 'Introducing N's flight [9M1][163] | Oliver on swing [7M3] | Mrs Bedwin's sentimentality [7M6] | Passage to O[liver]'s flight to London [4M1]'. (*B*) BL (Add. MS 54775); f. 26^v (26^r blank; part of a bifolium of which the second leaf is unfoliated); [1] p.; 24-staff paper (365 × 270). Pencil sketches for 10M2 and 11M1 (see **Synopsis** below). *Full score*: BL (Loan 91/3; owned by Oliver Neighbour, formerly by Dermot Bax and then by Barbara Bax, his widow); [55] ff.; 110 pp. (99 holograph, 11 non-autograph) + 12 blank (interspersed throughout); incomplete; for details of paper see **Synopsis** below; loosely inserted between card boards.

Of all Bax's MSS this is by far the most chaotic. As with most film scores, passages written for one scene were adapted for another; cuts were made at the recording session; some sections were repeated; some passages were added by Bax at the last minute. The score includes a few sections entirely in a copyist's hand and contains innumerable additions made by the

[160] Miss Gleaves misremembered the occasion as being the coronation of 1953, which neither Coward nor Bax attended.

[161] See Patric Stevenson, 'Some anecdotes about Arnold Bax', *Bax Society Bulletin*, 5 (May 1969), p. 79.

[162] Acquired together with Add. MS 54776.

[163] These are the music cue numbers, as listed in the **Synopsis** below, which refer to the order in which the music appears (or was intended to appear) in the film; thus '9M1' means the first section of reel 9.

conductor and copyists in blue and red pencil, as well as many alterations and adjustments in Bax's own hand. The pagination is incomplete and practically useless, since individual sections are separately paginated and have been moved from one part of the score to another. Inserted into the MS are a six-page dossier, dated 4 June 1948, on the 'Rights and Obligations' of the film company (Independent Producers Ltd.); four pages of music cue sheets (the first three in duplicate); and the holograph scores, both in pencil, of the two 'street band' arrangements by Fred Lewis: 'Smithfield Street Band' (4M2), pp. 3 + 4 blank; and 'Street Band' (7M5), pp. 4 + 3 blank; both 12-staff paper (303 × 238). Unpublished except for the *Two Lyrical Pieces* (see **375**). *Parts*: CH.

Performance: (1) *Soundtrack recording*: Harriet Cohen (pf.), Philharmonia Orchestra, Muir Mathieson; Denham Recording Theatre; *c.* 10-16 May 1948. (2) *Press show*: Odeon Theatre, Leicester Square; 22 June 1948. (3) *Film première*: Odeon Theatre, Marble Arch; 24 June 1948. The film was banned in the USA until February 1951 because the portrayal of Fagin was considered anti-Semitic. When it was shown at the Kurbel Cinema in Berlin in February 1949, Polish Jews stopped the performance, and there were demonstrations outside the cinema, resulting in baton charges, fire hoses and revolver shots.

Arrangement: (i) Suite arranged by Muir Mathieson in consultation with Bax: CH (MS 374), t.p. + 81 pp.; 24-staff transparency paper (362 × 266). The suite comprises 1. Prelude; 2. The Fight; 3. Two Piano Pieces: (a) Oliver's Sleepless Night, (b) Oliver and Brownlow; 4. The Chase; 5. Fagin's Romp; 6. Finale (with an ending different from that on the soundtrack). Of these sections only Nos. 2 and 3(a) are also found in the MS (the second piece not in Bax's hand). (ii) A second 'suite', compiled by Graham Parlett, was arranged from a photocopy of Bax's MS and is intended to provide additional movements rather than to be performed separately.

Adaptation: The first part of the finale was employed (though uncredited) for the opening titles of the film *The Browning Version* (1951), using the original 1948 soundtrack. The comedy film *The Happiest Days of your Life* (1950) contains a parody of the scene in which Oliver asks for more food, with Mischa Spoliansky serving up a few bars of imitation Bax.

Duration: (1) *Complete film*: *c.* 110'00. (2) *Music used on soundtrack*: *c.* 44'00.

Note: Despite his reservations about the melding of music and speech on film soundtracks, a problem to which Vaughan Williams, with his more flexible attitude to the technical problems involved, had more readily adjusted, Bax was coaxed into accepting a commission from David Lean to write the music for his film version of Dickens's *Oliver Twist*, which had begun production in 1947, with a screenplay by Lean and Stanley Hayes; and again it was Muir Mathieson who suggested Bax's name and who persuaded the composer to accept, although it is obvious from a letter dating from December 1947 that he did so reluctantly:

I have been inveigled (not to say bullied) into writing music for the Oliver Twist film. It is the book of Dickens that I most dislike, and there is no music in the subject at all.[164] So I must think up counterparts in sound of Gillray's and Rowlandson's savage cartoons. The première is supposed to be at the beginning of March (the usual inconsiderate rush) but I was *not* to be stampeded.

And a few months later he wrote:

I am still plagued by the 'Oliver Twist' film for which I struggled in agonies to provide music—a very thankless task as there is no music in the subject. I cannot imagine any subject more unsuited to me.

Similar complaints appear in a letter to May Harrison (January 1948):

I am at present distracted by having to write music for 'Oliver Twist' and lots of it. They could not have found a more unmusical subject and I don't know what will come of it.

In another letter to her dating from June he bemoans the fact that the première clashes with the Test Match at Lords: '. . . though that should not make much difference.' Nevertheless, the music was well received even by critics not normally sympathetic to the composer:

The utilisation and elaboration of the thematic material is, throughout the score, arresting. One hopes indeed that Bax will now continue to contribute to the film, ideally suited as his work is for exciting the cinema-goer's interest in good film music. For he is able to avail himself, to quite an extent, of a good old idiom, and yet to write good music.' (From Hans Keller, 'Bax's "Oliver Twist"', *Music Review*, August 1948, pp. 198-9.)

Bax's contribution to the film was written within ten weeks at The White Horse Hotel in Storrington, and in an article published three years later he is quoted as having in retrospect derived a special interest from the production and found the work challenging:

Composing for the film was hard work, and I found I had to adapt my normal musical approach quite a bit; it was nevertheless an interesting experience, and I was particularly impressed by the ingenuity and skill of the music director in the actual process of recording the music with the picture on the screen.[165]

After the uncongenial subject matter of *Oliver Twist*, Bax expressed his views on the possibility of writing film music again:

[164] The only published reference by Bax to Dickens occurs in Clifford Bax's *Ideas and People*, p. 195, where he expresses the opinion that 'Dickens was the first writer who took the poor in a serious spirit, and that may have been the cause of his tremendous popularity.' According to Mary Gleaves, Bax's favourite Dickens novel was *The Pickwick Papers*.

[165] John Huntley, 'The Music of "Hamlet" and "Oliver Twist"', *The Penguin Film Review*, 8 (London, 1949), p. 110.

I should like now to try my hand at a particular type of film which would really be in tune with the sort of thing I have tried to do in much of my music. A romantic subject, with beauty and poetry, with colour and gaiety, calm and green and pleasing, a subject that would be lyrical and full of the clean, country air.

Oliver Twist was made at Pinewood Studios at Iver Heath in Buckinghamshire by Cineguild Ltd., and the earliest mention of music in the production bulletins comes from January 1948. The use of a solo piano was suggested by David Lean, who felt that it 'emphasizes the isolation of the little boy in a world of bullying adults'. Not all of the music used in the film was written by Bax, the exceptions being six pieces of 'source' music: 'Sunday Night', a tavern song taken from a broadside of the period with music specially composed by Guy Warrack; 'He didn't know when to stop', with words by Ronnie Hill, music by Fred Lewis; 'Tippitiwitchet', a song made famous by Grimaldi; two 'street band' arrangements, one of them J. Munro's 'King George IV's Grand March'; and 'Carnival of Venice' ('old Italian tune') played on a hurdy-gurdy.

Bax's MS was sold by his daughter-in-law for £400 at Sotheby's, London, on 11 May 1977. The score is currently unbound, in poor condition and incomplete, though fortunately most of the missing sections are available in the form of Muir Mathison's concert suite. The only parts of the soundtrack that appear in neither the MS nor the suite are: 1. Oliver's pickpocketing lesson; 2. Pickpocketing (although the string parts are extant); 3. The evacuation of Fagin's hideout; 4. The church sequence following Nancy's death (although the parts are extant); 5. Finale (with its revised ending). On the other hand the MS includes several sequences that do not appear on the final soundtrack, though it is clear from marginalia that at least some of these were actually recorded at Denham during May 1948.

Synopsis:

The first synopsis shows the physical disposition of the MS as it was when inspected in 1991, except that a few sequences that had been inserted carelessly have been notionally restored to their rightful places. Since the MS is unfoliated and the various paginations chaotic, each section—apart from the first three (non-autograph) folios—is referred to by the reel cue number written on the first page of each section (sometimes in Bax's hand, sometimes not), although there are some discrepancies between these numbers and those listed on the music cue sheets, which are detailed in the second synopsis:

f. 1 Title page for Muir Mathieson's suite in blue pencil; 24-staff paper (363 × 266).

f. 1^{v} Blank except for '3M2', '3M2A' and a note that these two cues were recorded on 16 May 1948.

f. 2 Blank except for 'Piano Music | OLIVER TWIST'. 'Uncle Silas' [the title of a 1947 film] crossed through.

f. 2^{v}–3^{v} Copyist's score of 'Oliver's sleepless night'; 24-staff paper (358 × 261).

1M2 *Storm* (Allegro molto; 17 pp. + 1 blank; pp. 1-6, 14-17: 24-staff paper (364 × 269);[166] pp. 7-13 + 1 blank: ALP 29 paper (354 × 260). This section was omitted from the soundtrack, real sound effects being used instead, except at one point where the outline of a thorn bush is silhouetted against the sky. Here three chords for strings in natural harmonics are heard, deriving from the passage beginning at three bars after letter (E).[167] The Storm sequence has two separate openings in the MS, both of which (judging from marginalia) were recorded in May 1948, though not used.[168]

1M3 *The Locket, etc.*[169] (Molto moderato; 4 pp.; 24-staff paper). Both the 'Oliver' and 'Locket' themes make their second appearances in this section, having previously been heard in the Prelude, which is missing from the MS. Several cuts were made for the soundtrack.

1M4 This non-autograph sequence (1 p. + 1 blank; 20-staff paper (367 × 270)), comprises three separate cues (marked A, B and C), each consisting of a variant of the 'Oliver' theme. 1M4[B] (six bars) was used on the soundtrack.

2M1 [No title] (Moderato; 3 pp.; 24-staff paper). Again a few bars from this section were omitted from the soundtrack.

2M2 *Asks for more?* (Allegro moderato e feroce); 2 pp. (starting on the same page as the end of 2M1); 24-staff paper). The final two bars of this ten-bar sequence do not appear on the soundtrack.

2M3 *Oliver and Bumble walk to Sowerby's* [*sic*] (Moderato; 1 p. + 1 blank; 24-staff paper). This 24-bar section does not appear in the film, the journey to Mr Sowerberry's funeral parlour being accompanied instead by the first appearance of Bumble's theme.

2M4 *Oliver sent to bed under stairs* (Moderato; 6 pp.; pp. 1-2: HKS paper (369 × 273), pp. 3-6: 24-staff paper. Bax has inadvertently written the cue number '2M2', which has been corrected in another hand.) A few bars from this sequence were omitted from the soundtrack.

2M5 *Noah scrubbing in shop* (Molto energico; 1 p.; ALP 30 paper (355 × 261). The cue number is given as '2M5 & 3M1'). This purely descriptive passage was not used in the film, the scene being enacted without music.

3M1 *Oliver as funeral mute* (Moderate march time; 3 pp.; ALP 30 paper (355 × 261)). This music was originally intended to be used for 2M3, the walk to Sowerberry's. In the film the first part accompanies Oliver in a funeral cortège, which leads directly into the scene of *Mrs Thingummy seeking admission* [to the funeral parlour]. This sequence was originally intended to lead on directly from Noah scrubbing in the shop, but on the soundtrack it is introduced by two bars for two flutes playing the 'Oliver' theme; these

[166] These measurements apply to all the leaves of 24-staff paper noted below.

[167] 'The branch of a sharp prickly briar against the clouds. The wind shrieks out.' (Description of this close-up shot from Roger Manvell, *The Film and the Public*, Harmondsworth, 1955, p. 203, which also includes John Bryan's original sketches for the opening sequence of the film.)

[168] The original opening derives from section IV of *St George* (see **371**).

[169] The locket, which contains a portrait of Oliver's mother, plays an important part in the story since it is the only clue to his identity. The two principal musical motives devised by Bax are the 'Oliver' theme and the 'Locket' theme.

are written out (non-autograph) on the timp. line of the previous page. On the soundtrack the funeral procession leads straight into the next section, *Mrs Thingummy seeking admission* (2 pp.; 24-staff paper). At the foot of the second page Bax has written the opening three bars of the revised version of the *Storm* sequence, headed 'Oliver's mother sees the workhouse on hill', but the music was not used on the soundtrack.

3M2 *The Fight* (Allegro; 10 pp.; 24-staff paper). Again, only a few bars of this section—the fight between Oliver and Noah Claypole—were omitted from the soundtrack.

3M2A *Beadle music* (Pomposo; 2 pp.; 24-staff paper). On the soundtrack this passage has previously been heard in place of 2M3. As before, the first two bars and the final three are omitted.

3M3 [No title] (Poco lento; 3 pp.; 24-staff paper). This variation on the 'Oliver' theme was originally intended as cue 2M1A, a continuation of the oakum-picking scene. It seems then to have been considered for *Oliver's sleepless night*; and at the foot of the first page Bax has written '2nd part | Oliver at Mr | Brownlow's house'.

4M1 *(second part) Oliver's flight to London* ([No tempo]—Allegro moderato con vivacità; 3 pp.; 24-staff paper). This passage was intended to follow *Oliver's sleepless night* but was omitted from the soundtrack.

4M3 *'Rabbit Warren'* 1 (Allegro moderato; 7 pp. + 1 blank except for a pencilled note (non-autograph) about the images on the screen during the sequence; 24-staff paper). The music accompanies the Artful Dodger and Oliver on their way to Fagin's den. As usual, a number of cuts are made.

6M1 *Oliver faints in court* ([No tempo]; 1 p. (the reverse of a folio, on the obverse of which someone has written in the title, etc.; 24-staff paper)). A note at the top of the page indicates that this ten-bar sequence was recorded on 10 May 1948.

7M1&2 *Confession and death of Mrs Thingummy* (Lento; 3 pp.; 24-staff paper. The third page appears twice, the first copy holograph, the second non-autograph). On the soundtrack this passage is first heard between cues 3M1 and 3M2, though it appears originally to have been intended for the flashback to the earlier scene. The music is heard complete in the film and includes the 'Locket' theme.

7M3 *Oliver on swing, etc.* (Allegretto semplice; 2 pp.; 24-staff paper). A few bars are omitted from the soundtrack.

7M4 *Oliver turns to look at picture* (Lento; 1 p.; 24-staff paper). This passage, which accompanies the scene in which Oliver admires the portrait of his mother, Mr Brownlow's daughter, begins with a reference to the 'Oliver' theme and ends with the 'Locket' theme.

7M5 *Oliver walking to bookseller's shop* (Allegretto; 1 p.; 24-staff paper). In the MS this section leads directly into *Nancy's hysterical remonstrances* (Allegro agitato; 5 pp.) and illustrates the scene in which Nancy accosts Oliver in the street and ostentatiously pretends that he is her long-lost brother. In the film this sequence is played entirely without music.

7M6 *Mrs Bedwin on steps looking for Oliver* (Lento; 2 pp.; both 24-staff paper). Two versions of this cue are found in the MS, the first (7 bars) immediately after 7M5, the second after 7M6A. On the soundtrack the latter (9 bars) is used. Both cues are based on the 'Oliver' theme.

7M6A *2nd Rabbit Warren* (Allegro moderato; 3 pp. + 1 blank; 24-staff paper). This comprises a slightly modified version of the first 17 bars of cue 4M3 and depicts Oliver being taken back to Fagin's hideout. There are no cuts on the soundtrack, three of the bars in fact being repeated in order to make the music synchronize with the action. 7M6 (2nd version) appears at the foot of p. 3.

8M1 *Nancy attacks Fagin* (Allegro molto; 2 pp.; 24-staff paper). A note on the score mentions that this eight-bar sequence was recorded on 13 May 1948. The final bar does not appear on the soundtrack.

8M2 *Mr Brownlow grieving over chess-board* (Andante; 1 p.; 24-staff paper). This 17-bar sequence leads directly into the 'second part', *Oliver playing with a piece of wood* (Allegretto; 2 pp. + 1 blank; 24-staff paper). Only the first part is heard on the soundtrack.

9M1 *Dodger hiding in the cold rain* ([No tempo]; 10 bars). This brief passage leads into *Nancy's Flight in the rain* (Allegro; 5 pp. + 1 blank; 24-staff paper). In the MS this originally leads to a Poco lento section headed *Nancy['s] serious colloquy with Mr Brownlow*, but this was jettisoned and replaced on the soundtrack by a shorter, 15-bar passage that is loosely inserted at the end on an eight-staff scrap of paper.

10M2 *Sykes* [*sic*] *(Blast him!)* (Poco Lento (monotonous); 4 pp. + 2 blank; 24-staff paper). This illustrates Bill Sikes's 'dream montage'.

11M1 [No title] (Moderato; 5 pp. + 1 blank; 24-staff paper). Most of the last fifteen minutes or so of the film are played without any music on the soundtrack, and it is not clear exactly where this cue was originally intended to appear. In the event only the last thirteen bars were actually used, where the music accompanies the posting of bills offering a reward for the capture of Sikes.

The second synopsis derives from the music cue sheets and usefully gives the timings of the sections as they were recorded for the soundtrack:

1M1 Title music (1'11).
1M2 The thorn (0'3).
1M3 Mrs. Thingummy opens the shutters (1'31).
1M4 Oliver scrubbing (0'12).
2M1 Picking oakum (0'38).
2M2 Asks for more (0'24).
2M3 Oliver goes to Sowerberry's (0'24).
2M4 Oliver goes to bed (1'30).
2M5 The funeral (part 1) (0'15).
3M1 The funeral (part 2) (1'34).
3M2 Mrs. Thingummy's story (1'50).
3M3 The fight (0'55).
3M4 'Fetch the Beadle' (0'17).
4M1 Oliver goes to London (1'50).
4M2 King George IV's Grand March (1'12).
4M3 Oliver meets the Dodger (1'12).
4M4 Oliver's first lesson in picking pockets (1'44).
5M1 Oliver goes picking pockets (3'14).
6M1 Oliver faints in court (0'15).
6M2 The evacuation of Fagin's den (0'44).
6M3 Oliver's new home (3'45).

6M4	Carnival of Venice (old Italian tune) (on hurdy-gurdy) (0'55).
7M1	Mrs. Thingummy's death (1'6).
7M2	The locket (0'10).
7M3	Oliver on the swing (0'36).
7M4	The portrait (0'33).
7M5	He didn't know when to stop (1'22).
7M6	Oliver is taken to Fagin (1'30).
8M1	Nancy faints (0'14).
8M2	Brownlow's study (1'24).
8M3	Sunday Night (3'3).
9M1	Tippitiwitchet (2'50).
9M2	He didn't know when to stop (1'8).
9M3	Nancy's run to London Bridge (1'1).
10M1	Dawn (0'55).
10M2	After the murder (1'24).
11M1	Wanted for murder (0'27).
12M1	End titles.

The third synopsis is of the music as it was used in the film and is based on a conflation of Bax's original MS, Muir Mathieson's concert suite, and a recording of the film's soundtrack. The sections are arranged in the order in which they appear on the soundtrack, omitting those which were never used. Italicized titles appear on Bax's MS; those in inverted commas derive from the suite, the original commercial recordings of the music, or the music cue sheets. Where there is no title, the dialogue cue is given on its own. In cases where sections were used on the soundtrack for scenes other than those for which they had been written, the actual music cue number is followed in brackets by the original number.

1M1	'Title music' ('Prelude').[170]
1M2	*Storm* ('The thorn'). Only three notes from this (str. harmonics) appear on the soundtrack.
1M3/2M1A	*The Locket, etc.* ('Mrs. Thingummy opens the shutters'). Cue: 'It's all over, Mrs. Thingummy!'.[171]
1M4B	'Oliver scrubbing'. Cue: 'Let me see the boy'.
2M1	'Picking oakum'. Cue: 'You'll begin to pick oakum tomorrow morning at six o'clock'.
2M2	'Asks for more?' Cue: 'Please, Sir. I want some more'.
3M2A	*Beadle music.* Cue: 'I'll take him'.
2M4	*Oliver sent to bed under stairs.* Cue: 'No, Sir'.
3M1 [2M3]	'The funeral (part 1)'. *Oliver as funeral mute.* Cue: 'It would have a most superb effect'.
3M3 [2M1A, 3M1]	'The funeral (part 2)'. *Mrs Thingummy seeking admission.*
7M1 & 2 [3M2]	'Mrs. Thingummy's story'. *Confession and death of Mrs Thingummy.* Cue: 'It'll come soon enough for us all'.
3M2 [3M3]	*The Fight.* Cue: '. . . and it's a great deal better, Work'us, she died when she did . . .'.
3M2A [3M4]	*Beadle music.* Cue: 'Fetch the Beadle'.
4M1	'Oliver's sleepless night'. Cue: 'My porochial [*sic*] apologies, Sir'.

[170] David Lean's original notes for this sequence are quoted in Huntley, op. cit., p. 114.
[171] David Lean's original notes for this sequence are quoted in Huntley, op.cit., pp. 114-15.

4M2	Smithfield Street Band: King George IV's Grand March (arr. Fred Lewis).
4M3	'Oliver meets the Dodger'. *'Rabbit Warren'* 1. Cue: 'Follow me!'
4M4	'Oliver's pickpocketing lesson'.[172] Cue: 'Certainly, dear, certainly'.
5M1	'Pickpocketing'. 'The Chase'. Cue: 'Stop, thief!'
6M1	*Oliver faints in court.* Cue: 'Don't try and make a fool of me!'
6M2	'The evacuation of Fagin's den.' Cue: ''E'll blow on us, Fagin, for certain!'
6M3	'Oliver's new home' ('Oliver and Brownlow').
6M4	Monks and Bumble in the tavern: Carnival of Venice (on hurdy-gurdy).
7M1 & 2	[Flashback to] *Confession and death of Mrs Thingummy.* Cue: 'She asked that we should be alone'.
7M3	*Oliver on swing, etc.* Cue: 'It is'.
7M4	'The portrait'. *Oliver turns to look at picture* [of his mother]. Cue: '. . . even to myself'.
7M5	Street band: 'He didn't know when to stop' (arr. Fred Lewis).
7M6	*Mrs Bedwin on steps looking for Oliver.*
7M6A [7M6]	'Oliver is taken to Fagin'. *2nd Rabbit Warren.* [Oliver taken back to Fagin.]
8M1	'Nancy faints'. *Nancy attacks Fagin.* Cue: 'Day and night!'
8M2	'Brownlow's study'. Mr Brownlow grieving over chess-board.
8M3 [8M3, 9M1, 9M2]	At the Three Cripples Inn. Three songs performed: 'Sunday , Night', 'He didn't know when to stop' and 'Tippitiwitchet'.
9M1 [9M3]	*Dodger hiding in the cold rain—Nancy's Flight in the rain.*
10M1	'Dawn'.
10M2	'After the murder'. *Sykes* [*sic*] *(Blast him!).*
11M1	'Wanted for murder'. Cue: 'I no longer consider that promise binding'.
12M1	'End titles'.

The finale of the film, which is missing from Bax's MS, includes a broad melody taken from the orchestral work *In Memoriam* (**179**) of 1916. The ending of the finale as found in the copyist's score held by CH as part of Muir Mathieson's suite differs from that heard on the soundtrack, which concludes with triumphal statements of both the 'Oliver' and 'Locket' themes. It seems likely that Bax wrote the serene ending first but was later asked to provide music in a more heroic vein to bring the film to a rousing conclusion. Since Mathieson compiled the suite with Bax's assistance, we may assume that the composer preferred the quieter ending.

[172] David Lean's original notes for this sequence are quoted in Huntley, op. cit., pp. 115-16. See also Roger Manvell and John Huntley, *The Technique of Film Music* (London and New York, 1957), pp. 74–5.

375 TWO LYRICAL PIECES for piano

a. Oliver's sleepless night. **b.** Oliver and Mr. Brownlow.

Date: Some time between the completion of *Oliver Twist* (probably March 1948) and the end of the year (the date of publication).
Manuscript: Not traced.
Publication: CH (38932), 1948, 4to, 6 pp.
Duration: **a.** 2'10. **b.** 2'57.
Note: Arranged by Bax from *Oliver Twist* (**374**).

376 MAGNIFICAT for chorus (SATB) and organ

Date: Undated, but listed as 1948 in *Gr5*.
Dedication: *Printed score only*: 'To Dr Harold Darke'.
Text: St Luke's Gospel, I, 46-55.
Manuscript: ULY (Music Deposit No. 2); [4] ff.; 7 pp. + 1 blank; 24-staff paper (365 × 270); loose in leather, silk and paper portfolio; '. . . presented to the Music Library coupled with the name of Luther Noss [former Dean of the Yale School of Music] by Harriet Cohen on December 1, 1964'. *Negative photostat copy*: BL (MS Facs. 656).
Publication: CH (38928), 1949, 8vo, 8 pp.
Duration: 5'57.
Note: This is an arrangement of the 'Magnificat' for voice and piano dating from 1906 (**86**). Bax made it specifically for Dr Harold Darke, Organist of St Michael's, Cornhill, for fifty years and founder of the St Michael's Singers. 'Nor was it of any value to Darke, who did not like it, thinking it unworthy of its composer.' (LF, p. 348.)

1949

377 CONCERTANTE FOR THREE SOLO INSTRUMENTS AND ORCHESTRA for cor anglais, clarinet, horn and orchestra

I. Elegy (Lento). II. Scherzo (Allegro)—Allegretto semplice. III. Lento. IV. Allegro ma non troppo brillante.

Title: *MS*: Untitled. First performed with the above title. *Printed page of photostat of MS*: 'Concertante for Three ~~Solo~~ [*sic*] Wind Instruments'. On the first page of the score, the title 'Elegy' is followed in brackets by something that has been crossed through and is illegible, perhaps the 'hidden' title referred to in the letter to John Horgan quoted in the **Note** below.
Date: I. 'Nov 23rd 1948'; II. 'Dec 7th 1948'; III. 'Nov 29th 1948'; IV. 'Storrington | New | Year's | Day | 1949'.
Orchestra: I. c.a. solo, 1 tpt., 3 tbns., timp., 1 perc. (s.d., cym.), hp., str. II. cl. solo, 1 tpt., 3 tbns., timp., 2 perc. (b.d., t.d., cym.), str.

III. hn. solo, 1 tpt., 3 tbns., timp., hp., str.
IV. c.a., cl. and hn. soli, 2(1)222, 4230, timp., 3 perc. (b.d., s.d., tamb., gl.), hp., str.
Manuscript: *Sketch*: BL (Add. MS 54775); f. 28^{v}, [1] p.; 24-staff paper (365 × 270); sketch for part of movt. IV written in ballpoint. *Full score*: CH (MS 239): Destroyed by fire on 6 May 1964. *Photo-facsimile of full score*: CH (MS 442); [33] ff.; 66 pp. (1-11, 12-28, 29-38, 39-66; Bax has inadvertently omitted p. 48 from his pagin. and misnumbered pp. 48-66 as 49-67); 24-staff paper (original MS probably 365 × 270, as for that of **378** and **379** below); loose in brown paper wrappers. Movts. I–III appear from the facsimile to have been written with a ballpoint pen, but IV is clearly in ink. The final horn solo in III has an 8$^{vo....}$ inserted in another hand and the comment: 'with the composer's consent'. Unpublished. *Parts*: CH.
Performance: Helen Gaskell (c.a.), Ralph Clarke (cl.), Aubrey Thonger (hn.), BBC Symphony Orchestra, Sir Malcolm Sargent; Royal Albert Hall; 2 March 1949 (Sir Henry Wood Memorial Concert).
Duration: 27'13.
Note: This work was commissioned by the Henry Wood Concert Society, of which Bax was president. In a letter the composer referred to it as '. . . a kind of triple concerto in four movements (a) cor anglais and orchestra (b) clarinet and orchestra (c) horn and orchestra and (d) all three used as soloists together.' In another letter, dated 18 November 1948, Bax confessed that the score was giving him 'a good deal of trouble', although in the event the first three movements were completed within a fortnight of each other.

Writing to John Horgan, the Coroner of Cork, Bax revealed that the first movement 'is really entitled "Lament for Tragic Lovers 1803" [a reference to the tragic love-affair between Robert Emmet and Sarah Curran] . . . There is a two bar quotation played by solo violin at the end taken from "She is far from the land" [quoted between bars 4 and 8 after fig. (M)]'.[173] This letter is in UCC and is quoted in Aloys Fleischmann, 'The Arnold Bax Memorial', *UCC Record*, 31 (Cork, Easter 1956), p. 29, where the reference by Bax to his 'Concertante' is misinterpreted as being to the work for orchestra with piano (left hand) (**378**).

In a letter to Jessie Wood dated 2 February [1950] Bax wrote: 'I don't like the idea of the cor anglais piece [movt. I] being played by itself at a prom. It is disgraceful that a work so suitable for a prom has never been played again. I am sick to death . . . '.

[173] The words of this song are by Thomas Moore, but the tune quoted by Bax is not from the setting in Moore's *Irish Melodies*.

378 CONCERTANTE for piano (left hand) and orchestra

I. Allegro moderato. II. Moderato tranquillo. III. Rondo (Allegro moderato).

Title: *MSS*: Untitled. First performed as 'Concertante for Orchestra with Piano Solo (Left Hand)'. The title 'Concerto for left hand' is written in another hand on the title page of the facsimile of the full score MS.
Date: *Short score*: Undated. *Full score*: 'Storrington | June 3rd 1949'. According to Mary Gleaves, the score was completed at 'Widford', the house (belonging to Bax) in which she lived in Storrington.
Dedication: None on MSS, but written for Harriet Cohen.
Orchestra: 3(1) 2+1 2020, 4331, timp., 2 perc. (b.d., t.d., s.d., tamb., cym., gl.), str.
Manuscript: *Short score*: BL (Add. MS 54759); [10] ff.; 19 pp. (1-7, 8-12, 13-19 + 1 blank); 24-staff paper (365 × 270); p. 1 in ballpoint with ink and pencil additions; p. 2 has the first five systems (three-staff) mainly in ballpoint, the sixth system and the rest of the MS in ink with pencil annotations. *Full score*: Presumed to have been destroyed in Chappell's fire of 6 May 1964. *Photo-facsimile of full score*: CH (MS 431); [34] ff.; 68 pp. (1-28, 29-42, 43-69); 24-staff paper (original MS probably 365 × 270, as for that of **377** and **379**). *Copyist's 2-piano score*: CH; 49 pp.; TP paper (320 × 250).
Publication: *Full score (photocopy of MS)*: WC0511. See also **Arrangement**.
Performance: (1) Harriet Cohen (pf.), Hallé Orchestra, Sir John Barbirolli; Town Hall, Cheltenham; 4 July 1950 (Cheltenham Festival). (2) Harriet Cohen, BBC Symphony Orchestra, Sir Malcolm Sargent; Royal Albert Hall; 25 July 1950 (Promenade Concert). 'Bax must be quite our most static composer (and that's putting it moderately). This last work of his sounds not a note different to the music he was writing as a young man; he is now 76 [actually 66]. The kindest thing that can be said in the piece's favour: it was a gallant gesture made to a temporarily disabled musician.' (Donald Mitchell, *Music Survey*, III, 2, December 1950, p. 117).
Arrangement: Abridged arr. of movt. II for piano solo (both hands) by [William] Lloyd Webber, CH (40602), 1950, 4to, 7 pp. *Earliest performance traced*: John Simons; British Music Information Centre; 14 October 1983 (lecture-recital by Lewis Foreman, *et al.*).
Duration: 25'42.
Note: This work was written for Harriet Cohen after she had fallen 'carrying a tray of glass dishes into the kitchen of her London home in 1948 and cut the wrist of her right hand damaging the nerve and causing it to wither.' (Nicolas Slonimsky, *Music since 1900*, 4th edn., London, 1971, p. 897.) By a curious coincidence this accident followed Bax's refusal to marry Miss Cohen after she had found out that his wife had died the previous year and he had been forced to reveal the existence of Mary Gleaves. Bax appears to have had difficulty with the score. In a letter to the Dutch composer and cellist Henri van Marken he wrote: 'I find it terribly difficult to think of

anything effective for the one hand. But then I am very much out of practice in writing for the piano at all.' The copyist's two-piano score includes several optional and alternative passages for the soloist that derive from the short score but are not found in the full score. In a prefatory note to the copyist's score, it is stated that 'the more important of them . . . usually featured in Miss Cohen's performances', and this is confirmed by the only extant recording of her playing the work; but she also includes several passages that do not appear in the two-piano score.The percussion part that has been added to the opening of the third movement in the MS full score is not in Bax's handwriting; it is omitted in the recording by Margaret Fingerhut. The final two bars in the full score have been altered in another hand, though there is no reason to doubt their authenticity.

379 VARIATIONS ON THE NAME GABRIEL FAURÉ for harp and string orchestra

I. Prelude. II. Barcarolle. III. Polka. IV. Intermezzo (Storm). V. Finale (Quodlibet).

Title: 'Variations on the name | GABRIEL FAURÉ | for | String Orchestra and | Harp' (t.p.). 'Fauré Variations' (p. 1).
Date: 'Aug: 1949' (t.p.). 'Storrington | Sussex | Aug 28th 1949' (end of score).
Dedication: None in Bax's hand. 'To Boyd Neel' written on the t.p. in ballpoint by Harriet Cohen.
Manuscript: *Short score*: The original piano version (see **362** above). *Full score*: Malcolm Hunter (MS formerly owned by Boyd Neel); 46 pp. (t.p. + 1 blank except for Boyd Neel's signature in facsimile + 1-6, 7-14, 15-23, 24-32, 33-46: pagin. in pencil); 24-staff paper (365 × 270); loose in manila folder with Boyd Neel's handwriting in pencil on the front. Neel deposited the MS with the Royal Bank of Canada on 9 January 1980; it seems never to have been on loan to the library of Montreal University (as noted in LF, p. 427). *Photostat copy of full score*: BL (MS Facs. 695). *Copyist's score* (in the hand of Malcolm Hunter): Malcolm Hunter; 46 pp.; 12-staff manuscript music book with red wrappers. Unpublished. *Parts*: BBC; CH; Faculty of Music Library, University of Toronto.
Performance: Boyd Neel Orchestra, Dr Boyd Neel; br. on BBC Third Programme, 31 January 1961. A proposed second performance was due to be recorded by Neel with the BBC Symphony Orchestra in November 1977 but never took place.
Duration: 18'47.
Note: This is a transcription of the *Suite on the Name Gabriel Fauré* (**362**), the titles of the movements being identical in both versions. The only structural alterations occur in movts. I and V: in the orchestral version, there are eight additional introductory bars, in which the harp plays the theme unaccompanied; in V, fourteen bars are cut (bars 87-100 of the piano

score). A letter to Boyd Neel from Bax dated 1 August (no earlier than 1950, no later than 1953) is Sellotaped to the title page:

Many thanks for your letter and for your wish to have a look at the Fauré variations. They are for string orchestra and harp. I doubt whether they are any good, but it is long since I thought about them[.] Anyway I will hunt them out[.]

This seems to imply that the work was not written specifically for Neel but that Bax subsequently gave the MS to him. However, Neel is believed to have received the score only after Bax's death, and since the dedication is in Harriet Cohen's hand it was probably she who presented him with it.

1950

'I have written nothing for two years [actually seventeen months] and have lost the impulse . . .' (Bax writing to Beatrice Harrison on 6 January 1951.)

1951

380 TWO FANFARES FOR 'SHOW BUSINESS 1851-1951' for brass and percussion

a. Moderato. b. Allegro con brio.

Title: '2 Fanfares' ('Show Business' appended twice in different hands).
Date: **a.** 'March 31st 1951'. **b.** Undated.
Orchestra: 3 tpts., 2 ten. tbns., 1 b.tbn., s.d.
Manuscript: *Short score*: BL (Add. MS 54775): **a.** f. 19v; [1] p.; **b.** f. 21; [1] p. (excluding opening two bars); 20-staff paper (f. 19v: 359 × 260; f. 21: 357 × 262). *Full score*: BBC (MS 55422); [2] ff.; [4] pp. (18 and 11 bars respectively); 16-staff paper (350 × 251); stitched into limp grey covers with title on front cover (non-autograph). Unpublished.
Performance: Bax's original unperformed.
Arrangement: By 'Chappelle' (probably Frederick W. Chappelle) for 2 hns., 2 tpts. (in C; but separate parts written in B♭), 3 tbns., s.d.: BBC (MS 55422), **a.** [3] ff.; 5 pp. + 1 blank; 10-staff paper (146 × 278 cut down from larger sheets); **b.** [2] ff.; 3 pp. + 1 blank; BBC paper (307 × 233); in a different hand from **a.** *Script* (by John Watt): BBC (DLO. 88201). Unpublished. *Parts*: BBC. *Performance*: 'Billy Ternant and his Orchestra'; Æolian Hall; between 16 and 20 April 1951 (recording session); br. on BBC Home Service, 18 May 1951 (radio programme 'Show Business 1851-1951: Festival to Festival', produced by Michael North).
Duration: **a.** *c.* 0'45. **b.** *c.* 0'25.
Note: These two brief fanfares were written for a radio programme associated with the Festival of Britain that offered a concise history of light entertainment from the time of the Great Exhibition of 1851 to the present

day. The first fanfare was played immediately after the opening credits, and the second after an intervening four-line piece of dialogue; the first was used again after the announcements in Part 2.

381 JOURNEY INTO HISTORY: Film music for orchestra

Title: The film's original working title was 'Museums', and the original string parts for four of the sections are headed 'Museum Piece'; the rest of the parts and the full score are missing.
Date: In an internal BBC memorandum dated 9 August 1951, Kenneth Wright mentions that this score was written in the space of a fortnight 'last April'. The film was released in 1952.
Orchestra: Details unknown. Using the soundtrack as a guide, perhaps 3(1)2+1 2020, 4330, timp., 1 perc. (b.d., s.d., gl.), str.
Manuscript: *Short score*: BL (Add. MS 54775); ff. 14-19, 20, 21^v, 22; [15] pp.; ff. 14-17: 16-staff paper (356 × 253); f. 18: 24-staff paper (365 × *c.* 272); f. 19: 20-staff paper (359 × 260); f. 20: 20-staff paper (357 × 268); f. 21: 20-staff paper (357 × 262); f. 22: 24-staff paper (365 × 270); f. 14: Prelude [fair copy in ink]; f. 14^v: Allegretto [pencil sketch]; f. 15: Allegretto [fair copy in ink]; f. 15^v: unidentified nine-bar sketch (**382**); f. 16: Gavotte Measure [pencil sketch]; f. 16^v: blank except for three bars from Hogarth [pencil sketch]; f. 17-17^v: Gavotte Measure [fair copy in ink]; f. 18: 'It was an age of building' [fair copy in ink]; f. 18^v-19: Hogarth [fair copy in ink]; f. 19^v: pencil sketch for 'Show Business' Fanfare No. 1 (**380a**); f. 20 'It was an age of discovery' and 'It was an age of building' [pencil sketches]; f. 20^v: Hogarth [pencil sketch]; f. 21: pencil sketches for 'Show Business' Fanfare No. 2 (**380b**) and an unidentified melody on three single-staff lines (**382**) f. 21^v: 'It was an age of discovery' [fair copy in ink]; f. 22: Prelude [pencil sketch]; f. 22^v: an unidentified six-bar sketch on five staves (**382**).

Full score: Not traced. Unpublished. *String parts only* (for sections 2-5 in the **Synopsis** below): BBC.[174]
Performance: *Soundtrack recording*: Philharmonia Orchestra, Muir Mathieson; Riverside Studios, Hammersmith; *c.* May 1951.[175]
Duration: (1) *Complete film*: 10'31. (2) *Complete music*: 10'23.
Note: This documentary was directed by George Burgess and made by British Transport Films (now defunct). It was briefly described in their catalogue as follows:

[174] These parts are identified with letters: A = section 4; B = 3; C = 5; D = 2. This suggests the possibility that the four sections were extracted from the complete score to form a concert suite, but no trace of a performance has yet been found.

[175] The precise date of this session seems not to have been recorded either by the orchestra or the film company (the session notes have '1951' only). John Legard, who worked for British Transport Films, believes it took place in the spring of that year.

10 minutes. Colour. 16 & 35 mm. 1952. In the cities of Britain we can travel in time as well as space. This film chooses the England of Hogarth, Gainsborough, Robert Adam and Captain Cook, and as the camera moves across monuments to their achievements from Syon House to Greenwich, members of the Old Vic Company recite literature of the age. The music was specially composed by the late Sir Arnold Bax.

The music on the soundtrack falls clearly into nine sections, the last three being partial reprises of earlier ones. Comparison with the extant short score reveals a few cuts (noted below), but whether these were made by Bax when he orchestrated the music or by the conductor at the recording session is unknown. John Legard believes that Bax was present, since he recalls the editor of the film, Stewart McAllister, talking about him. (A recording of the session is extant, and after a particular take a high-pitched voice resembling Bax's can just be heard saying 'Yes, it was much better that time.')

In the **Synopsis** below, the titles in italics derive from the short score; those in brackets (possibly taken from the missing full score) from the session notes; and the quotations from the narration. References to systems are to those in the short score:

Synopsis:

1. *Prelude* [Introduction] (56M1): Opening titles and credits. This is recorded complete.
2. *Hogarth* (Allegro giocoso) (56M2): 'It was a rowdy age; Hogarth painted its lustiness'. Bars 7 and 8 of system 7 are omitted.
3. *Allegretto* [Age of Elegance] (56M3): ' . . . Gainsborough painted its elegance'. There is an extra bar at bar 3 of system 3; there is a cut from bar 3 of system 5 to bar 2 (inclusive) of system 7.
4. [Untitled] (56M4): 'It was an age of building'.
5. *Gavotte Measure* [China Figures] (56M5): 'It was an age of taste'.
6. [Sea Music] (56M6): 'It was an age of discovery'.
7. Partial reprise of *Hogarth* (56M2): 'It was an age of gusto'.
8. Extended reprise of *Prelude* [Finale] (56M7): Closing sequence.
9. Reprise of the final four bars of *Prelude*: End titles.

Bax is reported to have said of this score: 'It doesn't matter what one writes for these entertainments.' (CSS, p. 185.)

382 [UNTITLED]: Sketches

Note: These are to be found on ff. 15^v, 21 and 22^v of the short score of *Journey into History* (**381**). Although listed here as a single entry, they are not obviously related to each other, and none of the material appears in any extant score. They may, of course, be ideas intended for the film but never used.

383 HAPPY BIRTHDAY TO YOU: Song by Mildred J. Hill arranged for unaccompanied chorus (SATB)

Title: None on MS. The collection of which this is part has a title page in Samuel Barber's handwriting and is called 'Happy Birthday to Mary'; the third phrase of Bax's text is 'Happy Birthday Mrs Zimbalist'.
Date: Bax has written 'August 6th 1951' below his signature and above the dedication, but this is the date of the dedicatee's birthday. The piece was commissioned in the spring of 1951.
Dedication: 'To Mrs Zimbalist.'
Text: Patty Smith Hill, 'Happy Birthday to You' (first published with these words in *Union School Chorus Music*, 1935).[176]
Manuscript: *Holograph*: Not traced. *Negative photostat*: LC (ML 96.4.Z5); [1] f.; [1] p. + 1 blank; 9 bars; 8-staff paper (220 × 273). Unpublished.
Note: In the spring of 1951 Samuel Barber invited twenty-three composers to harmonize variations on 'Happy Birthday to You' in 'any shape, style, or variant which might amuse'[177] as a tribute to Mary Zimbalist (née Curtis Bok), the founder of the Curtis Institute of Music in Philadelphia, who was celebrating her seventy-fifth birthday on 6 August. As well as contributions from Bax and Barber himself, the album contains tributes from Bloch, Chávez, Copland, Dohnányi, Harris, Hindemith, Honegger, Martinů, Menotti, Milhaud, Piston, Pizzetti, Poulenc, Scalero,[178] Schuman, Sibelius, Stravinsky, Thomson, Vaughan Williams, Villa-Lobos, Walton, and the dedicatee's husband, Efrem Zimbalist.

c. 1951

384 [UNTITLED]: Sketch

Date: Undated but no earlier than September 1951 (see **Note** below).
Manuscript: UCC: Six bars on three single-staff lines written in pencil on the front free endpaper (184 × 122) of a humorous book formerly owned by Bax: George Mikes [Mikeš], *Down with Everybody!* (London: Allan Wingate, 1951). Unpublished.
Note: The book was published in September 1951, which provides a *terminus post quem* for these jottings: five bars of a melodic line in D followed by three chords. Although there is no tempo indication, the music could only be sprightly and sounds like the opening of an overture in the

[176] The song was originally published as 'Good morning to all' in *Song Stories for Kindergarten* (Chicago: Clayton F. Summy, 1893). In 1934 it appeared as a march called 'Happy Birthday'.

[177] Quoted in Barbara B. Heyman, *Samuel Barber: The Composer and His Music* (Oxford, 1992), p. 315.

[178] Rosario Scalero, Barber's composition teacher.

same vein as *Work in Progress* (**354**). It is probably far too fanciful to suggest a connection with Kenneth Wright's BBC memorandum of 9 August 1951 regarding the possibility of Bax's writing a signature tune for television (see Appendix 6).

1952

385 CORONATION MARCH for orchestra

Date: 'Nov 29th | 1952'. Begun after 7 August and before 8 November 1952 (see **Note** below).
Orchestra: 3(1)222, 4331, timp., 3 perc. (b.d., s.d., cym., gl., bells 'if possible'), str.
Manuscript: *Sketches*: BL (Add. MS 54775); f. 23-3v; [2] pp.; CH 26 paper (414 × 251); in pencil. *Full score*: CH (MS 238); [16] ff.; t.p. + 1 blank + 29 pp. (p. 1 unnumbered) + 1 blank; 24-staff paper (365 × 271); loose in fawn card folder. *Copyist's score*: CH; [15] ff.; 30 pp.; ARCO paper. Unpublished. *Parts*: CH.
Performance: (1) London Symphony Orchestra, Sir Malcolm Sargent; Kingsway Hall, London; 29 April 1953 (recording session for Decca). (2) Special Coronation Orchestra, Sir Adrian Boult; Westminster Abbey; 2 June 1953 (Coronation of Queen Elizabeth II). (3) RAM Orchestra, Clarence Raybould; RAM; 10 June 1953.
Arrangement: For organ by Garrett O'Brien. Unpublished but recorded.
Duration: 6'34.
Note: This was Bax's last orchestral work. The trio, like that of the *Victory March* of 1945 (**364**), was taken from the finale of the music for the film *Malta, G. C.* (**347**); the rest of the material was newly composed. The work was the last commissioned piece to be played at the ceremony. In a letter to Freda Swain dated 28 September 1952, Bax wrote that 'the Archbishop of Canterbury has, as it were, issued an edict that all the Coronation music is to be controlled by Dr. McKie, the organist of Westminster Abbey. I am supposed to be consulted, but I shall merely be in the position of a yesman.' On 6 August, McKie had written to Bax officially informing him of the arrangement and commenting that he had heard from Buckingham Palace that 'you had some thought of writing a Coronation March', adding that he had already been hoping that such a work might be produced. In his reply of 7 August, Bax wrote: 'It was very nice of you to think of asking me to write a march. Whether I shall be able to produce anything worth playing I don't know, for I have done nothing except a short it[em] of film music for three y[ears. I] can but try!'[179] Not surprisingly, Bax had little enthusiasm

[179] This has had a piece torn off it, and the letters enclosed here in brackets are missing.

for the commission, as he remarked in a letter to May Harrison dated 8 November, his sixty-ninth birthday: 'I am now engaged upon trying to write a Coronation March (funny [?] without being vulgar!) for the Abbey Service. I think the result will be that my reputation will be killed for all time. However I am old now and it does not matter.'

McKie visited Bax at Pulborough, near Storrington, on 25 October to discuss the coronation, and on 4 December Bax wrote that the programme of music 'seems to me excellently well-balanced'. He attended a committee meeting early in January 1953 to discuss the specially selected orchestra, and on 2 February he complained that he had 'been pestered by reporters, representing all sorts of papers . . .'. A meeting with McKie, Boult and Eugene Cruft (the Coronation Orchestral Committee) took place on 17 February at the Athenaeum Club, but Bax was unable to attend a further meeting on 3 March because of train problems at Pulborough; fog and an attack of gout prevented his attending another meeting in April. He received a letter and a telephone call from Sir Malcolm Sargent expressing horror that there was no Elgar on the programme (apart from *Nimrod*); and on 9 April he wrote to McKie expressing his own surprise that Sargent was due to record the march so soon (more than four weeks before the coronation). In the event, he was pleased with Sargent's performance, preferring it to Boult's, as he remarked in a letter to May Harrison dated 26 May: 'On Sunday I went to the Abbey [f]or the Coronation music rehearsal and heard Adrian play my new march much too fast!'

Bax did not attend the ceremony itself. Harriet Cohen told Clifford Gillam that he listened to it on the radio at her flat and was disappointed that his march was not included in the part that was broadcast. An article by Bax entitled 'Music at the Coronation' was published in *The National & English Review*, CXL (January–June 1953), pp. 345-7.

1953

386 WHAT IS IT LIKE TO BE YOUNG AND FAIR?: Part-song for unaccompanied chorus (SSAAT)

Title: 'Part-Song "What is it like to be young and fair?"'.
Date: 'Feb 1953'. Finished by 11 February (see **Note** below).
Dedication: The collection of which this is part is 'DEDICATED | BY GRACIOUS PERMISSION | TO | HER MAJESTY QUEEN ELIZABETH II'.
Text: Clifford Bax, 'What is it like to be young and fair?' (not otherwise published). *Holograph MS of poem*: BL (Add. MS 54775), f. 29; [1] p.; leaf of lined paper torn from a notebook (198 × *c.* 160).
Manuscript: *Sketches*: BL (Add. MS 54775); ff. 30 and 31 (30^v and 31^v blank; followed by 14 blank folios of MS paper); [2] pp; 24-staff paper (365 × 270).

Holograph score: Not traced. *Photostat copy of holograph score*: Graham Parlett (made from a copy formerly held by the Arts Council of Great Britain); [2] ff.; 3 pp. + 1 blank; 24-staff paper (*c.* 370 × 278); also in NYPL.
Publication: In *A Garland for the Queen*, SB (5347) (copyright by CH), 1953, 8vo, pp. 19-26. Published with part-songs by Berkeley, Bliss, Finzi, Howells, Ireland, Rawsthorne, Rubbra, Tippett and Vaughan Williams. The BL has a registration copy in fo. format printed from the original plates (H.3423.a.(21.)).
Performance: Cambridge University Madrigal Society, The Golden Age Singers, Boris Ord; Royal Festival Hall; 1 June 1953 ('Music for the Eve of Coronation Day' concert).
Duration: 2'15.
Note: The origins of Bax's swansong can be traced in the following excerpts from letters exchanged between John Denison (JD), Music Director of the Arts Council; a 'Mr. Williams' (W); and Arnold and Clifford Bax (AB and CB):

AB to JD (4 November 1952): 'I am fully in accord with the new Oriana Madrigal project and if it materializes I shall hope to contribute'.
JD to AB (4 December 1952): 'I now enclose a formal letter offering you a commission in connection with the Coronation scheme . . . The fee which the Council would be prepared to offer is fifty pounds . . .'.
AB to JD (6 December 1952): 'I accept the commission to write a madrigal . . . My brother Clifford Bax . . . will be the poet'.
W to CB (11 December 1952): 'I write on behalf of my Council to offer you a commission to write a text for setting to music by Sir Arnold Bax. . . . The fee which my Council would be prepared to offer is £25. . . . You will realize, of course, that the composer with whom you are collaborating will be unable to begin work until your contribution is ready. . . . The fee will paid as soon as Sir Arnold Bax has accepted the text.'
CB to W (15 December 1952): 'I sent off my lyric a few days ago, and am glad to say that my brother . . . likes it. Indeed, I hope he is busy finding a tune for it!' [The holograph poem in the BL has a note from CB to AB: 'Is this any better? Say what you like', implying that the first version was considered unsatisfactory.]
JD to AB (10 February 1953): 'I wonder if you could let me know when we can expect to receive your score of the Coronation piece . . . I hate to press you unduly but we have to make material available for the choirs to start rehearsing at a very early date'.
AB to JD (11th February 1953): 'My contribution to the madrigal collection is finished and you shall have it in a day or two'.
AB to JD (21 February 1953): 'Here is my part-song (for that is all it is!) . . .'.

An article by Clifford Bax on the collection ('Songs for the Queen') appeared in *Apollo*, LVII, 339 (May 1953), p. 171.

Bax appears to have composed nothing after early February 1953. He had declined to write incidental music for an Old Vic production of Shakespeare's *King Henry VIII* and was involved in preparations for the coronation on 2 June. He turned down an invitation from the BBC to broadcast a talk on his personal beliefs, and in a letter to Christopher Whelen dated 3 September he indicated that he was 'not writing anything at present'. A month later, on 3 October, he died in Cork. His last creative work was a speech in honour of Sir John Barbirolli completed shortly before his death.

ADDENDA

Sketches

Details of sketches containing material that found its way into completed works or that are written down on the MSS of other scores have been incorporated into the appropriate chronological sequence in the main part of the Catalogue. There are, however, a number of unidentified jottings and sketches that exist independently of extant scores and presumably represent ideas that never came to fruition. Handwriting and paper types can suggest an approximate date, and the presence of identifiable matter on some of the MSS can provide a clue. None of the MSS has foliation or pagination, and the medium is pencil unless otherwise noted.

1. Sketches bought anonymously at Sotheby's on 26 May 1994. Formerly owned by Harriet Cohen, then by Colin Scott-Sutherland.

Add. 1. [3] ff.; [5] pp. + 1 blank; two lines in ink; 2 pp. of ALM 18 (361 × 272), 1 of AL 16 paper (366 × 276). Contains material used in *The Truth about the Russian Dancers* (**220**) of 1920. AL 16 paper is otherwise attested only in the song 'Welcome Somer' (**158b**), which dates from 1914. The indication 'whooping and laughter' at one point suggests a dramatic work (see **170**). The final page is crossed through and contains no recognizable material.

Add. 2. [1] f.; [1] p. + 1 blank; 14-staff paper (358 × 276). Five bars only on the bottom two staves. In a childish hand but not remotely like the spidery writing of Bax's juvenilia. The music—whether by Bax or not—seems more sophisticated than the handwriting.

Add. 3. [2] ff. (a bifolium of which the second leaf has had the top five staves cut out); [1] p. + 3 blank; 26-staff paper (348 × 276). No identifiable material.

Add. 4. [2] ff.; [4] pp.; a few lines in ink; 1 p. of AL 12 (363 × 272), 1 p. of AL 18a paper (361 × 272). One fragment used in *The Truth about the Russian Dancers* (**220**), and thus probably no later than 1920; the rest of the material unidentifiable.

Add. 5. [1] f.; [1] p. + 1 blank; AL 18 paper (361 × 272). No identifiable material.
Add. 6. [1] f.; [2] pp.; AL 14c paper (361 × 271). Sketch for the song 'Eternity' (**273**), and thus no later than 1925; the rest of the material unidentifiable.
Add. 7. [2] ff.; [4] pp.; AL 14c paper (361 × 271). One fragment used in the *First Northern Ballad* (**309**), and thus no later than 1927; the rest of the material unidentifiable.
Add. 8. [2] ff.; [4] pp.; a few lines in ink; AL 14 paper (361 × 271). Mostly sketches for the *Second Northern Ballad* (**324**), and thus no later than 1933, plus some unidentifiable material.
Add. 9. [1] f.; [1] p. + 1 blank; AL 14c paper (361 × 271). Three systems, the first containing four bars in 5/4, the second five bars in 4/4, the third a six-chord continuation of the second. No identifiable material.
Add. 10. [2] ff. (a bifolium); [1] p. + 3 blank; ink; ALM 12 paper (363 × 272). Four lines of unidentifiable material, the first three on two staves, the fourth on one: mostly single melodic lines with a few chords, plus a squiggle where Bax was evidently testing his pen.
Add. 11. [2] ff. (a bifolium); [1] p. + 3 blank; ALM 8 paper (346 × 272; not otherwise attested among Bax's MSS). Seven two-staff bars of unidentifiable music and a single melodic line of nine bars. Other ALM types of paper date from 1905-19; the handwriting suggests a later rather than an earlier date.
Add. 12. [1] f.; [1] p. + 1 blank; AL 12 paper (363 × 272). A single two-staff fragment of four bars.
Add. 13. [1] f. (the top cut away); [1] p. + 1 blank; AL 12 paper (363 × 272). A single two-bar melodic fragment on the second line down.

2. Sketches owned by Clifford Gillam. Formerly owned by Harriet Cohen.

Add. 14. [1] f.; [2] pp.; AL 12 paper (363 × 272). Eight two-staff systems of unidentifiable material written in ink.
Add. 15. [2] ff.; [3] pp. + 1 blank; 16-staff paper (339 × 269). F. 1 contains unidentifiable sketches in pencil and ink; ff. 1^{v} and 2 are in pencil only; 'alla passacaglia' is written above the staff at the start of f. 2.
Add. 16. [1] f.; [2] pp.; AL 12 paper (363 × 272). Unidentifiable sketches in ink.
Add. 17. [2] ff.; [4] pp.; ALM 18 paper (361 × 272). F. 1 contains pencil sketches for *The Happy Forest* (**157**) of 1914. F. 2 is blank, and f. 2^{v} contains unidentified pencil sketches in pencil, written upside down on the paper.
Add. 18. [1] f.; [2] pp.; AL 14 paper (361 × 271). The recto has unidentifiable sketches in ink and pencil, the verso is in pencil only.
Add. 19. [2] ff.; [4] pp.; AL 12 paper (361 × 272). Four pages of unidentifiable sketches in ink (f. 2^{v} written upside down on the paper). F. 1 has

six two-staff systems, f. 1^v has four, f. 2 has two, and f. 2^v has four three-staff systems.
Add. 20. Fragment of manuscript paper (max. 54 × 271) cut from a larger sheet. Four staves: staff 1 has a melodic line; 2 and 3 consist of a single system; 4 is blank.

Unidentified

An unspecified work by Bax was used for a ballet entitled *Eve of Silence*, with choreography, costumes and scenery by Ron Sequoio. *Performance*: Members of the Greater Houston Civic Ballet: Pamela Royal, Sandy Whitaker, Steven Maynard; McFarlin Auditorium, Dallas, Texas; 31 March 1973 (part of the Southwest Regional Ballet Festival Gala). A video recording of this performance is in the New York Public Library, but the music is unidentified in the cataloguing data. *Duration*: 10'30.

Appendix 1

CLASSIFIED INDEX OF MUSIC

Titles are arranged chronologically within the following categories:

I. CONCERT WORKS FOR ORCHESTRA

II. DRAMATIC AND OCCASIONAL WORKS

- (a) Projected operas
- (b) Ballets
- (c) Plays
- (d) Films
- (e) Fanfares

III. WORKS FOR SOLO INSTRUMENTS WITH ORCHESTRA

IV. WORKS FOR INSTRUMENTAL GROUPS

- (a) Six–nine instruments
- (b) Quintets
- (c) Quartets
- (d) Trios
- (e) Violin with piano
- (f) Viola with piano (or harp)
- (g) Cello with piano
- (h) Flute with piano (or harp)
- (i) Clarinet with piano
- (j) Two pianos

V. WORKS FOR SOLO INSTRUMENTS

(a) Cello (b) Harp (c) Piano

VI. CHORAL WORKS

- (a) Soloists and chorus with orchestra
- (b) Chorus with orchestra
- (c) Chorus with organ
- (d) Chorus with other accompaniment
- (e) Unaccompanied chorus
- (f) Part-song and hymn

VII. WORKS FOR SOLO VOICE

- (a) Songs with orchestra
- (b) Songs with string quartet
- (c) Songs with piano
- (d) Traditional song and carol arrangements with piano
- (e) Recitations with piano

VIII. ARRANGEMENTS BY BAX OF OTHER COMPOSERS' WORKS

IX. ARRANGEMENTS OF BAX'S WORKS BY OTHERS

X. SKETCHES AND FRAGMENTS

1. The year given is the one in which the work was completed.
2. Only main titles are listed; for variants and subtitles see the individual Catalogue entries (numbers in **bold**).
3. An obelus (†) indicates an unfinished or unorchestrated work; a superscript nought (°) indicates a score known or believed to have been written but now missing.

I. CONCERT WORKS FOR ORCHESTRA

1898 †Symphonische Dichtung nach 'Rubaiyat' von Omar Khayyam **21**
1901 †Ballet Suite **50**
1902 †Love-Song **54**
1904 Variations **61**
1905 °A Connemara Revel **68**
Cathaleen-ni-Hoolihan **72** [orch. of movt. II from String Quartet in E]
°A Song of Life and Love **78**
A Song of War and Victory **79**
1907 †Symphony in F major and minor **95**
†Carnival **98** [sketches only; perhaps intended as incidental music]
1908 Into the Twilight **110**
1909 In the Faery Hills **114** [revised 1921]
1910 Rosc-catha **128**
1911 Festival Overture **134** [revised 1918; see also section IX (10)]
c. 1911 †Symphonietta **144**
1912 Christmas Eve on the Mountains **145** [revised *c.* 1921]
Prelude to Adonais **147**
1913 Four Orchestral Pieces **152** [1-3 revised 1928; see also section IX (15)]
Spring Fire **153**
1915 Nympholept **164** [see also **333**]
1916 The Garden of Fand **175**
In Memoriam **179** [see also section IX (16)]
1917 Scherzo **187** [revised 1933]
November Woods **191**
1918 Festival Overture **209** [revision]
1919 Tintagel **213**
Russian Suite **215** [see also section IX (24)]
1921 Summer Music **243** [revised 1932]
In the Faery Hills **245** [revision]
c. 1921 Christmas Eve **249** [revision]
1922 Symphony No. 1 **256**
Mediterranean **257**
The Happy Forest **260**
1925 Cortège **274**
1926 Symphony No. 2 **276**
Romantic Overture **277**
1927 Overture, Elegy and Rondo **288**
1928 Three Pieces for Small Orchestra **295** [revision]
1929 Symphony No. 3 **297**
1930 Overture to a Picaresque Comedy **305**
1931 Symphony No. 4 **307** [see also section IX (30)]

Northern Ballad No. 1 **309**
The Tale the Pine-Trees knew **310**
1932 Symphony No. 5 **313**
Summer Music **314** [revision]
Sinfonietta **315**
1933 Prelude for a Solemn Occasion **320**
Symphonic Scherzo **322** [revision]
1934 Northern Ballad No. 2 **324**
1935 Symphony No. 6 **331**
1936 Rogue's Comedy **335**
Overture to Adventure **339**
1937 London Pageant **340**
1938 Pæan **343**
1939 Symphony No. 7 **344**
1943 Work in Progress **354**
1944 A Legend **357**
1945 Victory March **364** [see also *Call to the Red Army* (**358**)]
1949 Variations on the name Gabriel Fauré **379** [arr. for hp. and str. of *Suite on the Name Gabriel Fauré* for pf.]
1952 Coronation March **385** [see also section IX (7)]

II. DRAMATIC AND OCCASIONAL WORKS

(a) Projected operas

1907 †Deirdre **106** [see also *Into the Twilight* (**110**), *Rosc-catha* (**128**), and *On the Sea-shore* (section IX (27))]
c. 1915 †Red Owen **170**

(b) Ballets

1911 †Tamara **138**
1917 From Dusk till Dawn **188**
1918 °The Frog-Skin **202**

(c) Plays

1920 The Truth about the Russian Dancers **220**
1945 Golden Eagle **366**

Note: For *St George* see section VI (a).

(d) Films

1942 Malta, G.C. **347** [see also section IX (17-19)]
1948 Oliver Twist **374** [for suites see section IX (26)]
1951 °Journey into History **381** [sh.sc., str. parts and recording extant]

(e) Fanfares

1921 Hosting at Dawn **244** [see also section IX (13)]
1930 Fanfare for a Cheerful Occasion **304**
1943 °Two Fanfares [for 'Red Army Celebration'] **351**
Salute to Sydney **353**

1947 Three Royal Wedding Fanfares [only two extant] **373** [see also section IX (28)]
1951 Two Fanfares [for 'Show Business'] **380** [see also section IX (8)]

III. WORKS FOR SOLO INSTRUMENTS WITH ORCHESTRA

1918 Symphonic Variations [piano] **210**
1920 Phantasy [viola] **235**
1930 Winter Legends [piano] **303**
1932 Cello Concerto **316** [see also section IX (6)]
Saga Fragment [piano] **317**
1938 Violin Concerto **342**
1939 †Concertino [piano] **346**
1946 Morning Song [piano] **369**
1949 Concertante [cor anglais, clarinet, horn] **377**
Concertante [piano (left hand)] **378** [see also section IX (4)]

Note: For Concerto for oboe and string orchestra (arr. of Oboe Quintet) see section IX (7).

IV. WORKS FOR INSTRUMENTAL GROUPS

(a) Six–nine instruments

1898 Menuet [fl., ob., cl., bn., str. qt.] **15**
1917 In Memoriam (1916) [c.a., hp., str. qt.] **190**
1930 Nonet [fl., ob., cl., hp., str. qt., d.b.] **302**
1934 Octet [hn., pf., str. sext.] **329**
1936 Threnody and Scherzo [bn., hp., str. sext.] **336**
Concerto [fl., ob., hp., str. qt.; arr. of Sonata for flute and harp] **337**

(b) Quintets

1908 String Quintet in G **107** [2 vns., 1 va., 2 vcs.; movt. II revised 1922 as *Lyrical Interlude* for 2 vns., 2 vas., 1 vc.]
1915 Piano Quintet **167**
1919 Harp Quintet **214**
1922 Lyrical Interlude **261** [revision]
Oboe Quintet **258** [see also section IX (7)]
1933 String Quintet **319**

(c) Quartets

1902 String Quartet in A **55**
1903 String Quartet in E **57** [movt. II orch. as *Cathaleen-ni-Hoolihan* and probably also arr. 2 vns. and pf.]
1918 String Quartet No. 1 **199**
1922 Piano Quartet in one movement **255** [arr. 1932 as *Saga Fragment* for piano and small orchestra]
1925 String Quartet No. 2 **271**
1936 String Quartet No. 3 **338**

(d) Trios

1901 †Trio in B♭ minor [violin, cello, piano] **47**
1904 °Cathaleen-ni-Hoolihan [two violins, piano] **64** [probably arr. of movt. II from String Quartet in E]
1906 Trio in one movement [violin, viola or clarinet, piano] **87**
1916 Elegiac Trio [flute, viola, harp] **178**
1946 Trio in B♭ [violin, cello, piano] **367**

(e) Violin with piano

1901 Sonata in G minor **49**
1904 Concert Piece **60** [arr. of *Concert Piece* for viola and piano]
1910 Sonata No. 1 **124** [revised 1915, 1920, 1945]
1915 Legend **165**
Sonata No. 1 **166** [first revision]
Sonata No. 2 **166** [revised 1921]
1916 Ballad **181** [revised *c.* 1929]
1920 Sonata No. 1 **236** [second revision]
1921 Sonata No. 2 **248** [revision]
1927 Sonata No. 3 **289**
1928 Sonata in F **292** [arranged 1930 as Nonet]
c. 1929 Ballad **300** [revision]
1945 Sonata No. 1 **361** [third revision]

(f) Viola with piano (or harp)

1904 Concert Piece **59**
1922 Sonata **251**
1927 Fantasy Sonata [with harp] **284** [see also section IX (10)]
1929 Legend **299**
1934 °[Sonata No. 2] **328** [only one folio extant]

(g) Cello with piano

1918 Folk-Tale **198**
1923 Sonata **265**
1933 Sonatina **321**
1943 Legend-Sonata **352**

(h) Flute with piano (or harp)

1912 Four Pieces **149** [arr. from the ballet *Tamara*]
1928 Sonata [with harp] **291** [arr. 1936 as Concerto for septet]

(i) Clarinet with piano

1901 Intermezzo **46**
1934 Sonata **327**

(j) Two pianos

1900 Fantasia **40**
1917 Moy Mell **180** [see also section IX (23)]
1927 Hardanger **287**

1928 The Devil that tempted St Anthony **293** [originally for solo piano]
The Poisoned Fountain **296**
1929 Sonata **298**
1931 Red Autumn **311** [originally for solo piano]

Note: For *Festival Overture* [arr. for two pianos] see section IX (11).

V. WORKS FOR SOLO INSTRUMENTS

(a) Cello

1939 Rhapsodic Ballad **345**

(b) Harp

1931 Valse **308**

Note: For 'Rizzio preludes on the lute' [solo harp] see *Golden Eagle* (**366**).

(c) Piano

1896 °Sonata **2**
1897 °Sonatas [three at least] **3-5**
†Variations on an Air in G minor **7**
†Variations in G minor **8**
1898 Minuet in E minor **9** [also arr. for fl., ob., cl., bn., str. qt.]
Two Hungarian Dances **10**
Three Mazurkas **11**
Two Scherzi **12**
Prelude in G major **13**
Nocturne in D major **14**
†Sonata in D minor ['No. 5'] **16**
†Sonata, Op. 1 **17**
1900 Marcia Trionfale **26**
[Funeral] March **41**
Sonata in D minor **42**
1910 °Sonata No. 1 **127** [revised 1917-21]
Concert Valse **125**
1911 °Sonata in D minor **137**
1912 Two Russian Tone-Pictures **146** [No. 1 orch. 1919 as part of *Russian Suite*; see also section IX (13, 25)]
Nympholept **148** [orchestrated 1915]
°Mask **150**
°Red Autumn **151** [arranged 1931 for two pianos]
1913 °Sonata in F **154** [only Scherzo extant; orchestrated 1917]
Toccata **155**
1914 In the Night **159**
The Happy Forest **157** [orchestrated 1921]
1915 The Princess's Rose Garden **161**
In a Vodka Shop **162** [orchestrated 1919 as part of *Russian Suite*]
The Maiden with the Daffodil **163**
Apple-Blossom-Time **168**

	Sleepy-Head **169**
	A Mountain Mood **172**
	Winter Waters **173**
1916	Dream in Exile **176**
	Nereid **177**
1918	On a May Evening **205**
	A Romance **206**
1919	Whirligig **216**
	Sonata No. 2 **217** [revised 1920]
	The Slave Girl **218**
	What the Minstrel told us **219**
1920	Ceremonial Dance **221** [arr. from *The Truth about the Russian Dancers*]
	Serpent Dance **222** [arr. from *The Truth about the Russian Dancers*]
	Water Music **223** [arr. from *The Truth about the Russian Dancers*]
	Lullaby **224**
	Sonata No. 2 **225** [revision]
	Burlesque **229**
	Country-Tune **230**
	°The Devil that tempted St Anthony **231** [arr. 1929 for two pianos]
	A Hill Tune **232**
	Mediterranean **233** [orchestrated 1922; see also section IX (21, 22)]
1921	Sonata No. 1 **240** [revision]
	Sonata in E♭ **242** [movts. I and III orch. 1922 for Symphony No. 1]
1926	Sonata No. 3 **279**
c. 1928	Pæan **294** [orchestrated 1938; see also section IX (29)]
1932	Sonata No. 4 **318**
1935	Legend **334**
1937	Sonata in B♭ **341**
1945	Suite on the Name Gabriel Fauré **362** [arr. 1949 for hp. and str. orch.]
	O Dame get up and bake your pies **365**
1947	[Four Pieces] **370**
1948	Two Lyrical Pieces **375** [arranged from *Oliver Twist*]

Note: For 'Dance' [harpsichord] see *Golden Eagle* (**366**); for Scherzo [arr. pianola] see **212**.

VI. CHORAL WORKS

(a) Soloists and chorus with orchestra

1907	°Fatherland [tenor solo] **92** [vocal score published; revised 1934]
1910	Enchanted Summer [two soprano solos] **129**
1924	To the Name above every Name [soprano solo] **264**
1926	Walsinghame [tenor solo] **278**
1934	Fatherland **325** [revision]
1944	To Russia [baritone solo] **356**
1947	†St George [bass solo] **371**

(b) Chorus with orchestra

1901 †Tegnér's Drapa **52**
c. 1901 °The Pied Piper of Hamelin **53** [precise medium unknown]
1923 St Patrick's Breastplate **267**
1935 The Morning Watch **332**
1942 Five Fantasies on Polish Christmas Carols [unis. Tr. with str. orch.] **350**

(c) Chorus with organ

1945 Te Deum [SATB] **359**
Nunc Dimittis [SATB] **360**
Gloria [SATB] **363**
1947 Epithalamium [SATB in unison] **372**
1948 Magnificat [SATB] **376** [originally for solo voice with piano]

(d) Chorus with other accompaniment

1920 Of a rose I sing a song [SATB, harp, cello, double bass] **234**
1921 Now is the Time of Christymas [TB, flute, piano] **247**

(e) Unaccompanied chorus

1921 Mater, ora Filium [SSAATTBB] **246**
1922 This Worldes Joie [SATB] **254**
1923 The Boar's Head [TTBB] **263**
1942 Five Greek Folksongs [SATB] **349**
1953 What is it like to be young and fair? [SSAAT] **386**

Note: For 'Happy Birthday to you' [arr. SATB] see section VIII (1951).

(f) Part-song and hymn

1923 I sing of a maiden that is makeless [SAATB] **266**
1930 Lord, Thou hast told us [SATB] **306**

VII. WORKS FOR SOLO VOICE

(a) Songs with orchestra

1905 °Two Songs **80** [piano version of *Viking-Battle-Song* (77) extant]
1911 †Three Nocturnes [soprano] **136** [see also *Aufblick*, section IX (2)]
1914 Three Songs [soprano] **156**
The Bard of the Dimbovitza [1-5: high voice; 6: bass] **160** [rev. 1946]
1934 A Lyke Wake [high voice] **326a**
Wild Almond [high voice] **326b**
°The Splendour falls [high voice] **326c**
Eternity [high voice] **330**
1946 The Bard of the Dimbovitza [mezzo-soprano] **368** [partial revision]

Note: For 'Rizzio's Song of Ronsard' [sop., alto, bar., hp., str.] see *Golden Eagle* (**366**).

(b) Songs with string quartet

c. 1921 My eyes for beauty pine **250a** [also with piano]
O Mistress mine **250b** [also with piano]

(c) Songs with piano

1896 °Butterflies all white **1**
1900 Wanting is—what? **23**
To Daffodils **24**
A Serenade of Spring-time **25**
I love thee! **27**
Cytherea's Day **28**
To the Moon **29**
[Archy's Song] **30**
To the Cuckoo **31**
[If I but knew] **32**
An Indian Serenade **33**
To Phyllis **34**
Phillida and Corydon **35**
[Why we love and why we hate] **36**
[Say, Myra!] **37**
Music when soft voices die **38**
The Soldier's Dream **39**
†[To the Virgins] **43**
1901 †Songs of the Four Seasons **48**
[I will dream] **51**
1903 The Grand Match **56**
1904 To my Homeland **62**
A Celtic Song-Cycle **63** [revised 1922]
1905 When we are lost **65**
From the Uplands to the Sea [with one or two pianos] **66, 67**
Leaves, Shadows and Dreams **69**
In the Silences of the Woods **70**
Green Branches **71**
The Fairies **73**
Golden Guendolen **74**
The Song in the Twilight **75**
°Rune of Age **76** [also with orchestra]
Viking-Battle-Song **77** [also with orchestra]
1906 A Hushing Song **81**
I fear thy kisses, gentle maiden **82**
Magnificat **86** [arranged 1948 for chorus with organ]
c. 1906 °Echo **88**
°For Love's Sake **89**
°Garden Song **90**
°Summer Night **91**
1907 The Fiddler of Dooney/The Enchanted Fiddle **93/94**
Longing **96**
The Flute **97**
Du Blomst i Dug **99**
From the Hills of Dream **100**
A Milking Sian **101**
Heart o'Beauty **103**

The White Peace **102** [see also section IX (34)]

°The Kingdom **104**

1908 A Lyke-Wake Dirge **105** [orchestrated 1934]

Landskab **108**

Shieling Song **109**

Isla **111**

°The Wood-Lake **112**

1909 Marguerite **113**

The Garden by the Sea **115**

A Christmas Carol **116** [orchestrated 1914; see also section IX (3)]

Aspiration **117** [for arr. with piano trio see section IX (1)]

°Beloved, even in Dreams **118**

°The Dance-Ring **119**

°Enlightenment **120**

°Home **121**

°Ideala **122**

°Love-Ode **123** [orchestrated version of 1911 extant]

1910 A Lullaby **126** [orchestrated 1914]

To Eire **132**

Frühlingsregen **130**

Treue Liebe **131** [possibly a folksong arrangement]

1911 Das tote Kind **133**

°The Bridal Prayer **139**

°Faith **140**

°Flight **141**

°Freimund **142**

°The Journey **143**

1914 Three Rondels **158**

1916 I know myself no more, my child **182**

A Leader **183**

O Mistress mine **184** [also with string quartet]

Parting **185**

1917 The Splendour falls **186** [orchestrated 1934]

°Go, lovely Rose **189**

1918 Far in a Western Brookland **201**

Green grow the Rashes O! **203**

°Midsummer **204**

When I was one-and-twenty **207**

Youth **208**

1920 A Rabelaisian Catechism **228**

c. 1920 My eyes for beauty pine **237** [also with string quartet]

1921 Five Irish Songs **238** [see also section IX (15)]

Glamour **239** [see also section IX (12)]

1922 Three Irish Songs **252**

The Market Girl **262**

Dermott Donn MacMorna **253**

A Celtic Song-Cycle **259** [revision]

1924 I heard a soldier **268**

Wild Almond **269** [orchestrated 1934]

1925 Carrey Clavel **272**
Eternity **273** [orchestrated 1934]
c. 1925? °Blow, northern wind **275**
1926 In the Morning **281**
On the Bridge **282**
Out and Away **283**
1927 Three Songs from the Norse **285**
c. 1931 Watching the Needleboats **312**
c. 1943 Dream Child **355**

Note: The existence of songs entitled 'Finland', 'Morfydd', 'A Patriot' and 'To an Isle in the Water' is dubious (see **92** and **268**).

(d) Traditional song and carol arrangements with piano

1918 I have house and land in Kent **192**
The Maid and the Miller **194**
O dear! what can the matter be? **195** [see also section IX (25, 26)]
Trois enfantines **196**
Variations sur 'Cadet-Rousselle' **197** [in collaboration with Bridge, Goossens and Ireland; see also section IX (32, 33)]
1920 Le Chant d'Isabeau **226**
Traditional Songs of France **227**
1926 °[Three Carols] **280** [No. 3 with piano, flute and tambourine]

Note: For the arrangement of 'Mo rùn geal, dìleas' [bar. and hp.] see *Golden Eagle* (**366**).

(e) Recitations with piano

1906 The Blessed Damozel **84** [possibly also with orchestra: see **83**]
The Twa Corbies **85**

VIII. ARRANGEMENTS BY BAX OF OTHER COMPOSERS' WORKS

1918 Thomas Campion, 'Jack and Jone': song with piano **193**
°Anatol Liadov, *Dance Prelude* and *Lament of the Swan-Princess*: orchestrations of *Prelude*, Op. 11 No. 1, and *Sur la prairie*, Op. 23 **200**
1921 °Frédéric Chopin, *Ballade in A♭*, Op. 47: transposed into A major and orchestrated **241**
1927 Antonio Vivaldi, Concerto for viola d'amore, lute and strings, RV 540: arranged for harp and string quartet **286**
J. S. Bach, *Fantasia in G* for organ, BWV 572: transcribed for piano **290**
1951 Mildred J. Hill, 'Happy Birthday to you': arranged for unaccompanied chorus (SATB) **383**

IX. ARRANGEMENTS OF BAX'S WORKS BY OTHERS

1. Aspiration: arr. for voice and piano trio; possibly by Bax himself, but MS not in his hand **117**.
2. Aufblick: arr. for voice and piano by Stephen Banfield **136a**.
3. A Christmas Carol: arr. for boys' voices and organ **116**.

4. Concertante for piano (left hand) and orchestra: slow movement abridged and arr. for piano solo (both hands) by William Lloyd Webber **378**.
5. Concertino for piano and orchestra: movt. III ed. and orch. by Graham Parlett (in preparation) **346**.
6 Concerto for cello and orchestra: arr. for viola and orchestra by Norman Carrell **315**.
7. Concerto for oboe and string orchestra: arr. by Sir John Barbirolli of the Oboe Quintet **258**.
8. Coronation March: arr. for organ by Garrett O'Brien **385**.
9. Fanfares for Show Business: arr. for 2 hns., 2 tpts., 3 tbns., s.d. by 'Chappelle' (probably Frederick W. Chappelle) **380**.
10. Fantasy Sonata: arr. for viola and piano by Charles Matthews **284**.
11. Festival Overture: arr. for two pianos; possibly by Bax himself, but MS not in his hand **134**.
12. Glamour: arr. for voice and orchestra by Rodney Newton **239**.
13. Gopak: arr. for violin and piano by Louis Godowsky **146b**.
14. Hosting at Dawn: orchestrated by (i) Arthur Cohn, (ii) Graham Parlett **244**.
15. I heard a piper piping: arr. for flute and guitar by John Harper **238c**.
16. In the Hills of Home: arr. for piano by Peter Warlock **152c**.
17. In Memoriam [Pádraig Pearse]: ed. and orch. by Graham Parlett (for Bax's own orchestration see section I) **179**.
18. Malta, G.C.: Funeral March arr. for organ by W. H. Harris **347**.
19. Malta, G.C.: March arr. for military band by W. J. Duthoit **347**.
20. Malta, G.C.: March arr. for piano by William Lloyd Webber **347**.
21. Mediterranean: arr. for violin and piano by Jascha Heifetz **232**.
22. Mediterranean: arr. for two pianos, three hands by H. Rich **232**.
23. Moy Mell: arr. for two pianos, three hands by Lionel Salter **180**.
24. Nocturne (May-Night in the Ukraine): orchestrated by Graham Parlett as movt. II of the Russian Suite **146a**.
25. 'O dear! what can the matter be?: arr. for piano trio by Gilbert Stacey **195**.
26. 'O dear! what can the matter be?: arr. for voice and wind band by Leonard B. Smith **195**.
27. Oliver Twist: concert suite arr. by Muir Mathieson; second suite arr. by Graham Parlett **374**.
28. On the Sea-shore ('Cuid 5' from Deirdre): ed. and orch. by Graham Parlett **106**.
29. Pæan: arr. for organ by William Barr **294**.
30. Royal Wedding Fanfares: arr. for 4 tpts., 3 tbns., s.d., cym. by Capt. Meredith Roberts **373**.
31. Symphony No. 4: arr. for two pianos by Walter Emery and William Cole **307**.
32. Variations sur 'Cadet-Rousselle': orchestrated 1930 (without voice) by Eugene Goossens (Op. 40) **198**.
33. Variations sur 'Cadet-Rousselle': arr. for solo male voice, men's chorus and orchestra by Max Saunders **198**.
34. The White Peace: arr. for solo piano by Ronald Stevenson **102**.

X. SKETCHES AND FRAGMENTS

Note: Further sketches, numbered **Add. 1-20**, are listed at the end of the main chronological sequence (pp. 275-7).

Appendix 2
CONCORDANCE OF MANUSCRIPTS

Repositories are listed alphabetically by country. The name of each institution is followed by the short titles of the works it houses preceded by their inventory numbers (if any) and followed by the Catalogue reference numbers. Manuscripts belonging to private individuals are noted anonymously at the end. Scores are in Bax's handwriting unless designated 'non-autograph'.

AUSTRALIA

Melbourne: Grainger Museum

MG C2/BAX-9-2 Symphony No. 6 [f.sc. of movts. II and III] **331**

DENMARK

Århus: Statsbiblioteket

Three Songs from the Norse [non-autograph] **285**

Copenhagen: Kongelige Bibliotek

C I, 370 Landskab [two copies, one incomplete] **108**
C I, 370 Three Songs from the Norse [non-autograph] **285**

FINLAND

Åbo (Turku): Sibeliusmuseum

Symphony No. 5 [pf.sc.] **313**

Helsinki: Sibelius-Akatemia

To the Name above every Name [f.sc.] **264**

FRANCE

Paris: Bibliothèque nationale de France

MS 9884 (1–5) Suite on the Name Gabriel Fauré **362**

GREAT BRITAIN

Aldeburgh: Britten-Pears Library

O Mistress mine! [pf. and str. qt. versions] **184 250b**
My eyes for beauty pine [str. qt. version] **250a**
[Golden Eagle] Two songs **366**

Bury St Edmunds: Chester Music Ltd.

The Fiddler of Dooney [mostly non-autograph] **93**
A Milking Sian [mostly non-autograph] **101**
The White Peace [mostly non-autograph] **102**
Shieling Song [mostly non-autograph] **109**
A Christmas Carol [mostly non-autograph] **116**
To Eire [mostly non-autograph] **132**
Dream in Exile **176**
Elegiac Trio [non-autograph parts with autograph title on cover] **178**
Moy Mell [non-autograph] **180**
I have house and land in Kent **192**
Jack and Jone **193**
The Maid and the Miller **194**
O dear! what can the matter be? **195**
Trois Enfantines **196**

Note: The last five MSS listed above are currently missing (see **192**). See also BL Loan 75/1–9 below.

Durham: University Library

Add. MS 814 (formerly BL Loan 53/26) Viola Sonata **251**

London: BBC Music Library

O dear! What can the matter be? [arr. pf. trio by Gilbert Stacey; now untraced] **196**
MS 2994 Salute to Sydney **353**
MS 55422 Two Fanfares for 'Show Business' [holograph and non-autograph arr.] **380**

London: British Library

Add. MSS.

Note: Add. MSS 54724–54780 were originally part of the Harriet Cohen Loan Collection. The original loan numbers are added in parentheses.

50173 Festival Overture [incomplete sh.sc.] **134**
50174 Festival Overture [f.sc. of 1st version] **134**
50175 Four Orchestral Pieces **152**
50176 The Happy Forest [pf. version] **157**
50177 The Happy Forest [f.sc.] **260**
50178 A Romance **206**
50179 To the Name above every Name [v.sc.] **264**
50180 Cello Sonata **265**
50181 Carrey Clavel **272**
53735 Moy Mell **180**
54395 Legend [vn. and pf.] **165**
54724 Symphony No. 1 [sh.sc.] (56/1) **242 256**
54725 Symphony No. 1 [f.sc.] (53/1) **256**
54726 Symphony No. 2 [sh.sc.] (56/2) **276**
54727 Symphony No. 2 [f.sc.] (53/2) **276**
54728 Symphony No. 3 [sh.sc.] (56/3) **297**
54729 Symphony No. 3 [f.sc.] (53/3) **297**

54730 Symphony No. 5 [f.sc.] (53/4) **313**
54731 Symphony No. 6 [sh.sc.] (53/5) **331**
54732 Ballet Suite; Tegnér's Drapa; Love-Song **50 52 54**
54733 In the Faery Hills [f.sc. of 1st version] **114**
54734 Rosc-catha [f.sc.] **128**
54735 Christmas Eve [f.sc. of 2nd version] (53/9) **249**
54736 Christmas Eve on the Mountains [f.sc. of 1st version] (53/10) **145**
54737 Nympholept [pf. version] **148**
54738 Spring Fire [sh.sc.] **153**
54739 Spring Fire [f.sc.] **153**
54740 Symphonic Variations [sh.sc. and f.sc. of Variation I] (56/4) **210**
54741 Symphonic Variations [non-autograph f.sc.] **210**
54742 Symphonic Scherzo (53/11) **322**
54743 November Woods [sh.sc.] (56/13) **191**
54744 The Truth about the Russian Dancers (56/14) **220**
54745 Phantasy for viola and orchestra [f.sc.] (56/9) **235**
54746 Summer Music [sh.sc.] **243**
54747 Saga Fragment [photostat of non-autograph f.sc.] **317**
54748 Romantic Overture [sh.sc.] (53/12) **277**
54749 Romantic Overture [f.sc.] (53/13) **277**
54750 Northern Ballad No. 1 [sh.sc.]; Prelude for a Solemn Occasion [sh.sc.] (56/15) **309 320**
54751 Winter Legends [sh.sc.] (56/5) **303**
54752 Winter Legends [f.sc.] (temp 4589) **303**
54753 The Tale the Pine-Trees knew [sh.sc.] (56/17) **310**
54754 The Tale the Pine-Trees knew [f.sc] (53/14) **310**
54755 Cello Concerto [f.sc.] (53/6) **316**
54756 Prelude for a Solemn Occasion [f.sc.] (53/15) **320**
54757 Violin Concerto [f.sc.] (53/7) **342**
54758 Concertino [sh.sc. of movts. I and II] (56/7) **346**
54759 Concertante for piano (left hand) [sh.sc.] (56/8) **378**
54760 Nonet (53/16) **302**
54761 Piano Quintet (53/17) **167**
54762 Piano Quartet (53/19) **255**
54763 String Quartet No. 2; String Quartet No. 3 (53/20, 21) **271 338**
54764 Piano Trio in B♭ (53/22) **367**
54765 Violin Sonata No. 1 [1st version; movts. I and II holograph, III non-autograph] (56/19) **124**
54766 Violin Sonata No. 2; Sonata in F (53/25) **248 289 292**
54767 Scherzo [pf. version]; Piano Sonata No. 2; Piano Sonata No. 3; Sonata in B♭ (56/22, 24, 53) **154 217 279 341**
54768 Clavierstücke **9-16**
54769 Marcia trionfale; In the Night; Berceuse; In a Vodka Shop; The Maiden with the Daffodil; A Mountain Mood; Ideala (Nereid); What the Minstrel told us (56/21, 23) **26 159 161 163 172 177 162 218**
54770 Suite on the Name Gabriel Fauré [non-autograph]; [Four Pieces] for pf. (56/27) **362 370**
54771 Enchanted Summer [f.sc.] (53/8) **129**
54772 Three Nocturnes; Slumber Song [f.sc.] **136 156c**

54773 The Bard of the Dimbovitza [f.sc. of 1st version] (56/10, 31, 38) **160**
54774 Walsinghame [v.sc.] (53/34); Eternity [f.sc.] (56/11) **278 331**
54775 St George; sketches for Journey into History, Two Fanfares for 'Show Business', Coronation March, Work in Progress, Oliver Twist, Concertante for three instruments and orchestra **371 381 380 385 354 374 377**
54776 Miscellaneous songs [1900–05] **23-25 27-39 48 51 69**
54777 Miscellaneous songs [1905–8] (56/33) **69-71 77 81 96 100-3 109 111**
54778 Miscellaneous songs [1905–10] (56/32) **65-6 82 93 97 99 105 108 113 115-16 126**
54779 Miscellaneous Songs [1911–27] (56/34) **133 160d, f 186 228 237 239 268 273 285**
54780 Concertino [sh.sc. of movt. III] (56/6) **346**
57523 Symphony No. 7 [f.sc.] **344**

Loans

Note: Nos. 75/1–9 are on loan from JWC; 91/3 is on loan from Oliver Neighbour.

75/1 A Celtic Lullaby [orch. version] **156a**
75/2 Roundel **158c**
75/3 A Mountain Mood **172**
75/4 Winter Waters **173**
75/5 Elegiac Trio **178**
75/6 Nereid **177**
75/7 Folk-Tale **198**
75/8 Whirligig **216**
75/9 Fatherland [f.sc. of 2nd version] **325**
91/3 Oliver Twist **374**

Photostat copies

MS Facs. 639 Octet [sh.sc and f.sc.] **329**
MS Facs. 656 Magnificat [SATB version] **376**
MS Facs. 695 Fauré Variations [f.sc.] **379**

London: Royal Academy of Music

MS 18 Tintagel [f.sc.] **213**
MS 19 Tintagel [sh.sc.] **213**
MS 317 Fantasia; [Funeral] March **40-1**
MS 319 Sonata in D minor **42**
MS 529 Symphony No. 4 [sh.sc.] **307**
MS 533 From Dusk till Dawn [sh.sc. and f.sc.] **188**

London: University of London Library

MS 435 A Lyke-Wake [incomplete sh.sc. and f.sc.] **105 326a**

London: Warner Chappell Music Ltd. (MSS stored in Kenley, Surrey)

MS 234 Symphonic Variations [f.sc.] **210**
MS 235 Festival Overture [2nd version] **209**
MS 236 Five Fantasies on Polish Christmas Carols [f.sc.] **350**
MS 237 Cortège **274**

MS 238 Coronation March **385**
MS 239 Concertante for three solo instruments and orchestra [destroyed by fire on 6 May 1964; photostat copy survives] **377**
MS 240 Concerto for fl., ob., hp. and str. qt. **337**
MS 241 The Bard of the Dimbovitza [f.sc. of 2nd version] **368**
MS 242 St Patrick's Breastplate [f.sc.] **267**
MS 243 Rogue's Comedy **335**
MS 244 Nympholept [orch. version] **164**
MS 245 Symphony No. 6 [f.sc. of movt. I] **331**
MS 246 Threnody and Scherzo **336**
MS 247 Three Pieces for small orchestra **295**
MS 249 To Russia [v.sc. and f.sc.] **356**
MS 251 Work in Progress **354**
MS 253 Northern Ballad No. 2 **324**
MS 254 Northern Ballad No. 1 **309**
MS 255 Pæan [orch. version] **343**
MS 256 The Morning Watch [f.sc.] **332**
MS 257 London Pageant **340**
MS 258 A Legend **357**
MS 259 Golden Eagle **366**
MS 260 Victory March **364**
MS 306 The Truth about the Russian Dancers [non-autograph; destroyed by fire on 6 May 1964; photostat copy survives] **220**
MS 374 Oliver Twist [non-autograph suites] **374**
MS 415 Symphony No. 3 [printer's pulls] **297**
MS 431 Concertante for piano (left hand) and orchestra [photostat copy of f.sc.; original probably destroyed by fire on 6 May 1964] **378**
MS 780 Symphony No. 2 [printer's pulls] **276**
MS 807 The Garden of Fand [printer's pulls] **175**

Russian Suite [movt. II non-autograph] **215**
Octet [non-autograph] **329**
Concerto for fl., ob., hp. and str. qt. [non-autograph] **337**
To the Name above every Name [non-autograph] **264**

London: Westminster Music Library

035718 The Maiden with the Daffodil **163**
035719 In a Vodka Shop [non-autograph] **162**
Moy Mell [non-autograph] **180**
Concert Valse [non-autograph] **125**

Oxford: Bodleian Library

MS. Don.c.48 Symphony No. 4 **307**
MS. Mus.c.370 Legend-Sonata **352**

Twickenham: Royal Military School of Music

Hosting at Dawn [non-autograph] **244**
Fanfare for a Cheerful Occasion [non-autograph] **304**
Two Royal Wedding Fanfares [non-autograph] **373**

IRELAND

Cork: University College (Boole Library)

Note: The MSS in this repository are listed below in the order in which they appear in Dr Jeremy Dibble's typescript 'Inventory of Bax Collection', compiled June 1988.

A

1 Concert Piece [for va. and pf.; non-autograph] **59**
2 Cathaleen-ni-Hoolihan **72**
3 Concert Piece [holograph part for vn. arr.] **60**
4 Green Branches **71**
5 Symphony in F [sh.sc.] **95**
6 Into the Twilight [f.sc.] **110**
7 Into the Twilight [sh.sc.] **110**
8 Aspiration [non-autograph version with pf. trio] **117**
9 Frühlingsregen **130**
10 Christmas Eve on the Mountains [sh.sc.; incomplete] **145**
11 Tamara [sh.sc.] **138**
12 The Garden of Fand [sh.sc.] **175**
13 In the Faery Hills [f.sc. of 2nd version] **245**
14 [lacking]
15 Miscellaneous juvenilia **6-8 17-22**
16 Deirdre [fragments] **106**
17 Oboe Quintet (formerly BL Loan 53/18) **258**
18 This Worldes Joie (formerly BL Loan 53/31) **254**
19 Fantasy Sonata **284**
20 Clarinet Sonata (formerly BL Loan 53/29) **327**
21 Rhapsodic Ballad **345**
22 Symphony No. 7 [discarded part of movt. I] **344**
23 Symphony No. 7 [sketches for part of movt. III] **344**
26 String Quartet No. 3 [corrected proofs] **338**
F (vii)
23 [Untitled sketch] **384**

Dublin: Trinity College

MS 4940/1 O Dame get up and bake your Pies [non-autograph] **365**

Dublin: University of Dublin Library

Note: These MSS were formerly numbered 19/1 to 19/6.

MS 26/1 In Memoriam [sh.sc.] **179**
MS 26/2 St Patrick's Breastplate [v.sc.] **267**
MS 26/3 A Leader **183**
MS 26/4 This Worldes Joie [corrected proofs] **254**
MS 26/5 Phantasy [non-autograph f.sc.] **235**
MS 26/6 Four Orchestral Pieces [non-autograph] **152**

ISRAEL

Jerusalem: Jewish National and University Library

4 MUS.2(2) Fantasia [after Bach] **290**

MALTA

Valletta: National Library of Malta

Malta, G.C. **347**

UNITED STATES OF AMERICA

New Haven: Yale University Library

Magnificat [SATB version] **376**

New York: BMI Archives

Violin Sonata No. 1 [signed quotation] **236**
[Fanfare] [fragment; signed quotation] **348**

New York: Public Library

Sonatina [vc. and pf.] **321**

Philadelphia: Edwin Fleisher Collection

Hosting at Dawn [non-autograph arr.] **244**

Southern California: University Library

fML 96 B35 Wild Almond [f.sc.] **326b**

Stanford: University (Memorial Library)

Symphony No. 3 [corrected proofs] **297**

Washington: Library of Congress

ML 29c.B34 Legend [va. and pf.] **299**
ML 29c.B34 Octet [sh.sc. and f.sc.] **329**
ML 96.4.Z5 Happy Birthday to you [negative photostat of Bax's arr. for SATB] **383**
ML 96.B36 Saga Fragment **317**
ML 96.B36 Symphony No. 7 [sh.sc.] **344**

PRIVATELY OWNED

Note: Where the owner has granted permission, his or her name will be found in the Catalogue entry.

Ballad [vn. and pf.] **181**
[Ballad] [sketch] **301**
The Blessed Damozel **84**
Carnival **98**
Cathaleen-ni-Hoolihan [orch.] **72**
Concerto [after Vivaldi] **286**
Corbies, The Twa **85**
Dermott Donn MacMorna **253**
In Memoriam [orch.] **179**
Intermezzo [cl. and pf.] **46**
Legend [pf.] **334**
Miscellaneous sketches **Add. 1-20**

Appendix 3
RECORDINGS

'The Gramophone is on the whole a ghastly invention . . .'
Arnold Bax writing to May Harrison in 1929

There are four sections:

I. COMMERCIAL RECORDINGS
II. RECORDINGS OF BAX PLAYING THE PIANO
III. RECORDINGS OF BAX SPEAKING
IV. BROADCAST PROGRAMMES ABOUT BAX

The first section lists all recordings known to have been intended for purchase (including one or two of dubious legality) together with a few samplers and free discs given away with magazines. Titles are arranged alphabetically with the medium specified only to avoid ambiguity. Recordings under each title are in chronological order of issue, and details comprise the names of the performers, the record company or label, the type of carrier (tape cassette, compact disc, etc.) and the record numbers. In addition to abbreviations found in the main body of the Catalogue, the following are used:

CD	compact disc
EP	extended-play microgroove record (7-inch; 45 rpm)
LP	long-play microgroove record (12-inch; 33⅓ rpm)
LP-10	long-play microgroove record (10-inch; 33⅓ rpm)
PP	player-piano (pianola)
PR	piano roll
SR	shellac record (twelve-inch; 78 rpm + a single 80 rpm recording)
SR-10	shellac record (ten-inch; 78 rpm)
ST	soundtrack (as part of a film for hire or purchase on video)
TC	tape cassette
TP	tape (seven-inch reel to reel)

Note: Recordings are stereophonic unless designated (m) for monaural or, in two instances, (m/st) for 'mono recording electronically reprocessed to give stereo effect' (early 1970s Decca Eclipse label only).

Every effort has been made to ensure that the information given is as comprehensive and accurate as possible, and with few exceptions record numbers have been taken down directly from actual copies of recordings rather than from catalogues or previous discographies (stops in prefixes having been omitted in accordance with current usage: e.g. NGS for N. G. S.). Nevertheless, it should be remembered that this appendix is the one most likely to be out of date before it appears in print: new recordings are coming on to the market all the time and old ones are being reissued with different numbers. No attempt has been made to indicate current availability, and the cut-off date for inclusion is 1 August 1998, though several forthcoming discs have also been listed.

The total number of performances commercially issued or due to be recorded at the time of writing is 469, ranging from piano rolls to compact discs. The most recorded work is the Clarinet Sonata, of which there are eleven versions. There have been ten recordings each of the *Elegiac Trio* and *Tintagel*, nine of the *Fantasy Sonata* and the Oboe Quintet, and seven of *Mater, ora Filium*, the Second Piano Sonata and the Viola Sonata. For further information about new recordings, see the Sir Arnold Bax Web Site compiled by Richard R. Adams and Rob Barnett: "http:// phobos.kiss. de: 81/ ~ adams/compact. html".

I. COMMERCIAL RECORDINGS

Apple-Blossom-Time: (1) Iris Loveridge. Lyrita LP: RCS 30 (m)—not issued. (2) Malcolm Binns. Pearl LP: SHE 565. (3) Eric Parkin. Chandos TC: ABTD 1372; CD: CHAN 8732.
Ballad: Henry Holst (vn.), Frank Merrick (pf.). Frank Merrick Society LP: FMS 18 (m).
Bard of the Dimbovitza, The: Jean Rigby (mezz.), BBC Philharmonic Orchestra, Vernon Handley. Chandos CD: forthcoming.
Berceuse: Megan Thomas (sop.), Geraldine Mason (pf.). Cabaletta LP: HRM 2001 (m).
Boar's Head, The: Baccholian Singers of London. HMV LP: CSD 3783; CD: EMI 7243 5 65125 2 8.
Burlesque: (1) Harriet Cohen. Duo-Art PR: 0357 (m). (2) Iris Loveridge. Lyrita LP: RCS 26 (m); Musical Heritage Society LP: MHS 7014 (m). (3) Richard Deering. Saga LP: Saga 5445. (4) Eric Parkin. Chandos TC: ABTD 1372; CD: CHAN 8732.
Celtic Song Cycle, A: Ellen Frohnmayer (sop. in Nos. 1-4), Philip Frohnmayer (bar. in No. 5), Logan Skelton (pf.). Centaur CD: CRC 2075.
Ceremonial Dance: (1) Iris Loveridge. Lyrita LP: RCS 10 (m). (2) Eric Parkin. Chandos CD: CHAN 9561.
Christmas Carol, A: (1) Jane Wilson (sop.), George Trovillo (pf.). US Decca LP: DL 9554 (m). (2) Dorothy Dorow (sop.), Susan Bradshaw (pf.). Jupiter EP: JEP OC33 (m). (3) Patricia Wright (sop.), Rosemary Barnes (pf.). Continuum CD: CCD 1046.
Christmas Carol, A [arr. chorus and organ]: Canterbury Cathedral Choir, Allan Wicks, Stephen Darlington (org.). Grosvenor LP: GRS 1034.
Christmas Eve: London Philharmonic Orchestra, Bryden Thomson. Chandos LP: ABRD 1192; TC: ABTD 1192; CD: CHAN 8480, CHAN 9168.
Concert Valse in E♭: Iris Loveridge. Lyrita LP: RCS 30 (m)—not issued.
Concertante for piano (left hand) and orchestra: (1) Harriet Cohen (pf.), Radio Symphonique de Paris, Tony Aubin. Connoisseur Cassettes TC: CPL3 (m). (2) Margaret Fingerhut (pf.), BBC Philharmonic Orchestra, Vernon Handley. Chandos CD: forthcoming.
Concerto for cello and orchestra: (1) Raphael Wallfisch (vc.), London Philharmonic Orchestra, Bryden Thomson. Chandos LP: ABRD 1204; TC: ABTD 1204; CD: CHAN 8494. (2) Beatrice Harrison (vc.), BBC Symphony Orchestra, Sir Henry Wood. Symposium CD: Symposium 1150 (m)—recording incomplete.

Concerto for seven instruments: Academy of St Martin-in-the-Fields Chamber Ensemble. Chandos CD: CHAN 9602; *finale only*: Free CD issued with the May 1998 issue of *The Gramophone* magazine: GCD0598.
Concerto for violin and orchestra: Lydia Mordkovitch (vn.), London Philharmonic Orchestra, Bryden Thomson. Chandos CD: 9003.
Coronation March: (1) London Symphony Orchestra, Sir Malcolm Sargent. Decca LP: LXT 2793 (m); ACL 137 (m); (Eclipse) ECS 649(m/st); US-London LP: LL804 (m); LD 9046 (m); CM 9070 (m); Everest LP: 3277E (m); LP-10: LW 5057 (m); Ditto TC: DTO 10119A (m); Decca CD: 425 662-2 (m); Beulah CD: 1PD13 (m). (2) London Festival Orchestra, Eric Rogers. Britannia LP: BRI 077. (3) London Philharmonic Orchestra, Charles Mackerras. Reader's Digest LP: RDS 8024, RDS 0001/0002.
Coronation March [arr. organ by Garrett O'Brien]: Christopher Herrick. Vista LP: VPS 1055.
Cortège: London Philharmonic Orchestra, Bryden Thomson. Chandos LP: ABRD 1204; TC: ABTD 1204; CD: CHAN 8494.
Country-Tune, A: (1) Homer Samuels. Ampico PR: 68031 (m). (2) Iris Loveridge. Lyrita LP: RCS 10 (m); Musical Heritage Society LP: MHS 7011 (m). (3) Eric Parkin. Chandos LP: ABRD 1206; TC: ABTD 1206; CD: CHAN 8496.
Cradle Song: (1) Anne Thursfield (sop.), [Anon.] (pf.). HMV SR-10: E 410 (m). (2) Kirsten Flagstad (sop.), Waldemar Almo (pf.). Golden Age of Opera LP: EJS338 (m); Simax CD: PSC 1824 (m). (3) Norma Burrowes (sop.), Noel Skinner (pf.). Bax Society LP: BAX LP 1 (m)—live recording. See also **Irish Songs, Three**.
Dance in the Sunlight: English Sinfonia, Neville Dilkes. HMV LP CSD 3696, (Greensleeves) ESD 7100; (Greensleeves) TC: TC-ESD 7100. See also **Pieces for small orchestra, Three**.
Dance of Wild Irravel, The: London Philharmonic Orchestra, Bryden Thomson. Chandos LP: ABRD 1165; TC: ABTD 1165; CD: CHAN 8454; CHAN 9168.
Devil that tempted St Anthony, The: (1) Ruth Harte, Vivian Langrish. Bax Society LP: BAX LP 1 (m). (2) Frank Merrick, Michael Round.[1] Cabaletta LP: HRS 2004; CDN 5002. (3) Seta Tanyel, Jeremy Brown. Chandos LP: ABRD 1295; TC: ABTD 1295; CD: CHAN 8603.
Dream in Exile: (1) Iris Loveridge. Lyrita LP: RCS 11 (m); Musical Heritage Society LP: MHS 7012 (m). (2) Eric Parkin. Chandos CD: CHAN 9561.
Elegiac Trio: (1) Martin Ruderman (fl.), Milton Thomas (va.), Lois Craft (hp.). Alco SR: AC 205 (m); LP: ALP 1007 (m). (2) Christopher Hyde-Smith (fl.), John Underwood (va.), Maria Robles (hp.). Argo LP: ZRG 574. (3) Lucien Grujon (fl.), Walter Mony (va.), Kathleen Alister (hp.). RPM LP: RPM 1038S; Westminster LP: WGS-8196. (4) Thomas Prevost (fl.), Jean Dupouy (va.), Martine Geliot (hp.). Quantum CD: QM 6898. (5) Megan Meisenback (fl.), Bruce Williams (va.), Mary Golden (hp.). Centaur CD: CRC 2114. (6) Maarika Järvi (fl.), Paul Cortese (va.), Marie-Pierre Langlamet. Chandos CD: CHAN 9395. (7) Nash Ensemble: Philippa Davies (fl.), Roger Chase (va.), Skaila Kanga (hp.). Hyperion CD: CDA66807. (8) Mallarmé Chamber Players. Capstone CD: CPS 8638. (9) Trio Turner: Philippe

[1] A recording by Frank Merrick and Angus Morrison of this and Bax's other works for two pianos was advertised in 1967 but never made. It would have been issued on the Frank Merrick LP label as FMS 22.

Pierlot (fl.), Sabine Toutain (va.), Isabelle Perrin (hp.). Arion CD: ARN 68423. (10) Alexa Still (fl.), Marcus Thompson (va.), Ann Hobson (hp.). Koch CD: forthcoming.

Enchanted Fiddle, The: Norma Burrowes (sop.), Noel Skinner (pf.). Bax Society LP: BAX LP 1 (m)—live recording.

Enchanted Summer: Anne Williams-King, Lynore McWhirter (sops.), Brighton Festival Chorus, Royal Philharmonic Orchestra, Vernon Handley. Chandos LP: ABRD 1314; TC: ABTD 1314; CD: CHAN 8625.

Enfantines, Trois see **Berceuse** [No. 2].

Epithalamium: (1) Rodolphus Choir, Ralph Allwood, Christopher Hughes (org.). Herald CD: HAVPCD 176. (2) The Ramsey Singers, Mark Fenton, Jeremy Filsell (org.). ASV CD: CD DCA 941 (English Church Music, vol. 5).

Eternity [with orchestra]: Martyn Hill (ten.), London Philharmonic Orchestra, Bryden Thomson. Chandos LP: ABRD 1317; TC ABTD 1317; CD: CHAN 8628, CHAN BM1 (sampler disc).

Eternity [with piano]: Patricia Wright (sop.), Rosemary Barnes (pf.). Continuum CD: CCD 1046.

Fairies, The: Christopher Gillett (ten.), David Owen Norris (pf.). Ensemble TC: TRI 002.

Fanfare for a Cheerful Occasion: Kneller Hall Trumpeters, Capt. H. E. Adkins. HMV SR: C 2445 (m).

Fanfares for the Royal Wedding see **Royal Wedding Fanfares, Two.**

Fantasies on Polish Christmas Carols, Five: (1) St Angela's Singers, Divertimenti, Peter Broadbent. Ensemble TC: ENS 112, ENS 136. (2) Bel Canto Voices, Plymouth Festival Orchestra, Philip Brunelle. Pro Arte LP: PAD-192.

Fantasy Sonata: (1) Raymond Jeremy (va.), Maria Korchinska (hp.). National Gramophonic Society SR: NGS 118/120 (m); *movementI only*: Pearl CD: GEMM CDS 9148. (2) Watson Forbes (va.), Maria Korchinska (hp.). Decca SR: AK 941/943 (m). (3) Emanual Vardi (va.), Margaret Ross (hp.). Musical Heritage Society LP: MHS 3613; TC: MHC 5613. (4) Milton Thomas (va.), Susann McDonald (hp.). Klavier LP: KS-570. (5) Michael Ponder (va.), Imogen Barford (hp.). Ensemble TC: ENS 123. (6) Rikva Golani (va.), Judy Loman (hp.). Marquis Classics CD: MAR 131. (7) Sabine Toutain (va.), Isabelle Perrin (hp.). Arion CD: ARN 68423. (8) Marcus Thompson (va.), Ann Hobson (hp.). Koch CD: forthcoming. (9) Marcia Dickstein (hp.), *et al.* RCM Records CD: forthcoming.

Fantasy Sonata [arr. viola and piano by Richard Crabtree]: Richard Crabtree (va.), Charles Matthews (pf.). Olympia CD: OCD 454.

Far in a Western Brookland: (1) Graham Trew (bar.), Roger Vignoles (pf.). Meridian LP: E 77031/2; TC: KE 77031/2. (2) Christopher Keyte (bar.), Rosemary Barnes (pf.). Continuum CD: CCD 1046.

Fatherland: Martyn Hill (ten.), Brighton Festival Chorus, Royal Philharmonic Orchestra, Vernon Handley. Chandos LP: ABRD 1314; TC: ABTD 1314; CD: CHAN 8625,

Femmes battez vos marys: Patricia Wright (sop.), Rosemary Barnes (pf.). Continuum CD: CCD 1046.

Festival Overture [revised version]: London Philharmonic Orchestra, Bryden Thomson. Chandos LP: ABRD 1278; TC: ABTD 1278; CD: CHAN 8586, CHAN 9168.

Flute, The: Patricia Wright (sop.), Rosemary Barnes (pf.). Continuum CD: CCD 1046.

Folk-Tale: (1) Florence Hooton (vc.), Wilfrid Parry (pf.). Lyrita LP RCS 7 (m); Musical Heritage Society LP: MHS 7016 (m). (2) Moray Welsh (vc.), Roger Vignoles (pf.). Pearl LP: SHE 571. (3) Bernard Gregor-Smith (vc.), Yolande Wrigley (pf.). ASV CD: CD DCA 896.

From Dusk till Dawn: London Philharmonic Orchestra, Bryden Thomson. Chandos TC: ABTD 1478; CD: CHAN 8863.

Frühlingsregen: Christopher Gillett (ten.), David Owen Norris (pf.). Ensemble TC: TRI 002.

Garden of Fand, The: (1) Royal Philharmonic Orchestra, Sir Thomas Beecham. HMV SR: DB 6654/5 (m); LP: HQM 1165 (m); Odeon PHQM 1165 (m); EMI CD: CDM 7 63405 2. (2) Hallé Orchestra, Sir John Barbirolli. Pye LP-10: CCT 31000 (m); LP: GGC 4061 (m); GSGC 14061, GSGC 15017, GSGC 2059; Mercury: MG 50115 (m); MG 90115; TC: ZGGC 2059; PRT CD: PVCD 8380; Nixa CD: NIXCD 6003. (3) London Philharmonic Orchestra, Sir Adrian Boult. Lyrita LP: SRCS 62; CD: SRCD 231; HNH LP: HNH 4034 (also in box HNH3-4080X); Musical Heritage Society LP: MHS 1769. (4) Ulster Orchestra, Bryden Thomson. Chandos LP: ABRD 1066; TC: ABTD 1066; CD: CHAN 8307. (5) Chicago Symphony Orchestra, Leonard Slatkin. CSO CD: CSO 90-07 (from CSO 90/12: 'The Chicago Symphony Orchestra—The First 100 Years')—live recording. (6) Royal Scottish National Orchestra, David Lloyd-Jones. Naxos CD: 8.553525.

Glamour [with piano]: Christopher Gillett (ten.), David Owen Norris (pf.). Ensemble TC: TRI 002.

Glamour [orch. by Rodney Newton]: Martyn Hill (ten.), London Philharmonic Orchestra, Bryden Thomson. Chandos LP: ABRD 1317; TC: ABTD 1317; CD: CHAN 8628.

Gloria: The Ramsey Singers, Mark Fenton, Jeremy Filsell (org.). ASV CD: CD DCA 941 (English Church Music, vol. 5).

Golden Eagle [excerpts]: London Philharmonic Orchestra, Bryden Thomson. Chandos CD: CHAN 9003.

Gopak [orchestra] see **Russian Suite**.

Gopak [piano]: Aeolian PP: T 23418 (m); Universal Music Co. Ltd. PP: S 9874 (m); Broadwood Piano Co. Ltd. PP: S 9874 (m); Artistyle PP: 92600 (m). See also **Russian Tone-Pictures, Two**.

Gopak [arr. violin and piano by Louis Godowsky]: Nicola Burton (vn.), Matthew Morley (pf.). Environs TC: ENV 015.

Greek Folksongs, Five: (1) BBC Northern Singers, Stephen Wilkinson. Hyperion LP: A66092. (2) Finzi Singers, Paul Spicer. Chandos CD: CHAN 9139.

Happy Forest, The: (1) London Symphony Orchestra, Edward Downes. RCA LP: RCA SB 6806; GL 42247. (2) Ulster Orchestra, Bryden Thomson. Chandos LP: ABRD 1066; TC: ABTD 1066; CD: CHAN 8307.

Hardanger: (1) Ethel Bartlett, Rae Robertson. National Gramophonic Society SR: NGS 158 (m). (2) Frank Merrick, Michael Round. Cabaletta LP: HRS 2004, CDN 5002. (3) Seta Tanyel, Jeremy Brown. Chandos LP: ABRD 1295; TC: ABTD 1295; CD: CHAN 8603.

Hill Tune, A: (1) Harriet Cohen. Columbia SR: DX 1109 (m). (2) Frank Merrick. Frank Merrick Society LP: FMS 8 (m); Rare Recorded Edition LP: SRRE 129 (m). (3) Iris Loveridge. Lyrita LP: RCS 10 (m); Musical Heritage Society LP: MHS 7012 (m). (4) Eric Parkin. Chandos LP: ABRD 1207; TC: ABTD 1207; CD: CHAN 8497.

I have house and land in Kent: Christopher Keyte (bar.), Rosemary Barnes (pf.). Continuum CD: CCD 1046.

I heard a piper piping: (1) Astra Desmond (con.), Gerald Moore (pf.). SR-10: Decca M 522 (m). (2) Norma Burrowes (sop.), Noel Skinner (pf.). Bax Society LP: BAX LP 1 (m)—live recording. (3) Elizabeth Harwood (sop.), John Constable (pf.). Conifer LP: CFRA 120; TC: MCFRA 120. (4) Patricia Wright (sop.), Rosemary Barnes (pf.). Continuum CD: CCD 1046.

I heard a soldier: Peter Savidge (bar.), David Owen Norris (pf.). Ensemble TC: TRI 002.

I sing of a maiden that is makeless: (1) Norwich Cathedral Choir, Michael Nicholas. Vista LP: VPS 1084. (2) BBC Northern Singers, Stephen Wilkinson. Hyperion LP: A66092. (3) Choir of King's College, Nicholas Cleobury. EMI LP: EL 270440-1; TC: EL 270440-4; CD: CDC 7 47663 2; CDM 5 65595 2. (4) Finzi Singers, Paul Spicer. Chandos CD: CHAN 9139. (5) Rodolphus Choir, Ralph Allwood. Herald CD: HAVPCD 176.

In Memoriam [orchestra]: BBC Philharmonic Orchestra, Vernon Handley. Chandos CD: forthcoming.

In Memoriam (1916) [sextet]: (1) Academy of St Martin-in-the-Fields Chamber Ensemble. Chandos CD: CHAN 9602. (2) Marcia Dickstein (hp.), *et al.* RCM Records CD: forthcoming.

In a Vodka Shop [orchestra] see **Russian Suite**.

In a Vodka Shop [piano]: (1) Iris Loveridge. Lyrita LP: RCS 12 (m); Musical Heritage Society LP: MHS 7013 (m). (2) Eric Parkin. Chandos LP: ABRD 1207; TC: ABTD 1207; CD: CHAN 8497. (3) Charles Matthews. Olympia CD: OCD 454.

In the Faery Hills: (1) Ulster Orchestra, Bryden Thomson. Chandos LP: ABRD 1133; TC: ABTD 1133, MBTD 6525; CD: CHAN 8367, CHAN 6525. (2) Royal Scottish National Orchestra, David Lloyd-Jones. Naxos CD: 8.553525.

In the Night: Eric Parkin. Chandos CD: CHAN 9561.

Into the Twilight: Ulster Orchestra, Bryden Thomson. Chandos LP: ABRD 1133; TC: ABTD 1133; CD: CHAN 8367.

Irish Landscape: Royal Philharmonic Orchestra, Vernon Handley. LP: Lyrita SRCS 99. See also **Pieces for small orchestra, Three**.

Irish Songs, Five see **I heard a piper piping** [No. 3].

Irish Songs, Three: Mary O'Brien (sop.), Lincoln Mayorga (pf.). Town Hall LP: S22. See also **Cradle Song** [No. 1] and **Rann of Exile** [No. 2].

Jack and Jone: Christopher Keyte (bar.), Rosemary Barnes (pf.). Continuum CD: CCD 1046.

Langueo d'amours: Patricia Wright (sop.), Rosemary Barnes (pf.). Continuum CD: CCD 1046.

Legend [orchestra]: London Philharmonic Orchestra, Bryden Thomson. Chandos CD: CHAN 9003.

Legend [piano]: (1) John McCabe. Continuum CD: CCD 1045. (2) Eric Parkin. Chandos CD: CHAN 9561.

Legend [viola]: (1) Watson Forbes (va.), Leonard Cassini (pf.). Delta LP: 12024 (m); SDEL 18024; Summit LP: LSU 3058 (m); TLS 6063; Concert Artist LP: SRCAM 5008; Dover LP: HCR 5260 (m); HCR-ST 7012; TC: ATL-TC-5001. (2) Esther Geldard (va.), Alison Proctor (pf.). Environs TC: ENV 009. (3) Paul Coletti (va.), Leslie Howard (pf.). Hyperion CD CDA66687. (4) Steven Dann (va.), Bruce Vogt (pf.). CBC CD: MVCD1072. (5) Richard Crabtree (va.), Charles Matthews (pf.). Olympia CD: OCD 454.

Legend [violin]: Henry Holst (vn.), Frank Merrick (pf.). Frank Merrick Society LP: FMS 21 (m).

Legend-Sonata: (1) Florence Hooton (vc.), Wilfrid Parry (pf.). Lyrita LP: RCS 6 (m); Musical Heritage Society LP: MHS 7015 (m). (2) Bernard Gregor-Smith (vc.), Yolande Wrigley (pf.). ASV CD: CD DCA 896. (3) Naxos CD: forthcoming.

Lord, Thou hast told us: Rodolphus Choir, Ralph Allwood. Herald CD: HAVPCD 176.

Lullaby [piano]: (1) Harriet Cohen. Duo-Art PR: 0355 (m). (2) Frank Merrick. Frank Merrick Society LP: FMS 7 (m). (3) Iris Loveridge. Lyrita LP: RCS 12 (m); Musical Heritage Society LP: MHS 7013 (m). (4) Eric Parkin. Chandos LP: ABRD 1206; TC: ABTD 1206; CD: CHAN 8496. (5) Charles Matthews. Olympia CD: OCD 454.

Lyke-Wake, A [with orchestra]: Martyn Hill (ten.), London Philharmonic Orchestra, Bryden Thomson. Chandos LP: ABRD 1317; TC: ABTD 1317; CD: CHAN 8628.

Magnificat [SATB and organ]: (1) Choir of Gloucester Cathedral, John Sanders, Mark Blatchly (org.). Priory TC: PRC 218; CD: PRCD 218. (2) Rodolphus Choir, Ralph Allwood, Christopher Hughes (org.). Herald CD: HAVPCD 176. (3) The Ramsey Singers, Mark Fenton, Jeremy Filsell (org.). ASV CD: CD DCA 941 (English Church Music, vol. 5). (4) *With organ part played on the piano*: BBC Northern Singers, Stephen Wilkinson, Keith Swallow (pf.). Hyperion LP: A66092.

Magnificat [solo voice and piano]: Patricia Wright (sop.), Rosemary Barnes (pf.). Continuum CD: CCD 1046.

Maiden with the Daffodil, The: (1) Iris Loveridge. Lyrita LP: RCS 12 (m); Musical Heritage Society LP: MHS 7013 (m). (2) Eric Parkin. Chandos TC: ABTD 1372; CD: CHAN 8732.

Malta, G.C.: (1) *Complete*: Royal Philharmonic Orchestra, Kenneth Alwyn. Cloud Nine LP: CN 7012; CD: ACN 7012; ASV TC: ZC WHL 2058; CD: CD WHL 2058; *'Quick (Gay) March', 'Intermezzo', 'March' only*: Cloud Nine CD: CNS 5446; *'March' only*: Silva Screen TC: SILVAC3002; CD: SILVAD3002. (2) *Substantially complete:* RAF Orchestra, Muir Mathieson. ST. (3) *'Quiet Interlude' (i.e. 'Intermezzo') and 'Gay March' only*: London Symphony Orchestra, Muir Mathieson. London SR-10: T 5054 (m). (4) *'Introduction and March' (i.e. the Lento non troppo and 'March' only)*: City of Birmingham Orchestra, Marcus Dods. HMV LP: ASD 3797, ED 290109-1; TC: TC-ASD 3797, ED 290109-4.

Market Girl, The: Richard Greager (ten.), Rosemary Barnes (pf.). Continuum CD: CCD 1046.

Mater, ora filium: (1) Leeds Festival Chorus (1925), Albert Coates. HMV SR: D 1044/5 (m). (2) BBC Chorus, Leslie Woodgate. Columbia SR: ROX 179/82 (m); ROX 8041/39 (m); US Columbia 11156/7D, set M 386 (m) (English Music Society, vol. 2) (3) BBC Northern Singers, Stephen Wilkinson. Hyperion LP: A66092. (4) John Oliver Chorale, John Oliver. Northeastern Records LP: NR 229. (5) Choir of King's College, Nicholas Cleobury. EMI LP: EL 27 0440 1; TC: EL 27 0440 4; CD: CDC 7 47663 2; CDM 5 65595 2; excerpt on CDZ 5 69599 2. (6) Finzi Singers, Paul Spicer. Chandos CD: CHAN 9139. (7) Rodolphus Choir, Ralph Allwood. Herald CD: HAVPCD 176.

May-Night in the Ukraine [orchestra] see **Russian Suite.**
May-Night in the Ukraine [piano] see **Russian Tone-Pictures, Two.**
Me suis mise en danse: Janet Baker (alto), Gerald Moore (pf.). EMI LP: ASD 2929; TC: TC-ESD 1024394.
Mediterranean [orchestra]: (1) New Symphony Orchestra, Eugene Goossens. HMV SR: C 1620 (m); US Victor SR: 9788 (m). (2) London Philharmonic Orchestra, Sir Adrian Boult. Lyrita LP: SRCS 62; CD: SRCD 231; Musical Heritage Society LP: MHS 1769; HNH LP: HNH 4034 (also in box HNH3-4080X). (3) London Philharmonic Orchestra, Bryden Thomson. Chandos LP: ABRD 1204; TC: ABTD 1204, MBTD 6538; CD: CHAN 6538, CHAN 8494; Conifer (Aspects) TC: ASPC 3061; CD: ASP 5061. (4) Northern Sinfonia of England, Richard Hickox. EMI CD: CDC 7 49933 2; CDM 5 66542 2. (5) London Philharmonic Orchestra, Sir Adrian Boult. BBC CD: BBCRD 9127—live recording.
Mediterranean [piano]: (1) Harriet Cohen. Duo-Art PR: 0355 (m). (2) Eugène d'Albert. Polydor SR: 66032 (m); LP: Veritas VM 110 (m); Concert Artist/Fidelio TC: CH4-TC-4013. (3) Iris Loveridge. Lyrita LP: RCS 10 (m); Musical Heritage Society LP: MHS 7011 (m). (4) Eric Parkin. Chandos CD: CHAN 9561.
Mediterranean [arr. 2 pianos, 3 hands by H. Rich]: Cyril Smith, Phyllis Sellick. LP: HMV CLP 3563 (m); CSD 3563.
Mediterranean [arr. violin and piano by Jascha Heifetz]: Jascha Heifetz (vn.), Emmanual Bay (pf.). Victor SR: 10-1293 (m); HMV LP: EC 193 (m), ARM 4-0946 (m); RCA CD: 09026 61737 2 (m).
Milking Sian, A: Patricia Wright (sop.), Rosemary Barnes (pf.). Continuum CD: CCD 1046.
Morning Song: (1) Harriet Cohen (pf.), [orchestra], Dr Malcolm Sargent. Columbia SR: DX 1361 (m); DX 1838 (m); LP: HMV HLM 7148 (m). (2) Margaret Fingerhut (pf.), London Philharmonic Orchestra, Bryden Thomson. Chandos LP: ABRD 1226; TC: ABTD 1226; CD: CHAN 8516.
Mountain Mood, A: (1) Harriet Cohen. Columbia SR: DX 1109. (2) John Clegg. Alpha LP: 148c (m). (3) Iris Loveridge. Lyrita LP: RCS 30 (m)—not issued. (4) Eric Parkin. Chandos CD: CHAN 9561.
Moy Mell: (1) Ethel Bartlett, Rae Robertson (pfs). National Gramophonic Society SR: NGS 102 (m). (2) Frank Merrick, Michael Round. Cabaletta LP: HRS 2004, CDN 5002. (3) Seta Tanyel, Jeremy Brown. Chandos LP: ABRD 1295; TC: ABTD 1295; CD: CHAN 8603.
Moy Mell [arr. 2 pianos, 3 hands by Lionel Salter]: Cyril Smith, Phyllis Sellick. MK LP: D-011283-4 (m); D-003150 (m).
Nereid: (1) Iris Loveridge. Lyrita LP: RCS 30 (m)—not issued. (2) Eric Parkin. Chandos TC: ABTD 1372; CD: CHAN 8732.
Nocturne [orchestra] see **Russian Suite.**
Nocturne [piano] see **Two Russian Tone-Pictures.**
Nonet: (1) Joseph Slater (fl.), Léon Goossens (ob.), Frederick Thurston (cl.), Maria Korchinska (hp.), Griller String Quartet, Victor Watson (d.b.). Columbia SR: ROX 182/4 (m) (English Music Society, vol. 2); Dutton CD: CDAX 8014 (m). (2) Harmonia Ensemble. Giulia CD: GS 201009; ASdisc CD: AS 5005; Arts Music CD: 47328-2. (3) Nash Ensemble: Philippa Davies (fl.), Gareth Hulse (ob.), Michael Collins (cl.), Skaila Kanga (hp.), Marcia Crayford (vn.), Elizabeth Wexler (vn.), Roger Chase (va.), Christopher van Kempen (vc.), Duncan McTier (d.b.), Ian Brown (cond.). Hyperion CD: CDA66807.

Northern Ballad No. 1: London Philharmonic Orchestra, Sir Adrian Boult. Lyrita LP: SRCS 62; CD: SRCD 231; Musical Heritage Society LP: MHS 1769; HNH LP: HNH 4034 (also in box HNH3-4080X).
Northern Ballad No. 2: (1) Royal Philharmonic Orchestra, Vernon Handley. Chandos LP: ABRD 1180; TC: ABTD 1180; CD: CHAN 8464. (2) BBC Philharmonic Orchestra, Edward Downes. BBC Radio Classics CD: 15656 9159-2.
'Northern Ballad No. 3' see **Prelude for a Solemn Occasion**.
November Woods: (1) London Philharmonic Orchestra, Sir Adrian Boult. Lyrita LP: SRCS 37; CD: SRCD 231; HNH LP: HNH 4038. (2) Ulster Orchestra, Bryden Thomson. Chandos LP: ABRD 1066; TC: ABTD 1066; CD: CHAN 8307. (3) Academy of St Martin-in-the-Fields, Sir Neville Marriner. Philips CD: 454 444-2. (4) Royal Scottish National Orchestra, David Lloyd-Jones. Naxos CD: forthcoming.
Now is the Time of Christymas: New York City Gay Men's Chorus, Gary Miller, John Blanchard (fl.), Dean X [*sic*] Johnson (pf.). Virgin Classics CD: VC7 59121-2 (0777 7591212 8).
Nunc Dimittis: (1) Choir of Gloucester Cathedral, John Sanders, Mark Blatchly (org.). Priory TC: PRC 218; CD: PRCD 218. (2) The Ramsey Singers, Mark Fenton, Jeremy Filsell (org.). ASV CD: CD DCA 941 (English Church Music, vol. 5).
Nympholept [orchestra]: London Philharmonic Orchestra, Bryden Thomson. Chandos LP: ABRD 1203; TC: ABTD 1203; CD: CHAN 8493, CHAN 9168.
O Dame get up and bake your pies: (1) Iris Loveridge (pf.). Lyrita LP: RCS 12 (m); Musical Heritage Society LP: MHS 7013 (m). (2) Eric Parkin. Chandos TC: ABTD 1372; CD: CHAN 8732.
O dear! what can the matter be?: (1) Megan Thomas (sop.), Geraldine Mason (pf.). Cabaletta LP: HRM 2001 (m). (2) Patricia Wright (sop.), Rosemary Barnes (pf.). Continuum CD: CCD 1046.
Octet: Margaret Fingerhut (pf.), Academy of St Martin-in-the-Fields Chamber Ensemble. Chandos CD: CHAN 9602.
Of a Rose I sing a Song: Charlotte Seal (hp.), David Fletcher (vc.), Jeffrey Box (d.b.), BBC Northern Singers, Stephen Wilkinson. Hyperion LP: A 66092.
Oliver Twist: (1) *Substantially complete*: Harriet Cohen (pf.), Philharmonia Orchestra, Muir Mathieson. Rank ST: Rank Video 0054; Rank / Carlton: RCC 3056. (2) *Excerpts only (taken from the original music tracks)*: Harriet Cohen (pf.), Philharmonia Orchestra, Muir Mathieson. Columbia SR: DX 1516/17 (m); American Columbia MX 330 (m); LP-10: ML 2092 (m); Ariel LP: CBF 13 (m). (3) *'Fagin's Romp' and 'Finale'*: Rank SR: FM 27-28 (m)—direct soundtrack recording.[2] (4) *'Fagin's Romp' and 'Finale'*: National Symphony Orchestra, Bernard Herrmann. Decca LP: PFS 4363; TC: KPFC 4363; LP: 411 837-1 1DV; TC: KPFC 4363, 411 837-4; London LP: SPC 21149; CD: 448 954-2 LPF. (5) *Muir Mathieson's Concert Suite and other excerpts*: Eric Parkin (pf.), Royal Philharmonic Orchestra, Kenneth Alwyn. Cloud Nine LP: CN 7012; CD: ACN 7012; ASV TC: ZC WHL 2058; CD: CD WHL 2058; *'Fagin's Romp' only*: Silva Screen TC: SILVAC 3002; CD: SILVAD3002.
On a May Evening: (1) Iris Loveridge. Lyrita LP: RCS 30 (m)—not issued. (2) Eric Parkin. Chandos TC: ABTD 1372; CD: CHAN 8732.

[2] '. . . not available commercially but . . . issued to the permanent record libraries of radio and television stations in about sixty countries.' (Roger Manvell and John Huntley, *The Technique of Film Music*, London and New York: Focal Press, 1957, p. 266.)

On the Sea-shore [ed./orch. by Graham Parlett]: Ulster Orchestra, Vernon Handley. Chandos LP: ABRD 1184; TC: ABTD 1184; CHAN 8473.

Orchestral Pieces, Four see **Dance of Wild Irravel, The** [No. 4]. See also **Pieces for small orchestra, Three** [rev. versions of Nos. 1-3].

Out and Away: Richard Greager (ten.), Rosemary Barnes (pf.). Continuum CD: CCD 1046.

Overture, Elegy and Rondo: Slovak Philharmonic Orchestra, Barry Wordsworth. Marco Polo CD: 8.223102.

Overture to Adventure: (1) Munich Symphony Orchestra, Douglas Bostock. Classico CD: forthcoming. (2) Royal Philharmonic Orchestra, Vernon Handley. Lyrita CD: forthcoming.

Overture to a Picaresque Comedy: (1) London Philharmonic Orchestra, Sir Hamilton Harty. Columbia SR: LX 394 (m); Dutton CD: CDLX 7016 (m). (2) New York Philharmonic-Symphony Orchestra, Dmitri Mitropoulos. Off the Air Club LP: 8 (m). (3) Royal Philharmonic Orchestra, Igor Buketoff. RCA Victor LP: RB-6730 (m); SB-6730; LM 3005 (m); LSC 3005. (4) London Philharmonic Orchestra, Bryden Thomson. Chandos LP: ABRD 1204; TC: ABTD 1204; CD: CHAN 8494. (5) Royal Scottish National Orchestra, David Lloyd-Jones. Naxos CD: forthcoming.

Pæan [orchestra]: London Philharmonic Orchestra, Bryden Thomson. Chandos LP: ABRD 1165; TC ABTD 1165; CD: CHAN 8454; CHAN 9168.

Pæan [piano]: (1) Harriet Cohen. Columbia SR-10: DB 1786 (m) (Columbia History of Music by Ear and Eye, vol. V). (2) Frank Merrick. Frank Merrick Society LP: [FMS] 3 (m). (3) Iris Loveridge. Lyrita LP: RCS 11 (m); Musical Heritage Society LP: MHS 7012 (m). (4) Eric Parkin. Chandos CD: CHAN 9561.

Phantasy for viola and orchestra: Rikva Golani (va.), Royal Philharmonic Orchestra, Vernon Handley. Conifer LP: CFC 171; TC: MCFC 171; CD: CDCF 171; excerpt on CDCF 706 (sampler disc); The Boots Company's Classical Collection TC: DDC 507; CD: DDD 507.

Pieces for flute, Four: (1) Kathleen Moy (fl.), John Simons (pf.). Ensemble TC: TRIAD 001. (2) Kenneth Smith (fl.), Paul Rhodes (pf.). ASV CD: CD DCA 768.

Pieces for small orchestra, Three: English Chamber Orchestra, Jeffrey Tate. EMI LP: EL 27 0592 1; TC: EL 27 0592 4; CD: CDC 7 47945 2, CDM 7 64200 2. See also **Irish Landscape** [No. 2] and **Dance in the Sunlight** [No. 3].

'Pièces sur le nom de Gabriel Fauré, Cinq' see **Suite on the Name Gabriel Fauré.**

Poisoned Fountain, The: (1) Arthur Whittemore, Jack Lowe. LP: Victor LM 1705 (m); EP: WDM 1705 (m); Capitol P 8550 (m); SP 8550. (2) Ruth Harte, Vivian Langrish. Bax Society LP: BAX LP 1 (m). (3) Frank Merrick, Michael Round. Cabaletta LP: HRS 2004, CDN 5002. (4) Seta Tanyel, Jeremy Brown. Chandos LP: ABRD 1295; TC: ABTD 1295; CD: CHAN 8603. (5) David Bradshaw, Cosmo Buono. Sync TC: C4171; Connoisseur Society CD: CD4171. (6) Joshua Pierce, Dorothy Jones. Koch CD: 3-7013-2.

Prelude for a Solemn Occasion: (1) London Philharmonic Orchestra, Bryden Thomson. Chandos LP: ABRD 1204; TC: ABTD 1204; CD: CHAN 8494. (2) BBC Philharmonic Orchestra, Edward Downes. BBC Radio Classics CD: 15656 9159-2.

Princess's Rose Garden, The: (1) Malcolm Binns (pf.). Pearl LP: SHE 565. (2) Eric Parkin. Chandos TC: ABTD 1372; CD: CHAN 8732.

Quartet for piano and strings: John McCabe (pf.), English String Quartet. Chandos LP: ABRD 1113; TC: ABTD 1113; CD: CHAN 8391.

Quartet No. 1 for strings: (1) Wilson String Quartet. National Gramophonic Society SR: [NGS] 153/5 (m). (2) Griller Quartet. Decca SR: AK 1009/12 (m). (3) English String Quartet. Chandos LP: ABRD 1113; ABTD 1113; CD: CHAN: 8391.
Quartet No. 2 for strings: Mistry String Quartet. Chandos TC: ABTD 1427; CD: CHAN 8795; excerpt on CHAN BM2 (sampler disc).
Quartet No. 3 for strings: Amici String Quartet. Gaudeamus LP: KRS 31.
Quintet for harp and strings: (1) Laura Newell (hp.), Stuyvesant String Quartet. Philharmonia LP: PH 102 (m); PH 119 (m). (2) Skaila Kanga (hp.), English String Quartet. Chandos LP: ABRD 1113; TC: ABTD 1113; CD: CHAN 8391. (3) Nash Ensemble: Skaila Kanga (hp.), Marcia Crayford (vn.), Iris Juda (vn.), Roger Chase (va.), Christopher van Kempen (vc.). Hyperion CD: CDA66807. (4) Marcia Dickstein (hp.), *et al.* RCM Records CD: forthcoming.
Quintet for oboe and strings: (1) Léon Goossens (ob.), International String Quartet. National Gramophonic Society SR (80 rpm): NGS 76/77 (m). (2) Earl Schuster (ob.), Classic String Quartet. Classic Editions LP: CE 1030 (m). (3) I. Wilson (ob.), Hoffman String Quartet. Brolga LP: BZM 06 (m). (4) Helen Powell (ob.), Sylvia Sutton (vn.), Avril MacLennon (vn.), Janet Schlapp (va.), Robert Glenton (vc.). Bax Society LP: BAX LP 1 (m)—live recording. (5) Bert Lucarelli (ob.), Manhatten String Quartet. Musical Heritage Society LP: MHS 3521; TC: MHC 5521. (6) Sarah Francis (ob.), English String Quartet. Chandos LP: ABRD 1114; TC: ABTD 1114; CD: CHAN 8392. (7) Pamela Woods (Pamela Pecha on Carlton reissue) (ob.), Audubon String Quartet. Telarc CD: CD-80205; IMP CD: IMP 30367 0103-2; Carlton CD: 30367 01032. (8) Nash Ensemble: Gareth Hulse (ob.), Marcia Crayford (vn.), Iris Juda (vn.), Roger Chase (va.), Christopher van Kempen (vc.). Hyperion CD: CDA66807. (9) Gordon Hunt (ob.), Tale Quartet. BIS CD: CD-763.
Quintet for piano and strings: Mistry String Quartet, David Owen Norris (pf.). Chandos TC: ABTD 1427; CD: CHAN 8795.[3]
Quintet for strings [1933]: Academy of St Martin-in-the-Fields Chamber Ensemble. Chandos CD: CHAN 9602.
Rann of Exile: (1) Anne Thursfield (sop.), [Anon.] (pf.). HMV SR-10: E 410 (m). (2) Peter Dawson (bar.), Gerald Moore (pf.). HMV SR-10 (m): B 8866 (m); LP: EX 29 0911 3 (m); TC: EX 29 0911 5 (m). (3) Peter Savidge (bar.), David Owen Norris (pf.). Ensemble TC: TRI 002. (4) Christopher Keyte (bar.), Rosemary Barnes (pf.). Continuum CD: CCD 1046. See also **Irish Songs, Three**.
Red Autumn: Seta Tanyel, Jeremy Brown. Chandos LP: ABRD 1295; TC: ABTD 1295; CD: CHAN 8603.
Rhapsodic Ballad: (1) Rohan de Saram. Pearl LP: SHE 547. (2) Raphael Wallfisch. Chandos LP: ABRD 1209; TC: ABTD 1209; CD: CHAN 8499.
Rogue's Comedy: Royal Philharmonic Orchestra, Vernon Handley. Lyrita CD: forthcoming.
Romance, A: (1) Iris Loveridge. Lyrita LP: RCS 26 (m); Musical Heritage Society LP: MHS 7014 (m). (2) Eric Parkin. Chandos TC: ABTD 1372; CD: CHAN 8732.
Romantic Overture: London Philharmonic Orchestra, Bryden Thomson. Chandos CD: CHAN 9003.

[3] A recording of this work with Frank Merrick as the pianist was advertised in 1967 but never made. It would have been issued on the Frank Merrick LP label as FMS 20.

Rosc-catha: Ulster Orchestra, Bryden Thomson. Chandos LP: ABRD 1133; TC: ABTD 1133, MBTD 6525; CD: CHAN 8367, CHAN 6525.
Roundel: Peter Savidge (bar.), David Owen Norris (pf.). Ensemble TC: TRI 002.
Royal Wedding Fanfares, Two [arr. by Capt. M. Roberts]: (1) Trumpeters of the Royal Military School of Music, Capt. M. Roberts. HMV SR-10: B 9616 (m). (2) *No. 1 only*: Band of H. M. Royal Marines, Lieut.-Colonel Sir Vivian Dunn. Columbia LP: TWO 285. (3) *No. 1 only*: Band of the Scots Guards, Capt. Duncan Beat. EMI LP: EMC 3179. (4) *No. 2 only*: Trumpeters of the Royal Military School of Music, Capt. M. Roberts. EMI LP: ALP 1043 (m)—brief excerpt from a recording of the actual ceremony. (5) *No. 2 only*: Philip Jones Brass Ensemble, Philip Jones. Decca LP: SDD 274, SPA 419; TC: SPA 500, Argo TC: KCSP 500; Decca CD: 430 369-2, 436 404-2.
Russian Suite: London Philharmonic Orchestra, Bryden Thomson. Chandos LP: ABRD 1356; TC: ABTD 1356; CD: CHAN 8669.
Russian Tone-pictures, Two: (1) Iris Loveridge. Lyrita LP: RCS 26 (m). (2) Eric Parkin. Chandos TC: ABTD 1372; CD: CHAN 8732. (3) Charles Matthews. Olympia CD: OCD 454. See also **Gopak [piano], Gopak [arr. violin and piano]** and **Russian Suite**.
Saga Fragment: Margaret Fingerhut (pf.), London Philharmonic Orchestra, Bryden Thomson. Chandos LP: ABRD 1195; TC: ABTD 1195; CD: CHAN 8484.
'Salzburg' Sonata see **Sonata in B♭**.
Sarabande: (1) Peter Savidge (bar.), David Owen Norris (pf.). Ensemble TC: TRI 002. (2) Patricia Wright (sop.), Rosemary Barnes (pf.). Continuum CD: CCD 1046.
Scherzo [piano]: Malcolm Binns. Pearl LP: SHE 565.
Scherzo [arr. player-piano]: Aeolian PP: T 951; Universal Music Co. Ltd. PP: S 13620; Broadwood Piano Co. Ltd. PP: S 13620; Artistyle PP: 93519.
Serpent Dance: (1) Iris Loveridge. Lyrita LP: RCS 10 (m). (2) Eric Parkin. Chandos CD: CHAN 9561.
Shieling Song: Patricia Wright (sop.), Rosemary Barnes (pf.). Continuum CD: CCD 1046.
Sinfonietta: Slovak Philharmonic Orchestra, Barry Wordsworth. Marco Polo CD: 8.223102.
Slave-Girl, The: (1) Iris Loveridge. Lyrita LP: RCS 30 (m)—not issued. (2) Malcolm Binns. Pearl LP: SHE 565 (title misprinted on sleeve as 'Slave Dance'). (3) Eric Parkin. Chandos CD: CHAN 9561.
Sleepy Head: (1) Iris Loveridge. Lyrita LP: RCS 26 (m). (2) Eric Parkin. Chandos TC: ABRT 1372; CD: CHAN 8732.
Slumber Song: Martyn Hill (ten.), London Philharmonic Orchestra, Bryden Thomson. Chandos LP: ABRD 1317; TC: ABTD 1317; CD: CHAN 8628.
Sonata for cello and piano: (1) Florence Hooton (vc.), Wilfrid Parry (pf.). Lyrita LP: RCS 7 (m); Musical Heritage Society LP: MHS 7016 (m). (2) Bernard Gregor-Smith (vc.), Yolande Wrigley (pf.). ASV CD: CD DCA 896. (3) Naxos CD: forthcoming.
Sonata for clarinet and piano: (1) Stanley Drucker (cl.), Leonid Hambro (pf.). Odyssey LP: Y 30492; Sony CD: SMK 58932; SBK 62750. (2) John Denman (cl.), Hazel Vivienne (pf.). Revolution LP: RCF 009; Concert Artist/Fidelio TC: FED-TC-038. (3) Janet Hilton (cl.), Keith Swallow (pf.). Chandos LP: ABRD 1078, DBRD 4001; TC: ABTD 1078, DBTD 4001; CD: CHAN 8683. (4) Murray Khouri (cl.), Peter Pettinger (pf.). Continuum CD: CCD 1038. (5) Emma Johnson (cl.), Malcolm Martineau (pf.). ASV TC: ZC DCA 891; CD: CD DCA 891. (6) John Denman (cl.), Paula Fan (pf.). British Music Label CD: BML 009. (7) Klara Stanic (cl.), Damjana

Zupan (pf.). Environs TC: ENV 028. (8) Heather Nicoll (cl.), Anna Rastoptchina (pf.). Environs TC: ENV 032. (9) John Leenders (cl.), Mariann Ábrahám (pf.). MP Classic CD: MPCD 9501. (10) Michael Collins (cl.), Ian Brown (pf.). Hyperion CD: CDA66807. (11) Paul Meyer (cl.), Eric Le Sage (pf.). Denon CD: DEN 18016.

Sonata for flute and harp: (1) Emily Beynon (fl.), Catherine Beynon (hp.). Metier CD: MSV CD92006. (2) Philippe Pierlot (fl.), Isabelle Perrin (hp.). Arion CD: ARN 68423. (3) Marcia Dickstein (hp.), *et al.* RCM Records CD: forthcoming.

Sonata for two pianos: (1) Ethel Bartlett, Rae Robertson. National Gramophonic Society SR: [NGS] 156/158 (m). (2) Frank Merrick, Michael Round. Cabaletta LP: HRS 2004, CDN 5002. (3) Seta Tanyel, Jeremy Brown. Chandos LP: ABRD 1295; TC: ABTD 1295; CD: CHAN 8603.

Sonata for viola and piano: (1) Lionel Tertis (va.), Arnold Bax (pf.). For details of this recording see section III below. (2) William Primrose (va.), Harriet Cohen (pf.). Columbia SR: ROX 179/182 (m); ROX 8039/45 (m) auto (English Music Society, vol. 2); US Columbia 11181/4D (m), set M 386; Pearl CD: GEMM CD 9453 (m). (3) Herbert Downes (va.), Leonard Cassini. Delta LP: DEL 12028 (m); Summit LP: LSU 3073 (m); Revolution LP: RCB 1. (4) Emanuel Vardi (va.), Abba Bogin (pf.). Musical Heritage Society LP: MHS 3613; TC: MHC 5613. (5) Milton Thomas (va.), Doris Stevenson (pf.). Klavier LP: KS-570. (6) Michael Ponder (va.), John Alley (pf.). Ensemble TC: ENS 123. (7) Duncan Ferguson (va.), Hester Dickson (pf.). Environs TC: ENV 010.

Sonata in B♭ for piano ('Salzburg'): *Movement II only:* Eric Parkin. Chandos CD: CD 9561.

Sonata in E♭ for piano: (1) Noemy Belinkaya. Ensemble TC: ENS 136; Bnai Brith TC: MSCB BB 104. (2) John McCabe. Continuum CD: CCD 1045. (3) *Movement II only:* John Simons. Ensemble TC: TRIAD 001. See also the orchestrated version: **Symphony No. 1**.

Sonata No. 1 for piano: (1) Iris Loveridge. Lyrita LP: RCS 10 (m); Musical Heritage Society LP: MHS 7011 (m). (2) Frank Merrick. Frank Merrick Society LP: FMS 7 (m). (3) Joyce Hatto. Revolution LP: RCF 010; Concert Artist/Fidelio TC: FED-TC-011. (4) Eric Parkin. Chandos LP: ABRD 1206; TC: ABTD 1206; CD: CHAN 8496. (5) Marie-Catherine Girod. Opès 3D CD: 3D 8008; 3D Classics 122184.

Sonata No. 2 for piano: (1) Frank Merrick. Frank Merrick Society LP: FMS 6 (m). (2) Iris Loveridge. Lyrita LP: RCS 11 (m); Musical Heritage Society LP: MHS 7012 (m). (3) Peter Cooper. Pye LP: GGC 4085 (m); GSGC 14085; GSGC 2061; TC: ZGGC 2061. (4) Malcolm Binns. Pearl LP: SHE 565. (5) Eric Parkin. Chandos LP: ABRD 1206; TC: ABTD 1206; CD: CHAN 8496. (6) John McCabe. Continuum CD: CCD 1045. (7) Marie-Catherine Girod. Opès 3D CD: 3D 8008; 3D Classics 122184.

Sonata No. 3 for piano: (1) Frank Merrick. Frank Merrick Society LP: FMS 7 (m). (2) Iris Loveridge. Lyrita LP: RCS 12 (m); Musical Heritage Society LP: MHS 7013 (m). (3) Eric Parkin. Chandos LP: ABRD 1207; TC: ABTD 1207; CD: CHAN 8497. (4) Marie-Catherine Girod. Opès 3D CD: 3D 8008; 3D Classics 122184.

Sonata No. 4 for piano: (1) Iris Loveridge. Lyrita LP: RCS 26 (m); Musical Heritage Society LP: MHS 7014 (m). (2) Frank Merrick. Frank Merrick Society LP: FMS 8 (m). (3) Joyce Hatto. Revolution LP: RCF 010; TC: FED-TC-011. (4) Eric Parkin. Chandos LP: ABRD 1207; TC: ABTD 1207; CD: CHAN 8497. (5) Marie-Catherine

Girod. Opès 3D CD: 3D 8008; 3D Classics 122184. (6) *Movement II only:* John McCabe. Decca LP: SDD 444.

Sonata No. 1 for violin and piano: (1) *1920 version*: Henry Holst (vn.), Frank Merrick (pf.). Concert Artist LP: LPA 1099 (m); Revolution LP: RCB 20; Concert Artist/Fidelio TC: ATL-TC-5005. (2) *1945 version*: Erich Gruenberg (vn.), John McCabe (pf.). Chandos TC: ABTD 1462; CD: CHAN 8845.

Sonata No. 2 for violin and piano: (1) Henry Holst (vn.), Frank Merrick (pf.). Frank Merrick Society LP: FMS 18 (m). (2) Erich Gruenberg (vn.), John McCabe (pf.). Chandos TC: ABTD 1462; CD: CHAN 8845.

Sonata No. 3 for violin and piano: (1) Henry Holst (vn.), Frank Merrick (pf.). Frank Merrick Society LP: FMS 18 (m). (2) Nicola Burton (vn.), Matthew Morley (pf.). Environs TC: ENV 015. (3) May Harrison (vn.), Charles Lynch (pf.). Symposium CD: Symposium 1075 (m)–recording incomplete.

Sonatina for cello and piano: (1) Florence Hooton (vc.), Wilfrid Parry (pf.). Lyrita LP: RCS 6 (m); Musical Heritage Society LP: MHS 7 (m). (2) Bernard Gregor-Smith (vc.), Yolande Wrigley (pf.). ASV CD: CD DCA 896.

Song in the Twilight, The: Patricia Wright (sop.), Rosemary Barnes (pf.). Continuum CD: CCD 1046.

Spring Fire: Royal Philharmonic Orchestra, Vernon Handley. Chandos LP: ABRD 1180; TC: ABTD 1180; CD: CHAN 8464.

Spring Rain see **Frühlingsregen**.

Suite on the Name Gabriel Fauré: Marie-Catherine Girod. Opès 3D CD: 3D 8008; 3D Classics 122184 (recorded as 'Cinq pièces sur le nom de Gabriel Fauré').

Summer Music: Ulster Orchestra, Bryden Thomson. Chandos LP: ABRD 1066; TC: ABTD 1066; CD: CHAN 8307.

Symphonic Scherzo: Royal Philharmonic Orchestra, Vernon Handley. Chandos LP: ABRD 1180; TC: ABTD 1180; CD: CHAN 8464.

Symphonic Variations: (1) Joyce Hatto (pf.), Guildford Philharmonic Orchestra, Vernon Handley. Revolution LP: RCF 001; Concert Artist/Fidelio TC: FED-TC-001. (2) Margaret Fingerhut (pf.), London Philharmonic Orchestra, Bryden Thomson. Chandos LP: ABRD 1226; TC: ABTD 1226; CD: CHAN 8516.

Symphony No. 1: (1) London Philharmonic Orchestra, Myer Fredman. Lyrita LP: SRCS 53; CD: SRCD 232; Musical Heritage Society LP: MHS 1586. (2) London Philharmonic Orchestra, Bryden Thomson. Chandos LP: ABRD 1192; TC: ABTD 1192; CD: CHAN 8480 (also in CHAN 8906-10). (3) Royal Scottish National Orchestra, David Lloyd-Jones. Naxos CD: 8.553525. See also the original piano version: **Sonata in E♭**.

Symphony No. 2: (1) London Philharmonic Orchestra, Myer Fredman. Lyrita LP: SRCS 54; Musical Heritage Society LP: MHS 1632. Lyrita CD: forthcoming. (2) London Philharmonic Orchestra, Bryden Thomson. Chandos LP: ABRD 1203; TC: ABTD 1203; CD: CHAN 8493 (also in CHAN 8906-10). (3) Royal Scottish National Orchestra, David Lloyd-Jones. Naxos CD: forthcoming.

Symphony No. 3: (1) Hallé Orchestra, John Barbirolli. HMV SR: C 3380/5 (m); C 7593/8 (m) (auto); EMI LP: EX 29 0107 3 (m); TC: 29 0107 5 (m); CD: CDH 7 63910 2 (m). (2) London Symphony Orchestra, Edward Downes. RCA LP: RCA SB 6806; GL 42247. (3) Sydney Symphony Orchestra, Myer Fredman. ABC LP: L38227; TC: C38227. (4) London Philharmonic Orchestra, Bryden Thomson. Chandos LP: ABRD 1165; TC ABTD 1165; CD: CHAN 8454 (also in CHAN 8906-10). (5) *Brief* *excerpt from rehearsal sequence*: BBC Symphony Orchestra, Sir Henry Wood. Symposium CD: Symposium 1150 (m). (6) Royal Scottish National Orchestra, David Lloyd-Jones. Naxos CD: forthcoming.

Symphony No. 4: (1) Guildford Philharmonic Orchestra, Vernon Handley. Concert Artist LP: LPA 1097 (m); SLPA 1097; Revolution LP: RCF 002; Concert Artist/Fidelio TC: FED-TC-009. (2)Ulster Orchestra, Bryden Thomson. Chandos LP: ABRD 1091; TC ABTD 1091; CD: CHAN 8312 (also in CHAN 8906-10). (3) Royal Scottish National Orchestra, David Lloyd-Jones. Naxos CD: forthcoming.

Symphony No. 5: (1) London Philharmonic Orchestra, Raymond Leppard. Lyrita LP: SRCS 58; Musical Heritage Society LP: MHS 1652; Lyrita CD: forthcoming. (2) London Philharmonic Orchestra, Bryden Thomson. Chandos LP: ABRD 1356; TC: ABTD 1356; CD: CHAN 8669 (also in CHAN 8906-10). (3) Royal Scottish National Orchestra, David Lloyd-Jones. Naxos CD: forthcoming.

Symphony No. 6: (1) New Philharmonia Orchestra, Norman Del Mar. Lyrita LP: RCS 35 (m); SRCS 35; Musical Heritage Society LP: MHS 1198; Lyrita CD: forthcoming. (2) London Philharmonic Orchestra, Bryden Thomson. Chandos LP: ABRD 1278; TC ABTD 1278; CD: CHAN 8586 (also in CHAN 8906-10). (3) Munich Symphony Orchestra, Douglas Bostock. Classico CD: forthcoming. (4) Royal Scottish National Orchestra, David Lloyd-Jones. Naxos CD: forthcoming.

Symphony No. 7: (1) London Philharmonic Orchestra, Raymond Leppard. Lyrita LP: SRCS 83; CD: SRCD 232; HNH LP: HNH 4010. (2) London Philharmonic Orchestra, Bryden Thomson. Chandos LP: ABRD 1317; TC ABTD 1317; CD: CHAN 8628 (also in CHAN 8906-10). (3) Royal Scottish National Orchestra, David Lloyd-Jones. Naxos CD: forthcoming.

Tale the Pine-trees knew, The: (1) Guildford Philharmonic Orchestra, Vernon Handley. Concert Artist LP: LPA 2002 (m); Revolution LP: RCF 003. (2) Ulster Orchestra, Bryden Thomson. Chandos LP: ABRD 1133; TC: ABTD 1133; CD: CHAN 8367. (3) Royal Scottish National Orchestra, David Lloyd-Jones. Naxos CD: forthcoming.

Targo, La: Christopher Keyte (bar.), Rosemary Barnes (pf.). Continuum CD: CCD 1046.

Te Deum: The Ramsey Singers, Mark Fenton, Jeremy Filsell (org.). ASV CD: CD DCA 941 (English Church Music, vol. 5).

This Worldes Joie: (1) BBC Northern Singers, Stephen Wilkinson. Hyperion LP: A66092. (2) Gloucester Cathedral Choir, John Sanders. Alpha LP: ACA 526. (3) Choir of King's College, Nicholas Cleobury. EMI LP: EL 27 0440 1; TC: EL 27 0440 4; CD: CDC 7 47663 2; CDM 5 65595 2. (4) Finzi Singers, Paul Spicer. Chandos CD: CHAN 9139. (5) Rodolphus Choir, Ralph Allwood. Herald CD: HAVPCD 176. (6) Schola Cantorum of Oxford, Mark Shepherd. Guild CD: GMCD 7139.

Threnody and Scherzo: Academy of St Martin-in-the-Fields Chamber Ensemble. Chandos CD: CHAN 9602.

Tintagel: (1) New Symphony Orchestra, Eugene Goossens. HMV SR: C 1619/20 (m); US Victor SR: 9787/8 (m). (2) London Symphony Orchestra, George Weldon. Columbia LP: 33SX 1019 (m); TP: CCT 655 (m); Dutton CD: CDCLP 4002 (m). (3) London Philharmonic Orchestra, Sir Adrian Boult. Decca LP: LXT 5015 (m); Decca (Ace of Clubs): ACL 113 (m); London LL 1169 (m); CM 9122 (m); Decca (Eclipse) EC2 647(m/st); Ditto TC: DTO 10119B (m); Belart CD: 461 3542 (m). (4) London Symphony Orchestra, Sir John Barbirolli. HMV LP: ALP 2305 (m), ASD 2305; (Greensleeves) ESD 7092; (Greensleeves) TC: TC-ESD 7092; Angel LP: S-36415; EMI

CD: CDC 7 47984 2, CDM 5 65110 2, HMV 5 68469 2. (5) London Philharmonic Orchestra, Sir Adrian Boult. Lyrita LP: SRCS 62; CD: SRCD 231; Musical Heritage Society LP: MHS 7016; HNH LP: HNH 4034 (also in box HNH3-4080X). (6) Ulster Orchestra, Bryden Thomson. Chandos LP: ABRD 1091; TC: ABTD 1091, MBTD 6538; CD: CHAN 6538, CHAN 8312, CHAN 9168; Conifer (Aspects) TC: ASPC 3061; CD: ASP 5061; excerpt on Technics CD: unnumbered sampler disc ('Music Lovers [*sic*] Choice—Vol. 1. A selection of classical music by the Critics of Gramophone Magazine' offered in a 1990 subscription promotion); excerpt on free CD issued with the June 1998 issue (No. 99) of *Classic CD*: CCD/99/06/98. (7) BBC Philharmonic Orchestra, Edward Downes. BBC Radio Classics CD: 15656 9159-2. (8) BBC Symphony Orchestra, Andrew Davis. BBC CD: MM63—live recording: free CD issued with the November 1997 issue of the *BBC Music Magazine*. (9) Munich Symphony Orchestra, Douglas Bostock. Classico CD: forthcoming. (10) Royal Scottish National Orchestra, David Lloyd-Jones. Naxos CD: forthcoming.

To Eire: (1) Peter Savidge (bar.), David Owen Norris (pf.). Ensemble TC: TRI 002. (2) Patricia Wright (sop.), Rosemary Barnes (pf.). Continuum CD: CCD 1046.

Toccata: (1) Iris Loveridge. Lyrita LP: RCS 30 (m)—not issued. (2) Joyce Hatto (pf.). Revolution LP: RCF 010; TC: FED-TC-011. (3) Eric Parkin. Chandos CD: CHAN 9561.

Traditional Songs of France see **Femmes battez vos marys, Langueo d'amours, Me suis mise en danse, Sarabande** and **La Targo**.

Treue Liebe: Peter Savidge (bar.), David Owen Norris (pf.). Ensemble TC: TRI 002.

Trio in B♭: (1) Borodin Trio. Chandos LP: ABRD 1205; TC: ABTD 1205; CD: CHAN 8495. (2) Pirasti Trio. ASV CD: CD DCA 925.

Trio in one movement: Elizabeth Holborn (vn.), Thomas Tatton (va.), Robert MacSparren (pf.). Ensemble TC: TRIAD 001.

Truth about the Russian Dancers, The: London Philharmonic Orchestra, Bryden Thomson. Chandos TC: ABTD 1478; CD: CHAN 8863.

Valse [harp]: Marcia Dickstein. RCM Records CD: forthcoming.

Walsinghame: Martyn Hill (ten.), Brighton Festival Chorus, Royal Philharmonic Orchestra, Vernon Handley. Chandos LP: ABRD 1314; TC: ABTD 1314; CD: CHAN 8625; excerpt on Albany CD: TROY 095 (sampler disc).

Water Music: (1) Iris Loveridge. Lyrita LP: RCS 10 (m). (2) Joyce Hatto. Revolution LP: RCF 010; TC: FED-TC-011. (3) Eric Parkin. Chandos LP: ABRD 1207; TC: ABTD 1207; CD: CHAN 8497.

What is it like to be young and fair?: (1) Cambridge University Madrigal Society, Boris Ord. Columbia LP: 33CX 1063 (m). (2) Exultate Singers, Garrett O'Brien. RCA LP: GL 25062; TC: GK 25062. (3) Bristol Bach Choir, Glyn Jenkins. Priory CD: PRCD 352. (4) Cambridge University Chamber Choir, Timothy Brown. Gamut CD: GAM CD 529, IMCD 703.

What the Minstrel told us: (1) Iris Loveridge (pf.). Lyrita LP: RCS 11 (m). (2) Charles Matthews. Olympia CD: OCD 454. (3) Eric Parkin. Chandos CD: CHAN 9561.

Whirligig: (1) Iris Loveridge. Lyrita LP: RCS 30 (m)—not issued. (2) Eric Parkin. Chandos CD: CHAN 9561.

White Peace, The: (1) John McCormack (ten.), Gerald Moore (pf.). HMV SR-10: DA 1791 (m); HMV Ireland IR 299 (m); LP: HQM 1176 (m); HLM 3037 (m); EX 29 0911 3 (m); TC: EX 29 0911 5 (m); Pearl CD: GEMMCDS9188 (m). (2) Kirsten Flagstad (sop.), Waldemar Almo (pf.). Golden Age of Opera LP: EJS 238 (m); Simax

CD: PSC 1824 (m). (3) Frederick Harvey (bar.), Gerald Moore (pf.). HMV LP: CLP 3587 (m); CSD 3587. (4) Norma Burrowes (sop.), Noel Skinner (pf.). Bax Society LP: BAX LP 1 (m)—live recording. (5) Patricia Wright (sop.), Rosemary Barnes (pf.). Continuum CD: CCD 1046.
Winter Legends: (1) Margaret Fingerhut (pf.), London Philharmonic Orchestra, Bryden Thomson. Chandos LP: ABRD 1195; TC: ABTD 1195; CD: CHAN 8484; *Epilogue only*: Free CD with the April 1997 issue of *The Gramophone* magazine: GCD0497. (2) Harriet Cohen (pf.), BBC Symphony Orchestra, 'Sir Adrian Boult' (but probably Clarence Raybould). Connoisseur Cassettes TC: CPL 5 (m).
Winter Waters: (1) Iris Loveridge. Lyrita LP: RCS 12 (m). (2) Eric Parkin. Chandos LP: ABRD 1206; TC: ABTD 1206; CD: CHAN 8496.
Work in Progress: Royal Philharmonic Orchestra, Vernon Handley. Lyrita CD: forthcoming.
Youth: Peter Savidge (bar.), David Owen Norris (pf.). Ensemble TC: TRI 002.

Note: Archival (non-commercial) recordings are held in the BBC Sound Archives, to which there is no public access, and in The National Sound Archive (96 Euston Road, London NW1 2DB), which has a computerized catalogue and offers free listening facilities by appointment.[4]

II. RECORDINGS OF BAX PLAYING THE PIANO

(1) **Bax: Sonata for viola and piano**: Lionel Tertis (va.), Arnold Bax (pf.). Columbia SR: WAX 4949/54 (m)—not issued; Pearl LP: GEMM 201 (m); CD: GEMM CD 9918 (m). Recorded on 27 May 1929, evidentally with some trepidation: 'I have to record my viola sonata with Tertis to-morrow (Oh help!!)'. (From a letter to May Harrison.)
(2) **Delius: Violin Sonata No. 1**: May Harrison (vn.), Arnold Bax (pf.). HMV SR: C 1749/50 (m); Pearl CD: GEMM CD 9436-8; Claremont CD: CD GSE 78-50-47 (m); Symposium CD: Symposium 1140. Recorded on 1 and 26 June 1929.
(3) **Delius: Violin Sonata No. 3**: May Harrison (vn.), probably Arnold Bax (pf.). Symposium CD: Symposium 1075 (m). This was a private recording dating from *c.* 1937 found amongst May Harrison's effects. The labels on the original discs do not give the performers' names, but on hearing the recording over fifty years later Eric Fenby had no hesitation in identifying the pianist as Bax, who had played the piano part at its first performance, on 6 November 1930 at the Wigmore Hall. If the pianist is not Bax, it may be Charles Lynch.

III. RECORDINGS OF BAX SPEAKING

(1) 'Sir Edward Elgar': First broadcast on 'Music Magazine', BBC Home Service, 14 July 1946 (MY1). Excerpt broadcast on 'Music Magazine', Radio 3, on 24 December 1972.
(2) An interview with Eamonn Andrews: Recorded in 1947. Rebroadcast by RTE, 6 November 1983.

[4] A recording of a *Peace Fanfare for Children* was formerly listed in the National Sound Archive catalogue as being by Bax, but the work is actually by Arthur Bliss.

(3) No. 3 in the series 'British Composers': A talk recorded at the Maida Vale Studios on 6 May 1949 (MY1 (X/13389)).[5] Date of first broadcast not traced. Rebroadcast on Radio 3, 3 October 1973. Excerpts broadcast on the Bax centenary programme, 'The Golden Age has Passed', first broadcast on Radio 3 on 6 November 1983. Revised versions rebroadcast on 7 November 1983 and 19 February 1984.

IV. BROADCAST PROGRAMMES ABOUT BAX

(1) '"The Music of Arnold Bax", an appreciation by Robin Hull': Broadcast on 'Music Magazine', BBC Home Service, 2 December 1945.
(2) Tribute to Bax by Julian Herbage: Broadcast on 'Music Magazine', BBC Third Programme, 11 October 1953.
(3) Tribute to Bax: Broadcast on 'Music Magazine', BBC Third Programme, 8 November 1953 (with contributions from Basil Cameron, Scott Goddard and Christopher Whelen).
(4) An introduction to Bax's orchestral music by Christopher Whelen: Broadcast on 'Music Magazine', BBC Third Programme, 17 June 1956.
(5) 'Brazen Romantic' by Lewis Foreman: Broadcast on BBC Radio 3, 8 November 1975.
(6) 'The Golden Age has Passed: A portrait of Sir Arnold Bax (1883-1953)' [centenary programme]: First broadcast on BBC Radio 3, 6 November 1983. Revised versions broadcast on 7 November 1983 and 19 February 1984.
(7) [Centenary tribute to Bax], with Robert Walker and Richard Baker: Broadcast on 'Omnibus', ITV, 6 November 1983.
(8) 'Wind Blown Music from the Sea' by Ian Lace: 'A [radio] programme developed for local broadcasting in Sussex in [September] 1982'.
(9) 'The Garden of Fand': Documentary film broadcast on Ulster Television in 1992. The television company cannot provide the date of this broadcast.
(10) 'The Secret Life of Arnold Bax': A film written and directed by and starring Ken Russell (as Bax), with Glenda Jackson (as Harriet Cohen). Broadcast on 'The South Bank Show', ITV, 22 November 1992. Dubbed into German and broadcast on the WDR Network, April/May1996.
(11) 'Arnold Bax: vom Überschwang zur Verzweiflung': A radio programme written and presented by Christoph Schlüren. Produced on 19 December 1994 and broadcast on 'Montagsthema', BR4, Munich, 16 January 1995.

[5] This is sometimes given as the date of its first broadcast (see Lewis Foreman, 'Arnold Bax: A Discography', *Recorded Sound*, January–April 1968, pp. 282). However, a note in the BBC Written Archives at Caversham indicates that the talk was recorded on that date.

Appendix 4

INDEX OF POETS

The authors of words set to music by Bax, with Catalogue numbers indicated.

Appendix 5
INDEX OF DEDICATEES

The dedicatees of Bax's music are listed alphabetically, with groups of people and some unidentified individuals noted at the end. A few entries have a *floruit* date representing a year or the earliest and latest years in which the person is known to have been alive; a plus sign after a year indicates that the person was then still living. Dedicatees are English unless otherwise indicated.

ALBANESI, Carlo (1856–1926): Italian composer and pianist **205**

ALEXANDER, Arthur (1891–1961): New Zealand composer and pianist **173**

ANTONIETTI, Olga (1889–1965): Anglo-Italian actress; the 'Fiammetta' of *FMY*, pp. 64 ff. **146a**

ATKINS, Sir Ivor (1869–1953): Composer, conductor, and Organist of Worcester Cathedral from 1897 to 1950 **332**

AUSTIN, Frederic (1872–1952): Composer and baritone **201**

AUSTIN, Richard (1903–89): Conductor; son of the preceding **339**

BARBIROLLI, Sir John (1899–1970): Conductor **310**

BARTLETT, Ethel (1900–78) *and* ROBERTSON, Rae (1893–1956): Anglo-Scottish piano duo **287 293 296 298 311**

BAX, Charlotte (1860–1940): Bax's mother **23**

BAX, Elsa (Elsita) (*c.* 1890–1947): Bax's wife **169**

BAX, Evelyn (1887–1984): Bax's sister **116**

BAX, Freda [Winifred Ada] (1883–1928): Bax's cousin **75**

BAYNES, [Helton] Godwin (1882–1943): Friend of Bax; later a disciple of Carl Jung **79**

BEECHAM, Sir Thomas (1879–1961): Conductor **314**

BENCKENDORFF, Count Constantine (Konstantin Kony) (1880–1959): Russian amateur flautist; son of the last Tsarist ambassador to Britain; husband of Maria Korchinska, the harpist **291 337**

BOCQUET, Roland (1878–1940+): Composer and poet (see *FMY*, pp. 36-8) **85**

BOULT, Sir Adrian (1889–1983): Conductor **331**

BRAITHWAITE, Sam Hartley ('Tim') (1883–1947): Composer and pianist **168**

CAMERON, Basil (1885–1975): Conductor **309 344** (original dedicatee)

CARSE, Adam (1878–1958): Composer **324**

CASALS, Pablo (Pau) (1876–1973): Spanish cellist, conductor and composer **321**

[1] The dedicatee's surname does not appear on the score, but in view of Mrs Jellinek's nationality it seems certain that she was the recipient of these *Three Songs from the Norse* (1927).

Collective Dedicatees

Unidentified

Appendix 6

UNFULFILLED PROJECTS AND COMMISSIONS

Bax was often asked to write works for specific occasions, especially after his appointment as Master of the King's Music in February 1942. The following is a chronological list (inevitably incomplete) of works requested or contemplated but never brought to fruition.

1905 Among the papers of Francis Colmer, formerly Bax's private tutor, there is a transcription of a postcard from 'Aureole' (Bax) to 'Col' (Colmer) dated 23 July 1905 in which the young composer thanks his mentor for sending him the words of a 'dramatic cantata' called *Carthon*. This was probably written by Colmer himself and based on the poem of the same title in James MacPherson's spurious *Poems of Ossian*. It tells of the hero Carthon, who is unwittingly slain by his own father, Clessámmor. Bax had presumably been asked by Colmer to set the verses to music. 'It looks very good', he replied, 'and well suited to musical treatment', but there is no evidence that he ever undertook the task.

1913 In a letter to Philip Heseltine dated 27 July 1913, his music teacher at Eton, Colin Taylor, mentioned that he had recently met Bax, who told him that he had 'a splendid "Book" for a ballet and he is longing to get to work on it'. There is no clue to the work's identity, and after *Tamara* (1911) Bax wrote no ballet until 1917. Since the latter was commissioned for a specific occasion it cannot be the one of which he spoke to Taylor.

1918 Bax was commissioned to write a prelude, a song and a ballet for a Plough Club production of Clifford Bax's four-act play *The Sneezing Charm* (1912) at the Royal Court Theatre on 9 June. However, his preoccupation with the break-up of his marriage prevented his complying, and Holst wrote the music instead (H. 143), later adapting it for his opera *The Perfect Fool*.

1921 An *Irish Suite* by Bax is among twenty-five symphonic interludes printed in a separate list of such pieces commissioned for the 1921 season of Diaghilev's Ballets Russes. In one copy of this list held in the Theatre Museum, Covent Garden, nine of the titles have been crossed through in pencil, including Bax's suite, which does not appear in any of the printed programmes relating to works actually performed; nor is there any other evidence to suggest that it was ever played or even written. The *Irish Suite* was evidently a commissioned work that failed to materialize.

c. **1924** In *A Bundle of Time* (p. 93) Harriet Cohen writes:

[Christen Jul] was slowly getting Arnold turned towards writing an opera and considered it of the greatest importance for him to do so 'to cope with something more than the things which only come from fancies and moods'. He thought that most of his friend's troubles had their roots in lack of connection with real life and pointed out that in opera writing there are plenty of practical things to put up with. 'He shall jolly well write a great and romantic opera and Dresden is the place to produce it'.

Christen Pedersen (better known as Christen Jul) was a Danish baritone and playwright, later manager-producer at the Theatre Royal, Copenhagen. His three-act play *Valkyrie* (Copenhagen, 1932) is dedicated to Bax. Nothing came of his plan.

1927 On 3 December the BBC requested Bax to write 'a military band piece in one movement, lasting from twelve to fifteen minutes in performance, in the form of a Concert Overture, a Fantasy, or Symphonic Poem'. In his reply of 5 December Bax wrote:

I fear that I must regretfully decline your invitation . . . I know nothing about this branch of musical composition except that it involves a very special kind of technique that cannot be acquired without an immense amount of practice. This being so I do not feel in any way qualified to accept your proposal.

?1930s In *My Record of Music* (London, 1955), p. 260, Compton Mackenzie recalled that 'Bax once suggested that I should write a libretto for an opera based on the West Highlands to which he was devoted, but I have always been deterred from the experiment of writing the libretto for an opera by the conviction that it would be drowned by over-orchestration or starved for lack of melody'. Bax also told Christopher Whelen that he had once thought of turning one of Clifford Bax's plays (possibly *The Rose without a Thorn*) into an opera.

1932 In a letter to May Harrison dated 4 November, Bax turned down the idea of writing her a violin concerto:

I don't feel that I could start something else in the thick of this cello concerto. Besides violin and orchestra is I think about the most difficult thing that a non-string player could make a mess of. The standard is so high, remembering the Brahms concerto. . . . Do you really think men look their best in bed? How unexpected!!

1936 On 28 August the BBC asked Bax if he would be willing to write an overture and 'perhaps two or three short interludes' for a 'poetic chronicle on the subject of the Knights of the Round table' as part of a Christmas broadcast. This was commissioned presumably on the strength of *Tintagel*, but Bax refused saying that he would 'find it very difficult to recover the peculiar mood of romanticism required', and added: 'I am rather tired musically and do not want to have to work at all strenuously this autumn'. The commission went to Britten on 12 February 1937, and the feature (*King Arthur*) was produced on the following St George's Day. (See also *London Pageant* (**340**) in the main Catalogue.)

1938 In a letter dated 2 May and addressed to a Mrs H. K. (Christine) Ryan, with whom he was having an affair, Bax writes: 'I am getting no ideas for that alarming commission though! But I did not expect to do so'. There is no indication what this might have been. In a letter to Mrs Ryan written eighteen days later, he mentions another unwelcome commission: 'I have just been visited by a perfectly enormous (and panting) French woman who wanted me to write a piece for her daughter who is an expert on the guitar—an instrument of which I know less than nothing. . . '.

1939 In a letter to Edwin Evans dated 24 July, Bax requested that he be released from an undertaking to compose a work for strings for an ISCM concert in December:

The reason is that I do not feel that I could do myself justice at the present time. The perpetual political tension is scarcely conducive to concentration upon creative work, and apart from that I feel that my imagination is getting somewhat weary and needs a rest.

Pre-1940 In his book *Some I knew well* (London, 1951), p. 68, Clifford Bax mentions that W. H. Davies (author of *Autobiography of a Super-Tramp*) once wrote the libretto for a 'Tramp's Opera', for which he considered asking Arnold to write the music, but it is not known whether the composer was approached.

1942 On 23 March Bax wrote to Arthur Bliss, Head of Music at the BBC:

I should like to assist in the brass band scheme by contributing some short piece, if I am able to do so. But I certainly could not undertake to score for the combination as I know nothing whatever about the technique.

Walton was also approached by Bliss, but his answer was much the same: 'I know precisely nothing about brass bands.'

1943 In a letter to Henry Wood dated 16 November (BL Add. MS 56419, f. 83) Bax wrote: 'I am not forgetting the anniversary next year and shall do my best'. This clearly refers to a possible commission for the fiftieth anniversary of the Promenade Concerts, but none was forthcoming.

1946 In an exchange of letters between Jessie Wood and Bax at the beginning of this year (BL Add. MS 56419, ff. 84-90), the possibility of his writing a 'memorial piece' for Sir Henry Wood is discussed. AB to JW (9 January):

. . . now I can get down to the memorial piece. I cannot say anything about it as yet, except that I don't think Masefield's poem is a success and is not long enough to make more than a five minutes or so setting. However I will have another look at it and see if anything occurs to me. I wish you could suggest an alternative. I don't see the necessity for a particularly large orchestra. It might even be for chorus, organ and strings.

In her reply (13 January) JW agrees about Masefield's poem: 'I think it is not a singable text'. AB to JW (21 January):

I am still utterly becalmed for lack of a suitable poem for the little cantata. It is particularly difficult as I am away from my own or any other serious library. So to-day I am writing to my brother—and two other literary friends—appealing for suggestions for the solution of a distinctly difficult problem. I have even suggested to Clifford that he should write a small ode himself, a thing he could do finely, although he does not write verse very often now-a-days. If nothing transpires from all this research I don't know what can be done. I don't suppose it would take me very long to write the music if only the right poem were forth-coming.

AB to JW (27 February):

I have been ill during a great part of this month and unable to do any work—nor have I been successful in finding any suitable poem for the suggested cantata. My brother's young poet sent me an excellent effort yesterday, but it is just not suitable for choral setting. And Clifford himself is seriously ill with two hospital nurses in attendance! So it occurs to me that a "Te Deum" and "Nunc Dimittis" which the BBC commissioned me to write early last year, but have never yet performed (!) might not be inappropriate. They are written for chorus and organ (for cathedral purposes) but could be orchestrated if required.

Although Jessie Wood thought this 'an excellent suggestion', the plan was never carried through (see **359** in the main Catalogue). Bax's suggestion that the slow movement of his Third Symphony might be played at the concert was rejected and Vaughan Williams's *Serenade to Music* was substituted. (For Walton's collaboration with Masefield on a similar project see Michael Kennedy, *Portrait of Walton*, Oxford, 1990, pp. 127-8.)

1940s Professor Aloys Fleischmann once asked Bax to write a work for his amateur orchestra. 'He said that he would like to, and wished he could, but that he was incapable of expressing himself in terms with which an amateur group could cope' ('Arnold Bax', *Recorded Sound*, 29-30, January–April 1968, p. 274, and confirmed in conversation with Professor Fleischmann in October 1991).

1950 An announcement was made in *The Times* for 25 April that Bax had been asked to write an overture for the Festival of Britain in the following year, but the work was never composed, as he explained in a letter to Beatrice Harrison dated 6 January 1951:

I am afraid that it is unlikely that I shall be able to turn out a new piece for you. I have written nothing for nearly two years and have lost the impulse. . . . I was commissioned to write a new orchestral work for the Festival of Britain but have been obliged to cry off as I cannot feel any urge. It is sad and part of getting old, no doubt.

Leaving Bournemouth after hearing his Third Symphony played in 1950, Bax leaned out of the train carriage window and said to the conductor Christopher Whelen: 'I ought perhaps to be thinking of an eighth'. But by this time his increasing reliance on whisky had undermined his ability to concentrate on large-scale composition.

1951 In an internal BBC memorandum dated 9 August, Kenneth Wright describes a visit to Bax to discuss the possibility of his writing something for television. After commenting that Bax had only ever seen television twice—the first time a pre-war transmission in which Harriet Cohen had appeared—Wright continued:

He *would like* to be invited to do something for us provided he has reasonable notice (i.e. a couple of months not a couple of weeks), and in fact became quite enthusiastic saying, 'I see that Television has a tremendously important future'. I suggest we bear him in mind when a suitable chance occurs. He might be worth considering for an important signature tune if Sir Arthur Bliss refuses—I am working on him first as I think he will be better.

In the event there is no evidence that Bax was commissioned.

1952 During the last year of Bax's life, Christopher Whelen, then Musical Director of the Old Vic Company, telephoned him to ask whether he would care to provide incidental music for a 'Coronation' production of Shakespeare's *King Henry VIII*, believed by some to have been written in collaboration with John Fletcher. Whelen recalled that the conversation went something like this:

— 'I have a great favour to ask. Would you consider writing the music for Tyrone Guthrie's production of Shakespeare's "Henry VIII" at the Old Vic?'
— 'I think not—after all he didn't write all of it himself, did he?'
— 'Well, it is rather an important occasion as the Queen is coming. Won't you at least think about it?'
— 'No, I feel I'm past it.'
— 'Are you sure?'
— 'Yes—not even if it was "Henry IX".'

The production finally went ahead with incidental music by Cedric Thorpe Davie.

Appendix 7

LITERARY WORKS AND OCCASIONAL WRITINGS

Titles are arranged chronologically within six broad categories, followed by an alphabetical index:

I. PLAYS

II. POEMS

(a) Published collections
(b) Individually published
(c) Unpublished

III. STORIES

(a) Published collections
(b) Individually published
(c) Unpublished

IV. AUTOBIOGRAPHY

V. MISCELLANEOUS AND OCCASIONAL WRITINGS

(a) About music
(b) About people
(c) Programme notes
(d) Forewords
(e) Book reviews
(f) Talks
(g) Speeches
(h) Interviews
(i) Miscellaneous

VI. LETTERS

VII. ALPHABETICAL INDEX OF LITERARY TITLES

Bax's earliest extant writings date from 1897, when he was fourteen; his last was a speech composed shortly before his death in October 1953. Apart from frivolous juvenilia, his earliest surviving poetry dates from December 1904, two years after his discovery of Yeats and the Celtic world, and can be found written in notebooks under the pseudonym 'Dermod McDermott', with variant spellings of the first name ('Dermid' and 'Dermot'). Two of these poems were published in June 1908 under the name 'Diarmid', but when a collected volume of his verse was published the following year it appeared under the final version of his pen-name, 'Dermot O'Byrne'. Although Bax wrote poems and short stories into the 1940s, the unpublished play *The Grey Swan* (dated spring 1919) seems to be his latest work to bear this name, and his final published collection of verse appeared anonymously in 1923 as *Love Poems of a Musician.* All of his non-fictional writings were written under his real name, with the possible exception of a single review in an Irish periodical (see V. (e) below).

In the following list, full bibliographical descriptions are given for books and significant MSS; briefer writings are noted more simply. In transcribing details of title pages and so forth, a single upright stroke | indicates the start of a new line, a double stroke || a more substantial space between lines.

I. PLAYS

(1) DEIRDRE

Title: 'DÉIRDRE. | A Saga-drama in Five Scenes and a Prologue. [typed] | by Arnold Bax [in Bax's hand]'. Elsewhere Bax writes 'Deirdre' rather than 'Déirdre'; the name can be spelled either way.
Date: 'Glencolumcille, Co. Donegal, | Nov. 18th 1907.' [typed at end of foreword].
Dedication: '"Old unhappy far-off things, | And battles long ago."[1] || TO THE SPIRITS ON THE ULSTER MOUNTAINS.'
Typescript: Lewis Foreman; [62] ff. with typing on the obverses only; [i]: dedication; [ii]: title page + [i]-xi: 'FORE-WORD' with date as noted above + [xii]: half-title page; [xiii]: blank + [1-107] + [ii]: notes on the characters + [ii]: [i] blank, [ii] bearing a pencil sketch of a conductor; the whole affixed by clips into a thin black cloth cover now ragged at the outer edges. Unpublished. For further details see **106** in the main Catalogue.

(2) THE SHADOW OF THE GLEN by J. M. Synge: unfinished translation into Irish Gaelic

Title: *MS A*: '"Sgáile an Ghleann" (Aistriughadh le Ardhgail Bacsa 'g Domhnaill Mac Giohis Easbóig)' ['"Shadow of the Glen" (translation by Arnold Bax and Donnall Gillespie)']. *MS B*: 'Sgáile an Ghleann' [in Irish script].
Manuscript: *MS A*: UCC; [18] ff. (writing on obverses of folios only); 9 pp.; plain paper (259 × 202); the title and translation are written entirely in Irish script. *MS B*: Privately owned (formerly owned by Harriet Cohen, then by Colin Scott-Sutherland, then sold at Sotheby's on 26 May 1994 and bought for an anonymous client by Bertram Rota); 7 ff; [13] pp; first three and a half lines in pencil, the rest in ink; f. 7^{v} has an untitled poem in Gaelic. The

[1] From William Wordsworth's 'The Solitary Reaper' in *Memorials of a Tour in Scotland* (1803).

MS is bound in after 'Told on a stormy night' (see III. (c) below). Unpublished.
Note: This undated attempt at a translation of Synge's play was started in collaboration with Donnall Gillespie, of whom Bax wrote: '[He] was a rather particular friend of mine when he was a "wee fella" . . .' (LF, p. 258; see also his poems 'To Donnall' and 'To my Little Friend Donnall Gillespie in Glencolumcille'); he later became a schoolmaster. When they met in Belfast in 1929, they had not seen each other since 1913, the latest year in which this translation could have been made.

(3) ON THE HILL

Title: 'ON THE HILL | *A Play in One Act* | *by DERMOT O'BYRNE*'.
Dedication: '*(To Molly and Padraic Colum)*'.
Publication: In *The Irish Review* (February 1913), pp. 648-63. In blue wrappers with yapped edges, uniform with all other issues of this periodical.

(4) RED OWEN

Title: *Upper cover*: 'RED OWEN | A PLAY IN 3 ACTS | By | Dermot O'Byrne' [upper cover]. *Title page*: 'RED OWEN | BY | DERMOT O'BYRNE | Author of | "Wrack," "Children of the Hills," etc.'
Dedication: 'TO | LENNOX ROBINSON'.
Publication: 'Dublin | The Talbot Press Limited | 89 Talbot Street | 1919.'; [1-4] + 5-51; p. [1]: dedication; [2]: blank; [3]: title page; [4]: list of characters. Issued in blue paper boards with blue-grey mottled wrappers. For further details see **170** in the main Catalogue.

(5) THE GREY SWAN

Title: 'THE GREY SWAN | By | DERMOT O'BYRNE. | Spring 1919' [typed].
Typescript: Privately owned; typed on the obverses only of each leaf; [vi] + [1], 2-25, [26] + [i]; [ii]: blank; [iii, v]: 'Note to "THE GREY SWAN".', the final paragraph written in Bax's hand; [iv, vi]: blank; [26] has the date April 29, 1919. At the top right-hand corner Bax has written in his Fellows Road address. Unpublished except for the introduction and final chorus: in Lewis Foreman (ed.), *Dermot O'Byrne: Poems by Arnold Bax* (London, 1979), pp. 14-15, 71.

Note: None of Bax's four completed plays has ever been staged or broadcast.

II. POEMS

(a) *Published collections*

(1) SEAFOAM AND FIRELIGHT

Title: *Upper cover*: 'THE ORPHEUS SERIES [space] NO.2 || SEAFOAM AND FIRELIGHT || BY | DERMOT O'BYRNE'. *Title page*: 'SEA-FOAM [*sic*]| AND | FIRELIGHT | BY | • DERMOT • O'BYRNE •' [the whole t.p. surrounded by a border with Celtic design].
Publication: 'W. BUDD & CO. | THE ORPHEUS PRESS | 68, ROSSLYN HILL, HAMPSTEAD, N.W.'; n.d. but 1909; [1-4] + 5-34 + [ii]: p. [1]: title page; [2]: '*Copyright.* | *Entered at Stationers' Hall.*'; [3]: contents page; [4]: dedication 'To G.' (perhaps Gladys Lees, for whom see Appendix 5); [i]: an asterisk only; [ii]: note about the Orpheus Series. Issued in pale blue-grey boards with canvas backing (priced 1/2d) and in dark green paper wrappers with Celtic design (priced 8d).[2]

Contents: In Carna (p. 5); To Ireland (p. 6); The Peasant (p. 8); By a Faery Lough (p. 11); A Poet's Immortality (p. 12); To Eire (p. 13); In Galway Bay (p. 14); To the Belovèd (p. 15); The Glen of Starry Peace (p. 17); Sonnet (p. 18); The Music of Man (p. 19); A Quiet Landscape (p. 21); On the Strand (p. 23); The Valley of the Bells (p. 24); The Proud Harper (p. 26); The Emigrants (p. 27); On Pipe-Music heard in a London Street (p. 28); A Country Song (p. 29); The Aran Islands (p. 30); Behind the Wind (p. 31); Fintan, the Spirit of Irish Song (p. 32); The Ships (p. 34).

Note: 'On Pipe-Music heard in a London Street' also in *Hallé Magazine* (August 1950), p. 24. A MS of 'Behind the Wind', formerly owned by Colin Scott-Sutherland, was sold at Sotheby's on 26 May 1994 and bought for an anonymous client by Bertram Rota.

(2) A DUBLIN BALLAD AND OTHER POEMS

Title: *Upper cover*: 'A Dublin Ballad | AND OTHER POEMS | BY DERMOT O'BYRNE'. *Title page*: 'A Dublin Ballad | and Other Poems | By Dermot O'Byrne'.
Publication: *Upper cover:* 'DUBLIN: THE CANDLE PRESS | PRICE ONE SHILLING'. *Title page*: 'The Candle Press | 44 Dawson Street, Dublin | 1918 (poetry booklets No. 2)'; *front paste-down endpaper*: 'Trí candle foro na each odorcha, fír, aicned, ecna. [in Irish script] | Three candles that light up every darkness: Truth, Nature, Knowledge. | The Triads of Ireland.' *Back of title page*: '*425 copies have been printed. The type has been distributed*[.] || PRINTED BY COLM O-LOCHLAINN, DUBLIN.' There is no contents page. Issued in brown card covers; sewn with thread.

[2] The bibliographical details are taken from a copy issued in boards; I have never seen a copy of the issue with wrappers.

Note: Although 425 copies were printed, this collection was suppressed by the British censor in Ireland and it was never officially published.

Contents: A Dublin Ballad—1916 (p. 5); In Memoriam My Friend Patrick H. Pearse (Ruler of Ireland for one week) (p. 8); After (p. 11); In Glencullen (p. 14); Shells at Oranmore (April 1916) (p. 16); Kilmasheogue—1916 (p. 17); Martial Law in Dublin (p. 19); The East Clare Election 1828-1917 (p. 20); The East Clare Election 1917 (p. 22).

Note: 'A Dublin Ballad—1916' also in Edna C. Fitzhenry (comp.), *Nineteen-Sixteen: An Anthology* (Dublin: Browne & Nolan Ltd., 1935, 1966), pp. 41-3; Padraic Colum (ed.), *An Anthology of Irish Verse* (New York: Liveright Publishing Corporation, 1948), pp. 372-3 (in this rev. edn. only); *Poetry Ireland,* 13 (April 1951), pp. 18-19; Donagh Mac Donagh and Lennox Robinson (comps.), *The Oxford Book of Irish Verse* (Oxford: OUP, 1958), pp. 205-7; Frank O'Connor, *A Book of Ireland* (London and Glasgow: William Collins Sons and Co. Ltd., 1959), pp. 123-5; Lewis Foreman (ed.), *Dermot O'Byrne: Poems by Arnold Bax* (London: Thames Publishing, 1979), p. 62; 'Shells at Oranmore' and 'Martial Law in Dublin' also in Padraic Colum, op. cit., pp. 44-5.; Lewis Foreman, op. cit., p. 65.

(3) LOVE POEMS OF A MUSICIAN

Title: 'Love Poems | of a Musician' [published anonymously].
Publication: 'Cecil Palmer | Forty-nine | Chandos | Street | W.C.2.'; *publisher's imprint*: 'FIRST| EDITION | 1923 | COPY | RIGHT'; [1-6], 7-53, [54]. Issued in pale grey paper-covered boards with a paper label on the front, a cream linen backing, and grey dust-jacket.

Contents: A Summer Memory (p. 9); To a Russian Girl (p. 11); Nympholept (p. 12); Mirrors (p. 14); In the Night (p. 15); Heart's Desire (p. 16); Sanctuary (p. 17); At 'Tristan and Isolde' (p. 18); At Parting (p. 19); The Battle of the Somme (p. 20); Stephen's Green (p. 22); In Donegal (p. 23); Love and Reason (p. 24); Woman and Artist (p. 25); The Immortality of Form (p. 26); The Guest House (p. 28); The Prison House (p. 29); Oblation (p. 30); A Moment (p. 32); Love (p. 33); Epithalamium (p. 34); A Ghost (p. 35); The Labour of Love (p. 36); Enigma (p. 37); Transitional (p. 38); Shiplake (p. 39); Consolation (p. 40); A Girl's Music (p. 41); Panic (p. 42); Irony (p. 43); Cherry Blossom (p. 44); Illusion (p. 45); Helplessness (p. 46); Tintagel Castle (p. 47); Too Late (p. 48); The Emigrant (p. 49); Glamour (p. 50); A Thought of Ireland at Sunset (p. 52); An Old Man's Chatter (p. 53).

Note: A MS of 'The Emigrant' formerly belonging to Colin Scott-Sutherland was sold at Sotheby's on 26 May 1994 and bought for an anonymous client by Bertram Rota.

(4) DERMOT O'BYRNE. POEMS BY ARNOLD BAX

Title: *Dust-jacket (upper cover)*: 'Dermot O'Byrne | Selected | poems | of | Arnold | Bax | edited by | Lewis Foreman'. *Spine (head to tail)*: 'Dermot O'Byrne poems by Arnold Bax Foreman (ed) Thames'. *Half-title page*: 'Dermot O'Byrne | Poems | by | Arnold Bax'. *Title page*: 'DERMOT O'BYRNE | poems by | Arnold Bax | *collected, selected and edited* | *by* | LEWIS FOREMAN || *together with two previously unpublished* | *songs by Bax to his own words*'.

Publication: 'Thames Publishing | London | 1979'; *verso*: publisher's imprint including ISBN number 0 905210 11 5; 'Printed by | Bookmag, Henderson Road, Inverness'; [1-6] + 7-96: [1]: half title; [2]: blank; [3]: title page; [4]: publisher's imprint; [5]: contents pages; [6]: list of illustrations; 7: acknowledgments; 8: note on 'Bax's spelling of Irish names'; 9-10: editor's foreword; 11-22: more preliminary sections.

Contents: Dedication (p. 23); A Summer Memory (p. 24); A Ghost (p. 26); The Aran Islands (p. 27); On the Strand (p. 28); A Poet's Immortality (p. 29); Déirdre's Spinning Song (p. 30); An Old Man's Chatter (p. 31); At the Last (p. 32; The Glen of Starry Peace (p. 33); The Lake of Stars (p. 34); Sundered Dreams (p. 35); The Song of the Old Fiddler (p. 36); The Emigrant (p. 37); By a Faery Lough (p. 38); To the Beloved (p. 39); From Old Days (p. 40); On Pipe-Music heard in a London Street (p. 41); Green Magic (p. 42); To my little Friend Donnall Gillespie (p. 43); Allurement (p. 44); To a Russian Girl (p. 45); Out of Faeryland (p. 46); In the Night (p. 47); A Lullaby (p. 48); A Summer in Exile (p. 49); Certainty (p. 50); The End of a Romance (p. 51); Morning in Connemara (p. 52); The Burden of Memory (p. 53); Woman and Artist (p. 53); Tryst (p. 54); Nympholept (p. 55); Consolation (p. 56); The New Devil (p. 57); A Girl's Music (p. 58); Crisis (p. 59); The Guest House (p. 60); The Irish Mail (p. 61); A Dublin Ballad–1916 (p. 62); In Glencullen (p. 64); Shells at Oranmore (p. 65); Kilmasheogue–1916 (p. 66); In a Back-Street (p. 67); Amersham (p. 68); Darkness (p. 69); Man and Wife (p. 69); Tintagel Castle (p. 70); The Grey Swan: final chorus (p. 71); To F (p. 72). Two songs by Bax to his own words (p. 73); Bax's settings of his own words (p. 74); When we are lost (p. 75); Glamour (p. 80).

(5) IDEALA (NEREID). SOME EARLY LOVE LETTERS AND POEMS BY ARNOLD BAX

Title: *Upper cover and title page*: 'IDEALA (Nereid) || Some early love letters and poems | by | Arnold Bax || edited with an introduction | by | COLIN SCOTT-SUTHERLAND || privately printed | Crail 1995' [two white labels pasted on]. Page with handwritten note from the editor dated February 1996. *Half-title page*: 'IDEALA | (Nereid) | Some early love | letters and poems | *** | ARNOLD BAX'.

Typescript/Photocopy: 84 ff. in all; 168 unnumbered pages, some with typed material, some with photocopied handwritten material, some with photocopied photographs (some in colour), some blank. This collection was privately issued (not for sale) in dark green paper wrappers with melanex outer wrappers and ring-binding.

Contents: Introductory essay by the editor; reproductions of photographs and printed programmes; poems by Bax extracted from the otherwise unpublished notebook described in II. (c) below: A Poet's Immortality, Ideala, When we are lost, In the House of Memory, A Girl's May-Eve, To an Irish child, Love in the Noonday, Intermezzo, The Isles of Arran, Flames, A Song of the Western Sea, To the Beloved, Flames and Dreams, Glencolumcille, Parenthesis, In an Orchard, A Donegal Twilight, In a Bohemian Forest, [A Sea Dream], Caoine for Eire, [Above the dark dome of the forest], The Eyes of the Stars, The Song of the Old Fiddler, [This for the Maiden with the Daffodil], A Girl's Music, Enigma, Transitional, Cherry-Blossom, A Ghost, Sanctuary, The Immortality of Form, Love and Reason, Sanctuary, In the Night, Heart's Desire, Shiplake, A Moment, In Donegal, Nympholept, A Thought of Ireland at Sunset, A Summer Memory; letters to Isobel Hodgson, Mary Field and Harriet Cohen; Gougane Barra and St Senans on the Shannon: extract from the memoirs of Tilly Fleischmann.

(b) *Individually published*

(1) The Soul's answer: *Orpheus*, 5 (January 1909), p. 16.
(2) Glamour: *Orpheus*, 12 (October 1910), pp. 202-3. Also in Lewis Foreman (ed.), *Dermot O'Byrne: Poems by Arnold Bax*, pp. 80-95.
(3) To Deirdre: *Orpheus*, 13 (January 1911), p. 249.
(4) Certainty: *Orpheus*, 14 (April 1911), p. 282.
(5) Exile: *The Irish Review* (April 1913), p. 68.
(6) In a Bohemian Forest: CSS, pp. 14-15 (extract only); also in Lewis Foreman (ed.), *Farewell, my Youth and Other Writings by Arnold Bax* , p. 173.
(7) Love and the Sea: CSS, pp. 70-1 (extract only).
(8) This for the maiden with the daffodil: CSS, p. 47.
(9) When we are lost: Lewis Foreman (ed.), *Dermot O'Byrne*, pp. 75-9.
(10) Leannán-Sídhe: This poem is found in a letter to Clifford Bax dated 6 March 1918 (see LF, pp. 159-60). It seems to be part of a longer poem based upon 'The Sickbed of Cuchulain'. The title is the Irish Gaelic for 'phantom lover'.
(11) Untitled limerick referring to Stacy Aumonier's cricketing prowess, beginning 'With regard to our free-hitting Stacy', and attributed to Arnold Bax in Clifford Bax's *Inland Far* (London, 1925), p. 182.
(12) 'The "Korshjem-Saga" translated from the Icelandic by A. B., with notes by Sir Gaga Thompson, F. R. S., F. S. A. &c.', Clifford Bax (ed.), *The Old Broughtonian Cricket Weeks*, 3 (London: The Favil Press, 1927), pp. 44-9. This is a parody of an Icelandic saga, with 'scholarly' notes at the end dated October 1926 and attributed to 'Gaga Thompson, *Dust and Cobweb Club, W. 1.*'
(13) To M. (poem beginning 'Ah why did summer stay so long?'): This occurs in a letter to Mary Gleaves dating from the 1930s (see LF, pp. 256-7).

(c) *Unpublished* [3]

(1) [NOTEBOOK]

Manuscript: Colin Scott-Sutherland; untitled bound volume containing 92 holograph poems written on both sides of 89 folios + 1 page blank; the pages are unnumbered. The volume is bound in red leather with the name 'Lorrie' embossed on the upper cover in gold. On the flyleaf is inscribed: 'Lorrie | from | June | Xmas 1904'.[4] The poems are dated between December 1904 and June 1907 and are mostly arranged in chronological order, suggesting that they are fair copies collected together at a later date and written into the blank volume that had been given to Bax as a Christmas present in 1904. Most of the poems are dated (see below), and many of them bear the name 'Dermod McDermott', with variant spellings 'Dermid', 'Dermot' or 'D. M^{c} D.' Some of the poems from this volume are reproduced in Colin Scott-Sutherland, *Ideala (Nereid)*. *Photocopy*: BL (MS FACS 834), from which the folio numbers listed below are derived.

Contents: Two Roundels (f. 2; 'December 23rd'); In the Forest (f. 2^{v}; 'Dec 4th'); To Donegal (ff. 3-4; 'Dec 26th 1904'); Villanelle (f. 4^{v}; 'Dec 29th'); Villanelle (f. 5; 'Dec 29th'); Dream in the Firelight (ff. 5^{v}-6^{v}; 'Dec 8th 1904'); Triolets (f. 7; 'SUNDAY EVENING. Jan 1. 1905.'); A Song of two Stars. Villanelle (f. 7^{v}; 'Freshwater. I.W. Jan 10th 1905.'); When we are lost (f. 8; 'Jan 24th 1905'); Flames (ff. 8^{v}-9; 'January 23rd 1905'); Ideala (ff. 9^{v}-10^{v}; 'Jan 31 [?] 1905'); A Song of two Hearts (f. 11; 'Feb 8th 1905'); Spring-Night (ff. 12-13; 'February 19th'); In the Hills of Dreamland (f. 13^{v}; 'Feb 22 [or 27?] 1905'); A God's Play (f. 14; 'March 3rd 1905'); A dreary Landscape (f. 14^{v}; 'March 5th 1905'); Intermezzo (f. 15; 'March 23rd 1905'); Perpetuum Mobile (f. 15^{v}; 'Aranmore. April 8th 1905'); Caoine for Eri (f. 16; 'Leanane [Leenane] April 23rd'); To + + + (f. 16^{v}; 'Dugoort Achill April 26th'); A Song of Mockery (f. 17; 'Sligo May 1st'); Midnight in the Forest (f. 17^{v}; 'Galloway April 9th'); The Lament of Aengus Ogue (f. 18; 'Letterfrack. Co Galway. April 14th'); A Sea-Dream (f. 19; 'Aranmore April 8th 1905'); To Frau Wittich (f. 20; 'To Frau Wittich as Isolde May 25th 1905'); The Question (f. 20^{v}; n.d.); The Eyes of the Stars (f. 21; 'June 18th'); Love in the Noonday (f. 22; n.d.); To the World-Goddess (ff. 22^{v}-23; 'June 23rd 1905'); The shadowy Sleepers (ff. 23^{v}-24; 'July 18th 1905'); The Army of the Dawn (f. 24^{v}; 'July 20th'); After Sunset in Connemara (f. 25^{v}; 'April 1905.'); The End of all the Dreams of the World (ff. 26-28^{v}; 'July 27th 1905'); To an Irish Child | I (f. 29; 'July 27th'); To an Irish Child | II (f. 29^{v}; July 31th [*sic*] 1905'); The Singing of the Wind (f. 30; 'Aug 3rd 1905'); To a Wayfarer (ff. 30^{v}-31; n.d.); The Song amid the Dew (ff. 31^{v}-32; 'Mallaig. Aug 13th 1905'); The Lake of Stars (f. 33; 'Mallaig Aug 14th 1905.'); Flaming Day (f. 34; n.d.); The everlasting Battle (ff. 34^{v}-35; 'August 1905 I o. Skye'); Fallen Gods (ff. 35^{v}-36;

[3] That is to say in this precise form; but some of the poems in the collections detailed here later appeared in published volumes of verse.

[4] Letters from Francis Colmer, the Bax children's private tutor, reveal that nicknames were rife in the family: Arnold was called 'Ozal', 'Aureole', 'Orrie' and 'Lorrie'; Clifford was called 'Budge'. 'June' (surname unknown) was one of several girls at the RAM with whom Bax became infatuated as a student.

'Tarbert Harris [n.d.]'); A Donegal Twilight (f. 36^{v}; 'Carrick, C^{o} Donegal Sept 25th 1905.'); Cross-roads (ff. 37-38; 'Nov 1905'); A Song from the Western Sea (Twelve line Roundel) (f. 38^{v}; 'Dec 7th 1905'); Two Improvizations [*sic*]: Winter Morning in the Garden (ff. 39-40^{v}; 'Jan 8th 1906') *and* In the Forest. Thursday afternoon Jan 4th 1906 ('To Godwin [Baynes]') (ff. 40^{v}-42; 'Jan. 1906'); The Return of St Bride (ff. 42^{v}-43^{v}; 'February 14th 1906'); In an Orchard (f. 44; 'February 16th 1906'); The Gift of God (f. 45; 'April 8th 1906'); The Isles of Arran (f. 46; 'Galway April 14th 1906'); Storm on the Lough (ff. 46^{v}-47; 'Connemara. April 1906'); The Island of Storms (ff. 47^{v}-48; 'Delphi. Connemara. April 1906.'); In Galway Bay (ff. 48^{v}-49; 'Galway April 10th 1906'); In the Meadows of Heartland (ff. 49^{v}-50; 'June 15th 1906.'); A Girl's May-Eve (ff. 50^{v}-52; 'Sligo April 1906'); A Lament (ff. 52^{v}-53; 'In the New Forest July [1906]'); Sea Spray (f. 53^{v}; 'Pollasuill Bay. Aug 12th 1906'); Sundered Dreams (f. 54; 'Tramore Strand Aug 13th'); Art and Imagination (ff. 54^{v}-55^{v}; 'Coleraine August 10th 1906'); The Reason Why (f. 56; 'Tramore Strand Aug. 13th 1906'); The Prayer of the Lay Brother on the Threshold (ff. 56^{v}-59^{v}; 'Dunfaneghy Aug 17th 1906'); The Ship of the Spirit (f. 60; 'Horn Head. August 18th 1906'); The Spirit's Companion (ff. 61-62; 'Dunfaneghy Aug 20th 1906.'); To the Beloved (ff. 62^{v}-63^{v}; 'Glenties August 27th 1906'); Dusk and Dawn (f. 64; 'Glencolumcille Sept 4th 1906'); Glencolumcille (ff. 65-67; 'Glencolumcille Sept 5th 1906'); In the House of Memory (f. 67^{v}; 'Sligo Sept 15th 1906.'); In the House of Memory II (BL copy misfoliated 68^{r}, 70^{v}, 71^{r}; 'Sept 24th 1906.'); Beneath the Hills of God (ff. 68^{v}-69; 'Dunfaneghy August 1906'); To a Dream-rhythym [*sic*] (ff. 69^{v}-70; 'Carrick Sept 1906'); Sonnet (f. 71^{v}; 'Nov 19th 1906'); Flames and Dreams (f. 72; 'Nov 24th 1906'); In the Lord's House (f. 73; 'Nov 29th 1906.'); The Secrets of the Sea (f. 74; 'Morthoe Dec 9th 1906'); A Snow-Dream (f. 75; 'Jan 5th 1907'); Parenthesis (f. 76; 'Jan 7th 1907'); 'Mademoiselle de Maupin' and her Lovers (f. 77; 'Jan 20th 1907'); In a Bohemian Forest (ff. 77^{v}-78^{v}; *Note*: BL copy incomplete); At Wendover (f. 79; 'Wendover October 1906'); The Spirit to the Body (f. 80; 'Dresden April 1907') The Home of the Heart (f. 80^{v}; 'Glenties June 8th 1907'); Into the Mist (f. 81; 'Glenties June 10th 1907'); The Voice of the Sea (f. 82; 'Glencolumcille June 10th 1907'); The Sea's Singer (f. 83; 'Glencolumcille June 11th 1907'); A Mad Song (f. 84; 'Glencolumcille June 10th 1907'); On a windy Night (f. 84^{v}; 'Glencolumcille, June 12th 1907'); A Poet's Immortality (f. 85; 'Glencolumcille June 13th 1907'); Love and the Sea (ff. 85^{v}-86; 'Glencolumcille June 14th 1907'); A Sea-Prayer (ff. 86^{v}-87; 'Glencolumcille June 15th 1907'); On a storm-night (f. 87^{v}; 'Glencolumcille June 15th 1907'); At the Last (f. 88; 'Glencolumcille June 16th 1907'); The Song of the Old Fiddle[r] (f. 89; 'Glencolumcille June 18th 1907').

(2) POEMS

Title: 'Poems.'

Manuscript/Typescript: *Carbon copy*: Privately owned (formerly by Gladys Lees, then by Evelyn Bax); bound volume containing 52 typescript and 26 handwritten poems. The typescript pages are on the obverse sides only of each leaf, the reverses blank; the handwritten pages occupy both sides of each leaf; t.p. + [1]-2 + 3-64 + [65-92]. The five classificatory title pages ('I. Songs of Quietness', etc.) are unnumbered. Total number of folios: 50 (including a p. '38a'). Pages [1]-2 contain a 'Dedication. (To C.L.B.)' [i.e. Clifford Lea Bax] in verse and dated 'Glencolumcille, June 21st 1907'. The handwritten poems are all separately dated, and since the chronology is without any kind of order they are all obviously fair copies made from earlier versions. A pocket is sewn into the back containing two extra manuscript poems. The volume is bound in light blue cloth with the initials G. N. L. (i.e. Gladys Noel Lees, for whom see Appendix 5) embossed diagonally on the lower right-hand corner of the upper cover. *Original typescript*: Privately owned (formerly by Dermot Bax, then sold at Sotheby's in 1977); this disbound top copy of the carbon copy detailed above lacks the handwritten additions. It is dated 'August 1907'.

Contents: Dedication (p. 1); Songs of Quietness: The Glen of Starry Peace (p. 3); In Galway Bay (p. 4); The Eyes of the Stars (p. 5); In the Hills of Dreamland (p. 6); To the Beloved (p. 7); A Poet's Immortality (p. 9); At the Last (p. 10); An English Landscape (Wendover) (p. 11); A Lament (New Forest) (p. 12); The Lake of Stars (A dawn-dream) (p. 14); In an Orchard (p. 15); The Gift of God (p. 16); After Sunset (Connemara) (p. 17); Songs of Storm: On a Windy Night (p. 18); On a Stormy Night (p. 19); The Everlasting Battle (p. 20); Flames and Dreams (p. 21); The Ship of the Spirit (p. 23); Our Home (p. 24); The Island of Storms (p. 25); Songs of the Western Seas: Sea Spray (p. 27); The Voice of the Sea (p. 28); Perpetuum Mobile (p. 29); The Flowers of the Sea (p. 30); Love and the Sea (p. 31); A Sea-Prayer (p. 32); The Sea's Singer (p. 33); The Secrets of the Sea (p. 34); From Irish Hills and Cabins: The Song of a Madman (p. 35); Fintan, the Spirit of Irish Song (p. 36); By a Faery Lough (p. 37); The Aran Islands (p. 38); A Donegal Twilight (p. 38a); The Singing in the Wind (p. 39): Into the Mist (p. 40); A Girl's May-Eve (p. 41); Sundered Dreams (p. 43); A Mad Song (p. 44); The Song of the Old Fiddler (p. 45);To a Wayfarer (p. 46); To an Irish Child (p. 47); Caoine for Eire (Salruck pipe-graveyard) (p. 49); Glencolumcille (p. 50); To a Dream-Rhythm (p. 52); The Rune of Columcille (p. 54); Hill-Magic (p. 56); Miscellaneous Lyrics: 'Half a Note from Blake' (p. 57); A Dreary Landscape (p. 58); To Frau Marie Wittich as 'Isolda' (p. 59); Hymn to Night (p. 60); Sonnet to a French Composer of Songs (p. 62); Shadowed Godhead (p. 63). *Manuscript additions*: To Deirdre ('In Russia June 12th 1910.'); Morning in Connemara ('March 22nd 1911.'); The Tower of Love ('Jan 5th 1910.'); Out of Faeryland ('Jan 10th 1910.'); In the Night ('Jan. 29th 1910.'); Heart's Desire ('Feb 8th 1910.'); In Sanctuary ('Feb 15th; 1910.') Dream Armour ('Jan 23rd | 1910.'); Undine ('Feb 1910.'); At 'Tristan und Isolde' (Covent Garden Feb. 1910) ('Feb 25th 1910.'); Lullaby ('March 21st 1910.'); Earth-Love ('March 30th 1910.'); Pastel. In Regent's Park ('Oct 22nd 1909.'). A Rain Dream ('Nov. 1908'); To my Little Friend Donnall Gillespie in Glencolumcille ('Dec 20th 1909.'); From Old Days ('Nov. 1908.'); In the After-time ('Sept. 1908.'); The End of a Romance ('July 5th | 1910.'); To Donnall ('Feb 20th 1911.'); The Shadow of Memory ('March 1911.'); Trance ('Feb 28th 1911.'); The Lost Ship ('May 26th 1911.'); In an Old Forest (unfinished) ('1910.'); Tryst ('Dec 1911.').

Loose in a pocket at the back: The Reproof ('March 18th'); The Twentieth Year ('June 26th').

(3) OTHER POEMS

(i) Parody of Sir Henry Newbolt's 'The Fighting Téméraire': This forty-eight-line burlesque occurs in a letter to Mary Field (for whom see **84**) dating from *c.* 1908. (See Richard MacNutt sale catalogue 102, p. 7, item 9.)
(ii) Mary Field informed Colin Scott-Sutherland that '[Bax] once told me he had written a poem about me in the lovely dress I wore for my first London recital [*c.* 1908-9]'. In the early 1940s Miss Field wrote to Bax asking if he could let her have a copy of it. On 29 June, in a letter 'written very badly with obviously a shaky hand on what looks like lavatory paper', he replied: 'I wish I could send you the poem about you in your white dress with the gold girdle: but I don't remember it in any sort of detail'.
(iii) Typewritten poems with the dedication 'For Rosalind [Thornycroft], March 25th 1913'. Typescript owned by Chloë Green (née Baynes); t.p. + 17 pp.; 4to paper. I am grateful to the owner for details of this collection, which I have not seen.

Contents: At 'Tristan und Isolde'; The Burden of Memory; Connemara; In Glencree; The Kingdom of the Daffodil; The Lost Ship; Morning in Connemara; Nympholept; Oblation; Sanctuary; Summer Memory; To a Child; To an Irish Child.

(iv) Two poems: (a) Thunderstorm; (b) Rue. *Date*: 'Storrington Aug 1945' (on each MS). Owned by Dennis Andrews (MS formerly owned by Christopher Whelen); each poem is written in ink on a sheet of writing paper (185 × 113). 'Thunderstorm' was published in LF, p. 337. These are Bax's latest known poems.

Note: Further miscellaneous unpublished poems are listed in the alphabetical index starting on p. 355.

III. STORIES

(a) *Published collections*

(1) CHILDREN OF THE HILLS

Title: *Title page*: 'CHILDREN OF | THE HILLS | TALES AND SKETCHES | OF WESTERN IRELAND IN THE | OLD TIME AND THE PRESENT DAY | DERMOT O'BYRNE'. *Label at head of spine*: '[rule] | CHILDREN | OF THE | HILLS | [ornament] | DERMOT | O'BYRNE | [rule]'.
Dedication: 'TO | ELSITA' [Elsa Bax, the author's wife]
Publication: 'MAUNSEL & CO. LTD. | DUBLIN AND LONDON' [n.d. but 1913]; [vii] + [1], 2-148: [i]: half-title page: '(CHILDREN OF | THE HILLS)'; [ii]: blank; [iii]: title page; [iv]: blank; [v]: dedication; [vi]: note about previous publication of some of the stories; [vii]: contents page; [viii]: blank; at the foot of p. 148 is printed 'WILLIAM BRENDON AND

SON, LTD. | PRINTERS, PLYMOUTH'. Issued in light brown boards with canvas backing.

Contents: Hunger (p. 1); Through the Rain (p. 20); The Call of the Road (p. 30); "Seanoidín" (p. 55); The Lifting of the Veil (p. 88); Ancient Dominions (p. 100); The Death of Macha Gold-Hair (p. 136).

Note: 'Hunger' previously published in *The Irish Review* (May 1912), pp. 140-51. 'Through the Rain' in *Orpheus*, 15 (July 1911), pp. 301-5. 'The Call of the Road' in *The Irish Review* (December 1912), pp. 519-33. 'The Lifting of the Veil' in *Orpheus*, 20 (October 1912), pp. 105-10; also in *Horror by Lamplight* (London: Chancellor Press, 1993). 'The Death of Macha Gold-Hair' in *Orpheus*, 12 (July 1910), pp. 211-17; also in Peter Haining (ed.), *Great Irish Tales of the Unimaginable* (London: Souvenir Press, 1994). 'Ancient Dominions' also in Lewis Foreman (ed.), *Farewell, my Youth and Other Writings by Arnold Bax*, pp. 135-57.

(2) THE SISTERS AND GREEN MAGIC

Title: *Upper cover*: 'THE SISTERS | AND | GREEN MAGIC. || DERMOT O'BYRNE.' *Spine (from tail to head)*: 'THE SISTERS AND GREEN MAGIC. DERMOT O'BYRNE.' [the whole embossed in gold]. *Title page*: 'THE ORPHEUS SERIES [space] No.VIII. || THE SISTERS | AND | GREEN MAGIC || by | DERMOT O'BYRNE'.
Date: 'The Sisters': 'ST. PETERSBURG. *April 23rd*, 1910.'; 'Green Magic': 'GWEEDORE, Co. DONEGAL. | *September*, 1909.'
Dedication: '*To A. E.*' (George Russell).
Publication: '[Orpheus Press] 3, Amen Corner | Paternoster Row, London, E. C.' [n.d. but 1912]; [1-4] + 5-76 + [ii]: [1]: title page; [2]: blank; [3]: dedication; [4]: blank; 5-49: The Sisters; 50-76: Green Magic; [i]: list of books in the Orpheus Series; [ii]: 'LONDON | WOMEN'S PRINTING SOCIETY, LTD., | BRICK STREET, PICCADILLY.' Issued in dark blue boards (priced 2/6d).

(3) WRACK AND OTHER STORIES

Title and publication: *Upper cover*: 'WRACK | AND OTHER STORIES || Dermot O'Byrne. [reproduction of Bax's pseudonymous signature] [rule]'. Spine (at head): 'WRACK | O'BYRNE || THE | TALBOT | PRESS'. *Dust-jacket (upper cover)*: 'By Dermot O'Byrne | [rule] | Wrack | and Other Stories | [16-line blurb about the stories].' *Dust-jacket (lower cover)*: Advertisement for 'NEW | TALBOT PRESS | BOOKS'. *Spine*: 'WRACK | AND OTHER | :: STORIES :: || DERMOT | O'BYRNE || 3/6 | NET || THE TALBOT | PRESS LTD | T. FISHER | UNWIN LTD.' *Title page*: 'WRACK | AND OTHER STORIES | BY | DERMOT O'BYRNE | [publisher's device with Celtic design] | DUBLIN | The Talbot Press Ltd. | 89 Talbot Street | LONDON | T. Fisher Unwin Ltd. | 1 Adelphi Terrace | 1918.'

Publication: [viii] + 1-195: [i]: half-title page; [ii]: titles of two other works '*By the same Author*'; [iii]: title page; [iv]: Printed at | THE TALBOT PRESS, LTD. | 89 Talbot Street, Dublin; [v]: dedication: 'TO | ERNEST A. BOYD'; [vi]: blank; [vii]: contents page; [viii]: blank. Issued in pale salmon boards with brown backing; light brown manila-style dust-jacket.

Contents: Wrack (p. 1); Before Dawn (p. 29); "From the Fury of the O'Flaherty's!" (p. 67); A Coward's Saga (p. 84); The Invisible City of Coolanoole (p. 127); The King's Messenger (p. 156); The Vision of St. Molaise (p. 172).

(b) *Individually published*

Note: The following four stories appeared in issues of *Orpheus* and were never reprinted. For the six titles that originally appeared in *The Irish Review* or *Orpheus* and were subsequently reprinted see *Children of the Hills* above.

(1) The End of Aodh Costello: *Orpheus*, 8 (October 1909), pp. 80-2; continued in *Orpheus*, 9 (January 1910), pp. 116-20.
(2) The Strayed Soul: *Orpheus*, 18 (April 1912), pp. 42-54. Dated 'Glencolumcille, December 1910'.
(3) The Servant of the Bishop: *Orpheus*, 16 (October 1911), pp. 345-54.
(4) The Birth of a Song: A Celtic Idyll: *Orpheus*, 24 (October 1913), pp. 113-25.

(c) *Unpublished*

(1) '"Told on a stormy night" [in pencil] | *Cormac Og* A phantasmagoria' [in ink]. Dated at end: 'October 2nd 1911 | Glencolumcille.' 14 ff. ; 14 pp. on recto of each folio only; lined paper from a notebook, now bound together with Bax's translation of part of Synge's *The Shadow of the Glen* (see above); ff. 11v and 12v have pencilled notes in Gaelic, and 14v a Gaelic vocabulary and Irish sayings. Formerly owned by Harriet Cohen, then by Colin Scott-Sutherland, then sold at Sotheby's on 26 May 1994 and bought for an anonymous client by Bertram Rota.
(2) 'The Horsemen.' 14 ff.; 14 pp. on recto of each folio only (the versos containing drafts for scene 2 of *Red Owen*); lined paper in a notebook with black covers. This story is undated, but previous pages in the notebook once contained another story, 'The Sisters', which was written in St Petersburg in April–May 1910; this has been torn out, presumably for publication in 1912, though the title page, written on the front paste-down end paper, is still extant. The final eight pages of the notebook contain an Irish Gaelic vocabulary (also in Bax's hand).
(3) Short stories: Unpublished and 'missing'. Christopher Whelen told me on several occasions that he owned some unpublished short stories, perhaps the eight written in the spring of 1942 that Harriet Cohen gave to Clifford

Bax and of which he wrote that 'for vigour and variety [they] could not easily be bettered' (from Clifford Bax's memoir, published in Lewis Foreman, *Farewell, my Youth and Other Writings by Arnold Bax*, p. xxviii). During the 1950s or '60s Whelen (who died in 1993) lent them to someone who never returned them to him and whose name he was unable to recall.

IV. AUTOBIOGRAPHY

FAREWELL, MY YOUTH

Half-title page: 'FAREWELL, MY YOUTH || BOOK | PRODUCTION | WAR ECONOMY | STANDARD [within a device consisting of an open book with a lion seated on the upper edges] | THIS BOOK IS PRODUCED IN | COMPLETE CONFORMITY WITH THE | AUTHORIZED ECONOMY STANDARDS'. *Title page*: 'Farewell, My Youth || BY | ARNOLD BAX || LONGMANS, GREEN AND CO. | LONDON ◇ NEW YORK ◇ TORONTO'. *Dedicatory page*: 'Many of my friends whose names appear in the | following pages are no longer in our world. To | their loved memory I dedicate this little book.' [1-4] + 5-112: [1]: half-title page; [2]: publisher's imprint including 'First published 1943' and a Code Number: '12408 | Printed in Great Britain | by Western Printing Services Ltd., Bristol'; [3]: title page; [4]: dedication; 5-6: Foreword (inscribed 'Morar, | Inverness-shire'). Issued in blue linen boards in blue and green dust-jacket with white lettering on the upper cover; blurb about Bax on the lower cover; gold lettering on upper cover and up spine; priced at 7/6d. New imprint 1943, 1944. New imprint by photolithography 1949; new light blue and fawn dust-jacket; same blurb on lower cover and with press opinions on front flap. Reprinted 1970: Westport, Connecticut: Greenwood Press Publishers (SBN 8371-32 46-0). Issued in blue-black boards with dust-jacket green on front and spine, white on back. 'Farewell | My Youth | by | Arnold Bax' in white on front.

Illustrated edition: Lewis Foreman (ed.), *Farewell, my Youth and Other Writings by Arnold Bax* (London: Scolar Press, 1992; now Aldershot: Ashgate Publishing Ltd.), pp. xxxi-ii, [1]-99. This edition was newly set up in print and contains seventy-nine illustrations. It will be referred to below as *FMY2*.

Extract: 'At Queen's Hall'. This is a slightly modified version of the chapter called 'Philharmonic' in the original edition (pp. 80-8) and is known to me only from a photocopy. It comes from a collection of writings by various authors, presumably post-1943, pp. 455-63, but it has not yet been possible to identify the source.[5]

[5] In 1997 I contacted Dr Alexander Comfort, one of whose short stories immediately precedes Bax's piece, but he was unable, after fifty-odd years, to recall details of the publication.

V. MISCELLANEOUS AND OCCASIONAL WRITINGS

(a) *About music*

(1) 'Arnold Bax' [untitled article about music], *The Musical Standard* (11 April 1914), p. 342. Also in *Bax Society Bulletin* (January 1973), p. 48, and in *FMY2*, pp. 103-5 with the title 'A Native British Art'.
(2) 'A British School of Composers', *The Musical Herald* (September 1915), p. 409. Also in *FMY2*, pp. 105-7.
(3) 'More "Victory" Year Messages From Eminent Musicians to the Readers of "The Musical Standard."', *The Musical Standard* (18 January 1919), p. 22.
(4) 'Harmony' [unspecified contribution to the article on this subject], A. Eaglefield-Hull (ed.), *A Dictionary of Modern Music and Musicians* (London and Toronto: J. M. Dent & Sons Ltd., 1924), pp. 214-24. An excerpt from *The Garden of Fand* appears on p. 222 (ex. 36) and is briefly discussed on p. 221, but none of the text can be definitely attributed to Bax. According to the dictionary's General Preface (p. vi), the article on harmony was written 'by various contributors who have met several times as a committee to discuss it by word of mouth, and have supplied material on various points to the General Editor.' The committee consisted of Hugh Allen, Béla Bartók, Arnold Bax, Eugene Goossens, Eaglefield-Hull, Donald Tovey and Vaughan Williams, with Granville Bantock as chairman.
(5) 'Arnold Bax | *Composer*' in Percy A. Scholes (comp.), *A Book of Greetings from British Musicians to their friends and colleagues members of the Music Supervisors National Conference Chicago,* [*18 April*] *1928* (OUP/ Aeolian Co., 1928), pp. 31-2.
(6) 'Bax defines his music—"I am a Brazen Romantic" he says', R. H. Wollstein, 'The Turn of the Dial', *Musical America* (7 July 1928), p. 9. Also in *FMY2*, p. 168.
(7) 'On Inspiration', *The Chesterian* (September–October 1928), pp. 2-3. Reprinted as 'Opinions: Arnold Bax', *On Inspiration* (JWC, [1929]), pp. 17-18 and in *FMY2*, pp. 109-10. Also in Gertrude Norman and Miriam Lubell Shrifte (comps.), *Letters of Composers: An Anthology 1603-1945* (New York: A. A. Kopf, 1946), pp. 358-9.
(8) 'Give British Music a Chance!', *The Radio Times* (6 April 1945), p. 3. Also in *FMY2*, pp. 117-20.
(9) 'My Strongest Musical Impression of 1946', *The Music Teacher and Piano Student* (January 1947), p. 13.
(10) Quotations in John Huntley, *British Film Music* (London: Skelton Robinson, 1947), p. 160.
(11) 'My Strongest Musical Impression of 1947', *The Music Teacher and Piano Student* (January 1948), p. 13.
(12) 'My Strongest Musical Impression of 1948', *The Music Teacher and Piano Student* (January 1949), p. 13.

(13) 'The Music of "Hamlet" [by Walton] and "Oliver Twist" [also *Malta, G.C.*]', *Penguin Film Review*, 8 (1949), pp. 110, 114; reprinted by Scolar Press, 1977. Contains quotations from Bax on writing film music.
(14) 'My Strongest Musical Impression of 1949', *The Music Teacher and Piano Student* (January 1950), p. 13.
(15) 'Music at the Coronation', *National and English Review*, CXL (January–June 1953), pp. 345-7.
(16) 'Bax, Sir Arnold', K. B. Sandved (ed.), *The World of Music* (London: Waverley Book Company, 1954), column 168. Contains brief quotations from Bax on his music.

(b) *About people*

(1) 'Lionel Tertis. | An Appreciation', *The Musical News and Herald* (27 May 1922), p. 656.
(2) 'Frederick Corder', *The Times* (27 August 1932). Also in *FMY2*, pp. 114-15.
(3) 'In Memoriam | Frederick Corder | Professor, Curator and Fellow | January 26 1852–August 21 1932', *R. A. M. Club Magazine*, 94 (November 1932), pp. 66-7.
(4) 'Sir E. Elgar: an artist of balance and finish', *The Daily Telegraph* (26 February 1934), p. 10.
(5) 'Dr. H. G. Baynes | An Appreciation', *The Times* (17 September 1943), p. 7.
(6) 'A Physical Giant', *Homage to Sir Henry Wood: A World Symposium*, 2nd enlarged edn. (L. P. O. Booklets, L. P. P. Ltd., [*c.* 1944]), pp. 13-14.
(7) 'He is a National Institution', Ralph Hill and C. B. Rees (eds.), *Sir Henry Wood: Fifty years of the Proms* (London: BBC Publications, [1944]), pp. 26-9.
(8) 'Edwin Evans: September 1, 1874–March 3, 1945', *The Musical Times* (April 1945), p. 107. Also in *FMY2*, p. 127.
(9) Contribution to 'Maitland as we knew him', in *Poems by Maitland Radford. With a Memoir by some of his Friends* (London: George Allen and Unwin Ltd., 1945; limited edn. of 500 copies), p. 15.
(10) 'Edward Elgar (1857-1934 Baronet—Order of Merit—Master of the King's Musick (1924-1934)': Introduction to the programme for the Elgar Festival, Royal Albert Hall (30 May–15 June 1949), pp. 2-5. Also in *FMY2*, pp. 123-7.
(11) 'Richard Strauss', Anna Instone and Julian Herbage (eds.), *Selections from the BBC Programme Music Magazine* (London: Rockliff Publishing Corporation Ltd., 1953), pp. 76-8. Also in *FMY2*, pp. 130-2.
(12) 'E. J. Moeran: 1894-1950', *Music and Letters*, XXXII, 2 (April 1951), pp. 125-7. Also in Lionel Hill, *Lonely Waters: The Diary of a Friendship with E. J. Moeran* (London: Thames Publishing, 1985), pp. 119-20, and *FMY2*, pp. 110-13.

(13) Tribute to Balfour Gardiner sent to Rolf Gardiner with a letter dated 14 April 1951 and included (in slightly abbreviated form) in the programme for the Memorial Concert on 23 April 1951.
(14) Brief contribution to: 'Arnold Schönberg: 1874-1951', *Music and Letters*, XXXII, 4 (October 1951), p. 307. Also in Nicolas Slonimsky, *Lexicon of Musical Invective* (Seattle and London: University of Washington Press, 1953), p. 166, and *FMY2*, p. 132.
(15) 'Ralph Vaughan Williams | A tribute on behalf of the Musicians of Britain', souvenir programme for a 'Celebration Concert on the occasion of the 80th birthday of Dr. Ralph Vaughan Williams O.M.', Royal Festival Hall (12 October [1952]), pp. 3-4. Also in *FMY2*, pp. 115-17.

(c) *Programme notes*

The programme notes and written introductions that Bax provided for some of his works are reproduced or quoted from in the main part of the Catalogue:

Concert Piece (**59**), Fatherland (**92**), Symphony in F (**95**), In the Faery Hills (**114**), Enchanted Summer (**129**), Festival Overture (**134**), Tamara (**138**), Christmas Eve on the Mountains (**145**), Four Orchestral Pieces (**152**), Spring Fire (**153**), The Happy Forest (**157**), Nympholept (**164**), The Garden of Fand (**175**), Moy Mell (**180**), November Woods (**191**), Tintagel (**213**), Phantasy (**235**), Violin Sonata No. 2 (**248**), Symphony No. 1 (**256**), Symphony No. 2 (**276**), Overture, Elegy and Rondo (**288**), Violin Sonata No. 3 (**289**), Symphony No. 3 (**297**), Nonet (**302**), Winter Legends (**303**), Northern Ballad No. 1 (**309**), The Tale the Pine-Trees Knew (**310**), Summer Music (**314**), Saga Fragment (**317**), String Quartet No. 3 (**338**), Violin Concerto (**342**), A Legend (**357**).

(d) *Forewords*

(1) The prospectus for the fifty-seventh season of Henry Wood Promenade Concerts, 1951, p. 3. Also in *FMY2*, pp. 108-9.
(2) 'Commemorative book of Programmes and Texts' for 'Eight Concerts of Music by English Composers 1300-1750' (Arts Council of Great Britain, 1951), p. [3].
(3) 'Eight Coronation Concerts': 'Eight Concerts of Choral and Orchestral Music Presented by the Royal Philharmonic Society in association with the Arts Council of Great Britain, the British Broadcasting Corporation and the London County Council to celebrate the Coronation of Her Majesty Queen Elizabeth the Second [in] The Royal Festival Hall' (Arts Council of Great Britain, 1953), p. ii.

(4) Aloys Fleischmann (ed.), *Music in Ireland: A Symposium* (Cork: Cork University Press, and Oxford: B. H. Blackwell Ltd., 1952), pp. iii-iv. Also in *FMY2*, pp. 132-4.

(e) *Book reviews*

(1) 'The Crock of Gold' [by James Stephens], 'by D. O'B.', in *The Irish Review* (December 1912), pp. 550-2. It is not certain that this is by Bax, but the language contains nothing inconsistent with his style, and the writer's mention of *Also sprach Zarathusthra* and the nineteenth-century Russian novelists (both favourites of Bax) as well as the characteristic use of the unusual spelling 'extatic' for 'ecstatic' suggest that the initials may well stand for 'Dermot O'Byrne'. The same issue also contains Bax's short story 'The Call of the Road'.
(2) 'Celtic Twilight in Moderation | Turf beneath my Feet. By Garry Hogg.', *National and English Review*, CXXXV (July–December 1950), pp. 510, 512.
(3) 'Tang of Turf-Smoke | Sweet Cork of Thee. By Robert | Gibbings. Dent. 16s.', *National and English Review*, CXXXVII (July–December 1951), pp. 237-8.
(4) 'New Light on a Genius | Letters of Richard Wagner. Burrell Collection. Gollancz. 42s.', *National and English Review*, CXXXVIII (January–June 1952), pp. 172-4. Also in *FMY2*, pp. 127-30.

(f) *Talks*

Note: Talks and speeches are listed here because they also exist (or existed) in script form; it has proved impossible to ascertain from the BBC which scripts are extant. For recordings of Bax's voice see Appendix 3.

(1) 'Sir Edward Elgar': For details see Appendix 3, section III (1).
(2) 'Richard Strauss (1864-1949)': First broadcast on 'Music Magazine', BBC Home Service, 2 October 1949. Published in Anna Instone and Julian Herbage (eds.), *Selections from the BBC Programme Music Magazine* (London: Rockliff Publishing Corporation Ltd., 1953), pp. 76-8. Also in *FMY2*, pp. 130-2.
(3) Talk in the series 'British Composers': For details see Appendix 3, section III (3). Published in *FMY2*, pp. 164-8, under the title 'A Radio Self-Portrait (1949)'.
(4) 'Greetings to Sibelius on his 85th birthday': Recorded in Studio 8, Bush House, between 4.00 and 4.15 p. m. on 2 December 1950 (rehearsal at 3.45) and broadcast on BBC European Service at 4 p.m. on 8 December 1950. Bax's fee was five guineas.
(5) 'Spike Hughes introduces Sir Arnold Bax . . . in *Records I like*': First broadcast on BBC Light Programme, 23 January 1951. The records chosen

by Bax included a comic song by Cicely Courtneidge and a piece by the musical caricaturist Beethove.

Bax also wrote two talks that were read over the air by Stuart Hibberd:

(6) 'Tribute to Sir Henry J. Wood': Broadcast on BBC Home Service, 4 March 1934. Published in *FMY2*, pp. 120-3.
(7) A talk on the Concertante for three solo instruments and orchestra: Broadcast on 2 October 1949.

(g) *Speeches*

Note: In a letter to Christopher Whelen dating from July 1951, Bax wrote: 'I could no more make a speech than play a stringed instrument!' He dreaded having to speak in public. In his 'Impressions—Sir Arnold Bax', *Musical Events* (November 1950), p. 14, C. B. Rees recalled a dinner party after a concert at which Bax was guest of honour:

> Warm tributes were paid to his music, and to himself as a distinguished figure in our musical annals. Admiration and enthusiasm ran high. He fidgeted. He was called upon to reply. He fidgeted more. But he got up on his feet, somewhat ponderously, surveyed the gathering with a disturbed glance, coughed, and said, 'Ladies and gentlemen, thank you.' We had hoped for a speech. But we had got something better. We had Arnold Bax's 'thank you'—which meant everything.

(1) On 5 November 1931 Bax was presented with the Gold Medal of the Royal Philharmonic Society: 'I had a most embarrassing time at the Philharmonic last week . . . I had to stand on the platform [of Queen's Hall] for about five minutes whilst Sir John McEwen talked about me and then I had to say something myself. I managed to survive but felt rather shattered afterwards.' (From a letter to Tilly Fleischmann. In another letter, to May Harrison, Bax mentions that McEwen made rather a hash of his eulogy.)
(2) On 6 November 1934 Bax was guest of honour at a Musicians' Club Dinner in the Wharncliffe Rooms, Hotel Great Central, London, and made a brief speech of thanks (see *Musical Opinion*, December 1934, p. 220).
(3) A page of notes apparently for a speech expressing sympathy with the plight of the Jews: 1 p.; 4to: a sheet of Harriet Cohen's headed notepaper. Formerly owned by Colin Scott-Sutherland and sold at Sotheby's on 26 May 1994, bought for an anonymous client by Bertram Rota.
(4) Speech in honour of John Barbirolli. This was completed very shortly before Bax's death on 3 October 1953 and was to have been given at a dinner in the conductor's honour. In it Bax claims that it is the first speech he would ever have made, which suggests that it was at least the longest and most fully prepared. It is quoted in the memoir that Clifford Bax wrote for Christopher Whelen, published in *FMY2*, pp. xxviii-xxix, but the original MS has not been traced.

(h) *Interviews*

(1) *The Musical Standard* (27 September 1913), p. 303: 'We had the pleasure of interviewing Mr. Bax very recently . . .', followed by quotations from the composer about his *Two Orchestral Sketches* (see **152**).
(2) Katharine Eggar, 'The Piano Pieces of Arnold Bax', *The Music Student*, XIV (November 1921), pp. 65-7, 78. Also in *FMY2*, pp. 161-2. This contains quotations from Bax about his music.
(3) Watson Lyle, 'Musician of the North', *The Bookman* (February 1932), p. 268. Also in *FMY2*, pp. 162-4.
(4) 'The Master of the King's Musick', *Picture Post* (28 March 1942), p. 21. Although not written as an interview, this contains information clearly extracted from a reluctant Bax: 'Yes, isn't that Picture Post stuff awful? I only allowed *one* press photographer (out of about twenty who asked me) to take pictures of me and then told him clearly which of his photo's I minded least; after which he chooses the most appalling!' (From a letter to May Harrison dated 4 April 1942.)

Note: For the only extant sound recording of an interview with Bax (a very brief one) see Appendix 3.

(i) *Miscellaneous*

(1) 'The Ladies own Book of Volcanoes': A pamphlet written by Bax at the age of nine (1892-3) for his mother and stitched together by the nursemaid (see CSS, p. 6, based on information from Clifford Bax). Not extant. Mention may also be made here of a photograph owned by Colin Scott-Sutherland showing a castle built by Bax as a child with toy bricks.
(2) 'The Universal | Edited by A. E. T. Bax | — | Volume I. No 1. | 1897. [four lines underneath] | October. [two curly lines underneath].' T.p. [the reverse blank] + 15 pp. + [1] p. containing the list of contents; written on lined paper (206 × 165); stitched without covers. *Contents* (derived from the main text, the wording on the contents page differing slightly): 'Notices. "Spot"' [a game played with billiard balls] (pp. 1-4); 'The Vulture and the Husbandman' [a parody of 'The Walrus and the Carpenter'] (pp. 5-9); 'A few puns' [e.g. 'Tired but never weary. A wheel'] (pp. 9-10); 'Halfda [originally 'Cedric']. A tale of the Norse sea-kings | Chapter 1' [first part of a story] (pp. 10-14); 'Our puzzle page' (p. 15); 'Contents for October' (p. [16]).
(3) 'THE IVY-BANK GAZETTE': A cover (203 × 163) for the first issue of this handwritten magazine devised by Bax is all that appears to be extant. It is dated 'March 1900' and priced at '2^{D}'. The design consists of a drawing of Charlotte Bax with ivy leaves surrounding it and was probably done either by Clifford Bax or by Francis Colmer, the Bax children's private tutor.

(4) Two notebooks in UCC:

(i) Notebook in use from 1899 to *c.* 1910: 67 ff. (including a few torn out) of lined paper (135 × 82) used vertically; bound in dark green boards with red leather spine and with a tape fastener on the outside. The contents are written partly in ink, partly in pencil, and consist mainly of cricket scores and batting averages, the earliest relating to family matches played in August 1899, the latest to one on 30 July 1910. Ff. 7^{v} and 8 contain a list of thirty-five song titles by Bax that include some not known from any other source (see **88-91** in the main Catalogue). Two other, shorter lists of songs appear on ff. 63^{v} and 66^{v}; f. 64^{r} has a list of songs by Wolf and Strauss; f. 67 has a list of names, including many musicians (e.g. Parry, Dale, Bell, the Sobrinos): perhaps a list of invitees to some function. The pastedown endpaper has sums in red ink and some musical notation entirely in crotchets.

(ii) Notebook in use from April 1909 to at least 4 September 1913, and later used by Clifford Bax: 60 ff. (including several torn out) of lined paper (131 × 84) used vertically; bound in dark green boards with patterned pastedown endpapers and with a tape fastener on the outside. The contents are written entirely in pencil and consist mainly of poems and poetic drafts. The following list is of complete poems only: 'A spring-day' (endpaper-f. 1^{v}; 'April 1909'); 'In Carna' (ff. 3-5^{r}); 'The hidden country' (ff. 5^{v}-6^{r}; 'Carna April 30th 1909'); 'The old men of the Twilight' (ff. 7^{v}-8^{r}; 'Renvyle May 5th'); 'And in that land were spirits pondering by the sea' (f. 12; 'Renvile [*sic*] May 8th'); ff. 56-60 have more drafts but starting on the back free endpaper and working towards the front: 'Homeward' (ff. 59^{r}-58^{v}); 'By a lake edge' (ff. 56^{v}-52^{r}; 'Renvyle May 4th'); f. 11^{v} has four single-staff systems containing the melody of an unidentified Irish folksong; ff. 13-25 have been torn out but one stub has the date 'Sept 4. 1913' at the top; ff. 26-35 contain, in Clifford Bax's hand, his translation of act 2 of Tasso's *L'Aminta*; another chorus from this play was later published as *The Age of Gold: A Chorus Translated out of Tasso's 'L'Aminta'* (Derby: The Grasshopper Press, March 1944; limited edn. of 250 copies).

(5) Three notebooks, formerly owned by Harriet Cohen and subequently by Colin Scott-Sutherland, which were sold at Sotheby's on 26 May 1994 and bought for an anonymous client by Bertram Rota:

(i) Notebook dating from Bax's schooldays containing 'Notes on Orchestral Instruments' (their compasses), notes on 'Scripture history', economic matters,[6] algebraic formulæ, a translation of a passage from Cicero's *Second*

[6] The page of economic notes is reproduced in Colin Scott-Sutherland's *Ideala (Nereid)* (Crail, 1995) and seems to be in the hand of Bax's tutor, Francis Colmer. At the bottom of the same page is a drawing of a male nude dated 'July 27.09.' (i.e. later than the other contents), which is by Clifford Bax. It may be that some of the other pages are also in Colmer's hand, but it was not possible to check this notebook very thoroughly before it went into anonymous private ownership.

Catilinarian Oration, translations into Latin, a transcription of Shelley's 'Queen Mab', cricket scores, doodles and sketches; *c.* 50 pp. + many blanks; boards; covers worn and coming loose; 8vo. Inscribed on upper cover 'A. E. T. Bax'.

(ii) Notebook dating from after 1902 containing a narrative fragment that begins 'She is gone. Gone away to-night with that Frenchman I met at the Embassy . . .'. It also contains some Irish observations and a list of countries (each followed by a number) arranged within broad geographical areas, beginning 'Oceana | Solomon Isles 2 | Cook— 1 | Fiji 5': perhaps a catalogue of a stamp collection with the number of stamps from each country listed;[7] 7 pp. torn loose; black oilskin boards; 4to.

(iii) Notebook containing poems and drafts, including 'The Sword of Tethra', 'The Dreamer', 'Narcissus the Mystic', 'Behind the Wind', 'The Emigrants', as well as a Gaelic vocabulary. Photographs (loosely inserted) of a landscape and of Bax taken at Cahirciveen, Co. Kerry, in 1937.[8] Also a letter from Harriet Cohen; 60 pp.; red paper wrappers (detached); 8vo.

(6) Bax's copy of Stewart MacPherson's *Practical Counterpoint* (London, 1900) in UCC has loosely inserted into it an RAM examination paper in the elements of music for the Lent Term 1902. Someone has filled in some of the answers in pencil, a few of them incorrectly. The handwriting cannot be positively identified as Bax's, but if it is his—though obviously not done as part of an examination—it would tend to corroborate Rebecca Clarke's statement in her unpublished autobiography that Bax once 'flunked his elements' and was denied the Certificate of Merit.

(7) Facetious concert programme devised by Bax on two sides of a folio of lined paper (212 × 153) torn from a notebook and found among sketches for *Tamara* (see (9) below): formerly belonging to Colin Scott-Sutherland, sold at Sotheby's on 26 May 1994 and bought for an anonymous client by Bertram Rota. The programme contains imaginary works by ten composers, including an 'Intermezzo Apoplectica [*sic*]' by Sir Hubert Parry, a 'Symphony in 10 movements (A hard week's work)' by York Bowen, and '17 serious variations on a theme taken down by Sir C. V. Stanford from the whistling of Brahms' housekeeper' by one 'S. Haliwell Bradley (A. R. C. M.)'—perhaps S. Hartley Braithwaite.[9] Three of the other items are

[7] Among Bax's books in UCC is *The Standard Catalogue of Postage Stamps* (1924), suggesting he had some interest in philately.

[8] This was the home of Herbert Hughes, the Irish composer and editor of *The Joyce Book* (see **312** in the main Catalogue).

[9] Stanford himself once concocted a similar spoof programme that included a 'Concerto for Penny Whistle and Tuba [by] A. Bax.' (Letter of 7 August 1910 to Herbert Thompson.)

reproduced in CSS (pp. 191-2). The final piece is a piano solo by Bax himself: 'Eire's welcome to the congested districts board'.[10]

(8) Notebook with writing in pencil: UCC. Most of the pages have been torn out leaving just four loose folios of lined paper (229 × 171)—ff. 1 and 3 being conjugate—and one of the black oilskin boards with lined paper on the reverse; f. 1 contains the words and music (on three single-staff systems) of an Irish folksong taken down by the composer from a native singer in Donegal, and then, written upside down, a list of twelve names of people and places (e.g. 'Maggie', 'Glen Head', 'view from window'). Some of the people can be identified as denizens of Glencolumcille in the 1900s (e.g. 'Paddy John [McNelis]', 'Sally Boyle': see *FMY*, pp. 48-56); perhaps it is a list of photographs taken by Bax; f. 1^v contains a three-staff variant of the folktune on the obverse; ff. $2\text{-}3^r$ contain the words of the song (written in Irish script) with the heading 'na bearla cruadh' (i.e. 'the harsh conditions'); f. 3^v is blank. The endpaper has a list of eleven names similar to the ones on f. 1, and then, written upside down, a few Irishisms (e.g. 'plubbering = chattering and arguing'), an astrological (?) symbol, and notes about the card game Twenty-five.

(9) Notebook in use *c.* 1911 from which the pages have been torn out leaving the black outer covers and the lined endpapers (230 × *c.* 175), on which Bax has written annotations in ink for the ballet *Tamara* (**138**). It also includes the following: 'Ah, there's music always in my head and there's only myself is hearing it. It's going up to the roof of the house now.' These are perhaps the original *ipsissima verba* of Paddy John McNelis, the publican in Glencolumcille, that were quoted in modified form some thirty-odd years later in *FMY*, p. 49.

(10) *Orpheus*, 12 (October 1910). In the absence of his brother, who was abroad, Bax edited this issue. He included his own poem 'Glamour' (pp. 202-3).

(11) 'Lúireach Naoimh Pádraig'. For the suggestion that Bax may have translated this Irish text into English in 1923 see *St Patrick's Breastplate* (**267**).

(12) 'At Melksham', Clifford Bax (ed.), *The Old Broughtonians Cricket Weeks*, 4 (London: The Favil Press Ltd., 1930), pp. 80-1. An account of a cricket match won by Clifford Bax's Old Broughtonians; the losers were a local team from Melksham in Wiltshire.

(13) 'Melksham', Clifford Bax (ed.), *The Old Broughtonians Cricket Weeks*, 5 (London: The Favil Press Ltd., 1933), pp. 56-7. A replay; the Melksham team was again defeated.

[10] The 'Congested Districts' of western Ireland were Donegal, Mayo, Galway and parts of Sligo and Kerry.

(14) Bax's will. This consists of two typed pages, signed and dated 10 February 1950, with two single-page codicils dated 23 April 1951 and 18 December 1951. His executors were Clifford Bax and Arthur Lockyer Rye.

VI. LETTERS

Seven letters written by Bax to newspapers or journals have been traced:[11]

(1) *Music News & Herald* (30 April 1921): About the journalistic habit of referring to composers' ages.
(2) *The Sackbut*, IV, 7 (February 1924), p. 214: Extracts from a letter about 'works I have written during the last year.'
(3) *The Irish Statesman* (11 September 1926), pp. 11-12: About proposals for an Irish national anthem.
(4) *The Gramophone* (February 1928), p. 397: Praising the recording by Ethel Bartlett and Rae Robertson of *Moy Mell* (**180**).
(5) *The Times* (16 December 1929), p. 13: 'Composers and the Bill: The Twopenny Fee': Attacking a proposed House of Commons bill to do with musical copyright; letter dated 13 December 1929 and signed by Bantock, Bax, Delius, German, Holst, McEwen and Vaughan Williams. Elgar wrote a similar letter published in *The Evening Standard* of 17 December 1929.
(6) *The Times* (9 April 1946): 'A Great Music Library': About the threat to remove the library of Paul Hirsch from Cambridge; letter signed by Bax, Boult, Dent, Dyson, Hess, Marchant and Vaughan Williams.
(7) *The Irish Times* (16 July 1947), p. 5: 'A Tribute' from Bax to his Irish friends after he had been awarded an honorary Mus.D. by the National University of Ireland; letter dated 'Dublin, July 12th, 1947' and reproduced in LF, p. 344.

Autograph letters are held in the following institutions:[12]

Australia

Grainger Museum, Melbourne: Letters to Percy Grainger.

England

(1) BBC Written Archives, Reading: Letters to Arthur Bliss, Adrian Boult, Victor Hely-Hutchinson and other BBC officials.

[11] LF (p. 408) lists another letter, believed to have been published in *The Daily Telegraph* for 13 January 1931, but I have been unable to trace it. It does not appear in the edition kept in the Newspaper Library at Colindale.

[12] There must have been extensive correspondence between Bax and his principal publisher, Murdoch (later Chappell), but no trace of it can be found in the archives of Warner Chappell Music Ltd.

(2) British Library, London:[13] Letters to Edward Clark, Cecil Gray, Philip Heseltine, Colin Taylor, Henry Wood, Jessie Wood.
(3) Britten–Pears Library, Aldeburgh: Letters to Benjamin Britten and Cecil Armstrong Gibbs.
(4) Cambridge University Library: One letter to William Gerhardie.
(5) Harrison Sisters Archive, Royal College of Music, London: Letters to Beatrice Harrison and May Harrison.
(6) Muniment Room and Library, Westminster Abbey, London: Letters to William McKie.
(7) Royal Archives, Windsor Castle, Windsor, Berkshire: Seven letters to Alan Lascelles (King George V's Private Secretary).
(8) Theatre Museum, Covent Garden: One letter to Paul Beard.

Ireland

(1) Trinity College Library, Dublin: One letter to Seumas O'Sullivan.
(2) University College, Cork: Letters to Aloys and Tilly Fleichmann[14] and to John Horgan; also an empty envelope addressed to 'Frieda' [Freda] Bax.

South Africa

J. W. Jagger Library, University of Cape Town: Letters to Erik Chisholm.

USA

(1) Broadcast Music, Inc. Archives, New York (collection of Carl Haverlin).
(2) Chicago Symphony Orchestra.
(3) Harry Ransom Humanities Research Center, The University of Texas at Austin: Letters to Charlotte Bax (1), Clifford Bax (45 + 1 postcard), Richard Church (3), John Masefield (2). This institution also has letters to Bax from James Joyce, Compton Mackenzie, W. Somerset Maugham and George Russell.
(4) Lauinger Library, Georgetown University, USA: One letter to James P. J. Murphy; also a signed photograph.
(5) Library of Congress, Washington D.C.: Letters to Philip Hale, Serge Koussevitzky, Nikolai Medtner.
(6) Lilly Library, University of Indiana, Bloomington: One letter to George Russell).
(7) New York Public Library: Thirty-one letters, mostly to Gertrude Norman (among the Van Dresser–Norman Papers).

[13] In 1967 Harriet Cohen bequeathed her papers (including, presumably, much Bax material) to the British Library on the condition that they were not to be looked at until thirty years after her death. By the time this catalogue was completed (July 1998), the material had not been made available.

[14] Further material from the personal collection of Professor Aloys Fleischmann is currently being catalogued.

(8) Northwestern University Library (Music Library), Evanston, Illinois: One letter to Ernest Newman.
(9) Pierpoint Morgan Library, New York: Three letters to 'Keith' (partly in Irish Gaelic; see **267**).
(10) University of Michigan (Department of Rare Books and Special Collections), Ann Arbor: Three letters to Frederick A. Stock.

There are also many letters and postcards in private hands, including the following:

(1) Dennis Andrews: Thirty-eight letters to Christopher Whelen and one to Whelen's mother. These are published in Dennis Andrews, *Cuchulan among the Guns* (Cumnor: privately published, 1998).
(2) Lewis Foreman: Letters to Arthur Alexander, Harry Farjeon, Mary Gleaves, Philip Heseltine, Harry Isaacs, Christine Ryan, John Simons, Winifred Small, Freda Swain, Rosalind Thornycroft, Richard Tildesley.
(3) Graham Parlett: Letters to 'Mr. Birkett', Basil Cameron, Francis Colmer, 'Lady Cynthia', 'Mr. [Walter?] Emery', Edwin Evans, Reginald Goodall, Katherine Goodson, Harry Isaacs, '[Alexander?] Pearson', Robert Ponsonby, 'Miss Thomas', and an anonymous official of the International Congress of Music in Florence.
(4) Colin Scott-Sutherland: Letters to Harriet Cohen, Mary Field and Isobel Hodgson. Letters to Padraic Colum, Molly Colum and Graham Royde Smith were sold at Sotheby's on 26 May 1994 and bought for an anonymous client by Bertram Rota.

For a list of Bax's letters that have been published in books see LF, p. 408.

VII. ALPHABETICAL INDEX OF LITERARY TITLES

There are three subdivisions: *Plays*, *Stories* and *Poems*. Bax's original spellings and punctuation are retained, but with definite or indefinite articles transposed to the end of the title. Inverted commas are in the original. Abbreviations following the title in the second and third categories indicate where the poem or story may be found (see entries above for full bibliographical details; single references are written out in full).

CH *Children of the Hills.*
DB *A Dublin Ballad.*
DO'B Lewis Foreman (ed.), *Dermot O'Byrne: Poems of Arnold Bax.*
FMY2 Lewis Foreman (ed.), *Farewell, my Youth and Other Writings by Arnold Bax.*
ID Colin Scott-Sutherland (ed.), *Ideala (Nereid): Some Early Love Letters and Poems by Arnold Bax.*

IR	*The Irish Review: A Monthly Magazine of Irish Literature, Art & Science.*
LPM	*Love Poems of a Musician.*
MS	Unpublished poem not in NB, *P* or UCC.
NB	Notebook: unpublished holograph collection.
NS	Edna C. Fitzhenry (comp.), *Nineteen-Sixteen: An Anthology.*
P	*Poems*: unpublished typescript collection with MS additions.
RT	'Rosalind Thornycroft': collection of typewritten poems dedicated to her.
SF	*Seafoam and Firelight.*
SGM	*The Sisters and Green Magic.*
TTAC	*Transactions of the Theosophical Art-Circle.*
UCC	Unpublished notebook in UCC containing mainly cricketing data.
W	*Wrack.*

Plays

Deirdre
Grey Swan, The
On the Hill
Red Owen
Shadow of the Glen, The (trans.)

Stories

Ancient Dominions: *CH*, *FMY2*
Before Dawn: *W*
Birth of a Song. A Celtic Idyll: *Orpheus*, 24 (October 1913), pp. 113-25
Call of the Road, The: *IR* (December 1912), pp. 519-33; *CH*
Cormac Og–A Phantasmagoria (Told on a stormy night): Unpublished
Coward's Saga, A: *W*
Death of Macha Gold-Hair, The: *Orpheus*, 12 (July 1910), pp. 211-17; *CH*; Peter Haining (ed.), *Great Irish Tales of the Unimaginable* (London: Souvenir Press, 1994)
End of Aodh Costello, The: *Orpheus*, 8 (October 1909), pp. 80-2, and 9 (January 1910), pp. 116-20
"From the Fury of the O'Flaherty's!": *W*
Green Magic: *SGM*
Horsemen, The: Unpublished
Hunger: *IR*, May 1912, pp. 140-51; *CH*
Invisible City of Coolanoole, The: *W*
King's Messenger, The: *W*
Lifting of the Veil, The: *Orpheus*, 20 (October 1912), pp. 105-10; *CH*; *Horror by Lamplight* (London: Chancellor Press, 1993)
"Seanoidín": *CH*
Servant of the Bishop, The: *Orpheus*, 16 (October 1911), pp. 345-54
Sisters, The: *SGM*
Strayed Soul, The: *Orpheus*, 18 (April 1912), pp. 42-54
Through the Rain: *Orpheus*, 15 (July 1911), pp. 301-5; *CH*
Vision of St Molaise, The: *W*
Wrack: *W*

Poems

Adventure: MS
After: *DB*
After Sunset (Connemara) *or* After Sunset in Connemara: NB, *P*
'Ah why did summer stay so long?': LF, pp. 256-7
Allurement: *DO'B*
Amersham: *DO'B*
And in that land were spirits: UCC

April Night (24 March 1918): MS
Aran Islands, The: *P*, *SF*, *DO'B* (also called The Isles of Arran [*sic*], q.v.)
Army of the Dawn, The: NB
Art and Imagination: NB
At Liberty's (June 1916): MS
At Parting: *LPM*
At the Last: NB, *P*, *DO'B*
At 'Tristan und Isolde' (Covent Garden Feb. 1910): *P*, RT, *LPM*
At Wendover: NB
Atlantic Cavern, An (1911): MS
Autumn Night (19 May 1908): MS
Battle of the Somme, The: *LPM*
Beauty (October 1916): MS
Behind the Wind: *SF*
Beneath the Hills of God: NB
Buckinghamshire: MS
Burden of Memory, The: *DO'B*, RT (also called The Shadow of Memory, q.v.)
By a Faery Lough: *P*, *SF*, *DO'B*
By a lake edge: UCC
Caoine for Eire (Salruck Pipe-Graveyard): NB, *P* (originally Caoine for Eri)
Caprice (February 1916): MS
Certainty: *Orpheus*, 14 (April 1911), p. 282; *DO'B*
Cherry Blossom: *LPM*
Circle, The (5 January 1915): MS
Confusion: MS
Connemara: RT
Consolation: *LPM*, *DO'B*
Cornish Night (4-30 September 1917): MS
Country Song, A: *SF*
Crisis: *DO'B*
Cross-roads: NB
Cry of the Heart, The (25 November 1913): MS
Cynics (13 November 1913): MS
Darkness: *DO'B*
Dedication. (To C.L.B.): *P*, *DO'B*
Deirdre's Spinning Song: *DO'B* (from the play *Deirdre*)
Dionysia (May 1909): MS
Disillusion (30 November 1913): MS
Donegal Twilight, A: NB, *P*
Dream Armour: *P*
Dream before Sleep (December 19-16): MS
Dream in the Firelight: NB
Dreamer, The: MS
Dreary Landscape, A: NB, *P*
Dublin Ballad—1916, A: *DB*, *NS*, *DO'B*; *Poetry Ireland*, 13 (April 1951), p. 18; Donagh MacDonagh and Lennox Robinson (eds.), *The Oxford Book of Irish Verse* (Oxford, 1958), pp. 205-7; Frank O'Connor (ed.), *A Book of Ireland* (London and Glasgow, 1959), pp. 123-5; Lewis Foreman (ed.), *Dermot O'Byrne* (London, 1979), p. 62
Dusk and Dawn: NB
Earth-Love: *P*
East Clare Election 1828-1917, The: *DB*, *NS*
East Clare Election 1917, The: *DB*
Emigrant, The: *LPM*, *DO'B* (also called Exile, q.v.)
Emigrants, The: *SF* (a different poem from the preceding)
Enchanted Fiddle, The: *DO'B*
End of a Romance, The: *P*, *DO'B*
End of all the Dreams of the World, The: *NB*
English Landscape (Wendover), An: *P*
Enigma: *LPM*
Epithalamium: *LPM*
Everlasting Battle, The: NB, *P*
Exile: *IR* (April 1913), p. 68 (also called The Emigrant, q.v.)
Eyes of the Stars, The: NB, *P*
Fallen Gods: NB
Fear (9 January 1915): MS
[Fighting Téméraire, The] Parody of: see II. (c) above
Fintan, the Spirit of Irish Song: *P*, *SF*
Flames: NB
Flames and Dreams: NB, *P*
Flaming Day: NB
Flowers of the Sea, The: *P*
From Old Days: *P*, *DO'B*

Gaelic (18 March 1909): MS
Garden Song: UCC (as song title only; see 90 in Catalogue of Music)
Ghost, A: *LPM*, *DO'B*
Gift of God, The: NB, *P*
Girl's May-Eve, A: NB, *P*
Girl's Music, A: *LPM*, *DO'B*
Glamour: *Orpheus*, 12 (October 1910), pp. 202-3; *LPM*, *DO'B*
Glen of Starry Peace, The: *Orpheus*, 4 (October 1908), p. 11; *P*, *SF*, *DO'B*
Glencolumcille: NB, *P*
God's play, A: NB
Green Magic: *DO'B* (from the short story *Green Magic*)
Grey Swan, The: *DO'B* (final chorus only from the play *The Grey Swan*)
Guest House, The: *LPM*, *DO'B*
'Half a Note from Blake': *P* (also called Parenthesis, q.v.)
Harp of Desire, The (November 1908): MS
Haunted Lake, The (February 1911): MS
Heart's Desire: *P*, *LPM*
Helplessness: *LPM*
Hidden country, The: UCC
Hill-Magic: *P*
Home of the Heart, The: MS
Homeward: UCC
Hunter, The (13 December 1913): MS
Hymn to Night: *P*
I am all broken up with love: MS
I will lift up mine eyes unto the hills (22 June 1910): MS
Ideala: NB
Illusion: *LPM*
Images (20 February 1911): MS
Immortality of Form, The: *LPM*
Improvizations [*sic*], Two: NB
In a Back-Street: *DO'B*
In a Backwater (5 December 1913): MS
In a Bohemian Forest: NB, MS, *ID*; CSS, pp. 14-15 (excerpt only)
In an Old Forest (Unfinished): *P*
In an Orchard: NB, *P*
In Carna: UCC; *Orpheus*, 7 (June 1909), p. 60; *SF*
In Donegal: *LPM*
In Dublin Bay (4 December 1913): MS
In Flight: MS
In Galway Bay: NB, *P*, *SF*, *Orpheus*, 6 (April 1909), p. 33
In Glencree: RT
In Glencullen: *DB*, *DO'B*
In Memoriam My Friend Patrick H. Pearse (Ruler of Ireland for one week): *DB*
In Sanctuary: *P*
In September (30 September 1917): MS
In the After-Time: *P*
In the Forest: NB
In the Hills of Dreamland: NB, *P*
In the House of Memory: NB
In the Lord's House: NB
In the Meadows of Heartland: NB
In the Night: *P*, *LPM*, *DO'B*
Innermost, The: MS
Intermezzo: NB
Into the Mist: NB, *P*
Irish Mail, The: *DO'B*
Irony: *LPM*
Island of Storms, The: NB, *P*
Isles of Arran, The: NB (also called The Aran Islands, q.v.)
Kilmasheogue: *DB*, *NS*, *DO'B*
Kingdom of the Daffodil, The: RT
Korshjem-Saga, The: Clifford Bax (ed.), *The Old Broughtonian Cricket Weeks*, 3 (London, 1927), pp. 44- 9.
Labour of Love, The: *LPM*
Lake of Stars (A Dawn-Dream), The: NB, *P*, *DO'B*
Lament (New Forest), A: NB, *P*
Lament of Aengus Ogue, The: NB
Leannán-Sídhe: LF, p. 160.
Lost Ship, The: *P*, RT
Lost Soul, A (May 1908): MS
Love: *LPM*
Love and Reason: *LPM*
Love and the Sea: NB, *P*; CSS, p. 70-1 (excerpt only)

Love in the Noonday: NB
Lullaby: *P*, *DO'B*
Mad Song, A: *NB*, *P*
Magh Mell (8 May 1909): MS
'Mademoiselle de Maupin' and her Lovers: NB
Maiden with the Daffodil, The (October 1916): MS (also called This for the Maiden with the Daffodil, q.v.)
Man and Wife: *DO'B*
Martial Law in Dublin: *DB*, *NS*
Masks (22 June 1916): MS
Midnight in the Forest: NB
Mirrors: *Orpheus*, 26 (January 1914), p. 34; *LPM*
Moment, A: *LPM*
Morning in Connemara: *P*, *DO'B*, RT
Music of Man, The: *Orpheus*, 6 (April 1909), p. 43; *SF*
Narcissus the Mystic: MS
Nature (May 1918): MS
New Devil, The: *DO'B*
Nostalgia: MS
Nympholept: *LPM*, RT, *DO'B*
Oblation: RT, *LPM*
Old Man's Chatter, An: *LPM*, *DO'B*
Old Men of the Twilight, The: UCC
On a Stormy [*or* Storm-] Night: NB, *P*
On a Windy Night: NB, *P*
On Pipe-Music heard in a London Street: *SF*, *DO'B*; *Hallé Magazine*, 27 (August 1950), p. 24
On the Heights (7 December 1913): MS
On the Strand: *SF*, *DO'B*
Our Home: *P*
Out of Faeryland: *P*, *DO'B*
Pain in Youth (26 November 1913): MS
Panic: *LPM*
Paradox: MS
Parenthesis: NB (also called 'Half a Note from Blake', q.v.)
Passion (August 1917): MS
Pastel. In Regent's Park: *P*
Pastime (28 November 1913): MS
Peasant, The: *TTAC*, 3 (26 June 1908), p. 15; *SF*
Perpetuum Mobile: NB, *P*
Poet despairs of images, The (November 1916): MS
Poet's Immortality, A: NB, *P*, *SF*, *DO'B*
Prayer of the Lay Brother on the Threshold, The: NB
Prison House, The: *LPM*
Proud Harper, The: *SF*
Question, The: NB
Quiet Landscape, The: *SF*
Rain in the Twilight (29 July 1908): MS
Reason Why, The: NB
Reproof, The: *P*
Return (2 November 1909): MS
Return of St. Bride, The: NB
Revolt in Spring (1912): MS
Roundels, Two: NB
Rue ('Storrington Aug 1945'): MS
Rune of Columcille, The: *P*
Sacred Love (April 1915): MS
Sanctuary: RT, *LPM*
Sea-Dream, A: NB
Sea-Prayer, A: NB, *P*
Sea Spray: NB, *P*
Sea's Singer, The: NB, *P*
Secrets of the Sea, The: NB, *P*
Sentimentalist, The (February 1918): MS
Shadow of Memory, The: *P* (also called The Burden of Memory, q.v.)
Shadowed Godhead: *P*
Shadowy Sleepers, The: NB
Shells at Oranmore (April 1916): *DB*, *NS*, *DO'B*; *Éire: Weekly Bulletin of the Department of External Affairs*, 729 (15 February 1966), p. 4 (excerpt only)
Ship of the Spirit, The: NB, *P*
Shiplake: *LPM*
Ships, The: *SF*
Singing in [*or* of] the Wind, The: NB, *P*
Snow-Dream, A: NB

Snow on the Hills (18 November 1909): MS
Song amid the Dew, The: NB
Song from the Western Sea (Twelve line Roundel), A: NB
Song of a Madman, The: *P*
Song of Mockery, A: NB
Song of the Old Fiddler, The: NB, *P*, *DO'B*
Song of two Hearts, A: NB
Song of two Stars, A: NB
Sonnet: NB (see also the variant titles in the next two entries)
Sonnet (To a Foreign Singer): *SF*
Sonnet to a French Composer of Songs [Gabriel Fauré]: *P*; *TTAC*, 3 (26 June 1908), p. 18
Soul's Answer, The: *Orpheus*, 5 (January 1909), p. 16
Spirit to the Body, The: NB
Spirit's Companion, The: NB
Spring-Day, A: UCC
Spring-Night: NB
Stephen's Green: *LPM*
Storm on the Lough: NB
Summer Memory, A: RT, *LPM*, *DO'B*
Summer Night: UCC (as song title only; see **91** in the Catalogue of Music)
Sun-horses (February 1918): MS
Sundered Dreams: NB, *P*, *DO'B*
Sword of Tethra, The: MS
This for the Maiden with the Daffodil: CSS, p. 47 (also called The Maiden with the Daffodil, q.v.)
Thought of Ireland at Sunset, A: *LPM*
Thunderstorm ('Storrington Aug 1945'): MS
Tintagel Castle: *LPM*, *DO'B*
To + + +: NB
To a Child: RT
To a Dream-Rhythm: NB, *P*
To a Friend (July 1910): MS
To a Russian Girl: *LPM*, *DO'B*
To a Wayfarer: NB, *P*
To an Irish Child: NB, *P*, RT
To Deirdre: *P*; *Orpheus*, 13 (January 1911), p. 249
To Donegal: NB
To Donnall: *P*
To Eire: *SF*
To F (with a brief book of Irish verse banned by the censor [i.e. *A Dublin Ballad*]) : *DO'B*
To Frau Marie Wittich as 'Isolda': *NB*, *P*
To Ireland: *SF*
To M: LF, pp. 256-7
To my Little Friend Donnall Gillespie in Glencolumcille: *Orpheus*, 10 (April 1910), p. 144; *P*, *DO'B*
To the Beloved: NB, *P*, *SF*, *DO'B*
To the World-Goddess: NB
Too Late: *LPM*
Tower of Love, The: *P*
Trance: *P*
Transitional: *LPM*
Trevor's Ballades: MS
Triolets, [Two]: NB
Tryst: *P*, *DO'B*
Twentieth Year, The: *P*
Under the Sea: NB
Undine: *P*
Vain Dream, A (To G): *P*
Valley of the Bells, The: *SF*
Villanelle [I]: NB
Villanelle [II]: NB
Voice of the Sea, The: NB, *P*
Well-meaning One, The (February 1916): MS
When we are lost: NB, *DO'B* (see also **65** in the Catalogue of Music)
Winter-night (January 1915): MS
Winter Sunlight: MS
'With regard to our free-hitting Stacy': Clifford Bax, *Inland Far* (London, 1925), p. 182; LF, p. 87
Woman and Artist: *LPM*, *DO'B*

Appendix 8

PHOTOGRAPHS, PORTRAITS AND PERSONALIA

Photographs

'A photographer's studio is to me only second in horror to the dentist's chair.'

Bax's reply to a request in 1932 for a signed portrait

Well over a hundred black and white photographs of Bax exist, many of them published, but a large number of informal pictures, including holiday snaps, are in private possession. The earliest is reproduced in Lewis Foreman, *Farewell, my Youth and Other Writings by Arnold Bax* (pl. 1), and shows Bax at the age of one (1884/5) being held by his grandmother. The last photographs were probably those taken by Yevonde Middleton at Clifford Bax's Albany flat in September 1953, less than a month before the composer's death. One of the pictures is reproduced in CSS (the penultimate plate between pp. 110 and 111). Two photographs taken by Bax himself are reproduced in Foreman's biography (LF).

Three colour photographs of Bax are known. The earliest was taken *c.* 1907 by Paul Corder, who had developed his own colour process, and is reproduced (in black and white only) as the frontispiece to Lewis Foreman's edition of *Farewell, my Youth*. Forty-odd years later, in November 1948, Messrs. Tunbridge made two colour portraits of Bax at the request of Percy Grainger, who had asked several of his composer friends to have their faces photographed to support his curious notion that all true creative artists have blue eyes. Original prints of these two photographs are in the Grainger Museum, Melbourne, and in private hands. One of them was reproduced on the sleeve of the Cloud Nine recording of *Malta, G.C.* and *Oliver Twist*.The other has been published in monochrome in the June 1986 (p. 1) and February 1987 (p. 1109) issues of *The Gramophone*.

Although Bax attended at least two public functions at which film cameras were present (the royal wedding in 1947 and the funeral of King George VI in 1952), no film footage of him has been traced.

Portraits

Many line drawings and caricatures of Bax have appeared in print over the years, mostly based on existing photographs, and there are several original portraits done from life: A red crayon drawing signed 'Wilson' and dating from 1931 is reproduced on the sleeves of the Chandos recordings of Bax's two-piano works and of Eric Parkin's volumes of the solo piano music. The RAM owns a portrait in oils by his sister-in-law, Vera Bax, dated 1933, which is reproduced on the sleeve of the Chandos recording of *Enchanted*

Summer and also in David Fraser (ed.), *Fairest Isle* (London, 1995), p. 78. A pencil drawing by Powys Evans in the National Portrait Gallery is reproduced in Frank Howes, *The English Musical Renaissance* (London, 1966), pl. 8, the *Arnold Bax Society Bulletin*, 1 (February 1968), front cover, and in CSS, p. xvii. A Vorticist-style drawing of Bax appeared in *The Radio Times* for 15 March 1935, p. 15, and was reproduced in *BMS News*, 67 (September, 1995), p. 153. A drawing by Robert Sherriffs appeared in *The Radio Times* for 7 September 1945, p. 5. Another drawing is part of the Harrison Sisters Archive in the RCM. Milein Cosman (the wife of Hans Keller) drew Bax in 1948, and this is reproduced in Arthur Jacobs (comp.), *Music Lover's Anthology* (London, 1948), opp. p. 113, and in *The Radio Times* for 16 October 1953, p. 3. In the summer of 1952 Richard Walker visited Bax at Storrington, where he made several sketches and subsequently a small painting in oils.

No sculptures of Bax are known to exist, but the Boole Library, University College, Cork, has his death mask (made by Seamus Murphy), which formerly hung in the Bax Memorial Room. There is also a plaster cast of his left hand, and a large bronze medallion with a portrait in low relief of the composer (based on a photograph taken *c.* 1920) and bearing his titles and the legend: 'In Memory of Clifford Bax'. The medallion is reproduced on the front of the booklet of the Olympia recording of the *Fantasy Sonata* (arr. viola and piano).

Personalia

A lock of Bax's hair given to Harriet Cohen is in private ownership, as are the composer's cricket bat and a silver box presented to him as a twenty-first birthday present. Other personal effects—pens, pencils, spectacles, pipes, wallets, certificates, chess set, knightly insignia, knick-knacks, and so forth—are in the Boole Library, which also has his collection of scores and some of his books, mostly those on music and the Irish language but including ordnance survey maps of Ireland and some works of literature; the rest of Bax's library is in University College, Dublin, the vast majority of the books dealing with aspects of Irish culture, history and literature, over half of them being in Irish Gaelic. (Bax was an omnivorous reader and his literary tastes were wide, ranging from Sophocles' *Oidiopús i gColón*, in Irish, to *Lady Chatterleys Elsker*, in Danish.) The Bax Memorial Room in the Music Department of University College, Cork, formerly housed a grand piano belonging to him that had been presented by Harriet Cohen; according to the late Aloys Fleischmann, this was sold in the early 1980s by one of his successors as Professor of Music.

Bax's addresses

Although Bax's adult life was always spent in rented accomodation, he owned at least three houses: 1 Abercorn Place, St John's Wood, London NW8 (leasehold), which was occupied by Harriet Cohen from 1934 until its destruction by two incendiary bombs on 11 September 1940; 8 Gloucester Place Mews, Gloucester Place, Portman Square, London W1 (leasehold), in which Miss Cohen lived from July 1942 until her death in 1967; and 'Widford', Fern Road, Storrington, Sussex (freehold), in which Mary Gleaves lived from the 1940s until the late 1970s. Many letters also exist written by Bax from a wide variety of temporary addresses (mostly hotels) in Britain and Ireland. In the following list, details of the early addresses in south London are based on the researches of John Cresswell of the Streatham Society.

1883–4: 'Heath Villa', 13 Angles Road, Streatham, Surrey. In 1993 English Heritage erected a blue plaque outside this house.
1884–6: 'Hazeldean', 15 Angles Road, Streatham, Surrey. This road was renamed Pendennis Road on 18 July 1884, and Streatham is now London SW16.
1886–88/9: 'Holmewood', Balham High Road, Upper Tooting, London SW[12]. Part of Du Cane Court now stands on this site.
1888/9–1897: 'Marlborough House', [4] Balham Hill, London SW[12]. House demolished in the 1930s.
1897–1911: Ivy Bank, Haverstock Hill, Hampstead, London NW[3]. House bought by Alfred Bax in 1893 and demolished in 1911. A model of Ivy Bank is owned by the local history department of Camden Public Libraries. When visiting Glencolumcille (on and off between 1903 and 1930), Bax stayed in the local pub.
1911: 1a Chester Terrace, Regents Park, London NW[1]. Bax's parents moved in February of this year to 7 Cavendish Square, London W1.
1911–spring 1914: 'Yeovil', 10 Bushy Park Road, Rathgar, Co. Dublin, Ireland. This house still exists.
Spring 1914–15: Elm Corner, Marlow Common, Buckinghamshire.
1915–18: 'The Crossways', Station Rise, Marlow on Thames, Buckinghamshire. Bax also writes it as 'The Crossways Riversleigh Beaconsfield. Marlow on Tham[es] Bucks.' though Beaconsfield is actually some distance from Marlow.
1918–September 1939: 155 Fellows Road, Swiss Cottage, London NW3. House demolished in 1968. Bax retained his rooms at this address after his move to Sussex in 1939.
Winter 1928–January 1940: Yearly winter visits to Station Hotel, Morar, Inverness-shire, Scotland. Now called the Morar Hotel.
September–December1939: Several temporary addresses in Sussex: Roundabout Hotel, Storrington; Warnes Hotel, Worthing; Railway Hotel, Pulborough.
1940–1953: The White Horse Hotel, Storrington, Sussex. A commemorative plaque was erected outside in 1983. Bax died at the home of Professor Aloys Fleischmann: Glen House, Ballyvolane, Cork, Ireland.

BIBLIOGRAPHY

This contains details of all the major writings on Bax and a fair proportion of the innumerable minor and ephemeral articles that have appeared over the years, the cut-off date for inclusion being 1 July 1998. Lewis Foreman's *Bibliography of Writings on Arnold Bax* (1970) and the bibliography in his *Bax: A Composer and his Times* (1983, rev. 1988) have proved invaluable. A few articles that are currently on the Internet have also been included; these are on the Sir Arnold Bax Web Site compiled by Richard R. Adams and Rob Barnett: "http://phobos.kiss.de:81/~adams/welcome.htm"; also on "http://www.edu.coventry.ac.uk/music/bax/welcome.htm".

Abraham, G. E. H., 'Six British Piano Sonatas: 3. The Two Bax Sonatas', *The Music Teacher* (July 1926), pp. 418-19.

Alexander, Arthur, 'Arnold Bax: Some Personal Recollections': Unpublished essay.

Allen, David Rayvern, *A Song for Cricket* (London: Pelham Books Ltd., 1981), pp. 74, 76. Includes the 'Old Broughtonians' Battle-Song' of 1924.

Alwyn, William, 'The Music of Arnold Bax', *R. A. M. Magazine*, 157 (January 1954), pp. 6-8.

Anderson, Colin, 'Vernon Handley interviewed by Colin Anderson', *Strictly Off the Record: Live Music in View*, 6 (autumn 1994), pp. 8-10.

Anderson, W. R., 'Symphony No. 3', *The Gramophone* (February 1944), pp. 134-5.

—— 'Some Modern Masters: 10. Arnold Bax (Born 1883)', *The Music Teacher* (September 1947), pp. 341, 334 [*sic*].

—— 'Obituary: Sir Arnold Bax (6 [actually 8] November 1883—3 October 1953)', *The Musical Times*, (November 1953), pp. 528-9.

Andrews, Dennis, *Cuchulan among the Guns* (Cumnor: privately published, 1998; limited edn. of 250 copies). Essays by Christopher Whelen and letters written to him by Bax.

Angles, R., 'Brazen Romantic', *Records and Recordings* (February 1965), p. 13.

Antcliffe, H., 'Boughton, Holst and Bax', *The Musical News and Herald* (19 January 1924), pp. 60-1.

Aprahamian, Felix, 'An English master ripe for reprise', *The Sunday Times* (4 June 1989). The photograph accompanying this article is of Moeran not Bax.

Baker, T., 'Sir Arnold Bax', *Baker's Biographical Dictionary of Musicians*, 5th edn. rev. by Nicolas Slonimsky (New York: G. Schirmer, Inc., 1958), pp. 102-3.

Balanchine, G. and Mason, F., 'Picnic at Tintagel', *Balanchine's Festival of Ballet* (London, 1978), pp. 429-32.

Banfield, Stephen, 'Bax as Song Composer', *The Musical Times* (November 1983), pp. 666-9.

—— 'The Celtic Twilight', *Sensibility and English Song*, I (Cambridge: CUP, 1985), pp. 248-74.

—— (ed.), *Music in Britain: The Twentieth Century*, The Blackwell History of Music in Britain (general ed. Ian Spink), 6 (Oxford: Basil Blackwell Ltd., 1995).

Bannard, Y., 'Arnold Bax, Magician', *The Musical Standard* (13 October 1917).

Barnett, Rob, 'Rob Barnett interviews Myer Fredman', The Sir Arnold Bax Web Site (1998).

—— 'Composer John McCabe on Arnold Bax', The Sir Arnold Bax Web Site (1998).

Barrie, J. M., 'The Truth about the Russian Dancers: Introduced by Tamara Karsavina', *Dance Perspectives*, 14 (spring 1962). Reprinted by the Johnson Reprint Corp., New York, 1970.

Barrington, Jonah, *And Master of None* (London: Walter Edwards Ltd., n.d. [*c.* 1947])

Bax, Clifford, *Inland Far* (London: William Heinemann Ltd., 1925; Lovat Dickson Ltd., 1933).

—— *Ideas and People* (London: Lovat Dickson Ltd., 1936).

—— 'Silver and Bronze Trumpets', *The National & English Review* (June 1948), pp. 500-6.

—— 'Clifford Bax on Arnold Bax', *Crescendo*, 12 (November 1948), pp. 5-6.

Bax Society Bulletin (London and Philadelphia: Bax Society), 1968-73.

'Bax Symphonies, The', *BMS News* [newsletter of the British Music Society], 74 (June 1997), pp. 35-40. Contributions from David Lloyd-Jones, Vernon Handley, Colin Scott-Sutherland, Lewis Foreman, Robert Walker, Eric Fenby, *et al.*

'Bax's Third Symphony', *Bax Society Bulletin*, 6 (August 1969), pp. 102-7.

Beechey, G., 'The Legacy of Arnold Bax (1883-1953)', *Musical Opinion* (August 1983), pp. 348-51; (September 1983), pp. 357-63, 383.

Benjamin, Arthur, 'Arnold Bax: 1883-1953', *Music & Letters* (January 1954), pp. 1-5.

Bennett, R., 'Arnold Bax', *The Bookman* (September 1922), pp. 266-8.

Blake, Andrew, *The Land without Music: Music, Culture and Society in twentieth-century Britain*' (Manchester and New York: Manchester University Press, 1997).

Bliss, Arthur, 'Recent Works of Arnold Bax', *The Musical News and Herald* (21 May 1921), p. 625.

—— 'Berners and Bax', *The League of Composers Review* (February 1924), pp. 26-7.

—— 'Arnold Bax: 1883-1953', *Music & Letters* (January 1954), pp. 1-14.

Block, Maxine (ed.), *Current Biography: Who's News and Why 1943* (New York: The H. W. Wilson Company, 1944), pp. 31-3.

Blom, Eric, 'Arnold Bax', *Chesterian* (February 1920), pp. 136-9; excerpt also in Norman Demuth (ed.), *An Anthology of 'Musical Criticism* (London: Eyre & Spottiswoode, 1947), pp. 358-9.

—— 'Studies at Random: XVI. A Revival of the Carol', *Musical Opinion* (November 1922), p. 144.

—— *Programme of Concert of Recent Works of Arnold Bax*, Queen's Hall, 13 November 1922, vii + 24 pp.

—— 'Arnold Bax's [First] Symphony', *The Manchester Guardian* (14 January 1924). Reprinted in *Bax Society Bulletin*, 3 (October 1968), pp. 44-5.

—— 'The Carol Revived', *Stepchildren of Music* (London: G. T. Foulis [1926]), pp. 277-83.

—— *A General Index to Modern Musical Literature in the English Language* (London, 1927).

—— 'Bax's Symphony No. 2', *The Music Teacher* (April 1931), pp. 195-6.

—— 'Arnold Bax's Piano Sonatas', *The Listener* (12 October 1944), p. 417.

Bowen, York, 'Arnold Bax: 1883-1953', *Music & Letters* (January 1954), pp. 5-7.

Boyd, Ernest, *Ireland's Literary Renaissance* (Dublin and London, 1916), pp. 386-7, 407.

Bradbury, E. 'Music and Musicians: Bax the Brazen Romantic', *Yorkshire Post* (12 October 1965).
—— 'Celtic Soul of Bax laid bare', *Yorkshire Post* (25 June 1983).
Brian, Havergal, 'The First Symphony of Arnold Bax', *Musical Opinion* (December 1922), pp. 253-4. Reprinted in Malcolm MacDonald (ed.), *Havergal Brian on Music: Selections from his Journalism, I: British Music* (London: Toccata Press, 1986), pp. 233-40.
—— 'Bax's Third String Quartet', *Musical Opinion* (July 1941), p. 445. Reprinted in Malcolm MacDonald (ed.), op. cit., 240-1.
British Musician and Musical News, 'Musicians: X. Arnold Bax' (August 1930), pp. 210-12.
Brooke, Donald, 'Sir Arnold Bax', *Composer's Gallery* (London: Rockliff Publishing Corporation Ltd., 1946), pp. 16-19.
[Butterworth, Arthur] 'Déjà vu? Composer Arthur Butterworth muses on Sir Arnold Bax', The Sir Arnold Bax Web Site (1998).
Capell, Richard, 'Bax as Man and Artist: The Celtic Fancy', *The Daily Telegraph* (10 October 1953).
Cardus, Nevil, 'Bax's Third Symphony', *The Manchester Guardian* (19 November 1930). Reprinted in *Bax Society Bulletin*, 6 (August 1969), pp. 104-5.
—— 'Through a Dark Haze', *The Guardian*, 3 November 1965.
Chappell & Co. Ltd., *The Chappell Orchestral Hire Library* [catalogue] (October 1971).
Chappell Music Ltd., *Sir Arnold Bax 1883-1953* (1983): Centenary folder of leaflets including 'Sir Arnold Bax' by Lewis Foreman, 'A Guide to the Music of Arnold Bax' by Christopher Palmer, and 'A Catalogue of Works' [by Graham Parlett].
Chester, J. & W., *Arnold Bax* (Miniature Essay Series), 1921, 16 pp. In English and French. German translation published in the programme for the International Society for Contemporary Music on the occasion of the performance of Bax's First Symphony in Prague on 1 June 1924.
Chesterian, The, 'Arnold Bax: Album of Seven Selected Songs' (April 1919), pp. 274-5.
Chisholm, Diana, 'Sir Arnold Bax' : Unpublished essay, *c.* November1963(?), held by the J. W. Jagger Library, University of Cape Town.
Chisholm, Erik, 'Arnold Bax': Script for an unpublished talk, *c.* 1963(?), held by the J. W. Jagger Library, University of Cape Town.
Chislett, W. A., 'Neglected Composers. V. Arnold Bax', *The Gramophone* (July 1927), p. 77.
Church, Richard, 'The Story of Tintagel in a Bax Tone Poem', *Musical Masterpieces of the Week: XXIV*, *The Radio Times* (24 April 1931), p. 189.
—— *The Voyage Home* (London: William Heinemann Ltd., 1964), pp. 50-3.
Clarke, G., 'Arnold Bax: sonata for viola and harp', *Canon* (November 1949), pp. 223-4.
Coates, Eric, 'Arnold Bax: 1883-1953', *Music & Letters* (January 1954), p. 7.
Cohen, Harriet, 'Arnold Bax. Nereid', *Music's Handmaid* (London: Faber & Faber Ltd., 1936), pp. 153-60.
—— *A Bundle of Time* (London: Faber & Faber Ltd., 1969).
Colmer, Francis, 'A few remarks on certain traits of character belonging to Arnold and Clifford Bax': unpublished notes sent to Colin Scott-Sutherland in May 1963.

Colum, Mary, *Life and the Dream* (London: Macmillan Publishers Ltd., 1947), pp. 103, 185, 188, 301-2, 421.

Cooper, Martin, 'John Ireland et Arnold Bax', *Les Musiciens anglais d'aujourd'hui* (Paris: Librairie Plon, 1952), pp. 61-73.

—— 'The Dream World of Arnold Bax', *The Daily Telegraph* (19 May 1973).

Cox, David, 'Arnold Bax', *The Symphony*, ed. Robert Simpson, 2 (Harmondsworth: Penguin Books Ltd., 1967), pp. 153-65.

[Cresswell, John], *The Birthplace of Sir Arnold Bax: 13 Pendennis Road London SW 16* (London: Streatham Society, [1988]).

Crichton, Ronald, 'A Centenary of Bax', *The Financial Times* (23 September 1983), p. 19.

Cronin, Sister K., 'The Celtic Literary Influence in the Songs of Arnold Bax', M.A. thesis (Mt St Mary College, Los Angeles, July 1967).

—— 'Bax in the modern media', *Bax Society Bulletin*, 4 (February 1969), pp. 57-60.

Crowley, Anne, 'Arnold Bax': Unpublished notes sent to Graham Parlett in 1975.

Curran, Tim, 'Concert hall—in Cyril's semi!', *Argus Weekender* (8 May 1982). About the Brighton and Hove Gramophone Orchestral Society of which Bax was President.

Daily Telegraph, The, 'Italian Critics of Bax' (25 November 1935). Reprinted in the *Bax Society Bulletin*, 6 (August 1969), pp. 103-4.

Dale, S. S., 'Contemporary Cello Concerti XVI—Sir Arnold Bax', *The Strad* (February 1974), pp. 591, 593 and 595.

Day, Christine, 'Friendly ghost mystery at the White Horse', *West Sussex County Times* (28 December 1979). This and the next entry refer to reported sightings of Bax's ghost.

—— 'Guests fall "victim" to hotel ghost', *West Sussex County Times* (11 January 1980).

Demuth, Norman, 'The Garden of Fand', *Record Collector's Series No. 1: Suggestions for forming a basic record library* (EMI, 1950), pp. 57-8.

—— 'Bax-Symphony No. 3 in C', *Record Collector's Series No. 2: Symphonies* (EMI, 1950), pp. 54-8.

—— 'Sir Arnold Bax', *Musical Trends in the Twentieth Century* (London: Rockliff Publishing Corporation Ltd., 1952), pp. 155-67.

—— 'Sir Arnold Bax', *Musical Opinion* (April 1957), pp. 401 and 403.

Dent, Edward J., 'Arnold Bax', *The National and Athenaeum* (25 November 1922), pp. 328-30. Reprinted in Hale (see below).

Dibble, Jeremy, 'Inventory of Bax Collection' (Cork: Music Department, University College, June 1988) [unpublished typescript].

Eggar, Katharine E., 'The Piano Pieces of Arnold Bax', *The Music Student* (November 1921), pp. 65-7, 78.

—— 'Recent Chamber Works by Bax', *The Music Bulletin* (November 1927), p. 339.

Elkin, R., 'Symphonic Poems of Bax', *The Stories behind Music* (London: Rider & Co., 1949), pp. 23-6.

Elliott, C. K., 'Rosalind and Godwin Baynes: A Wisbech Vignette 1913-15', *The Wisbech Society: 46th Annual Report* (1985), pp. 7-10

Evans, Edwin, 'Arnold Bax's Piano Music', *The Chesterian* (June 1918), pp. 213-16.

—— 'Modern British Composers. II. Arnold Bax', *The Musical Times* (1 March 1919), pp. 103-5; (1 April 1919), pp. 154-6.

—— 'November Woods', *The Sackbut* (February 1922), pp. 33-4.
—— 'Arnold Bax', *The Musical Quarterly* (April 1923), pp. 167-80.
—— 'Bax, Arnold Edward Trevor', *A Dictionary of Modern Music and Musicians*, ed. A. Eaglefield-Hull, *et al.* (London: J. M. Dent & Sons Ltd., 1924), pp. 32-4.
—— 'Arnold Bax', *Modern Music* (November–December 1927), pp. 25-30.
—— 'Bax', *Cobbett's Cyclopaedic Survey of Chamber Music*, 1 (Oxford: OUP, 1929; 2nd edn. 1963), pp. 67-78.
—— 'Master of the King's Musick', *Time & Tide* (28 February 1942), p. 172.
—— 'The Bax Symphonies', *The Listener* (29 October 1942), p. 573.
—— 'Arnold Bax, Hunter of Dreams', *The Listener* (4 January 1945), p. 25.
—— 'Bax', *Grove's Dictionary of Music and Musicians*, 5th edn., 1 (London: Macmillan & Ltd., 1954), pp. 509-12; also *Supplement* (1961), p. 27.
Ewen, D., *Composers of today* (New York: The H. W. Wilson Company, 1934), pp. 15-16.
—— *The Complete Book of 20th Century Music* (London: Anthony Blond Ltd., 1952, 1959), pp. 17-19.
—— 'Sir Arnold Bax', *European Composers Today* (New York: The H. W. Wilson Company, 1954), pp. 23-4.
—— 'Arnold Bax', *The Home Book of Twentieth Century Music* (New York: Arco, 1956), pp. 17-19.
—— 'Sir Arnold Bax', *The World of Twentieth Century Music* (New York: Robert Hale, 1969), pp. 45-9.
Ezcurdia, H. de, 'Arnold Bax', *Orientación Musical* (October 1946), pp. 5-6.
Farjeon, Eleanor, *Edward Thomas: The Last Four Years* (Oxford: OUP, 1958). Revised by Anne Harvey (Phoenix Mill, Thrupp, Stroud: Sutton Publishing Ltd., 1997).
Fawkes, Richard, 'Bax on the box', *Classical Music* (14 November 1992), p. 34. About Ken Russell's television film on Bax.
Fleischmann, Aloys, 'The Arnold Bax Memorial', *UCC Record*, 31 (Cork, Easter 1956), pp. 25-30.
—— 'Arnold Bax', *Recorded Sound* (January–April 1968), pp. 273-6.
—— 'In Conversation with Michael Dawney', *The Composer*, 56 (winter 1975-6), pp. 29-31.
Fleischmann, Tilly, 'Some reminiscences of Arnold Bax': Unpublished typescript in UCC, August 1955.
Fleury, Michel, *L'impressionisme et la musique* (Paris: Fayard, 1996).
Flothuis, Marius, *Modern British Composers* (Stockholm: The Continental Book Company A. D. and London: Sidgwick & Jackson, n.d. [1950?].
Foreman, Lewis [R.L.E.], 'The Unperformed Works of Sir Arnold Bax', *Musical Opinion* (July 1966), pp. 598-9.
—— 'Arnold Bax: A Discography', *Recorded Sound* (January–April 1968), pp. 277-83.
—— 'Spring Fire: A major unperformed work by Sir Arnold Bax', *Bax Society Bulletin*, 2 (June 1968), pp. 30-5.
—— 'Catalogue of the Unrecorded Works of Arnold Bax', *BIRS* (August 1968), 8 pp.
—— 'A Time for Bax', *Records and Recordings* (October 1968), pp. 20-1.
—— 'The Garden of Fand: A study of Arnold Bax', *Audio and Record Review*, (January 1969), pp. 19, 78.

—— 'Sir Arnold Bax's Rhapsodic Ballad', *The Strad* (April 1969), pp. 50, 507.

—— 'The Quest for Bax', *Brio* (autumn 1969), pp. 28-31.

—— 'Bax, the Symphony and Sibelius', *Musical Opinion* (February 1970), pp. 245-6.

—— 'Bax and the score of Malta G.C.', *Bax Society Bulletin*, 8 (April 1970), pp. 7-9.

—— 'Bibliography of Writings on Arnold Bax', *Current Musicology*, 19 (1970), pp. 124-40.

—— 'The Musical Development of Arnold Bax', *Music & Letters* (January 1971), pp. 59-68.

—— 'Symphonic Variations', *Musical Opinion* (March 1971), pp. 291, 293.

—— 'A Catalogue of Autograph Manuscript Sources of Music by Sir Arnold Bax', *RMA Research Chronicle*, 12 (1974), pp. 91-105.

—— 'Bax and the Ballet', *Proceedings of the RMA*, 104 (1977-8), pp. 11-19.

—— (ed.), *Dermot O'Byrne: Poems by Arnold Bax* (London: Thames Publishing, 1979).

—— 'Arnold Bax', *International Music Guide 1983* (London: The Tantivy Press Ltd., 1982), pp. 26-7.

—— *Bax: A Composer and his Times* (London: Scholar Press, 1983; 2nd edn. 1988; now Aldershot: Ashgate Publishing Ltd.).

—— 'Arnold Bax at the RAM', *The Royal Academy of Music Magazine*, 233 (autumn 1983), pp. 11-17

—— 'Spring Fire', programme note for a Royal Philharmonic Society Concert (5 October 1983).

—— 'Celtic Nympholept', *The Listener* (3 November 1983), p. 36.

—— 'Building a Career', *The Gramophone* (February 1987), p. 1096. Interview with Margaret Fingerhut about *Winter Legends*.

—— (ed.), *From Parry to Britten: British Music in letters 1900-1945* (London: B. T. Batsford Ltd., 1987).

—— ['Arnold Bax']: booklet for *The Complete Symphonies* [boxed set of CDs: CHAN 8906-10] (Colchester: Chandos Records Ltd., 1990), pp. 5-15; with translations into German and French.

—— *Music in England 1885-1920* (London: Thames Publishing, 1994).

—— 'Heirs and Rebels: The Wars and Between 1914-1945', David Fraser (ed.), *Fairest Isle: BBC Radio 3 Book of British Music* (London: BBC Radio 3, 1995), pp. 77-81.

[Forsyth, J. A.], 'Pen Pictures of Personalities Past & Present: No. 4 Arnold Bax', *R. A. M. Magazine*, 78 (June 1927), pp. 3-4.

Foss, Herbert, 'Some Chamber Music by Arnold Bax', *The Dominant* (December 1927), pp. 16-19.

—— 'Arnold Bax's Third Violin Sonata', *Gamut* (March–April 1929), pp. 40-1.

—— 'Sir Arnold Bax: Master of the King's Music', *Music in Schools* (March–April 1942), p. 377.

Frank, Alan, 'Sir Arnold Bax: A Portrait of the Man and his Music', *Music Teacher* (September 1952), pp. 412, 416. Revised as 'Sir Arnold Bax', *Modern British Composers*, Student's Music Library Series (London: Dennis Dobson Ltd., 1953), pp. 21-7.

G., E. [Edward Greenfield], [tribute], *The Times* (20 October 1953).

Gillam, C. W., 'A Lost Work by Bax', *Bax Society Bulletin*, 3 (October 1968), p. 40. About the *Prelude to Adonais*.

Gilman, Lawrence, 'Some Celtic Music old and new', *North American Review* (May 1921), pp. 697-704.
—— 'Music: Two Novelties by Arnold Bax', *New York Herald Tribune* (24 November 1933). Reprinted in *Bax Society Bulletin*, 5 (May 1969), pp. 81-2.
Glock, William, 'Malta G. C.', *The Observer* (28 February 1943), p. 2.
Goddard, Scott, 'London Letter', *The Chesterian* (January 1954), p. 31.
Goossens, Eugene, *Overture and Beginners: A Musical Autobiography* (London: Methuen & Co. Ltd., 1951).
Gramophone, The (February 1987). This issue features the Chandos recording of *Winter Legends* on the front cover and contains several articles and reviews of Baxian interest.
Green, D. M., 'Oliver Twist: Music for the Film', *Music in Education* (September–October 1948), p. 123.
Green, L. Dunton, 'New Music Reviewed: Arnold Bax's latest Published Works', *The Chesterian* (June 1922), pp. 244-6.
H., C., 'Mr. Arnold Bax in a Celtic Fog', *The Spectator* (25 November 1922), pp. 764-5.
Hadley, Patrick, [tribute], *The Times* (20 October 1953).
—— ['Arnold Bax: 1883-1953'], *Music & Letters* (January 1954), pp. 8-9
Hale, Philip, 'Arnold Bax' [programme note to first performance of Second Symphony by the Boston Symphony Orchestra] (13 December 1929), pp. 610-34. Includes reprint of Dent (see above).
Handley, Vernon, 'Conducting Bax's Music', *Bax Society Bulletin*, 5 (May 1969), pp. 74-6.
—— 'Back to Bax', *The Musical Times* (August 1992), pp. 377-8.
Hawkins, D., 'Master of the Queen's Musick', *Music Making*, 24 (spring 1954), p. 14.
Heim, N. M., 'Sonata for Clarinet and Piano by Arnold Bax' in his 'The Use of the Clarinet in Published Sonatas for Clarinet and Piano by English Composers . . .', M.M. thesis (Eastman School of Music, Rochester, 1954), pp. 124-58.
Henry, Leigh, 'Contemporaries: Arnold Bax', *Musical Opinion* (May 1920), pp. 629-31.
—— 'Arnold Bax: The New Publications', *British Music Bulletin* (May 1921), pp. 109-11.
—— 'Arnold Bax', *The Music Bulletin* [of the British Music Society] (August 1923), pp. 240-3.
Herbage, Julian, 'Hail, Bright Cecilia', *The Radio Times* (19 November 1943), p. 4. About Bax's Violin Concerto.
—— 'Sir Arnold Bax', *British Music in our Time*, ed. A. L. Bacharach (Harmondsworth: Penguin Books Ltd., 2nd edn., 1951), pp. 11-26.
—— 'The Music of Arnold Bax', *The Music Times* (December 1953), pp. 555-7.
—— 'Bax, Sir Arnold Edward Trevor', *Dictionary of National Biography* (Oxford: OUP, 1971), pp. 75-7.
Heward, Leslie H., 'Arnold Bax', *Voorslag*, 1, 10 (March–April 1927), pp. 15-18.
Hill, Ralph, 'Master of the King's Music', *The Radio Times* (13 March 1942).
—— 'Music of Sir Arnold Bax', *The Radio Times* (7 May 1943), p. 4.
—— 'Colour Impressionism', *The Radio Times* (13 August 1943), p. 4.
—— 'Arnold Bax: The Man and his Music', *The Radio Times* (5 January 1945), p. 5.

—— 'Arnold Bax: Master of the King's Musick', *Hinrichsen's Musical Year Book*, 2-3 (1945-6), pp. 17-22.

Hoffpauir, J. C., 'Three Tone-Poems by Arnold Bax', M.M. thesis (University of Missouri, Kansas City, 1981).

Holbrooke, Joseph, 'Arnold Bax', *Contemporary British Composers* (London: Cecil Palmer, 1925), pp. 53-60.

Holquist, R. A., 'An Analytical Study of Choral Music of Arnold Bax (1883-1953)', M.S. thesis (Wisconsin State University, Eau Claire, 1971).

Howes, Frank, 'The Late Romantics', *English Music Renaissance* (London: Secker & Warburg, 1966), pp. 214-22.

Hughes, Herbert, 'Arnold Bax's new Concerto for Violoncello', *The Saturday Review* (28 October 1933), p. 444.

Hull, Robert H. ['Robin Hull' for the last three entries], 'Bax's Third Symphony', *The Musical Times* (March 1930), pp. 217-20.

—— 'Arnold Bax's Third Symphony', *The Monthly Musical Record* (September 1930), pp. 259-60.

—— 'In the Vanguard of British Composers', *The Radio Times* (11 July 1930), p. 66.

—— 'Arnold Bax', *The Contemporary Review* (March 1931), pp. 343-8.

—— *A Handbook on Arnold Bax's Symphonies* (London: Murdoch, Murdoch & Co., [1932]), 51 pp.

—— 'Bax's Fourth Symphony', *The Spectator* (9 December 1932), p. 827.

—— 'Arnold Bax's Fourth Symphony', *The Musical Mirror and Fanfare* (December 1932), pp. 77-8.

—— 'Arnold Bax: Chamber Music', *The Musical Mirror and Fanfare* (June 1933).

—— 'Arnold Bax's Fifth Symphony', *The Monthly Musical Record* (January 1934), pp. 7-9. Reprinted in *Bax Society Bulletin*, 4 (February 1969), pp. 61-5.

—— 'Arnold Bax's Fifth Symphony', *The Daily Telegraph* (13 January 1934).

—— 'About 'Cello Concertos', *The Radio Times* (15 March 1935), p. 15.

—— 'Bax's Sixth Symphony', *Musical Opinion* (November 1935), pp. 115-16.

—— 'Approach to Bax's Symphonies', *Music & Letters* (April 1942), pp. 101-15.

—— 'Arnold Bax' [booklet issued with *The English Music Society*, 2, Columbia Records, *c*. 1942].

—— 'Composers of To-day: 3. Sir Arnold Bax', *Our Time*, 5, 9 (April 1946), pp. 187-8.

Hull, Robin *see* Hull, Robert H.

Huntley, John, 'The Film Music of Arnold Bax', *The Cinema Studio*, I, 10 (2 June 1948), p. 5.

—— 'The Film Music of Bax—Fanfares and Anthems—The M. K. M. writes them from a room over the saloon bar', *Musical Express* (25 June 1948), p. 2.

—— 'Music by Appointment', *Band Wagon* (August 1948), p. 36.

—— 'The Music of "Hamlet" and "Oliver Twist"', *Penguin Film Review*, 8 (1949), pp. 110-16.

—— 'Oliver Twist', *Film Music Notes* (September–October 1951), pp. 20-2.

Inman, Daniel, 'The Truth about the Russian Dancers', *Bax Society Bulletin*, 2 (June 1968), pp. 21-3.

James, Burnett, 'Sir Arnold Bax . . .', *The Gramophone* (November 1953), p. 179; (December 1953), pp. 221-2.

—— 'New Recognition for Bax', *Audio and Record Review* (January 1965), pp. 25-6.

—— 'Arnold Bax and the Concerto', *Bax Society Bulletin*, 8 (April 1970), pp. 4-6.

Kalisch, Alfred, 'Arnold Bax: A British Musical Genius', *The Daily News* (5 December 1922). Reprinted in *Bax Society Bulletin*, 1 (February 1968), pp. 8-9.

Kedge, Don, 'Sir Arnold Bax', *Streatham and the Famous*, 6 (Streatham Society, 1988).

Keener, Andrew, 'Arnold Bax', in John Lade (ed.), *Building a Library: A Listener's Guide to Record Collecting* (London: OUP, 1979), pp. 144-7.

Keller, Hans ['H.K.'], 'Bax's Oliver Twist', *The Music Review* (August 1948), pp. 198-9. Reprinted in *Bax Society Bulletin*, 9 (November 1970), pp. 22-3.

Kendell, A., 'Arnold Bax: Individualist', *Canon* (November 1949), pp. 231-3.

Kennedy, Michael, 'State of Bax Britannica', *The Daily Telegraph* (25 July 1981).

—— 'Reviving the best of Bax', *The Daily Telegraph* (25 June 1983), p. 11.

Lace, Ian, 'The Bax Symphonies', *BMS News*, 74 (June 1997), pp. 35-9. Reprinted in *Fanfare*, 21, 5 (May/June 1998), pp. 22, 25-6, 28-32, 34, 38-9. Also on The Sir Arnold Bax Web Site (1998).

—— 'Bax and Elgar', The Sir Arnold Bax Web Site (1998).

—— 'Following Bax to Morar', *BMS News*, 75 (September 1997), pp. 70-2. Also on The Sir Arnold Bax Web Site (1998).

—— 'Bax and Harriet Cohen', *BMS News*, 75 (September 1997), pp. 84.

Latham, Peter, 'Arnold Bax: 1883-1953', *Music & Letters* (January 1954), pp 10-12.

Layton, Robert, 'The Symphony in Britain', Layton, Robert (ed.), *A Companion to the Symphony* (London: Simon & Schuster, 1993), pp. 436-8.

Lee, E. M., 'The Amateur's Repertoire' [on Bax's Irish songs], *Musical Opinion* (April 1931), p. 603.

—— 'The Student Interpreter: Fourth Piano Sonata', *Musical Opinion* (December 1935), p. 219; (January 1936), p. 312.

Lloyd, Stephen, 'Symphony No.7', *Bax Society Bulletin*, 11 (January 1973), pp. 46-7.

—— *H. Balfour Gardiner* (Cambridge: CUP, 1984).

—— *Sir Dan Godfrey: Champion of British Composers* (London: Thames Publishing, 1995).

Longmire, John, 'Bax and John Ireland', *Bax Society Bulletin*, 6 (August 1969), pp. 99-101. Also on The Sir Arnold Bax Web Site (1998).

Lyle, Watson, 'Musician of the North', *The Bookman* (February 1932), p. 268.

McCabe, John, 'The John McCabe Interview', *BMS News*, 75 (September 1997), pp. 72-4. *See also* Barnett, Rob, 'Composer John McCabe on Arnold Bax'.

MacDonald, Calum, 'Burgeoning Bax', *The Listener* (18 October 1984), pp. 41-2.

McNaught, William, 'Arnold Bax', *The Monthly Musical Record* (May 1930), pp. 129-30.

—— '[Arnold Bax]', *Modern Music and Musicians* (London: 2nd edn., 1938), pp. 38-40.

Maine, Basil, 'Arnold Bax', *Morning Post* (21 August 1931).

—— 'On Arnold Bax', *New Paths in Music* (London, etc.: Thomas Nelson & Sons Ltd., 1940), pp. 29-30.

Mann, William, 'Some English Concertos: Arnold Bax Violin Concerto', Ralph Hill (ed.), *The Concerto* (Harmondsworth: Penguin Books Ltd., 1952), pp. 405-9.

Manvell, Roger and Huntley, John, *The Technique of Film Music* (London and New York: Focal Press, 1957), pp. 75, 98, 197, 233-4.

May, Frederick, 'The Late Sir Arnold Bax', *The Bell*, XIX, 3 (February 1954), pp. 37-40.

Mayfield, Connie E., 'The Structural Function of Motives in the Piano Sonatas of Arnold Bax', Ph.D. thesis (University of Kansas, 1993).

Mellers, Wilfred H., 'Comments and Reviews: Master of the King's Musick', *Scrutiny* (1942), pp. 376-80. Revised as 'Master of the King's Musick', *Studies in Contemporary Music* (London: Dennis Dobson Ltd., 1947), pp. 179-86.

Miller, Geoffrey, *The Bournemouth Symphony Orchestra* (Milborne Port, Sherborne: Dorset Publishing Co., 1970).

Montague-Nathan, M., 'Reminiscences of Arnold Bax', *The Musical Times* (November 1953), pp. 507-8.

Monthly Music Broadsheet [of the British Council], 'British Composers: Arnold Bax, Master of the Queen's Music', 23 (July 1953), pp. 14-15

Moore, Gerald, 'The White Peace', *Singer and Accompanist* (London, 1953), pp. 1-4.

Morris, Margaret, *The Art of J. D. Fergusson* (Glasgow and London: Blackie, 1974), pp. 102, 135-6.

Murdoch, Murdoch & Co., *Catalogue of Arnold Bax's Compositions* (London, [1933?]), 32 pp.

Musical Standard, The, 'Arnold Bax' (13 October 1917), pp. 241-2.

Myers, Rollo, *Music since 1939: The Arts in Britain: No. 7* (London: Longmans, Green & Co. for The British Council, 1947). Reprinted in *Since 1939: Ballet, films, music, painting* (London: Phoenix House Ltd., 1948).

Newman, Ernest, 'The Art of Mr. Arnold Bax', *The Sunday Times* (19 November 1922).

—— 'The Happy Forest', *The Sunday Times* (27 September 1925).

—— 'Bax's New Work [Winter Legends]', *The Sunday Times* (14 February 1932).

—— 'The Week's Music: Bax and the Promenades', *The Sunday Times* (30 August 1936).

Newmarch, Rosa, 'Symphonic Variations in E' [note to the first performance], Queen's Hall (23 November 1920). Reprinted in *Bax Society Bulletin*, 8 (April 1970), pp. 10-12, and in her *Concert Goer's Library of Descriptive Notes*, V (Oxford, 1938), pp. 5-7.

Newstone, Harry, 'Two First Recordings', *Disc* (winter 1949), pp. 32-4.

O'Connell, C., 'Symphony in E♭ minor', in his *The Victor Book of Symphonies* (New York: Simon & Schuster, rev. edn. 1948), pp. 27-31.

Palmer, Christopher, 'The Post-Impressionists in England' , *Impressionism in Music* (London: Hutchinson University Library, 1973), pp. 167-72.

—— 'England', *Delius: Portrait of a Cosmopolitan* (London: Gerald Duckworth & Co. Ltd., 1976), pp. 151-3.

Parker, D. C., 'Arnold Bax: Peter Pan of Music', *Musical America* (November 1922), p. 5.

Parlett, Graham, 'Bax's Viola Concerto', *Bax Society Bulletin*, 2 (June 1968), pp. 25-7.

—— 'Deirdre and Rosc-catha', *Bax Society Bulletin*, 9 (November 1970), pp. 18-21.

—— *Arnold Bax: A Catalogue of his Music* (London: Triad Press, 1972; limited edn. of 150 copies).

—— 'Bax's Overtures', *Bax Society Bulletin*, 11 (January 1973), pp. 38-9.

—— 'The Music of Arnold Bax: Documentation and Analysis', Ph.D. thesis (University of London, 1994).

—— 'The Unwritten Operas of Arnold Bax', *BMS News*, 67 (September, 1995), pp. 152-5. Also on The Sir Arnold Bax Web Site but with footnotes omitted (1998).

—— 'Bax's stellar hatstand', *BMS News*, 76 (December 1997), p. 123.

Payne, Anthony, 'Problems of a Lyric Composer', *Music & Musicians* (January 1965), p. 17.

—— 'Bax, Sir Arnold (Edward Trevor)', *The New Grove*, 2 (London: Macmillan & Sons, 1980, pp. 306-10.

—— 'Bax: A Centenary Assessment', *Tempo*, 180 (September 1984), pp. 29-32.

Peterkin, H., 'The Songs of Arnold Bax', *Musical Opinion* (September 1920), pp. 958-9.

Picture Post, 'The Master of the King's Music' (28 March 1942), p. 21.

—— 'Bax composes a Royal Fanfare' (22 November 1947), p. 47.

Pirie, Peter J., 'The Nordic Element: Bax and Sibelius', *Musical Opinion* (February 1957), pp. 277-8.

—— 'The Odd Case of Sir Arnold Bax', *The Musical Times* (September 1961), pp. 559-60.

—— 'The "Georgian" Composers', *Music in Britain*, 69 (summer 1965), pp. 23-7.

—— 'The Unfashionable Generation', *High Fidelity Magazine* (January 1966), pp. 59-62.

—— 'Some Thoughts on hearing "The Truth about the Russian Dancers"', *Bax Society Bulletin*, 2 (June 1968), pp. 20-1.

—— 'More than a Brazen Romantic', *Music & Musicians* (January 1971), pp. 32-6, 38.

—— *The English Musical Renaissance* (London: Victor Gollancz, 1979).

Podro, Paul, 'Bax and his Critics', *Bax Society Bulletin*, 1 (February 1968), pp. 4-6.

Pope, Michael, 'Bax and the Royal Philharmonic Society': In the programme booklet for an RPS concert held at the Royal Festival Hall on 5 October 1983, pp. 10-11.

Protheroe, G., 'The Choral Music of Arnold Bax (1883-1953)', *Chorale* (March–April 1983), pp. 6-9.

[Prowse, J.], 'Bax on 78s'; 'Instrumentalists connected with Bax'; 'Composers connected with Bax', Decso Epsom Ltd., *Collectors List*, 39 (summer 1984), pp. 65-8.

Puffett, Derrick, 'In the Garden of Fand—Arnold Bax and the "Celtic Twilight"', *Art Nouveau, Jugendstil und Musik*, Jürg Stenzl (ed.) (Zürich: Atlantis Verlag, 1980), pp. 193-210.

—— 'The Master in faeryland', *Times Literary Supplement* (29 July 1983). Review of Foreman's biography of Bax.

Rawlinson, Harold, 'Movie Maker's Notebook: Music and the Films' [on *Oliver Twist*], *The British Journal of Photography* (6 August 1948), p. 317.

Redlich, Hans F., 'Bax, Sir Arnold Edward Trevor', in *Musik in Geschichte und Gegenwart*, 1 (Leipzig: Bärenreiter-Verlag, 1949), cols. 1427-31.

Rees, C. B., 'Impressions: Sir Arnold Bax', *London Musical Events* (November 1950), pp. 14-16.

Reynolds, Peter, 'Changing Performance Practice in British Orchestral Music', *British Music: The Journal of the British Music Society*, 17 (1995), pp. 22-34.

Rivers, Joseph LaRoche, 'Formal Determinants in the Symphonies of Arnold Bax', Ph.D. thesis (University of Arizona, 1982).

Rockwell, John, 'Arnold Bax: Dowdy, Yes, But Dazzling', *The New York Times* (22 March 1987), section H, p. 23.

Rothstein, E., 'The Two-Piano Music of Arnold Bax', thesis (Eastman School of Music, Rochester, 1945), 50 pp.

Rowe, Basil, 'Bax's Second String Quartet', *Bax Society Bulletin*, 6 (August 1969), pp. 94-8.

Rubbra, Edmund, 'Arnold Bax's Technics: A New Flowering of Old Traditions', *The Daily Telegraph* (14 October 1933). Reprinted with minor alterations as 'Arnold Bax's Music: A New Flowering of Old Traditions', *Bax Society Bulletin*, 1 (February 1968).

Rutland, Harold, 'Notes and Comments: Sir Henry Wood and Bax', *The Musical Times* (September 1957), p. 486.

Sack, Joe, 'Musical Surprises', *Rand Daily Mail* (8 June 1968). Reprinted in *Bax Society Bulletin*, 3 (October 1968), pp. 49-50.

Sandved, K. B., 'Bax, Sir Arnold', *The World of Music*, 1 (London: Waverley Book Co., 1954), pp. 167-8.

Saul, G. B., 'Of Tales Half Forgotten', *Arizona Quarterly* (summer 1962), pp. 151-4. About Bax's short stories.

Schaawächter, Jürgen, *Die britische Sinfonie 1914-1945* (Cologne: Verlag Christoph Dohr, 1995). Revised and amended extract: 'British Symphonists: Arnold Bax', The Sir Arnold Bax Web Site (1998).

Scherek, J., 'Arnold Bax', *Canon* (November 1949), pp. 221-2.

Schlüren, Christoph, *Arnold Bax: vom Überschwang zur Verzweiflung* ([Munich]: privately printed, 1995). Script of a radio programme (see Appendix 3, section IV).

Scholes, Percy A., 'Arnold Bax', *The Observer* (19 November 1922).

—— *The Mirror of Music 1844-1944*, 2 vols. (London: Novello & Co. Ltd. and OUP, 1947).

Scott-Sutherland, Colin, 'The Symphonies of Arnold Bax', *The Music Review* (February 1962), pp. 20-3. Also on The Sir Arnold Bax Web Site (1998).

—— 'Morar and the Master of the Queen's Music', *Scotland's Magazine* (November 1962), pp. 20-3.

—— 'Arnold Bax 1883-1953', *The Musical Times* (October 1963), p. 706.

—— 'Some Unpublished Works of Arnold Bax', *The Music Review* (November 1963), pp. 322-6. Also on The Sir Arnold Bax Web Site (1998).

—— 'Sir Arnold Bax: Symphonic Variations', *The Music Review* (May 1967), pp. 156-7.

—— 'Bax and Melody', *Bax Society Bulletin*, 4 (February 1969), pp. 54-7.

—— *Arnold Bax* (London: J. M. Dent & Sons Ltd., 1973).

—— 'Arnold Bax and Dermot O'Byrne', *Book and Magazine Collector*, 150 (September 1996), pp. 68-76.

Sear, H. G., 'Bax and his Orchestra', *The Monthly Musical Record* (June 1948), pp. 115-19.

—— 'Sir Arnold Bax', *The Symphony*, Ralph Hill (ed.) (Harmondsworth: Penguin Books Ltd., 1949), pp. 402-16.

Shera, F.H., [Bax's symphonies], *Grove's Dictionary of Music and Musicians*, 8, 5th edn. (London: Macmillan & Co. Ltd., 1954), p. 248.

Shore, Bernard, 'Arnold Bax' and 'Bax's Third Symphony' in his *Sixteen Symphonies* (London: Longmans, Green & Co., 1949), pp. 341-8, 349-65.

—— ['Arnold Bax: 1883-1953'], *Music & Letters* (January 1954), p. 12-13.

Smith, Mark, 'Magister: In Search of Arnold Bax: The Genesis of a Magical Novel', the Infinity Plus Web Site (1997): "http://www.users.zetnet.co.uk/iplus/". See also Wylie, Jonathan.

Sommerich, P., 'Bax to the Fore: Briefly', *Hampstead & Highgate Express* (11 November 1983), p. 20.

Stevenson, Patric, 'Some Anecdotes about Arnold Bax', *Bax Society Bulletin*, 5 (May 1969), pp. 77-80.

Stevenson, Ronald, 'The Truth about Bax', *Radio 3 Magazine* (November 1983), pp. 2-3.

Streatham Society *see* [Cresswell, John].

Suchy-Pilalis, Jessica R., 'The Use of the Harp in the Chamber Music of Arnold Bax', thesis in partial fulfilment for D.Mus. (Indiana University, August 1990).

Suckling, Norman, 'Bax and his Piano Sonatas', *The Listener* (17 June 1954), p. 1069.

Swynnoe, Jan G., 'Brief Encounter: British Composers and the Seventh Art (British Film Music 1930-1960)', Ph.D. thesis (University of Wales, Bangor, 1997).

Taylor, J. R., 'Arnold Bax', *Music & Musicians* (November 1983), pp. 12-13.

Taylor, S., 'The Motets of Arnold Bax', *The Music Mirror and Fanfare* (June 1931), pp. 187, 189.

Thistlethwaite, Bernard, *The Bax Family* (London: Headly Brothers, 1936).

Thomson, Oscar, *The International Cyclopedia of Music and Musicians*, 9th edn., ed. R. Sabin (London: J. M. Dent & Sons Ltd., 1964), pp. 161-4.

Thornycroft, Rosalind, completed by Chloë Baynes, *Time which spaces us apart* (Batcombe: Chloë Baynes, 1991; limited edn. of 100 copies).

The Times, 'Concerts: Mr. Arnold Bax's Compositions' (20 July 1908), p. 6 [early edn. only].

—— 'Sir Arnold Bax, the Master of the Queen's Musick' [obituary] (5 October 1953).

Upton, G. P., and Borowski, Felix, *The Standard Concert Guide* (London: Garden Publications, rev. edn. 1947), pp. 22-3.

Vaughan Williams, Ralph, ['Arnold Bax: 1883-1953'], *Music & Letters* (January 1954), pp. 13-14.

Walker, R. A., 'Reminiscences of Bax', *Bax Society Bulletin*, 3 (October 1968), pp. 41-3.

Walton, William, ['Arnold Bax: 1883-1953'], *Music & Letters* (January 1954), p. 14.

Warner Chappell Music Ltd., *Catalogue of Music for Hire* (London, [1990]).

Watt, D., 'Musical Events—Nothing Gained', *The New Yorker* (8 March 1952), pp. 91-2.

Whelbourne, H., 'Arnold Edward Trevor Bax', *Standard Book of Celebrated Musicians Past and Present* (London: T. Werner Laurie Ltd., 1937), pp. 32-3.

Whelen, Christopher, 'Bax's Third Symphony', *Youth and Music: Musica-Viva* (March 1950).

—— 'An Approach to Bax', *The Mercury* (Winter Gardens Society, Bournemouth), 8 (July 1950), pp. 5-10.

—— 'A Tribute to Sir Arnold Bax', *Music & Musicians* (December 1953), p. 12.

—— 'Arnold Edward Trevor Bax', *The Music Masters*, ed. A. L. Bacharach, 4: *The Twentieth Century* (London: Cassell & Co. Ltd., 1954; Harmondsworth: Penguin Books Ltd., 1957), pp. 26-34. Also on The Sir Arnold Bax Web Site (1998).

White, Felix, 'Arnold Bax's [First] Violin Sonata', *The Musical News and Herald* (14 January 1922), pp. 49-50.
Whitwell, D., '20th-century English composers: Their Music for Winds', *The Instrumentalist* (November 1968), pp. 47-50.
Wiborg, F., 'Bax, Berners and Bliss', *Arts and Decoration* (June 1925), p. 20.
Willetts, Pamela J., 'Autograph Music Manuscripts of Sir Arnold Bax', *British Museum Quarterly*, XXIII (1960-1), pp. 43-5.
[Williams, John McLaughlin], 'Conductor/violinist John McLaughlin Williams discusses Bax and his American premiere performance of the Violin Concerto', The Sir Arnold Bax Web Site (1998).
Williams, L. H., 'The Philosopher's Musician', *Sackbut* (March 1931), pp. 216-19. Partly reprinted in Norman Demuth (ed.), *An Anthology of Musical Criticism* (London: Eyre & Spottiswoode, 1947), pp. 359-62.
Wilson, Colin, 'Some English Music' in his *Brandy of the Damned* (London: John Baker Publishers Ltd., 1964), pp. 148-9.
—— 'Arnold Bax: A Music Lover's Musician', *Bax Society Bulletin*, 7 (November 1969), pp. 113-14.
Wilson, D., 'The Orchestral Development of Arnold Bax', M.A. thesis (University of Wales, 1975).
Wollstein, R. H., 'Bax defines his music—"I am a Brazen Romantic" he says', 'The Turn of the Dial', *Musical America* (7 July 1928), p. 9. Reprinted in FMY2, p. 168.
Wortham, H. E., 'Music of the Month', *Apollo* (March 1928), pp. 143-4.
'Wych Elm', 'Airing our Views: Symphony No. Four by Sir Arnold Bax', *Canon* (November 1948), pp. 189-90.
Wylie, Jonathan [pseud. of Mark and Julia Smith], *Magister* (London: Orbit, 1997). A fantasy novel about Bax. Extract published on the Infinity Plus Web Site (1997): "http://www. users.zetnet. co.uk/iplus/". See also Smith, Mark.
Young, B. A., 'Back to Bax', *The Financial Times* (25 February 1984).
Young, Percy M., 'Bax, Arnold Edward Trevor', *Critical Dictionary of Composers and their Music* (London: Dennis Dobson Ltd., 1954), pp. 42-3.
—— 'Romanticism still prevalent', *A History of British Music* (London: Ernest Benn Ltd., 1967), pp. 570-73.

INDEX OF TITLES AND FIRST LINES

Main titles, subtitles, and the first lines of word-settings are listed with Catalogue numbers indicated. Inverted commas enclose the first line of a poem except when it doubles as the title (e.g. 'She cometh no more' but Far in a Western Brookland). It should be noted that Bax sometimes modified the original title of a poem (e.g. On the Bridge instead of Sitting on the Bridge) and was not always accurate in transcribing texts. Articles and numerals are transposed to the end of the line in titles but not in the few cases where they occur as the first word of a poem set (e.g. Tote Kind, Das but 'Das Heilige, womit sich lange mein Herz getröstet'). For untitled fragments see Appendix 1 (section X), and for literary titles see Appendix 7.

GENERAL INDEX

References are to page numbers.